Fifth Edition

The Little, Brown Handbook

(Brief Version)

第 5 版

李特-布朗英文写作手册

简明版

〔美〕简·E.阿伦（Jane E. Aaron） 编著

（北京大学）刘瑾　张敏　王伶　译

著作权合同登记号 图字:01-2014-5535

图书在版编目(CIP)数据

李特-布朗英文写作手册:简明版:第 5 版/(美)简·E. 阿伦(Jane E.Aaron)编著;刘瑾,张敏,王伶译.— 北京:北京大学出版社,2022.8
ISBN 978-7-301-32734-0

Ⅰ.①李… Ⅱ.①简… ②刘… ③张… ④王… Ⅲ.①英语-写作-手册 Ⅳ.① H315-62

中国版本图书馆 CIP 数据核字(2021)第 257392 号

Authorized translation from the English language edition, entitled THE LITTLE, BROWN HANDBOOK, 5th Edition, Brief Version by JANE E. AARON, published by Pearson Education, Inc, Copyright © 2012 Jane E. Aaron
ISBN: 978-0-321-89666-7

All rights reserved. No part of this book may be reproduced or transmitted in any form or by any means, electronic or mechanical, including photocopying, recording or by any information storage retrieval system, without permission from Pearson Education, Inc.

CHINESE SIMPLIFIED language edition published by PEKING UNIVERSITY PRESS LTD., Copyright © 2022.
本书中文简体字版经授权由北京大学出版社限在中华人民共和国境内(不包括香港特别行政区、澳门特别行政区和台湾)独家出版发行。

本书封面贴有 Pearson Education(培生教育出版集团)激光防伪标签。
无标签者不得销售。

书　　　名	李特-布朗英文写作手册(简明版)第 5 版 LITE-BULANG YINGWEN XIEZUO SHOUCE (JIANMING BAN) DI-WU BAN
著作责任者	〔美〕简·E. 阿伦(Jane E. Aaron) 编著;刘瑾　张敏　王伶　译
责 任 编 辑	李书雅
标 准 书 号	ISBN 978-7-301-32734-0
出 版 发 行	北京大学出版社
地　　　址	北京市海淀区成府路 205 号　100871
网　　　址	http://www.pup.cn　新浪微博:@北京大学出版社　@阅读培文
电 子 信 箱	pkupw@qq.com
电　　　话	邮购部 010-62752015　发行部 010-62750672　编辑部 010-62766820
印 刷 者	天津光之彩印刷有限公司
经 销 者	新华书店
	660 毫米 ×960 毫米　16 开本　40 印张　935 千字 2022 年 8 月第 1 版　2022 年 8 月第 1 次印刷
定　　　价	158.00 元(精装版)

未经许可,不得以任何方式复制或抄袭本书之部分或全部内容。
版权所有,侵权必究
举报电话:010-62752024　电子信箱:fd@pup.pku.edu.cn
图书如有印装质量问题,请与出版部联系,电话:010-62756370

前言　致学生

　　《李特–布朗英文写作手册（简明版）》（以下简称《简明版》）包含你在校内外写作需要的基本信息。从这本书中你可以了解怎样获得想法、使用标点、搜寻网络、引用文献、写简历，等等——所有这些都在一本方便好用的小书里。

　　本书主要是一本工具书，供你需要时查找。你可能不需要从头到尾阅读本书，也不一定会用到本书中的每一项内容，因为，不管你是否意识到，你已经了解了其中很多内容。关键在于弄清楚你不了解的——从自己的写作经历中，从别人的评价中，得到提示——然后在本书中找到你的问题的答案。

　　使用本书之前，可能需要先清除头脑中一个常见的误解：写作只是，或主要是，正确与否的问题。没错，如果语法、标点等正确，任何写作都会更具可读性。但是，这些事情应该是写作过程中更靠后一些的问题，首先你得弄清楚你要说什么，在这个过程中放手去犯错。正如一个作家所说，先得把陶泥放在转轮上，才能把它塑成碗的形状；先得塑成碗的形状，才能把它完善。所以，先把你的陶泥放在转轮上吧，然后加工，直到它有碗的样子。这之后再操心正确与否的问题。

找到你所需要的内容

　　有许多方法可以在本书中找到你所需要的内容：
- **使用目录**。简明目录有简短的内容提要，列出了本书各部分和各章的内容。详细目录有更详细的内容提要，列出了每一章的小标题。
- **使用词语用法汇编**。"词语用法汇编"（pp. 523–535[2]）讲解了二百五十多个容易混淆和误用的词语。
- **使用索引**。本手册有大量的索引，列出了本书提到的话题、易出现问题的词语或短语。
- **使用清单**。本书最后有一个很有用的帮助清单：CULTURE LANGUAGE "语言文化提示"

1　此边码为英文原版书页码。

2　本书以p.或pp.标注的页码均为边码。

面向把标准美式英语作为第二语言或第二方言的学生，汇总了书中所有相关材料。

- **使用书页中的各种元素。** 如图例所示，手册的每一页都告诉你在那里能够找到什么。

» **本手册页面元素**

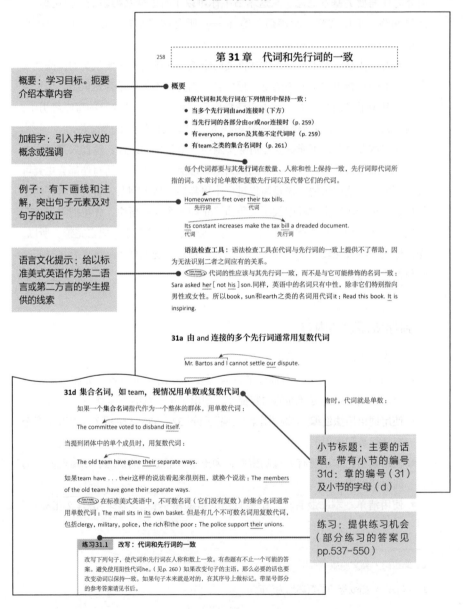

前言　致老师

《简明版》为写作者提供可靠、好用、实惠的参考。本手册沿袭其父版《李特–布朗英文写作手册》的权威，采用简明的格式，解答关于写作过程、批判性阅读、语法和文体、研究性写作及文档等问题。它具有跨学科的视野、方便易用的形式，并且几乎不要求读者有先期的写作经验或曾经读过写作手册。不论学生有什么样的兴趣和技能，《简明版》都能有所帮助。

本版新在何处

《简明版》发挥了《李特–布朗英文写作手册》的长处，又随着写作及其教学的迅速发展与时俱进。本手册具有许多方面的参考功能，而接下来的几页将用"NEW"突出标注本版最重要的补充及改变。

学术写作入门

本手册向学生介绍了大学写作的目标和要求。

- **NEW** 新增加的第9章"加入学术圈"，为写作者提出了一些建议，以期帮助学生在面授课堂和在线课堂取得成功，以及写文章进行学术探讨。
- **NEW** 本手册以重要章节讨论加强学术操守和避免抄袭。其中新增的第9章和原有的第10章讨论学术写作，第54章讨论避免抄袭。手册的其他章节也不断加强这两点。
- **NEW** 在讲写作过程和学术写作的章节中，会着重讲述学术写作的常见类型。全书包含学术写作类型的十个范例。（列表见p.102）
- **NEW** 在本手册各种文章范例的基础上，新增了一些写作的新鲜例作，包括一篇说明文、一篇文学叙事、一篇研究计划及一篇文学评论。
- **NEW** 关于批判性思维与阅读的第10章中，新增了关于写总结的重点讲述。
- 本手册也特别重点讨论了综述文章的写法，以帮助学生平衡自己与他人的观点，如怎样写读后感。
- 第七部分在论文写作方面能给学生打下坚实的基础，有多个章节讨论了MLA（现代语言协会）和APA（美国心理学协会）的必备资料及格式。

论文写作指导

本手册始终密切重视论文写作和文献引用，提供了详细建议和MLA及APA格式的论文范例。本书重点讨论了网络图书馆的使用、信息的管理、文献的评价和综合、文献资料的融合及抄袭的避免。手册全面论及MLA和APA文档格式，体现了每种格式的新版本。

- **NEW** 为了帮助学生对研究的问题形成自己的视角，本手册强调了如何提出问题、如何与文献对话交流，及如何公正负责地呈现多种观点。
- **NEW** 本手册提供了一份带注释的学生写的参考目录范例，包括对文献的评价，展示了如何做初步的文献评价。
- **NEW** 本手册讨论了图书馆的门户网站，内容涵盖研究资源指引、集中式搜索引擎，并更新了数据库的资料，展示了学生搜寻文献的各种方法。
- **NEW** 本手册就网络资源的可信度评价进行了广泛讨论——包括网络站点、社交网站、博客、维基百科（允许访问者添加或修改资料的网站）、多媒体，帮助学生辨识资料的意图、分辨可靠与不可靠资源。
- 本手册提供了资料评估的案例分析，展示如何将评判标准运用到范例文章和网络文档。
- **NEW** 本手册修改了关于避免抄袭和参考文献的章节，对于故意和非故意的抄袭给出了更多的例子，对于必须引用的资料给出了新的例子，对于如何避免抄袭网络资源给出了更新的建议。
- 本手册提供的一篇关于green consumerism的研究论文正在进行中，它跟随学生完成研究过程并最终得出结论，以MLA格式给出参考文献。

文献的参考

本手册广泛涉及MLA和APA格式的参考文献，反映了各自的最新版本，并提供了许多引用电子资源的例子。

- **NEW** 本手册采用了更新的、带注释的参考文献范例，举例说明了MLA和APA格式的参考文献，告诉学生如何找到所需的书目信息来做这两种格式的引用。
- 本手册突出展示了所有的参考文献范式，便于读者掌握作者、标题、日期及其他引用元素。

写作进程的指导

本手册采用简明实用的方式讲解写作的情境、想法的激发、主题句的形成、修改，以及写作进程的其他元素。

- **NEW** 本手册提供了新的类别，将写作主题、写作意图及读者融合为每一个写作情境的关键元素，以便影响内容、形式及读者的期待。
- **NEW** 本手册用单独一章讲解如何修改，着重讨论不同于校订和校阅的修改。
- **NEW** 本手册第7章的内容是段落的写作，以讨论文章中各段落的联系开始，给出了许多新的例子。
- **NEW** 本手册有一章全面讲解写作的展示，包括纸版和电子版文档的设计、图像及其他媒介在多模式写作中的创造和使用，以及网络写作。

用法、语法和标点的指导

本手册的核心参考材料简明而可靠地解释了写作的基本概念和常见错误，给出了数百个带注释的例子，并在相关讨论中提供了丰富的练习。

- **NEW** 第三部分的内容是"明晰与风格"，这部分给出了许多新的例子，讨论了在线词典和类语词典，也对如何避免使用缩略语、残缺句及其他网络用语提出了建议。
- **NEW** 在原有的一百多个练习集的基础上，本手册又提供了超过十五个新的练习集和改编过的练习集，供学生练习用法、语法、标点、文字处理细节，也练习如何写主题句及如何改述句子。这些练习相互呼应，其主题涵盖整个大纲。在本书末尾有大约半数练习的答案。
- 本手册提供数以百计的带有下画线的例子，以清楚展示各种错误及其修正方法。

对语言文化背景各异的写作者的指导

本手册中，有些注释和小节上标注了 CULTURE LANGUAGE。在这些地方，本手册为母语或方言不是标准美式英语的作者在修辞和语法上提供了各种帮助。

- 本书不是采用单独的章节，而是结合多个章节在这方面提供帮助，这样，学生不必知道自己与以标准美式英语为母语者有何共同与不同的问题，就可以找到自己所需要的帮助。

- pp. 592–593提供了"(CULTURE LANGUAGE)语言文化提示",可以帮助学生找到关于标准美式英语的建议,并且把各章节的相关内容集中起来。
- **NEW** 全书中有许多带有(CULTURE LANGUAGE)的注释,它们使用的是简单的语言,并且增加了例句。

图像资料的指导

在图像资料的处理、图像资料在写作中的有效使用方面,本手册为学生提供了帮助。

- **NEW** 本手册第8章的内容是关于写作的展示,第52章的内容是关于寻找资料,这两章都为学生在大学写作任务中如何创造、选择和使用图像资料与多媒体资料提供了实用的建议。
- 本手册第10章的内容是关于批判性阅读,第53章的内容是关于如何使用资源,这两章就如何批判性地阅读广告和其他图像资料进行了充分的讨论。
- 手册中一些学生论文的插图展示了用视觉信息支持书面观点的各种方法。

特别好用的参考

《简明版》用心面对学生,使用多种手段来帮助学生找到自己所需要的,然后使用自己所找到的。

- **NEW** 本手册提供简洁的目录,使读者对内容一目了然,而又提供了详细的目录。
- **NEW** 在每一章开头的"概要"部分,本手册给出了学习目标,使学生对本手册的关键内容有一个大致的了解。
- 本手册的结构直接清晰,便于学生掌握各个主题。
- 在规则和其他标题中,本手册尽可能少使用术语,用例子替代术语、对术语做补充说明。
- 本手册中有将近五十个清单和小结,突出展示了关键的参考信息,比如关于读者群的问题、逗号的使用,以及参考文献的索引。
- 本手册对文字和图像例子都做了注释,使得概念和例证得以统一。
- 本手册强调了参考文献的样式,突出了各个重要元素。
- 本手册的索引采用词典风格,便于读者找到所需条目。
- 致学生的前言概述了本手册的内容、给出了详细的参考帮助,并解释了页面的版式。

致 谢

《简明版》之所以能保持新鲜与有用，得益于教师与出版商的销售代表和编辑谈话、完成问卷、写详细的反馈并给我个人写信。

说到本手册的第5版，我特别感激如下教师，是他们的洞见和经验使得你手中的这本书得以改进。William R. Black III, Weatherford College; Randy Boone, Northampton Community College; Linda Boynton, Oakland Community College; Nancy C. DeJoy, Michigan State University; Susan Denning, Clark College; Kristen Garrison, Midwestern State University; Loren C. Gruber, Missouri Valley College; Kimberly Hall, Harrisburg Area Community College; Gregg W. Heitschmidt, Surry Community College; David Hennessy, Broward College, Central Campus; Cary Henson, University of Wisconsin, Oshkosh; Calley Hornbuckle, Columbia College; Cynthia Kimball, Portland Community College; Lawrence Morgan, University of Wisconsin, Stevens Point; Andrew J. Pegman, Cuyahoga Community College; and James Price, Navarro College.

与这些深入思考的批评者相应的，我还得到了几位独具创意的人士的帮助。University of Michigan的Aaron McCullough引导我走过现代图书馆的迷宫。Marilyn Hochman的建议帮助我改善了给母语和方言不是标准美式英语的学生写的注释。Tufts University的Sylvan Barnet一直以他的专长帮我改善"文学阅读与写作"，这一章改编自他（与William Burto和William E. Cain合作）的著作*Short Guide to Writing about Literature*。Ellen Kuhl在论文写作的材料方面提供了独有创意、耐心细致、无价的帮助。还有，Carol Hollar-Zwick是我必不可少的且才华横溢的发起人、宣传者、批判者、协调者、研究者、出版人，以及朋友。

还要感谢这本书无敌的出版团队。Pearson的编辑Joe Opiela和Anne Brunell Ehrenworth在教师和学生的需求上给了我高明的洞见，而Kelly Connors高效而愉快地回应了我所有的要求。Kathy Smith和Vernon Nahrgang准确而仔细地分别做了编修和校对工作。Jerilyn Bockorick和Alisha Webber使得这本书的使用令人舒心，而Susan McIntyre总是以她的平静（并且令人平静）而神奇的时间规划和管理让这本书得以出版。我对所有这些合作者表示感谢。

简明目录

前言　致学生 / iii

前言　致老师 / v

001　第一部分　写作过程

第1章　写作情境 …………………………… 003
第2章　创作 ………………………………… 011
第3章　主题和组织 ………………………… 017
第4章　打草稿 ……………………………… 028
第5章　修改 ………………………………… 032
第6章　校订、定格式和校对 ……………… 039
第7章　段落 ………………………………… 046
第8章　提交终稿 …………………………… 071

085　第二部分　大学内外的写作

第9章　加入学术圈 ………………………… 087
第10章　批判性思维与阅读 ………………… 092
第11章　学术写作 …………………………… 108
第12章　撰写论述文 ………………………… 120
第13章　文学阅读与写作 …………………… 140
第14章　大众写作 …………………………… 146

155 第三部分 明晰与风格

- 第15章 强调 ········· 157
- 第16章 平行结构 ········· 167
- 第17章 变化与细节 ········· 171
- 第18章 恰当而准确的用词 ········· 175
- 第19章 完整 ········· 194
- 第20章 简明 ········· 195

203 第四部分 句子成分和句型

基本语法 / 205
- 第21章 词性 ········· 205
- 第22章 句子 ········· 213
- 第23章 短语和从句 ········· 221
- 第24章 句子类型 ········· 228

动词 / 230
- 第25章 动词的词形 ········· 230
- 第26章 动词时态 ········· 246
- 第27章 动词语气 ········· 254
- 第28章 动词的语态 ········· 256
- 第29章 主谓一致 ········· 259

代词 / 267
- 第30章 代词的格 ········· 267
- 第31章 代词和先行词的一致 ········· 274
- 第32章 代词对先行词的指向 ········· 278

修饰语 / 283
- 第33章 形容词和副词 ········· 283
- 第34章 错置修饰语和垂悬修饰语 ········· 295

句子中的错误 / 302
- 第35章 残缺句 ········· 302
- 第36章 逗号拼接句和融合句 ········· 307
- 第37章 杂糅句（混合句） ········· 314

第五部分 标点符号 — 319

- 第38章 句末标点 — 321
- 第39章 逗号 — 323
- 第40章 分号 — 339
- 第41章 冒号 — 343
- 第42章 撇号 — 346
- 第43章 引号 — 352
- 第44章 其他标点 — 356

第六部分 拼写和文字处理细节 — 363

- 第45章 拼写 — 365
- 第46章 连字符 — 371
- 第47章 大写字母 — 373
- 第48章 斜体或下画线 — 377
- 第49章 缩略语 — 381
- 第50章 数字 — 384

第七部分 研究和文献记录 — 389

- 第51章 研究策略 — 391
- 第52章 寻找原始资料 — 399
- 第53章 处理原始资料 — 417
- 第54章 抄袭的避免和原始资料的引用 — 445
- 第55章 撰写论文 — 454
- 第56章 MLA原始资料来源的标注与格式 — 457
- 第57章 APA原始资料来源的标注与格式 — 516

词语用法汇编 / 543

带星号练习题答案 / 558

索引 / 573

CULTURE LANGUAGE 语言文化提示 / 613

详细目录

前言　致学生 / iii

前言　致老师 / v

001 第一部分 写作过程

第1章　写作情境 ·················· 003
　　1a　分析写作情境 / 003
　　1b　选择适合任务的题材 / 005
　　1c　确定写作目的 / 007
　　1d　考虑读者对象 / 008
　　1e　了解体裁 / 010

第2章　创作 ······················· 011
　　2a　记写作日记 / 012
　　2b　观察周围环境 / 013
　　2c　自由写作 / 013
　　2d　头脑风暴 / 014
　　2e　组织观点 / 015
　　2f　提问 / 016

第3章　主题和组织 ················ 017
　　3a　写出主题句 / 017
　　3b　组织观点 / 021

第4章　打草稿 ···················· 028
　　4a　开始动笔 / 029
　　4b　保持良好势头 / 029
　　4c　初稿范例 / 030

第5章 修改 ········ 032
- 5a 批判性地阅读你的作品 / 033
- 5b 合作修改 / 034
- 5c 写标题 / 036
- 5d 修改样文 / 037

第6章 校订、定格式和校对 ········ 039
- 6a 校订修改后的草稿 / 039
- 6b 定格式和校对终稿 / 043
- 6c 终稿样例 / 044

第7章 段落 ········ 046
- 7a 让文中段落产生关联 / 047
- 7b 围绕中心论点保持段落完整 / 048
- 7c 实现段落连贯 / 051
- 7d 展开中心思想 / 058
- 7e 撰写开头段和结尾段 / 067

第8章 提交终稿 ········ 071
- 8a 给各学科学术写作适当制定格式 / 071
- 8b 将图像和其他媒体适当用于多模式写作 / 076
- 8c 为网络写作时考虑设计 / 082

085 第二部分 大学内外的写作

第9章 加入学术圈 ········ 087
- 9a 从大学课程中获得最大收益 / 087
- 9b 成为一名学术作者 / 088
- 9c 树立学术操守 / 089
- 9d 在学术环境中进行有效沟通 / 090

第10章 批判性思维与阅读 ········ 092
- 10a 使用批判性阅读的技巧 / 092
- 10b 总结文章 / 098
- 10c 形成批判性反应 / 100

10d 批判性地观看图像 / 103

第11章 学术写作 ··· 108
　　　11a 确定写作目的、目标读者和文章体裁 / 109
　　　11b 撰写对文章的反应 / 110
　　　11c 选择结构和内容 / 113
　　　11d 使用学术语言 / 114
　　　11e 批判性反应的范例 / 116

第12章 撰写论述文 ··· 120
　　　12a 使用论述文的元素 / 120
　　　12b 理性写作 / 124
　　　12c 有效组织论述文 / 134
　　　12d 论述文范例 / 135

第13章 文学阅读与写作 ·· 140
　　　13a 边阅读文学作品边写作 / 140
　　　13b 批判性阅读文学作品 / 141
　　　13c 文学作品分析范例 / 143

第14章 大众写作 ··· 146
　　　14a 使用商务信函和简历的固定格式 / 147
　　　14b 撰写目标明确的备忘录 / 150
　　　14c 为社区工作创建有效的文件 / 152

第三部分 明晰与风格　155

第15章 强调 ··· 157
　　　15a 使用主语和动词来表达施动者和动作 / 157
　　　15b 使用句子的开头和结尾 / 159
　　　15c 同等重要的思想用并列结构 / 162
　　　15d 使用从属来强调一些思想 / 164

第16章 平行结构 ··· 167
　　　16a 使用带and, but, or, nor和yet的平行结构 / 168

16b 使用带both...and, not...but，或别的关系连词的平行
　　结构 / 169

16c 在比较中使用平行结构 / 169

16d 在列表、标题和提纲中使用平行结构 / 169

第17章 变化与细节 171

17a 变化句子长度 / 172

17b 变化句子结构 / 172

17c 增加细节 / 174

第18章 恰当而准确的用词 175

18a 选择恰当的词语 / 176

18b 选择准确的词语 / 183

第19章 完整 194

19a 要写完整的复合结构 / 194

19b 补上必要的词语 / 194

第20章 简明 195

20a 注重主语和动词 / 196

20b 删除空洞词语 / 197

20c 去掉不需要的重复 / 198

20d 让修饰语紧凑 / 199

20e 修改there is 或 it is 结构 / 199

20f 合并句子 / 200

20g 避免使用行话 / 200

第四部分　句子成分和句型　203

基本语法 / 205

第21章 词性 205

21a 学会识别名词 / 205

21b 学会识别代词 / 206

21c 学会识别动词 / 206

21d 学会识别形容词和副词 / 209

21e 学会识别连接词：介词和连词 / 210

21f 学会识别感叹词 / 213

第22章 句子 ·········· 213

22a 学会识别主语和谓语 / 213

22b 学会基本的谓语结构 / 216

22c 学会其他句型 / 218

第23章 短语和从句 ·········· 221

23a 学会识别短语 / 221

23b 学会识别从句 / 225

第24章 句子类型 ·········· 228

24a 学会识别简单句 / 228

24b 学会识别并列句 / 228

24c 学会识别复合句 / 228

24d 学会识别并列复合句 / 229

动词 / 230

第25章 动词的词形 ·········· 230

25a 正确使用sing/sang/sung及其他不规则动词的词形 / 230

25b 分辨sit和set，lie和lay，rise和raise / 234

25c 正确使用动词的-s和-ed形式 / 235

25d 正确使用与主要动词连用的助动词 / 237

25e 在动词后正确使用动名词和不定式 / 241

25f 正确使用双词动词的分词形式 / 244

第26章 动词时态 ·········· 246

26a 注意现在时态的特殊用法（sing）/ 247

26b 注意完成时态的用法（have/had/will have sung）/ 248

26c 注意进行时态的用法（is/was/will be singing）/ 249

26d 保持时态一致 / 250

26e 使用恰当的动词时态呼应 / 251

第27章 动词语气 254
27a 正确使用动词虚拟语气，如I wish I were / 254
27b 保持语气一致 / 255

第28章 动词的语态 256
28a 优先使用主动语态 / 256
28b 当施动者不明或不重要时，或者当指明施动者可能有所冒犯时，使用被动语态 / 257
28c 保持语态一致 / 258

第29章 主谓一致 259
29a 名词和动词的词尾-s及-es作用不同 / 260
29b 即使有别的词插在主谓之间，主谓也需要保持一致 / 261
29c 由and连接的主语通常用复数动词 / 261
29d 当主语的各部分由or或nor连接时，动词与较近的部分保持一致 / 262
29e 主语是everyone和其他不定代词时，视情况用单数或复数动词 / 262
29f 集合名词，如team，依其意思而用单数或复数动词 / 263
29g who，which和that接的动词与它们的先行词保持一致 / 263
29h news和其他一些以-s结尾的单数名词用单数动词 / 264
29i 即使动词在主语之前，也要与主语保持一致 / 264
29j is，are和其他系动词与主语保持一致，而不是与主语补足语保持一致 / 265
29k 头衔和被定义的词用单数动词 / 265

代词 / 267

第30章 代词的格 267
30a 区分复合主语和复合宾语：she and I 与 her and me / 268
30b 在主语补足语中使用主格：It was she. / 269
30c 用who还是whom取决于代词在句子中的功能 / 270
30d 在其他结构中使用正确的格 / 272

第31章 代词和先行词的一致 …… 274

- 31a 由and连接的多个先行词通常用复数代词 / 274
- 31b 当先行词的各部分由or或nor连接时,代词与就近的部分保持一致 / 275
- 31c 有everyone,person和其他先行词时,视情况用单数或复数代词 / 275
- 31d 集合名词,如team,视情况用单数或复数代词 / 277

第32章 代词对先行词的指向 …… 278

- 32a 使代词清楚地指向一个先行词 / 279
- 32b 把代词放在离先行词足够近的位置,以确保指代清晰 / 279
- 32c 使代词指向一个确定的,而不是暗示的先行词 / 279
- 32d 指代"你,读者"时,只能用"you" / 281
- 32e 保持代词一致 / 281

修饰语 / 283

第33章 形容词和副词 …… 283

- 33a 形容词只用来修饰名词和代词 / 284
- 33b 在系动词后使用形容词修饰主语,用副词修饰动词 / 284
- 33c 正确使用形容词和副词的比较级、最高级形式 / 285
- 33d 当心双重否定 / 287
- 33e 区分现在分词形容词和过去分词形容词 / 288
- 33f 正确使用a, an, the和其他限定词 / 289

第34章 错置修饰语和垂悬修饰语 …… 295

- 34a 重置错置修饰语 / 295
- 34b 让垂悬修饰语与句子关联 / 300

句子中的错误 / 302

第35章 残缺句 …… 302

- 35a 检验你的句子是否完整 / 303
- 35b 改写残缺句 / 304
- 35c 注意一些非完整句的可以接受的用法 / 305

第36章 逗号拼接句和融合句 ·· 307
  36a 把没有由and, but或别的并列连词分开的主句分开 / 308
  36b 把由however, for example等连接的主句分开 / 310

第37章 杂糅句（混合句）·· 314
  37a 使主谓在意义上相匹配 / 314
  37b 理清楚语法上杂糅的句子 / 315
  37c 句子的各部分，比如主语，只说一次 / 317

319
第五部分 标点符号

第38章 句末标点 ·· 321
  38a 大多数句子后面，许多缩略语后面，用句号 / 321
  38b 在直接疑问句的末尾用问号，有时也用问号表示存疑 / 322
  38c 在强调声明、感叹词或命令的后面，用感叹号 / 322

第39章 逗号 ··· 323
  39a 在连接主句的and, but或其他并列连词之前使用逗号 / 325
  39b 用逗号把大多数引入成分与主句分开 / 326
  39c 用一个或多个逗号把非重要的成分与主句隔开 / 328
  39d 在一系列项目之间使用逗号 / 332
  39e 在平等修饰同一个词的多个形容词之间用逗号 / 332
  39f 在日期、地址、地名和长数字上用逗号 / 334
  39g 按照标准做法在引用语中使用逗号 / 335
  39h 删掉不需要的逗号 / 336

第40章 分号 ··· 339
  40a 在不由and, but或其他并列连词连接的主句之间使用分号 / 339
  40b 在由however, for example等连接的主句之间使用分号 / 340
  40c 在主句之间使用分号或者在一系列含逗号的项目之间使用分号 / 341
  40d 删除或替换无用的分号 / 342

第41章 冒号 ··· 343

41a 在结论性的解释、系列或同位语,以及一些引语之前使用冒号 / 343

41b 公文信件的致意之后,标题和副标题之间,以及时间的分隔之间,使用冒号 / 344

41c 删除或替换无用的冒号 / 344

第42章 撇号 ··· 346

42a 用撇号表示所有 / 347

42b 删除或取代复数名词、单数动词或人称代词所有格中误用的撇号 / 349

42c 使用撇号构成缩略形式 / 350

42d 缩略语、日期和词形本身的复数形式中,撇号可要可不要 / 351

第43章 引号 ··· 352

43a 用双引号括住直接引语 / 352

43b 用单引号括住引语里的引语 / 353

43c 是更大作品的一部分的作品的标题,前后要用引号 / 353

43d 引号可用来括住用在特殊意义上的词语 / 354

43e 删除不需要的引号 / 354

43f 按照标准做法把其他标点放在引号之内或之外 / 354

第44章 其他标点 ··· 356

44a 用一个或多个破折号表示转换以及把一些句子成分隔开 / 356

44b 用括号把句中的插入性短语和列表标记括起来 / 358

44c 用省略号表示引文中的省略 / 358

44d 用方括号表示引文的改动 / 361

44e 在多个选择之间、诗歌各行之间,用斜线 / 362

第六部分 拼写和文字处理细节 363

第45章 拼写 365
45a 对典型拼写错误要有所预期 / 365
45b 遵循拼写规则 / 368

第46章 连字符 371
46a 在某些复合词中使用连字符 / 371
46b 使用连字符断开行末的单词 / 372

第47章 大写字母 373
47a 每句话的第一个字母要大写 / 373
47b 专有名词、专有形容词和用作专有名词的重要部分的词，要首字母大写 / 374
47c 标题和副标题中的大部分词都要首字母大写 / 376
47d 网络通信中，按惯例使用大写 / 376

第48章 斜体或下画线 377
48a 单独出现的作品标题 / 378
48b 船只、飞机、航天器和火车的名字，用斜体或下画线 / 379
48c 不是英语的一部分的外语词，用斜体或下画线 / 379
48d 当作字符用的词或字母，用斜体或下画线标记 / 379
48e 偶尔也用斜体或下画线表示强调 / 380
48f 在网络通信中，用其他做法替代斜体或下画线 / 380

第49章 缩略语 381
49a 大多数写作中，可以接受常见的缩略语和首字母 / 382
49b 通常把度量单位、地名、日历名称、人名和课程完全拼写出来 / 382
49c 通常拉丁缩略语只用在引文出处和括号内的解释中 / 382
49d 在紧挨专有名词之前及之后的头衔中使用标准缩略语 / 383
49e 只有在特定日期和数字之前或之后才使用BC, BCE, AD, CE, AM, PM, no.及$ / 383
49f 只在公司的官方名称中才使用Inc., Bros., Co.或&(and) / 383

第50章 数字 384
50a 按你所在领域的标准用法使用数字 / 385

50b 对于日期、地址和其他信息，按照惯例来使用数字 / 386

50c 把句首的数拼写出来 / 386

第七部分 研究和文献记录 389

第51章 研究策略 ………………………………………… 391

51a 规划研究过程 / 391

51b 撰写研究日记 / 392

51c 寻找可研究的主题和问题 / 392

51d 设定关于原始资料的目标 / 394

51e 记录带有注释的参考目录 / 396

第52章 寻找原始资料 ………………………………………… 399

52a 从图书馆网址入手 / 399

52b 规划电子搜索 / 400

52c 查阅参考作品 / 403

52d 查阅书籍 / 403

52e 查阅期刊 / 404

52f 搜索网络 / 408

52g 查找社交媒体 / 411

52h 查阅政府出版物 / 412

52i 查找图像、音频和视频资料 / 413

52j 形成自己的原始资料 / 415

第53章 处理原始资料 ………………………………………… 417

53a 评估原始资料 / 417

53b 合成原始资料 / 429

53c 从原始资料中收集信息 / 431

53d 总结、改述和引用 / 432

53e 将原始资料融入文章中 / 439

第54章 抄袭的避免和原始资料的引用 ………………………… 445

54a 避免有意和无意的抄袭 / 446

54b 了解不需要标明出处的材料 / 448

54c 了解必须标明出处的材料 / 448

　　　　54d 发表作品时获得许可 / 451

　　　　54e 认真标注原始资料来源 / 452

第55章 撰写论文 454

　　　　55a 整理并组织论文 / 454

　　　　55b 草稿、修改、校订和论文格式 / 456

第56章 MLA原始资料来源的标注与格式 457

　　　　56a 在文章中使用MLA文内引文注释 / 458

　　　　56b 准备MLA格式的参考目录 / 466

　　　　56c 用MLA格式撰写论文 / 503

　　　　56d 用MLA格式写成的论文范例 / 505

第57章 APA原始资料来源的标注与格式 516

　　　　57a 在文章中使用APA文内引文注释 / 517

　　　　57b 准备APA格式的参考目录 / 520

　　　　57c 用APA格式撰写论文 / 535

　　　　57d APA格式的论文范例 / 538

词语用法汇编 / 543

带星号练习题答案 / 558

索引 / 573

　　CULTURE LANGUAGE 语言文化提示 / 613

第一部分
写作过程

第1章 · 写作情境

第2章 · 创作

第3章 · 主题和组织

第4章 · 打草稿

第5章 · 修改

第6章 · 校订、定格式和校对

第7章 · 段落

第8章 · 提交终稿

第 1 章　写作情境

概要

开始写作任务时，需要响应写作情境：
- 分析情境（下方）
- 选择适合任务的题材（p. 4）
- 确定写作目的（p. 6）
- 考虑读者对象（p. 7）
- 了解体裁（p. 9）

响应写作情境通常是写作过程的第一步——写作过程包括从动笔到最后完成作品所进行的全部脑力和体力活动。写作过程因人而异：没有两个写作者写作方式完全相同，即便是一个独立的个体写作者也会以他或她自己独特的方式完成手头的写作任务。不过，更多的写作者会经历几个重复循环的阶段：先明确写作情境（本章），继而创作和布局谋篇（第2章和第3章），然后打草稿、修改和编辑（第4—6章）。当你完成了各种写作任务，并尝试过本书中介绍的许多技巧之后，你就会形成自己的写作步骤。

1a 分析写作情境

你为别人进行的任何写作活动都处在这样一个写作情境之下，它既限制了你的选择，又使你的选择变得明晰。你在一个特定的环境下，就一个特定的题材，为一个具体的原因，与一个特定的读者群进行交流。这也许要求你以一种特定的体裁写作。你也许需要进行调查研究。你或许会遇到篇幅长度和截稿日期的要求。而且，你也许需要以某种格式和方法提交你的文章。

在写作任务初始阶段就分析写作情境对你如何进行写作大有裨益。（讨论下列要素时参考所列页码）

任务（pp. 4-5）
- 基本要求是什么？需要对题材、目的、读者、体裁和所做研究的要求加以考虑。你有什么发挥余地？
- 你还有什么其他必须满足的要求？文章写多长？何时交稿？任务是否明确或允许以什么格式提交——打印版，网页，还是口头演讲？

3   题材（pp. 4-6）
- 你的写作任务要求你写些什么？如果没有具体任务，你想写些什么？
- 题材哪些方面使你感兴趣？你在哪些方面已经有了想法或者想了解更多？

目的（pp. 6-7）
- 你的任务指定的目的是什么？例如，是否要求你解释什么或围绕某观点进行辩论？
- 你为什么要写作？你想要你的文章达到什么目的？你想要你的文章对读者产生什么样的影响？
- 你如何最大限度地达到你的目的？

读者（pp. 7-9）
- 你文章的读者是谁？
- 对你的题材，读者已经了解些什么，看法是什么？你具备什么能影响读者的特质，比如，教育背景、专业经历或者政治观点，使得读者能接受你的文章？
- 你在文章中如何表现自己？在与读者的关系上，你应该扮演什么角色？应该提供什么信息？你的文章应该有多正式或多随意？
- 读者读完你的文章后，你想让他们做什么，想什么？

体裁（pp. 9-10）
- 写作任务要求用什么体裁或写作形式？你要写的是一篇分析文章、一个报告，还是一份提案，或是某种别的形式？或者，你是否可以随意选择写作的体裁？
- 你所用体裁的传统写作方法是什么？例如，读者也许期待的是附有证据的宣言，对既定问题的解决方案，清晰的说明或容易找到的信息。

调研（pp. 370-434）
- 什么样的证据最大限度地契合你的题材、目的、读者以及体裁？什么样的事实、事例以及专家观点组合起来能支持你的论点？
- 你的写作任务需要调研吗？你需要查阅信息来源或以采访、调查、实验等形式进行其他调研吗？
- 即使不需要调研，你还需要什么其他信息来扩展你的题材？你将如何得到这些信息？

- 你应该使用什么形式来引用你的来源？（学术界注明参考资料来源，见 pp. 432–434）

展示
- 写作任务明示或暗示了什么格式或展示方法？（学术写作见 pp. 63–76，商务和其他大众写作见 pp. 135–142）
- 你如何使用标题、列表、插图、视频以及其他元素来达到你的目的？（见 pp. 66–75）

> **练习 1.1　分析写作情境**
>
> 下方是心理学概论课程的作业。就写作情境要素而言，该作业明示或暗示了什么？如果要你完成这个作业，你如何回答以上问题？
>
> When is psychotherapy most likely to work? That is, what combinations of client, therapist, and theory tend to achieve good results? In your discussion, cite studies supporting your conclusions. Length: 1500 to 1800 words. Post your paper online to me and your discussion group by March 30.

1b 选择适合任务的题材

一个写作题材具有几个基本要求：
- 题材应该契合目的、读者以及任务体裁。
- 考虑到指定的截稿日期和篇幅长度，题材应该既不太宽泛，也不太局限。
- 题材应该是你愿意进一步了解的，甚至是你所关心的。

1 ▪ 响应特定任务写作

当你收到一项写作任务时，要研究它的措辞及写作情境的启示，以便指导你题材的选择：

- **要你做什么？** 许多写作任务包含这样的字眼，如**讨论**、**描述**、**分析**、**报告**、**阐释**、**解释**、**定义**、**议论**或**评价**。这些字眼详细表明了你着手处理题材的方法、你应具有什么样的想法以及你的一般目的。（见 pp. 6–7）
- **写给谁看？** 许多任务会明确让你知道读者是谁，但有时你不得不自己判定读者是什么人，以及他们想从你这里得到什么。（见 pp. 7–9，获得更多关于分析读者方面的信息）
- **需要做什么样的研究？** 写作任务会标明你应该查阅的资料，你可以用此类信息选择题材。（如果你不确定是否需要调研，和你导师商量）

- **题材需要凝缩吗？** 为了在规定的篇幅和时间内把题材论述清楚，你经常需要控制题材范围。（见下方）

2 ■ 凝缩一般性题材

回答以上关于写作任务的问题有助于为选定题材设限。这样你就可以挖掘你自己的兴趣点和亲身经历，缩小题材范围，以便在有限的空间和时间里充分展开论述。面向大学生的联邦援助可以成为一本书的题材；可以得到什么样的援助或者说为何政府应该增加援助等，都可以成为更合适的题材，写上四页纸，一周内提交。

凝缩题材的一个有效手段是围绕题材，集中问问题，找出适合写作任务的题材，并确保该题材在写作过程中自始至终能抓住你的兴趣。下方的例子表明，如何通过问问题，将宽泛的题材凝缩成具体、可控的题材：

宽泛题材	具体题材
Social-networking sites	What draws people to these sites?
	How do the sites alter the ways people interact?
	What privacy protections should the sites provide for users?
Mrs. Mallard in Kate Chopin's "The Story of an Hour"	What changes does Mrs. Mallard undergo?
	Why does Mrs. Mallard respond as she does to news of her husband's death?
	What does the story's irony contribute to the character of Mrs. Mallard?
Lincoln's weaknesses as President	What was Lincoln's most significant error as commander-in-chief of the Union army?
	Why did Lincoln delay emancipating the slaves?
	Why did Lincoln have difficulties controlling his cabinet?

根据以下指导，凝缩宽泛题材：
- 围绕宽泛题材，你能想到多少问题，就问多少问题。列出一份清单。
- 对每一个引起你兴趣的和适合写作任务的问题，粗略地概括出主要观点。考虑一下你需要多少段落，或者需要多少具体事实、事例以及其他细节来把以上观点锁定。这个想法会使你大概知晓你的工作量是多少，以及你终稿的篇幅有多长。
- 把过于宽泛的问题进一步切分，重复以前的步骤。

因特网也可以帮助你控制一般性题材。浏览类似INFOMINE（infomine.ucr.edu）这样的目录，搜索不断变窄的目录，以便找到适当圈定了范围的话题。

> **练习1.2　凝缩题材**
>
> 在以下宽泛题材中选出三个题材，然后使用上文的指导，将每一个题材凝缩成至少一个具体问题，该问题可用三四页纸来回答。
>
> 1. Use of cell phones
> 2. Training of teachers
> 3. Dance in America
> 4. The history of women's suffrage
> 5. Food additives
> 6. Immigrants in the United States
> 7. Space exploration
> 8. African Americans and civil rights
> 9. Child abuse
> 10. Successes in cancer research
> 11. Reality TV shows
> 12. Women writers
> 13. Campaign finance reform
> 14. Genetic engineering
> 15. Trends in popular music

1c 确定写作目的

写作**目的**是你就题材与特定读者群沟通的主要理由。你的大部分作品具有以下四个主要目的之一：
- 为读者提供娱乐。
- 表达你的情感和观点。
- 向读者做阐释（说明）。
- 说服读者接受或者按照你的意见去做（议论）。

这些目的在一篇文章里经常重叠，但通常主要目的只有一个。而且，这个主要目的会影响你对题材的看法，影响你选择的细节，甚至措辞。

许多写作任务用一个词语凝缩写作目的，如下所示：
- **报告**：调查、组织，并客观呈现题材中可获得的证据。
- **概括**：简明陈述在课文、论述文、理论及其他文本中的主要论点。
- **讨论**：仔细检查题材中的主要论点、对立的观点或启示。
- **比较和对比**：解释两个议题之间的相同点和不同点。（见p. 57）

- **下定义**：阐明一个术语或概念的意思，其与众不同的特性、界线等。（见 pp. 55–56）
- **分析**：找出题材元素，并讨论这些元素是如何布局成篇的。（见 pp. 58–59，及 p. 92）
- **阐释**：推断题材的意思和含义。
- **评价**：判断题材的质量和意义，兼顾正、反两方面。（见 pp. 93–94）
- **论述**：在文章中选定立场，然后用证据支持你的立场。（见 pp. 111–125）

你也可以以这种方式更具体地设想你的目的，即体现你的特定题材，达到你想要的结果：

To explain the steps in a new office procedure so that staffers will be able to follow it without difficulty.

To analyze how Annie Dillard's "Total Eclipse" builds to its climax so that readers appreciate the author's skill.

To persuade readers to support the college administration's plan for more required courses.

To argue against additional regulation of handguns so that readers will perceive the potential disadvantages for themselves and for the nation as a whole.

1d 考虑读者对象

在写作任务中，有可能看到你文章的读者，即你的读者对象，常常是明确的或隐含的。当你为学生刊物写社论时，你的读者对象就是你的同学。当你在文学课上分析诗歌时，你的读者对象就是你的老师，也许还有你的同学。p. 8 的方框内罗列了一些问题，这些问题有助于你在更多的写作情境下确定读者对象。

具有读者对象意识将影响你写作的三个主要方面：

- **用来吸引和保持读者注意力、引导读者接受你的结论的特定信息。** 这个信息也许包含细节、事实、事例以及其他证据，以上种种使得你观点清晰，为你的主张提供支持，并使读者需求得到满足。
- **在与读者的交互中你选择扮演的角色。** 鉴于你的目的，你会希望读者以某种方式感知你的存在。可能扮演的角色很多，而且各式各样——比如，学者、讲故事的人、演讲者、向导、记者、倡议者、激励者等。
- **使用的语气。** 写作中的语气是通过词和句子结构传递出的一种态度。鉴于你的目标以及你认为读者的期待和反应，你的语气既可以正式，也可以随意。你传递给读者的态度可以严肃或轻松，强烈或镇定，恼怒或愉快。

有关读者对象的问题

身份和期望
- 我的读者是谁？
- 我的读者从我的写作体裁中期待什么？他们期待类似特殊结构和格式的特征、与众不同的证据，还是某种形式的参考资料来源注明？
- 读者读完我的作品后，我想要他们了解什么或做什么？我该如何让他们明白这一点？
- 我应该让读者如何解读我？他们希望我的体裁有多正式或者多随意？我的角色和语气如何确定？

特征、知识和态度
- 读者什么样的特征与我的题材和目的相关？例如：
  年龄和性别
  职业：学生、专业同行等
  社会或经济角色：汽车购买者、未来雇主等
  经济或教育背景
  种族背景
  政治、宗教或道德信仰及价值观
  爱好或活动
- 读者特征如何影响他们对我的题材的态度？
- 读者对我的话题已经知道或不知道什么？我必须告诉他们多少？我题材的什么方面会引起他们的兴趣以及与他们相关？
- 我应该如何处理那些专业术语？读者知道这些术语吗？如果不知道，我是否应该解释这些术语？
- 什么样的观点、争论或者信息可能会使读者震惊、激动或者冒犯到他们？我应该如何处理这些难点？
- 读者对我的题材或者说我，可能会有什么错误概念？我如何消除这些错误概念？

用途和格式
- 读者拿我的文章用来做什么？我是否应该指望他们从头逐字阅读，浏览信息，或者寻找结论？我是否可以给读者提供概要、标题、插图或者其他帮助，以便帮助他们理解？（见pp. 63–75，提交终稿）

信息、角色以及语气构成作者的语调：你自己在你文章中的投影。你的语调传达了你对这个世界的感知，这种感知在特定的写作情境中得到了应用：这个题材、这个目的、这个读者群。因此，语调在不同写作情境之中发生变化，正如下方留言所示。这两份留言有着相同的主题和同样的目的，但是对话的读者群体不同。

第一部分　写作过程

写给同事

Ever notice how much paper collects in your trash basket every day? Well, most of it can be recycled with little effort, I promise. Basically, all you need to do is set a bag or box near your desk and deposit wastepaper in it. I know, space is cramped in these little cubicles. But what's a little more crowding when the earth's at stake? . . .

声音：	体贴、开朗、富有同情心的同行
信息：	员工如何处理回收；没有提到成本
角色：	同事
语气：	非正式的、个人的（Ever notice；Well；you；I know，space is cramped）

写给管理部门

In my four months here, I have observed that all of us throw out baskets of potentially recyclable paper every day. Considering the drain on our forest resources and the pressure on landfills that paper causes, we could make a valuable contribution to the environmental movement by helping to recycle the paper we use. At the company where I worked before, the employees separate clean wastepaper from other trash at their desks. The maintenance staff collects trash in two receptacles, and the trash hauler (the same one we use here) makes separate pickups. I do not know what the hauler charges for handling recyclable material. . . .

声音：	有思想、有责任感、认真的下属
信息：	具体原因；对公司整体的看法；提及另一家公司；成本问题
角色：	员工
语气：	正式、严肃（Considering the drain；forest resources；valuable contribution；没有you）

CULTURE LANGUAGE 如果英语不是你的母语，那么在写作时，你也许不习惯于向读者发出呼吁。例如，在一些文化当中，读者也许不加质疑就接受作者的观点。那么当你用英语写作时，一定要努力以这种姿态迎接读者，即用词准确、立场公正、幽默风趣以及语言清晰。

1e 了解体裁

写作者使用熟悉的体裁，或者说写作形式，用以表达自己的思想。你可以识别出许多体裁：诗歌和文学小说，商务写作中的简历，还有体育赛事的新闻报道等。大学会要求你用各种不同的体裁写作，比如，分析性文章、实验室报告、评论、提案、口头演讲，甚至博客帖子。

简言之，体裁就是在一定的语境下，写作所采取的一种惯用形式。在学术写作中，体裁惯用形式有助于实现专业领域的目标；例如，一份化学实验室报告呈现的特性阐明了科学研究中的步骤、结果及结论。此外，这些惯用形式还有助于促进写作者和读者之间的沟通，因为写作者清楚读者的需求，而且读者也能预知他们将在文章中读到什么方面的内容。

当你接受写作任务时，确定你熟知与体裁有关的所有要求：

- **写作任务是否指定了特定的体裁？** 需要你完成的写作任务，比如分析、议论或报告等，已经明确了你需要使用的体裁。
- **该体裁的惯用形式是什么？** 你的导师或教科书也许会把要求为你罗列出来。你也可以通过阅读该体裁样例的方法了解该体裁的要求。请查看本手册p. 102列出的样例范文。
- **你具有哪些灵活发挥的空间？** 在惯用形式范围内，大多数体裁仍然为你选取的角度和语调留有大量发挥空间。同样，通读范文对你的选择性发挥大有裨益。

第 2 章　创作

概要

为构思成文，可使用以下一个或多个创作技巧：

- 记写作日记（p. 11）
- 观察周围环境（p. 12）
- 自由写作或头脑风暴（pp. 12–13）
- 组织观点（p. 14）
- 提问（p. 15）

写作者使用上方列出的技巧为自己的写作主题进行创作或发现思路和信息。**无论你使用哪种创作技巧，都要落实在书面，而不是只停留在脑子里。** 这样，这些思路就变得一目了然，而且亲自动笔写作本身将给你带来全新的见解。

CULTURE LANGUAGE　这里提倡的发现过程对快速写作非常有益，你不必事先绞尽脑汁去想写什么内容以及如何写。如果你的母语不是标准美式英语，你不妨最初用母语或方言做这种探索性写作，然后把有用的材料译成标准美式英语供起草使用。这样的过程很有效，但是需要做额外的工作。你可以在初始阶段这样做，然后逐渐过渡到用标准美式英语完成写作全过程。

2a 记写作日记

写作日记是指将自己的想法记录在纸上或电脑上。它给你提供了一个地方，记录你的反应和思想，并记录你对自己所见、所闻、所涉猎或所经历的观察。它也可以为写作提供思路。由于你是写给自己看的，因此可以在没有"无处不在的"读者的压力的情况下产生创作灵感，这些"无处不在的"读者总是对你的逻辑性，或组织能力，或者正确性做出评价。如果你每天如此，即便只写几分钟，这个习惯将会提升你的写作能力，增强写作信心。

写作日记用途很广：吐露情感，探究内心世界对电影和其他传播媒介的感想，练习某种写作形式（如诗歌或新闻报道），从课程里探寻思路，或者对所阅读物进行批判性思考。一个叫作Katy Moreno的学生的写作日记就是出于最后一个目的。她的写作导师布置了这样一个题目："毕竟世界是平的"（"It's a Flat World, after All"），这是Thomas L. Friedman关于全球化和就业市场的一篇文章。导师布置了下面的作业，要求写读后感：

> In "It's a Flat World, after All," Thomas L. Friedman describes today's global job market, focusing not on manufacturing jobs that have been "outsourced" to overseas workers but on jobs that require a college degree and are no longer immune to outsourcing. Friedman argues that keeping jobs in the United States requires that US students, parents, and educators improve math and science education. As a college student, how do you respond to this analysis of the global market for jobs? What do you think today's college students should be learning?

读第一遍，Moreno认为该文章令人信服，因为Friedman对就业市场的描述跟她家庭的实际情况相符：她母亲就因为工作被外包给了印度而失了业。然而，读了第二遍之后，Moreno便不再相信加强数学和科学学科的教育就一定能增加就业机会，并给未来就业打包票。她把Friedman的建议和她从母亲的经历中回想起的细节进行了对比后，在写作日记中回应道：

12　　Friedman is certainly right that more jobs than we realize are going overseas—

that's what happened to Mom's job and we were shocked! But he gives only one way for students like me to compete—take more math and science. At first I thought he's totally right. But then I thought that what he said didn't really explain what happened to Mom—she had lots of math + science + tons of experience, but it was her salary, not better training, that caused her job to be outsourced. An overseas worker would do her job for less money. So she lost her job because of money + because she wasn't a manager. Caught in the middle. I want to major in computer science, but I don't think it's smart to try for the kind of job Mom had—at least not as long as it's so much cheaper for companies to hire workers overseas.

（更多Moreno的写作范文将在接下来的四章中出现）

CULTURE LANGUAGE 记写作日记对母语不是标准美式英语的人尤其有帮助。你可以通过练习写作，提高流畅程度，探索句型和词的运用。同样重要的是，你可以试着把自己从语言实践中领会的内容应用到阅读和观察中。

2b 观察周围环境

有时可以通过观察周围，找到好的题材，或者就一个题材收集信息，这种观察不是指我们大多数人在日常生活中东奔西走时的那种心不在焉，而是有意为之的、全神贯注的那种观察。比如，在公交车上，是否有一些特定类型的乘客？公交司机又在想什么呢？为尽可能从观察中受益，要随身带笔记本、笔或者其他工具，便于随时做笔记和写随笔。回到书桌旁以后，要研究这些笔记和随笔，以便写下奇闻逸事，或者将一些模式留存下来，待以后进一步探索。

2c 自由写作

1 ▪ 写到一个题材上去

许多作家通过**自由写作**找到题材或产生观点，即不停地写，达到一定的时间（比如十分钟），或者达到一定的长度（比如一页）。自由写作的目的，是通过搜寻大脑中那块不想写或者想不出到底写些什么的区域，从内心深处产生想法和信息。要让文字本身激发出其他更多的文字。写什么并不重要，重要的是坚持写。不要停下来，尽管那意味着在新的内容到来之前，一直在重复写着同样的内容。不要回去重读，不要审查那些看似跑题或重复的观点，尤其是不要停下来做任何修正：语法、标点、拼写等在这个阶段都无关紧要。

如果你可以把电脑显示器调暗或者关掉，那你在自由写作时就可以尝试**隐形书写**，以便不停地写下去。当你面对黑屏打字的时候，电脑会将你打字的内容记录下来，但又使你无法看到，因此阻止了你去修改。隐形书写最初会令你感到不舒服，但它可以让你放飞思绪，产生非常有创意的结果。

(CULTURE LANGUAGE) 如果你对用标准美式英语写作很不自在，而且你往往担心在写作中出错，那么隐形书写就非常有帮助：空白电脑显示屏使得你别无选择，只能探索思路，不会再考虑表达。如果你决定开着显示屏写作，那就把精力放在你想说什么，而不是怎样说。

2 ▪ 有主题的自由写作

有主题的自由写作的过程更集中：从对议题提出的问题入手，不间断地回答这个问题，比如连续进行十五分钟或写满一页纸。在所有自由写作中，你奋力绕开构思障碍和自我意识，不考虑说什么或者校正已写完的内容。在有主题的自由写作过程中，写作这个体力活动带你进入并融入主题之中了。

关于有主题的自由写作的范例可以在 Katy Moreno 的写作日记中找到，这是她为 Thomas L. Friedman 的文章 "It's a Flat World, after All" 写的读后感，登在前面。由于她对 Friedman 的文章已经形成了自己的观点，因此 Moreno 就可以做到胸有成竹，并对自己的观点加以扩充。

2d 头脑风暴

类似于自由写作的一个方法是头脑风暴——全部精力集中在一个主题上，时间固定（比如十五分钟），使自己奋力列出每一个出现在脑海里的想法和细节。像自由写作一样，头脑风暴也需要你关掉内心的编辑器，这样你的思路就能保持连续不中断。（上方描述的在电脑上隐形书写的技巧可以帮助你不中断地写下去）

以下是头脑风暴的范例，是一个叫 Johanna Abrams 的学生写的，主题是关于暑期打工能教会我们什么：

summer work teaches—
    how to look busy while doing nothing
    how to avoid the sun in summer
    seriously: discipline, budgeting money, value of money

which job? Burger King cashier? baby-sitter? mail-room clerk?
mail room: how to sort mail into boxes: this is learning??
how to survive getting fired—humiliation, outrage
Mrs. King! the mail-room queen as learning experience
the shock of getting fired: what to tell parents, friends?
Mrs. K was so rigid—dumb procedures
initials instead of names on the mail boxes—confusion!
Mrs. K's anger, resentment: the disadvantages of being smarter than your boss
the odd thing about office work: a world with its own rules for how to act
the pecking order—big chick (Mrs. K) pecks on little chick (me)
a job can beat you down—make you be mean to other people

2e 组织观点

许多写作者通过使用**聚类法**或**画构想图**找到观点。正如自由写作和头脑风暴，该技巧将自由联想以及快速产生的、未经编辑修订的思路框架聚集成图，但同时又着重于观点之间的关系。从主题开始，并从一个中心点向外辐射。一个观点出现时，用树状结构寻求相关观点，直到穷尽。然后对其他观点同样处置，对链接保持开放，不停地通过分枝或画箭头建立联系。下面的范例展示一名学生是如何运用聚类法探索作为掩饰手段的写作的：

» 聚类或构想图

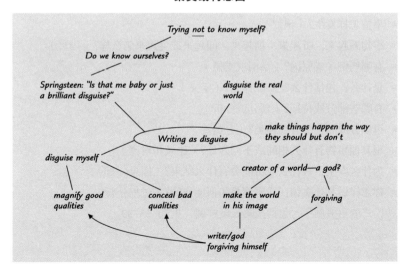

可使用构想图软件画这种图表。该软件允许你将观点直接键入类似图表中，然后重新排列、删除，并在写作过程中的任何节点添加新的观点。

2f 提问

对主题进行提问并写出答案可以帮助你客观地看待这个话题，并可发现新的可能性。

1 ▪ 使用记者式问题

记者为写新闻报道，会提出一系列问题：

- 谁牵涉其中？
- 发生了什么，有什么结果？
- 何时发生？
- 在哪里发生？
- 为何发生？
- 怎样发生？

这些问题对探究文章主题同样有用，特别是叙述故事或调查因果关系时。

2 ▪ 模式问题

我们通过模式思考和理解各式各样的主题，这些模式包括记叙、分类及比较和对比。基于模式的提问可以帮助你从许多角度审视你的话题。有时，你可能仅想用一种模式展开全文。

- 事情怎样发生？（记叙）
- 事物看起来、听起来、摸起来、闻起来或尝起来怎么样？（描写）
- 有哪些例子或原因？（举例或支持）
- 是什么？包括什么？排除什么？（定义）
- 有哪些部分或特征？（划分或分析）
- 可以分成哪些部分或种类？（分类）
- 跟其他事物有什么相同或不同之处？（比较和对比）
- 为什么发生？有什么或可能会有什么结果？（因果分析）
- 你怎样做某件事情，或事情是如何运作的？（过程分析）

这些模式的更多例子，包括段落长度样例，见 pp. 53–59。

第 3 章　主题和组织

概要

形成观点需要：
- 写出主题句（下方）
- 组织观点（p. 20）

通过以上两个主要写作步骤你就会形成大致的观点。找到主题或主旨大意，这会给你提供重心和方向。组织初始写作素材有助于你澄清不相干的观点、发现可能出现的不一致，使主题鲜明突出。

3a　写出主题句

读者希望文章紧扣一个主旨或**主题**。在终稿时，往往可通过一个**主题句**把这个主题表示出来，通常在引言的末尾。可以想出一个主题句，这样既公示了文章的主题，又向读者承诺主题以何种方式展开。文章接下来就会完成公示、兑现承诺。

1 ▪ 主题句的功能

如以下方框所示，主题句具有四个主要功能和一个次要功能。

主题句

- 把你的主题限定为一个单一的中心思想，这恰是你想要读者从文中得到的。
- 给你的主题下一个明确、有意义的断言，这个断言需要得到支持。
- 传达你的意图，你写作的原因。
- 给文章定基调，表明你对主题的态度以及你在读者面前担任的角色。
- 常常简明扼要地安排论点，因此也可有助于你组织文章。

（CULTURE LANGUAGE）在一些文化中，写作者对自己的观点或中心思想直言不讳，会被看作没有必要或缺乏礼貌。但出于学业或工作的目的用美式英语写作时，你可以假定读者希望在文章开头部分看到明确的主题思想。你这样做不会被认为是粗鲁。

2 ▪ 评价主题句

在写作过程的初始阶段，你最后的主题句可能还没有在你头脑中闪现。开始时你可能只想传达某种观点，但你需要对那个观点加以精练，以符合所写文章的现实。你常常不得不写了又写，直到得出结论为止。

尽管可能会有变化，但你对主题的感觉会在写作过程中给你指明方向。试着草拟一个暂定的主题句，或者构想出一个带有引领作用的**主题问句**。当你努力凝缩你的主题时（p. 5），这个问句就会出现，而且当你论述观点时，这个问句就会变得更清晰。最终你就可以用主题句来回答这个问句。

下方就是问句和回答性主题句的样例。作为断言，每个主题句包含一个话题（通常称为一般性主题）和关于话题的断言。**注意**：每一个主题句是如何同时又表达了目的的。主题句1—3是**解释性**的：写作者主要向读者做解释，比如服兵役的好处。主题句4—6是**议论性**的：写作者主要想要读者相信某事，比如立法禁止司机使用手机的必要性。你在大学论文里写的大部分主题句，不是解释性的就是议论性的。

主题问句	解释性主题句
1. What are the advantages of serving in the US military?	Military service teaches teamwork, discipline, and job-related skills that transfer well to civilian life. [主题：military service。声称：teaches skills that transfer to civilian life。]
2. What steps can prevent juvenile crime?	Juveniles can be diverted from crime by active learning programs, full-time sports, and intervention by mentors and role models. [主题：juvenile crime。声称：can be prevented in three ways。]
3. Why did Abraham Lincoln delay emancipating the slaves?	Lincoln delayed emancipating any slaves until 1863 because his primary goal was to restore and preserve the Union, with or without slavery. [主题：Lincoln's delay。声称：was caused by his goal of preserving the Union。]

主题问句	议论性主题句
4. Why should drivers' use of cell phones be banned?	Drivers' use of cell phones should be outlawed because people who talk and drive at the same time cause accidents. [主题：drivers' use of cell phones。声称：should be outlawed because it causes accidents。]
5. Which college students should be entitled to federal aid?	As an investment in its own economy, the federal government should provide a tuition grant to any college student who qualifies academically. [主题：federal aid。声称：should be provided to any college student who qualifies academically。]
6. Should the state government play a role in moving consumers to hybrid cars?	Each proposal for the state to encourage purchase of hybrid cars—advertising campaigns, trade-in deals, and tax incentives—needlessly involves government in decisions that consumers are already making on their own. [主题：proposals to encourage hybrid cars。声称：needlessly involve government in consumer decisions。]

注意主题句1、2和6清楚地预示出接下来文章的组织结构。

3 ▪ 修改主题句

在主题句最后确定下来之前，问以下几个问题。

- 主题句对主题是否下了一个简洁的断言？即，它是否表明了一种观点？

  原句：Toni Morrison won the Nobel Prize in Literature in 1993.

  原句表明的是一个事实，而不是一种关于Morrison作品的观点。下面的修改句则是一个断言，表明了获奖的意义：

  修改：Toni Morrison's 1993 Nobel Prize in Literature, the first awarded to an African American woman, affirms both the strength of her vivid prose style and the importance of her subject matter.

- 这个断言是否被限定成一个单一的具体观点？

  原句：Diets are dangerous.

原句太过宽泛以至于看起来无法忍受。修改句限定了饮食种类以及功效：

修改：Fad diets can be dangerous when they deprive the body of essential nutrients or rely on excessive quantities of potentially harmful foods.

下方原句仍过于宽泛，而修改句则明确指出了它们的不同和意义：

原句：Televised sports are different from live sports.

修改：Although television cannot transmit all the excitement of being in a crowd during a game, its close-ups and slow-motion replays reveal much about the players and the strategy of the game.

- 主题句是否一致以至于句子各成分之间明显相互关联？

原句：Cell phones can be convenient, but they can also be dangerous.

由于两个事实被but连接，原句朝两个方向走，而不是一个。修改句明确了各分句和它们的意义之间的关系：

修改：The convenience of cell phones does not justify the risks of driving while talking or texting.

- 主题句是否至少隐含了你的目的？

原句：Educators' motives for using the Internet vary widely.

原句没有携带写作者探索主题的原因的暗示。相比之下，修改句暗示了这样一个目的，即反对因利益驱动将因特网用于教育。

修改：Too often, educators' uses of the Internet seem motivated less by teaching and learning than by saving money.

- 主题句是否传递出你的基调？

原句：Television viewing can reduce loneliness, cause laughter, and teach children.

原句缺少基调感。修改句表明了写作者对主题的态度以及在读者面前担任的角色：

修改：Despite its many faults, television has at least one strong virtue: it can ease loneliness, spark healthful laughter, and even educate young children by providing voices that supplement our own.

练习3.1　评价主题句

评价下方主题句，考虑一下是否每句都是被充分限定了的、具体的和一致的断言。如需要，重写主题句，以达到以上目的。

1. Aggression usually leads to violence, injury, and even death, and we should use it constructively.
2. The religion of Islam is widely misunderstood in the United States.
3. One evening of a radio talk show amply illustrates both the appeal of such shows and their silliness.
4. Good manners make our society work.
5. The poem is about motherhood.
6. I disliked American history in high school, but I like it in college.
7. Cell phones are useful for adults who have busy schedules, but they can be harmful for children.
8. Drunken drivers, whose perception and coordination are impaired, should receive mandatory suspensions of their licenses.
9. Business is a good major for many students.
10. The state's lenient divorce laws undermine the institution of marriage, which is fundamental to our culture, and they should certainly be made stricter for couples who have children.

3b 组织观点

多数文章都有一个基本模式：引言（申明主题）、正文（扩展主题）和结论（将文章所有观点汇集在一起）。引言和结论在pp. 60–63讨论。在正文内，每个段落都在扩展文章主题的一些方面。见pp. 41–42，Katy Moreno的文章，注释部分突出显示了正文对主题句的支持。

（CULTURE LANGUAGE）如果你不习惯阅读美国学术性文章，那么这种"引言、正文、结论"的模式以及这里讨论的组织策划对你来说也许很不熟悉。例如，你也许习惯于那种能和读者建立起个人关系的开头，而不是那种迅速将重心移到话题和主题上的引言。你也许习惯于不带支持的一般性陈述（因为写作者会假定读者自己提供证据），或者习惯于不带解释的证据（因为写作者假定读者能推断出一般的观点），而不是那些先强调一般性观点，然后再用具体证据支持这些观点的正文段落。撰写美国学术性文章时，你需要考虑读者的期待，他们希望直截了当的表述以及对一般性观点的陈述和支持。

1 ▪ 一般和特殊

为一篇文章组织材料，需要区分一般和特殊观点，并看清观点之间的关系。**一般**和**特殊**是指包含在一组里的几个例子或对象，这个组由一个词来表明。下方的"阶梯"按从一般到特殊的顺序给出。

最一般

▲ life form
　plant
　flowering plant
　rose
▼ Uncle Dan's prize-winning American Beauty rose

最特殊

组织材料时，找出一般性观点，然后找出支持一般观点的特殊观点。把与中心论点无关的观点放到一边。在电脑上，你可以很容易地试着对一般性观点和支持性信息进行各种安排整理：保存总清单，复制，然后使用剪切和粘贴功能移动材料内容。

2 ▪ 组织文章的方法

一篇文章的正文可以以许多读者熟悉的形式安排。选择哪种形式取决于主题、目的和读者。

- **空间**：在描述人、地点或东西时，按部就班地在空间中移动，从起点到其他特征，例如，从顶部到底部，由近到远，从左到右。
- **时间顺序**：依次列举一系列事件时，依照事件实际发生的时间从头到尾安排事件。
- **从一般到特殊**：先对主题进行全面探讨，然后加入细节、事实、例子以及其他支持。
- **从特殊到一般**：先提供支持，然后从中引出结论。
- **递进**：按照主题重要性递增或读者兴趣递增的顺序安排观点。
- **从问题到解决方案**：先列出需要解决的问题，然后提出解决方案。

你可将这些方法用于不同的写作形式，这些形式在本书第11–14章都已探讨。例如，论述文也许会采用"从问题到解决方案"的方法，加入一个关键元

素，即对可能出现的反对意见的回应。（见pp. 124–125）

3 ▪ 提纲

在起草文章之前，精心拟出一份详细的提纲并不重要；事实上，在起草阶段，过分详细的计划反而妨碍你去发现观点。然而，即使是一份草拟的计划也可以向你展示出一般观点和特殊观点的模式、显示比例，提醒涵盖范围内的漏洞和重叠部分。

提纲有若干种。有些提纲相较其他更灵活。

草稿提纲或非正式提纲

草稿提纲或非正式提纲包括关键的一般观点，并可显示具体证据。以下是Katy Moreno的主题句和关于全球就业市场的草稿提纲：

主题句

Friedman overlooks that technical training by itself can be too narrow to produce the communicators and problem solvers needed by contemporary businesses.

草稿提纲

Mom's outsourcing experience
  Excellent tech skills
  Salary too high compared to overseas tech workers
  Lack of planning + communication skills, unlike managers who kept jobs
Well-rounded education to protect vs. outsourcing
  Tech training, as Friedman says
  Also, communication, problem solving, other management skills

草稿提纲或非正式提纲可以是你开始打草稿的全部需要。当然，有时这个引导显得过于吝啬，你也许想将其扩展成一个更为详细的提纲。Katy Moreno用她的草稿提纲作为更详细的正式提纲（p.23）的基础，此举给了她更明确的方向感。

树形图

在树形图中，观点和细节按特殊性递增的顺序展开。与许多线性提纲不同的是，该图可以无尽地补充和扩展，因此很容易修改。从Johanna Abrams的关于暑期打工（pp. 13–14）的头脑风暴来看，她写出以下主题句，并画出下方树形图。

主题句

Two months working in a large agency taught me that an office's pecking order should be respected.

» 树形图

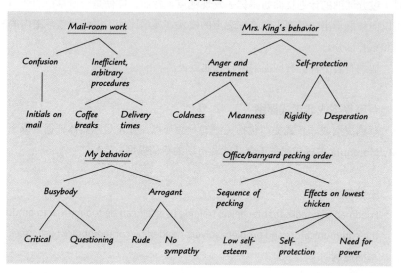

23　正式提纲

正式提纲不仅列出主要观点及其论据，也显示出文中所有要素的相对重要性。在上面Katy Moreno的草稿提纲的基础上，她为自己那篇关于全球就业市场的文章，准备了详细的正式提纲。

主题句

Friedman overlooks that technical training by itself can be too narrow to produce the communicators and problem solvers needed by contemporary businesses.

正式提纲

I. Summary of Friedman's article

　　A. Reasons for outsourcing

　　　　1. Improved technology and access

　　　　2. Well-educated workers

　　　　3. Productive workers

　　　　4. Lower wages

  B. Need for improved technical training in US

 II. Mother's experience

  A. Outsourcing of job

   1. Mother's education, experience, performance

   2. Employer's cost savings

  B. Retention of managers' jobs

   1. Planning skills

   2. Communication skills

 III. Conclusions about ideal education

  A. Needs of US businesses

   1. Technical skills

   2. Management skills

    a. Communication

    b. Problem solving

    c. Versatility

  B. Personal goals

   1. Technical training

   2. English and history courses for management skills

  这个范例列出了撰写提纲的几个原则，这些原则可确保提纲结构完整、详略得当、关系清晰：

- 提纲的所有部分都系统地缩进和标记：罗马数字（I, II）为主要分隔；缩进的大写字母（A, B）为次要分隔；进一步缩进的阿拉伯数字（1, 2）为支持性样例；小写字母（a, b）用于细节。
- 提纲把材料分成几组内容。一长串同类型的观点应该打散，按观点密切相关性重组。
- 同一概括等级的话题以平行标题出现，同样用缩进、编号或用字母表示。
- 所有再分的标题都至少分为两部分。从逻辑上说，一个话题不能只分为一部分。
- 所有标题都用平行的语法结构表达——比如，词组都用名词加修饰语组成。

  注意：上面，Katy Moreno 的提纲是**话题提纲**，标题就用词组表示。至于**句子提纲**的范例，标题都用完整句子表达，见 p. 487。

完整性和连贯性

有效写作的两个特质与组织有关：完整和连贯。当你感觉某人的文章"流畅"时，你正欣赏的就是这些特质。

为检验提纲或草稿的**完整性**，需要问这些问题：
- 每个主要部分都与全文的中心思想（主题）相关吗？
- 在主要部分中，是否每个例子或细节都支持那部分的主要观点？

为检验提纲或草稿的**连贯性**，需要问以下问题：
- 观点是否以清晰的顺序排列？
- 文章的各部分是不是很有逻辑地连接在一起？
- 连接是否清晰和顺畅？

以下文章说明了实现统一性和连贯性的一些方法（在边注中突出显示）。

Who Benefits from the Money in College Football?

确立文章主题的引言

Anyone who follows Division 1-A college football cannot fail to notice the money that pours into every aspect of the sport—the lavish stadiums, corporate sponsorships, televised games, and long post-season bowl series. The influx of money may seem to benefit the players, but in reality the institutions that promote college football, not the players, have gotten rich. College football is a multimillion-dollar industry not for the players but for the colleges and universities, conferences, and television networks.

主题句

段落中心句，与主题句相连接

Colleges and universities are major players in the for-profit football industry. A vibrant football program attracts not only skilled coaches and talented players but also wealthy, sports-minded donors who give money for state-of-the art stadiums and facilities. These great facilities in turn attract fans, some of whom are willing to pay high ticket prices to watch games in luxurious sky boxes and thus generate more profits for the schools' athletic departments.

围绕支持中心句的论据而展开的段落

段落中心句，与主题句相连接

The athletic conferences to which the schools belong—such as the Big Ten, the Atlantic Coast Conference, and the PAC-12—reap financial rewards from college football. Each conference maintains a Web site to post schedules and scores, sell tickets and merchandise, and promote interest in its teams. However, the proceeds from ticket and merchandise sales surely pale in comparison to the money generated by the annual Bowl Championship Series—the three-week-long post-season football extravaganza. Each game is not only televised but also carries the name of a corporate sponsor that pays for the privilege of having its name attached to a bowl game.

Like the schools and athletic conferences, the television networks profit from football. Networks sell advertising slots to the highest bidders for every televised game during the regular season and the Bowl Championship Series, and they work to sustain fans' interest in football by cultivating viewers on the Web. For instance, one network generates interest in up-and-coming high school players through *Scout.com*, a Web site that posts profiles of boys being recruited by colleges and universities and that is supported, at least in part, through advertising and paid subscriptions.

Amid these money-making players are the actual football players, the young men who are bound by NCAA rules to play as amateurs and to receive no direct compensation for their hours of practice and field time. True, their generous athletic scholarships cover tuition, room and board, and expenses such as uniforms, medical care, and travel. Yet compared to the millions of dollars spent on promoting football, the scholarships seem rather quaint and old-fashioned.

Many critics have pointed out the disparity between players' rewards and the profits made by the industry and have called for allowing players to receive compensation in one form or another. But so far the schools, conferences, and networks have ignored these calls for change and have perpetuated a system that benefits everyone except the players.

—Terrence MacDonald (student)

关于段落的完整与连贯还可见 pp. 45–52。

> **练习3.2** **组织观点**
>
> 下方的一系列观点是一个美国学生从他的自由写作中提取的,他写的是一篇关于足球的短文。以他的主题句作为引导,挑出一般性观点,并在这些观点下方排列相关的具体论点。在某些情况下,你不得不推断出一般性观点,以涵盖列表中的具体观点。
>
> **主题句**
>
> Although its growth in the United States has been slow and halting, professional soccer may finally be poised to become a major American sport.
>
> **观点列表**
>
> In countries of South and Latin America, soccer is the favorite sport.
>
> In the United States the success of a sport depends largely on its ability to attract huge TV audiences.
>
> Soccer was not often presented on US television.
>
> In 2006 and 2010, the World Cup final was broadcast on ABC and on Spanish-language Univision.
>
> In the past, professional soccer could not get a foothold in the United States because of poor TV coverage and lack of financial backing.
>
> The growing Hispanic population in the United States could help soccer grow as well.
>
> Investors have poured hundreds of millions of dollars into the top US professional league.
>
> Potential fans did not have a chance to see soccer games.
>
> Failures of early start-up leagues made potential backers wary of new ventures.
>
> Recently, the outlook for professional soccer has changed dramatically.
>
> The US television audience for the 2010 US-Ghana match was larger than the audience for baseball's World Series.

第 4 章　打草稿

概要

打草稿需要:

- 开始动笔(下页)

- 保持良好势头（下方）

打草稿是一种探索的机会。不要指望把实际的想法一转到纸上就立刻妙笔生花。反之，就让打草稿这个行为本身帮助你发现和形成意图。

4a 开始动笔

万事开头难，即便对于写作老手来说，开始打草稿也需要一定的勇气。拖延也许确实有用，如果你在等待想法厚积薄发的话。但是，在某一时刻，你不得不面对白纸和空屏而无法落笔。以下技巧可以帮助你开始：

- 把已经写好的 —— 笔记、提纲等 —— 通读一遍，头脑中一有想法就立即开始打草稿。
- 自由写作。（见 pp. 11–12）
- 胡乱写或随意敲（键盘），直到可用的话开始出现。
- 假设在给朋友写关于你的主题的内容。
- 描述一个可以代表你的主题的形象 —— 一个物品、一个面部表情、两个争论不休的人、为采矿凿挖地球的大型机械，凡此种种。
- 跳过开头，从中间开始写，或先写结论。
- 写一个段落。解释你认为你的作品在完稿时是关于什么内容的。
- 从你理解得最好或感觉最强烈的部分开始写起。用提纲把作品分成几块 —— 比如，一块是引言，另一块是第一点，如此等等。这些大块的某一部分就会呼之欲出，跃然纸上。

4b 保持良好势头

打草稿需要激情：这种向前冲的动力令你才思泉涌。为保持这种动力，尝试运用以下一个或更多技巧：

- 给自己留出足够的时间。一篇短文的初稿通常至少需要一两个小时。
- 在一个安静的地方写。
- 让自己觉得舒服。
- 如果必须停止工作，记下你下一步想做什么。这样很容易再把它捡起来，把中断影响降为最低。
- 尽可能灵活。顺其自然将你对主题的态度通过句子自然显露出来。
- 坚持写。跳过卡壳部分；找不到合适的词就先空着；暂时把替代的想法或措辞放在括号里，供你以后考虑。如果一个莫名的想法突然冒了出来，但似乎又不太合适，立即记下来，或把它写进草稿里和括号里，或用黑体标注，以便以后再看。
- **不要苛求自己。** 不要担心形式、语法、拼写、标点等。不要担心读者会怎么想。这些虽然是非常重要的事情，但还是把它们留到修改阶段再说。
- **使用主题句和提纲。** 它们可以提醒你已计划好的写作目的、组织和内容。然而，如果写作把你引到了一个你更感兴趣的方向，那么就跟着走下去。

4c 初稿范例

以下两页刊登了 Katy Moreno 写的关于 Thomas L. Friedman 的 "It's a Flat World, after All" 一文的读后感初稿。（前两段包含了 Friedman 文章的页码，Moreno 就是从这篇文章中总结素材的）作为作业的一部分，Moreno 把草稿给她的四个同学看了，他们把修改建议写在了草稿页边空白处。他们使用了微软文字处理软件的评论功能，该功能允许使用者加批注评论，而不会把文字插到文档文本中去。（需要注意的是，她的同学们忽略了语法和标点方面的错误，而是去关注更大的问题，比如，主题、观点清晰度和完整）

Title?

In "It's a Flat World, after All," Thomas L. Friedman argues that, most US students are not preparing themselves as well as they should to compete in today's economy. Not like students in India, China, and other countries are (34-37). My mother lost her job because it was outsourced to India, but not all technical jobs in her company were outsourced. Thomas L. Friedman's advice to improve students' technical training is too narrow.

Friedman describes a "flat" world where technology like the Internet and wireless communication makes it possible for college graduates all over the globe, in particular in India and China, to get jobs that once were gotten by graduates of US colleges and universities (37). He argues that US students need more math and

评论 [Jared]：你母亲的工作被外包这件事很有趣，但是你的引言似乎有些太过匆忙。

评论 [Rabia]：你的主题句的结尾部分不够清晰——太窄了怎么办？

评论 [Erin]：你能否把 Friedman 给出的关于海外学生成功的原因包括进来？

science in order to compete (37).

  I came to college with first-hand knowledge of globalization and outsourcing. My mother, who worked for sixteen years in the field of information technology (IT), was laid off six months ago when the company she worked for decided to outsource much of its IT work to a company based in India. My mother majored in computer science, had sixteen years of experience, and her bosses always gave her good reviews. She never expected to be laid off and was surprised when she was. She wasn't laid off because of her background and performance. In fact, my mother had a very strong background in math and science and years of training and job experience. The reason was because her salary and benefits cost the company more than outsourcing her job did. Which hurt my family financially, as you can imagine.

评论 [Nathaniel]：这段是否可以紧凑点以避免重复？还有，你母亲的经历与Friedman以及你的主题有什么关系？

  A number of well-paid people in the IT department where my mother worked, namely IT managers, were not laid off. As my mother explained at the time, they kept their jobs because they were better at planning, and they communicated better, they were better writers and speakers than my mother.

评论 [Erin]：经理们在计划什么方面做得更好？

  Like my mother, I am more comfortable in front of a computer than I am in front of a group of people. I planned to major in computer science. Since my mother lost her job, though, I have decided to take courses in English and history too, where the classes will require me to do different kinds of work. When I enter the job market, my well-rounded education will make me a more attractive job candidate, and, will help me to be a versatile, productive employee.

评论 [Nathaniel]：你能更具体地说说你将需要从事的工作吗？

评论 [Rabia]：你能把这一点加到你的主题里去吗？

  We know from our history that Americans have been innovative, hard-working people. We students

> have educational opportunities to compete in the global economy, but we must use our time in college wisely. As Thomas L. Friedman says, my classmates and I need to be ready for a rapidly changing future. We will have to work hard each day, which means being prepared for class, getting the best grades we can, and making the most of each class. Our futures depend on the decisions we make today.

评论 [Jared]：结论似乎有些跑题。Friedman提到了努力工作，但这一直都不是你的重点。

评论 [Rabia]：不要忘了你引用的著作。

第 5 章　修改

概要

文章修改需要：
- 批判性地阅读你的作品（p. 30）
- 使用修改检查单（p. 31）
- 合作修改（p. 32）

对精品创作而言，修改工作是一项非常重要的任务。在修改过程中——准确地说，就是"再看一遍"——你把重心从自己和主题上移开，转移到外在的读者身上，重点放在如何帮助读者对你的作品做出回应。许多写作者把修改分为两个阶段：首先，他们把文章作为一个整体看待，对文章的整体意思和结构进行评价和改进（本章）；然后，他们对句子的措辞、语法、标点、拼写等等进行编辑（下一章）。

修改文章时，你可以独自为战，或者，可以从导师和/或合作团队中的其他同学处得到意见和反馈。无论你是对自己的评价做出回应，还是对读者的，你都需要重新考虑你的主题，移动或删除整个段落，厘清观点是否和主题相关，或者用细节以及进一步调研支持观点。由于知道你下一步将对文章进行编辑，因此你就可以超越纸质文本或电脑显示屏的边框，把文章作为一个整体来看。

5a 批判性地阅读你的作品

修改文章的第一步应该是检查文章整体方面的问题，比如你的目的和主题对读者是否清晰，主题是否在草稿中得到了充分的论述。以这种方式评价你的文章，你则需要批判性地阅读你的作品，这意味着你不得不与你的草稿保持一定的距离。以下技巧会有助于你客观地看待自己的作品：

- **完成草稿后先放一下**。也许几个小时足矣，一整夜或一整天更好。
- **请人读你的草稿，并做出评价**。如果你的导师鼓励学生之间合作，那就一定要充分利用这个机会，听取别人的意见和建议。（见pp. 32–33，查看更多关于合作的信息）
- **以新的方式读草稿**。键入手写草稿或打印出文字处理过的草稿，可以显露出你在原稿中没有发现的弱点。
- **给草稿列提纲**。把支持主题的主要观点用高亮标出，然后以提纲的形式把这些句子分别写下来。然后检查你所列的提纲是否在逻辑顺序、漏洞、跑题等方面存在问题。一份正式提纲因其精心的结构而格外具有启发意义。（见pp. 23–24）
- **把草稿读出声来听**。把草稿高声读出来给自己、朋友或同学听，录下来听，或者让别人念给你听。
- **使用修改检查单**。不要试图立即把你的草稿从头到尾再看一遍。用下面的修改检查单，把每项仔细过一遍。

全文修改检查单

任务
你如何回应这份写作任务？确保你的主题、目的及体裁与任务要求相符合。

目的
写作目的是什么？这个目的符合任务要求吗？是不是整篇文章都围绕这个目的？（见pp. 6–7）

读者
文章是以什么方式与既定读者对话的？文章是如何满足读者对主题的可能的期待的？读者在什么地方还需要更多信息？

体裁
你的文章是如何做到符合你文章体裁的传统特点的，比如组织、证据、语言和格式？

（续表）

主题
文章的主题是什么？在哪里可以清晰地看出来？主题和文章匹配程度如何：文章的一些部分有没有偏离主题？文章是否完成了主题的承诺？（见pp. 16–19）

组织
文章的要点是什么？（罗列出来）每个论点在支持主题方面做得如何？为达到文章的目的，论点的排列有多么卓有成效？（见pp. 20–24）

展开
细节、例子和其他论据是不是很好地支持每个要点？有没有什么地方读者会觉得论据不足或理解困难？如果有，在哪里？（见pp. 6–7, pp. 53–59）

完整性
每句话、每一段都说明了主题的什么方面？有没有跑题？哪里跑题了？应该把它们删掉还是重写以支持主题？（见p. 24, pp. 45–46）

连贯性
行文是不是清晰流畅？什么地方看起来粗略或累赘？过渡的地方还能不能改进？（见p. 24, pp. 46–52）

题目、引言、结论
题目是不是精确、有趣地反映了文章的内容？（见p. 34）引言有没有很好地吸引和集中读者的注意力？（见pp. 60–62）结论有没有成功地给人论文已完成的感觉？（见pp. 62–63）

用文字处理器来处理草稿

当你在电脑上修改时，采取几个预防措施来保存草稿，以防丢失：

- **在你最新完成的草稿上做改动**。这样原文将保持原样不变，直到你真正完成。在这个文件上，你可使用文字处理器的追踪修订功能，该功能可以显示你原文件中出现的变化，使得你能够接受或拒绝以后的修改。
- **保存草稿并以"草稿"为文件名**。由于观点和措辞的原因，你也许需要查看更早前的草稿。
- **每五到十分钟保存一下文档**。
- **完成计划中的任何一项主要工作，都要创建该文档的备份版本**。

5b 合作修改

在许多写作课程中，学生一起学习，经常互相交换文章，以便帮助修改。这种合作性写作可提供用批判性眼光阅读文章和通过文章了解别人的经历。这种合作可以通过将大家分成小组面对面，把草稿和点评落实在纸上来进行，或者通过以下方式在线进行，即通过课程管理系统，比如Blackboard或Moodle教学平台，或者通过班级博客、电子邮件列表或维基百科。

无论哪种合作媒介，遵循一些准则将帮助你从别人的评论中获得更多，成为一个更有建设性的读者。

从别人的评论中获益

- **把你的读者看成咨询师或教练。** 他们可以帮助你看清你文章中的优点和瑕疵，使你对读者的需求更明确。
- **仔细阅读或倾听评论。**
- **弄懂评论的内容。** 如果你需要更多信息，开口询问，或者查看本指南的相关部分。
- **不要采取防卫姿态。** 对他人评论产生冒犯感只会在改进你的写作方面竖起一道障碍。正如一位写作教师建议的："把你的自我抛到脑后。"
- **依照恰当的评论修改你的作品。** 你从修改本身学到的东西会更多，相比于仅仅考虑改动。
- **记住，你才是为你文章做最终裁定的人。** 应该对建议保持开放心态，但如果你认为不合适，你可以拒绝采纳建议。
- **把别人指出的优点和弱点都记录下来。** 那么，在以后的作业中，你就会促成你的成功，并且对出问题区域格外注意。

评论别人的写作

- **确定你知道作者在说什么。** 如果需要，对文章进行总结，以便理解它的内容。（见pp. 89–91）
- **只提出你对作品的最有意义的看法。** 将注意力集中在其他作者草稿，特别是早期草稿的那些深刻的问题上：主题、目的、读者、组织和主题论据。判别是否有意义的标准见p. 31上的修改检查单。除非另有要求，忽略语法、标点、拼写等错误。（如果作者对标准美式英语不如你的经验丰富，那么想把注意力集中在这类错误上的诱惑力就特别强烈）强调错误对帮助作者修改几乎没有意义。
- **牢记你是读者，而不是作者。** 不要校订句子，增加细节，或者假定你对文章负有责任。
- **评论时措辞要谨慎。** 避免做出太过自信的评论而产生误会，这种做法既明确，又值得敬佩。如果你是用书面或在线做回应，而不是和作者面对面，那就记住作者除了你写下来的文字，没有别的东西可参考。他或她无法要求你立即做澄清，也不能从你的手势、面部表情，以及声调判断你的态度。

- **要具体。** 如果有什么使你感到困惑，说为什么。如果你不同意某个结论，说为什么。
- **不仅要诚实，还要支持作者。** 告诉作者你喜欢文章的哪些方面。评论时措辞要积极正面：不要说"这段引不起我的兴趣"，而是说"你这里有一个有趣的细节，我差点错过"。质疑作者时，要以强调文章对你这个读者的影响这种方式进行："这个段落使我困惑，因为……"而且要避免对照外部标准对文章进行评价："这篇文章结构很糟糕。你的主题句不够充分。"
- **读他人文章时，把你的评论写下来。** 即便你很快就会亲自送上你的评论，书面记录也会帮助你回想起你当时的想法。
- **把评论与文中具体部分联系起来。** 特别是当你在电脑上阅读文章时，要清楚文章的每一条评论和什么有关系。你可以使用文字处理器的评论功能给文档加批注。

34　（CULTURE LANGUAGE）在一些文化中，写作者不会料到会从读者处听到批评，读者对他们所读之物也不会带有批判性思考。例如，读者不会去质疑一个不清晰的主题，或者去评价一篇议论文中的证据。如果在你的文化中批判性回应不普遍的话，那么合作刚开始对你来说可能就不舒服。作为写作者，应该这样去考虑，即读者对你的草稿或你的终稿做回应，更多的是作为对一种观点的探讨，而不是对你的主题有决定权，这样，你也许就更能接受读者的建议了。作为读者，允许自己带着怀疑的眼光去接触一篇文本，即问有关重点、内容，及组织结构的问题，例如，"这个一般性陈述是如何为主题提供支持的"或者"这个例子是如何支持一般性陈述的"，要知道你机智的问题和建议将通常被认为是恰当的。

5c 写标题

修改阶段是考虑标题的好时机，因为试图用一个词组给你的文章做总结可以把你的注意力高度集中在主题、目的和读者上。

以下是给文章加题目的建议：

- **描述性标题清晰和准确地通告主题。** 这种标题几乎总是恰如其分，通常用于学术性写作。Katy Moreno最后确定的标题就是个例子，她的标题是："Can We Compete? College Education for the Global Economy"。
- **提示性标题暗示主题并引发好奇心。** 这类标题在通俗杂志上很常见，而且可能更适合非正式性写作。Moreno或许可以选择类似这样的提示性标题："Training for the New World"或者"Education for a Flat World"（呼应Thomas L. Friedman的标题）。

有关文章标题的更多信息，见p. 358（标题大部分词首字母要大写），p. 484（MLA标题格式）和p. 516（APA标题格式）。

5d 修改样文

Katy Moreno对她的初稿很满意：观点排列有序，安排符合逻辑。然而，从修改检查单中，她知道草稿需要加工，她同学的评论（pp. 28–29）明显标注出她需要重点关注的。以下是她修改草稿的前半部分，页边注释凸显出改动部分。Moreno使用了她文字处理器中的追踪修订功能，这样，删除部分被画掉，增加部分用加粗标出。

Can We Compete?
College Education for the Global Economy
~~Title?~~

Today's students cannot miss news stories about globalization of the economy and outsourcing of jobs, but are students aware of how these trends are affecting the job market? In "It's a Flat World, after All," Thomas L. Friedman argues that most US students are not preparing themselves as well as ~~they should to compete in today's economy. Not like~~ students in India, China, and other countries ~~are~~ **to compete in today's economy, which requires hard-working, productive scientists and engineers** (34-37). **The article speaks to me because my mother recently lost her job when it was outsourced to India, but Friedman does not explain why many technical jobs are not outsourced. He overlooks that technical training by itself can be too narrow to produce the communicators and problem solvers needed by contemporary businesses.** ~~My mother lost her job because it was outsourced to India, but not all technical jobs in her company were outsourced. Thomas L. Friedman's advice to improve students' technical training is too narrow.~~

> 35 描述性题目点明了话题，并预示了文章走向。

> 扩展了的引言把读者吸引到Moreno的话题中，明确表明了她和Friedman一致的观点，并提出她修改后的主题。

> 扩展后的对Friedman文章的概述列举了海外劳工的特点。

Friedman describes a "flat" world where technology like the Internet and wireless communication makes it possible for college graduates all over the globe, in particular **to compete for high paying jobs that once belonged to graduates of US colleges and universities (34). He focuses on workers** in India and China, **who graduate from college with excellent educations in math and science, who are eager for new opportunities, and who are willing to work exceptionally hard, often harder than their American counterparts and, for less money** to get jobs that once were gotten by graduates of US colleges and universities (37). He **Friedman argues that US students must be better prepared academically, especially in** need more **math and science, so that they can get and keep jobs that will otherwise go overseas** in order to compete (37).

> 新的起始句与引言和主题句相关联，再次提出与Friedman一致和不一致的观点。

I came to college with first hand knowledge of globalization and outsourcing. My mother, who worked for sixteen years in the field of information technology (IT), was laid off six months ago when the company she worked for decided to outsource much of its IT work to a company based in India. My mother **At first glance, my mother's experience of losing her job might seem to support the argument of Friedman that better training in math and science is the key to competing in the global job market. Her experience, however, adds dimensions to the globalization story, which Friedman misses. First my mother had the kind of strong background in math and science that Friedman says, today's workers need. She** majored in computer science, **rose within the information technology (IT) department of a large company,** had sixteen years of experience, **and her bosses always gave her good performance reviews. Still, when her employer decided to outsource most of its IT work, my mother lost her job.** She never expected to be laid off and was surprised when she was. She wasn't laid off because of her background and performance. In fact, my mother had a very strong background in math and science and years of training and job experience.

> 修改稿压缩了关于母亲经历的长篇幅的例子。

The reason was**n't** because her **technical skills were inadequate. Instead,** her salary and benefits cost the company more than outsourcing her job did. **Until wages rise around the globe, jobs like my mother's will be vulnerable. No matter how well you are trained.** ~~Which hurt my family financially, as you can imagine.~~

> 段落结论句强化了论点，并和主题句相关联。

第 6 章　校订、定格式和校对

概要

完成写作需要：

- 校订修改后的草稿（下方）
- 使用校订检查单（下方）
- 定格式和校对终稿（p. 40）

完成文章修订，所有内容都合适之后，需要转到重要的工作上来，将可能影响读者理解或欣赏你的观点的那些表面问题去除。

6a 校订修改后的草稿

校订时，先使句子清晰、有效、流畅。然后检查句子是否正确。用下面的校订检查单中列出的问题帮助你校订。

1 ▪ 发现需要校订的内容

使用这些方法，以找到文章中可能的错误：

- 休息一下。即使十五或二十分钟也可以令你头脑清醒。

校订检查单

我的句子是否清晰
词和句子是不是很好地传达了它们应该表达的意思？有没有意思模糊的地方？特别注意检查文章的以下方面：
语言准确（pp. 171–179）

（续表）

平行结构（pp. 155–157）
修饰语清楚（pp. 278–284）
代词指代清楚（pp. 263–266）
句子完整（pp. 285–288）
句子正确分隔（pp. 290–295）

我的句子有效吗
词和句子是不是很好地吸引和抓住了读者的注意力？有没有什么地方显得啰唆、不连贯或者乏味？特别注意检查文章的以下方面：

语调表达（pp. 8-9）
强调主要观点（pp. 144–153）
顺畅、提示性的过渡（pp. 50–52）
句子长度和结构富于变化（pp. 159–162）
得体的语言（pp. 163–170）
简明的句子（pp. 183–187）

我的句子有错误吗
表面上的错误在什么地方会影响表达的清晰和有效？特别注意检查文章的以下方面：

- 拼写错误（pp. 348–352）
- 句子不完整（pp. 285–288）
- 逗号粘连（pp. 290–295）
- 动词错误

  动词形式，尤其是-s和-ed结尾的形式，不规则动词的正确形式，以及合适的助动词（pp. 214–229）

  动词时态，特别注意前后一致（pp. 230–236）

  主谓一致，尤其是主谓之间有插入成分或主语是each, everyone或类似词时（pp. 243–249）

- 代词错误

  代词形式，尤其是用主格（he, she, they, who）还是宾格（him, her, them, whom）（pp. 251–257）

  代词和先行词一致，尤其是先行词包含或先行词是each, everyone, person或类似词时（pp. 258–261）

- 标点错误

  逗号，尤其是有逗号分隔句子时（pp. 290–295），有and或but时，有引入性成分时，有非本质成分时，以及有系列时（pp. 306–315）

  在非复数名词中表示所有格的撇号（Dave's / witches）以及在非所有格人称代词的缩写中的撇号（it's / its）（pp. 329–333）

- 如果可能，在双倍行距的纸版上改。许多人发现，在电脑显示屏上发现错误比在纸上难得多。

- **放慢速度读草稿，读你确实看到的文字**。否则，你很有可能读到你最初打算写但又没有写的东西。如果你慢下来有困难，那么就逐句从后往前读草稿。
- **把草稿读出声来听**。大声朗读草稿，录下来听回放，或者使用文本转语音软件做成一个语音版本。要警惕蹩脚的节奏，重复的句型和没有过渡。
- **请同学、朋友或亲戚读你的作品**。确信你理解并考虑了读者的建议，尽管你决定不采纳这些建议。
- **从自己的经验中学习**。把自己的常见问题做一个记录 —— 某些拼写错误，there is使用过多，类似the fact that这种短语用得过多等 —— 对照这个记录检查自己的作品。使用文字处理器的寻找命令，迅速找到问题。

2 ▪ 校订段落样例

下方是Katy Moreno校订草稿的第三段。在改动中，她精练了措辞，改进了平行结构（用了consistently received），改正了几个逗号错误，修复了最后的句子片段。

At first glance, my mother's experience of losing her job might seem to support ~~the~~ **Friedman's** argument ~~of Friedman~~ that better training in math and science is the key to competing in the global job market. **However,** ~~H~~**h**er experience~~, however,~~ adds dimensions to the globalization story~~, which~~ **that** Friedman misses. First, my mother had the kind of strong background in math and science that Friedman says~~,~~ today's workers need. She majored in computer science, rose within the information technology (IT) department of a large company, and **consistently received** ~~her bosses always gave her~~ good performance reviews. Still, when her employer decided to outsource most of its IT work, my mother lost her job. The reason wasn't ~~because~~**that** her technical skills were inadequate. Instead, her salary and benefits cost the company more than outsourcing her job did. Until wages rise around the globe, jobs like my mother's will be vulnerable~~,~~**.** ~~N~~**n**o matter how well ~~you are~~ **a person is** trained.

3 ▪ 使用拼写和语法/形式检查器

拼写检查器和语法/形式检查器可以很有帮助，如果你在它们限定的范围内使用。这个程序会放过很多问题，甚至会在实际正确的项目上做标记。而且，它们对你的文章无法做出重要决定，因为它们对你的主题、目的以及读者都一无所知。使用这些工具一定要谨慎。

- 亲自通读自己的文章，确保文章内容清晰且没有错误。

- 仔细考虑检查器的建议，对照你的意图逐个权衡。如果你不能确定是否接受检查器的建议，查阅字典、写作手册或其他资料。你的版本也许没问题。

使用拼写检查器

你的文字处理拼写检查器可以是个非常棒的助手：它会把拼错的词标注出来，而且通常会把与你打出的词相像的拼写，作为可替代的选择提供给你。然而，这个助手也具有暗中给你帮倒忙的潜在弊端。

- 检查器可能会把你拼写正确的词标注出来，只因为这个词没有在它的字典里面出现过。
- 检查器提供的选择可能不正确。在为你的词提供一长串可供选择的拼写的时候，检查器会将它认为最有可能是正确的词突显出来。例如，如果你将definitely拼错，打成definately，检查器会将defiantly作为正确选项突显出来。你需要证实检查器提供的选择确实是你在选择前就确定想要的。当你对检查器提供的选择不能确定时，查阅在线字典或纸版字典。（见 pp. 171–172）
- 更重要的是，拼写检查器不会把在它字典出现过但被你用错了的词标记出来。下方展示的顺口溜作为对拼写检查器的警告广为流传。（还可见p. 353 关于使用拼写检查器的练习）

» **拼写检查器**

拼写检查器未能抓住顺口溜中十三个错误中的任何一个。你能发现这些错吗？

I have a spelling checker,
It came with my PC;
It plainly marks four my revue
Mistakes I cannot sea.
I've run this poem threw it,
I'm sure your please too no.
Its letter perfect in it's weigh,
My checker tolled me sew.

你可以安装一个拼写检查器，但要保留一个你常出的拼写错误的文件夹，然后选择编辑菜单下的寻找功能，以便检查这些错误。但是，最终唯一使你文章不出拼写错误的办法就是你亲自校对你的文章。校对技巧见下页。更多关于拼写的建议，见第45章。

使用语法/形式检查器

语法/形式检查器可以标记出不正确的语法或标点，以及冗长或蹩脚的句子。然而，这些程序只能把你的注意力吸引到可能出错的文本。它们会错过很多错误，因为它们还不能分析如此错综复杂的语言。（例如，它们不能准确识别单词的词性，因为存在不同的可能性，正如 light 可以是名词、动词或形容词）而且它们还常常质疑根本不需要校订的文本，比如一个恰当的被动式动词，或者故意的、为加重语气使用的重复。

作为一个写作者，你可以定制一个语法/形式检查器，以适应你的需要和习惯。大多数检查器允许你指定是否仅检查语法，还是既检查语法又检查形式。一些形式检查器可以设置你想达到的写作等级，比如正式、标准和非正式。（学术写作，选择正式）你还可以命令检查器将困扰你的具体语法和形式问题标注出来，如复数名词的所有格的撇号，过度使用的被动态，或 its 和 it's 之间使用的混乱。

6b 定格式和校对终稿

文章修订完之后，在提交给导师之前，对其定格式和校对。遵循文件格式要求，如 MLA（pp. 484–486）或 APA（pp. 516–519），也可见 pp. 63–75 获得文件设计方面的帮助。

一定要反复几次校对终稿，以发现和纠正错误。为增加校对的准确性，你需要尝试一些方法，使自己不会因文章的节奏和内容而产生懈怠感。以下是几种技巧，包括一些专业校对者使用的技巧：

- **阅读打印稿**，尽管最后以电子版形式提交稿子。许多人在纸版上校对比在电脑显示屏上校对更准确。（同时，不要以为打印出的版本看起来很干净就一定没有错误。看起来干净的纸版稿子仍然会有错误存在）
- **出声朗读文稿**，速度要慢，而且要明确无误地把你看到的读出来。
- **用一把尺子**，在稿子上随阅读行移动。
- **"比对着"读稿**，逐句对照终稿和校订稿。
- **忽略内容**。校对时，为避免稿子内容分散你的注意力，从后往前倒读文稿，把每句话都作为一个独立的单元检查。或者利用文字处理器，把每一段打在另一页上，使其和文稿上下文隔离开来。（当然，在提交文稿之前，要把这些段落重新组合起来）

6c 终稿样例

下方是Katy Moreno的终稿,除了页码,均以MLA格式呈现。页边空白处的评论指明了稿子内容的主要特征。

Katy Moreno

Professor Lacourse

English 110

14 February 2012

Can We Compete?

College Education for the Global Economy

> 描述性题目

> 引言

Today's students cannot miss news stories about globalization of the economy and outsourcing of jobs, but are students aware of how these trends are affecting the job market? In "It's a Flat World, after All," Thomas L. Friedman argues that most US students are not preparing themselves as well as students in India, China, and other countries to compete in today's economy, which requires hard-working, productive scientists and engineers (34-37). The article speaks to me because my mother lost her job when it was outsourced to India, but Friedman does not explain why many technical jobs are not outsourced. He overlooks that technical training by itself can be too narrow to produce the communicators and problem solvers needed by contemporary businesses.

> 引用了Friedman的总结,使用MLA格式插入页码(p. 439)

> 主题句:与Friedman的基本分歧

Friedman describes a "flat" world where technology like the Internet and wireless communication makes it possible for college graduates all over the globe to compete for high-paying jobs that once belonged to graduates of US colleges and universities (34). He focuses on workers in India and China who graduate from college with excellent educations in math and science, who are eager for new opportunities, and who are willing to work exceptionally hard, often harder than their American counterparts, and for less money (37). Friedman argues that US students must be better prepared academically, especially in math

> 对Friedman文章的总结

and science, so that they can get and keep jobs that will otherwise go overseas (37).

  At first glance, my mother's experience of losing her job might seem to support Friedman's argument that better training in math and science is the key to competing in the global job market. However, her experience adds dimensions to the globalization story that Friedman misses. First, my mother had the kind of strong background in math and science that Friedman says today's workers need. She majored in computer science, rose within the information technology (IT) department of a large company, and consistently received good performance reviews. Still, when her employer decided to outsource most of its IT work, my mother lost her job. The reason wasn't that her technical skills were inadequate; instead, her salary and benefits cost the company more than outsourcing her job did. Until wages rise around the globe, jobs like my mother's will be vulnerable, no matter how well a person is trained.

  The second dimension that Friedman misses is that a number of well-paid people in my mother's IT department, namely IT managers, were not laid off. As my mother explained at the time, they kept their jobs because they were experienced at figuring out the company's IT needs, planning for changes, researching and proposing solutions, and communicating in writing and speech—skills that her more narrow training and experience had missed. Friedman misses these skills by focusing only on technical training. Without the ability to solve problems creatively and to communicate, people with technical expertise alone may not have enough to save their jobs, as my mother learned.

  Like my mother, I am more comfortable in front of a computer than I am in front of a group of people, and I had planned to major in computer science. Since my mother lost her job, however, I have decided to take courses in English and history as well. Classes in these subjects will require me to read broadly, think critically, research, and communicate ideas in writing—in short, to develop skills that make managers. When I enter the job market, my well-rounded education will make me a more attractive job candidate and will help me to become the kind of forward-thinking manager that companies will always need to employ here in the United States.

> 对最后观点的解释

Many jobs that require a college degree are indeed going overseas, as Thomas L. Friedman says, and my classmates and I need to be ready for a rapidly changing future. But rather than focus only on math and science, we need to broaden our academic experiences so that the skills we develop make us not only employable but also indispensable.

> 结论：扼要重述与 Friedman 相同和不同观点，并总结全文

[New page.]

Work Cited

Friedman, Thomas L. "It's a Flat World, after All." *New York Times Magazine* 3 Apr. 2005: 32-37. Print.

> 以MLA格式引用的文章（p. 448）

第 7 章　段落

概要

段落写作需要：

- 每段都与文章整体相关联（下页）
- 每段统一围绕一个主题（p. 45）
- 每段都要连贯（p. 46）
- 展开每段的中心思想（p. 53）
- 创建开头段和结尾段，以开始和完成写作（p. 60）

段落给你提供了一种方法，可使你一步接一步、一个论点接一个论点地去扩展文章中心思想（主题）。段落帮助你的读者认清你的观点，跟上你的组织结构，并且可让读者在阅读长篇大论中休息片刻。在文章的主体部分，你可以将段落用于以下任何一种目的：

- 引入一个支持文章主题的主要观点，并给予论据。见 pp. 16–19 关于文章主题的讨论。

- 在一组阐述一个观点的段落中，展开一个主要例子或其他重要论据。
- 转换思路——如从赞同到反对，从问题到解决，从提问到回答。
- 用序列标示进展，比如从一个原因转到下一个原因，或从一步转到下一步。

CULTURE LANGUAGE 并不是所有文化都具有美国学术写作的段落写作传统。在一些别的语言中，页面上字的移动方式和英语不同——不是从左到右，而是从右到左，或者从上到下。即便那些页面字的移动方式和英语一样的语言，写作者也许根本不使用段落。或者，他们也许使用段落，但并不点明中心思想或提供过渡性表达，以向读者展示句子之间关联。如果你的母语不是英语，写段落有困难，那么在打草稿过程中不要担心段落问题，而是要在修改文章时的独立步骤里，把你论述主要观点的文本分成几部分，然后用首行缩进的形式把这几段标示出来。

7a 让文中段落产生关联

段落不是孤立存在的：它是长篇文章中重要组成部分。尽管你独立起草段落，它也需要和你的中心思想或主题相联系——对主题进行解释和挖掘。段落聚在一起，流水般从一段流向另一段，这样读者很容易抓住你的要点，并清楚每个观点是如何对全文起到推动作用的。

修改段落检查单

- 每段是否对文章整体连贯起到作用？每段是否支持文章的中心思想，或主题？段与段之间是否有关联？（见上方和下方）
- 每段是不是前后一致？每段是否集中在一个中心论点上，这个论点不是通过主题句表达了，就是非常之明显？（见p. 45）
- 每段是不是连贯？句子是否排列清晰有序？句子是否用平行、重复、重述、代词、一致以及过渡性表达适当连接？（见p. 46）
- 每段有没有充分展开？段落大意是否得到具体论据的有力支持，如细节、事实、例子以及理由？（见p. 53）

为看清主体段落是如何有效地帮助写作者和读者的，看一下上一章Katy Moreno 的文章"Can We Compete?"的第四段。为了回应Thomas L. Friedman 的文章，Moreno在支持她的主题，即Friedman忽略了科技人员应成为良好的沟通者和解决问题高手的需要。

> The second dimension that Friedman misses is that a number of well-paid people in my mother's IT department, namely IT managers, were not laid off. As my mother explained at the time, they kept their jobs because they were experienced at figuring out the company's IT needs, planning for changes, researching and proposing solutions, and communicating in writing and speech—skills that her more narrow training and experience had missed. Friedman misses these skills by focusing only on technical training. Without the ability to solve problems creatively and to communicate, people with technical expertise alone may not have enough to save their jobs, as my mother learned.

— 连接上一段和主题的新论点

— 支持新论点的细节

— 总结段落，连接上一段及主题的结论句

练习7.1　分析文章段落

分析Katy Moreno文章的第三和第五段，在第6章pp. 41–42。她是如何把这两段与主题句和其他段落相联系的？

7b 围绕中心论点保持段落完整

正如读者希望段落和文章主题清晰地相关一样，他们通常也希望每一段都保持**完整**——也就是说，只阐述一个观点。这个观点常常是通过一个**主题句**来表述的。举个例子，再看一下上面Katy Moreno写的段落：开头的陈述传递了Moreno的承诺，即她将对Friedman论点中缺失的东西做出解释，而且接下来的句子履行了这个承诺。但是假设Moreno写下这样的一个段落，效果会怎样呢？

> The second dimension that Friedman misses is that a number of well-paid people in my mother's IT department, namely IT managers, were not laid off. As my mother explained at the time, they kept their jobs because they were experienced at figuring out the company's IT needs, planning for changes, researching and proposing solutions, and

— 主题句：总述

— 支持主题句的细节

> communicating in writing. Like my mother, these managers had families to support, so they were lucky to keep their jobs. Our family still struggles with the financial and emotional effects of my mother's unemployment.

—— 跑题

该段落偏离了为什么一些经理人仍然持有工作的主题，因此未能履行主题句的承诺。

中心论点必须永远把控段落内容，就像门口处站立的卫兵一样，但事实上，段落往往不用主题句开头。你也许想先从上一段来一个过渡，直到第二句或第三句才表明中心论点。你也许打算先为你的观点提供论据，最后才让它构建成主题句，正如下方关于美国内战时William Tecumseh Sherman将军的例子：

> Sherman is considered by some to be the inventor of "total war": the first general in human history to carry the logic of war to its ultimate extreme, the first to scorch the earth, the first to consciously demoralize the hostile civilian population in order to subdue its army, the first to wreck an economy in order to starve its soldiers. He has been called our first "merchant of terror" and seen as the spiritual father of our Vietnam War concepts of "search and destroy," "pacification," "strategic hamlets," and "free-fire zones." As such, he remains a cardboard figure of our history: a monstrous arch-villain to unreconstructed Southerners, and an embarrassment to Northerners.
>
> —Adapted from James Reston, Jr., "You Cannot Refine It"

—— 支持并构建主题句的信息

—— 主题句

即使中心论点落到了段落结尾处，它也必须把控前面出现的所有细节。

有时，你也许根本不把段落中心论点明示出来，特别是在记叙文和描写文中，论点在细节里面变得清晰。但是，无论论点明示与否，这个论点必须清晰。

练习7.2　把段落修改完整

以下段落包含观点和细节，但不支持中心论点。在段落中找出主题句，并删除无关部分。

In the southern part of the state, some people still live much as they did a century ago. They use coal- or wood-burning stoves for heating and cooking. Their homes do not have electricity or indoor bathrooms or running water. The towns they live in don't receive adequate funding from the state and federal governments, so the schools are poor and in bad shape. Beside most homes there is a garden where fresh vegetables are gathered for canning. Small pastures nearby support livestock, including cattle, pigs, horses, and chickens. Most of the people have cars or trucks, but the vehicles are old and beat-up from traveling on unpaved roads.

练习7.3　写一个完整的段落

将下列主题句扩展成一个完整的段落，使用支持性陈述句中的相关信息。删除每个与主题句不直接相关的陈述句，然后重写，并把句子适当连接。将主题句放在看起来最有效的位置。

主题句

Mozart's accomplishments in music seem remarkable even today.

支持性信息

Wolfgang Amadeus Mozart was born in 1756 in Salzburg, Austria.

He began composing music at the age of five.

He lived most of his life in Salzburg and Vienna.

His first concert tour of Europe was at the age of six.

On his first tour he played harpsichord, organ, and violin.

He published numerous compositions before reaching adolescence.

He married in 1782.

Mozart and his wife were both poor managers of money.

They were plagued by debts.

Mozart composed over six hundred musical compositions.

His notable works include operas, symphonies, quartets, and concertos.

He died at the age of thirty-five.

7c 实现段落连贯

如果段落**连贯**，读者就能看出该段是如何环环相扣构成一个整体的：句子有逻辑地、顺畅地从一句进入下一句。下面是一个不连贯段落的例子：

The ancient Egyptians were masters of preserving dead people's bodies by making mummies of them.	主题句
Mummies several thousand years old have been discovered nearly intact. The skin, hair, teeth, finger- and toenails, and facial features of the mummies were evident. It is possible to diagnose the diseases they suffered in life, such as smallpox, arthritis, and nutritional deficiencies. The process was remarkably effective. Sometimes apparent were the fatal afflictions of the dead people: a middle-aged king died from a blow on the head, and polio killed a child king. Mummification consisted of removing the internal organs, applying natural preservatives inside and out, and then wrapping the body in layers of bandages.	句子都与主题句有关但彼此不连贯

该段落很难读懂。句子磕磕绊绊，而不是一个论点接一个论点顺畅展开。

下面是上面段落的本来面目。该段落很清晰，因为作者以不同的方式排列信息，而且在句子之中建立了连接，因此进展顺畅：

- 在主题句中表明了中心论点之后，作者移动到两个具体解释处，并且用四个句子举例说明第二个解释。
- 浅灰色字体重复或（以另一种形式）重述关键词语或概念。
- 深灰色字体连接句子，并澄清关系。
- 下画线短语是并列语法形式，以表达类似的内容。

The ancient Egyptians were masters of preserving dead people's bodies by making mummies of them.	主题句
Basically, mummification consisted of removing the internal organs, applying natural preservatives inside and out, and then wrapping the body in	解释1：木乃伊是什么

layers of bandages. And the process was remarkably effective. Indeed, mummies several thousand years old have been discovered nearly intact. Their skin, hair, teeth, finger- and toenails, and facial features are still evident. Their diseases in life, such as smallpox, arthritis, and nutritional deficiencies, are still diagnosable. Even their fatal afflictions are still apparent: a middleaged king died from a blow on the head; a child king died from polio.

——Mitchell Rosenbaum (student),
"Lost Arts of the Egyptians"

> 解释2：为什么埃及人精于做木乃伊
>
> 解释2的具体例子

1 ▪ 段落组织

连贯的段落将信息组织起来，使读者轻松阅读。以下是常用段落设计：

- **从一般到特殊**：句子从比较一般的陈述缓缓移动到更具体的陈述。（见上面Mitchell Rosenbaum的段落）
- **高潮式**：句子的戏剧性或趣味性不断增强，达到高潮。（见下页Lawrence Mayer的段落）
- **空间式**：句子审视人、场景或物体，从顶部到底部，从一边到另一边，或者以一些别的近似于人们观察事物的方式进行。（见p. 54，Virginia Woolf的段落）
- **按时间顺序**：句子按事情发生的先后顺序排列。（见p. 50，Kathleen LaFrank的段落）

2 ▪ 并列

并列有助于句子紧密相连。下段中下画线的并列结构连接了第一个句子之后的所有句子，同时，并列结构还出现在许多句子中（如第八句的He served..., survived..., and earned）。此段选自一个学生关于Ronald Reagan的简介。

Ronald Reagan holds a particularly interesting place in American history, combining successful careers in show business and in politics. After graduating from college in 1932, he worked as a radio sports announcer with an affinity for describing game details. He then launched a successful film career, starring in dozens of movies. After a stint in the US Army, he assumed the role of host for *General*

Electric Theater, a weekly TV program that ran from 1953 to 1962. He first entered politics by supporting candidates and making speeches in the 1950s and early 1960s. He became governor of California in 1966 and served for eight years. He ran unsuccessfully for the US presidency in 1976 and then won the job in 1980, when he became the fortieth President. He served two terms, survived an assassination attempt, and earned a popularity that most politicians can only envy.

　　　　　　　　—William Brooks (student), "Ronald Reagan, the Actor President"

3 ▪ 重复和（以另一种形式）重述

重复和（以另一种形式）重述关键词有助于段落连贯，并且提醒读者主题是什么。在下方段落中，注意下画线重复的词sleep以及（以另一种形式）重述的词adults。

Perhaps the simplest fact about sleep is that individual needs for it vary widely. Most adults sleep between seven and nine hours, but occasionally people turn up who need twelve hours or so, while some rare types can get by on three or four. Rarest of all are those legendary types who require almost no sleep at all; respected researchers have recently studied three such people. One of them—a healthy, happy woman in her seventies—sleeps about an hour every two or three days. The other two are men in early middle age, who get by on a few minutes a night. One of them complains about the daily fifteen minutes or so he's forced to "waste" in sleeping.

　　　　　　　　—Lawrence A. Mayer, "The Confounding Enemy of Sleep"

4 ▪ 代词

由于代词指代名词，所以代词可以把句子联系起来。在上面William Brooks的段落中，he就起到这个作用，替代Ronald Reagan。

5 ▪ 一致

一致（或不一致）主要出现在动词时态以及名词和代词的人称和数中。任何并非出于语意需要的不一致都会影响读者追踪论点展开的能力。

在下方段落中，不一致出现在有下画线的词语中：

时态转换

In the Hopi religion, water <u>is</u> the driving force. Since the Hopi <u>lived</u> in the Arizona desert, they <u>needed</u> water urgently for drinking, cooking, and irrigating crops. Their complex beliefs <u>are</u> focused in part on gaining the assistance of supernatural forces in obtaining water. Many of the Hopi kachinas, or spirit essences, <u>were</u> directly concerned with clouds, rain, and snow.

数转换

<u>Kachinas</u> represent spiritually the things and events of the real world, such as cumulus clouds, mischief, cornmeal, and even death. A <u>kachina</u> is not worshiped as a god but regarded as an interested friend. <u>They</u> visit the Hopi from December through July in the form of men who dress in kachina costumes and perform dances and other rituals.

人称转换

Unlike the man, the Hopi <u>woman</u> does not keep contact with kachinas through costumes and dancing. Instead, <u>one</u> receives a tihu, or small effigy, of a kachina from the man impersonating the kachina. <u>You</u> are more likely to receive a tihu as a girl approaching marriage, though a child or older woman may receive one, too.

语法检查器：语法检查器不能帮你查找句子中的时态、数或人称的转换。转换有时是必要的，（当时态变化表示时间上实际的不同时）而且即便带有不必要的转换的短文也许语法上仍然正确，正如前面的那些短文一样。

6 ▪ 过渡语

过渡语，比如therefore, in contrast以及meanwhile可以在句子之间产生特定的连接。注意同一段落两个版本的区别：

Medical science has succeeded in identifying the hundreds of viruses that can cause the common cold. It has discovered the most effective means of prevention. One person transmits the cold viruses to another most often by hand. An infected person covers his mouth to cough. He picks up the	段落不连贯，难以读下去

telephone. His daughter picks up the telephone. She rubs her eyes. She has a cold. It spreads. To avoid colds, people should wash their hands often and keep their hands away from their faces.

  Medical science has thus succeeded in identifying the hundreds of viruses that can cause the common cold. It has also discovered the most effective means of prevention. One person transmits the cold viruses to another most often by hand. For instance, an infected person covers his mouth to cough. Then he picks up the telephone. Half an hour later, his daughter picks up the same telephone. Immediately afterward, she rubs her eyes. Within a few days, she, too, has a cold. And thus it spreads. To avoid colds, therefore, people should wash their hands often and keep their hands away from their faces.
—Kathleen LaFrank (student),
"Colds: Myth and Science"

过渡语（标灰部分）消除了不连贯，清楚地表明相互关系

  注意过渡语既可以连接句子，也可以连接段落。在LaFrank段落的第一句，thus这个词表示出本段与前一段讨论结果的关系。见pp. 43–44，查看这种过渡的更多信息。

  下方方框内列出了许多过渡语以及它们的功能。

过渡语

追加或表示次序
again, also, and, and then, besides, equally important, finally, first, further, furthermore, in addition, in the first place, last, moreover, next, second, still, too

类比
also, in the same way, likewise, similarly

第一部分　写作过程　　055

（续表）

对比
although, and yet, but, but at the same time, despite, even so, even though, for all that, however, in contrast, in spite of, nevertheless, notwithstanding, on the contrary, on the other hand, regardless, still, though, yet

举例或强化
after all, an illustration of, even, for example, for instance, indeed, in fact, it is true, of course, specifically, that is, to illustrate, truly

指示地点
above, adjacent to, below, elsewhere, farther on, here, near, nearby, on the other side, opposite to, there, to the east, to the left

指示时间
after a while, afterward, as long as, as soon as, at last, at length, at that time, before, earlier, eventually, formerly, immediately, in the meantime, in the past, lately, later, meanwhile, now, presently, shortly, simultaneously, since, so far, soon, subsequently, suddenly, then, thereafter, until, until now, when

重复、概述或下结论
all in all, altogether, as has been said, in brief, in conclusion, in other words, in particular, in short, in simpler terms, in summary, on the whole, that is, therefore, to put it differently, to summarize

表明原因或结果
accordingly, as a result, because, consequently, for this purpose, hence, otherwise, since, then, therefore, thereupon, thus, to this end

注意：从这串过渡语清单里抽词使用时要谨慎，因为每一个组里的词都不可互换使用。例如，besides，finally和second都可以用来补充信息，但是每个词都有它自己不同的意思。

52　CULTURE LANGUAGE　如果过渡语在你的母语中不常使用，你可能会在英语写作时，用在句首添加连接词的方法对此加以补偿。但是这种显而易见的过渡语并不是哪里都需要，而且过多使用会形成干扰并显得别扭。当插入过渡语时，要考虑读者需要信号的要求：通常，通过上下文，句子之间的连接已经很清晰了，或者通过更紧密地联系句子内容，句子之间的连接已经变得清晰。（见pp. 146–148）当你确实需要过渡语时，试着在句中变换它们的位置，正如p. 50 LaFrank段落中所列举的一样。

练习7.4　保持句子的连贯性

在主题句（句子1）之后，下方这个学生写的段落中的句子被打乱了，变得不连贯。使用主题句和其他线索作为引导，将句子重新组合，使其成为一个有序的、连贯的段落。

Although some people argue that television ruins the minds of children, 1
others point to the benefits of educational programming. Even some cartoons 2
familiarize children with the material of literature. Many programs for school- 3
age children teach worthwhile lessons. Thus it is important to evaluate actual 4
programming rather than dismiss television for children as uniformly unhealthy.
For example, some after-school shows, such as *Sid the Science Kid*, stress 5
academic skills, while other shows, such as *Arthur*, emphasize social skills.

练习7.5　分析段落的连贯性

通过Hillary Begas（pp. 53–54）和Freeman Dyson（p. 55）写的段落，研究作者为达到连贯所使用的技巧。特别要注意观察组织、并列结构和观点、重复和（以另一种形式）重述、代词以及过渡语。

练习7.6　写一个连贯的段落

根据下列信息，写一个连贯的段落，如必要，合并和改写句子。首先，用给出的主题句开头，按高潮式顺序组织支持句。然后，合并和重写支持句，通过引入重复和（以另一种形式）重述、并列、代词、一致以及过渡语的方法，帮助读者看到连接。

主题句

Hypnosis is far superior to drugs for relieving tension.

支持性信息

Hypnosis has none of the dangerous side effects of the drugs that relieve tension.

Tension-relieving drugs can cause weight loss or gain, illness, or even death.

Hypnosis is nonaddictive.

Most of the drugs that relieve tension do foster addiction.

Tension-relieving drugs are expensive.

Hypnosis is inexpensive even for people who have not mastered self-hypnosis.

7d 展开中心思想

有效的、论述充分的段落总是会提供给读者需要和期待的明确信息，以便使读者理解和对你说的保持兴趣。段落长度可以粗略地衡量发展情况：任何比75个单词短得多的内容都可能让读者感到不完整。看一下这个例子：

> Untruths can serve as a kind of social oil when they smooth connections between people. In preventing confrontation and injured feelings, they allow everyone to go on as before.

一般性论述，需要例子使其清晰和可信

这个段落缺少扩展或完整。它没有提供足够的信息让我们评价，甚至关注作者的主张。为了对这个段落加以改进，作者需要用具体的例子来支持这些一般性陈述，就像下方修改的那样：

> Untruths can serve as a kind of social oil when they smooth connections between people. Assuring a worried friend that his haircut is flattering, claiming an appointment to avoid an aunt's dinner invitation, pretending interest in an acquaintance's children—these lies may protect the liar, but they also protect the person lied to. In preventing confrontation and injured feelings, the lies allow everyone to go on as before.
>
> —Joan Lar (student), "The Truth of Lies"

详细说明谎言种类和结果的例子

为扩展或形成一个段落的中心思想，一个或更多的以下模式会有帮助。（这些模式也可用来扩展整篇文章，见p.15）

1 ▪ 记叙

记叙常常按事件发生的顺序（即时间顺序）重述一个有意义的事件序列。叙述者不仅只关注事件序列，而且还关注事件的结果以及事件对整体的重要性。

Jill's story is typical for "recruits" to religious cults. She was very lonely in college and appreciated the attention of the nice young men and women who lived in a house near campus. They persuaded her to share their meals and then to move in with them. Between intense bombardments of "love," they deprived her of sleep and sometimes threatened to throw her out. Jill became increasingly confused and dependent, losing touch with any reality besides the one in the group. She dropped out of school and refused to see or communicate with her family. Before long she, too, was preying on lonely college students.

> 按时间顺序排序的重要事件

—Hillary Begas (student),
"The Love Bombers"

2 ▪ 描写

描写提供关于一个人、地点、事物或感情的感官性质的细节，使用具体、明确的词来传达一种主要的情绪，举例说明一个观点，或者达到某种其他目的。在下方段落中，几乎每个词都有助于在读者脑海中产生一个画面：

The sun struck straight upon the house, making the white walls glare between the dark windows. Their panes, woven thickly with green branches, held circles of impenetrable darkness. Sharp-edged wedges of light lay upon the window-sill and showed inside the room plates with blue rings, cups with curved handles, the bulge of a great bowl, the criss-cross pattern in the rug, and the formidable corners and lines of cabinets and bookcases. Behind their conglomeration hung a zone of shadow in which might be a further shape to be disencumbered of shadow or still denser depths of darkness.

> 感官细节的具体记录

—Virginia Woolf, *The Waves*

3 ▪ 举例或支持

观点可以通过几个具体例子展开,就像p. 48的William Brooks和p. 53的Joan Lar使用的例子一样。或者观点也可以通过一个单一的、拉长的例子展开,如下方段落所示:

> The experience is a familiar one to many emergency-room medics. A patient who has been pronounced dead and unexpectedly recovers later describes what happened to him during those moments—sometimes hours—when his body exhibited no signs of life. ⎤ 主题句
>
> According to one repeated account, the patient feels himself rushing through a long, dark tunnel while noise rings in his ears. Suddenly, he finds himself outside his own body looking down with curious detachment at a medical team's efforts to resuscitate him. He hears what is said, notes what is happening but cannot communicate with anyone. Soon his attention is drawn to other presences in the room—spirits of dead relatives or friends—who communicate with him nonverbally. Gradually he is drawn to a vague "being of light." This being invites him to evaluate his life and shows him highlights of his past in panoramic vision. The patient longs to stay with the being of light but is reluctantly drawn back into his physical body and recovers. ⎤ 单一的、详细的例子
>
> —Kenneth L. Woodward, "Life after Death?"

有时你可以通过提供你尝试一个大致想法的理由来展开一段。例如:

> There are three reasons, quite apart from scientific considerations, that mankind needs to travel in space. The first reason is the need for ⎤ 主题句

garbage disposal: we need to transfer industrial processes into space, so that the earth may remain a green and pleasant place for our grandchildren to live in. The second reason is the need to escape material impoverishment: the resources of this planet are finite, and we shall not forgo forever the abundant solar energy and minerals and living space that are spread out all around us. The third reason is our spiritual need for an open frontier: the ultimate purpose of space travel is to bring to humanity not only scientific discoveries and an occasional spectacular show on television but a real expansion of our spirit.

—Freeman Dyson, "Disturbing the Universe"

> 三个理由，依照不断增加的戏剧性和重要性的顺序安排

4 ▪ 定义

给一个复杂的、抽象的、有争议的词语下定义，常常需要长长的解释。下方quality一词的定义来自一篇文章，它宣称"quality in product and effort has become a vanishing element of current civilization"。注意观察作者是如何通过提供例子和与质量缺失相对照的方法，表明自己的意思的：

In the hope of possibly reducing the hail of censure which is certain to greet this essay (I am thinking of going to Alaska or possibly Patagonia in the week it is published), let me say that quality, as I understand it, means investment of the best skill and effort possible to produce the finest and most admirable result possible. Its presence or absence in some degree characterizes every man-made object, service, skilled or unskilled labor—laying bricks, painting a picture, ironing shirts, practicing medicine, shoemaking, scholarship, writing a book. You do it well or you do it half-well. Materials are sound and durable or they are sleazy; method is painstaking or

> 一般性定义
>
> 可能涉及质量的活动

whatever is easiest. Quality is achieving or reaching for the highest standard as against being satisfied with the sloppy or fraudulent. It is honesty of purpose as against catering to cheap or sensational sentiment. It does not allow compromise with the second-rate.　　有质量的和无质量的对比

　　—Barbara Tuchman, "The Decline of Quality"

5 ▪ 划分或分析

　　所谓划分或分析，就是把某事物分成要素，从而更好地理解它。例如，你可以把一张报纸分成几个部分，比如国内新闻、地区新闻、生活方式等。在下方段落中，你仍然可以解读经你划分出的元素的意思和意义。

Reality TV shows are anything but "real."	主题句
Participants are selected from thousands of applicants, and they have auditioned to prove themselves to be competent in front of a camera.	元素： 精心挑选出的参加者
The settings for the action are often environments created especially for the shows.	制造出的环境
Scenes that seem unscripted are often planned to capture entertaining footage. The wardrobes of the participants may be designed to enhance participants' "characters" and to improve their looks on camera.	策划出的场景
And footage is clearly edited to create scenes that seem authentic and tell compelling stories.	剪辑出的片段

　　—Darrell Carter (student), "(Un) Reality TV"

　　分析是批判性阅读的关键技能。见p. 92。

6 ▪ 分类

　　当你把很多事物分成几组时，你就把事物分了类，以便清楚地看到它们之间的关系。下方段落分出三组，或三类父母：

In my experience, the parents who hire daytime sitters for their school-age children tend to fall into one of three groups. The first group includes parents who work and want someone to be at home when the children return from school. These parents are looking for an extension of themselves, someone who will give the care they would give if they were at home. The second group includes parents who may be home all day themselves but are too disorganized or too frazzled by their children's demands to handle child care alone. They are looking for an organizer and helpmate. The third and final group includes parents who do not want to be bothered by their children, whether they are home all day or not. Unlike the parents in the first two groups, who care for their children whenever and however they can, these parents are looking for a permanent substitute for themselves.

—Nancy Whittle (student), "Modern Parenting"

主题句

三组：
在一方面相似（都雇佣临时看管小孩的人）
各组之间不重合（每组态度都不同）
种类：根据戏剧性增加的顺序划分

7 ▪ 比较和对比

比较和对比可以分别或同时使用来展开一个观点。下方段落举例说明了两个常见的组织比较和对比的方法之一：**把每个话题逐个展开**，先展开一个，然后进行下一个。

Consider the differences also in the behavior of rock and classical music audiences. At a rock concert, the audience members yell, whistle, sing along, and stamp their feet. They may even stand during the entire performance. The better the music, the more active they'll be. At a classical concert, in contrast, the better the performance, the more *still* the audience is. Members of the classical audience are so highly

话题：摇滚和古典音乐观众

摇滚音乐观众

disciplined that they refrain from even clearing their throats or coughing. No matter what effect the powerful music has on their intellects and feelings, they sit on their hands.

— 古典音乐观众

—Tony Nahm (student),
"Rock and Roll Is Here to Stay"

下一个段落举例说明了另一个常见的组织方法：**把每一点逐个展开，两个话题相提并论，话题对话题，特征对特征**：

Arguing is often equated with fighting, but there are key differences between the two. — 话题：辩论和争论

Participants in an argument approach the subject to find common ground, or points on which both sides agree, while people engaged in a fight usually approach the subject with an "us-versus-them" attitude. — 接近话题的方式：辩论，争论

Participants in an argument are careful to use respectful, polite language, in contrast to the insults and worse that people in a fight use to get the better of their opponents. — 语言：辩论，争论

Finally, participants in an argument commonly have the goal of reaching a new understanding or larger truth about the subject they're debating, while those in a fight have winning as their only goal. — 目标：辩论，争论

—Erica Ito (student),
"Is an Argument Always a Fight?"

8 ▪ 因果分析

当你用分析来解释为什么某事发生，或发生了什么事，或者什么事可能发生时，我们就在确定因果关系。在下方段落中，作者观察了一个结果的原因——日本的集体主义：

> This *shinkansen* or "bullet train" speeds across the rural areas of Japan giving a quick view of cluster after cluster of farmhouses surrounded by rice paddies. This particular pattern did not develop purely by chance, but as a consequence of the technology peculiar to the growing of rice, the staple of the Japanese diet. The growing of rice requires the construction and maintenance of an irrigation system, something that takes many hands to build. More importantly, the planting and the harvesting of rice can only be done efficiently with the cooperation of twenty or more people. The "bottom line" is that a single family working alone cannot produce enough rice to survive, but a dozen families working together can produce a surplus. Thus the Japanese have had to develop the capacity to work together in harmony, no matter what the forces of disagreement or social disintegration, in order to survive.
>
> —William Ouchi, *Theory Z*

- 结果：日本农作模式
- 原因：日本依赖大米，需要集体的力量
- 结果：在田间和睦劳作

9 ▪ 过程分析

当你分析怎样做某事或某事物怎样运作时，就在解释一个过程。以下样例展示了一个过程，描述了所需设备，详述了过程中的步骤：

> As a car owner, you waste money when you pay a mechanic to change the engine oil. The job is not difficult, even if you know little about cars. All you need is a wrench to remove the drain plug, a large, flat pan to collect the draining oil, plastic bottles to dispose of the used oil, and fresh oil. First, warm up the car's engine so that the oil will flow more easily. When the engine is warm, shut it off and remove its oil-filler cap (the owner's manual shows where this cap is). Then locate the drain plug under the engine

- 过程：换机油
- 所需设备
- 过程中的步骤

(again consulting the owner's manual for its location) and place the flat pan under the plug. Remove the plug with the wrench, letting the oil flow into the pan. When the oil stops flowing, replace the plug and, at the engine's filler hole, add the amount and kind of fresh oil specified by the owner's manual. Pour the used oil into the plastic bottles and take it to a waste-oil collector, which any garage mechanic can recommend.

—Anthony Andres (student),
"Do-It-Yourself Car Care"

练习7.7　分析和修改未充分展开的段落

以下段落没有充分展开。重写一个充分展开的段落，用你自己具体的细节或例子来支持一般性陈述。

1. One big difference between successful and unsuccessful teachers is the quality of communication. A successful teacher is sensitive to students' needs and excited by the course subject. In contrast, an unsuccessful teacher seems uninterested in students and bored by the subject.

2. Gestures are one of our most important means of communication. We use them instead of speech. We use them to supplement the words we speak. And we use them to communicate some feelings or meanings that words cannot adequately express.

练习7.8　用不同的展开模式进行写作

写出至少三个重点突出、连贯的、充分展开的段落，每段用不同模式展开。从这里提取话题，或者选出你自己的话题。

1. 记叙：an experience of public speaking, a disappointment, leaving home, waking up

2. 描写：your room, a crowded or deserted place, a food, an intimidating person

3. 举例或支持：study habits, having a headache, the best sports event, usefulness (or uselessness) of a self-help book

4. 定义：humor, an adult, fear, authority

5. 划分或分析：a television news show, a barn, a Web site, a piece of music

6. 分类：factions in a campus controversy, styles or playing poker, types of Web sites, kinds of teachers

7. 比较和对比：using *Facebook* and watching TV, AM and FM radio announcers, high school and college football, movies on TV and in a theater
8. 因果分析：connection between tension and anger, causes of failing a course, connection between credit cards and debt, causes of a serious accident
9. 过程分析：preparing for a job interview, setting up a blog, protecting your home from burglars, making a jump shot

7e 撰写开头段和结尾段

开头段给文章开头，可激发读者对你话题的兴趣。结尾段给文章收尾，给读者一个完成的感觉。

1 ▪ 开头

开头段把读者从他们的世界拉进你的世界：

- 开头把读者的注意力集中到主题上，并唤起他们对于你要说的内容的好奇心。
- 开头明确指出你的话题，并暗示你的态度。
- 通常，开头包含你的主题句。（见 p.16）
- 开头要简洁和真诚。

为集中读者注意力，你有许多选择：

开头策略

- 提问题。
- 讲一件事。
- 一个生动的引用。
- 提供出乎意料的统计数字或其他事实。
- 陈述与你的主题相关的观点。
- 提供背景信息。

- 创造代表你的主题的意象。
- 做历史比较或对比。
- 列出问题或困境。
- 定义你的主题的中心词。
- 在一些商务或技术写作中，总结你的论文。

(CULTURE LANGUAGE) 如果你的母语不是英语，撰写开头的这些选择也许不是你的习惯做法。在其他文化中，读者也许会从作者的开头部分寻求一种熟悉或安心，或者他们也许更喜欢间接地去接近主题。然而，在学术和商务英语中，作者和读者更喜欢原创以及简洁的、直截了当的表达。

有效的开头

非常常见的开头以对文章的一般性主题的陈述开篇,用一句或几句阐明或限制主题,然后在主题句里提出文章观点。以下是两个例子:

Can your home or office computer make you sterile? Can it strike you blind or dumb? The answer is, probably not.	与读者经历相关的主题
Nevertheless, reports of side effects relating to computer use should be examined, especially in the area of birth defects, eye complaints, and postural difficulties.	阐明主题:通往主题句的过渡
Although little conclusive evidence exists to establish a causal link between computer use and problems of this sort, the circumstantial evidence can be disturbing.	主题句

—Thomas Hartmann,
"How Dangerous Is Your Computer?"

The Declaration of Independence is so widely regarded as a statement of American ideals that its origins in practical politics tend to be forgotten.	关于主题的陈述
Thomas Jefferson's draft was intensely debated and then revised in the Continental Congress. Jefferson was disappointed with the result.	阐明主题:通往主题句的过渡
However, a close reading of both the historical context and the revisions themselves indicates that the Congress improved the document for its intended purpose.	主题句

—Ann Weiss (student), "The Editing of the Declaration of Independence"

在很多大众写作中,立即告诉读者你的观点是什么比试图吸引他们更为重要。这个简短备忘录的开头迅速概括了问题,并且(在主题句中)提出了解决问题的方法:

Starting next month, staff vacations will leave our department short-handed. We need to hire two or perhaps three temporary keyboarders to maintain our schedules for the month. —— 主题句

有效开头的其他例子在本手册到处可见。在p. 24，p. 41，p. 109，p. 125和p. 133，查看完整的写作范例。

开头勿用

撰写和修改你的开头时，避免以下这些方法，因为这些方法可能会使读者厌烦或使读者质疑你的真诚或控制力：

- **模糊的概括或真理**。不要天南地北扯太远，比如：Throughout human history . . . 或者In today's world . . . 你也许需要一个预热的段落，以便打草稿，但是读者可以不需要它。
- **平淡的表述**。不要这样开头：The purpose of this essay is . . . , In this essay I will . . . , 或者任何类似的有关意图或话题的表述。
- **指代文章题目**。文章的第一句不要指代文章的标题——例如：This is a big problem或者This book is about the history of the guitar.
- **引用词典条目**。不要拿引用字典定义开头。定义可以成为有效的文章开头，但是这种导入由于过度使用而变得索然无味。
- **道歉**。不要对自己的观点或认知带有责备的口吻，如：I'm not sure if I'm right, but I think . . . , I don't know much about this, but . . . , 或者类似的表述。

2 ▪ 结尾

结尾收束全文，并告诉读者你的最终目的。结尾回答了"那又怎么样"的问题。

有效的结尾

结尾通常自成一段，可以包含一个单句或一组句子。可采取以下方法之一或更多：

结尾策略

- 推荐一套行动方案。
- 总结全文。
- 呼应开头。
- 重申主题并思考它的含意。
- 提出希望或道出遗憾。
- 给出象征性或强有力的事实或其他细节。
- 举一个非常吸引人的例子。
- 创造代表你的主题的意象。
- 引用。

以下段落给一篇关于 Declaration of Independence 的文章收尾（开头见 p. 61）：

> The Declaration of Independence has come to be a statement of this nation's political philosophy, but that was not its purpose in 1776. Jefferson's passionate expression had to bow to the goals of the Congress as a whole to forge unity among the colonies and to win the support of foreign nations.
>
> —Ann Weiss (student), "The Editing of the Declaration of Independence"

呼应开头：过去和现在之间的对比

对主题的重述和详述

在下一篇样例里，作者以对公众行动的呼吁给涉及环境保护的文章结尾：

> Until we get the answers [about the effects of pollutants], I think we had better keep on building power plants and growing food with the help of fertilizers and such insect-controlling chemicals as we now have. The risks are well known, thanks to the environmentalists. If they had not created a widespread public awareness of the ecological crisis, we wouldn't stand a chance. But such awareness by itself is not enough. Flaming manifestos and prophecies of doom are no longer much help, and a search for scapegoats can only make matters worse. The time for sensations and manifestos is about over.

总结和观点

呼吁行动起来

Now we need rigorous analysis, united effort and very hard work.

　　　　　　—Peter F. Drucker,"How Best to Protect
　　　　　　　　　the Environment"

不好的结尾

以下几种结尾非常糟糕：

- **重复开头**。不要只是重复开头。结尾应该就正文所有段落对开头的补充内容加以总概括。
- **转向一个新的方向**。不要引入和你文章主题不同的主题。
- **过度概括**。不要对超出你提供的证据之外的东西进行概括。如果你的文章是关于你试图铲掉一个违章停车罚单的令人抓狂的经历，你不能概括为当地所有警察局都纠缠于繁文缛节而不为人民服务。
- **道歉**。不要让自己的文章疑云密布。不要说：Even though I'm no expert 或 This may not be convincing, but I believe it's true等类似的话。而是，为赢得读者的信任，你需要展示信心。

第 8 章　提交终稿

概要

清晰有效提交终稿需要：

- 遵照你所在学科的格式（下方）
- 多模式写作恰当使用图像和其他媒体 (p. 68)
- 网络写作需要考虑设计 (p. 75)

提交终稿给你提供了以迷人的、可读的格式，展示你辛勤耕耘的机会。这个机会也常常伴随挑战：完成任务要求、体裁惯例以及读者期待。

8a 给各学科学术写作适当制定格式

64

大学里很多作业需要你以纸版或电子版提交写下来的文本——例如，附在电子邮件上或网页课程上。对这样的论文，本章指南将帮助你以迷人的、可读的格式提交作业。此外，许多学术形式的指南还推荐了具体的格式。本书详述了两种格式：

- **MLA格式**，用于英语、其他外语以及其他一些人文学科。下方举例说明了MLA格式，pp. 484–486将有详细讨论。
- **APA格式**，用于社会科学，在pp. 516–519讨论。APA格式在标题页、章节标题形式以及其他特征方面与MLA格式不同。

其他学术格式可在pp. 433–434上的格式指南中找到。一定要与导师沟通核实，如果你对他或她要求的格式有任何问题。

有些学术写作作业完全是电子的，比如自传体博客帖子，或者一个提供校园某项服务的网页。下方许多设计指南也适用于类似项目，但在pp. 75–76中会

» MLA格式样例文章

作者的姓和页码	Torres 1
注明：作者姓名，导师姓名，课程题目，日期	Mia Torres Mr. O'Donnell English 131 14 March 2012
标题居中	Creating the Next Generation of Smokers
自始至终双倍行距	Parents warn their children not to smoke. Schools teach kids and teens about the dangers of smoking. States across the country have enacted smoking bans, making it illegal for adults to smoke in restaurants, bars, workplaces, and public buildings. Yet despite these efforts, smoking among teens and young adults continues, and it does so in part because the film industry creates movies that promote smoking.
在顶部、底部和两边各空1英寸（2.54厘米）	According to the organization Smoke Free Movies, a group based in the School of Medicine at the University of California, San Francisco, tobacco companies and filmmakers collaborate to promote smoking: tobacco companies pay filmmakers to feature their products, and filmmakers show celebrity actors smoking in movies and portray smoking as glamorous and socially acceptable (4-5). Stopping young people's exposure to images of smoking in movies requires stopping each of these activities.
MLA格式的原始资料引用（见p. 439）	Despite proof that showing smoking in movies encourages young people to start smoking, more than half of movies feature well-known stars smoking (Fox). As fig. 1 shows, cigarettes often figure prominently, with the cigarette held close to the celebrity's head so that it is an integral part of the shot.
引入图片，表明意思和目的	[照片：Scarlett Johansson]
和正文分开，可单独阅读的图片说明	Fig. 1. The actress Scarlett Johansson in *Black Dahlia*, one of many movies released each year in which characters smoke. From *Daily Mail*; Associated Newspapers, 2006; Web; 9 Mar. 2012.

受到单独的关注。

1 ▪ 设计原则

许多设计原则顺应了我们的阅读方式。比如空格使我们眼部放松，有助于我们通读全文。分类或列清单表明相互关系。图像和色彩增加了多样性，并有助于强调重要元素。

设计自己的文件时，要依照作业要求，考虑你的目的和读者期待，以及读者在电脑显示屏或纸上，将如何阅读文稿。考虑一下下方有关设计的一般原则，注意下一节讨论的一些元素不适用于所有学术形式，比如标题和列表。

- **在文稿中引导读者**。用标题、列表以及其他元素，在纸版页面或电脑显示屏上建立一种流畅感，即有利于眼睛跟随的模式。
- **运用空格缓解拥挤并集中读者注意力**。提供足够的页边空白，给标题、列表以及其他元素以喘息的空间。即使那些表示段落的空间（缩进或一行额外空间）也会给读者一个间歇，使他们确信观点被分成可控的几大块。
- **把信息分组，以表明相互关系**。使用标题（如本章所示）和列表（如你正在阅读的所示）来表达文稿部分中的相同点和不同点。
- **标准化创建，并满足期待**。帮助直接的读者通读你的文章，可采用以下方法，例如，对重要性等级相同的标题，使用相同字号和颜色。标准化也可减少混乱，使读者更易判定各部分的重要性。
- **强调重要元素**。用字体、字号、标题、缩进、颜色、方框以及空格等，建立信息等级。例如，在本书中，从字体和装饰性元素中，比如标题8a上方的空距，标题的重要性就一目了然。

2 ▪ 设计元素

页边、行距和字体，也许还包括强调、标题、清单、颜色以及插图都应该应用前述的原则。许多作业都会对你应该使用的格式加以规定。如果你的读者有视力障碍，那么也需要考虑p. 68方框中的要点。

页边空白

在纸版页面的顶部、底部及两边留出空白，以防页面布局太满给读者带来不快。多数学术文章四边使用1英寸（2.54厘米）空白。

行距

许多大部头纸版学术论文使用双倍行距，段落首行缩进，还有许多通过电脑显示屏阅读的论文是单倍行距，段落之间额外空行。无论是前者还是后者，双倍或三倍行距把标题分开。

字体和字号

文本可读性部分来自字体（或字形）和字号。学术和商务文本通常选择标准字体，如下所示：

10-point Cambria   10-point Arial
12-point Cambria   12-point Arial

像 Cambria 这样的字体有**衬线**——字符收尾处的细线，比如说这个 T 字顶部向下的部分。衬线字体适于正式写作，且适于大多数人纸版阅读。无衬线（sans serif，sans 为法语的"没有"）字体，比如上方的 Arial，通常更容易在电脑显示屏上阅读，而且对那些有视力障碍的读者来说，该字体在纸版上阅读更清晰。（见 p. 68）一般情况下，要避免使用装饰性字体，比如：**Comic Sans**，*Freestyle Script* 和 **Impact**。

字体的磅值对实际字体的大小并没有什么指导作用，但是最标准的字体以 10 或 12 磅为易读。如果你用 PowerPoint 幻灯片口头提交文稿，那你需要使用更大号字体。

强调

在一个文档文本中，<u>下画线</u>、*斜体*和**黑体**可以强调关键词或句子。在打印版中，你有时可以使用黑体来表示强调——例如，给一个词语下定义。在网络文档中，黑体和下画线通常用来表示媒体和其他网页的链接。

作为一般规则，选择性地使用强调，对你要表达的思想进行补充，而不仅仅是修饰性地给文章增色。许多读者发现字体装饰令人分心。

标题

标题的作用如同路标：引导读者注意文档中最重要的内容。在电子项目中，标题既具功能性又具装饰性，以大字号、大量空格和非常规的字体，吸引读者注意力。然而，在学术写作中，标题更单纯具有功能性。标题可以把长文本分成独立的部分，强调重点，并引导读者。

当你在学术写作中使用标题时，遵循以下要领：

- **使用一、二或三级标题**，取决于材料需要和文档篇幅。每两页左右出现某级标题有助于读者跟紧作者不跑偏。

- 创建文档提纲来计划在哪里添加标题。把一级标题留给要点（和主要章节）。使用二级或三级标题来标注带有支持性信息的子章节。
- 尽可能使标题简短，同时使标题对接下来的内容有明确提示。
- 标题语言一致——例如，都用疑问句（What Is the Scientific Method?），都用带有-ing的词组（Understanding the Scientific Method），或者都用名词词组（The Scientific Method）。
- 指示标题的相对重要性，用字号、位置和强调，比如大写或黑体。

一级标题

二级标题

三级标题

通常，你可以使用与文本相同的字体和大小作为标题。

- 不要在标题后换页。把标题推到下一页。

注意：心理学以及其他一些社会科学，文档格式需要对标题进行特殊处理，见p. 518。

清单

清单从视觉上加强了相同项目之间的关系——例如，一个过程的步骤或一项提案的要素。清单比段落容易读，并且增添了空白。

清单中的项目在语言上应该是并列的——例如，都使用完整的句子或者都使用词组。（还可见p. 157）清单上下都要留有空间。给项目编号，或者用项目标号做标记：圆点或其他图形，比如用于下方关于颜色清单的方点。在许多文字处理器上，你可以使用格式菜单自动创建清单。

为有视力障碍的读者做设计

如果你的读者包括视力低下、色觉有问题，或者处理视觉信息有困难的读者，那么让你的设计符合这些读者的需要：

- **使用大号字体。**许多指引语需要14磅号字，或者更大。
- **使用标准字体。**许多视力低下的人发现，看Arial这样的无衬线字体比看衬线字体更容易。避免使用带有不同寻常的回旋状花纹的装饰性字体，即便是用于标题。
- **避免将词全部大写。**
- **避免仅仅依靠颜色来区分元素。**给元素做标记，然后通过位置或字号识别它们。
- **选择性使用红和绿。**对那些红绿色盲读者来说，这些颜色将会以灰色、黄色或蓝色阴影出现。

(续表）

- **使用对比鲜明的颜色。**为使颜色便于区分，从色谱中挑选对比鲜明的颜色——例如，紫和黄，或者橙和蓝。
- **仅使用浅色作为字体后面的色调。**使字体本身为黑色或非常深的颜色。

颜色

网络文档和其他数字项目几乎总是需要使用颜色，但是传统的学术写作除了图像极少使用颜色。（找导师询问他或她的意见）如果你的确要在学术文档里使用颜色，遵循以下要领：

- 只用黑色打印文本。
- 确定有颜色的标题颜色足够深，以利阅读。
- 对同级别的标题使用相同颜色——例如，主要标题用红色，次要标题用黑色。
- 对项目标号、线和其他非文本元素使用颜色。但是使用的颜色不要超过三种，以使页面保持清晰。
- 使用颜色区分插图的不同部分。尽量根据需要使用颜色，以使插图清晰。

8b 将图像和其他媒体适当用于多模式写作

学术写作常常是**多模式**的——也就是说，它包括不止一种媒体，无论是文本、图表、照片、视频或音频，都可以。简单的多模式文稿只包含两种媒体——主要是嵌入了插图的文本。在线提交的文稿会添加音频或视频文件的链接。本小节为你写作提供了选择和使用这种媒体的应用指南。

注意：你写作中包含或链接的任何视频或媒体文件，都需要列出同样详尽的出处。见pp. 425–431，获得更多关于标明出处的信息。

1 ▪ 选择图像和其他媒体

根据写作情境，你可使用表、条形图、视频等，以支持写作。以下几页将对几种选择进行介绍和举例说明。

注意：网络对图像、音频和视频来说是绝佳的资源库。（见 pp. 392–394）你的电脑会包含这样的程序，可以制作表、图以及其他插图，或者你也可以使用类似 Excel（用于图和图表）或 Adobe Illustrator（用于图表、地图等）等程序。在口头演示时，使用 PowerPoint 或者类似的程序展示图像。

表

表通常展示原始数据，使复杂的信息变得容易为读者所理解。数据显示变量之间的关系，或者两个或两个以上群组进行对照，如下所示。

» 表

描述性题目列在表之上。	横排和竖列布局清晰：标题和数据对齐，数字和竖列对齐。
标题标明横排和竖列。	

Table 1
Public- and private-school enrollment of US students age five and older, 2011

	Number of students	Percentage in public school	Percentage in private school
All students	74,603,000	85	15
Kindergarten through grade 8	39,179,000	88	12
Grades 9-12	16,332,000	92	8
College (undergraduate)	16,366,000	77	23
Graduate and professional school	2,737,000	50	50

Source: Data from *Digest of Education Statistics: 2011*; Natl. Center for Educ. Statistics, Apr. 2012; Web; 10 May 2012; table 2.

饼状图

饼状图显示一个整体中各部分之间的关系。整体合计百分之百，每个饼形切片的大小和它在整体中所占份额成比例。当份额，而不是基本数据，成为关注焦点时，饼状图才有意义。

» 饼状图

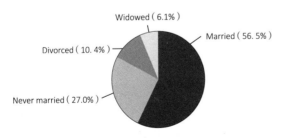

	颜色阴影标明饼状图各个部分。
	各部分百分比总计达百分之百。
	每部分都有标注。
	饼状图下方的说明解释了该图，并注明了出处。

Fig. 1. Marital status in 2010 of adults age eighteen and over. Data from *2012 Statistical Abstract*; US Census Bureau, Dec. 2011; Web; 7 Mar. 2012.

条形图

条形图以数量或频率为尺度，在群组或时间周期之间进行比较。当相对的大小尺寸变得重要时，条形图才有意义。条形图总是从左下角零点开始，这样纵轴上的数值就很清晰。

» 条形图

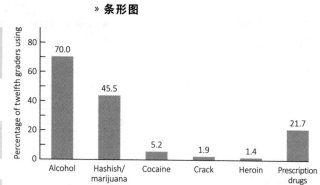

纵坐标显示并清楚标出测量的数值。零点使数值清晰。

横坐标显示并清楚标出对照群组。

条形图下方的说明解释了该图，并注明了出处。

Fig. 2. Lifetime prevalence of use of alcohol and other drugs among twelfth graders in 2011. Data from *Monitoring the Future: A Continuing Study of American Youth*; U of Michigan, 22 Feb. 2012; Web; 10 Apr. 2012.

线形图

线形图显示一个或一个以上研究对象随着时间发生的变化。线形图以一种经济的、高度可视化方式将许多数据点进行比较。线形图总是从左下角零点开始，这样纵轴上的数值就很清晰。（见下页图）

图表

图表从视觉上显示概念，比如一个组织的结构、某物运作方式或看起来的样子，或者研究对象之间的关系。通常，图表显示的是不能言简意赅地用文字描绘出的东西。（见下页图）

图像：照片、美术品、广告和漫画

有时你的整篇文章也许都用来批判性地分析一个图像，比如一幅油画或一个广告。更经常的是，你会使用图像来支持你在论文或演讲中提出的观点。你也许会用一幅土星照片（见第80页）来使一个信息量大的宇航员的报告更清晰，用复制一幅画面或照片的方法来加强对一部漫画小说的分析，提供一个20世纪50年代的广告作为断定该年代一种态度的证据，或者用一幅漫画捕捉一场政治辩论的关键。

» **线形图**

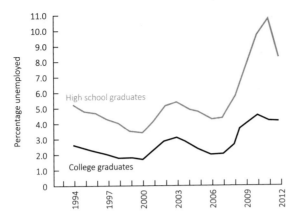

Fig. 3. Unemployment rates of high school graduates and college graduates, 1994-2012. Data from *Economics News Release*; US Dept. of Labor, Bureau of Labor Statistics, 3 Feb. 2012; Web; 6 June 2012.

纵坐标显示并清楚标出测量的数值。零点使数值清晰。

标签把被比较的研究对象区分开来。如果你的文稿不带颜色的话，可以使用打点的黑色虚线或深浅不同的线。

横坐标显示并清楚标出日期范围。

线形图下方的说明解释了该图，并注明了出处。

» **图表**

Fig. 4. *MyPlate*, a graphic representation of daily food portions required for a healthy diet. From *ChooseMyPlate.gov*; US Dept. of Agriculture, 2011; Web; 8 July 2012.

图表使概念变得容易理解。

图表下方的说明解释了该表，并注明了出处。

视频和音频

如果你数字化地展示你的作品——例如，一个网页或博客——你也许会选择用插入或链接视频和音频文件的方法来强调或举例说明你文中的观点。例如，你也许会用一个展示一件事情如何运转的视频来解释某个过程，用一场演出的视频来支持对一个剧本的解读，或者用链接一场面试的方法来阐明一个人的简况。下页的显示屏上显示了一篇在线文章中的一段文本，该文章链接到诗人Rita Dove，正在朗读她的诗作"American Smooth"。

> **照片**

照片比文字更经济、更引人注目地显示了物体。

图像下方的说明解释了该图,并注明了出处。

Fig. 5. View of Saturn from the *Cassini spacecraft*, showing the planet and its rings. From *Cassini-Huygens: Mission to Saturn and Titan*; US Natl. Atmospheric and Space Administration, Jet Propulsion Laboratory, 24 Feb. 2005; Web; 26 June 2012.

> **链接到视频文件**

Often a reading by the poet reinforces both the sound and the meaning of the poem. In Rita Dove's "American Smooth," two people move self-consciously through an intricate dance, smiling and holding their bodies just so, when suddenly they experience a moment of perfection: they nearly float. When Dove reads the poem aloud, she builds to that moment, allowing listeners to feel the same magic (http://www.poetryfoundation.org/features/video/267).

2 ▪ 有效使用图像和其他媒体

图像或视频剪辑可以吸引读者的注意力,但如果过多的话,将会变成装饰,或者更糟糕的是,将把读者的注意力从你作品的内容上移开。使用任何图像和其他媒体之前,要考虑它们是否符合你任务的需要,是否能达到目的,是否对读者合适。

考虑写作情境的需求和局限

你正在进行的写作类型和它的格式所允许的范围是什么?仔细观察类似写作的范例,以估计读者期待的媒体种类,如果有的话。但以下事情也很重要,即,你如何呈现你的作品:经PowerPoint演示的,或网上的一个短的动画可以做到精美绝伦，但打印的版本需要照片、图画以及其他静态的解释方法。

让图像和其他媒体支持你的写作

确认你使用的任何图像与你文章中的论点直接相关，对该论点有所补充，而且引发读者思考。在对一个广告的评价中，广告本身就支持你对该广告所做的断言。在一篇论证地震防备的文章中，一张照片就可以提供关于地震灾害的可视性报告，一张图表就可以显示出当前防备的级别。

负责任地使用图像和其他媒体

使用图像和其他媒体需要特别注意，以避免歪曲，并确保诚实使用其他媒体。

- **仔细创建并评价表、图表以及图。** 要核实你使用的数据是准确的，你所强调的变化、关系以及趋势反映了现实。例如，在线形图中，在零点处开始的纵轴把线放到了真实的背景之中。（见前面的例子）
- **对网络上找到的图像持怀疑态度。** 修改了的照片经常被挂在网上，且广泛流传。如果照片显得不真实，核查其来源或者干脆不用。
- **提供来源注解。** 无论你何时使用别人的数据创建图像，在你文档中插入别人的图像，或者链接别人的媒体文件，你必须注明出处。每个学科都有略微不同的来源注解格式：在pp. 69–73插图中的来源注解是MLA格式。还可见第56和57章。
- **如果必要，需要征得许可。** 对那些将驻留在网络上的项目来说，你使用图像或媒体文件需要经过版权持有者的许可。见pp. 431–432关于版权和许可的讨论。

下页两张图像支持了带有这个主题的文章：*By the mid-1960s, depictions of women in advertising reflected changing attitudes toward the traditional role of homemaker.*

让图像和其他媒体融入你的写作

读者应该理解你为什么要在文章中加入图像和其他媒体以及它们与整个项目有什么关系：

- **在插入图像的项目里，把图像和文本连在一起。** 当你在写作中加入了图像，要适时提及这些图像，读者也可以通过查阅这些图像受益——例如，"见图2"或"见表1"。把图和表分别编号。（图1，图2等；表1，表2等）一定要把说明包括进来，因为说明明确地把图像和文本连在一起——这样读者就不会对你的意图感到困惑——而且说明还提供来源信息。
- **在使用了音频和视频的在线项目里，把这些文件或链接加入你的文本中。** 读者应该知道你想要媒体展示什么，你是否从一个文本文件链接到一幅照

> **作为支持的图像**

图像例子支持主题：对作为家庭主妇的妇女不断变化的态度。

说明解释了图像，让图像和文本密不可分，并提供来源信息。

Fig. 6. An advertisement from 1945 (left) and a brochure illustration from 1965 (right) showing a change in the relationship between homemaking women and their appliances. Left: Hoover advertisement; 1945; print. Right: *Electric Ranges by Frigidaire*; 1965; print.

片上，或者你将文本、声音、静态图像以及视频加入一个复杂的网络项目中了。例如，在p. 73的样例中，插入的链接邀请读者去阅读和聆听Rita Dove朗读她的诗作"American Smooth"。

8c 为网络写作时考虑设计

网络项目的许多创建者上传文件到现存表格里，使得设计变得相当容易。即便你使用这样的软件，你仍将不得不就这些元素做出选择，比如字体、颜色、布局、标题等。pp. 64–68的学术写作设计指南可以帮助你做出这些决定，下方关于学术网络作品的讨论也可以，比如网站或者挂在博客或维基百科上的多模式项目。

1 ▪ 网站

设计网站时，要知道读者的阅读模式通常是在浏览页面亮点和专心关注文本的一个章节之间交替进行。为给这种阅读提供方便，你会想要一种既清晰又

易于导航的设计,如下方截屏所示:

» **网站主页**

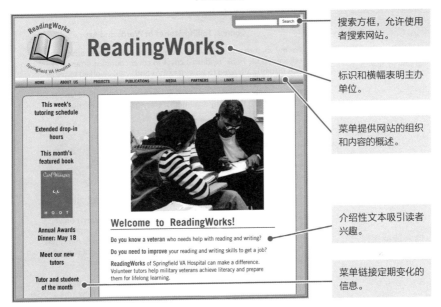

2 ▪ 博客或维基百科

作为学术作业,你可创建博客或维基百科,这样你将需要决定网站作为一个整体的外观。然而,对大多数学术博客或维基百科写作来说,你将张贴文章草稿,并且需要对同学的作业给予评论。你可以在文字处理器上撰写和校订你的文本,然后把文本张贴在博客或维基百科上面。届时,你将有机会为你的帖子写一个描述性标题,上传图像和其他媒体,并且添加链接到其他网站。你也可以在公开发布之前预览这个帖子。

下页例子展示了一个学生个人随笔的草稿,他把这个草稿张贴在他的班级博客上。

» 张贴在博客上的文章

描述性标题为帖子提供背景。

可读性标准字体。

插图支持帖子的一个论点。

插入链接到另一个网站。

FRIDAY, FEBRUARY 17, 2012
Literacy narrative draft

Comics: Telling Stories in Words and Art

For my seventh birthday, I received a Calvin and Hobbes comic book. I devoured the book, reading it cover to cover countless times, and was instantly attracted to how drawings and words worked together to tell very funny stories about the characters. I didn't always understand the vocabulary, the jokes, and references to the 1980s, but I laughed at what I did get: the funny arguments, crazy games, and hilarious schemes.

The summer after my birthday I began drawing my own comics. I created two characters modeled on Calvin and Hobbes—a boy  named Timmy and his dog Snuffy. Over the next five years, I drew hundreds of comics about Timmy, Snuffy, and Timmy's family and friends. I drew the strip shown here, about one of Timmy's many mishaps, when I was ten. I have this strip and some of my other favorites posted on my personal blog: johnsdoodles@blogger.com.

Timmy experienced much of what I did over the next several years. He went on vacation to places I visited with my family, like New York and San Francisco. He visited aunts, uncles, and grandparents. He exasperated his parents, annoyed his sister, learned to play an instrument, and dreamed of being a pilot. He also did things I had not experienced: he once trained for the school marathon and came in third, dreamed of going to the prom like his sister, and slid down what seemed like a mile-long hill on a sled. Through Timmy, I used language and drawing to explore ideas, dreams, and experiences, and feelings, all the time trying to make them funny.

Although I still draw and write, I left Timmy behind the summer I turned twelve. However, occasionally I look back at my Timmy comics and find it interesting to see how I used words and images to develop and display my sense of place in the world.

Posted by John Heywood at 4:23 PM.

第二部分
大学内外的写作

第9章 · 加入学术圈
第10章 · 批判性思维与阅读
第11章 · 学术写作
第12章 · 撰写论述文
第13章 · 文学阅读与写作
第14章 · 大众写作

第 9 章　加入学术圈

概要

加入学术圈：
- 从面授和在线课堂中获得最大收益（下方）
- 成为一名学术作者（p. 79）
- 树立学术操守（p. 80）
- 与老师和同学进行有效沟通（p. 82）

9a 从大学课程中获得最大收益

如果你积极参与课堂活动，你就会喜欢上每一门课，并从中获得更大收益。遵循以下准则，为你的大学课程做准备并为之做出贡献。

- **参与课堂活动**。无论是面授，还是在线课程，要消除其他顾虑，从而做到集中精力听课、提问、记笔记并参与讨论。（见 p. 79 加框文字中关于参加在线课程的贴士）
- **记笔记**。将课堂笔记与课程的所有要素相结合。课程要素包括老师对原始资料的观点和处理方法、你自己的想法以及指定的阅读材料（即便是你已经读过的材料）。上课时，要用自己的话尽可能完整地记笔记。要区分主要观点、次要观点和支撑观点。如有遗漏，要留出空间以便日后添加。课后要立即复习笔记内容以强化学习。
- **完成指定的阅读任务**。大学课程的指定阅读（如教材、期刊文章、论文和文学作品）要求你更多地关注理解和记忆，而不是娱乐或获得实用信息。下一章中描述的活动进程将帮助你成为一名既有效率又有效力的读者。
- **对新观点持开放态度**。大学课程不但应该增加知识，而且应该引发思考。如果你对新观点很好奇并对它持开放态度，你将会从大学经历中获益良多。
- **诚信学习**。你在大学的所有行为都向老师、同学及整个大学社区展现你是什么样的人。不论是上课、考试或撰写论文，你都要诚实认真，以此表示对他人和自己的尊重。详见 p. 80 学术操守。

> **参加在线课程**
>
> 本章节和本手册中的建议适用于面授或在线课程。但是对于在线课程，你通常是独自一人按照自己的节奏学习。以下的贴士可以帮助你取得成功。
>
> - **研究教学大纲**。课程大纲将告诉你课程目标、阅读和写作任务。大纲一般是课程预期的唯一提示。
> - **要有纪律性**。制订一份定期学习计划并遵守，这样你就不至于落后。做功课时，要关闭所有干扰物，如手机、电视和音乐播放器。
> - **参与课程学习**。如果课程涉及与他人的合作，你要积极参与。如果你有疑问或要对课程资料发表意见或想知道你在课上的表现，你要去问老师。
> - **备份你的学习**。对于在线学习和交流来说，电脑死机是灾难性的。按照惯例，将笔记、草稿和已完成的作业保存在闪存盘、外置硬盘或在线存储服务器上。

- **必要时寻求帮助**。大多数老师每周都会有与学生面谈的时间，许多老师还有在线面谈时间。另外，大多数学校有写作中心、辅导中心、图书馆导览和其他服务。

9b 成为一名学术作者

作为一名大学生，你或许要完成大量的写作任务。当然，学术写作任务根据学科、课程和老师会有所不同。但是，即便是有所不同，你也可以关注以下的关键目标，从而让自己适应每一项写作任务。本书的其他章节将会对每一个目标展开更为详尽的讨论。

- **了解任务要求**。大多数写作任务至少会暗示一个可能的主题、写作目的、读者、体裁（或论文类型），会明确文章的长度和截止日期。在这种情况下，你在写作过程中要提炼你的主题、目的和目标读者。（详见pp. 4–9）
- **确定并组织写作**。大多数学术论文围绕着主要论点或主题展开，并用证据支撑该主题。确定主题和组织文章详见pp. 16–24。
- **综合自己与他人的观点**。大学写作通常包括研究他人的作品并与之互动：对他人观点持开放态度，对他人观点做出反应，质疑并比较他人观点，以及使用他人观点回答问题。这些互动要求你进行批判性阅读（下一章内容），综合他人观点或将他人观点融入自己的观点中。观点综合详见p. 93和pp. 103–104。
- **使用学术语言**。使用正式而标准的英语，避免非正式和网络语言，例如，缩略语和不完整的句子，除非老师另有要求。pp. 105–108和pp. 163–170有学术语言的详尽介绍。
- **修改并校订论文**。大学的写作任务要求认真写作。你要留出足够的时间来修改和校订，这样读者就能明白你的主要观点，跟随你的思路，并读懂你的句子。修改和校订论文见pp. 29–34和pp. 36–38。
- **引用原始资料**。正如下面将要谈到的，学术作者通过完整标注所引用的观点和信息而依赖他人的作品。记录你所查阅的任何资料的出版信息。这样，如果你在写作中要用的话，你就可以引用它。

9c 树立学术操守

学术操守是构建学术知识大厦的基础。信任彼此的诚实让学生和学者得以细阅并拓展其他学者的作品，也使得老师可以指导并评估学生的学习进程。

作为一名学生，你在准备和参与课程学习中、在考试中，尤其是在写作中有机会树立并展示你的学术操守。许多写作任务要求你查阅原始资料，如期刊文章、网站和书籍。这些作品属于原创者。如果你能诚信地引用这些作品，你就可以自由地引用。这意味着要准确描述原始资料，不要误解或歪曲原始资料。这还意味着要标明原始资料的出处而不是抄袭，或以你是原创者的口吻展示原始资料和信息。在大多数大学校园，抄袭是该受惩罚的违法行为。

抄袭可以是有意的，也可以是无意的。故意抄袭是彻头彻尾的欺骗：抄袭其他作者的句子并当成是自己的句子而蒙混过关，从网上购买文章，或让他人代写论文。无意抄袭在学生中更为常见，通常源自在处理原始资料时的粗心大意和缺乏经验。例如，你可能将原始资料信息剪切并粘贴到自己的观点中，而没有明确是谁说了什么；或者你总结了原始资料，却没有标明部分内容其实是引用的。在这些情况下，抄袭是无意的，但依旧是抄袭。

通过形成自己的观点并负责任地处理原始资料，你就可以树立自己的学术操守。以下的贴士会有所帮助。更多信息，见pp. 425–431。

获取观点

开始研究之前，你要考虑你对某个主题的已有知识和观点。这样的事先筹划可以让你更容易地识别其他作者的观点，并在自己的写作中公正应对。（不论你是否同意这些观点）

- **查阅原始资料之前，评估你所知道的信息并思考主题**。在查阅他人观点之前，给自己时间了解自己的想法。之后，你就可以思考原始资料如何强化、否定或扩展你的已有知识。

- 认真评估原始资料。作者通常从某个特定角度来写作，有些人的偏见比其他人明显。你没有必要因为原始资料带有偏见而拒绝之。通常，你想要考虑多种观点。但是，你需要辨认并权衡作者的立场。见 pp. 397–409 关于评估原始资料的讨论。
- 公正处理原始资料。原封不动地再现作者的观点和角度，不要有任何误解或歪曲。在改写和总结时要小心谨慎，不要篡改作者的意思。编辑引文时，不要遗漏重要单词。

组织原始资料

通过认真记录所查阅的原始资料，记录影响思维的观点和所引用的单词与句子，并在写作中谨慎引用原始资料，你就可以避免抄袭。如果你不熟悉这些习惯，请在手边放置以下清单。

- 记录所阅读的原始资料信息。养成经常记录原始资料的出版信息（作者、标题、日期等）和在阅读原始资料时获得的观点的习惯。见 p. 377 的加框文字。
- 谨慎引用。如果你将文章、网站或其他原始资料的部分内容剪切并粘贴到自己的文档中，你必须加上引号，这样你就不会意外混淆自己的文字和原始资料的文字。检查你在写作中使用的引文是否有与原始资料相悖的地方。如何引用原始资料详见 pp. 416–418。
- 用自己的话改写或总结。改写或总结展示了原始资料的观点，但没有用原来的文字，也没有用引号。如果你在根据记忆写下原始资料时没有查看原始资料，你就不大可能使用原始资料作者的文字（因而也就不会抄袭）。不过，你依旧必须标注总结或改写的原始资料，就像你在引用时一样。如何总结并改述原始资料详见 pp. 413–416。
- 标注原始资料的来源。在打草稿时，你要意识到什么时候用了原始资料信息，并小心谨慎地明确标出引用的资料源自何处。在终稿中，你要在论文中使用特定的引文格式来列出论文最后详尽的参考目录。本书展现两种引文格式：MLA 关于英语和其他人文学科的论文格式（pp. 439–483）及 APA 关于社会科学的论文格式（pp. 497–516）。

9d 在学术环境中进行有效沟通

作为一名学术社区的成员，你不仅要写论文和计划书，还要通过电子邮件、课程博客或者课程管理系统，直接与老师、同学和学校的其他人进行文字交流。虽然这类交流不像指定写作那样正式，但它也不像给朋友的短信、推特上的帖子或Facebook上的评论那样不正式。

即便在简短的电子邮件中，如果你很好地展示自己并向读者表明你的敬意，你的信件也会获得更好的关注。下面的信件说明了在给老师写电子邮件时如何恰当融合正式和非正式语言。

» 电子邮件信息

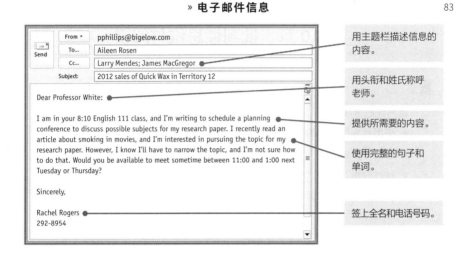

以下是这类交流的准则：

- **使用老师推荐的媒介**。不要发短信、推特或使用社交网站，除非你受邀这么做。
- **姓名的使用**。如果可能的话，在正文中，用姓名称呼读者。在姓氏前加上教授、博士、女士或先生，除非老师另有要求。结尾处签上自己的姓名和联系方式。
- **注意语气**。不要从头到尾都使用大写字母。小心使用反语或讽刺。在缺乏面部表情的情况下，反语或讽刺都会导致误解。
- **注意准确性**。避免使用缩写和推特体，如不完整的句子和缩略词（u代替you，r代替are等），尤其是在给老师写信时。（见pp. 106–107关于学术语言的讨论）检查有无语法、标点符号和拼写上的错误。
- **只给需要的人写信**。原则上，不要同时给多个收信人写信，如一门课的所有学生，除非信件内容适合所有收信人。在点击"回复所有人"之前，要确保"所有人"都想看到你的回信。
- **保护自己与他人的隐私**。在线工具可以让我们发布关于他人的有害信息，也可以让他人对我们做同样的事情。在发送有关自己或他人的信息之前，要考虑不论是现在还是将来，是否值得这么做、谁会看到这个信息。在转发信息时，要确保不要误发之前的个人信息。

- **不要写任何你不会当面说或不会在纸版信件中书写的内容。** 电子信息可以被保存、转发并在涉及成绩和其他事件的争议中被恢复。

第 10 章　批判性思维与阅读

概要

批判性思维和阅读：
- 使用批判性阅读的技巧（下方）
- 总结（p. 89）
- 通过分析、解释、综合与评估形成批判性反应（p. 91）
- 批判性地观看图像（p. 94）

整个大学期间以及大学毕业以后，人们会要求你进行评判性的思考、阅读和写作。这里的批判性不是指"否定的"而是指"怀疑的""好奇的""创造性的"。每天，在你弄明白为什么事情会发生在你身上或者你所经历的意味着什么时，你就已经在进行批判性活动了。它帮助你明白哪些观点是有用的、公平而明智的，哪些观点不是。

注意：批判性思维在研究性写作中起到重要作用。有关印刷版原始资料和在线原始资料的评估，见pp. 397–409。关于资料的合成，见pp. 409–410。

10a 使用批判性阅读的技巧

在大学和工作中，大多数的批判性思维关注书面文本（短篇小说、期刊文章、博客）或视觉物体（照片、图表、电影）。和所有值得进行批判性思考的题材一样，这类作品至少在三个层面上运行：(1) 原创者真正阐述或展示的内容；(2) 原创者没有阐述或展示但又（有意或无意）融入作品中的内容；(3) 你的想法。发现作品（即便是视觉作品）每一层面的内容涉及四个主要步骤：预览材料、积极阅读、总结和形成批判性的反应。

CULTURE LANGUAGE 如果你本国文化中的读者更倾向于寻求理解或同意，而不是参与他们所阅读的内容，那么批判性阅读的想法可能需要你做出一些调整。英语读者出于各种原因（包括娱乐、巩固记忆和获取信息）而使用作品，但是他们也都是带着问题阅读，试图揭示作者的意图（这位作家的倾向是什么），验证他们自己的观点（我能像这位作家那样很好地支撑我的观点吗）并形成新的知识（为什么作者的证据那么有说服力）。

1 ▪ 预览材料

在阅读文学作品，如短篇小说或诗歌时，通常最好是一头扎进去，不停地读。但是，对其他作品进行批判性阅读时，在逐字逐句阅读之前最好先浏览一遍，以便对作品有所预期，甚至形成一些初步问题。预览材料可以使你的阅读更加见闻广博且富有成效。

- **预估时间和水平**。材料是否简短易懂，这样你就可以一口气看完或者需要更长的时间？
- **检查出版信息**。出版日期显示材料是流行还是过时？出版商或出版物专攻学术文章、流行书籍或者其他？对于网络出版物来说，谁或者什么资助了网站？个人？非营利组织？政府机构？学院或大学？
- **查找内容线索**。题目、介绍、标题、插图、结论和其他特征告诉你哪些关于主题、作者方法和主要观点的内容？
- **了解作者**。传记告诉你作者的出版作品、兴趣、倾向及在该领域的声望了吗？如果没有传记，你从作者的文字中可以收集哪些关于作者的信息？使用网络搜索、查找不熟悉的作者。
- **思考你的初步反应**。你对主题知道些什么？对于主题或作者的方法，你有什么问题？影响你对作品阅读的个人倾向是什么？例如，好奇或者厌烦与作者相似或相反的观点。

> **练习10.1　预览文章**
>
> 下面是经济学家Thomas Sowell的一篇论文。他撰写过经济学、政治学和教育学方面的文章。这篇论文首次发表于20世纪90年代，但是关于学生贷款的争议一直没有平息。Sowell写完该论文后，身背贷款债务的大学毕业生人数增加了三分之一，他们所欠的平均金额几乎翻了三倍。使用前面所提到的准则预览该论文，然后阅读一或两遍，直到你认为自己理解作者说了些什么。记下你的问题和想法。
>
> Student Loans
>
> The first lesson of economics is scarcity: There is never enough of anything to fully satisfy all those who want it.

The first lesson of politics is to disregard the first lesson of economics. When politicians discover some group that is being vocal about not having as much as they want, the "solution" is to give them more. Where do politicians get this "more"? They rob Peter to pay Paul.

After a while, of course, they discover that Peter doesn't have enough. Bursting with compassion, politicians rush to the rescue. Needless to say, they do not admit that robbing Peter to pay Paul was a dumb idea in the first place. On the contrary, they now rob Tom, Dick, and Harry to help Peter.

The latest chapter in this long-running saga is that politicians have now suddenly discovered that many college students graduate heavily in debt. To politicians it follows, as the night follows the day, that the government should come to their rescue with the taxpayers' money.

How big is this crushing burden of college students' debt that we hear so much about from politicians and media deep thinkers? For those students who graduate from public colleges owing money, the debt averages a little under $7000. For those who graduate from private colleges owing money, the average debt is a little under $9000.

Buying a very modestly priced automobile involves more debt than that. And a car loan has to be paid off faster than the ten years that college graduates get to repay their student loans. Moreover, you have to keep buying cars every several years, while one college education lasts a lifetime.

College graduates of course earn higher incomes than other people. Why, then, should we panic at the thought that they have to repay loans for the education which gave them their opportunities? Even graduates with relatively modest incomes pay less than 10 percent of their annual salary on the loan the first year—with declining percentages in future years, as their pay increases.

Political hysteria and media hype may focus on the low-income student with a huge debt. That is where you get your heart-rending stories— even if they are not all that typical. In reality, the soaring student loans of the past decade have resulted from allowing high-income people to borrow under government programs.

Before 1978, college loans were available through government programs only to students whose family income was below some cut-off level. That cut-off level was about double the national average income, but at least it kept out the Rockefellers and the Vanderbilts. But, in an era of "compassion," Congress took off even those limits.

That opened the floodgates. No matter how rich you were, it still paid to borrow money through the government at low interest rates. The money you had set aside for your children's education could be invested somewhere else, at higher interest rates. Then, when the student loan became due, parents could pay it off with the money they had set aside— pocketing the difference in interest rates.

To politicians and the media, however, the rapidly growing loans showed what a great "need" there was. The fact that many students welshed when time came to repay their loans showed how "crushing" their burden of debt must be. In reality, those who welsh typically have smaller loans, but have dropped out of college before finishing. People who are irresponsible in one way are often irresponsible in other ways.

No small amount of the deterioration of college standards has been due to the increasingly easy availability of college to people who are not very serious about getting an education. College is not a bad place to hang out for a few years, if you have nothing better to do, and if someone else is paying for it. Its costs are staggering, but the taxpayers carry much of that burden, not only for state universities and city colleges, but also to an increasing extent even for "private" institutions.

Numerous government subsidies and loan programs make it possible for many people to use vast amounts of society's resources at low cost to themselves. Whether in money terms or in real terms, federal aid to higher education has increased several hundred percent since 1970. That has enabled colleges to raise their tuition by leaps and bounds and enabled professors to be paid more and more for doing less and less teaching.

Naturally all these beneficiaries are going to create hype and hysteria to keep more of the taxpayers' money coming in. But we would be fools to keep on writing blank checks for them.

When you weigh the cost of things, in economics that's called "trade-offs." In politics, it's called "mean-spirited." Apparently, if we just took a different attitude, scarcity would go away.

—Thomas Sowell

2 ▪ 阅读

阅读本身不是一步即成的过程。你要理解作品的第一层含义（作者真正表达的内容），然后形成自己的印象。

第一遍阅读

第一遍阅读新材料时，要尽量平稳而顺畅地阅读，努力了解作者的要点。

- **在可以集中精力的地方阅读。**选择安静、远离干扰（如音乐或谈话）的环境。
- **给自己留出时间。**催促自己或心系自己要做的其他事情会妨碍你理解正在阅读的材料。
- **努力喜欢所阅读的作品。**寻找作品与现有知识之间的联系，欣赏新的信息、有趣的关系、有说服力的写作、幽默和不错的例子。
- **第一遍阅读时，做少量的笔记。**标出主要的难点，比如你不理解的段落。再次阅读之前努力解决之。

（CULTURE LANGUAGE）如果英语不是你的第一语言而你又遇到不熟悉的单词，不要停下来查字典。停下来查字典会干扰你对作品的整体理解。努力通过上下文线索（如例子和单词的同义词）猜测单词的意思。记得圈出这些生词，稍后再查。你可以在单词本上记下单词、词义及其所在的句子。

再次阅读

第一遍阅读之后，至少要再读一遍。这一遍，你要慢慢地读，主要关注文章内容与结构。这意味着，如果你没有明白的话，要再读一遍，或者查字典以了解生词的意思。

自由使用钢笔、铅笔或键盘突显并提炼文章：

- **区分主要观点和支撑观点。**寻找中心思想（主题），每一段或每一部分的主要观点以及支撑这些观点的证据。
- **了解重要术语。**理解它们的意思与用法。
- **辨别观点之间的关系。**确保自己明白作者为什么从观点A转到观点B再转到观点C以及这些观点如何相互关联从而支撑中心思想。这通常有助于概述或总结作品。（见p. 89）
- **区分事实与观点。**尤其是在阅读论述文时，要梳理事实和作者的观点。这些观点可能基于事实，也可能不基于事实。（事实与观点详见pp. 112–113）
- **添加自己的评论。**在页边的空白处或别的地方，记录下其他阅读材料或课堂讨论的链接、需要进一步探索的问题、自己写作的可能话题以及你认为的优点或弱点。

批判性阅读的范例

以下范例显示了一名叫Charlene Robinson的学生如何处理Thomas Sowell的"Student Loans"一文。在第一遍阅读之后，她以较慢的速度再次阅读该文，并添加了自己的评论和问题。以下是加了她注释的文章的前四段：

The first lesson of economics is scarcity: There is never enough of anything to fully satisfy all those who want it.	*fact*
The first lesson of politics is to disregard the first lesson of economics. When politicians discover some group that is being vocal about not having as much as they want, the "solution" is to give them more. Where do politicians get this "more"? <u>They rob Peter to pay Paul.</u>	*opinion—basic contradiction between economics and politics* ← *biblical reference?*
After a while, <u>of course,</u> they discover that Peter doesn't have enough. <u>Bursting with compassion,</u> politicians <u>rush to the rescue.</u> <u>Needless to say,</u> they do not admit that robbing Peter to pay Paul was a <u>dumb idea</u> in the first place. On the contrary, they now rob Tom, Dick, and Harry to help Peter.	*ironic and dismissive language*
The latest chapter in this <u>long-running saga</u> is that politicians have now <u>suddenly discovered</u> that many college students graduate heavily in debt. To politicians it follows, as the night follows the day, that the government should come to their rescue with the taxpayers' money.	*politicians = fools? or irresponsible?*

在读完文章后，Robinson在电脑上的日记中对该文进行了描述。她将日记分成两栏，一栏是文本，另一栏是她的想法。以下是与上述段落有关的部分。

Text	Responses
Economics teaches lessons (1), and politics (politicians) and economics are at odds.	Is economics truer or more reliable than politics? More scientific?
Politicians don't accept econ. limits—always trying to satisfy "vocal" voters by giving them more of what they want (2).	Politicians do spend tax money, but do they always disregard economics? Evidence?
"Robbing Peter to pay Paul" (2)—the Bible (the Apostles)?	

Politicians support student-loan program with taxpayer refunds bec. of "vocal" voters (2-4): another ex. of not accepting econ. limits.	I support the loan program, too. Are politicians being irresponsible when they do? (Dismissive language underlined on copy.)

你应该努力回答你在边注和日记中提出的关于含义的问题，回答需要再次阅读或发掘其他原始资料（比如词典和百科全书）。在日记中记录你认为作者的哪些观点将帮助你理解文本。尝试总结文章的帮助会更大。（见下文）这样的努力会让你不再感到迷茫，并让你充满自信地说，你的困惑是作者的错，而不是读者的错。

> **练习10.2 阅读文章**
>
> 阅读pp. 85–87，Sowell的论文，直到你认为自己理解作者说了些什么。在页边空白处或其他地方，像Charlene Robinson处理前四段文章那样记下你的问题和想法。查字典了解生词的含义，并回答自己的问题。你也可以和同学讨论该文。

10b 总结文章

掌握文章内容、明白文章优缺点的一个好办法就是总结，用自己的话提炼文章的主要观点。除了明晰文章意思外，总结支撑文章的批判性分析。见pp. 109–110，Charlene Robinson的文章。

以下加框文字提供了一个总结文章的方法：

> **撰写总结**
>
> - **了解意思**。查字典了解你不知道的单词或概念的意思，从而理解作者的句子意思以及句子之间的联系。
> - **了解结构**。通读文章以便辨别文章的各个部分，（一个段落一个话题，还是一组段落一个话题）了解各部分之间的关系，试着画树状图或列出提纲。详见pp. 21–24。
> - **提炼每一部分**。用一个或两个句子总结每一部分。关注该部分的主要观点，删除例子、事实和其他支撑证据。
> - **陈述主要观点**。用一个或两个句子把握作者的中心思想。
> - **支撑主要观点**。以中心思想为开篇写一个完整的段落（必要的话，可写多个段落），用总结性的句子支撑这一段落。该段落应该简洁而精确地陈述整篇文章的要点。
> - **使用你自己的语言**。用自己的方式再创造文章的意思。避免抄袭。
> - **引用原始资料**。如果你在写作中使用了他人文章的总结，你要标明原始资料。

甚至是对一段文章的总结也会很棘手。下面，我们看一下对以下材料的总结。该材料来自一本生物学的入门教材。

原始文本

As astronomers study newly discovered planets orbiting distant stars, they hope to find evidence of water on these far-off celestial bodies, for water is the substance that makes possible life as we know it here on Earth. All organisms familiar to us are made mostly of water and live in an environment dominated by water. They require water more than any other substance. Human beings, for example, can survive for quite a few weeks without food, but only a week or so without water. Molecules of water participate in many chemical reactions necessary to sustain life. Most cells are surrounded by water, and cells themselves are about 70–95% water. Three-quarters of Earth's surface is submerged in water. Although most of this water is in liquid form, water is also present on Earth as ice and vapor. Water is the only common substance to exist in the natural environment in all three physical states of matter: solid, liquid, and gas.

—Neil A. Campbell and Jane B. Reece, *Biology*

对该段落的首次总结尝试了准确复述原文中的两个观点，但是它并没有提炼出该段落的精华。

总结草稿

Astronomers look for water in outer space because life depends on it. It is the most common substance on Earth and in living cells, and it can be a liquid, a solid (ice), or a gas (vapor).

天文学家的工作以及水的三种状态给原文增添了色彩和质感，但是它们偏离了水因其在生命中的作用而维持生命这一主要概念。以下的修改稿将总结的范围缩小到了这一概念上：

修改后的总结

Water is the most essential support for life, the dominant substance on Earth and in living cells and a component of life-sustaining chemical processes.

当Charlene Robinson总结Thomas Sowell的"Student Loans"时，她在第一稿中用这个句子总结了该文的前四段。

总结草稿

As much as politicians would like to satisfy voters by giving them everything they ask for, the government cannot afford a student loan program.

读了这个句子和Sowell的段落后，Robinson发现这个草稿误解了文章，断言政府无法承担学生贷款。她意识到Sowell的观点更为复杂，因而重写了一遍总结。

修改后的总结

As their support of the government's student loan program illustrates, politicians ignore the economic reality that using resources to benefit one group (students in debt) involves taking the resources from another group (taxpayers).

注意：用自己的话撰写总结不仅帮助你了解意思，而且是避免抄袭的第一步。第二步就是在写作中使用了他人文章的总结时，你要引用原始资料。见pp. 425–431。

注意：总结在网上找到的文章或拷贝到电脑上的文章时，不要依靠文字处理系统中的自动总结功能。这样的总结通常不准确，而且你得不到靠自己的力量与文本进行沟通的经验。

> **练习10.3　总结文章**
>
> 从Thomas Sowell论文的第五段开始，用自己的话总结整篇论文。你的总结不能超过一个段落。（关于总结的其他练习，见pp. 418–419）

10c 形成批判性反应

一旦你了解所阅读文本的内容（作者说了些什么），你就可以转而去理解作者没有直接说明但又暗示、隐含或无意中吐露的内容。在这一阶段，你要关注作者的目的或意图，以及作者的表达方式。

批判性思维和阅读由四个相互重叠的步骤构成：分析、解释、综合和评估。

分析

分析是指将阅读的文章分成部分或元素,以便理解文章。要明白这些元素,首先要解决体现阅读目的的问题:你为什么对它感到好奇或者你想明白它的哪些方面。这些问题起到放大镜的作用,突出了某些特征。

分析 Thomas Sowell 的 "Student Loans"(pp. 85–87),你或许会问下列问题:

分析问题	元素
What is Sowell's attitude toward politicians?	References to politicians: content, words, tone
How does Sowell support assertions about the loan program's costs?	Support: evidence, such as statistics and examples

解释

辨别文章的各个元素仅仅是解释的开端:你还需要解释各个元素的含义或各元素和整篇文章的重要性。解释通常要求你推断作者的假设,也就是对现有事实或可能或应该的情况的意见或看法。(推断指的是根据证据得出结论)

假设无处不在:我们都坚持某些价值观、想法和观点。但是,假设并不总是直截了当地表述出来。说话者和作者或许认为听众或读者已经明白并接受他们的假设。他们甚至可能不清楚他们的假设,或者他们可能因为担心听众或读者的不赞同而故意克制着不说出他们的假设。作为一个具有批判性思维的读者,你的任务就是解释这些假设。

Thomas Sowell 的 "Student Loans" 一文基于某些或明或暗的假设。正如之前提到的,如果你要分析 Sowell 对政客的态度,你就要关注他对政客的陈述。Sowell 说,政客"漠视经济学的第一课"。(第二段)这句话暗示政客忽视重要原理。(在知道 Sowell 本人就是一名经济学家后,得出这一假设也就合乎情理了)Sowell 还说,政客"借债还钱"是"同情心突发"。"他们不承认那是个愚蠢的想法。"他们是一部"长期上演的冒险故事"里的人物。他们得出结论,认为使用税收就像"白天过后是夜晚一样"是不可避免的。(第二至四段)从这些陈述中,你可以得出以下推论:

> Sowell assumes that politicians become compassionate when a cause is loud and popular, not necessarily just, and they act irresponsibly by trying to solve the problem with other people's (taxpayers') money.

第二部分　大学内外的写作

综合

如果你止步于分析和解释，批判性思维和阅读可能会给你留下一堆元素和可能的意思，你却无法获得完整的看法。综合就是建立各部分或者各整体之间的联系。通过得出关于各部分之间联系和暗示的结论，你用自己的观点（你的知识和想法）创建一个全新的整体。

作为学术阅读和写作的一个关键元素，综合将在下一章（pp. 103–104）和研究性写作的背景（pp. 409–410）中得到关注。有时候，你会对文章做出直接反应，就像下面关于Thomas Sowell的"Student Loans"一文的陈述那样。该陈述将Sowell关于政客的假设与文章所暗示的一个更大的观点联系了起来：

> Sowell's view that politicians are irresponsible with taxpayers' money reflects his overall opinion that the laws of economics, not politics, should drive government.

通常，综合让你脱离于文本。以下的问题能帮助你了解作品的语境：

- **如何对比该作品与他人的作品？** 例如，其他作者如何对Sowell关于学生贷款的观点做出反应？
- **该作品如何融入同一个作者或团体的其他作品语境？** Sowell关于学生贷款的观点如何成为他关于政治和经济问题的文章的代表？
- **哪些文化、经济或政治力量影响了该作品？** Sowell可以用来阐释其经济学而非政治学应该决定政府开支这一观点的其他例子是什么？
- **哪些历史力量影响了该作品？** 大学生债务在过去四十年发生了什么变化？

评估

批判性阅读和写作通常以综合收尾：形成并解释你对作品表达和未表达内容的理解。如果你还需要评估作品，你就要进一步判断作品的质量和重要性。你可能要评估你在研究中发现的原始资料（见pp. 397–409），或者你可能要完成一项旨在说明和支持某个判断或陈述的任务，例如，Thomas Sowell没有收集证据来支持他的观点。你可以阅读pp. 109–110，Charlene Robinson对Thomas Sowell的"Student Loans"一文的批判性分析。

评估需要一定的信心才能完成。你或许认为你缺乏对他人作品进行判断的经验，尤其是在该作品难以判断或者作者非常出名的情况下。诚然，你的学识越广，你越会成为更好的批判性读者。但是，与你独特的经历、观察和态度相比，谨慎阅读和分析将给予你判断一部作品的内在权威。

> **练习10.4　批判性地阅读一篇文章**
>
> 重读Thomas Sowell的"Student Loans"（pp. 85–87），形成你自己的批判性回应。把注意力集中在你对文本提出的任何问题上：可能包括假设、证据、组织、语言的使用、语气、对教育或学生的看法。一定要在阅读和思考的同时进行写作：你的笔记将有助于你的分析并提高你的创造力，它们在写作选择时是必不可少的。
>
> （见练习11.2，p. 111）

10d　批判性地观看图像

每天，我们都面临图像的狂轰滥炸：广告牌上的照片、电视里的广告、报纸和教材里的曲线图和图表，仅举几例。大多数图像都是一闪而过，我们不会去考虑它们。但是有时候，图像甚至要比文章更能悄悄地影响我们。它们的创作者所表述的目的，有些有价值，有些没价值。理解这些目的就需要批判性阅读。方法与前面提到的批判性阅读文章一样：浏览、阅读理解、分析、解释、综合和评估。

1 ▪ 浏览图像

探索图像的第一步就是对其起源和目的形成初步印象，并记录明显特征。这一浏览过程和浏览文章的过程一样（p. 85）：

- 你见到了什么？图像给人最深的印象是什么？主题是什么？文字或符号的要旨是什么？图像的总体效果是什么？
- 出版信息是什么？你第一次是在哪儿见到该图像？你认为图像是专门为该场合而创作的，还是可以适用于其他场合？你能说出哪些关于图像创作时的信息？
- 你对创作图像的人物或团体了解多少？例如，创作者是艺术家或学者或新闻团体或公司？创作者的目的是什么？
- 你的初步反应是什么？图像的哪些方面让你感兴趣、迷惑或感到困扰？形式、内容和主题是否熟悉？你的知识、经验和价值观如何影响你对图像的感受？

可能的话，复印图像或将它扫描到你的阅读日记中，在页边空白处或其他地方写下你的评论。

2 ▪ 研究图像

研究图像需要像阅读文章一样集中精力。以下插图显示的是一名学生

» 广告注释

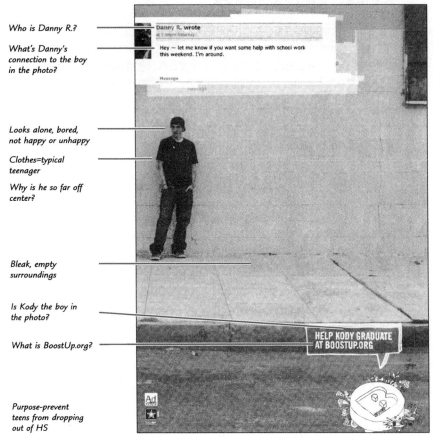

Advertisement for *BoostUp.org*

Matthew Greene在阅读一份广告时所做的笔记。

像Matthew Greene那样做笔记可以帮助你回答以下关于图像的问题。如果有些问题此时还不清楚，可以留待以后解决。

- **目的是什么？** 图像主要是解释性的（传递信息）还是说理式的（试图让读者相信某件事情或说服他们采取某种行动）？图像想要传递什么信息或观点？
- **谁是目标观众？** 图像的原始资料（包括出版信息）提及哪些关于创作者对读者的知识、兴趣和态度的预期？图像本身的特征给你留下哪些印象？
- **文字或符号增加了哪些信息？** 图像中或图像外（如标题中）的文字或符号增加了信息、吸引你的注意力或改变了你的印象吗？

- 图像展示了哪些行为、变化、任务、地点或事物？图像讲的是一个故事？你是否熟悉图像中的人物或其他特征？
- 图像的形式是什么？它是照片、广告、绘画、图表、卡通，还是其他？其内容、目的和观众如何与形式相联系？

3 ▪ 分析图像

分析元素

和分析文字作品时一样，你通过辨别其元素从而分析图像。以下加框文字列举了你要考虑的图像元素。记住，图像是一个作品，其每一个元素可能反映一个经过深思熟虑的沟通尝试。但是，极少有图像包括所有元素。你可以通过阅读的图像提出一个问题从而进一步减少问题清单。详见下方。

图像元素

- **重点。**大多数图像将你的视线集中在某些特征上：急剧上升的曲线、引起争议的人物、明亮的色彩、粗线等。照片的剪裁或表格中日期的排列也会反映哪些才是原创者认为重要的。
- **叙述。**无论是系列作品（电视广告或显示一段时间变化的图表）或单幅作品（照片、绘画或饼状图），大多数图像讲述的是故事。有时候，对话或标题或文字说明促成了故事的叙述。
- **观点。**图像的创作者考虑了观众与主题的物理联系（如正面观看或俯视）以及观众对主题的现有态度，以此影响观众的反应。
- **布局。**颜色或形式之间的模式、前景和背景的人物以及并列或分开的元素促成了作品的意思和影响。
- **颜色。**颜色能够引导观众的注意力，传递创作者对主题的态度。颜色还可能暗示情绪、时代、文化联系或其他形态。
- **人物塑造。**图像中的人物和物体有某些品质（是否具有同情心，是否令人满意等）。他们的特征反映他们在图像故事中所起的作用。
- **语境。**不论是学术期刊上的图表还是沙滩上的汽车照片，图像的原始资料或背景影响其含义。
- **张力。**图像通常传递问题，用一些似乎错误的特征（例如，拼错或未对齐的文字、扭曲的人物或人物之间富有争议的关系）抓住观众的注意力。
- **影射。**影射涉及一些观众可能会识别或反馈的内容，包括类似美元符号的文化象征、类似独角兽的神话人物或熟悉的电影人物。

分析问题

通过将对图像的主要兴趣设计成问题，你就可以聚焦自己的元素分析。Matthew Greene 提出了关于 BoostUp.org 广告的问题：广告让读者更多了解

BoostUp.org吗？它们如何帮助青少年毕业？这些问题让Greene关注该广告的某些元素：

Elements of the ad	Responses
Emphasis	The emptiness and the placement of Kody at the far left put primary emphasis on the boy's isolation. Danny R.'s message receives secondary emphasis.
Narration	The taped-on message suggests a story and connection between Kody and Danny R. Danny R. might be a friend, relative, or mentor. Based on the direct appeal in the word bubble at the bottom, it appears that Danny R. is trying to help Kody graduate by offering to help him with schoolwork.
Arrangement	The ad places Danny R. and Kody together on the left side of the page, with Danny's message a bright spot on the dull landscape. The appeal to help Kody graduate is subtle and set on its own—the last thing readers look at. It also pulls the elements together so that the ad makes sense.
Characterization	Kody is a sympathetic figure, a lonely-looking teen who would probably benefit from the help Danny R. is offering through *BoostUp. org*.

图像的分析范例

下一页的图像让你有机会分析一张照片的元素。试着回答注释中的问题。

4 ▪ 解释图像

解释图像的方法和解释文章一样。（pp. 92–93）在这一过程中，你更加深入地了解各个元素，思考它们与创作者可能的假设和意图之间的关系。你的目的在于得出关于图像为什么如此的合理推断，例如，关于p. 95 BoostUp.org广告的推断：The creators of the *BoostUp.org* ad assume that readers want students to graduate from high school. 该广告的文字支撑了此陈述。

5 ▪ 综合关于图像的观点

正如p. 93所讨论的，通过综合，你进一步分析和解释图像，从而思考作品

» 照片中的元素

重点：照片的焦点是什么？你的视线集中在哪里？

塑造：这个人的感受是什么？特别考虑他的嘴巴和眼睛。

叙述：照片可能讲的是什么故事？

布局：各元素的布局有什么有趣的地方？

颜色：这是一张黑白照。这样的表现方式对图像有什么帮助？如果是全色，会有什么不同？

影射：你看到了哪种象征符号？它给予照片什么意义？

Steve Simon拍摄

的各元素与所暗示的假设之间的关系以及作品所传递的全部信息。你也可能扩大综合范围，在一个更大的语境中观看整个图像：作品如何纳入其他作品的语境？影响作品的文化、经济、政治或历史因素是什么？

将图像放在一个语境中观看通常需要一些研究工作。例如，为了更好地了解BoostUp.org广告所暗示的假设和更大规模广告活动的目的，Matthew Greene访问了BoostUp.org网站和该广告的赞助商之一广告理事会的网站。下面这条来自他阅读日记的文字，综合了此研究以及他对该广告的观点：

> The *BoostUp.org* magazine ad that features Kody is part of a larger campaign designed to raise public awareness about high school dropouts and encourage pubic support to help teens stay in school. Sponsored by the US Army and the nonprofit Ad Council, *BoostUp.org* profiles high school seniors who are at risk of dropping out and asks individuals to write the students personal messages

of support. Ads like "Kody" are the first point of contact between the public and the teens, but they don't by themselves actually help the teens. For that, readers need to visit *BoostUp.org*. Thus the ad's elements work together like pieces of a puzzle, with the solution to be found only on the Web site.

6 ▪ 评估图像

如果你的批判性阅读进入评估阶段，你就会对图像的质量和重要性形成判断：图像的信息是准确公正的还是歪曲有偏见的？你能支撑、反驳或评估信息吗？图像实现其显性目的了吗？其目的有价值吗？图像如何影响了你？

> **练习10.5　批判性地观看图像**
>
> 回顾pp.96–97的图像元素列表，然后再仔细看看p.95的BoostUp.org广告或后面的图片。使用前几页的指导方针，对其中一个视觉效果得出你自己的结论。在阅读和思考的同时写作，帮助自己集中精力和发展想法。p.111练习11.3中有基于此活动的写作建议。

第 11 章　学术写作

概要

在学术环境中写作：

- 确定任务所规定的写作目的、目标读者和文章体裁（下页）
- 撰写对文章的反应（p. 102）
- 选择合适的结构和内容（p. 104）
- 使用学术语言（p. 105）

学术学科的主题和方法截然不同，但它们有共同的目标：通过质疑、研究和沟通建构知识。学科的区别主要在于问题的种类、解决问题的研究种类及用以沟通的写作体裁，如案例分析、研究报告、文学分析和对他人作品的评论。

11a 确定写作目的、目标读者和文章体裁

与任何形式的写作一样,学术写作在特定的环境下发生。该环境由写作任务及主体、写作目的、目标读者和文章体裁决定。每个项目的写作任务和主题会有所不同,但是可以对其他元素做一些归纳总结。(如果你还没有这么做,关于写作环境及其元素,请阅读pp. 2–10)

1 ▪ 写作目的

大多数学术写作的一般目的主要是解释性或辩论性的。通过对主题的分析、描述或报告,你的目的在于澄清主题,这样读者能和你一样理解主题。或者,你的目的在于让读者赞同与主题相关的可争议的观点。(见pp. 6–7一般目的和pp. 111–125论述文)

学术写作的特定目的(包括主题以及你对读者的预期反应)取决于文章的体裁,也就是写作类型。(见p.101)例如,在生物课的文献综述中,你希望读者明白你所从事的研究领域、研究者所取得的最新成就、需要进一步研究的问题以及你所查询的原始资料。巧合的是,这些话题正好是文献综述的主要部分。通过采用标准格式,你既可以明确你的目的,还可以达到学科(及老师的)要求。

特定目的也可以更为复杂。你选修一门课程是为了了解该课程以及专家对该课程的思考方法。作为回报,写作通过发现知识和观点角度对学科做出贡献。同时,作为学生,你想通过研究、证据、格式以及学科的其他要求展示自己的能力。

2 ▪ 目标读者

许多学术写作任务指定或假设一个有教养的读者或学术读者。这样的读者想看到文字清晰、观点公正、结构有序且推理严密的文章。其他的写作任务会指定或假设主题的专家读者;这些读者想看到一篇能满足主题需要的文章,想从中获取主张与证据、组织、语言、格式及其他特征。

除了你以外,你的大多数学术文章通常只有一个读者:教授课程的老师。作为读者,老师承担两个主要角色:

- **他们代表文章的读者**。事实上,在你向学术读者或主题专家致辞时,他们或许是听众成员。或者在阅读你的文章时,他们可能会想象自己是你的听众成员,如同他们坐在市政厅一样。他们对你如何进行有效写作很感兴趣。

- **他们充当教练**，指导你完成课程目标和构建并交流知识的学术目标。

与其他人一样，老师也有偏好和怨恨，但是试图揣测老师的偏好和怨恨浪费时间和精力。要关注任务的书面和口头指令。但是在其他场合，要将老师看成你为之撰稿的社团代表。他们的反应受社团的目标、预期及教授知识的愿望所引导。

3 ▪ 文章体裁

许多学术写作任务会暗示写作的格式，即写作的类型和/或格式。有时候，格式是规定好了的，例如，文献综述就有其标准内容和格式。其他的写作任务隐含写作的格式，例如，那些要求你分析、解释、比较或争辩的写作任务。在这些情况下，你的反应很有可能是想到传统的学术论文：引言、主题陈述、支撑段落、结论，加上对主题的分析、对比、解释或争辩。

不论写作任务明确抑或暗示了文章的格式，你都得展示你用该格式写作的能力。如果你不熟悉，你就需要花时间去了解其特征和规则。本书包含以下格式的范例。研究这些范例以及相邻的解释和注释会让你明白其他作家是如何在格式规则的范围内写作的。

 告知性文章（p. 24）
 对文章的个人反应（p. 41）
 告知性网站（p. 75）
 博客上的个人故事帖（p. 76）
 文章评论（p. 109）
 论述性文章（p. 125和p. 133）
 文学分析（p. 133）
 附有注释的参考目录（p. 378）
 研究论文（p. 488）
 研究报告（p. 519）

另外，第14章包含了大众写作中使用的格式范例：申请函和简历、备忘录和时事通信。

11b 撰写对文章的反应

学术知识的建立取决于阅读、分析和扩展他人的作品。因此，许多学术写作任务要求你对一篇或多篇文章（不仅包括写作成品，如故事和期刊文章，还包括视觉传播，如图像、图表、电影和广告）做出反应。在对文章形成反应时，你综合或融合文章的观点和信息。在撰写反应意见时，你通过从文章中引用证据来支撑你对文章的观点。

注意：平常的学术任务（即研究论文）要求你查阅并对多篇文章做出反应，以便支撑并拓展你的观点。详见第51—55章。本部分关注对单篇文章的直接反应，但是相关的技巧也适用于研究性写作。

1 ▪ 决定如何反应

当写作任务要求你对文章做出直接反应时，你可以采用以下的方法（注意，**作者**一词可以指写作者，也可以指摄影者、绘画者或其他创作者）：

- 同意并拓展作者的观点，探究相关的观点并提供额外的范例。
- 在某些方面同意作者的观点，但在其他方面不同意。
- 在一个或多个关键点上不同意作者的观点。
- 解释作者如何达到特定效果，例如，再现历史时期或平衡对立观点。
- 分析文章的总体效果，例如，作者如何用令人信服的证据很好地支撑主题，或者广告是否实现其未明确说明的目的。

2 ▪ 形成反应

对所分析的一些文章，你可能至少会有一个直接反应：你可能强烈同意或反对作者的观点。但是对于其他的反应，你可能需要时间和思索来决定作者的观点和你的看法。

不论什么样的写作任务，你的第一项任务就是完整阅读文章，确保明白作者所明确表达和假设或暗示的信息。使用前一章中提到的批判性阅读方式来记笔记、总结并形成批判性反应。然后，在写作的过程中，使用以下贴士将你的反应传递给读者。

对文章的反应

- **确保你的文章有一个要点**：聚焦反应的核心观点或主题。（形成主题见pp. 16–19）
- **如果读者不熟悉你的主题，你的文章需要有一个非常简要的总结。但是请记住，你的工作是从你的批判性角度来对作品进行反应，而不仅仅汇报作品说了些什么。**（见pp. 89–91总结）

（续表）

- 每一段文章围绕着一个观点展开。通常这个观点必须是你自己的，必须能支撑你的主题。用自己的话明确陈述你的观点。
- 用原文中的证据支撑每一段的观点：引用、改写、抓细节和举例。
- 用你对证据的理解来得出每一段的结论。一般来说，要避免用原始资料的证据来给段落收尾；相反，用至少一个解释证据的句子收尾。

3 ▪ 在反应中强调对文章的综合

遵守以上加框文字的建议可以让你向读者展示你通过批判性思考文章而形成的综合观点。也就是说，为了支撑你对作品得出的结论，你融合了自己的观点与作者的观点。

综合的关键就是如何在你的写作中展示你在阅读和观察中获得的证据。尤其是在撰写相对不熟悉的主题时，你可能受到诱惑。通过广泛的总结或引用，你可能会让原文或其他原始资料做你的代言人。但是，学术写作的读者希望看到你驾驭观点和信息，从而形成自己的观点。因此，以文本为基础的典型段落应该以你自己的观点为开篇，然后提供文本中的证据，最后根据你对证据的阐释得出结论。从下面的段落中，你可以看到此模式。该段落来自本章结尾出现的一篇文章（pp. 109–110）。

作者的观点

证据和解释

The most fundamental and most debatable assumption underlying Sowell's essay is that higher education is a kind of commodity that not everyone is entitled to. In order to diminish the importance of graduates' average debt from education loans, Sowell claims that a car loan will probably be higher (131). This comparison between education and an automobile implies that the two are somehow equal as products and that an affordable higher education is no more a right than a new car is. Sowell also condemns the "irresponsible" students who drop out of school and "the increasingly easy availability of college to people who are not very serious about getting an education" (132). But he overlooks the value of encouraging education, including the education of those who don't finish college or who aren't scholars. For many in the United States, education has a greater value than that of a mere commodity like a car. And even from an economic perspective such as Sowell's, the cost to society of an uneducated public needs to be taken into account. By failing to give education its due, Sowell undermines his argument at its core. 作者的结论

注意：有效的综合要求谨慎处理文本的证据（引用和改写），以使证据能顺畅地融入你的句子中，但又能有别于你自己的观点。详见pp. 419–422融合借用的材料。

11c 选择结构和内容

许多学术写作任务至少隐含你应该如何组织你的论文，甚至你应该如何展开你的观点等要求。和文献综述一样，所要求的论文类型分成独立的部分，每一部分都有内容上的要求。

不论写作任务明确了哪种论文类型，建立和交流知识的学术大目标决定了跨学科常见的特征。遵守以下学术写作的一般准则：

- **形成论文的主要论点**。通常，主要论点是声明或主题，但是在有些格式中，它可能是基于你所进行的初步研究的结果或结论的摘要，如实验、观察、调查或采访。（详见pp. 16–19主题陈述）
- **用证据支撑主要论点**。证据通常源自阅读、个人经验或原始研究。这类证据取决于学科和论文类型。
- **综合**。通过批判性思维让原始资料为你所用。用自己的话将原始资料融入自己的观点中。（详见pp. 103–104综合和pp. 409–410研究性写作）
- **完整引用原始资料，包括在线资料**。不标明原始资料破坏了学术写作的知识分享基础，也构成了抄袭。那是要受到惩罚的。（pp.425–431）详见pp. 433–434格式指导和第56章及第57章引用文献资料的原则和范例。
- **在论文格式的框架内清晰地组织资料**。按照写作目的和论文内容的要求，简单而直接地展开你的观点。清晰表述句子、段落和部分，这样读者能跟上论文的进展。

（CULTURE LANGUAGE）这些特征不是通用的。在有些文化中，学术作者不需要标注他人的观点，或通过提供原始资料的引用来树立文章的可靠性。了解本土文化与美国文化在这方面的差异有助于你适应美式学术写作。在自己的写作中，你可以使用前面提到的一般准则作为核对清单。

11d 使用学术语言

美式学术写作依赖于一种被称为标准美式英语的方言。这种方言也用于商务、各行各业、政府、媒体,其他社会和经济场合。在这些场合中,不同背景的人们必须彼此沟通。它之所以成为"标准",不是因为其优于别的英语形式,而是因为它被认可为通用语言,就像美元被认可为通用货币一样。

在写作中,标准美式英语有多种风格,从正式的学术研究报告到本手册中使用的更为轻松的语言,再到公司同事间非正式的电子邮件。正如下面两篇同一话题的文章所显示的,即便是学术写作,标准美式英语也为作者的语气和文体提供了很大的空间:

更为正式

Responsibility for the widespread problem of obesity among Americans depends on the person or group describing the problem and proposing a solution. Some people believe the cause lies with individuals who make poor eating choices for themselves and parents who feed unhealthy foods to their children. Others take strong issue with the food industry, citing food manufacturers and fast-food chains that create and advertise food that is high in sugar, fat, and sodium. Still others place responsibility on American society as a whole for preferring a sedentary lifestyle centered on screen-based activities such as watching television and using computers for video games and social interaction.

> 更长的措辞,例如,widespread problem of obesity among Americans。
>
> 更复杂的句子结构,例如,take strong issue with the food industry, citing food manufacturers and fast-food chains that create and advertise …
>
> 更正式的词,例如,responsibility, children, television。

不太正式

Who or what is to blame for the obesity epidemic depends on who is talking and what they want to do about the problem. Some people blame eaters for making bad choices and parents for feeding their kids unhealthy foods. Others

> 更多的非正式的措辞,例如,obesity epidemic。

demonize food manufacturers and fast-food chains for creating and advertising sugary, fatty, and sodium-loaded food. Still others point to Americans generally for spending too much time in front of screens watching TV, playing video games, or going on *Facebook*.

> 不太复杂的句子结构，例如，demonize food manufacturers and fast-food chains for creating and advertising...
>
> 更多的非正式的词，例如，blame, kids, TV。

虽然它们有所不同，但是这两个范例说明了学术语言的共同特征：

- 遵循标准美式英语的语法和用法规则。这些规则在本书中被描述为标准美式英语的指南。
- 使用标准词，而不是仅有一些团体明白的词，如俚语、种族或地区方言或另一种语言。（见p. 164和pp. 165–166）
- 不使用非正式的日常用语、短信和实时信息，包括不完整的句子、俚语、无大写字母和单词缩写（例如，u代替you，b4代替before，thru代替through等）。（见pp. 164–165更多此类形式）
- 通常使用第三人称（he，she，it，they）。第一人称I有时候适用于表述个人观点，但是学术作者倾向于不用它，而是让结论为自己辩护。第一人称we可以连接读者，并邀请读者一起思考，但是同样，许多学术作者不用它。第二人称you只有在直接向读者致辞时才适用。即便那样，它似乎很居高临下或者过于亲密。在对话中，要明确避免使用或暗示you，例如，You know what I mean和Don't take this the wrong way。
- 具有权威性和中立性。在p.106的范例中，作者充满信心而不是如Explaining the causes of obesity requires the reader's patience because... 等怯懦地表达自己的观点；他们也抑制了如The food industry's callous attitude toward health... 这样的敌意，还抑制了如The food industry's clever and appealing advertisements... 这样的热情。

学术写作的不同要求可能会让你探索合适的文体。在努力显得清新而自信的时候，你可能写得过于随意，就像你和朋友家人说话那样：

过于随意

Getting the truth about the obesity epidemic in the US requires some heavy lifting. It turns out that everyone else is to blame for the problem— big eaters, reckless corporations, and all those Americans who think it's OK to be a couch potato.

在努力显得"学术性"的时候,你可能造出一些冗长而笨拙的句子:

冗长而笨拙
The responsibility for the problem of widespread obesity among Americans depends on the manner of defining the problem and the proposals for its solution. In some discussions, the cause of obesity is thought to be individuals who are unable or unwilling to make healthy choices in their own diets and parents who similarly make unhealthy choices for their children. (这个例子中的被动语态 —— cause . . . is thought to be代替people blame —— 增加了它的冗长和间接。有关动词语态的更多信息,请见pp.240–241)

避免写作过于随意或过于僵硬的解决方法是阅读学术文章,使自己熟悉学术语言和风格,同时编辑自己的文章,使它看上去不陌生。(见pp. 36–38)

CULTURE LANGUAGE 如果你的第一语言不是英语或者是标准美式英语之外的英语方言,你就能明白与相同语言的人进行沟通的重要性。学习用标准美式英语写作并不是要你放弃自己的第一语言。和大多数多语言的人一样,你或许能够根据环境需要熟练地进行语言转换:例如,用一种语言和亲戚交谈,用另一种语言和老板交谈。随着你练习学术写作,你也会拥有相同的灵活性。

> **练习11.1　使用学术语言**
>
> 修改下面的段落,使语言更加学术化,同时保持事实信息一致。带星号部分的参考答案请见书后。
>
> 　　*If you buy into the stereotype of girls chatting away on their cell phones, you should think again. *One of the major wireless companies surveyed 1021 cell phone owners for a period of five years and—surprise!—reported that guys talk on cell phones more than girls do.In fact, guys were way ahead of girls, using an average of 571 minutes a month compared to 424 for girls. That's 35% more time on the phone! The survey also asked about conversations on land lines, and while girls still beat the field, the guys are catching up.

11e 批判性反应的范例

下面的文章举例说明常见的学术写作任务,即对文本的批判性反应或评论。在文章中,Charlene Robinson对Thomas Sowell的"Student Loans"一文(pp. 85–87)做了反应。前一章中提到,Robinson进行了批判性阅读、收集并组织了自己的观点、形成了关于Sowell文章的主题（该主题综合了Sowell和她本人的观点）、起草并修改直到她认为自己充分使用了源于自己经验和Sowell文章的证据来支撑自己的主题。通过这些步骤，Robinson得出了自己的反应，即论点。

Robinson没有假设她的读者会在Sowell的文章中发现同样的东西或分享她的观点，因此，她的文章用直接引用、总结和改写（用自己的话重述）的方式提供关于Thomas Sowell观点的证据。Robinson用MLA的格式来记录这些来自Thomas Sowell文章的引用：圆括号里的数字是刊载Sowell文章的书籍页码，在文章最后列为"参考目录"。（见第56章MLA格式）

注意：批判性写作不是总结。Robinson总结了Sowell的文章，为的是让自己明白作者的观点。（p. 91）她在引言中简单总结了Sowell的论点。但是，她的批判性写作超越了总结，为Sowell的作品赋予了自己的观点。

Weighing the Costs

In the essay "Student Loans," the economist Thomas Sowell challenges the US government's student-loan program for three main reasons: a scarce resource (taxpayers' money) goes to many undeserving students, a high number of recipients fail to repay their loans, and the easy availability of money has led to both lower academic standards and higher college tuitions. Sowell wants his readers to "weigh the costs of things" (133) in order to see, as he does, that the loan program should not receive so much government funding. Sowell wrote his essay in the 1990s, but the argument he makes is still heard frequently today and is worth examining. Does Sowell provide the evidence of cost and other problems to lead the reader to agree with his argument? The answer is no, because hard evidence is less common than debatable and unsupported assumptions about students, scarcity, and the value of education.

Sowell's portrait of student-loan recipients is questionable. It is based on averages, some statistical and some not, but averages are often deceptive. For example, Sowell cites college graduates' low average debt of $7,000 to $9,000 (131) without giving the full range of statistics or acknowledging that when he was writing

引言

总结Sowell的文章

Robinson的批判性问题

主题句

第一个主要论点

第一个论点的证据：源自Sowell文章的改写和引文

many students' debt was much higher. (Today the average debt itself is much higher.) Similarly, Sowell dismisses "heart-rending stories" of "the low-income student with a huge debt" as "not at all typical" (132), yet he invents his own exaggerated version of the typical loan recipient: an affluent slacker ("Rockefellers" and "Vanderbilts") for whom college is a "place to hang out for a few years" sponging off the government, while his or her parents clear a profit from making use of the loan program (132). Although such students (and parents) may well exist, are they really typical? Sowell does not offer any data one way or the other—for instance, how many loan recipients come from each income group, what percentage of loan funds go to each group, how many loan recipients receive significant help from their parents, and how many receive none. Together, Sowell's statements and omissions cast doubt on the argument that students don't need or deserve the loans.

Another set of assumptions in the essay has to do with "scarcity": "There is never enough of anything to fully satisfy all those who want it," Sowell says (131). This statement appeals to readers' common sense, but the "lesson" of scarcity does not necessarily apply to the student-loan program. Sowell omits many important figures needed to prove that the nation's resources are too scarce to support the program, such as the total cost of the program, its percentage of the total education budget and the total federal budget, and its cost compared to the cost of defense, Medicare, and other expensive programs. Moreover, Sowell does not mention the interest paid by loan recipients, even though the interest must offset some of the costs of running the program and covering unpaid loans. Thus his argument that there isn't enough money to run the student loan program is unconvincing.

The most fundamental and most debatable assumption underlying Sowell's essay is that higher education is a kind of commodity that not everyone is entitled to. In order to diminish the importance of graduates' average debt from education loans,

Sowell claims that a car loan will probably be higher (131). This comparison between education and an automobile implies that the two are somehow equal as products and that an affordable higher education is no more a right than a new car is. Sowell also condemns the "irresponsible" students who drop out of school and "the increasingly easy availability of college to people who are not very serious about getting an education" (132). But he overlooks the value of encouraging education, including the education of those who don't finish college or who aren't scholars. For many in the United States, education has a greater value than that of a mere commodity like a car. And even from an economic perspective such as Sowell's, the cost to society of an uneducated public needs to be taken into account. By failing to give education its due, Sowell undermines his argument at its core.

Sowell writes with conviction, and his concerns are valid: high taxes, waste, unfairness, declining educational standards, obtrusive government. However, the essay's flaws make it unlikely that Sowell could convince readers who do not already agree with him. He does not support his portrait of the typical loan recipient, he fails to demonstrate a lack of resources for the loan program, and he neglects the special nature of education compared to other services and products. Sowell may have the evidence to back up his assumptions, but by omitting it he himself does not truly weigh the costs of the loan program.

[New page.]

Work Cited

Sowell, Thomas. "Student Loans." *Is Reality Optional? and Other Essays.* Stanford: Hoover, 1993. 131-33. Print.

—Charlene Robinson (student)

111

练习11.2　撰写关于文章的批判性论文

根据你自己对Thomas Sowell的"Student Loans"（练习10.4，p. 94）的批判性阅读写一篇文章。你的评论可能与 Charlene Robinson 的完全不同，或者你可能会得出一些相同的观点。如果有相似之处，它们应该以你自己的方式表达和支持，在你自己的批判性观点的背景下。

练习11.3　撰写关于图像的批判性论文

根据你对p.95的BoostUp.org广告或p.99照片的批判性阅读，写一篇文章。（练习10.5，p. 99）

第 12 章　撰写论述文

概要

撰写有说服力的论述文：
- 使用论述文的组成元素：主题、主张、证据和假设（下方）
- 理性写作：有逻辑思维、恰当的诉求，承认对立的观点且没有谬误 (p. 114)
- 有效地组织材料 (p. 124)

论述文写作试图解决问题、向读者展示观点、改变读者的观点或让读者采取行动。使用不同的技巧，你就可以让读者发现共同之处并缩短你与他们在观点上的距离。

（CULTURE LANGUAGE）如果你的本土文化对论述文的构思和写作的方法与本书描写的不一样，你或许会在一开始感到不舒服。比如，有些文化可能会要求作者别开门见山、避免直接表达个人观点、将传统诉求视作证据，或达成妥协而不是对某个立场进行辩论。在美国的学术和商业环境中，作者尊重读者及其观点，但是有说服力的写作目的有利于作者清晰地陈述观点、从众多资料中收集证据并对观点进行直接而简洁的辩论。

12a 使用论述文的元素

人们通常认为论述文有四个主要元素：主题、主张、证据和假设。（后三个元素改编自英国哲学家Stephen Toulmin的作品）

1 ▪ 主题

论述文以主题开篇，通常也以对主题的观点（也就是促使你撰写该主题的观点）开篇。例如，你可能认为你的学校应该在节约能源方面做得更多一些，或者学校的化学实验室是个耻辱。（如果你没有主题或你不知道自己对主题的看法，尝试一下pp. 10–15提到的创作技巧）

你的最初观点应该满足几个要求：

- 它可以被争论：理智的人们可以不赞同它。
- 它会被争论：它现在是有争议的。
- 它的范围小得足以在目前的时间和空间内进行辩论。

在这些要求的另一面，因为涉及诸如人类肝脏功能等无可争议的事实、诸如对素食主义的道德信念等个人偏爱或信仰，或者诸如家庭安全的价值观等几乎没有人反对的观点，有些主题不适合作为论述文的出发点。

> **练习12.1　测试论述文的主题**
>
> 分析下面的每一个主题，以确定它是否适合辩论。解释你在每种情况下的理由。
>
> 1. Granting of athletic scholarships
> 2. Care of automobile tires
> 3. Censoring the Web sites of hate groups
> 4. History of the town park
> 5. Housing for the homeless
> 6. Billboards in urban residential areas or in rural areas
> 7. Animal testing for cosmetics research
> 8. Cats versus dogs as pets
> 9. Ten steps in recycling wastepaper
> 10. Benefits of being a parent

2 ▪ 主张

主张是需要支撑的观点陈述。在论述文中，你将话题演化成中心思想或主题，以**主题句**（p. 16）的形式直截了当地表述出来。这个中心思想是论述文的关键。

主题句通常是观点，是基于事实的判断；在事实基础上，它是可以论证的。它可能是：

- 关于过去或目前现实的主张：

  In both its space and its equipment, the college's chemistry laboratory is outdated.

  Academic cheating increases with students' economic insecurity.

- 关于价值观的主张：

  The new room fees are unjustified given the condition of the dormitories.

  Computer music pirates undermine the system that encourages the very creation of music.

- 一连串行动的推荐意见，通常是问题的解决之道：

  The college's outdated chemistry laboratory should be replaced incrementally over the next five years.

  Schools and businesses can help to resolve the region's traffic congestion by implementing car pools and rewarding participants.

论述文的支柱由支撑主题句的明确主张构成。它们可能是观点的陈述，也可能属于以下两类中的一类：

- **事实的陈述**，包括众所周知或可以验证的事实（如学校的学费）以及可以从可验证事实中推断出的事实（如大学教育的货币价值）。
- **信仰的陈述**，基于个人信仰或价值观的信念（例如，政府的首要目标应该是为所有人提供均等机会）的陈述。尽管看似可论证，但是信仰的陈述并不基于事实，所以不能在事实的基础上进行争辩。

> **练习12.2　构思主题句**
>
> 将练习12.1中每个有争议的主题缩小为一个具体的观点，并为每个主题起草一个初步的主题陈述。让每个主题陈述一个关于过去或现在的现实的声明，一个价值的声明，或一个行动方针的建议。

3 ▪ 证据

通过用证据支撑主张，你展示了主张的正确性。为了支撑上面提到的化学实验室过时了这一主张，你可能要提供目前实验室的年限、设备和仪器的详细目录、化学教授的证词，并对比最新仪器。

证据的类型：
- **事实**，其真实性是可以被证实或推断的文字陈述：Poland is slightly smaller than New Mexico.
- **统计数据**，用数字表示的事实：Of those polled, 22% prefer a flat tax.
- **例子**，可以得出观点的明确事例：Some groups, such as graduate and undergraduate students, would benefit from this policy.
- **专家意见**，主题方面的权威人士根据他们对事实的检验而形成的判断：Affirmative action is necessary to right past injustices, a point argued by Howard Glickstein, a past director of the US Commission on Civil Rights.
- **对读者的信仰或需求的契合**，要求读者接受主张的文字陈述，部分原因是它陈述了某些在没有证据的情况下，读者就已经认可为真实的事情：The shabby, antiquated chemistry lab shames the school, making it seem a second-rate institution.

证据必须可靠到具有说服力。关于证据，可以提出以下问题：
- **它是准确的吗？** 是值得相信、精确且未失真的吗？
- **它是相关的吗？** 是具有权威性、中肯且流行的吗？
- **它是有代表性的吗？** 真实反映语境，没有过分表达或未充分表达样本元素吗？
- **它是充分的吗？** 是丰富且详细的吗？

4 ▪ 假设

假设是联系证据与主张的观点、原则或意见：假设解释了为什么某个特定证据和某个特定主张有关。

　　　　主张：The college's chemistry laboratory is outdated.

证据（部分）：The testimony of chemistry professors.

　　　假设：Chemistry professors are the most capable of evaluating the present lab's quality.

假设不是论述文中的瑕疵而是必需品：我们都需要形成世界观的意见和观点。诠释作品的假设是批判性阅读（p. 92）的重要部分，而确认自己的假设是批判性论述文写作的关键。如果你的读者没有分享你的假设，或者他们认为你没有直接表达你的偏爱，他们不大会接受你的论点。（见下页关于合理性的讨论）

» 归纳推理法

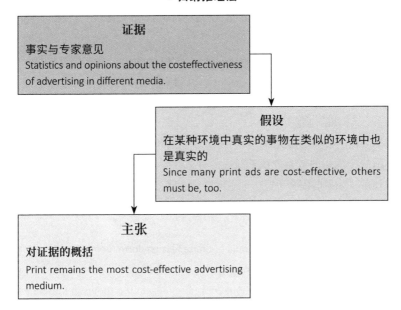

» 演绎推理法

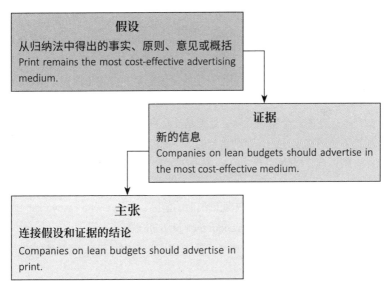

的房租，你的演绎论证可以用以下三段论的方式表达：

前提：The administration should not raise fees on dorm rooms in poor condition.（你认为是真实的概括或意见）

前提：The rooms in Maroni Hall are in poor condition.（新的信息：第一个前提的具体例子）

结论：The administration should not raise fees on the rooms in Maroni Hall.（你的主张）

117 只要三段论的前提是真实的，就会得出合乎逻辑和肯定的结论。

演绎推理法的效力取决于前提的可靠性以及在得出结论过程中对前提的谨慎使用。如果前提合乎逻辑地引向结论，那么推理过程是有效的。如果前提是可信的，那么推理过程就是真实的。有时候，推理是真实的，但却不是有效的：

前提：The administration should not raise fees on dorm rooms in bad condition.

前提：Maroni Hall is a dormitory.

结论：The administration should not raise fees on the rooms in Maroni Hall.

在上述例子中，两个前提都是真实的，但是第一个前提并不一定适用于第二个前提，所以结论是无效的。同样有时候，推理是有效的，但却不是真实的：

前提：All college administrations are indifferent to students' needs.

前提：The administration of Valley College is a college administration.

结论：The administration of Valley College is indifferent to students' needs.

这个三段论是有效的，但却是不真实的：第一个前提不是真实的假设，所以整个推理就是不真实的。无效和不真实的三段论是许多逻辑谬误（见pp. 120-123）的基础。

演绎推理法的一个特别危险之处就是没有言明的前提：连接证据和结论的基本前提不是明确表述的，而是暗示的。下面的例子中，没有言明的前提是可靠的而且论点是合理的：

Ms. Stein has worked with drug addicts for fifteen years, so she knows a great deal about their problems.（未明确说明的前提：Anyone who has worked fifteen years with drug addicts knows about their problems.）

但当没有言明的前提是错误的或者是没有事实根据时，那么论点就是错误的。例如：

Since Jane Lightbow is a senator, she must receive money illegally from lobbyists.（未明确说明的前提：All senators receive money illegally from lobbyists.）

2 ▪ 诉求

理性和感性诉求

在大多数论述文中,你要结合对读者逻辑推理能力的**理性诉求**和对读者的信仰和感情的**感性诉求**。在下面的例子中,第二个句子提出了理性诉求(对经济获益的逻辑性),第三个句子提出了感性诉求(对公正性和开放性的观念):

> Advertising should show more people who are physically challenged. The millions of Americans with disabilities have considerable buying power, yet so far advertisers have made little or no attempt to tap that power. Furthermore, by keeping people with disabilities out of the mainstream depicted in ads, advertisers encourage widespread prejudice against disability, prejudice that frightens and demeans those who hold it.

感性诉求要获得成功,对于读者和论点来说,它必须是恰当的:
- 它必须正确判断读者的真实情感。
- 它必须提及与主张和证据相关的情感问题。见 p. 122 关于具体的不恰当诉求(如时尚潮流和人身攻击)的讨论。

道德诉求

作为对读者的第三种诉求,道德诉求是你作为一个有能力、公正且值得关注的人所具有的意识。理性诉求和恰当的感性诉求会促成你的道德诉求,你对对立观点的承认也是如此。(见下页)一篇行文简洁且拼写、语法和其他方面准确的论述文会突显你的能力。另外,真挚而平和的语气会让读者相信你是有条不紊的,并且想和他们讲道理。

真挚而平和的语气并不排除带有感性诉求的语言,例如,上述关于广告的例子结尾中 frightens 和 demeans 等词。但是,要避免使用一些让你显得不公正的表达方式:
- **侮辱性单词**,如 idiotic 或 fascist。
- **歧视性语言**,如 fags 或 broads。(见 pp. 167–170)
- **讽刺**,例如,用 What a brilliant idea 来表示对该主意及其创作者的蔑视。
- **感叹号**!它们让你的文章"听"上去很刺耳!

3 ▪ 承认对立的观点

你如何处理可能的异议可以很好地检测你在论述文中是否公正。假设你的主题的确有商榷的余地,其他人就会整理出他们自己的证据来支持不同的观点。通过正当地处理这些对立的观点,你表示了自己的诚实和公正。你强化了自己的道德诉求,因而也加强了整篇论述文的效果。

在撰写草稿之前或之时,列出你能想到的所有对立的观点。通过与朋友和同学交谈以及批判性地思考自己的观点,你会在研究中发现这些对立的观点。你也可以在与主题相关的在线讨论中寻找一些观点。你可以从以下两个网站开始寻找:groups.yahoo.com上的雅虎讨论组档案和blogsearch.google.com上的谷歌博客目录。

处理对立观点的常见方法是陈述这些观点,驳斥你能驳斥的观点,承认其他观点的正确性,并说明为什么虽然对立的观点具有正确性但却比你自己的观点不那么令人信服。心理学家Carl Rogers提出的另一种不同方法强调对共同点的研究。按照Rogers的观点,你可以先在文章中展示你对读者观点的理解,指出你和读者同意和反对的地方。在你预计读者会抵制你的观点时,通过这种方式建立的联系尤其有帮助,因为在你阐释你的主张时,这种联系能让读者听完你的阐释。

练习12.3　使用归纳推理法

研究下面的事实,然后评估每个编号后的结论。根据证据,哪些概括是合理的,哪些是不合理的?为什么?带星号部分的参考答案请见书后。

In 2011 each American household viewed a weekly average of 58 hours and 54 minutes of television (including on DVRs and DVD players).

Each individual viewed an average of 34 hours and 39 minutes per week.

Those viewing the most television per week (50 hours and 28 minutes) were women over age 65.

Those viewing the least television per week (23 hours and 41 minutes) were teens, ages 12 to 17.

Households earning under $30,000 a year watched an average of 59 hours and 57 minutes a week.

Households earning more than $60,000 a year watched an average of 56 hours and 32 minutes a week.

*1. Households with incomes under $30,000 tend to watch more television than average.

*2. Women watch more television than men.

3. Nonaffluent people watch less television than affluent people.

4. Women over age 65 tend to watch more television than average.

5. Teens watch less television than critics generally assume.

> **练习12.4** 使用演绎推理法

将下列语句转换为三段论。（你必须声明一些未声明的假设）使用三段论来评估这个陈述的有效性和真实性。带星号部分的参考答案请见书后。

例子：

DiSantis is a banker, so he does not care about the poor.

前提：Bankers do not care about the poor.

前提：DiSantis is a banker.

结论：Therefore, DiSantis does not care about the poor.

这个结论不真实，因为第一个前提不真实。

*1. The mayor opposed pollution controls when he was president of a manufacturing company, so he may not support new controls or vigorously enforce existing ones.

*2. Information on corporate Web sites is unreliable because the sites are sponsored by for-profit entities.

3. Schroeder is a good artist because she trained at Parsons, like many other good artists.

4. Wealthy athletes who use their resources to help others deserve our particular appreciation.

5. Jimson is clearly a sexist because she has hired only one woman.

> **练习12.5** 识别各种诉求

将下面的每一篇文章区分为主要是理性诉求还是情感诉求。哪些段落也有强烈的道德诉求？带星号部分的参考答案请见书后。

*1. The Web may contribute to the global tendency toward breadth rather than depth of knowledge. Using those most essential of skills—pointing and clicking—our brightest minds may now never even hear of, much less read, the works of Aristotle, Shakespeare, and Darwin.

*2. Thus the data collected by these researchers indicate that a mandatory sentence for illegal possession of handguns may lead to reduction in handgun purchases.

3. Most broadcasters worry that further government regulation of television programming could breed censorship—certainly, an undesirable outcome. Yet most broadcasters also accept that children's television is a fair target for regulation.

4. Anyone who cherishes life in all its diversity could not help being appalled by the mistreatment of laboratory animals. The so-called scientists who run the labs are misguided.

5. Many experts in constitutional law have warned that the rule violates the right to free speech. Yet other experts have viewed the rule, however regretfully, as necessary for the good of the community as a whole.

4 ▪ 谬误

谬误——论点中的错误——要么规避论点中的问题，要么认为论点要比实际简单得多。

规避

有效的论点直面核心事物或问题。无效的论点用以下的方式躲避问题：

- **回避问题**：将值得质疑的观点视为人们赞同或反对的观点。从本质上说，作者恳求读者从一开始就接受他或她的主张。

  The college library's expenses should be reduced by cutting subscriptions to useless periodicals.〔回避的问题：Are some of the library's periodicals useless? Useless to whom?〕

  The fact is that political financing is too corrupt to be reformed.〔回避的问题：How corrupt is political financing? Does corruption, even if extensive, put the system beyond reform?〕

- **不合逻辑的推论**：将两个或多个事实上没有逻辑关系的观点联系在一起。通常，问题是联系观点的未明确说明的假设，但却是错误的。

  She uses a wheelchair, so she must be unhappy.〔未阐明的假设：People who use wheelchairs are unhappy.〕

  Kathleen Newsome has my vote for mayor because she has the best-run campaign organization.〔未阐明的假设：A good campaign organization means that the candidate is well qualified for the job.]

- **红鲱鱼**：引入会干扰读者对相关问题注意力的无关事物。(红鲱鱼是一种用来干扰狗的嗅觉的鱼)
  A campus speech code is essential to protect students, who already have enough problems coping with rising tuition. [Tuition costs and speech codes are different subjects. What protections do students need that a speech code will provide?]
  Instead of developing a campus speech code that will infringe on students' First Amendment rights, administrators should be figuring out how to prevent another tuition increase. [Again, tuition costs and speech codes are different subjects. How would the code infringe on rights?]

- **假权威**：将专业知识值得怀疑或没有专业知识的人视作专家。
  Jason Bing, a recognized expert in corporate finance, maintains that pharmaceutical companies do not test their products thoroughly enough. [Bing's expertise in corporate finance bears no apparent relation to the testing of pharmaceuticals.]
  According to Helen Liebowitz, the Food and Drug Administration has approved sixty dangerous drugs in the last two years alone. [Who is Helen Liebowitz? On what authority does she make this claim?]

- **激起读者的恐惧或怜悯**：用情感代替推理。
  By electing Susan Clark to the city council, you will prevent the city's economic collapse. [Trades on people's fears. Can Clark single handedly prevent economic collapse? Is collapse even likely?]
  She should not have to pay taxes because she is an aged widow with no friends or relatives. [Appeals to people's pity. Should age and loneliness, rather than income, determine a person's tax obligation?]

- **讲究派头的诉求**：让读者接受某个主张，以便让其能等同于读者钦佩的人。
  Angelina Jolie has an account at Big City Bank, and so should you. [A celebrity's endorsement does not guarantee the worth of a product, a service, an idea, or anything else.]

- **潮流**：让读者接受一个大家都接受的主张。
  As everyone knows, marijuana use leads to heroin addiction. [What is the evidence?]

- **诉诸群情**：让读者接受一个基于共同价值或者甚至是偏见的结论。
  Any truly patriotic American will support the President's action. [But why is the action worth taking?]

- **人身攻击**：攻击持对立观点的人的品质而不是观点本身。
  One of the scientists has been treated for emotional problems, so his pessimism about nuclear waste merits no attention. [Do the scientist's previous emotional problems invalidate his current views?]

过于简单化

在劳而无功地试图创建完全令人信服的事情时，无效的观点可能用以下的方式掩盖或忽视问题的复杂性：

- **仓促归纳**：在证据不足的情况下得出主张。
  It is disturbing that several of the youths who shot up schools were users of violent video games. Obviously, these games can breed violence, and they should be banned. [A few cases do not establish the relation between the games and violent behavior. Most youths who play violent video games do not behave violently.]

  From the way it handled this complaint, we can assume that the consumer protection office has little intention of protecting consumers. [One experience with the office does not demonstrate its intention or overall performance.]

- **笼统归纳**：得出没有根据的论点。有些笼统归纳是绝对陈述，使用了诸如 all，always，never 和 no one 等具有绝对含义的词。有些是刻板印象，即对某一群体的传统而过于简化的性格描述。

  People who live in cities are unfriendly.
  Californians are fad-crazy.
  Women are emotional.
  Men can't express their feelings.

（见 pp. 167–170 性别歧视和其他歧视语言）

- **简化了的谬误**：简化因果关系（使因果关系变弱）。
  Poverty causes crime. [If so, then why do people who are not poor commit crimes? And why aren't all poor people criminals?]
  The better a school's athletic facilities are, the worse its academic programs are. [The sentence assumes a direct cause-and-effect link between athletics and scholarship.]

- **事后归因谬误**：认为因为A在B之前，所以A一定引起B。
  In the two months since he took office, Mayor Holcomb has allowed crime in the city to increase 12%. [The increase in crime is probably attributable to conditions existing before Holcomb took office.]
  The town council erred in permitting the adult bookstore to open, for shortly afterward two women were assaulted. [It cannot be assumed without evidence that the women's assailants visited or were influenced by the bookstore.]

- **非此即彼的谬误**：认为复杂的问题只有一个好的和一个坏的答案、两个好的答案或两个坏的答案。
  City police officers are either brutal or corrupt. [Most city police officers are neither.]
  Either we permit mandatory drug testing in the workplace or productivity will continue to decline. [Productivity is not necessarily dependent on drug testing.]

- **错误的类比**：认为因为两个事物在某个方面相似，所以它们在其他方面也一定相似。当相似之处是合理时，类比在论述文中非常有用。例如，"禁毒之战"将与敌人的战争和根除（或至少减少）非法毒品的销售及使用相提并论：两个都涉及敌人、预期目标、身穿制服的官员和其他特征。但是，下面文章中的类比错到了极致：
  To win the war on drugs, we must wage more of a military-style operation. Prisoners of war are locked up without the benefit of a trial by jury, and drug dealers should be, too. Soldiers shoot their enemy on sight, and officials who encounter big drug operators should be allowed to shoot them, too. Military traitors may be executed, and corrupt law enforcers could be, too.

练习12.6　辨别并修改谬误

找出下列每句话中至少一个谬误，然后修改句子，使其更合理。带星号部分的参考答案请见书后。

*1. A successful marriage demands a maturity that no one under twenty-five possesses.

*2. Students' persistent complaints about the grading system prove that it is unfair.

*3. The United States got involved in World War II because the Japanese bombed Pearl Harbor.

*4. People watch television because they are too lazy to talk or read or because they want mindless escape from their lives.

*5. Racial tension is bound to occur when people with different backgrounds are forced to live side by side.

6. Emerging nations should not be allowed to use nuclear technology for creating energy because eventually they will use it to wage war.

7. Mountain climbing has more lasting effects than many people think: my cousin blacked out three times after he climbed Pikes Peak.

8. Failing to promote democracy throughout the Middle East will lose the region forever to American influence.

9. She admits to being an atheist, so how could she be a good philosophy teacher?

10. Teenagers are too young to be encouraged to use contraceptives.

12c 有效组织论述文

所有的论述文包括相同的几个部分：

- **引言确定主题的重要性并提供背景信息**。引言一般包括主题陈述，但是如果你认为读者在明白一些支撑证据之前难以接受主题陈述时，你可以将之延后。（见pp. 60–62引言）
- **正文陈述支撑主题的主张，并展开论述**。每一个主张占用一个或多个段落的篇幅。
- **详述并处理对对立观点的反应**。或者说明自己观点的优势，或者承认对方的观点。（见pp. 118–119承认对立观点）
- **结论使论述文变得完整**：再次陈述主题，总结支撑性主张，并对读者做最后的诉求。（见pp. 62–63结论）

正文的结构和对对立观点的反应取决于你的主题、写作目的、目标读者和推理的形式。以下是几种常用的方案：

常用方案	变体
Claim 1 and evidence	Claim 1 and evidence
Claim 2 and evidence	Response to opposing views
Claim X and evidence	Claim 2 and evidence
Response to opposing views	Response to opposing views
	Claim X and evidence
	Response to opposing views

Rogers方案	问题解决方案
Common ground and concession to opposing views	The problem: claims and evidence
Claim 1 and evidence	The solution: claims and evidence
Claim 2 and evidence	Response to opposing views
Claim X and evidence	

12d 论述文范例

学生Aimee Lee就下面的写作任务撰写了论述文：

Select an issue that can be argued, that you care about, and that you know something about through experience, reading, observation, and so on. As you plan and draft your argument, keep the following in mind:

Narrow and shape your subject into a specific thesis statement.

Gather and use evidence to support your claim.

Be aware of assumptions you are making.

Present your claims and evidence reasonably, attempting to establish common ground with your readers.

Acknowledge and try to refute opposing views.

Organize your argument paper straightforwardly and appropriately for your purpose.

The paper should be 900–1200 words in length.

Lee对该任务的反应阐释了本章中讨论的原则。要特别注意结构、主张与支撑证据之间的关系、Lee做出的诉求种类以及她处理对立观点的方法。

Awareness, Prevention, Support:
A Proposal to Reduce Cyberbullying

引言：明确问题

My roommate and I sat in front of her computer staring at the vicious message under her picture. She quickly removed the tag that identified her, but the comments already posted on the photo proved that the damage was done. While she slept, my roommate had become the victim of a cyberbully. She had joined an increasing number of college students who are targeted in texts, e-mails, social-networking sites, and other Web sites that broadcast photographs, videos, and comments. My roommate's experience alerted me that our campus needs a program aimed at awareness and prevention of cyberbullying and support for its victims.

主题句：提出问题的解决之道

问题的证据：已发表的研究

Although schoolyard bullying typically ends with high school graduation, cyberbullying continues in college. According to data gathered by researchers at the Massachusetts Aggression Reduction Center (MARC) of Bridgewater State College, cyberbullying behavior decreases when students enter college, but it does not cease. Examining the experiences of first-year students, the researchers found that 8% of college freshmen had been cyberbullied at college and 3% admitted to having cyberbullied another student (Englander, Mills, and McCoy 217-18). In a survey of fifty-two freshmen, I found further evidence of cyberbullying on this campus. I asked two questions: (1) Have you been involved in cyberbullying as a victim, a bully, or both? (2) If you answered "no" to the first question, do you know anyone who has been involved in cyberbullying as a victim, a bully, or both? While a large majority of the students I surveyed (74%) have not been touched by cyberbullying, a significant number (26%) have been involved personally or know someone who has, as shown in fig. 1. Taken together, the evidence demonstrates

问题的证据：学生自己的研究

that cyberbullying is a problem in colleges and specifically on our campus.

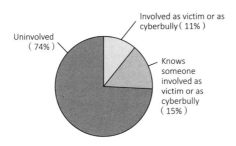

饼状图显示学生研究的结果

Fig. 1. Involvement in cyberbullying among fifty-two first-year students.

The proposed "Stop Cyberbullying" program aims to reduce the behavior through a month-long campaign of awareness, prevention, and support modeled on the college's "Alcohol Awareness Month" program. The program can raise awareness of cyberbullying by explaining what cyberbullying is and by informing students about the college's code of conduct, which prohibits cyberbullying behavior but which few people read. The program can work to prevent cyberbullying by appealing to students to treat those around them respectfully. And, with the participation of the counseling department, the program can provide support for victims, their friends, and others involved in the behavior.

解释问题的解决之道：活动的目的

If adopted, the program can use online and print media to get the message out to the entire college community. For instance, an extensive brochure distributed to first-year students and available through the counseling center can describe cyberbullying and how it violates the college's code of conduct, give strategies for avoiding it, and provide resources for help. During the month-long campaign, flyers posted on campus (see fig. 2) can also raise awareness of the problem, and brief postings to the college's Web site, *Facebook* page, and *Twitter* feed can reach students who take online and hybrid classes as well as those in traditional classes.

解释问题的解决之道：详细的行动

活动宣传的图像证据

Fig. 2. Sample flyer for proposed "Stop Cyberbullying" program.

对于反对意见的预期：行为准则的充足性

  Because this college already has a code of conduct in place and because the state has recently enacted anti-bullying legislation that includes cyberbullying, some students and administrators may contend that enough is being done to deal with the problem. To the administration's credit, the code of conduct contains specific language about online behavior, but promises of punishment for proven allegations do not address several aspects of the problem.

对于反对意见的反应：网络暴力的匿名性

  First, cyberbullies are sometimes anonymous. To accuse another student of cyberbullying, the victim needs to know the identity of the bully. While postings on *Facebook* are attached to real names, most college gossip sites are anonymous. On such sites, a cyberbully can post photographs, videos, and aggressive messages under the cover of anonymity.

对于反对意见的反应：问题的隐蔽性

  Second, even when the identities of cyberbullies are known, the bullying is often invisible to those in a position to take action against it. According to Ikuko Aoyama and Tony L. Talbert at Baylor University, cyberbullying occurs frequently in groups of people who know each other and who attack and retaliate: students are rarely "pure bullies" or "pure victims" but instead are often part of a "bully-victim group" (qtd. in Laster). Moreover, even if students want to separate from bullying groups, Englander, Mills, and McCoy found that they probably will not report cyberbullying incidents to authorities because students generally believe that administrators are unlikely to do anything about cyberbullying (221). Thus counselors and administrators who may be interested in helping students to cope are often unaware of the problem.

Third, conduct codes rarely affect cyberbullying. While some cyberbullying has resulted in tragedy, many aggressive incidents do not rise to the level of punishable offenses ("Cyberbullying"). More often they consist of a humiliating photograph or a mean message—hurtful, to be sure, but not necessarily in violation of the law or the code of conduct. Indeed, the hurdles to getting recourse through official channels are fairly high.

> 对于反对意见的反应：行为准则的无效性

Given its hidden nature and the inability of punitive measures to stop it, cyberbullying needs another approach—namely, a program that teaches students to recognize and regulate their own behavior and provides help when they find themselves in a difficult situation. This program will not heal the wound suffered by my roommate, nor will it prevent all cyberbullying. But if adopted, the program will demonstrate to the college community that the administration is aware of the problem, eager to prevent it, and willing to commit resources to support students who are affected by it.

> 结论

[New page.]

Works Cited

"Cyberbullying Goes to College." *Bostonia*. Boston U, Spring 2009. Web. 18 Feb. 2012.

Englander, Elizabeth, Elizabeth Mills, and Meghan McCoy. "Cyberbullying and Information Exposure: User-Generated Content in Post-Secondary Education." *Violence and Society in the Twenty-First Century*. Spec. issue of *International Journal of Contemporary Sociology* 46.2 (2009): 213-30.

> 用MLA格式标注参考目录

Web. 21 Feb. 2012.

Laster, Jill. "Two Scholars Examine Cyberbullying among College Students." *Chronicle of Higher Education*. Chronicle of Higher Education, June 2010. Web. 18 Feb. 2012.

—Aimee Lee (student)

第 13 章　文学阅读与写作

Sylvan Barnet 撰

概要

分析小说、诗歌、戏剧或其他文学作品：
- 边阅读文学作品边写作（下方）
- 批判性阅读以解释人物、意象和其他元素的意思（p. 130）

文学作品（故事、小说、诗歌和戏剧）的作者关注如何具体地呈现人类经历，给读者一种人生体验感而非讲述人生故事。因此，文学阅读与写作要求特别仔细地关注单词的感觉。例如，Robert Frost 的"Stopping by Woods on a Snowy Evening"中，woods 一词具有 forest 所没有的乡村而朴素的特质。许多类似的细微差异形成了诗歌的效应。

在阅读文学作品时，你要阐释这些差异，从而形成对作品的看法。当你就文学作品撰写文章时，你的观点就是你要陈述的主题，并用作品中的证据支撑该主题。（见 pp. 16–19 主题陈述）

注意：就文学作品撰写文章不仅仅是总结文学作品。你的主题是关于文学作品的含义或效应的主张，而不是其情节的陈述。你的论文是主题的展示，而不是作品变迁或事件的重述。

13a 边阅读文学作品边写作

如果你边阅读边写的话，你就会更加积极地参与到文学作品的阅读中。如果你拥有正在阅读的书籍，可以立即在你特别感兴趣的段落处画线或标示记号，立即在页码空白处注释，标明你的喜悦、哀伤或不确定的地方。如果你不是书籍的主人，可以在纸张或电脑上记笔记。

与作品进行互动的有效方法就是记阅读日记。阅读日记不是记录你所作所为的日记。相反，它是形成并存储你对所读作品反思的地方，例如，回答你在文章的页码空白处标注的问题或对课上观点做出反应。你或许想思考为什么你的观点与其他同学的观点不同。你甚至可能以给作者写信或者以一个人物给另一个人物写信的形式建立一个条目。（见pp. 11–12撰写阅读日记）

13b 批判性阅读文学作品

批判性阅读文学作品指的是与作品进行互动，并非为了做出否定判断，而是为了理解作品并评估其重要性或品质。与浏览报纸或看电视不一样，这样的互动是积极的。它是一个参与的过程，是潜入文字中的过程。

1 ▪ 文学作品中的含义

分析任何一个文学作品，你会立刻面临含义这个问题。读者向来对文学作品的含义意见不一，部分是因为文学作品往往只是展示而非讲述：它提供虚构的人类经历的具体形象，但通常没有说明我们该如何去理解这些形象。另外，读者在阅读过程中带入自己的不同经历，因此对作品做出不同的理解。在就文学作品撰写文章时，我们只能提供我们对作品含义的解读而不是含义本身。大多数人仍然赞同解释是有限度的：它必须由证据支撑，而这些证据即便不是完全令人信服，理性读者也会认为至少是貌似有理的。

2 ▪ 文学分析的问题

对含义的解释千差万别，一个原因就是读者用不同的方法处理文学作品，关注某些元素，并差异性地解释这些元素。例如，历史或文化评论考虑作者所处的环境对作品的影响，女权主义者或性别评论关注作品中的性别表达，而读者反应评论则强调作品对读者的影响。

本章着重讨论所谓的形式主义评论，也就是首先要理解文学作品本身。这种评论模式让读者直接关注文学作品，而不要求广泛的历史或文化背景。它引入了所有评论方法都探讨的文学传统元素，尽管它们看待元素的方法不同。以下的目录就每一个元素提出了问题。它们会帮助你富有建设性和充满想象力地思考你所阅读的作品。

- **情节：事件的关系和模式**。甚至是诗歌也有故事情节。如，情绪从悲伤转变为顺从。

发生了什么事?

发生了什么冲突?

事件之间如何联系? 事件和整个作品如何联系?

131
- **人物:作者创造的人物形象,**包括故事的讲述者或诗歌的朗诵者。

  作品的主人公是谁?

  他们如何互动?

  他们的行为、语言和思想展示了自己和他人的哪些性格?

  人物有没有变化? 为什么?

- **角度:诗歌朗诵者或故事讲述者的角度或态度。**角度可以是第一人称(参与者,使用I)或第三人称(he,she,it,they)。第一人称讲述者可能是故事的主要或次要人物,可能是可靠的,也可能是不可靠的(无法完整或准确报道事件)。第三人称讲述者可能是无所不知的(明白所有人物的所思所想)、认知有限的(只知道一两个人物的所思所想)或客观的(只知道人物外部的事情)。

  讲述者(或诗歌的朗诵者)是谁?

  讲述者的角度如何影响故事的叙述?

- **语气:讲述者或朗诵者的态度,**可以通过文字感知(如开心、痛苦或自信)。

  你听到了什么样的语气? 如果有变化的话,你如何解释?

  讲述者的语气(比如自信)与你认为的作者态度(如对人类过分自信的怜悯)之间有反讽对比吗?

- **意象:视觉、听觉、触觉、嗅觉、味觉所形成的文字图像或细节。**

  作者使用了哪些形象? 这些形象利用了哪些感觉?

  这些形象中(如宗教或商业形象),哪些模式是显而易见的?

  意象的重要性是什么?

- **象征主义:代表更大或更抽象观点的具体事物。**例如,美国国旗可能象征自由,或者凋谢的花朵可能象征死亡的命运。

  作者使用了哪些象征? 它们的重要性如何?

  象征主义如何与作品主题相关?

- **场景**：事件发生的场所。
   场所对作品有什么作用？
   场景的改变很重要吗？

- **形式**：作品的形态或结构。
   作品的形式是什么？（例如，故事可能在中间突然从开心转为悲伤）
   形式强调了作品的哪些部分？为什么？

- **主题**：整个作品所暗示的关于人类经历的主要观点。主题不是故事情节（发生了什么），也不是话题（如哀悼或婚姻）。主题是作者通过关于话题的故事情节所要表达的内容。
   你能用一句话陈述主题吗？避免提到具体的人物或行为；相反，记录下适用于整个人类的观察。
   有些单词、对话或描写段落，或情景是否清晰地反映了主题？
   作品的元素如何结合在一起详尽描述了主题？

- **吸引力**：作品让你满意的程度。
   你特别喜欢或特别不喜欢作品的哪个部分？为什么？
   你认为你的反应是独特的还是与大多数读者相似？为什么？

13c 文学作品分析范例

以下几页呈现了一首诗歌和一名学生所写的关于该诗歌的论文。这名学生Jessie Glenn对该诗歌的一个特定解释写了一篇论述文，详细描述了主题，并用源自该诗歌（第一手资料）的引文、改写和总结支撑其中心思想。Glenn还利用第二手资料（其他评论家的观点）来检测或进一步支撑自己的观点。

注意Glenn论文中的下列特点：

- 作者没有只进行作品总结。她进行了简要总结，以明确含义，但是她的论文主要由分析构成。
- 作者使用了许多源自文学作品的引文。引文为作者的观点提供证据，让读者听到作品的声音。
- 作者顺畅地将引文融入自己的句子中。见pp. 419–422。
- 作者使用了一般现在时态（critics interpret；speaker reflects）来描述诗人的作品和作品的行为。

至于文学论文的格式，请查阅本书的其他部分：
- 采用MLA文档格式处理页边空白、引文和其他元素。（pp. 484–486）
- 用MLA格式引用原始资料：在括号内标示文内引用，列出参考目录。（pp. 439–483）
- 标出对引文所做的编辑。用省略号表示引文中删除的内容。（pp. 341–343）用方括号表示引文中增加或修改的内容。（p. 344）

诗歌

Agha Shahid Ali

Postcard from Kashmir

Kashmir shrinks into my mailbox,
my home a neat four by six inches.
I always loved neatness. Now I hold
the half-inch Himalayas in my hand.

This is home. And this the closest 5
I'll ever be to home. When I return,
the colors won't be so brilliant,
the Jhelum's waters so clean,
so ultramarine. My love
so overexposed. 10

And my memory will be a little
out of focus, in it
a giant negative, black
and white, still undeveloped.

使用第二手资料撰写的一篇关于诗歌的论文

Past and Future in Agha Shahid Ali's "Postcard from Kashmir"

Most literary critics interpret Agha Shahid Ali's "Postcard from Kashmir" as a longing for a lost home, a poetic expression of the heartbreak of exile. For instance, Maimuna Dali Islam describes the speaker's futile effort "to capture his homeland" (262). However, such a reading of the poem seems too narrow. "Postcard from

Kashmir" does evoke the experience of being displaced from a beloved home, but the speaker does not seem to feel an intense loss. Instead, he seems to reflect on his position of having more than one home.

Ali's brief poem consists of three stanzas and divides into two parts. In the first half, the speaker examines a postcard he has received from his former home of Kashmir (lines 1-6). In the second half, the speaker looks forward, imagining how Kashmir will look the next time he sees it and assuming that the place will be different from the idealized view of the postcard and his memory (6-14). The geography is significant. Kashmir has been in the news for many years as the focus of territorial conflict, often violent, among the bordering nations of India, Pakistan, and China. Many residents of the region have been killed, and many have left the region. One of the exiles was Ali: he moved to the United States in 1976 and lived here until his death in 2001, but he also regularly visited his family in Kashmir (Benvenuto 261, 263).

In the context of Kashmir, the literary theorist Jahan Ramazani concludes that the poem "dramatizes the . . . condition" of losing one's homeland to political turmoil (12). Yet several lines in the poem suggest that the speaker is not mourning a loss but musing about having a sense of home both in Kashmir and in the United States. This sense is evident in the opening stanza: "Kashmir shrinks into my mailbox, / my home a neat four by six inches" (1-2), with "my mailbox" conveying his current residence as home and "my home" referring to Kashmir. The dual sense of home is even more evident in the lines "This is home. And this is the closest / I'll ever be to home" (5-6). Although Maimuna Dali Islam assumes that "This" in these lines refers to the Kashmir pictured on the postcard (262), it could also or instead refer to the home attached to the mailbox.

The speaker also seems to perceive that his dual sense of home will continue into the future. The critics do not mention that the second half of the poem is written in the future tense. Beginning with "When I return" (6), the speaker makes it clear that he expects to find himself in Kashmir again, and he imagines how things will be, not how they were. Islam takes the image on the postcard as proof that "there is a place that *can* be captured in a snapshot" (263), but the speaker compares photography to memory, characterizing both as flawed and deceptive with terms such as "overexposed" (10) and "out of focus" (12). He acknowledges that the place won't be like the photograph: "the colors won't be so brilliant, / the Jhelum's waters so clean, / so ultramarine" (7-9). Kashmir still exists, but not as any photograph or memory has recorded it. And the speaker's relationship to his original home, his "love" (9), is changing with the place itself.

In "Postcard from Kashmir" the speaker reflects on home and displacement as he gazes into a representation of his past and considers the future. If the poem mourns a loss, as the critics suggest, it is a loss that has not happened yet, at least not completely. More convincingly, the poem captures a moment when the two homes and the past, present, and future all meet.

Works Cited

Ali, Agha Shahid. "Postcard from Kashmir." *The Half-Inch Himalayas.* Middletown: Wesleyan UP, 1987. 1. Print.

Benvenuto, Christine. "Agha Shahid Ali." *Massachusetts Review* 43.1 (2002): 261-73. Web. 7 Mar. 2012.

Islam, Maimuna Dali. "A Way in the World of an Asian American Existence: Agha Shahid Ali's Transimmigrant Spacing of North America and India and Kashmir." *Transnational Asian American Literature: Sites and Transits.* Ed. Shirley Lim et al. Philadelphia: Temple UP, 2006. 257-73. Print.

Ramazani, Jahan. *The Hybrid Muse: Postcolonial Poetry in English.* Chicago: U of Chicago P, 2001. Print.

—Jessie Glenn(student)

第 14 章　大众写作

概要

在校园外进行有效沟通：
- 使用商务信函和简历的固定格式（p. 136）
- 撰写有明确目标的备忘录（p. 139）
- 为社区工作创建有效的文件（p. 141）

在很多方面，给校园外的公众写文章与学术写作相似。它通常涉及写作的基本过程（pp. 2–42）：评估写作环境、形成自己的观点、在草稿中表述自己的意思、修改并编辑以实现你的目的。它通常涉及研究（pp. 370–434），而且简洁扼要，使用恰当而准确的语言，运用正确的语法和用法（第15—50章）。

但是，根据你的写作内容和写作原因，大众写作也有其惯例。本章涵盖大众写作的几种类型：商务信函和简历、备忘录、时事通信和社区工作的其他文件。

CULTURE LANGUAGE 美国的大众写作，尤其是商务写作，强调效率。对比你的本土文化的大众写作，它可能会显得唐突或没有礼貌。例如，其他地方的商务信函可能要求在一开始礼貌地询问收信人的情况或恭维收信人所在的公司，而美国的商务信函则要求开门见山。

14a 使用商务信函和简历的固定格式

当你出于商业目的而写作时，你是在与大忙人说话。他们想很快地知道你为什么写作以及他们应该如何回复。请遵守以下商业写作的一般准则：

- 开篇就陈述你的目的。
- 要直截了当、清晰、简洁、客观，而且有礼貌。
- 遵守语法和用法规则。这让你的写作条理分明，用你的谨慎给读者留下印象。

1 ▪ 商务信函格式

商务信函要么使用8.5英寸（21.59厘米）×11英寸（27.94厘米）规格的空白纸或者使用顶端印有地址的信纸。行间距为单倍行距，各要素之间用双倍行距，单面打印。

p. 137为常用商务信函格式的图例：

- **寄信人地址信头**显示你的地址和写信日期。不包括你的姓名。如果你使用的信笺上有打印的信头，你只需要提供写信日期。
- **信内地址**显示收信人的姓名、头衔和完整的地址。
- **称呼语**向收信人表示敬意。可能的话，称呼语要明确具体的收信人。（联系公司或部门，询问收信人的姓名）如果你找不到收信人的姓名，则使用职务头衔（Dear Human Resources Manager, Dear Customer Service Manager）或使用一般的称呼语（Dear Smythe Shoes）。对于没有其他头衔的女性，或当你不知道她希望用什么方式称呼时，或者在你知道她愿意你用女士称呼她时，请使用女士相称。
- **正文**包括信函内容。段落之间空一行，而不是每一段首行缩进。
- **结束语**应该反映称呼语中的正式程度。Respectfully, Cordially, Yours truly, Sincerely是更为正式的结束语；Regards和Best wishes则不是那么正式。

- 签名有两个部分：你的姓名在结束语之后占四行，在空出的地方手签自己的姓名。信函的签名要与你签写支票和其他文件时一致。
- 在签名的下方输入附加信息。例如，Enc.（内附）（显示信函的附件）或 cc:Margaret Zusky（抄送：玛格丽特·祖斯基）（显示发送副本给此人）。

所用的信封应该能装下水平折三折的信函。信封的左上角应该显示你的姓名和地址。信封中部应该显示收信人的姓名、头衔和地址。为方便机器阅读，美国邮政总局推荐使用大写字母，且不标注标点符号（每一行的空格分

» 商业信函（求职信）

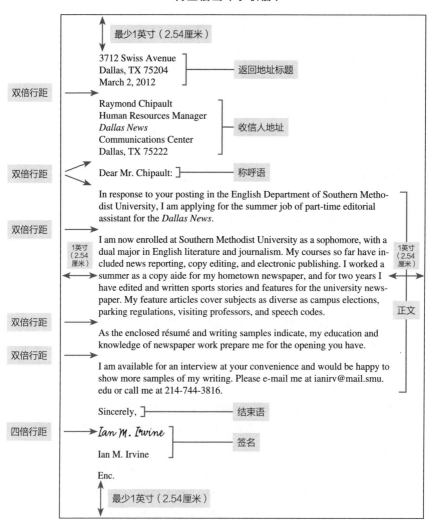

隔各元素）。如下所示：

RAYMOND CHIPAULT
HUMAN RESOURCES MANAGER
DALLAS NEWS
COMMUNICATIONS CENTER
DALLAS TX 75222-0188

2 ▪ 工作申请函

前面的范例说明了工作申请函的关键特征：

- **为特定的工作解释你的简历。** 不要详细描述你的完整简历，不要列举你的全部工作经历。相反，要突出并重塑仅与此工作相关的内容。
- 开篇就声明你要申请的工作以及你是如何听说相关信息的。
- 包含你申请工作的特殊原因，比如明确的职业目标。
- **总结你适合此工作的资格条件**，包括相关的教育和就业经历，强调所取得的突出成绩。要提到附带的简历中会有附加信息。
- **提供联系方式。** 信件的最后，要提到你随时可以在收信人方便的时候参加面试，或者明确说明什么时候可以找到你。

3 ▪ 简历

申请函附带的简历应该以表格的形式提供信息，这样潜在的雇主就可以很快评估你的资格条件。简历应该包含你的姓名和地址、你申请的职位、你的教育和工作经历、你拥有的特殊技能或者获得的奖励，以及如何获得你的推荐信。所有这些信息应该打印在一张纸上，但又不显拥挤，除非你的教育和工作经历非常丰富。见下页关于提交纸版简历的书写和格式规则。

雇主可能将你的简历添加到申请人的电子数据库中。他们可能扫描你的纸版简历，以便将它转变成电子文档，然后保存在合适的数据库中，或者他们可能要求你将简历嵌入电子邮件。为了制作可扫描的简历或电子简历，请遵守以下准则并查询 p.140 的范例：

- **保持简单的设计，以便准确扫描或电子传输。** 避免出现图像，异常文字，多栏、垂直或水平线，斜体字和下画线。
- **使用简洁而明确的文字来描述你的技能和经历。** 雇主的电脑可能使用关键词（通常是名词）来辨别合适岗位候选人的简历，而你要确保你的简历包含恰当的关键词。为你的特殊技能命名（如你能操作的电脑程序），使

» **简历（纸版）**

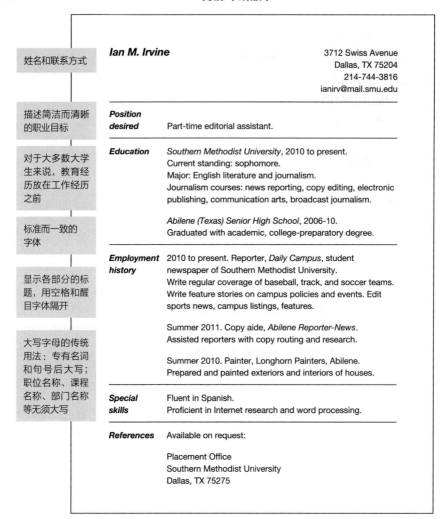

用诸如manager（而不是person with responsibility for）和reporter（而不是staff member who reports）等具体词。在你找到的雇主发布的工作描述中寻找可能的关键词。

14b 撰写目标明确的备忘录

商务备忘录的读者通常是同一机构的人员。大多数备忘录简略处理具体话

» 简历（扫描版或电子版）

Ian M. Irvine
3712 Swiss Avenue
Dallas, TX 75204
214-744-3816
ianirv@mail.smu.edu

KEYWORDS: Editor, editorial assistant, publishing, electronic publishing.

OBJECTIVE
Part-time editorial assistant.

EDUCATION
Southern Methodist University, 2010 to present.
Major: English literature and journalism.
Journalism courses: news reporting, copy editing, electronic publishing, communication arts, broadcast journalism.

Abilene (Texas) Senior High School, 2006-10.
Academic, college preparatory degree.

EMPLOYMENT HISTORY
Reporter, Daily Campus, Southern Methodist University, 2010 to present.
Writer of articles for student newspaper on sports teams, campus policies, and local events. Editor of sports news, campus listings, and features.

Copy aide, Abilene Reporter-News, Abilene, summer 2011.
Assistant to reporters, routing copy and doing research.

Painter, Longhorn Painters, Abilene, summer 2010.
Preparation and painting of exteriors and interiors of houses.

SPECIAL SKILLS
Fluent in Spanish.
Proficient in Internet research and word processing.

REFERENCES
Available on request:
Placement Office
Southern Methodist University
Dallas, TX 75275

> 准确的关键词可以让雇主将简历储存到恰当的数据库中

> 简单的设计，避免异常文字、斜体字、多栏、装饰性字行和图像

> 标准字体便于扫描仪扫描

> 每一行左对齐

题，例如回答一个问题或一项评估。

　　备忘录的格式和结构的设计都是为了切入主题和快速处理。（见下页的范例）在第一句话中陈述你的写作原因。第一段简要说明你的答案、结论或评价。备忘录的其他部分解释你的推理或证据。用恰当的标题或条目突出关键信息。

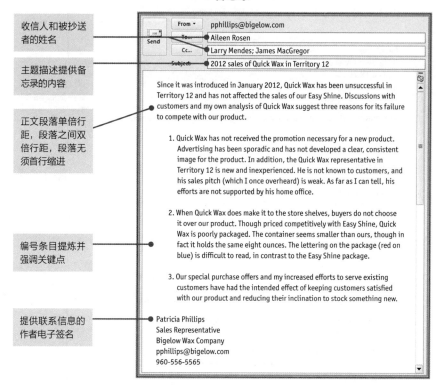

14c 为社区工作创建有效的文件

在人生的某些时候，你可能在社区机构（比如流动厨房、日托中心或文学项目组）当志愿者。许多大学课程包含服务学习。在这些课程中，你可以从事志愿工作、就课程经历撰写文章以及为服务的机构撰写文章。

你为社区团体撰写的文章种类从传单到经费申请报告不等。下页的时事通信是为一个文学项目而准备的。以下两个准则尤其有助于你为撰写高效的计划书做准备：

- **根据目的和读者起草文件。**你尝试和读者一起达到一个具体的目标，而你使用的方法和语气将影响读者的反应。例如，如果你给本地企业写信为流浪汉庇护所筹款，你要想着谁会看到你的信。你如何用最佳方式说服那些读者捐款。

- **期待与他人合作。**很多大众写作是多人合作的产物。即使你独立起草文件，其他人也会检查文件的内容、语气和构思。类似的合作是有益的，但有时候它要求耐心和善意。见pp. 32–33合作建议。
再见pp. 136–141信件和备忘录。

» 时事通信

Springfield Veterans Administration Hospital **SUMMER 2012**

From the director

Can you help? With more and more learners in the ReadingWorks program, we need more and more tutors. You may know people who would be interested in participating in the program, if only they knew about it.

Those of you who have been tutoring VA patients in reading and writing know both the great need you fulfill and the great benefits you bring to the students. New tutors need no special skills—we'll provide the training—only patience and an interest in helping others.

We've scheduled an orientation meeting for Friday, September 14, at 6:30 PM. Please come and bring a friend who is willing to contribute a couple of hours a week to our work.

Thanks,
Kate Goodman

IN THIS ISSUE	
First Annual Awards Dinner	1
New Guidelines on PTSD	1
Textbooks	2
Lesson Planning	2
Dyslexia Workshop	2
Support for Tutors	3
Writing by Students	3
Calendar of Events	4

FIRST ANNUAL AWARDS DINNER

A festive night for students and tutors

The first annual Reading-Works Awards Dinner on May 18th was a great success. Springfield's own Golden Fork provided tasty food and Amber Allen supplied lively music. The students decorated Suite 42 on the theme of books and reading. In all, 127 people attended.

The highlight of the night was the awards ceremony. Nine students, recommended by their tutors, received certificates recognizing their efforts and special accomplishments in learning to read and write:

Ramon Berva
Edward Byar
David Dunbar
Tony Garnier
Chris Guigni
Akili Haynes
Josh Livingston
Alex Obeld
B. J. Resnansky

In addition, nine tutors received certificates commemorating five years of service to ReadingWorks:

Anita Crumpton
Felix Cruz-Rivera
Bette Elgen

Kayleah Bortoluzzi
Harriotte Henderson
Ben Obiso
Meggie Puente
Max Smith
Sara Villante

Congratulations to all!

PTSD: New Guidelines

Most of us are working with veterans who have been diagnosed with post-traumatic stress disorder. Because this disorder is often complicated by alcoholism, depression, anxiety, and other problems, the National Center for PTSD has issued some guidelines for helping PTSD patients in ways that reduce their stress.

- The hospital must know your tutoring schedule, and you need to sign in and out before and after each tutoring session.
- To protect patients' privacy, meet them only in designated visiting and tutoring areas, never in their rooms.
- Treat patients with dignity and respect, even when (as sometimes happens) they grow frustrated and angry. Seek help from a nurse or orderly if you need it.

单个页面上的多栏格式为标题、文章和其他元素提供空间

两栏标题强调主条目

帮助读者浏览以了解重点元素：行距、变化的字体、字行和符号列表

字体让读者集中注意力于大字标题、标题和目录

活泼但又整齐的总体外观

左栏的方框突出目录

第三部分
明晰与风格 3

第15章·强调

第16章·平行结构

第17章·变化与细节

第18章·恰当而准确的用词

第19章·完整

第20章·简明

第 15 章 强调

概要
- 使用主语和动词来表达施动者和动作（下方）
- 使用句子的开头和结尾（p. 146）
- 同等重要的思想用并列结构（p. 149）
- 次要思想用从属结构（p. 152）

当你说话时，你的语调、表情，甚至手势，都会配合话语传达意义。但当你写作时，就全靠你的词句了。要准确地遣词达意，请看本章建议，在句中强调你的主要意思。第 20 章关于简明的讲解，对此也有裨益。

语法检查工具： 语法检查工具可以找出关于强调的一些问题，比如由动词转换来的名词、被动语态、拖泥带水的短语，还有松散没有重点的长句。但是，没有哪个语法检查工具能够帮你识别句子中的重要思想，或者告诉你那些思想是否得到了如你之意的适当强调。

15a 使用主语和动词来表达施动者和动作

每个句子的核心是其主语和谓语动词，主语指明施动者，谓语明确主语的动作：Children [主语] grow [动词]。如果主语和谓语没有给出句子的关键施动者和动作，读者就只能去句子的别处寻找，句子就会冗长而没有重点。

下面的句子中，用下画线标出了主语和动词：

无重点： The <u>intention</u> of the company <u>was</u> to expand its workforce. A <u>proposal</u> was also <u>made</u> to diversify the backgrounds and abilities of employees.

这样的句子没有重点，因为它们的关键思想没有出现在主语和动词中。修改后，句子不仅更清楚，而且更精练了：

修改： The <u>company</u> <u>intended</u> to expand its workforce. <u>It</u> also <u>proposed</u> to diversify the backgrounds and abilities of employees.

下面及 p. 146 讨论的结构常常会削弱句子主语和动词的意义。

由动词而来的名词

使用由动词转换而来的名词会使句子的关键动作模糊不清而且增加用词。

12b 理性写作

为了在你和读者之间建立共同基础，你的论点必须是合理的。读者希望看到逻辑思维、恰当诉求、公平对待对立观点，并在综合上述方面的基础上正确写作。

1 ▪ 进行逻辑思维训练

论述文的主题是你对证据进行推理之后得出的结论。即便你不熟悉术语，你也知道推理的两个过程：归纳和演绎。

归纳

当你要购买二手车时，你会咨询朋友、亲戚和消费者指南，然后决定购买哪一类型的车。使用归纳或归纳推理法，你可以详细观察汽车（证据）并归纳或推断出概括性主张：X汽车很可靠。这一概括是以观察为支撑的主张。

你也可能在有关平面广告的学期论文中使用归纳推理法：

证据：Advertisements in newspapers and magazines

证据：Comments by advertisers and publishers

证据：Data on the effectiveness of advertising

概括或主张：Print remains the most cost-effective medium for advertising.

归纳推理法始于支撑主张的证据，并结合连接证据和主张的假设。这样，归纳法从现有知识中创建了新知识。（见下页图）

当你进行归纳推理时，你通过假设在某种环境中真实的事物在类似的环境中也是真实的，从而连接证据和概括。你积累的证据越多，你的概括就越有可能是真实的。但是要注意，绝对肯定是不可能的。同时，你必须假定你的证据向你自己以及读者证明了你的概括是正当的。

归纳推理中的大多数错误涉及对证据或概括的过分简化。见pp. 120–123。

演绎

在你从概括（在你想买二手车的特定情况下，你概括出X汽车是最可靠的二手车）入手，得出你应该购买X汽车的结论时，你使用的就是演绎或演绎推理法。在演绎推理法中，你的假设是你认为的真实的概括、原则或意见。你将之运用到证据（新的信息）中，以便得出你的主张（你得出的结论）。关于演绎推理法的图解与关于归纳推理法的图解一致，以平面广告为例。（见下页）

演绎论证的传统表现方式是三段论。如果你希望校方暂不提高某幢宿舍楼这样的名词包括intention（来自intend），proposal（来自propose），decision（来自decide），expectation（来自expect），persistence（来自persist），argument（来自argue），以及inclusion（来自include）。

无重点：After the company made a <u>decision</u> to hire more workers with disabilities, its next step was the <u>construction</u> of wheelchair ramps and other facilities.

修改：After the company <u>decided</u> to hire more workers with disabilities, it next <u>constructed</u> wheelchair ramps and other facilities.

弱动词

弱动词，如上面无重点句子中的made和was，会削弱句子，埋没关键动作。

无重点：The company <u>is</u> now the leader among businesses in complying with the 1990 disabilities act. Its officers <u>make</u> frequent speeches on the act to business groups.

修改：The company now <u>leads</u> other businesses in complying with the 1990 disabilities act. Its officers frequently <u>speak</u> on the act to business groups.

各种词形的be，have和made常常是弱动词，但也不要想把它们的所有用法都去掉：be和have作为助动词是非常重要的（<u>is</u> going，<u>has</u> written）：be联系主语和描述它们的词语（Planes <u>are</u> noisy）；have和make有它们独立的意思（比如"拥有"和"迫使"）。但是，如果be，have和make后的词语本身可以变成一个动词，那就确实可以考虑那么做，如下例：

无重点	有重点
was influential	influenced
have a preference	prefer
had the appearance	appeared, seemed
made a claim	claimed

被动语态

被动语态中的动词表明主语接受而不是发出的动作。所以说，被动语态弱化了句子的真正施动者，有时候完全省略了施动者。一般来说，最好使用主动语态，由主语实施动作。

无重点：The 1990 <u>law is seen</u> by most businesses as fair, but the <u>costs of</u>

complying have sometimes been objected to.

有重点： Most businesses see the 1990 law as fair, but some have objected to the costs of complying.

关于被动语态的恰当使用及怎样修改，见pp.240–241。

> **练习15.1　改写：主语和动词的强调**
>
> 改写下列句子，使主语和动词表达的是关键施动者及动作。带星号部分的参考答案请见书后。
>
> 例子：
>
> The issue of students making a competition over grades is a reason why their focus on learning may be lost.
>
> Students who compete over grades may lose their focus on learning.

*1. The work of many heroes was crucial in helping to emancipate the slaves.

*2. The contribution of Harriet Tubman, an escaped slave herself, included the guidance of hundreds of other slaves to freedom on the Underground Railroad.

3. A return to slavery was risked by Tubman or possibly death.

4. During the Civil War she was also a carrier of information from the South to the North.

5. After the war, needy former slaves were helped by Tubman's raising of money.

15b 使用句子的开头和结尾

读者很自然地会到句子的主句中寻找作者的主要意思，即到指明施动者的主语和明确动作的谓语动词（p. 144）中去寻找。所以，为了帮助读者理解你想要表达的意思，作者应当控制主语的信息、控制主句和修饰语的关系。

旧信息与新信息

通常，读者期待句首包含他们已知的信息或你已经交代的信息，然后会期待句末包含新信息。在下面这个没有重点的段落里，第二句和第三句话都是以新话题开头，而旧话题出现在句子的末尾。这样段落的形式是A→B，C→B，D→A。

　　　　　　　　　　A　　　　　　　　　B
无重点：Education often means controversy these days, with rising costs and constant complaints about its inadequacies. But the value of schooling should not be obscured by the controversy. The single best means of economic advancement, despite its shortcomings, remains education.

在下面更有重点的修改版里，旧信息在每个句子的开头，新信息在句子的末尾。段落的形式是A→B, B→C, A→D。

修改：Education often means controversy these days, with rising costs and constant complaints about its inadequacies. But the controversy should not obscure the value of schooling. Education remains, despite its shortcomings, the single best means of economic advancement.

累计句和圆周句

你可以把需要读者注意的信息放在句首或句尾，把次要信息放在中间。

无重点：Education remains the single best means of economic advancement, despite its shortcomings. [强调不足之处]

修改：Despite its shortcomings, education remains the single best means of economic advancement. [强调进步而不是不足]

修改：Education remains, despite its shortcomings, the single best means of economic advancement. [弱化不足之处]

以主句开头然后加上修饰语的句子叫作累积句，因为它在句子的进行过程中累积各种信息：

累计句：Education has no equal in opening minds, instilling values, and creating opportunities.

累计句：Most of the Great American Desert is made up of bare rock, rugged cliffs, mesas, canyons, mountains, separated from one another by broad flat basins covered with sunbaked mud and alkali, supporting a sparse and measured growth of sagebrush or creosote or saltbush, depending on location and elevation.

　　　　　　　　　　　　　　　　　　　　——Edward Abbey

相对的句子类型称为圆周句（也叫掉尾句、紧凑句），它把主句留到最后，句号（the period）的前面。主句之前的一切都指向主语：

圆周句：In opening minds, instilling values, and creating opportunities, education has no equal.

圆周句：With people from all over the world—Korean doctors, Jamaican cricket players, Vietnamese engineers, Indian restaurant owners—the American mosaic is continually changing.

圆周句把重要信息留到句子末尾，因而给读者造成悬念。但读者也应该已经对句子的主语有所了解了，因为它在之前的句子里出现过，所以读者知道句子开头的修饰语描写的是什么。

练习15.2　句子合并：开头和结尾

找到下面各组带序号的句子中的主要思想。然后把每组句子合并为一个句子，在句首或句尾强调它的主要思想。对于第2—5组句子，决定主要思想的位置时，请考虑它与前面句子的关系。假如主要思想接续之前的话题，把它放在句首。假如主要思想是增加新的信息，把它放在句尾。带星号部分的参考答案请见书后。

例子：

The storm blew roofs off buildings. It caused extensive damage. It knocked down many trees. It severed power lines.

主要思想在句首：<u>The storm caused extensive damage</u>, blowing roofs off buildings, knocking down many trees, and severing power lines.

主要思想在句尾：Blowing roofs off buildings, knocking down many trees, and severing power lines, <u>the storm caused extensive damage</u>.

*1. Pat Taylor strode into the room. The room was packed. He greeted students called "Taylor's Kids." He nodded to their parents and teachers.

*2. This was a wealthy Louisiana oilman. He had promised his "Kids" free college educations. He was determined to make higher education available to all qualified but disadvantaged students.

3. The students welcomed Taylor. Their voices joined in singing. They sang "You Are the Wind beneath My Wings." Their faces beamed with hope. Their eyes flashed with self-confidence.

4. The students had thought a college education was beyond their dreams. It seemed too costly. It seemed too demanding.

5. Taylor had to ease the costs and the demands of getting to college. He created a bold plan. The plan consisted of scholarships, tutoring, and counseling.

15c 同等重要的思想用并列结构

用并列结构来表示句中的两个或更多元素在意义上同等重要,这样能使它们之间的关系清楚明白:

- 用逗号和并列连词连接两个主句,如and或but。

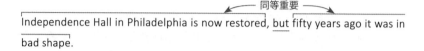
Independence Hall in Philadelphia is now restored, but fifty years ago it was in bad shape.

- 只用分号或用分号加连接副词连接两个主句,如however。

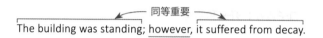
The building was standing; however, it suffered from decay.

- 在主句中,用并列连词连接多个词或短语,如and或or。

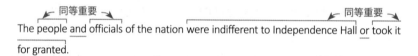
The people and officials of the nation were indifferent to Independence Hall or took it for granted.

- 用关系连词连接多个主句、词语或短语,如not only . . . but also。

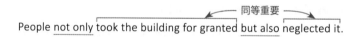
People not only took the building for granted but also neglected it.

关于并列成分的标点问题,请看p.308(逗号及并列连词),p.320(只用并列连词),及pp.323–324(只用分号或分号加连接副词)。

语法检查工具:语法检查工具可以查出并列成分标点问题上的一些错误,也能查出可能过度使用连词的长句,但是除此之外,它们对于并列没有什么帮助,因为它们无法识别句子中各个思想之间的关系。

1 ▪ 并列使句子顺畅

并列表示各成分之间的平等关系,如上述例子所示。同时,并列也能使意思清楚明白,它能使下面这样磕磕绊绊的句子变得顺畅:

磕绊的句子:We should not rely so heavily on oil. Coal and uranium are also overused. We have a substantial energy resource in the moving waters of our rivers. Smaller streams add to the total volume of water. The resource renews itself. Coal and oil are irreplaceable. Uranium is also irreplaceable. The cost of water does not increase much over time. The costs of coal, oil, and Uranium rise dramatically.

下面修改版把coal，oil及uranium归为一类，并将其与water清楚对照（连接词用下画线标记出来了）：

多个思想并列起来：We should not rely so heavily on coal, oil, <u>and</u> Uranium, <u>for</u> we have a substantial energy resource in the moving waters of our rivers <u>and</u> streams. Coal, oil, <u>and</u> Uranium are irreplaceable <u>and</u> thus subject to dramatic cost increases; water, <u>however</u>, is self-renewing <u>and</u> more stable in cost.

2 ▪ 有效使用并列

并列只用来表示多个思想或细节的平等关系。一系列并列的成分，特别是主句，表示这些点都是同等重要的：

过多的并列词：The weeks leading up to the resignation of President Nixon were eventful, and the Supreme Court and the Congress closed in on him, and the Senate Judiciary Committee voted to begin impeachment proceedings, and finally the President resigned on August 9, 1974.

这样的句子需要改写，以强调主句中的重要内容（在下面用下画线标记），并弱化非重要信息：

修改：<u>The weeks leading up to the resignation of President Nixon were eventful,</u> as the Supreme Court and the Congress closed in on him and the Senate Judiciary Committee voted to begin impeachment proceedings. <u>Finally, the President resigned on August 9, 1974.</u>

即便在单个句子中，并列也应当是表达各个思想之间的逻辑平等：

错误：John Stuart Mill was a nineteenth-century utilitarian, and he believed that actions should be judged by their usefulness or by the happiness they cause.［这两个句子并非分离而平等：第二句是对第一句的扩展，解释了像Mill这样的功利主义者会相信什么］

修改：John Stuart Mill, <u>a nineteenth-century utilitarian,</u> believed that actions should be judged by their usefulness or by the happiness they cause.

第三部分　明晰与风格

练习15.3　改写：过度或错误的并列

改写下列句子，去掉过度或错误的并列，可以用增加或降格信息的办法，或者用形成多个句子的办法。每个题可能有多个答案。带星号部分的参考答案请见书后。

例子：

My dog barks, and I have to move out of my apartment.

<u>Because my dog's barking disturbs my neighbors</u>, I have to move out of my apartment.

*1. Often soldiers admired their commanding officers, and they gave them nicknames, and these names frequently contained the word *old*, but not all of the commanders were old.

*2. General Thomas "Stonewall" Jackson was also called "Old Jack," and he was not yet forty years old.

3. Another Southern general in the Civil War was called "Old Pete," and his full name was James Longstreet.

4. The Union general Henry W. Halleck had a reputation as a good military strategist, and he was an expert on the work of a French military authority, Henri Jomini, and Halleck was called "Old Brains."

5. General William Henry Harrison won the Battle of Tippecanoe, and he received the nickname "Old Tippecanoe," and he used the name in his presidential campaign slogan, "Tippecanoe and Tyler, Too," and he won the election in 1840, but he died of pneumonia a month after taking office.

15d 使用从属来强调一些思想

用<u>从属结构</u>表示句子中的一些成分在意义上不如另一些重要。通常，主要思想出现在主句中，而次要思想出现在从属结构中。

- 使用以although, because, if, until, who（whom）, that, which或别的从属词开头的从句：

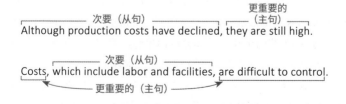

- 使用短语：

Despite some decline, production costs are still high.

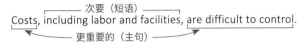
Costs, including labor and facilities, are difficult to control.

- 使用单个词语：

Declining costs have not matched prices.

Labor costs are difficult to control.

给从属成分加标点，请看 pp. 309–310（逗号与引入性成分）和 pp. 311–314（逗号与中断性成分）。

语法检查工具：语法检查工具能找出从属成分的标点问题中的一些错误，通常也能查出可能含有过度从属的长句。但是除此之外，它对从属的使用没有什么帮助，因为它无法识别句子中各个思想之间的关系。

1▪用从属来辨别重要的思想

一系列主句会使文中的一切显得同等重要，如下例所示：

一系列主句：Computer prices have dropped, and production costs have dropped more slowly, and computer manufacturers have struggled, for their profits have been declining.

强调来自各归其位：重要信息在主句中（见下，用下划线标记），次要信息在从句中。

改写：Because production costs have dropped more slowly than prices, <u>computer manufacturers have struggled with declining profits</u>.

2▪有效使用从属

在句子中使用从属时，要注意把关系理清楚：

- 只把句中的次要信息放在从属位置。错误的从属颠倒了读者所期待的依附关系。

  错误：Ms. Angelo was in her first year of teaching, although she was a better instructor than others with many years of experience.［这句话暗示了Angelo的缺乏经验是主要意思，而作者想强调她的技巧，尽管她缺乏经验］

修改：Although Ms. Angelo was in her first year of teaching, <u>she was a better instructor than others with many years of experience.</u>

- 避免把松散联系的一堆细节塞到一个长句里。

  过载的句子：The boats that were moored at the dock when the hurricane, which was one of the worst in three decades, struck were ripped from their moorings, because the owners had not been adequately prepared, since the weather service had predicted that the storm would blow out to sea, as storms do at this time of year.

  修改：Struck by one of the worst hurricanes in three decades, <u>the boats at the dock were ripped from their moorings.</u> The owners <u>were unprepared</u> because the weather service had said that hurricanes at this time of year blow out to sea.

- 避免垂悬修饰语，即没有合理地与句子其他部分发生联系的修饰语。（见 pp. 283–284）

  垂悬修饰语：Driving through the region, the destruction from the storm was everywhere.

  修改：Driving through the region, <u>we saw</u> destruction from the storm everywhere.

练习15.4　改写：错误或过度的从属

改写下列句子，去掉错误或过度的从属，以达到恰当的强调。带星号部分的参考答案请见书后。

例子：

Terrified to return home, he had driven his mother's car into a cornfield.

Having driven his mother's car into a cornfield, he was terrified to return home.

*1. Genaro González is a successful writer, which means that his stories and novels have been published to critical acclaim.

*2. He loves to write, although he has also earned a doctorate in psychology.

3. His first story, which reflects his growing consciousness of his Aztec heritage and place in the world, is titled "Un Hijo del Sol."

4. González wrote the first version of "Un Hijo del Sol" while he was a sophomore at the University of Texas–Pan American, which is in the Rio Grande Valley of southern Texas, which González calls "el Valle" in the story.

5. González's latest book, which is about a teenager and is titled *A So-Called Vacation*, is a novel about how the teen and his family live for a summer as migrant fruit pickers, which was the experience his father had when he first immigrated from Mexico.

练习15.5　改写：并列与从属

下面段落完全由简单句组成。用并列或从属的办法合并句子，以有效地强调主要意思。带星号部分的参考答案见书后。

*Sir Walter Raleigh personified the Elizabethan Age. *That was the period of Elizabeth I's rule of England. *The period occurred in the last half of the sixteenth century. *Raleigh was a courtier and poet. *He was also an explorer and entrepreneur. *Supposedly, he gained Queen Elizabeth's favor. *He did this by throwing his cloak beneath her feet at the right moment. * She was just about to step over a puddle. There is no evidence for this story. It does illustrate Raleigh's dramatic and dynamic personality. His energy drew others to him. He was one of Elizabeth's favorites. She supported him. She also dispensed favors to him. However, he lost his queen's goodwill. Without her permission he seduced one of her maids of honor. He eventually married the maid of honor. Elizabeth died. Then her successor imprisoned Raleigh in the Tower of London. Her successor was James I. The king falsely charged Raleigh with treason. Raleigh was released after thirteen years. He was arrested again two years later on the old treason charges. At the age of sixty-six he was beheaded.

第 16 章　平行结构

概要

- 使用带and, but, or, nor和yet的平行结构（下页）
- 使用带both . . . and, not . . . but, 或别的并列连词的平行结构（p. 156）
- 在比较、列表、标题和提纲中使用平行结构（p. 156, p. 157）

错误：Given training, workers can acquire the skills and interest in other jobs.
　　　［成语规定skills和interest使用不同的介词］
修改：Given training, workers can acquire the skills for and interest in other jobs.

16b 使用带 both ... and, not ... but, 或别的关系连词的平行结构

关系连词强调各成分之间的平等和平衡。平行结构加强了平等。

It is not a tax bill but a tax relief bill, providing relief not for the needy but for the greedy.

— Franklin Delano Roosevelt

用关系连词时，第二个连接词之后的成分必须与第一个连接词之后的成分相匹配。

不平行：Huck Finn learns not only that human beings have an enormous capacity for folly but also enormous dignity.［第一个元素包括human beings have；第二个元素没有］

修改：Huck Finn learns that human beings have not only an enormous capacity for folly but also enormous dignity.［human beings have的重新定位使得这两个元素平行］

16c 在比较中使用平行结构

在用than或as来进行比较的两个成分之间，平行结构加强了它们的相似或不同。

不平行：Huck Finn proves less a bad boy than to be an independent spirit. In the end he is every bit as determined in rejecting help as he is to leave for "the territory."

修改：Huck Finn proves less a bad boy than an independent spirit. In the end he is every bit as determined to reject help as he is to leave for "the territory."

（关于做合乎逻辑的比较，见pp.270–271）

16d 在列表、标题和提纲中使用平行结构

列表或提纲中的各项是并列关系，应当使用平行结构。在把一篇论文

分为各部分的各个标题中，以及在正式的提纲中，都必须使用平行结构。（见 pp. 23–24）

不平行	修改
Changes in Renaissance England	Changes in Renaissance England
1. Extension of trade routes	1. Extension of trade routes
2. Merchant class became more powerful	2. <u>Increased power</u> of the merchant class
3. The death of feudalism	3. <u>Death</u> of feudalism
4. Upsurging of the arts	4. <u>Upsurge</u> of the arts
5. Religious quarrels began	5. <u>Rise</u> of religious quarrels

练习16.1　改写：平行结构

改写下列句子，如果语法或连贯上需要的话，使用平行结构。必要的时候增删词或改换措辞。带星号部分的参考答案请见书后。

例子：

After emptying her bag, searching the apartment, and she called the library, Jennifer realized she had lost the book.

After emptying her bag, searching the apartment, and <u>calling</u> the library, Jennifer realized she had lost the book.

*1. The ancient Greeks celebrated four athletic contests: the Olympic Games at Olympia, the Isthmian Games were held near Corinth, at Delphi the Pythian Games, and the Nemean Games were sponsored by the people of Cleonae.

*2. Each day the games consisted of either athletic events or holding ceremonies and sacrifices to the gods.

*3. In the years between the games, competitors were taught wrestling, javelin throwing, and how to box.

*4. Competitors participated in running sprints, spectacular chariot and horse races, and running long distances while wearing full armor.

*5. The purpose of such events was to develop physical strength, demonstrating skill and endurance, and to sharpen the skills needed for war.

6. Events were held for both men and for boys.

7. At the Olympic Games the spectators cheered their favorites to victory, attended sacrifices to the gods, and they feasted on the meat not burned in offerings.

8. The athletes competed less to achieve great wealth than for gaining honor both for themselves and their cities.

9. Of course, exceptional athletes received financial support from patrons, poems and statues by admiring artists, and they even got lavish living quarters from their sponsoring cities.

10. With the medal counts and flag ceremonies, today's Olympians sometimes seem to be proving their countries' superiority more than to demonstrate individual talent.

练习16.2　句子合并：平行结构

把下列各组句子合并为一个简明的句子，使用平行结构来表达平行的成分。你可能会需要增删、改变措辞或重新安排词语。每道题可能有多个答案。带星号部分的参考答案请见书后。

例子：

The new process works smoothly. It is efficient, too.

The new process works smoothly and <u>efficiently</u>.

*1. People can develop post-traumatic stress disorder (PTSD). They develop it after experiencing a dangerous situation. They will also have felt fear for their survival.

*2. The disorder can be triggered by a wide variety of events. Combat is a typical cause. Similarly, natural disasters can result in PTSD. Some people experience PTSD after a hostage situation.

3. PTSD can occur immediately after the stressful incident. Or it may not appear until many years later.

4. Sometimes people with PTSD will act irrationally. Moreover, they often become angry.

5. Other symptoms include dreaming that one is reliving the experience. They include hallucinating that one is back in the terrifying place. In another symptom one imagines that strangers are actually one's former torturers.

第 17 章　变化与细节

概要

- 变换句子长度（下页）

- 用从属、合并、改变句子开头的办法变换句子结构（下方）
- 增加相关及翔实的细节（p. 162）

清晰而有趣的写作至少有两个特点：句子的长度及结构适合于句子的意思和重要性，有丰富的细节提供信息和质感。

语法检查工具：有一些语法检查工具能查出长句，然后你可以检查这些句子是否有恰当的变化。但通常来说这些工具无法帮你看到何处需要变化，因为它们无法识别你的思想的关系和复杂性，也无法对何处需要增加细节提出建议。

17a 变化句子长度

在当代写作中，句子一般在10到40个词之间，平均在15到25个词之间。如果你的句子都很长或都很短，读者可能会很难抓住你的重点并看到句子间的关系。

- **长句**：如果你的多数句子含35个词甚至更多，你的主要思想会湮没于细节而不能突显。要使主要思想得到更多的强调，需要把它从细节中分离出来，把长句打散成更短更简单的句子。
- **短句**：如果你的大部分句子包含的词少于15个，甚至10个，你的所有思想可能会显得都同样重要，它们之间的关联可能会不清楚。可以用并列（p. 149）和从属（p. 152）的办法合并句子，以表现关系，并使主要意思得到强调，突出于次要思想。

17b 变化句子结构

如果句子都是同样的句式，文章会很单调，就像队伍里的士兵。要变化结构，可以用从属、合并、变化句子开头及改变词序的办法。

1 ▪ 从属

一连串简单句或复合句会很笨拙：

单调：The moon is now drifting away from the earth. It moves away at the rate of about one inch a year. This movement is lengthening our days. They increase a thousandth of a second every century. Forty-seven of our present days will someday make up a month. We might eventually lose the moon altogether. Such great planetary movement rightly concerns astronomers, but it need not worry us. It will take 50 million years.

要让这样的句子生动起来——并使句子的主要意思得以突出，可以把不那么重要的信息放在从属性的句子和短语里。在下面的修改版中，下画线标出了由原来的主句改成的从属结构：

修改：The moon is now drifting away from the earth <u>about one inch a year. At a thousandth of a second every century,</u> this movement is lengthening our days. Forty-seven of our present days will someday make up a month, <u>if we don't eventually lose the moon altogether.</u> Such great planetary movement rightly concerns astronomers, but it need not worry us. It will take 50 million years.

2 ▪ 合并句子

如前例所示，使用从属结构来增加句式变化时，常常会需要把短句合并为长句，从而把相关信息联系起来并强调主要信息。下面再来一个句子合并的例子：

单调：Astronomy may seem a remote science. It may seem to have little to do with people's daily lives. Many astronomers find otherwise. They see their science as soothing. It gives perspective to everyday routines and problems.

把五个句子合并为一个，下面的改写比原句清晰而易读。下画线标出了所做的改变。

修改：Astronomy may seem a remote science <u>having</u> little to do with people's daily lives, <u>but</u> many astronomers <u>find their science soothing</u> <u>because</u> it gives perspective to everyday routines and problems.

3 ▪ 改变句子的开头

英语句子常以主语开头，通常主语可以从之前的句子抓取旧信息（见 pp. 146–147）：

The defendant's <u>lawyer</u> was determined to break the prosecution's witness. <u>He</u> relentlessly cross-examined the stubborn witness for a week.

但是，如果一连串句子全是以主语开头，很快就会显得单调乏味。

单调：The defendant's lawyer was determined to break the prosecution's witness. He relentlessly cross-examined the witness for a week. The

第三部分　明晰与风格

witness had expected to be dismissed within an hour and was visibly irritated. She did not cooperate. She was reprimanded by the judge.

如果用别的表达改写其中一些句子，会使句子清晰而易读。

修改：The defendant's lawyer was determined to break the prosecution's witness. <u>For a week</u> he relentlessly cross-examined the witness. <u>Expecting to be dismissed within an hour</u>, the witness was visibly irritated. She did not cooperate. <u>Indeed</u>, she was reprimanded by the judge.

下画线标出的表达代表了改变句子开头的最常见的选择：

- 副词修饰语，例如，For a week（修饰动词cross-examined）。
- 形容词修饰语，例如，Expecting to be dismissed within an hour（修饰witness）。
- 过渡语，例如，Indeed。（过渡语列表见p. 51方框）

〔CULTURE LANGUAGE〕在标准美式英语中，有一些否定的副词修饰语放在句首时，需要用问句的语序，动词或动词的一部分要放在主语的前面。这样的副词修饰语有never, rarely, seldom, 以及以no, not since和not until开头的副词短语。

    副词 主语 动词短语
错误：Seldom <u>a witness</u> <u>has held</u> the stand so long.

     助动词
   副词 主语 动词短语
修改：Seldom <u>has</u> <u>a witness</u> <u>held</u> the stand so long.

4 ▪ 改变语序

有时，可以用颠倒正常语序的办法来增加句子的变化并加以强调：

A dozen witnesses testified for the prosecution, and the defense attorney barely questioned eleven of them. <u>The twelfth, however, he grilled.</u>〔正常语序：He grilled the twelfth, however.〕

如果并非必要而使用倒装，句子会显得做作。只有当需要强调的时候才用倒装的手法。

17c 增加细节

相关的细节，比如事实和例子，可以让句子获得质感和活力，从而抓住读者注意力，帮他们掌握你的意思。注意下面两个例句的不同：

  平淡：Constructed after World War II, Levittown, New York, consisted of thousands of houses in two basic styles. Over the decades, residents have altered the houses so dramatically that the original styles are often unrecognizable.

有丰富细节：Constructed <u>on potato fields</u> after World War II, Levittown, New York, consisted of <u>more than seventeen thousand</u> houses in <u>Cape Cod and ranch</u> styles. Over the decades, residents have <u>added expansive front porches, punched dormer windows through roofs, converted garages to sun porches,</u> and otherwise altered the houses so dramatically that the original styles are often unrecognizable.

注意：修改版里的细节很有效果，因为它们与作者的观点相关，并使作者观点更清楚。不能支持和澄清作者观点的细节很可能会使读者分心或烦心。

练习17.1　改写：变化

下面的段落中的句子全以主语开头。使用本章讲到的技巧来给句子增加变化。可以增删词语或重新安排词语，以使句子好读，并突出重点。带星号部分的参考答案请见书后。

　　*The Italian volcano Vesuvius had been dormant for many years. *It then exploded on August 24 in the year AD 79. *The ash, pumice, and mud from the volcano buried two busy towns. *Herculaneum is one. *The more famous is Pompeii. *Both towns lay undiscovered for many centuries. *Herculaneum and Pompeii were discovered in 1709 and 1748, respectively. The excavation of Pompeii was the more systematic. It was the occasion for initiating modern methods of conservation and restoration. Herculaneum was simply looted of its more valuable finds. It was then left to disintegrate. Pompeii appears much as it did before the eruption. A luxurious house opens onto a lush central garden. An election poster decorates a wall. A dining table is set for breakfast.

第 18 章　恰当而准确的用词

概要

- 选择适合你的写作情境的词语（下页）
- 避免有性别歧视和偏见的语言（p. 167）
- 选择能准确表达你的意思的词语（p. 171）

为了写出清楚而有表现力的句子，要选择既符合你的写作情境又符合你想表达的意思的词语。

18a 选择恰当的词语

恰当的词语要适合你的写作情境——你的话题、目的和对象。在大多数学校写作和职业写作中，你应当依靠所谓标准美式英语，这是学校、商业、政府和媒体通常所用的英语。(关于它在学术写作中的作用的更多内容，请看 pp. 105–108)

书面标准美式英语的词汇量极大，可以表达无限思想和情感。但它不包括只有部分人使用、懂得或不觉得有冒犯性的词汇。它也不包括那些虽然在口语中常用但因不够准确而不用在书面语中的词汇。如果你不确定某个词的状况，查字典。(pp. 171–173) 如果有"非标准""俚语"或"口语"的标签，就说明这个词通常不适合用在学术或公文写作中。

语法检查工具：语法检查工具可以设置为能查出可能不恰当的词，比如非标准美式英语、口语及与性别有关的词 (manmade, mailman)。但是语法检查工具只能查出列在它的字典中的词，例如，它会把 A successful businessman puts clients first 中的 businessman 作为可能与性别有关的词标记出来，但不会标出 A successful businessperson listens to his clients. 使用语法检查工具复查语言，你仍需自己判断你的措辞是否适合于写作情境。

1 ▪ 非标准方言 CULTURE LANGUAGE

跟许多国家一样，美国包括几十种区域性、社会性或种族性的群体，他们都有自己独特的方言或英语变体。标准美式英语是方言之一，非洲裔美国人的白话英语、阿巴拉契亚英语、克里奥尔英语及缅因州英语也都是方言。所有这些英语方言都有许多共同特点，但每一种也都有自己的词汇、发音和语法。

如果你说标准美式英语之外的英语方言，要注意不要在标准美式英语是通用做法的情境使用方言，比如学术写作或公文写作。方言本身并没有错，但将一种方言输入进另一种方言的语言形式可能会被认为是不清楚或不正确。如果你知道人们的期待是标准美式英语，请删除与标准美式英语不同的方言表达，比如 theirselves, hisn, them books，以及其他字典上标记为"非标准"的表达。这些非标准表达还可能包括一些动词形式，如 pp. 219–224 所讨论的那些。要识别和改正非标准语言请看本书的 CULTURE LANGUAGE 。

加入标准美式英语的圈子并不要求你放弃自己的方言。你可以在给自己的写作中使用方言，比如日记、笔记和草稿，那些就该自由书写。你也可以在学术文章中引用方言，例如，当分析或转述方言对话时。当然，你也可以和其他使用这种方言的人说它。

2 ▪ 在线交流的缺点

电子邮件、短信或即时通信工具的迅速交流催生了一些非正式表达，这些不适合于学术写作。如果你常使用这些媒介，可能会需要特别检查你的学术文章，识别和修改如下错误：

- **残缺句**。确保每个句子都有主语和谓语。避免类似于Observing the results 或After the meeting这样的残缺句。（见pp. 285–288）
- **遗漏标点**。在句子间和句子内，使用标准标点符号。特别检查是否丢句中的逗号、所有格及缩略形式里的撇号。（见pp. 306–319和pp. 329–333）
- **遗漏大写字母**。句首、专用名词、专有形容词和标题用大写字母。（pp. 356–359）
- **不标准的缩写和拼写**。写出大部分单词，避免使用2表示to或too，b4表示before，bc表示because，ur表示you are或you're，+或&表示and。（见pp. 348–352和pp. 363–365）

3 ▪ 俚语

俚语是一群人——比如音乐家或程序员——使用的语言，反映他们共同的经历，可用于高效谈论技术。下面的例子来自一篇关于俚语"skaters"（skateboarders）的文章：

> Curtis slashed ultra-punk crunchers on his longboard, while the Rube-man flailed his usual Gumbyness on tweaked frontsides and lofty fakie ollies.
>
> —Miles Orkin, "Mucho Slingage by the Pool"

在听得懂的人群里，俚语很生动很有表现力。俚语常出现在对话中，偶尔出现的俚语可以让一篇非正式的文章生动起来，但是大多数俚语太过轻浮而含混，无助于有效交流，而且通常俚语也不适合大学或公文写作。注意下面修改版中严肃性和准确性的提高。

俚语：Many students start out <u>pretty together</u> but then <u>get weird</u>.

修改：Many students start out <u>with clear goals</u> but then <u>lose their direction</u>.

4 ▪ 口语

口语是日常生活使用的口头语言，包括get together，go nuts和chill out

第三部分　明晰与风格

这样的表达。

给朋友和家人非正式写作时，口语能带来一种随意轻松的谈话效果。但在学术和职业写作中，口语不足以准确地表达意思。在正式写作中可以偶尔来上一个口语表达，以获得想要的效果，但通常应该避免使用任何字典上标注为"非正式"或"口语"的词语和表达。

口语： According to a Native American myth, the Great Creator <u>had a dog hanging around with him</u> when he created the earth.

修改： According to a Native American myth, the Great Creator <u>was accompanied by a dog</u> when he created the earth.

注意： 关于正式和非正式语言在学术写作中的运用的讨论，见pp. 106–108。

5 ▪ 技术词汇

所有学科和职业都有自己特别的语言，使其成员得以准确而高效地交流。例如，化学家有自己的phosphatides（磷脂），文学批评家有自己的motifs（母题）和subtexts（潜文本）。没有解释的话，技术词汇对于非专业人士是无意义的。当你给非专业人士写作时，需要避免不必要的技术词汇，对必须使用的那些也要仔细地给出定义。

6 ▪ 拐弯抹角和装腔作势的写作

在大多数写作中，简短、朴素、直接的词语比含糊其词或华而不实的词语更受欢迎。要特别注意避免使用委婉语、指东说西和装模作样的写作。

委婉语是据推测没有冒犯性的词语，用来代替被认为有冒犯性，或者太过唐突的词，比如用passed away替代died，用misspeak替代lie，或者remains替代corpse。只有当你知道那些唐突的真话会不必要地伤害或冒犯听众时才使用委婉语。

有一种委婉语是故意回避事实，称为"**指东说西**"（也叫"**双言巧语**"或"**黄鼠狼话**"），其目的就是使人迷惑、让人误解。很不幸，现在指东说西在政治和广告中很普遍——revenue enhancement实际上是说"税收"，peace-keeping function其实就是发起战争，所谓biodegradable袋子其实是最不容易降解的。诚实的写作里没有这种语言的位置。

与委婉语和"指东说西"形影相随的，是拐弯抹角、花哨的语言，话说得比实际需要更复杂。写作措辞的目标是准确和经济。大词、花哨词可能会很诱人，但是不要用。读者会感激你的。

装腔作势： Hardly a day goes by without a new revelation about the devastation of the natural world, and to a significant extent our dependence on the internal combustion engine is the culprit. Respected scientific minds coalesce around the argument that carbon dioxide emissions, such as those from automobiles imbibing gasoline, are responsible for a gradual escalation in temperatures on the earth.

修改：Much of the frequent bad news about the environment can be blamed on the internal combustion engine. Respected scientists argue that carbon dioxide emissions, such as those from gas-powered cars, are warming the earth.

7 ▪ 性别歧视及其他带偏见的语言

即便不是故意，我们的语言也可能会反映出伤人的偏见。这样的偏见语言可能很明显——比如nigger, honky, mick, kike, fag, dyke和broad；也可能很微妙，会一概而论某些人群，其做法我们可能熟视无睹但其实并不准确也不公平。

偏见语言反映出的是使用者的不好，而不是这种语言所误刻画或侮辱的人。无偏见的语言不会错误地将人归类，而是以尊重待人，不给人贴上他们不喜欢的标签。

关于种族、民族、宗教、年龄和其他特征的成见

成见是没有什么根据的一概而论，是一种理解事物的模式，是仅仅根据人们所在的群体而评判人的做法：

Men are uncommunicative.
Women are emotional.
Liberals want to raise taxes.
Conservatives are affluent.

偏见的最好之处在于能暴露作者的不具有批判性，暴露作者的思考不能超越从别人那里得到的概念。你写作的时候，要当心不要写出对整体人群一概而论的陈述。

成见：Elderly drivers should have their licenses limited to daytime driving only. [声称所有的老人都是差劲的夜间驾驶员]

修改：Drivers with impaired night vision should have their licenses limited to daytime driving only.

第三部分　明晰与风格

当句子中的多个思想具有同样的功能和重要性时，可以用平行结构来表示它们之间的关系，如：

The air is dirtied by factories belching smoke and cars spewing exhaust.

使用平行结构，你可以用同样的语法形式来表达同等重要的思想。在上面的例子中，下画线标记的两个短语拥有同样的功能和重要性（空气污染的两个来源），所以它们也具有同样的句法结构。

语法检查工具：语法检查工具无法识别错误的平行结构，因为它无法识别各个思想之间的关系。

16a 使用带 and，but，or，nor 和 yet 的平行结构

并列连词 and，but，or，nor 和 yet 总是标示着有必要使用平行结构，如下例所示：

The industrial base was shifting and shrinking.［平行的词语］
Politicians rarely acknowledged the problem or proposed alternatives.［平行的短语］
Industrial workers were understandably disturbed that they were losing their jobs and that no one seemed to care.［平行的从句］

如果用并列连词连接的句子成分在结构上不平行，那么这个句子就很别扭而且让人看不懂。

不平行：The reasons steel companies kept losing money were that their plants were inefficient, high labor costs, and foreign competition was increasing.

修改：The reasons steel companies kept losing money were inefficient plants, high labor costs, and increasing foreign competition.

不平行：Success was difficult even for efficient companies because of the shift away from all manufacturing in the United States and the fact that steel production was shifting toward emerging nations.

修改：Success was difficult even for efficient companies because of the shift away from all manufacturing in the United States and toward steel production in emerging nations.

依照成语或语法要求有的词语必须用复合结构表示（见 p. 181）：

有一些成见已成为语言的一部分，但仍然具有冒犯性：

成见：The administrators <u>are too blind</u> to see the need for a new gymnasium.
　　［将视力损失与理解力缺乏等同起来］

修改：The administrators <u>do not understand</u> the need for a new gymnasium.

性别歧视的语言

最微妙而最顽固的歧视语言之一是对男性和女性的担当的角色、位置及在社会中的价值表现出狭隘的观念。和其他成见一样，性别歧视的语言也会伤害或激怒读者，而且它也显示出作者的不周和不公。下表列出了改掉性别歧视语言的一些方法。

去除性别歧视语言

■ **避免使用降低身份或高人一等的语言：**
性别歧视：<u>Dr. Keith Kim</u> and <u>Lydia Hawkins</u> coauthored the article.
修改：Dr. Keith Kim and Dr. Lydia Hawkins coauthored the article.
修改：<u>Keith Kim</u> and <u>Lydia Hawkins</u> coauthored the article.
性别歧视：<u>Ladies</u> are entering almost every occupation formerly filled by men.
修改：<u>Women</u> are entering almost every occupation formerly filled by men.

■ **避免职业和社会成见**
性别歧视：The considerate doctor commends a nurse when <u>she</u> provides <u>his</u> patients with good care.
　　修改：The considerate doctor commends a nurse <u>who provides good care for patients</u>.
性别歧视：The grocery shopper should save <u>her</u> coupons.
　　修改：<u>Grocery shoppers</u> should save <u>their</u> coupons.

■ **避免不必要地提到性别**
性别歧视：Marie Curie, <u>a woman chemist</u>, discovered radium.
　　修改：Marie Curie, <u>a chemist</u>, discovered radium.
性别歧视：The patients were tended by <u>a male nurse</u>.
　　修改：The patients were tended by <u>a nurse</u>.

但也不要矫枉过正，不敢适当地提及性别：Pregnant <u>women</u> [not <u>people</u>] should avoid drinking alcohol and smoking cigarettes.

■ **避免使用man或含man的词语来指称所有人。下面有一些替代办法：**

businessman	businessperson
chairman	chair, chairperson
congressman	representative, congressperson, legislator
craftsman	craftsperson, artisan

（续表）

```
layman        layperson
mankind       humankind, humanity, human beings, humans
manmade       handmade, manufactured, synthetic, artificial
manpower      personnel, human resources
policeman     police officer
salesman      salesperson
```

性别歧视：<u>Man</u> has not reached the limits of social justice.
修改：<u>Humankind [or Humanity]</u> has not reached the limits of social justice.
性别歧视：The furniture consists of <u>manmade</u> materials.
修改：The furniture consists of <u>synthetic</u> materials.

- 避免用男性代词he指代男女两性。（见pp. 259–261）
  性别歧视：The newborn child explores <u>his</u> world.
  修改：<u>Newborn children</u> explore <u>their</u> world. [代词及其所指都用复数]
  修改：The newborn child explores <u>the</u> world. [干脆避免用代词]
  修改：The newborn child explores <u>his or her</u> world. [代之以男性加女性代词]

最后一个办法要少用——一组句子里只用一次，并且只用来强调单数个体。

(CULTURE LANGUAGE) 称呼的形式在各个文化中不同。比如在有些文化中，对所有年长妇女都按已婚的方式称呼，用Mrs.的对应词，以表示敬意。在美国，渐渐改成了称呼时不对对方的婚姻状况、职业或其他方面做假设——例如，称呼女性为Ms.，除非知道她更喜欢Mrs.或Miss。

恰当的标签

我们常常会需要给群体加标签：swimmers, politicians, mothers, Christians, Westerners, students。但是标签很容易会成为偏见，让人们看见被贴上标签的人却忽视了群体成员本身的喜好。虽然有时候人们把对标签保持敏感贬之为"不关心政治正确"，但这样做不会伤害任何人，而且能赢得读者的信任和尊重。

- 避免（有意或无意）伤人的标签。有情感问题的人不是a mental patient（精神病人），罹患癌症的人不是a cancer victim（癌症受害者），使用轮椅的人不是wheelchair-bound（拴在轮椅上的人）。
- 指称种族、民族及其他群体时，用他们的成员喜欢的名字，至少是他们中大多数人喜欢的。现行的例子有，用African American（非洲裔美国人）而不是black（黑人），用people with disabilities（障碍人士）而不是the disabled（残废）或the handicapped（残疾）。但是标签也常常变化。要了解一个群体的成员希望被怎样称呼，可以直接问他们、采用声誉好的杂志上的说法，或者查查新近出的字典。

170 ■ 除非某人所在群体与你讨论的问题相关，否则不要指认其所在群体。要考虑标签的上下文：标签是必要的信息吗？如果不是，不要用它。

一个有用的参考指南：加州大学戴维斯分校的跨文化中心ccc.ucdavis.edu/bias_free_communication.pdf（因某些原因可能无法访问）

> **练习18.1　改写：恰当的用词**
>
> 按照标准美式英语改写下列句子，着重关注不恰当的俚语、技术语言、矫饰语言或偏见语言。必要的时候查字典以确定用词是否恰当并找到合适的替代语。带星号部分的参考答案请见书后。
>
> 例子：
>
> If negotiators get hyper during contract discussions, they may mess up chances for a settlement.
>
> If negotiators <u>become excited or upset</u> during contract discussions, they may <u>harm</u> chances for a settlement.
>
> *1. Acquired immune deficiency syndrome (AIDS) is a major deal all over the world.
>
> *2. The disease gets around primarily by sexual intercourse, exchange of bodily fluids, shared needles, and blood transfusions.
>
> *3. Those who think the disease is limited to homos, mainliners, and foreigners are quite mistaken.
>
> *4. Stats suggest that in the United States one in every five hundred college kids carries the HIV virus that causes AIDS.
>
> *5. A person with HIV or full-blown AIDS does not deserve to be subjected to exclusionary behavior or callousness on the part of his fellow citizens. Instead, he has the necessity for all the compassion, medical care, and financial assistance due those who are in the extremity of illness.
>
> 6. An HIV or AIDS victim often sees a team of doctors or a single doctor with a specialized practice.
>
> 7. The doctor may help his patients by obtaining social services for them as well as by providing medical care.
>
> 8. The HIV or AIDS sufferer who loses his job may need public assistance.
>
> 9. For someone who is very ill, a home-care nurse may be necessary. She can administer medications and make the sick person as comfortable as possible.

10. Some people with HIV or AIDS have insurance, but others lack the bucks for premiums.

练习18.2　改写：性别歧视语言

改写下列句子，去除性别歧视语言。如果把单数名词或代词改为复数，要在动词或其他代词上做相应改动。带星号部分的参考答案请见书后。

例子：

The career placement officer at most colleges and universities spends part of his time advising students how to write successful résumés.

<u>Career placement officers</u> at most colleges and universities <u>spend</u> part of <u>their</u> time advising students how to write successful résumés.

*1. When a person applies for a job, he should represent himself with the best possible résumé.

*2. A person applying for a job as a mailman should appear to be honest and responsible.

*3. A girl applying for a position as an in-home nurse should also represent herself as honest and responsible.

*4. Of course, she should also have a background of capable nursing.

*5. The businessman who is scanning a stack of résumés will, of necessity, read them all quickly.

6. The person who wants his résumé to stand out will make sure it highlights his best points.

7. The Web designer will highlight his experience with computers.

8. Volunteer work may be appropriate, too, such as being chairman of a student organization.

9. If the student has been secretary for a campus organization, she could include that volunteer experience in her résumé.

10. If the applicant writing a résumé would keep in mind the man who will be reading it, he might know better what he should include.

18b 选择准确的词语

要想表达清楚而有力，需要找到能精确表达你的意思、准确传达你的态度的词语。

语法检查工具：语法检查工具在查找不准确语言上能提供一点帮助，比如，你可以把它设置为标记那些容易混淆的词语（如continuous/continual）、成语中容易用错的介词（如把accuse for错写成accuse of），以及陈腐词。但是工具无法找出不恰当的言外之意、过度的抽象或者本章将讨论的其他问题。

1 ▪ 词语意思及同义词

要准确表达，词典必不可少，类语词典也很有帮助。

词典

词典定义词语、提供其发音、语法功能、词源（词的历史）以及其他信息。下面例子来自 *Merriam-Webster's Collegiate Dictionary*。

» 纸质词典条目

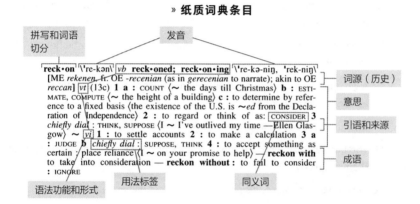

以上例子来自纸质词典，*Merriam-Webster* 及其他词典也有在线词典，提供同样的信息，形式不这么压缩，你还可以听到词的发音。下一页有来自 *Merriam-Webster* 在线词典（merriam-webster.com）的reckon条目的一部分。

其他有用的网址有 Dictionary.com（dictionary.com）和 The Free Dictionary（thefreedictionary.com），它们同时提供好几本词典的条目。

如果你更喜欢纸质词典，除了 *Merriam-Webster's Collegiate* 之外，好词典还有 *American Heritage College Dictionary*，*Random House Webster's College Dictionary*，以及 *Webster's New World College Dictionary*。其中有一些还有CD版本。

 如果英语不是你的母语，你可能需要一本特别为英语作为第二语言（ESL）的学生准备的词典。这样的词典包含关于介词、可数与不可数名词的信息，以及许多其他信息。下面是一些可靠的纸质ESL词典，括号中是它们的在线版本的网址：*Longman Dictionary of Contemporary English*（ldoceonline.com），

» 在线词典条目的一部分

```
reck·on 🔊 verb \re-kən\
reck·oned | reck·on·ing 🔊
Definition of RECKON
transitive verb
1  a : COUNT <reckon the days till Christmas>
   b : ESTIMATE, COMPUTE <reckon the height of a building>
   c : to determine by reference to a fixed basis <the existence
       of the United States is reckoned from the Declaration of
       Independence>
2 : to regard or think of as : CONSIDER
3  chiefly dialect : THINK, SUPPOSE <I reckon I've outlived my
   time — Ellen Glasgow>
```

Oxford Advanced Learner's Dictionary（oxfordadvancedlearnersdictionary.com），*Merriam-Webster Advanced Learner's English Dictionary*（learnersdictionary.com）。

类语词典

要找到一个准确表达你的微妙含义的词，你会需要参考类语词典，或叫同义词（具有接近或相同意思的词语）词典。纸质或在线类语词典都给几千个词列出了你想得到的绝大多数同义词。例如，在Thesaurus.com上，reckon一词有差不多五十个同义词，包括account、evaluate和judge。

类语词典的目的是提供多种可能性，所以它列出的同义词有意思很精确的，也有只是接近的。但类语词典并不给同义词下定义，也不做辨析，所以你需要一本词典来了解词语的准确意思。通常来说，不要直接从类语词典里搬词去用 —— 就算你喜欢那个词的读音也不行 —— 除非你很有把握它接近你要表达的意思。

2 ▪ 正确表达你的意思的词语

所有的词语都有一个或多个基本意义，称为"**指称意义**"，即列在词典中的意义，不涉及情感。要想读者能理解你，你使用词语时就必须用大家都接受的意义。

- 不确定一个词的意义时，务必查词典。
- 要区分音相近而意相远的词语：

  不准确：Older people often suffer infirmaries [places for the sick]．

准确：Older people often suffer infirmities [disabilities].

有些词语听起来一样但意思不同，这样的词语叫同音词，如 principal/principle 或 rain/reign/rein。（容易混淆的同音词，请看 pp. 348–349 列表）

- 区分意义相关但不同的单词：

  不准确：Television commercials continuously [unceasingly] interrupt programming.

  准确：Television commercials continually [regularly] interrupt programming.

除了无感情的意义之外，很多词语具有能引发特定情感的意义。这种内涵意义能影响读者的反应，是作者的一个强大工具。下列的各组词具有相近的指称意义，但有非常不同的内涵意义。

pride: sense of self-worth
vanity: excessive regard for oneself

firm: steady, unchanging, unyielding
stubborn: unreasonable, bullheaded

lasting: long-lived, enduring
endless: without limit, eternal

enthusiasm: excitement
mania: excessive interest or desire

词典能帮你追溯到你想要的有准确内涵意义的词语。除了提供意义之外，词典还会列出同义词并加以辨析，以指导你的选择。类语词典也能帮助你措辞，如前面所说。

> **练习18.3　改写：指称意义**
>
> 改写下列句子中用下画线标出的用得不正确的词语。如果对词的准确含义没有把握，查词典。带星号部分的参考答案请见书后。
>
> 例子：
>
> Sam and Dave are going to Bermuda and Hauppage, respectfully, for spring vacation.
>
> Sam and Dave are going to Bermuda and Hauppage, respectively, for spring vacation.
>
> *1. Maxine Hong Kingston was rewarded many prizes for her first two books, *The Woman Warrior* and *China Men*.

*2. Kingston sites her mother's tales about ancestors and ancient Chinese customs as the sources of these memoirs.

*3. Two of Kingston's progeny, her great-grandfathers, are focal points of *China Men*.

*4. Both men led rebellions against suppressive employers: a sugarcane farmer and a railroad-construction engineer.

*5. In her childhood Kingston was greatly effected by her mother's tale about a pregnant aunt who was ostracized by villagers.

6. The aunt gained avengeance by drowning herself in the village's water supply.

7. Kingston decided to make her nameless relative infamous by giving her immortality in *The Woman Warrior*.

8. Kingston's novel *Tripmaster Monkey* has been called the premier novel about the 1960s.

9. Her characters embody the principles that led to her own protest against the Vietnam War.

10. Kingston's innovative books infer her opposition to racism and sexism both in the China of the past and in the United States of the present.

练习18.4　考虑词语的内涵意义

从括号中选取最恰当的词填入下列句子的空格。必要的时候查词典。带星号部分的参考答案请见书后。

例子：

Channel 5 _____ Oshu the winner before the polls closed. (*advertised, declared, broadcast, promulgated*)

Channel 5 declared Oshu the winner before the polls closed.

*1. AIDS is a serious health _____. (*problem, worry, difficulty, plight*)

*2. Once the virus has entered the blood system, it _____ T-cells. (*murders, destroys, slaughters, executes*)

3. The _____ of T-cells is to combat infections. (*ambition, function, aim, goal*)

4. Without enough T-cells, the body is nearly _____ against infections. (*defenseless, hopeless, desperate*)

5. To prevent exposure to the disease, one should be especially _____ in sexual relationships. (*chary, circumspect, cautious, calculating*)

3 ▪ 具体和特定的词

抽象、笼统的词语可以概述事物，清楚、确切的词语可以详述事物，二者相互平衡。

- **抽象词语**（abstract words）命名概念：beauty, inflation, management, culture, liberal。**具体词语**（concrete words）命名品质和可以用五官来感受（看、听、触、尝、闻）的事物：sleek, humming, rough, salty, musty。
- **笼统词语**（general words）命名事物的类别或组别，例如，buildings, weather 或 birds，表示同一类中的各种变体。**具体概念词语**（specific words）命名同一类事物中的一个变体，例如，skyscraper 或 my house on Emerald Street，从而限制该笼统类别。

写宽泛的陈述，给写作定大方向的时候，抽象笼统的词有用：

The wild horse in America has a romantic history.

Relations between the sexes today are more relaxed than they were in the past.

但是这样的陈述需要进一步用具体确切细节加以发展。细节可以把模糊的句子变得精确：

模糊：The size of his hands made his smallness real.［他的手有多大？个子有多小？］

精确：Not until I saw his delicate, doll-like hands did I realize that he stood a full head shorter than most other men.

注意：如果你是在电脑上写作，可以利用"搜索"功能找出并修改容易过度使用的抽象笼统词。这样的词有 nice, interesting, things, very, good, a lot, a little 和 some。

练习18.5　改写：具体确切词

改写下列段落，选择恰当的细节扩展句子，使段落生动。用具体确切的词汇取代下画线标出的抽象笼统词。

I remember clearly how awful I felt the first time I attended Mrs. Murphy's second-grade class. I had recently moved from a small town in Missouri to a crowded suburb of Chicago. My new school looked big from the outside and seemed dark inside as I walked down the long corridor toward the classroom. The class was noisy as I neared the door; but when I entered, everyone became quiet and looked at me. I felt uncomfortable and wanted a place to hide. However, in a loud voice Mrs. Murphy directed me to the front of the room to introduce myself.

4 ▪ 成语

成语是任何语言都有的表达，它们不符合意义和语法的规则。例如，put up with, plug away at, make off with。

带介词的成语可能特别令人困惑，对母语者和非母语者都一样。下表列出了一些带介词的成语。（更多请看pp. 228–229）

带介词的成语

abide by a rule	identical with or to
in a place or state	impatient for a raise
according to	with a person
accords with	independent of
accuse of a crime	infer from
accustomed to	inferior to
adapt from a source	involved in a task
to a situation	with a person
afraid of	oblivious of or to one's surroundings
agree on a plan	of something forgotten
to a proposal	occupied by a person
with a person	in study
angry with	with a thing
aware of	opposed to
based on	part from a person
capable of	with a possession
certain of	prior to
charge for a purchase	proud of
with a crime	related to
concur in an opinion	rewarded by the judge
with a person	for something done
contend for a principle	with a gift
with a person	similar to
dependent on	sorry about an error
differ about or over a question	for a person
from in some quality	superior to
with a person	wait at a place
disappointed by or in a person	for a train, a person
in or with a thing	in a room
familiar with	on a customer

（CULTURE LANGUAGE）如果你在学习标准美式英语，你可能会对介词感到困难：它们的意思会根据上下文而变化，又有许多约定俗成的用法。掌握英语介词时，大概

免不了要记忆。不过你可以把相关的介词放在一起记忆，让事情容易一点。

at, in, 或on用在表时间的短语中
- 在具体的钟表时间之前，用at：at 8:30。
- 在月、年、世纪或时期之前，用in：in April, in 2013, in the twenty-first century, in the next month。
- 在天或日期之前，用on：on Tuesday, on August 3, on Labor Day。

at, in, 或on用在表地点的短语中
- 在具体的地点或地址之前，用at：at the school, at 511 Iris Street。
- 在有限制的地点之前，或在城市、州、国家或大陆之前，用in：in the house, in a box, in Oklahoma City, in China, in Asia。
- 用on表示"得到支撑"或"触碰表面"：on the table, on Iris Street, on page 150。

for或since用在表时间的短语中
- 在一个时间段之前，用for：for an hour, for two years。
- 在一个特定的时间点之前，用since：since 1999, since Friday。

二语英语词典是介词含义的最佳来源，见P. 173的建议。

> **练习18.6　使用成语中的介词**
>
> 在下列句子中插入介词以正确完成成语。必要的时候参考p. 177的表格或词典。带星号部分的参考答案请见书后。
>
> 　　例子：
>
> 　　I disagree _____ many feminists who say women should not be homemakers.
>
> 　　I disagree with many feminists who say women should not be homemakers.
>
> *1. Children are waiting longer to become independent _____ their parents.
>
> *2. According _____ US Census data for young adults ages eighteen to twenty-four, 57% of men and 47% of women live full-time with their parents.
>
> 3. Some of these adult children are dependent _____ their parents financially.
>
> 4. In other cases, the parents charge their children _____ housing, food, and other living expenses.
>
> 5. Many adult children are financially capable _____ living independently but prefer to save money rather than contend _____ high housing costs.

练习18.7　　使用成语中的介词　CULTURE LANGUAGE

从at, by, for, from, in, of, on, to, with中，选取恰当的介词填空，完成下列句子。带星号部分的参考答案请见书后。

例子：

The most recent amendment to the US Constitution, ratified ＿＿＿＿ May 18, 1992, was first proposed ＿＿＿＿ 1789.

The most recent amendment to the US Constitution, ratified <u>on</u> May 18, 1992, was first proposed <u>in</u> 1789.

*1. The Eighteenth Amendment ＿＿＿＿ the Constitution ＿＿＿＿ the United States was ratified ＿＿＿＿ 1919.

*2. It prohibited the "manufacture, sale, or transportation ＿＿＿＿ intoxicating liquors."

3. It was adopted ＿＿＿＿ response ＿＿＿＿ a nationwide crusade ＿＿＿＿ temperance groups.

4. The amendment did not prevent Americans ＿＿＿＿ drinking, and the sale ＿＿＿＿ alcoholic beverages was taken over ＿＿＿＿ organized crime.

5. Wide-scale smuggling and bootlegging came ＿＿＿＿ the demand ＿＿＿＿ liquor.

5 ▪ 形象化语言（修辞）

形象化语言（修辞）与词语的字面意思不同，通常是将非常不同的事物相比较：

字面：As I try to write, I can think of nothing to say.

修辞：As I try to write, <u>my mind is a slab of black slate</u>.

相比字面语言，形象化语言表情达意更为准确也更有情感。下面是技术性写作中的形象化语言的一个例子（解释物理学家Edward Andrade的话）：

The molecules in a liquid move continuously like couples on an overcrowded dance floor, jostling each other.

最常见的修辞是明喻和暗喻。它们都在不同类别的事物之间做比较，通常一个抽象一个具体。明喻是明白直接地做比较，通常以like或as开始：

Whenever we grow, we tend to feel it, <u>as</u> a young seed must feel the weight and inertia of the earth when it seeks to break out of its shell on its way to becoming a plant.

—Alice Walker

暗喻声称两个事物相同，但省略了like和as之类的词语：

A school is a hopper into which children are heaved while they are young and tender; therein they are pressed into certain standard shapes and covered from head to heels with official rubber stamps.

—H. L. Mencken

成功的修辞新颖无拘，使人注意到作者的意图而不是修辞本身。要当心，不要使用混合比喻，即两个或更多的不互相通的形象混合在一起。

混合：Various thorny problems that we try to sweep under the rug continue to bob up all the same.

改进：Various thorny problems that we try to weed out continue to thrive all the same.

> **练习18.8　使用形象化语言**
>
> 用自己创作的明喻或暗喻描写下列各场景或品质，然后在句子中使用该比喻。
>
> 例子：
>
> The attraction of a lake on a hot day
>
> The small waves like fingers beckoned us irresistibly.
>
> 1. The sound of a kindergarten classroom
> 2. People waiting in line to buy tickets to a rock concert
> 3. The politeness of strangers meeting for the first time
> 4. A streetlight seen through dense fog
> 5. The effect of watching television for ten hours straight

6 ▪ 陈词滥调

陈词滥调，或陈腐套话，是指那些老话套话，因为被重复了太多次数而了无新意。有以下这些：

add insult to injury	green with envy
better late than never	hard as a rock
crushing blow	heavy as lead
easier said than done	hit the nail on the head
face the music	hour of need
few and far between	ladder of success

moving experience	shoulder the burden
needle in a haystack	shoulder to cry on
point with pride	sneaking suspicion
pride and joy	stand in awe
ripe old age	thin as a rail
rude awakening	tried and true
sadder but wiser	wise as an owl

要改掉陈词滥调，你可以把你的文章念出来听，找出那些以前听过或用过的表达。也可以使用文体检查工具，它能查出老话套话。找到以后，代之以自己的新颖表达，或者用平实的语言重新说。

练习18.9　改写：陈词滥调

改写下列句子，去除陈词滥调。带星号部分的参考答案请见书后。

例子：

The basketball team had almost seized victory, but it faced the test of truth in the last quarter of the game.

The basketball team <u>seemed about to win</u>, but the <u>real test</u> came in the last quarter of the game.

*1. The disastrous consequences of the war have shaken the small nation to its roots.

*2. Prices for food have shot sky high, and citizens have sneaking suspicions that others are making a killing on the black market.

*3. Medical supplies are so few and far between that even civilians who are as sick as dogs cannot get treatment.

*4. With most men fighting or injured or killed, women have had to knuckle down and bear the men's burden in farming and manufacturing.

*5. Last but not least, the war's heavy drain on the nation's pocketbook has left the economy in shambles.

6. Our reliance on foreign oil to support our driving habit has hit record highs in recent years.

7. Gas-guzzling vehicles are responsible for part of the increase.

8. In the future, we may have to bite the bullet and use public transportation or drive only fuel-efficient cars.

9. Both solutions are easier said than done.

10. But it stands to reason that we cannot go on using the world's oil reserves at such a rapid rate.

第 19 章　完整

概要
- 复合结构要写完整（下方）
- 漏掉的词语要补起来（下方）

有时候，如果漏掉了of或in之类的小词，句子会不清楚。修改的时候，检查你的句子，确保所有需要的词都在句子里。更多关于完整句子的内容，请看第35章关于残缺句的讲解。

语法检查工具：本章所讲述的大多数不完整的句子，语法检查工具都查不出来。

19a 要写完整的复合结构

如果省略之后不会造成读者困惑不解，可以从复合结构中省略词语：
Environmentalists have hopes for alternative fuels and [for] public transportation.
Some cars will run on electricity and some [will run] on hydrogen.

只有当要省略的词对于复合结构的各部分是公用的时候，才可以省略。如果各部分的词在任何方式上有不同，那么不能省略，所有的词都必须保留在各部分。

One new hybrid car gets eighty miles per gallon; some old cars get as little as five miles per gallon. [一个动词是单数，另一个是复数]

Environmentalists believe in and work for fuel conservation. [成语需要用不同的介词来表示believe和work]

19b 补上必要的词语

不要在仓促和疏忽之间遗漏了句子明晰所必要的词语。

不完整：Regular payroll deductions are a type painless savings. You hardly notice missing amounts, and after period of years the contributions can add a large total.

修改：Regular payroll deductions are a type <u>of</u> painless savings. You hardly notice <u>the</u> missing amounts, and after <u>a</u> period of years the contributions can add <u>up to</u> a large total.

对于这种遗漏，仔细的校阅是唯一保障。仔细校阅你的所有文章，关于这方面的建议请看pp. 40–41。

(CULTURE LANGUAGE) 如果你的母语不是英语，也许你会对冠词a，an和the的使用感到困难。关于冠词使用的指导，请看pp. 273–275。

练习19.1　改写：完整

给下列句子补充词语，使句子完整清晰。带星号部分的参考答案请见书后。

例子：

The fruit this plant is edible.

The fruit <u>of</u> this plant is edible.

*1. The first ice cream, eaten China in about 2000 BC, was lumpier than modern ice cream.

*2. The Chinese made their ice cream of milk, spices, and overcooked rice and packed in snow to solidify.

3. In the fourteenth century ice milk and fruit ices appeared in Italy and the tables of the wealthy.

4. At her wedding in 1533 to the king of France, Catherine de Médicis offered several flavors fruit ices.

5. Modern sherbets resemble her ices; modern ice cream her soft dessert of thick, sweetened cream.

第 20 章　简明

概要

- 注重主语和动词（下页）
- 删除空洞词语和不需要的重复（p. 186）
- 让修饰语紧凑（p. 186）

- 改写there is或it is结构（p. 186）
- 合并句子（p. 187）
- 避免使用行话（p. 187）

简明的写作让每一个字都重要。简明不仅仅是简短：删除不需要的词语时，不应把细节和独到之处也删掉。简明是指表达的长度应适合于思想。

你可能会发现，对话题没有把握的时候、自己的想法一团乱麻的时候，文章就写得啰唆。写草稿的时候，磕磕绊绊、摸索来摸索去没什么，甚至是必要的。但是，修改和编辑的时候，应当理清楚你的想法，删除啰唆之处。

语法检查工具： 语法检查工具至少能查出一些啰唆的结构，比如重复的用词、无力的动词，以及被动态。但是它们查不出所有的啰唆结构，也没法判断一个结构是否适合你的思想。

啰唆不是不正确的语法：一个句子可以语法上完全正确但是仍然包含不需要的用词，这些词使得句子别扭、意思不清楚。

20a 注重主语和动词

用句子的主语和动词表示主要的施动者和动作，可以减少用词，强调重要思想。（更多关于这个话题的内容，请看pp. 144–146）

啰唆： The reason why most of the country shifts to daylight time is that summer days are much longer than winter days.

简明： Most of the country shifts to daylight time because summer days are much longer than winter days.

注重主语和动词还可以帮你避免另外几种啰唆（见pp. 144–146）的形成。

来自动词的名词

啰唆： The occurrence of the winter solstice, the shortest day of the year, is an event taking place about December 22.

简明： The winter solstice, the shortest day of the year, occurs about December 22.

弱变化动词

啰唆： The earth's axis has a tilt as the planet is in orbit around the sun so that the northern and southern hemispheres are alternately in alignment toward the sun.

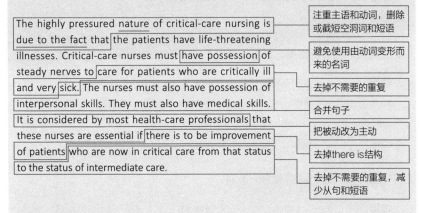

简明：The earth's axis tilts as the planet orbits around the sun so that the northern and southern hemispheres alternately align toward the sun.

被动语态
啰唆：During its winter the northern hemisphere is tilted farthest away from the sun, so the nights are made longer and the days are made shorter.

简明：During its winter the northern hemisphere tilts away from the sun, which makes the nights longer and the days shorter.

如上面的例子，被动语态变主动语态，见pp. 240–241。

20b 删除空洞词语

空洞词语空占位置，与句子的意思毫无补益。其中许多可以完全删掉。下面是几个例子：

all things considered	in a manner of speaking
as far as I'm concerned	in my opinion
for all intents and purposes	last but not least
for the most part	more or less

其他空洞词语也可以删除，通常连带它们前后的一些词语：

angle	character	kind	situation
area	element	manner	thing
aspect	factor	nature	type
case	field		

还有一些可以由几个词缩减为一个词：

啰唆	替换为
at all times	always
at the present time	now, yet
because of the fact that	because
by virtue of the fact that	because
due to the fact that	because
for the purpose of	for
in order to	to
in the event that	if
in the final analysis	finally
in today's society	now

删减这样的词语和短语可以让你的文章进展更快、效果更好。

啰唆：<u>In my opinion</u>, the council's proposal to improve the city center is inadequate, <u>all things considered</u>.

简明：The council's proposal to improve the city center is inadequate.

20c 去掉不需要的重复

特意的重复和重述能联系多个句子，让文章更连贯。（见 p. 48）但是不必要的重复会削弱句子：

啰唆：Many <u>unskilled</u> workers <u>without training in a particular job</u> are unemployed and do not have any work.

简明：Many unskilled workers are unemployed.

要特别当心那些把一件事说了两次的短语。下面的例子中，用下画线标记出了不必要的词语。

circle <u>around</u>
consensus <u>of opinion</u>
cooperate <u>together</u>
<u>final</u> completion
frank and honest exchange
the future <u>to come</u>

important [basic] essentials
puzzling <u>in nature</u>
repeat <u>again</u>
return <u>again</u>
square [round] <u>in shape</u>
<u>surrounding</u> circumstances

🌐 前面的短语是累赘的，因为其中的主要词语已经隐含了下画线标出的词语的意思。词典会告诉你一个词有什么隐含意义。例如，assassinate 的意思是"murder someone well known"，所以下列句子就是累赘的：Julius Caesar was <u>assassinated and killed</u> in 44 BCE.

20d 让修饰语紧凑

修饰语可以被扩展也可以被压缩，取决于你想要什么样的重点。编辑句子时，要考虑有没有哪个修饰语可以被压缩而无损于重点或清晰。

啰唆：The weight-loss industry faces new competition from lipolysis, <u>which is</u> a cosmetic procedure <u>that is</u> relatively noninvasive.

简明：The weight-loss industry faces new competition from lipolysis, <u>a relatively noninvasive cosmetic procedure</u>.

20e 修改 there is 或 it is 结构

可以用 there 和 it 把句子的主语后置：<u>There are</u> three points made in the text. <u>It</u> was not fair that only seniors could vote. 强调主语的时候（如第一次引出主语的时候），或者表示方向上的改变的时候，这些**填充**结构是有用的。但大多数时候它们只是增加字数、削弱句子。

啰唆：<u>There is</u> a completely noninvasive laser treatment <u>that</u> makes people thinner by rupturing fat cells and releasing the fat into the spaces between cells. <u>It is</u> the expectation of some doctors <u>that</u> the procedure will replace liposuction.

简明： <u>A completely noninvasive laser treatment</u> makes people thinner by rupturing fat cells and releasing the fat into the spaces between cells. <u>Some doctors expect</u> that the procedure will replace liposuction.

(CULTURE LANGUAGE) 使用填充结构的时候，别忘了there或it。只有命令和一些问题可以用动词开头。

20f 合并句子

两三个句子中的信息常常可以合并到一个紧凑的句子中：

啰唆： People who receive fat-releasing laser treatments can lose inches from their waists. They can also lose inches from their hips and thighs. They do not lose weight. The released fat remains in their bodies.

简明： People who receive fat-releasing laser treatments can lose inches from their <u>waists, hips, and thighs;</u> <u>but</u> they do not lose weight <u>because</u> the released fat remains in their bodies.

（关于合并句子以增加变化，见pp. 160–161）

20g 避免使用行话

行话可以是任何学科或职业的特殊词汇。（见p. 166）但它也可以形容那些模糊、浮夸，太过复杂甚至无法理解的语言。如果这样的语言出自政府，我们称之为官僚腔。

行话： The necessity for individuals to become separate entities in their own right may impel children to engage in open rebelliousness against parental authority or against sibling influence, with resultant bewilderment of those being rebelled against.

翻译： Children's natural desire to become themselves may make them rebel against bewildered parents or siblings.

练习20.1　改写：简洁写作

把下列句子改写得简洁明了。带星号部分的参考答案请见书后。

例子：

It is thought by some people that there is gain from exercise only when it involves pain.

<u>Some people think</u> that <u>gain comes</u> from exercise only <u>with</u> pain.

*1. If sore muscles after exercising are a problem for you, there are some measures that can be taken by you to ease the discomfort.

*2. First, the immediate application of cold will help to reduce inflammation.

*3. Blood vessels are constricted by cold. Blood is kept away from the injured muscles.

*4. It is advisable to avoid heat for the first day.

*5. The application of heat within the first twenty-four hours can cause an increase in muscle soreness and stiffness.

6. There are two ways the application of cold can be made: you can take a cold shower or use an ice pack.

7. Inflammation of muscles can also be reduced with aspirin, ibuprofen, or another anti-inflammatory medication.

8. There is the idea that muscle soreness can be worsened by power lifting.

9. While healing is occurring, you need to take it easy.

10. A day or two after overdoing exercise, it is advisable for you to get some light exercise and gentle massage.

练习20.2　改写：简明

让下面段落尽可能简洁明了。要毫不留情地改。带星号部分的参考答案请见书后。

　　*At the end of a lengthy line of reasoning, he came to the conclusion that the situation with carcinogens [cancer-causing substances] should be regarded as similar to the situation with the automobile. *Instead of giving in to an irrational fear of cancer, we should consider all aspects of the problem in a balanced and dispassionate frame of mind, making a total of the benefits received from potential carcinogens (plastics, pesticides, and other similar products) and measuring said total against the damage done by such products. This is the nature of most discussions about the automobile. Instead of responding irrationally to the visual, aural, and air pollution caused by automobiles, we have decided to live with them (while simultaneously working to improve on them) for the benefits brought to society as a whole.

第四部分
句子成分和句型

4

基本语法

动词

代词

修饰语

句子中的错误

基本语法

语法描述语言之运作。了解语法才能说出、写出清楚而准确的句子。本章解释句子中的各种词语（第21章），以及怎样写出基本的句子（第22章），扩展之（第23章），并归类之（第24章）。

语法检查工具：语法检查工具能给我们帮助，但也会造成问题。在本章及下两章，可以找到关于怎样使用语法检查工具的提醒和建议。关于语法检查的更多信息，见p. 40。

第 21 章　词性

概要

- 学会识别名词和代词（下方和p. 191）
- 学会识别动词（p. 192）
- 学会识别形容词和副词（p. 194）
- 学会识别介词、连词和感叹词（p. 195, p. 197）

英语词语可分为八类，或者说八种词性，如名词、动词、形容词和副词。一个词的词性决定了它的形式和在句子中的位置。同一个词在不同的句子中可以是不同的词性，如下列例子：

The government sent <u>aid</u> to the city.［aid是名词］
Governments <u>aid</u> citizens.［aid是动词］

一个词在句子中的功能决定了它在那个句子中的词性。

21a 学会识别名词

名词者，名也。它们命名某人（Helen Mirren, Jay-Z, astronaut）、某物（chair, book, Mt. Rainier）、某性质（pain, mystery, simplicity）、某地（city, Washington, ocean, Red Sea），或某概念（reality, peace, success）。

名词的形式，部分取决于它们属于哪一类，例如下面列出的各类。正如例子所示，同一个名词可能出现在多个类别中。

- **普通名词**　命名事物的通用类别，不以大写字母开头：earthquake，citizen，

earth, fortitude, army。
- **专有名词**　命名特定的人、地、物，以大写字母开头：Angelina Jolie，Washington Monument, El Paso, US Congress。
- **可数名词**　命名英语中认为可以数清楚的事物。大多数以加-s或-es来区别单数和复数：citizen, citizens；city, cities。有些可数名词形成不规则复数：woman, women；child, children。
- **不可数名词**　命名英语中认为不可以数清楚的事物（earth, sugar）或性质（chaos, fortitude）。不可数名词没有复数形式。
- **集合名词**　在形式上是单数，但给群体命名：army, family, herd, US Congress。

另外，大多数名词以加-'s形成**所有格**来表述所属（Nadia's books, citizen's rights）、来源（Auden's poems）和其他一些关系。

21b 学会识别代词

多数代词用来取代名词，在句子中的功用如同名词。Susanne Ling enlisted in the Navy when she graduated.

代词按形式和功能分为几类：
- **人称代词**指的是某特定之人或多人。I, you, he, she, it, we和they。
- **不定代词**，如everybody和some，不是指代特定的默认名词，虽然其功能如同名词。（Everybody speaks.）
- **关系代词**who, whoever, which, that，将某些词与名词或其他代词联系起来。（The book that won is a novel.）
- **疑问代词**，如who, which和what，引出问题。（Who will contribute?）
- **指示代词**，包括this, that和such，指向名词。（This is the problem.）
- **强势代词**，人称代词加上-self或-selves（himself, ourselves），强调一个名词或者其他代词。（He himself asked that question.）
- **反身代词**，与强势代词词性相同，但意指句子的主语也是动词的受动者。（They injured themselves.）

人称代词（I, he, she, we, they）和关系代词（who, whoever）的词性随它们在句子中的功能而变。（见第30章）

21c 学会识别动词

动词表示动作（bring, change, grow, consider）、出现（become, happen,

occur）或存在（be, seem, remain）。

1 ▪ 动词的词形

动词有五种不同的词形。如果一个词能有下述变形，那它就是动词：

- **原形**是动词在词典里的形态。主语是复数名词或人称代词I, we, you 或 they时，动词的原形表示动作在现在发生、习惯性发生或是通常真实。

  A few artists <u>live</u> in town today.

  They <u>hold</u> classes downtown.

- **-s 形式**以-s 或-es结尾。主语是单数名词、everyone之类的人称代词，或者 he, she, it之类的人称代词时，-s形式表示动作在现在发生、习惯性发生或是通常真实。

  The artist <u>lives</u> in town today.

  She <u>holds</u> classes downtown.

- **过去时**表示动词的动作在现在之前发生。通常在原形后加-d或-ed构成，虽然大多数不规则动词有不同的形式。（见pp. 214–217）

  Many artists <u>lived</u> in town before this year.

  They <u>held</u> classes downtown.[不规则动词]

- **过去分词**通常与过去时词形相同，除大多数不规则动词之外。它与have或be的各种形式连用（has <u>climbed</u>, was <u>created</u>），或者自己单独修饰名词和代词（the <u>sliced</u> apples）。

  Artists have <u>lived</u> in town for decades.

  They have <u>held</u> classes downtown.[不规则动词]

- **现在分词**在动词原形后加-ing。它与be的各种形式连用（is <u>buying</u>），修饰名词和代词（the <u>boiling</u> water）或者当名词用（<u>Running</u> exhausts me）。

  A few artists are <u>living</u> in town today.

  They are <u>holding</u> classes downtown.

大多数动词有五种词形，但be动词有八种词形：

原形：be

现在分词：being

过去分词：been

	I	he, she, it	we, you, they
现在时：	am	is	are
过去时：	was	was	were

2 ▪ 助动词

有些动词形式与**助动词**连用，表示时间、可能性、义务、必要性，及其他一些意思：<u>can</u> run, <u>was</u> sleeping, <u>had been</u> working。在这些**动词词组**中，run, sleeping 和 working 是**主要动词**——它们表达主要意思。

动词词组

助动词	主要动词
Artists <u>can</u>	<u>train</u> others to draw.
The techniques <u>have</u>	<u>changed</u> little.

下表列出大多数常用助动词。关于助动词的更多内容，见 pp. 220–224。

常用助动词

be 的各种形式：be, am, is, are, was, were, been, being
have 的各种形式：have, has, had, having
do 的各种形式：do, does, did

be able to	could	may	ought to	used to
be supposed to	had better	might	shall	will
can	have to	must	should	would

> **练习 21.1** 识别名词、代词和动词
>
> 识别下列句中用作名词（N）、代词（P）和动词（V）的词语。带星号部分的参考答案请见书后。
>
> 例子：
>
>   N   N   V   N
> <u>Ancestors</u> of the gingko <u>tree</u> <u>lived</u> 175 to 200 million <u>years</u> ago.
>
> *1. The gingko tree, which is one of the world's oldest trees, is large and picturesque.
>
> *2. Gingko trees may grow to over a hundred feet in height.
>
> *3. Their leaves look like fans and are about three inches wide.
>
> *4. The leaves turn yellow in the fall.
>
> *5. Because it tolerates smoke, low temperatures, and low rainfall, the gingko appears in many cities.
>
> 6. A shortcoming, however, is the foul odor of its fruit.

194

7. Inside the fruit is a large white seed, which some people value as food.

8. The fruit often does not appear until the tree is twenty years old.

9. The tree's name means "apricot" in the Japanese language.

10. Originally, the gingko grew only in China, but it has now spread throughout the world.

21d 学会识别形容词和副词

形容词描述或修饰名词和代词，说明是哪一个、什么品质或有多少。

副词 描述或修饰动词、形容词、其他副词，以及词群。副词说明什么时候、在哪儿、怎样及到什么程度。

词尾-ly常常是副词的标志，但并不总是这样。friendly是形容词，never是副词。判定一个词是形容词还是副词的唯一办法是看它修饰的是什么。

形容词和副词有三种形式：**原形**（green, angrily）、**比较级**（greener, more angrily）、**最高级**（greenest, most angrily）。

关于形容词和副词的更多内容，见第33章。

> **练习21.2　识别形容词和副词**
>
> 识别下列句子中的形容词（ADJ）和副词（ADV），把a, an和the 标记为形容词。带星号部分的参考答案请见书后。
>
> 例子：
>   ADV
> Stress can hit people when they least expect it.
>
> *1. You can reduce stress by making a few simple changes.
>
> *2. Get up fifteen minutes earlier than you ordinarily do.
>
> *3. Eat a healthy breakfast, and eat it slowly so that you enjoy it.

*4. Do your more unpleasant tasks early in the day.

*5. Every day, do at least one thing you really enjoy.

6. If waiting in lines is stressful for you, carry a book or magazine when you know you'll have to wait.

7. Make promises sparingly and keep them faithfully.

8. Plan ahead to prevent the most stressful situations.

9. For example, carry spare keys so you won't be locked out of your car or house.

10. See a doctor and a dentist regularly.

21e 学会识别连接词：介词和连词

连接词大多是小词，连接句子各部分。它们不变形。

1 ▪ 介词

介词把名词或代词（加上任何修饰语）连成词群，称为**介词词组**：about love，down the stairs。这些词组通常在句子中充当修饰语，如The plants trailed down the stairs.（见p.206）

常见介词

about	before	except for	of	throughout
above	behind	excepting	off	till
according to	below	for	on	to
across	beneath	from	onto	toward
after	beside	in	on top of	under
against	between	in addition to	out	underneath
along	beyond	inside	out of	unlike
along with	by	inside of	outside	until
among	concerning	in spite of	over	up
around	despite	instead of	past	upon
as	down	into	regarding	up to
aside from	due to	like	round	with
at	during	near	since	within
because of	except	next to	through	without

英语介词的意义和使用可能不容易掌握。关于成语中的介词——如proud of和angry with——的讨论，见pp. 176–178。想了解包含介词的双词

动词，如look after和look up，见pp. 228–229。

2 ▪ 从属连词

从属连词把多个句子连成句群，称为从句，例如，<u>when</u> the meeting ended。从句是句子的一部分：Everyone was relieved <u>when the meeting ended</u>.（关于从句的更多内容，见pp. 209–211）

常见的从属连词

after	even if	rather than	until
although	even though	since	when
as	if	so that	whenever
as if	if only	than	where
as long as	in order that	that	whereas
as though	now that	though	wherever
because	once	till	whether
before	provided	unless	while

(CULTURE LANGUAGE) 了解从属连词的意义有助于清楚表达自己的意思。注意，每个从属连词独立表达自己的意思，不需要别的功能词——如并列连词and，but，for或so——的帮助：

错误：<u>Even though</u> the parents are illiterate, <u>but</u> their children may read well.
〔even though和but有相同的意思，所以两者取其一〕

正确：<u>Even though</u> the parents are illiterate, their children may read well.

3 ▪ 并列连词和关联连词

并列连词和关联连词把同类的词或词群——如名词、形容词或句子——连接起来。

并列连词由一个词组成：

并列连词

and	nor	for	yet
but	or	so	

Biofeedback <u>or</u> simple relaxation can relieve headaches.
Relaxation works well, <u>and</u> it is inexpensive.

关联连词是并列连词和其他词的组合：

常见的关联连词

both . . . and
not only . . . but also
not . . . but
either . . . or

neither . . . nor
whether . . . or
as . . . as

197　Both biofeedback and relaxation can relieve headaches.

The headache sufferer learns not only to recognize the causes of headaches but also to control those causes.

练习21.3　加上连接词

在下列句中的空格里填上适当的连接词：介词、从属连词或并列连词。如果需要帮助可以参考前两页的表格。带星号部分的参考答案请见书后。

例子：

A Trojan priest warned, "Beware _____ Greeks bearing gifts."（介词）

A Trojan priest warned, "Beware of Greeks bearing gifts."

*1. Just about everyone has heard the story _____ the Trojan Horse.（介词）

*2. This incident happened at the city of Troy _____ was planned by the Greeks.（并列连词）

*3. The Greeks built a huge wooden horse _____ a hollow space big enough to hold many men.（介词）

*4. At night, they rolled the horse to the gate of Troy _____ left it there filled with soldiers.（并列连词）

*5. _____ the morning, the Trojans were surprised to see the enormous horse.（介词）

6. They were amazed _____ they saw that the Greeks were gone.（从属连词）

7. _____ they were curious to examine this gift from the Greeks, they dragged the horse into the city and left it outside the temple.（从属连词）

8. In the middle of the night, the hidden Greeks emerged _____ the horse and began setting fires all over town.（介词）

9. _____ the Trojan soldiers awoke and came out of their houses, the Greeks killed them one by one.（从属连词）

10. By the next morning, the Trojan men were dead _____ the women were slaves to the Greeks.（并列连词）

21f 学会识别感叹词

感叹词表达情感或唤起注意。学术写作和商务写作中很少使用感叹词。

<u>Oh</u>, the meeting went fine.
They won seven thousand dollars! <u>Wow</u>!

第 22 章　句子

概要

- 学会识别主语和谓语（下方）
- 学会基本的谓语结构（p. 200）
- 学会其他句型（p. 203）

句子是表达的基本单位，形成一个完整的思想。句子的主语和谓语通常是施动者和动作。

22a 学会识别主语和谓语

大多数句子做出陈述。首先**主语**指名某事物，然后**谓语**对主语做出表述或描述主语的动作。

　　　　　主语　　谓语
　　　　　Art　　thrives.

简单主语由一个或多个名词或代词构成，而**复合主语**还包括各种修饰语。**简单谓语**由一个或多个动词构成，而**复合谓语**还包括用来完备动词意义的任何词以及任何修饰语。

有时，就像在简短的例子 Art thrives 中一样，简单而完整的主语和谓语是一样的。更常见的是，它们是不同的：

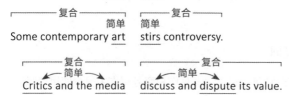

在第二个例子中，简单主语和简单谓语都是**复合词**：主语和谓语中，由并列连词and连接的两个词都起同样的作用。

🌐 英语的主语可以是名词（art）或者指向名词的代词（it），但不能两者并用。（见p. 301）

错误：Art it can stir controversy.
改写：Art can stir controversy.
改写：It can stir controversy.

---

199 **用验证的办法找出主语和谓语**

以下面句子为例：
Art that makes it into museums has often survived controversy.

识别主语
- 问一问，句中是谁或什么在施动或被描述。
  复合主语：art that makes it into museums
- 去掉修饰语，分离出简单主语 —— 去掉那些并不指明句子的施动者而只是提供关于施动者信息的词或词群。在例子中，词群that makes it into museums就不指明施动者，而只是修饰它。
  简单主语：art

识别谓语
- 问一问，句子对主语做了什么表述：主语有什么动作，在什么状态？在例子中，关于art的表述是has often survived controversy。
  复合谓语：has often survived controversy
- 用改变主语动作时间的办法分离出动词，简单谓语。随之而变化的词或词群就是谓语。
  例子：Art . . . has often survived controversy.
  现在：Art . . . often survives controversy.
  将来：Art . . . will often survive controversy.
  简单谓语：has survived

识别句子的主语和谓语时,要注意有些英语词可以当名词也可以当动词。如下面例子:

She <u>visits</u> the museum every Saturday.[动词]

Her <u>visits</u> are enjoyable.[名词]

注意:如果句子含有 that makes it into museums 或 because viewers agree about its quality 这样的词群,你可能会想把这个词群中的主语和动词标记为句子的主语和动词。但是,这些词群是从句,它们开头的 that 和 because 使得它们成为修饰语。从句不是句子。更多关于从句的内容,见 pp. 209–211。

> **练习22.1** 识别主语和谓语
>
> 在下列句子中,在复合主语和复合谓语之间插入一条竖线。给简单主语标单下画线,给简单谓语标双下画线。带星号部分的参考答案请见书后。
>
> 例子:
>
> The <u>pony</u>, the light <u>horse</u>, and the draft <u>horse</u> | <u><u>are</u></u> the three main types of domestic horses.
>
> *1. The horse has a long history of service to humanity but today is mainly a show and sport animal.
>
> *2. A member of the genus *Equus*, the domestic horse shares its lineage with the ass and the zebra.
>
> *3. The domestic horse and its relatives are all plains-dwelling herd animals.
>
> *4. The modern horse evolved in North America.
>
> *5. It migrated to other parts of the world and then became extinct in the Americas.
>
> 6. The Spaniards reintroduced the domestic horse to the Americas.
>
> 7. North American wild horses are actually descended from escaped domestic horses.
>
> 8. An average-sized adult horse may require twenty-six pounds or more of pasture feed or hay per day.
>
> 9. According to records, North Americans hunted and domesticated horses as early as four to five thousand years ago.
>
> 10. The earliest ancestor of the modern horse may have been eohippus, approximately 55 million years ago.

22b 学会基本的谓语结构

英语句子通常可归入下面五种句型，各自在复合谓语（动词及其后跟随的词语）上相区别。

🌐 英语句子中的词序可能与你的母语或方言不同。例如，有些语言喜欢把动词放在句首，而英语几乎总是把主语放在句首。

句型1: The earth trembled.

在最简单的句型中，谓语只包含一个**不及物动词**，即无须接别的词来表达完整意思的动词。

主语	谓语
	不及物动词
The earth	trembled.
The hospital	may close.

句型2: The earthquake destroyed the city.

在句型2中，动词后面跟有一个**直接宾语**，即一个名词或代词，来表明是谁或什么接受了动词的动作。需要后接直接宾语的动词来表达完整意思的动词叫作**及物动词**。

主语	谓语	
	及物动词	直接宾语
The earthquake	destroyed	the city.
Education	opens	doors.

🌐 只有及物动词可以用被动语态: The city was destroyed by the earthquake. 你的字典会告诉你一个动词是及物动词还是不及物动词，通常会用缩写，比如tr.或intr.。有些动词（begin, learn, read, write等）既可以是及物动词，也可以是不及物动词。

句型3: The result was chaos.

在句型3中，动词后面跟有一个**主语补足语**，即一个重述主语或者描写主语的词语。这种句型中的动词叫作**系动词**，因为它把主语和后面的描述联系起来。系动词包括be, seem, appear, become, grow, remain, stay, prove, feel, look, smell, sound和taste。主语补足语通常是名词或形容词。

主语	谓语	
	系动词	主语补足语
The result	was	chaos. [名词]
The man	became	an accountant. [名词]
The car	seems	expensive. [形容词]

句型4：The government sent the city aid.

在句型4中，动词后面跟有一个直接宾语和一个**间接宾语**，即一个表明动词的动作是向谁或为谁发出的词语。直接宾语和间接宾语指的是不同的事物、人或地方。

主语	谓语		
	及物动词	间接宾语	直接宾语
The government	sent	the city	aid.
One company	offered	its employees	bonuses.

有许多动词可以接间接宾语，包括 allow, bring, buy, deny, find, get, give, leave, make, offer, pay, read, sell, send, show, teach 和 write。

有些动词表达的是动作向谁或为谁发生，其间接宾语必须转换成以 to 或 for 开头的短语。另外，这个短语必须接在直接宾语的后面。有这样的要求的动词包括 admit, announce, demonstrate, explain, introduce, mention, prove, recommend, say 和 suggest。

　　　　　　　　　　　间接宾语　　　直接宾语
错误：The manual explains workers the new procedure.

　　　　　　　　　　　　　　直接宾语　　以to开头的短语
改写：The manual explains the new procedure to workers.

句型5：The citizens considered the earthquake a disaster.

在句型5中，动词后面跟有一个直接宾语和一个**宾语补足语**，即一个重述或描写直接宾语的词语。宾语补足语可以是名词或形容词。

主语	谓语		
	及物动词	直接宾语	宾语补足语
The citizens	considered	the earthquake	a disaster.
Success	makes	some people	nervous.

> **练习22.2** 识别句子成分

在下列句子中，识别主语（S）和动词（V），以及直接宾语（DO）、间接宾语（IO）、主语补足语（SC）或宾语补足语（OC）。带星号部分的参考答案请见书后。

例子：
$\quad$ S $\quad$ V $\quad$ V $\quad$ DO
Crime statistics can cause surprise.

*1. The number of serious crimes in the United States decreased.

*2. A decline in serious crimes occurred each year.

*3. The Crime Index measures serious crime.

*4. The FBI invented the index.

*5. The four serious violent crimes are murder, robbery, forcible rape, and aggravated assault.

6. The Crime Index calls auto theft, burglary, arson, and larceny-theft the four serious crimes against property.

7. The Crime Index gives the FBI a measure of crime.

8. The index shows trends in crimes and criminals.

9. The nation's largest cities showed the largest decline in crime.

10. However, crime actually increased in smaller cities, proving that the decline in crime is unrepresentative of the nation.

22c 学会其他句型

大多数英语句子首先在主语中指明施动者，然后在谓语中对施动者做出表述。但是有四种句子与这个基本结构不同。

1 ▪ 问句

下面是最常见的几种由陈述而提问的方式。记住问句以问号结尾。（见 p. 305）

- 把动词或者动词的一部分提到句首。这些问句能用是或否来回答。动词可以是 be 的某种形式。

    The rate is high. $\qquad$ Is the rate high?

    或者动词可以包含一个助动词和一个主要动词。然后把助动词，或者第一个助动词——假如有多个的话——提到句首。

    Rates can rise. $\qquad$ Can rates rise?

Rates have been rising.　　　　Have rates been rising?

- 以do的某种形式开始问句，并使用动词的原形。在这种问句中，动词必须只有一个词，并且不能是be动词。这样的问句可以用是或否来回答。

Interest rates rose.　　　　　Did interest rates rise?

- 在是—否问句的开头加上一个疑问词。这些疑问词是how，what，who，when，where，which和why。这些问句需要有解释性的回答。

Did rates rise today?　　　　Why did rates rise today?
Is the rate high?　　　　　　Why is the rate high?

- 在问句的开头加上who，what或which作为主语。主谓的顺序和陈述句相同。

Something is the answer.　　　What is the answer?
Someone can answer.　　　　Who can answer?

2 ▪ 命令句

204

把句子的主语去掉即构成命令句。

Think of options.　　　　　　Eat your spinach.
Watch the news.　　　　　　Leave me alone.

3 ▪ 被动句

在基本的主谓结构中，主语发出动词的动作。动词是**主动态**。

　　　　主动态
　主语　动词　　宾语
Kyong wrote the paper.

而在**被动态**中，主语接受动词的动作。

　　　　被动态
　主语　　动词
The paper was written by Kyong.

在被动态中，主动态动词的宾语（paper）称为被动态动词的主语。

被动态动词总是由be的某种形式加上主要动词的过去分词构成（paper was written，absences were excused）。实际的施动者（发出动词的动作的人或物）可以用短语来表达（如上例中的by Kyong），也可以完全省略掉——假如它不明确或者不重要的话，如The house was flooded。

更多关于被动态的形成和使用的内容，见pp. 240–241。

4 ▪ 主语后置的句子

有两种句子把主语放在谓语的后面。其一，颠倒正常语序是为了强调，例如：

The cause of the problem lies here.［正常语序］
Here lies the cause of the problem.［颠倒语序］

其二，句子以there或it开头，主语后置：

　　　　动词　　　　　　主语
There will be eighteen people at the meeting.［正常语序：Eighteen people will be at the meeting.］

　　动词　　　　　　　　　　主语
It was surprising that Marinetti was nominated.［正常语序：That Marinetti was nominated was surprising.］

这些句子中的there和it是**填补语**。它们只起到后置主语的作用。填补语是有用的，（见pp. 186–187）但常常是冗余的。

🌐 CULTURE LANGUAGE 使用填补语结构时，要包含there或it。只有命令句和一些问句能以动词开头。（见前几页）

错误：No one predicted the nomination. Were no polls showing Marinetti ahead.

改写：No one predicted the nomination. There were no polls showing Marinetti ahead.

> **练习22.3　改写被动句和填补语结构**
>
> 把下列被动句改写为主动句，把填补语结构改写为正常主谓语序。带星号部分的参考答案请见书后。更多关于被动态和填补语结构的联系，见p. 146, p. 188和p. 242。
>
> 例子：
>
> All the trees in the park were planted by the city.
>
> The city planted all the trees in the park.
>
> *1. The screenplay for *Monster's Ball* was cowritten by Milo Addica and Will Rokos.
>
> *2. The film was directed by Marc Foster.
>
> 3. There was only one performance in the movie that received an Academy Award.
>
> 4. It was Halle Berry who won the award for best actress.

5. Berry was congratulated by the press for being the first African American to win the award.

第 23 章　短语和从句

概要
- 学会识别短语：介词短语，动词短语，独立主格结构，同位语（下方）
- 学会识别从句（p. 209）

大多数句子都包含一些当作形容词、副词或名词使用的词群。这些短语和从句丰富了句子的色彩和意义，但它们不能作为完整的句子独立存在。（关于非完整句，见第35章）

23a 学会识别短语

短语要么缺少主语，要么缺少谓语，或者二者都缺少：in a panic（介词短语），fearing an accident（动词短语），alarms having sounded（独立主格结构），night, that dark blanket（同位语）。

1 ▪ 介词短语

介词短语包含一个介词加上一个被称为**介词宾语**的名词、代词或者当作名词使用的词群。介词包括 about, at, by, for, to, under 和 with。更完整的列表见 p. 195。

介词	宾语
of	spaghetti
on	the surface
with	great satisfaction
upon	entering the room
from	where you are standing

介词短语通常用作形容词或副词，作用是补充细节和使句子对于读者更有意思。形容词短语通常紧跟在它修饰的词后面，但副词短语不需要紧跟。

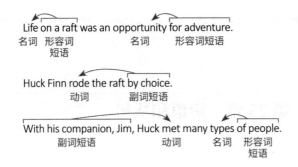

Life on a raft was an opportunity for adventure.
名词　形容词　　　名词　　形容词短语
　　　短语

Huck Finn rode the raft by choice.
　　　　　　动词　　　副词短语

With his companion, Jim, Huck met many types of people.
　　副词短语　　　　　动词　　名词　形容词
　　　　　　　　　　　　　　　　　短语

2 ▪ 动词短语

一些特定形式的动词，称为**非谓语动词**，可以用作修饰语或名词。在**动词短语**中，这些非谓语动词常常有自己的修饰语和宾语。

注意：非谓语动词不能在句中单独充当谓语。The sun rises over the dump 是个句子，而The sun rising over the dump是个非完整句。（见p. 286）

分词短语

现在分词以-ing结尾：living, walking。**过去分词**通常以-d或-ed结尾：lived, walked。**分词短语**以分词加上修饰语和宾语构成。分词和分词短语通常用作形容词，有时也用作副词。

Strolling shoppers fill the malls.
　形容词　　名词

They make selections determined by personal taste.
　　　　　　名词　　　　　形容词短语

Visiting stores, shoppers consider the merchandise for sale.
　副词短语　　　　　　动词

注意：不规则动词的过去分词可能有不同的词尾，例如：hidden funds。（见pp. 214–215）

（CULTURE LANGUAGE）表达情感的动词的现在分词和过去分词分别有不同的意思。现在分词修饰引发情感的事物：It was a boring lecture. 过去分词修饰经历此情感的人或事物：The bored students slept.（见p. 272）

动名词短语

动名词短语是用作名词的动词-ing形式。动名词和动名词短语能替代名词，完全起到名词的作用。

句子主语
　Shopping satisfies personal needs.
　　　名词

　　　　　　　　　　　　→ 介词
　　　　　　　　　　　　　宾语
　Malls are good at creating such needs.
　　　　　　　　　　　　名词短语

不定式短语

不定式短语由动词原形加上to构成：to hide。不定式和不定式短语用作形容词、副词或名词。名词或名词短语可以取代名词。

　　─ 句子主语 ─　　　　─ 主语补足语 ─
　To design a mall is to create an artificial environment.
　　　名词短语　　　　　　　　名词短语

副词或副词短语修饰动词、形容词、其他副词或整个词群，可以靠近也可以远离所修饰的词。

　To achieve this goal, designers emphasize the familiar.
　　　副词短语　　　　　　　　　　　动词

　Malls are designed to make shoppers feel safe.
　　　　动词　　　　　　　副词短语

形容词或形容词短语修饰名词、代词，通常紧跟所修饰的词语。

　The environment supports the impulse to shop.
　　　名词　　　　　　　　　　　名词　形容词

（CULTURE LANGUAGE）有些动词可以后接不定式和动名词，有些动词不可以。一个动词后的不定式和动名词可能有不同的意义：

　The cowboy stopped to sing.［他停下来去做活动］
　The cowboy stopped singing.［他完成了活动］

（见pp. 225–227）

3 ▪ 独立主格结构

独立主格结构包含一个名词或代词，一个分词，再加上任何修饰语。它修饰句子的其余部分，可以在句子多处出现。

Their own place established, many ethnic groups are making way for new arrivals.
　　独立主格结构

独立主格结构不同于分词短语，它总是包含充当主语的名词：

Learning English, many immigrants discover American culture.
　　分词短语

Immigrants having learned English, their opportunities widen.
　　独立主格结构

4 ▪ 同位语

同位语通常是重述另一个名词的名词。同位语短语也含有修饰语。同位语和同位语短语通常紧跟在所重述的名词后面。

Bizen ware, a dark stoneware, is produced in Japan.
　名词　　　同位语短语

同位语和同位语短语有时以that is，such as，for example 或 in other words开头。

Bizen ware is used in the Japanese tea ceremony, that is, the Zen Bud-dhist observance that links meditation and art.
　　　　　　　　　　　　　　　　　　　　　　名词　　同位语短语

练习23.1　**识别短语**

识别下面每个句子中的非谓语动词、同位语、动词短语、同位语短语、介词短语和独立主格结构。所有的句子都包含至少两个这样的词或词语。带星号部分的参考答案请见书后。

例子：
　　　　　　　　　　　　　　　　　　　　分词短语
　　Modern English contains words borrowed from many sources.
　　　　　　　　　　　　　　　　　　　　　　　介词短语

*1. With its many synonyms, or words with similar meanings, English can make choosing the right word a difficult task.

*2. Borrowing words from other languages such as French and Latin, English acquired an unusual number of synonyms.

*3. Having so many choices, how does a writer decide between *motherly* and *maternal* or among *womanly, feminine,* and *female*?

*4. Some people prefer longer and more ornate words to avoid the flatness of short words.

*5. During the Renaissance a heated debate occurred between the Latinists, favoring Latin words, and the Saxonists, preferring Anglo- Saxon words derived from Germanic roots.

6. Students in writing classes are often told to choose the shorter word, generally an Anglo-Saxon derivative.

7. Better advice, wrote William Hazlitt, is the principle of choosing "the best word in common use."

8. Keeping this principle in mind, a writer would choose either *womanly*, the Anglo-Saxon word, or *feminine*, a French derivative, according to meaning and situation.

9. Synonyms rarely have exactly the same meaning, usage having created subtle but real differences over time.

10. To take another example, *handbook*, an old English word, has a slightly different meaning than that of *manual*, a French derivative.

23b 学会识别从句

从句是包含主语和谓语的一个词群。主句和从句之间的区别很重要：

- 主句做一个完整的陈述，可以单独作为句子存在：The sky darkened.
- 从句和主句一样，但以从属词开头：when the sky darkened；whoever calls。
从属词把句子从一个完整的陈述降格为单个的形容词、副词或名词。
注意：作为一个句子的从句是一个句子片段。（见p. 287）

形容词性从句

形容词短语修饰名词或代词，通常以关系代词who，whom，whose，which或that开头，但也可以以where，when或why开头。形容词性从句通常紧跟所修饰的词语。

Parents who cannot read may have bad memories of school.
名词　　　形容词短语

Children whom the schools fail sometimes have illiterate parents.
名词　　　　形容词短语

One school, which is open year-round, helps parents learn to read.
　　名词　　　　形容词短语

The school is in a city where the illiteracy rate is high.
　　　　　　　　名词　　　　　形容词短语

在前三个例子里，关系代词who, whom和which指的是从句修饰的名词（Parents, Children, school）。关系代词充当从句的主语（who cannot read, which is open year-round）或宾语（whom the shcools fail）。在最后一个例子中，where替代in which（a city in which the illiteracy rate is high）。

关于形容词性从句怎样加标点，见pp. 312–313。

副词性从句

副词性从句修饰动词、形容词、另一个副词或者整个的词群。它总是以从属连词开头，如after, although, as, because, even though, how, if, until, when 或while。（更完整的列表见p. 196）副词性从句可以在句子中多处出现，但关于其限制见pp. 279–281。

The school began teaching parents when adult illiteracy gained national attention.
　　　动词　　　　　　　　　　　　　　副词性从句

At first the program was not as successful as its founders had hoped.
　　　　　　　　　　　　　　　形容词　　　　副词性从句

Because it was directed at people who could not read, advertising had to be inventive.
　　　　　　　副词性从句　　　　　　　　　　　　　　　主句

名词性从句

名词性从句取代句中名词用作主语、宾语或补足语。它以that, what, whatever, who, whom, whoever, whomever, when, where, whether, why 或 how 开头。

　　　　　　　　　句子主语
Whether the program would succeed depended on door-to-door advertising.
　　　　名词性从句

　　　　　　　　　　　　　　　动词宾语
Teachers explained in person how the program would work.
　　　　　　　　　　　　　　　名词性从句

```
            ┌─── 句子主语 ───┐
```
Whoever seemed slightly interested was invited to an open meeting.
        名词性从句

```
                                  ┌──── 介词宾语 ────┐
```
A few parents were anxious about what their children would think.
                             名词性从句

```
                         ┌──── 宾语补足语 ────┐
```
The children's needs were what the parents asked most about.
                       名词性从句

练习23.2　识别从句

用下画线标注下列句子中的从句，然后根据其在句中的功用辨识它们是形容词性（ADJ）、副词性（ADV）还是名词性（N）从句。带星号部分的参考答案请见书后。

例子：

          N
Whoever follows the Koran refers to God as *Allah*, the Arabic word for his name.

*1. The Prophet Muhammad, who was the founder of Islam, was born about 570 CE in the city of Mecca.

*2. He grew up in the care of his grandfather and an uncle because both of his parents had died.

*3. His family was part of a powerful Arab tribe that lived in western Arabia.

*4. When Muhammad was about forty years old, he had a vision while he was in a cave outside Mecca.

*5. He believed that God had selected him to be the prophet of a true religion for the Arab people.

6. Throughout his life he continued to have revelations, which have been written in the Koran.

7. The Koran is the sacred book of Muslims, who as adherents of Islam view Muhammad as God's messenger.

8. When he no longer had the support of the clans of Mecca, Muhammad and his followers moved to Medina.

9. There they established an organized Muslim community that sometimes clashed with the Meccans and with Jewish clans.

10. Throughout his life Muhammad continued as the religious, political, and military leader of Islam as it spread in Asia and Africa.

第 24 章　句子类型

概要
- 学会识别简单句（下方）
- 学会识别并列句（下方）
- 学会识别复合句（下方）
- 学会识别并列复合句（p. 213）

这四种句式所包含的从句数量各个不同。它们对句子中的主要信息和次要信息的强调也各个不同。

24a 学会识别简单句

简单句包含一个简单主句，不包含从句：

　　　　　　— 主句 —
Last summer was unusually hot.

　　　　　　　　　　　— 主句 —
The summer made many farmers leave the area for good or reduced them to bare existence.

24b 学会识别并列句

并列句包含两个或多个主句，不包含从句。

　　— 主句 —　　— 主句 —
Last July was hot, but August was even hotter.

　　— 主句 —　　　　— 主句 —
The hot sun scorched the earth, and the lack of rain killed many crops.

24c 学会识别复合句

复合句包含一个主句及一个或多个从句。

　— 主句 —　　— 从句 —
Rain finally came, although many had left the area by then.

[主句] Those who remained were able to start anew [从句] because the government came [从句] to their aid.

24d 学会识别并列复合句

并列复合句兼具并列句和复合句的特点，含两个或多个主句，至少一个从句。

[从句] When government aid finally came, [主句] many people had already been reduced to poverty and [主句] others had been forced to move.

练习24.1　识别句子结构

标出下列句子中的主句和从句，然后识别它们是简单句、并列句、复合句还是并列复合句。带星号部分的参考答案请见书后。

例子：

[主句] The human voice is produced in the larynx, [从句] which has two bands called vocal chords.［复合句］

*1. Our world has many sounds, but they all have one thing in common.

*2. The one thing that all sounds share is that they are produced by vibrations.

*3. The vibrations make the air move in waves, and these sound waves travel to the ear.

*4. When sound waves enter the ear, the auditory nerves convey them to the brain, and the brain interprets them.

*5. Sound waves can also travel through other material, such as water and even the solid earth.

6. Some sounds are pleasant, and others, which we call noise, are not.

7. Most noises are produced by irregular vibrations at irregular intervals; an example is the barking of a dog.

8. Sounds have frequency and pitch.

9. When an object vibrates rapidly, it produces high-frequency, high-pitched sounds.

10. People can hear sounds over a wide range of frequencies, but dogs, cats, and many other animals can hear high frequencies that humans cannot.

动词

动词表达动作、处境或状态。动词的基本使用和形式见 pp. 192–193。本部分解释和解决动词的词形（第25章）、时态（第26章）、语气（第27章）和语态（第28章）的最常见问题，并讲解怎样保持动词与主语的一致（第29章）。

第 25 章　动词的词形

概要

- 正确使用 sing/sang/sung 及其他不规则动词的词形（下方）
- 分辨 sit 和 set, lie 和 lay, rise 和 raise（p. 217）
- 正确使用动词的 -s 和 -ed 形式（p. 219）
- 正确使用与主要动词连用的助动词（p. 220）
- 在动词后正确使用动名词和不定式（p. 225）
- 正确使用双词动词的分词形式（p. 228）

动词的五种基本形式已在 p. 192 列出。本章着重讲解最常造成困难的动词形式。

25a　正确使用 sing/sang/sung 及其他不规则动词的词形

大多数动词是**规则动词**：在原形上加 -d 或 -ed 来构成过去时和过去分词。

原形	过去时	过去分词
live	lived	lived
act	acted	acted

英语的**不规则动词**大约有两百个：它们的过去式和过去分词以不规则方式构成，对动词的变形有疑问的时候，可在词典上其原形的条目下查找它们的变

化。词典会把不规则动词的原形、过去时和过去分词按顺序列出（go，went，gone）。如果词典只给出两种形式（如think，thought），那么过去时和过去分词形式相同。

常见不规则动词

原形	过去时	过去分词
arise	arose	arisen
be	was, were	been
become	became	become
begin	began	begun
bend	bent	bent
bid	bid	bid
bite	bit	bitten, bit
blow	blew	blown
break	broke	broken
bring	brought	brought
build	built	built
burst	burst	burst
buy	bought	bought
catch	caught	caught
choose	chose	chosen
come	came	come
cut	cut	cut
dig	dug	dug
dive	dived, dove	dived
do	did	done
draw	drew	drawn
dream	dreamed, dreamt	dreamed, dreamt
drink	drank	drunk
drive	drove	driven
eat	ate	eaten
fall	fell	fallen
find	found	found
fly	flew	flown
forget	forgot	forgotten, forgot
freeze	froze	frozen
get	got	got, gotten
give	gave	given
go	went	gone
grow	grew	grown
hang (suspend)	hung	hung
hang (execute)	hanged	hanged
have	had	had

（续表）

原形	过去时	过去分词
hear	heard	heard
hide	hid	hidden
hold	held	held
hurt	hurt	hurt
keep	kept	kept
know	knew	known
lay	laid	laid
lead	led	led
leave	left	left
let	let	let
lie	lay	lain
lose	lost	lost
pay	paid	paid
read	read	read
ride	rode	ridden
ring	rang	rung
rise	rose	risen
run	ran	run
say	said	said
see	saw	seen
set	set	set
shake	shook	shaken
shrink	shrank, shrunk	shrunk, shrunken
sing	sang, sung	sung
sink	sank, sunk	sunk
sit	sat	sat
sleep	slept	slept
speak	spoke	spoken
stand	stood	stood
steal	stole	stolen
swim	swam	swum
swing	swung	swung
take	took	taken
teach	taught	taught
tear	tore	torn
throw	threw	thrown
wear	wore	worn
write	wrote	written

语法检查工具：语法检查工具可能会标出不规则动词的错误形式，但也可能标不出。例如，语法检查工具会标出 The runner stealed（stole 才是正确的）second base，但标不出 The runner had steal（stolen 才是正确的）second base。对不规则动词的词形有疑问的时候，查找前面列表或者参考词典。

CULTURE LANGUAGE 有些英语方言使用的动词词形不同于标准美式英语，例如，不用 dragged而用drug，不用grew而用growed，不用came而用come，不用gone而用went。在需要使用标准美式英语的时候，用前面列表或词典里列出的词形。

错误：They have went to the movies.

改写：They have gone to the movies.

练习25.1　使用不规则动词

给出括号中不规则动词的过去时或过去分词，确认你用的是什么词形。带星号部分的参考答案请见书后。

例子：

Though we had [hide] the cash box, it was [steal].

Though we had hidden the cash box, it was stolen. [两个过去分词]

*1. The world population has [grow] by two-thirds of a billion people in less than a decade.

*2. Recently it [break] the 7 billion mark.

*3. Experts have [draw] pictures of a crowded future.

*4. They predict that the world population may have [slide] up to as much as 10 billion by the year 2050.

*5. Though the food supply [rise] in the last decade, the share to each person [fall].

6. At the same time the water supply, which had actually [become] healthier in the twentieth century, [sink] in size and quality.

7. The number of species on earth [shrink] by 20%.

8. Changes in land use [run] nomads and subsistence farmers off the land.

9. Yet all has not been [lose].

10. Recently human beings have [begin] to heed these and other problems and to explore how technology can be [drive] to help the earth and all its populations.

11. Some new techniques for waste processing have [prove] effective.

12. Crop management has [take] some pressure off lands with poor soil, allowing their owners to produce food.

13. Genetic engineering could replenish food supplies that have [shrink].

14. Population control has [find] adherents all over the world.

15. Many endangered species have been [give] room to thrive.

25b 分辨 sit 和 set，lie 和 lay，rise 和 raise

sit和set，lie和lay，以及rise和raise容易混淆。

原形	过去时	过去分词
sit	sat	sat
set	set	set
lie	lay	lain
lay	laid	laid
rise	rose	risen
raise	raised	raised

这三对容易混淆的词，每一对中其一是不及物动词（不带宾语），其二是及物动词（带宾语）。更多关于这个区别的内容，见pp. 200–201。

不及物动词

The patients lie in their hospital beds.［lie的意思是recline，不带宾语］
Visitors sit with them.［sit的意思是be seated或be located，不带宾语］
Patients' temperatures rise.［rise的意思是increase或get up，不带宾语］

及物动词

Nursing aides lay the dinner trays on tables.［lay的意思是place，这里带宾语trays］
The aides set the trays down.［set的意思是place，这里带宾语trays］
The aides raise the patients' beds.［raise的意思是lift或bring up，这里带宾语beds］

注意：动词lie意为to tell an untruth时，是不规则动词，其过去时和过去分词均为lied：Nikki lied to us. She has lied to us for many years.

练习25.2　分辨sit和set，lie和lay，rise和raise

从括号中选择正确的动词，然后依题意给出其过去时或过去分词。带星号部分的参考答案请见书后。

例子：

After I washed all the windows, I [lie, lay] down the squeegee and then I [sit, set] the table.

After I washed all the windows, I laid down the squeegee and then I set the table.

*1. Yesterday afternoon the child [lie, lay] down for a nap.

*2. The child has been [rise, raise] by her grandparents.

3. Most days her grandfather has [sit, set] with her, reading her adventure stories.

4. She has [rise, raise] at dawn most mornings.

5. Her toys were [lie, lay] on the floor.

25c 正确使用动词的 -s 和 -ed 形式

某些英语方言或非英语母语者有时会漏掉标准美式英语中要求有的动词词尾的-s和-ed。

注意：如果你写作时常会漏掉这些词尾，可以试试读书说话时把正确的动词念出声来，比如下面例子中的动词，这样能帮助你写作时记住词尾。

语法检查工具：语法检查工具会标出漏掉词尾-s和-ed的动词，如he ask和was ask中的动词，但也会遗漏很多错误而不标记。

1 ▪ 不可少的-s词尾

在下面两种情况**都**有的时候，使用动词的-s结尾：

- **主语是单数名词（boy）、不定代词（everyone）或he, she, it**。这些主语是第三人称，谈及某人某物时使用。
- **动词的动作出现在现在。**

The letter asks [不是 ask] for a quick response.

Delay costs [不是 cost] money.

要特别注意这些动词的-s形式：be (is)，have (has) 和do (does, doesn't)。在现在时态使用第三人称单数主语的时候，总是要用这些词形。

The company is [不是 be] late in responding.

It has [不是 have] problems.

It doesn't [不是 don't] have the needed data.

The contract does [不是 do] depend on the response.

另外，在过去时态使用I和第三人称单数主语时，be要用-s形式。

The company was [不是 were] in trouble before.

除了过去时的I was之外，代词I和you以及所有复数主语都不用动词的-s形式。

I am [不是 is] a student.

You are [不是 is] also a student.

They are [不是 is] students, too.

2 ▪ 不可少的-ed和-d词尾

下列所有情形中，动词必须使用-ed或-d形式。

- 动词的动作出现在过去：

The company asked [不是 ask] for more time.

- 动词的变形用作修饰语：

The data concerned [不是 concern] should be retrievable.

- 动词的词形与be或have的某种形式连用：

The company is supposed [不是 suppose] to be the best.

It has developed [不是 develop] an excellent reputation.

特别要注意发音不很清楚时的-ed或-d词尾，比如asked, discussed, mixed, supposed, walked及used。

练习25.3　使用-s和-ed词尾

给出括号中动词的正确形式。注意别忘了标准美式英语中需要有的-ed或-d词尾。带星号部分的参考答案请见书后。

例子：

Unfortunately, the roof on our new house already [leak].

Unfortunately, the roof on our new house already leaks.

*1. A teacher sometimes [ask] too much of a student.

*2. In high school I was once [punish] for being sick.

*3. I had [miss] a week of school because of a serious case of the flu.

*4. I [realize] that I would fail a test unless I had a chance to make up the class work.

*5. I [discuss] the problem with the teacher.

6. He said I was [suppose] to make up the work while I was sick.

7. At that I [walk] out of the class.

8. I [receive] a failing grade then, but it did not change my attitude.

9. I [work] harder in the courses that have more understanding teachers.

10. Today I still balk when a teacher [make] unreasonable demands or [expect] miracles.

25d 正确使用与主要动词连用的助动词

助动词在动词短语中与主要动词连用：The line should have been cut. Who was calling?

语法检查工具：语法检查工具常常能查出遗漏的助动词以及连用的主要动词的错误形式，但有时候也查不出来，比如会查出 Many been fortunate，但查不出 The conference will be occurred。

1 ▪ 不可少的助动词

标准美式英语在如下情形要求有助动词：

- **主要动词以-ing结尾**：
  Researchers are conducting fieldwork all over the world. [不是 Researchers conducting . . .]

- **主要动词是 been 或 be**：
  Many have been fortunate in their discoveries. [不是 Many been . . .]
  Some could be real-life Indiana Joneses. [不是 Some be . . .]

- **主要动词是过去分词形式，例如 talked，begun 或 thrown**：
  Their discoveries were covered in newspapers and magazines. [不是 Their discoveries covered . . .]
  The researchers have given interviews. [不是 The researchers given . . .]

遗漏助动词会造成非完整句或**句子片段**，因为现在分词（conducting）、不规则动词的过去分词（been）或动词原形 be 不能单独充当句子中的唯一动词。（见 p. 286）要做句子中的动词，这些词形需要助动词。

2 ▪ 助动词与主要动词的连用

助动词和主要动词以特定方式连用形成动词短语。

注意：动词短语中的主要动词不随主语或时间的改变而改变：she has sung, you had sung。只需要变化助动词。

"be+现在分词"形式

进行时态表示动作正在进行中，以 be, am, is, are, was, were 或 been 后面

加上主要动词的现在分词构成。

She is working on a new book.

222　be和been要求有额外的助动词来构成进行时态。

can	might	should		have	
could	must	will	be working	has	been working
may	shall	would		had	

构成进行时态时，主要动词一定要使用-ing形式。

错误：Her ideas are grow more complex. She is developed a new approach to ethics.

改写：Her ideas are growing more complex. She is developing a new approach to ethics.

"be+过去分词"形式

动词的被动态表示主语接受动词的动作。被动态以be，am，is，are，was，were，being或been后面加上及物动词的过去分词构成。

Her latest book was completed in four months.

be，being和been要求有额外的助动词来构成被动态：

have		am		
has	been completed	is	was	being completed
had		are	were	

will be completed

在被动态中，要确保使用主要动词的过去分词形式：

错误：Her next book will be publish soon.

改写：Her next book will be published soon.

注意：只有及物动词才能构成被动态。

错误：A philosophy conference will be occurred in the same week that the book comes out.［occur不是及物动词］

改写：A philosophy conference will occur in the same week that the book comes out.

223　关于怎样使用被动态和避免错误，见pp. 240–241。

have的几种形式

have作为助动词使用有四种形式：have, has, had, having。其中任何一种加上主要动词的过去分词形式，就构成完成时，表示动作在另一个确定的时间或动作之前就已经完成。

Some students have complained about the laboratory.

Others had complained before.

will和其他助动词有时与have的完成时态连用：

Several more students will have complained by the end of the week.

do的几种形式

do, does和did作为助动词有三种用法，总是和主要动词的原形连用。

- **构成问句**：How did the trial end?
- **强调主要动词**：It did end eventually.
- **与not或never连用，否定主要动词**：The judge did not withdraw.

与do的任何形式连用时，主要动词总是要用原形。

错误：The judge did remained in court.

改写：The judge did remain in court.

情态动词

情态动词包括can, may, should, would和几个两三个词的组合，如have to和be supposed to。（见p. 193）

情态动词表达多重意义，下面是最常用的几种：

- **能力**：can, could, be able to

  The equipment can detect small vibrations.［现在］

  The equipment could detect small vibrations.［过去］

  The equipment is able to detect small vibrations.［现在。过去：was able to。将来：will be able to］

- **可能性**：could, may, might；could/may/might have + 过去分词

  The equipment could fail.［现在］

  The equipment may fail.［现在或将来］

  The equipment might fail.［现在或将来］

  The equipment may have failed.［过去］

- 必要性或义务：must, have to, be supposed to

  The lab must purchase a backup. [现在或将来]

  The lab has to purchase a backup. [现在或将来。过去：had to]

  The lab will have to purchase a backup. [将来]

  The lab is supposed to purchase a backup. [现在。过去：was supposed to]

- 允许：may, can, could

  The lab may spend the money. [现在或将来]

  The lab can spend the money. [现在或将来]

  The lab could spend the money. [现在或将来，更没把握]

  The lab could have spent the money. [过去]

- 意图：will, shall, would

  The lab will spend the money. [将来]

  Shall we offer advice? [将来。用 shall 提问，寻求观点或赞同]

  We would have offered advice. [过去]

- 要求：could, can, would

  Could [或 Can 或 Would] you please obtain a bid? [现在或将来]

- 劝告和建议：should, had better, ought to, should have + 过去分词

  You should obtain three bids. [现在或将来]

  You had better obtain three bids. [现在或将来]

  You ought to obtain three bids. [现在或将来]

  You should have obtained three bids. [过去]

- 过去的习惯：would, used to

  In years past we would obtain five bids.

  We used to obtain five bids.

练习25.4　使用助动词 (CULTURE LANGUAGE)

在下列句子中加上助动词。带星号部分的参考答案请见书后。

例子：

The school be opened to shelter storm victims.

The school will be opened to shelter storm victims.

*1. For as long as I can remember, I been writing stories.

*2. While I living with my grandparents one summer, I wrote mystery stories.

3. Nearly every afternoon I sat at the computer and wrote about two brothers who solved mysteries while their mother be working.

4. By the end of the summer, I written four stories.

5. I was very happy when one of my stories published in the school newspaper.

练习25.5　改写：助动词+主要动词 (CULTURE LANGUAGE)

改写下列句子，正确使用助动词和主要动词。如果句子是正确的，在句子前的序号上做标记。带星号部分的参考答案请见书后。

例子：

The college testing service has test as many as five hundred students at one time.

The college testing service has tested as many as five hundred students at one time.

*1. A report from the Bureau of the Census has confirm a widening gap between rich and poor.

*2. As suspected, the percentage of people below the poverty level did increased over the last decade.

3. The richest 1% of the population is make 17% of all the income.

4. These households will keeping an average of $1.3 million each after taxes.

5. The average middle-income household will retain about $55,000.

25e 在动词后正确使用动名词和不定式 (CULTURE LANGUAGE)

非英语母语者可能会拿不准动词后面究竟要用动名词还是不定式。动名词和不定式能跟在一些动词后面，但不能跟在另一些动词后面。有时，同一个动词与动名词或不定式连用会改变动词的意义。

语法检查工具：语法检查工具能找出与动词连用的动名词或不定式的一些错误，但也会有遗漏。例如，能查出 I adore to shop，但查不出 I practice to swim 或 I promise helping out。使用下面列表和英语二语词典来确定究竟该用动名词还是不定式。（英语二语词典列表见 p.173）

1 ▪ 动名词或不定式都可以

下列动词后面可以接动名词也可以接不定式，意思没有重要区别。

begin	continue	intend	prefer
can't bear	hate	like	start
can't stand	hesitate	love	

The pump began working. The pump began to work.

2 ▪ 动词后可以用动名词或不定式，但意义不同

下面四个动词接动名词或不定式会有很不同的意义。

forget	stop
remember	try

The engineer stopped eating.［工程师不再吃东西了］
The engineer stopped to eat.［工程师停下来吃］

3 ▪ 只能接动名词，不能接不定式

下列动词后面不能用不定式：

admit	discuss	mind	recollect
adore	dislike	miss	resent
appreciate	enjoy	postpone	resist
avoid	escape	practice	risk
consider	finish	put off	suggest
deny	imagine	quit	tolerate
detest	keep	recall	understand

错误：He finished to eat lunch.
改写：He finished eating lunch.

4 ▪ 只能接不定式，不能接动名词

下列动词后面不能用动名词：

agree	claim	manage	promise
appear	consent	mean	refuse
arrange	decide	offer	say
ask	expect	plan	wait
assent	have	prepare	want
beg	hope	pretend	wish

错误：He decided <u>checking</u> the pump.
改写：He decided <u>to check</u> the pump.

5 ▪ 名词或代词+不定式

有些动词后面可以单接一个不定式，也可以接一个名词或代词加不定式。名词或代词的存在改变了意思。

ask	dare	need	wish
beg	expect	promise	would like
choose	help	want	

He expected <u>to watch</u>.
He expected <u>his workers to watch</u>.

有些动词后面必须接名词或代词加不定式：

admonish	encourage	oblige	require
advise	forbid	order	teach
allow	force	permit	tell
cause	hire	persuade	train
challenge	instruct	remind	urge
command	invite	request	warn
convince			

He instructed <u>his workers to watch</u>.

不定式跟在下列动词加名词或代词后面时，不要to：

feel   make ("force")
have   see
hear   watch
let

He let his workers learn by observation.

> **练习25.6   改写：动词加动名词或不定式** CULTURE LANGUAGE
>
> 改写下列句子，正确使用动名词或不定式。如果句子是正确的，在它前面的序号上做标记。带星号部分的参考答案请见书后。
>
> 例子：
>
> A politician cannot avoid to alienate some voters.
>
> A politician cannot avoid alienating some voters.
>
> *1. A program called *Boostup.org* encourages students to finish high school.
>
> *2. People supporting this program hope that students will at least postpone to drop out of school.
>
> 3. Adults who want to help can promise mentoring a student.
>
> 4. Because of *Boostup.org*, many students who might have dropped out now plan going to college.
>
> 5. The organization persuades volunteers signing up via its Web site, *Facebook* page, and *Twitter* feed.

25f 正确使用双词动词的分词形式 CULTURE LANGUAGE

标准美式英语里有一些动词，它们包含两个词，动词本身及一个影响动词意义的虚词、介词或副词。例如：

Look up the answer.［寻求答案］
Look over the answer.［检查答案］

这些双词动词的意义通常与构成它们的单个词的意义有很大的不同。（还有一些由三个词组成的动词，如look out for，put up with和run out of）

英语二语词典会解释这些双词动词，也会说明它们在句子中能不能分开，如下所示。（关于英语二语词典，见p. 173）语法检查工具很少能查出这些动词的错误使用。

注意：许多双词动词在口语中比在正式的学术或大众写作中更常见。对于正式写作，考虑用research代替look up，用examine或inspect代替look over。

1 ▪ 不可分开的双词动词

动词与虚词不能被任何词分开的有下列这些：

catch on	go over	play around	stay away
come across	grow up	run into	stay up
get along	keep on	run out of	take care of
give in	look into	speak up	turn up at

错误：Children grow quickly up.

改写：Children grow up quickly.

2 ▪ 可分开的双词动词

大多数带直接宾语的双词动词可以被宾语分开。

Parents help out their children.

Parents help their children out.

如果直接宾语是代词，该代词**必须**插在动词和虚词之间。

错误：Parents help out them.

改写：Parents help them out.

可分开的双词动词有如下这些：

bring up	give back	make up	throw out
call off	hand in	point out	try on
call up	hand out	put away	try out
drop off	help out	put back	turn down
fill out	leave out	put off	turn on
fill up	look over	take out	turn up
give away	look up	take over	wrap up

练习25.7　改写：动词加虚词

下列句子中的双词动词或三词动词用下画线标出来了，有些对，有些不对，要看它们该或者不该被其他词分开。改写错误的动词和其他词。必要的时候查看前面列表或英语二语词典来确认哪些能被分开。带星号部分的参考答案请见书后。

例子：

Hollywood producers never seem to come up with entirely new plots, but they also never run new ways out of to present old ones.

Hollywood producers never seem to come up with [correct] entirely new plots, but they also never run out of new ways to present old ones.

*1. American movies treat everything from going out with someone to making up an ethnic identity, but few people look their significance into.

*2. While some viewers stay away from topical films, others turn at the theater up simply because a movie has sparked debate.

3. Some movies attracted rowdy spectators, and the theaters had to throw out them.

4. Filmmakers have always been eager to point their influence out to the public.

5. Everyone agrees that filmmakers will keep creating controversy on, if only because it can fill up theaters.

第 26 章　动词时态

概要

- 注意现在时态的特殊用法（sing）（下页）
- 注意完成时态的用法（have/had/will have sung）（p. 232）
- 注意进行时态的用法（is/was/will be singing）（p. 232）
- 保持时态一致（p. 233）
- 使用恰当的动词时态呼应（p. 234）

时态表示动词动作的时间。p. 231的方框内列出了规则动词的各种时态。（不规则动词有不同的过去时和过去分词形式。见pp.214–217）

语法检查工具：在动词时态和时态呼应上，语法检查工具提供不了什么帮助，因为正确的使用取决于意义。

【CULTURE LANGUAGE】在标准美式英语中，动词通过其形式表达时间和顺序。在某些别的语言和方言中，可能会有除动词词形之外的其他标志来表达动作的时间。例如，非洲裔美国人的英语口语中，I be attending class on Tuesday的意思是说话人每周二上课。但是对于不了解这种方言的人来说，这个句子的意思可能指上个周二、这个周二，或每周二。在标准美式英语中，想表达的意思由动词时态表示。

I attended class on Tuesday.（过去时意指上个周二）
I will attend class on Tuesday.（将来时表示下个周二）
I attend class on Tuesday.（现在时表示习惯性动作，每个周二）

26a 注意现在时态的特殊用法（sing）

现在时态有几种不同的用法：

现在发生的动作
She understands the problem.
We define the problem differently.

习惯性或反复发生的动作
Banks regularly undergo audits.
The audits monitor the banks' activities.

普遍真理
The mills of the gods grind slowly.
The earth is round.

规则动词的时态（主动语态）

现在时：动作正在发生、习惯性出现，或是普遍真理

一般现在时：原形或-s形式
I walk.
You/we/they walk.
He/she/it walks.

现在进行时：am/is/are+-ing形式
I am walking.
You/we/they are walking.
He/she/it is walking.

过去时：在此之前发生的行为

一般过去时：过去时（-d或-ed）
I/he/she/it walked.
You/we/they walked.

过去进行时：was/were+-ing形式
I/he/she/it was walking.
You/we/they were walking.

将来时：动作在将来发生

一般将来时：will + 原形
I/you/he/she/it/we/they will walk.

将来进行时：will be+-ing形式
I/you/he/she/it/we/they will be walking.

现在完成时：动作在过去发生，联系到现在	
现在完成时：have/has +过去分词 I/you/we/they have walked. He/she/it has walked.	现在完成进行时：have been/has been +-ing形式 I/you/we/they have been walking. He/she/it has been walking.
过去完成时：动作在另一个过去时间之前就已经完成	
过去完成时：had + 过去分词（-d/-ed） I/you/he/she/it/we/they had walked.	过去完成进行时：had been +-ing形式 I/you/he/she/it/we/they had been walking.
将来完成时：动作在将来的另一个时间之前就会完成	
将来完成时：will have + 过去分词（-d/-ed） I/you/he/she/it/we/they will have walked.	将来完成进行时：will have been +-ing形式 I/you/he/she/it/we/they will have been walking.

232　**讨论文学作品、电影等**

Huckleberry Finn has adventures we all envy.

In that article the author examines several causes of crime in very rural areas.

将来的时间

Next week we draft a new budget.

Funding ends in less than a year.

现在时态用上述例子中的表达来表示将来时间：next week，in less than a year。

26b 注意完成时态的用法（have/had/will have sung）

完成时态由某个形式的have加动词的过去分词（closed, hidden）构成。完成时态表示一个动作在某个特定时间或动作之前已经完成。现在完成时也用来表示一个过去开始的动作持续至今。

　　　　　现在完成时
The dancer has performed here only once.[动作在陈述的时候就完成了]

　　　　　　现在完成时
Critics have written about the performance ever since.[行动开始于过去，并继续到现在]

过去完成时
The dancer had trained in Asia before his performance.［该动作在另一个过去动作之前完成］

将来完成时
He will have danced here again by the end of the year.［动作开始于现在或未来，并将在未来的特定时间完成］

CULTURE LANGUAGE 在现在完成时态中，since 和 for 后面跟不同的信息。since 之后是一个特定的时间点：The play has run since 1989. 而 for 后面是一个时间段：It has run for decades.

26c 注意进行时态的用法（is/was/will be singing）

进行时态表示动作的持续（所以叫"进行"时），由 be 的某种形式加动词 -ing 形式（现在分词）构成。（be 和 been 必须与其他助动词连用。见 p. 222）

现在进行时
The team is improving.

过去进行时
Last year the team was losing.

将来进行时
The owners will be watching for signs of improvement.

现在完成进行时
Sports writers have been expecting an upturn.

过去完成进行时
New players had been performing well.

将来完成进行时
If the season goes badly, fans will have been watching their team lose for ten years straight.

注意：有些动词表达的是不变的状况（特别是精神状态）而不是物理状态，它们通常不用进行时态。这些动词包括 adore, appear, believe, belong, care, hate, have, hear, know, like, love, mean, need, own, prefer, remember, see, sound, taste, think, understand 和 want。

错误：She is wanting to study ethics.
改写：She wants to study ethics.

26d 保持时态一致

在一个句子中，动词的时态和形式不需要保持一样，只要它们反映的是现实的时间变化。Ramon will graduate from college thirty years after his father arrived in America. 在口语中，我们常常会转换时态，即使它们并不反映时间的变化。但是写作的时候，这样随意的时态转换会令读者困惑不解。

不一致的时态：Immediately after Booth shot Lincoln, Major Rathbone threw himself upon the assassin. But Booth pulls a knife and plunges it into the major's arm.

改写：Immediately after Booth shot Lincoln, Major Rathbone threw himself upon the assassin. But Booth pulled a knife and plunged it into the major's arm.

不一致的时态：The main character in the novel suffers psychologically because he has a clubfoot, but he eventually triumphed over his disability.

改写：The main character in the novel suffers psychologically because he has a clubfoot, but he eventually triumphs over his disability.
［在讨论文学作品、电影等内容时使用现在时］

练习26.1　改写：保持一致的过去时态

对下面段落里动词的时态做必要的改写，使之保持一致的一般过去时态。带星号部分的参考答案请见书后。

*The 1960 presidential race between Richard Nixon and John F. Kennedy was the first to feature a televised debate. *Despite his extensive political experience, Nixon perspires heavily and looks haggard and uneasy in front of the camera. *By contrast, Kennedy was projecting cool poise and providing crisp answers that made him seem fit for the office of President. The public responded positively to Kennedy's image. His poll ratings shoot up immediately, while Nixon's take a corresponding drop. The popular vote was close, but Kennedy won the election.

练习26.2　改写：保持一致的现在时态

对下面段落里的动词进行必要的改写，使之保持一致的一般现在时态。带星号部分的参考答案请见书后。

*E. B. White's famous children's novel *Charlotte's Web* is a wonderful story of friendship and loyalty. *Charlotte, the wise and motherly spider, decided to save her friend Wilbur, the young and childlike pig, from being butchered by his owner. *She made a plan to weave words into her web that described Wilbur. She first weaves "Some Pig" and later presented "Terrific," "Radiant," and "Humble." Her plan succeeded beautifully. She fools the humans into believing that Wilbur was a pig unlike any other, and Wilbur lived.

26e 使用恰当的动词时态呼应

时态的呼应指主句中动词时态与从句中动词时态的关系。主从句的时态常常不同，以反映相对时间的不同：

Ramon's father arrived in the United States thirty years ago, after he had married, and now Ramon has decided that he will return to his father's homeland.

英语时态的呼应即使对于英语母语者也可能很棘手，更不用说对于非母语者了。下面讨论主要的难点。

1 ▪ 主句用过去时或过去完成时

当主句中的动词用过去时或过去完成时的时候，从句中的动词也必须是过去时或过去完成时。

主句：过去时　　　　从句：过去时
The researchers discovered that people varied widely in their knowledge of public events.

主句：过去时　　　　　　从句：过去完成时
The variation occurred because respondents had been born in different decades.

主句：过去完成时　　　　从句：过去时
None of them had been born when Eisenhower was President.

例外：普遍真理总是用现在时态，比如：The earth is round.

主句：过去时　　　　从句：现在时
Most understood that popular Presidents are not necessarily good Presidents.

2 ▪ 条件句

条件句表达因果之间的事实关系、做出预测，或者推测将会发生什么。这样的句子通常含有一个以 if, when 或 unless 开头的从句，以及一个陈述结果的主句。这三种条件句各自使用不同的动词。

表达事实关系

陈述某事物发生则另一事物必然会发生，主句、从句都用现在时态。

　　　　　从句：现在时　　　　　主句：现在时
When a voter casts a ballot, he or she has complete privacy.

如果相关的两件事都发生在过去，则主句、从句都用过去时。

　　　　　从句：过去时　　　　　主句：过去时
When voters registered in some states, they had to pay a poll tax.

预测

做预测时，通常在从句中用现在时态，而在主句中用将来时态。

　　　　　从句：现在时　　　　　主句：将来时
Unless citizens regain faith in politics, they will not vote.

有时候主句中的动词由may，can，should或might加上动词的原形构成：If citizens regain faith, they may vote.

推测

推测主要有两种，每一种有自己的动词范式。对于那些客观上有可能而实际上不太可能的事情，在从句中用过去时态，而在主句中用would，could或might加动词原形：

　　　　从句：过去时　　　　　主句：would+动词
If voters had more confidence, they would vote more often.

主语是I，he，she，it或单数名词时，用were而不用was。（更多关于这种特殊动词形式的内容，见pp. 238–239）

　　　　从句：过去时　　　　　主句：would+动词
If the voter were more confident, he or she would vote more often.

对于那些现在不可能的事情，与事实相反的事情，使用与上述相同的时态（包括在适用的情况下也用特别的were）。

　　　从句：过去时　　主句：might+动词
If Lincoln were alive, he might inspire confidence.

对于那些在过去不可能的事情，在从句中用过去完成时，而在主句中用would，could或might加现在完成时。

　　　从句：过去完成时　　　　主句：might+现在完成时
If Lincoln had lived past the Civil War, he might have helped stabilize the country.

> **练习26.3**　调整时态的呼应：过去时或过去完成时

下面句子中的时态有正确的呼应。按要求改变一个动词的时态，然后据此改变另一个动词的时态，以维持动词的呼应。带星号部分的参考答案请见书后。

例子：

Delgado will call when he reaches his destination.（变will call成called）

Delgado called when he reached [or had reached] his destination.

*1. Diaries that Adolf Hitler is supposed to have written have surfaced in Germany.（变have surfaced成had surfaced）

*2. Many people believe that the diaries are authentic because a well-known historian has declared them so.（变believe成believed）

3. However, the historian's evaluation has been questioned by other authorities, who call the diaries forgeries.（变has been questioned成was questioned）

4. They claim, among other things, that the paper is not old enough to have been used by Hitler.（变claim成claimed）

5. Eventually, the doubters will win the debate because they have the best evidence.（变will win成won）

> **练习26.4**　改写：带条件句的时态呼应

给出下面括号里的每个动词的正确时态。带星号部分的参考答案请见书后。

例子：

If Babe Ruth or Jim Thorpe [be] athletes today, they [remind] us that even sports heroes must contend with a harsh reality.

If Babe Ruth or Jim Thorpe were athletes today, they might [or could or would] remind us that even sports heroes must contend with a harsh reality.

*1. When an athlete [turn] professional, he or she commits to a grueling regimen of mental and physical training.

*2. If athletes [be] less committed, they [disappoint] teammates, fans, and themselves.

*3. If professional athletes [be] very lucky, they may play until age forty.

*4. Unless an athlete achieves celebrity status, he or she [have] few employment choices after retirement.

*5. If professional sports [be] less risky, athletes [have] longer careers and more choices after retirement.

6. If you think you [be] exposed to the flu in the winter, you [get] a flu shot.

7. If you are allergic to eggs, you [have] an allergic reaction to the flu shot.

8. If you get the flu after having a flu shot, your illness [be] milder.

9. If you had had a flu shot last year, you [avoid] the illness.

10. If you [be] not so afraid of shots, you [will] get a flu shot every year.

第 27 章　动词语气

概要

- 正确使用虚拟语气，如I wish I were（p. 238）
- 保持语气一致（p. 239）

英语动词有三种可能的语气：**陈述语气**表述事实或观点，或提出问题：The theater needs help. Can you help the theater? **祈使语气**表达命令或给出指示，它省略句子的主语you：Help the theater. 更复杂的是**虚拟语气**，它表达愿望、建议和其他态度，使用he were和其他特别的动词形式，如下所述。

语法检查工具：语法检查工具能查出虚拟语气中的一些简单错误，但会遗漏其他错误。例如，能查出I wish I was home（应该是were home），但查不出If I had a hammer, I will hammer in the morning（应该是would hammer）。

27a 正确使用动词虚拟语气，如 I wish I were

虚拟语气表达建议、要求、愿望或与事实相反的条件（即想象或假设）。

- **有些动词表示要求或规定**，如ask, insist, urge, require, recommend和suggest。这些动词后面常跟以that开头、含有要求或规定意义的从句。不管主语是什么，that从句里的动词都用原形。

  　　　　　　　　　　　　　原形
  Rules require that every donation be mailed.

- **与事实相反的从句**表示想象或假设的状况，通常以if或unless开头，或者跟在wish之后。对于现在与事实相反的从句，用动词的过去时态（对于be动词，不论主语是什么都用过去时were）：

　　　　　　　过去时　　　　　　　　　　　　过去时
If the theater were in better shape and had more money, its future would be assured.

　　　　　　过去时
I wish I were able to donate money.

对于过去分词从句，用had加动词的过去分词：

　　　　　　　　　　　　　　　　　　　过去完成时
The theater would be better funded if it had been better managed last year.

注意：不要在以if开头的与事实相反的从句中使用助动词would或could。

不要用：Many people would have helped if they would have known.

而要用：Many people would have helped if they had known.

更多关于与事实相反的句子中的动词时态，见p. 236。

27b 保持语气一致

一个句子中或几个相关句子中语气的变换会令人困惑。这样的转换最常见于指令。

语气不一致：Cook the mixture slowly, and you should stir it until the sugar is dissolved.［语气从祈使语气转变为陈述语气］

改写：Cook the mixture slowly, and stir it until the sugar is dissolved.［语气一致］

练习27.1　改写：虚拟语气

以恰当的虚拟语气动词形式改写下列句子。带星号部分的参考答案请见书后。

例子：

I would help the old man if I was able to reach him.

I would help the old man if I were able to reach him.

*1. If John Hawkins would have known of all the dangerous side effects of smoking tobacco, would he have introduced the dried plant to England in 1565?

*2. Hawkins noted that if a Florida Indian man was to travel for several days, he would have smoked tobacco to satisfy his hunger and thirst.

3. Early tobacco growers feared that their product would not gain acceptance unless it was perceived as healthful.

4. To prevent fires, in 1646 the General Court of Massachusetts passed a law

requiring that colonists smoked tobacco only if they were five miles from any town.

5. To prevent decadence, in 1647 Connecticut passed a law mandating that one's smoking of tobacco was limited to once a day in one's own home.

第 28 章　动词的语态

概要

- 优先使用主动语态（下方）
- 当施动者不明或不重要时，使用被动语态（下页）
- 保持语态一致（p. 241）

动词的**语态**表明句子的主语是发出动作（主动），还是接受动作（被动）。

主动语态：She wrote the book. [主体执行动作]
　　　　　主语　动词

被动语态：The book was written by her. [主体接受动作]
　　　　　主语　　动词

被动语态总是由 be 的某种形式加主要动词的过去完成时构成：Rents are controlled. 对于 be，being 和 been，需要用其他的助词：Rents will be controlled. Rents are being controlled. Rents have been controlled. 被动语态中只能使用及物动词（带宾语的动词）。（见 p. 201）

28a 优先使用主动语态

主动语态通常比被动语态更清楚、更简洁、更直接。

弱表达被动态：The library is used by both students and teachers for studying and research, and the plan to expand it has been praised by many.

强表达主动态：Both students and teachers use the library for studying and research, and many have praised the plan to expand it.

28b 当施动者不明或不重要时，或者当指明施动者可能有所冒犯时，使用被动语态

当不能或不想指明施动者时，被动语态就有用了。

- 施动者不明、不重要或不如动作的接受者重要时用被动语态。在下列句子中，作者想要强调the Internet而不是the actors。

  The Internet was established in 1969 by the US Department of Defense.

  The network has been extended internationally to governments, universities, corporations, and private individuals.

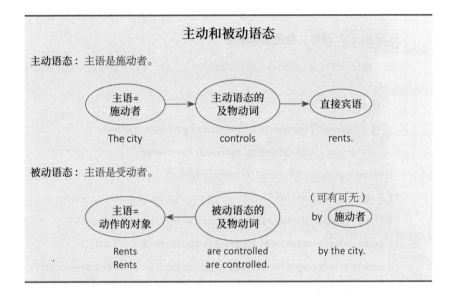

在下一个例子中，做实验的人，也许就是作者，不如过程重要。科技写作中普遍使用被动态。

  After the solution had been cooled to 10℃, the acid was added.

- 施动者对于动作应当是中立的。特别是在敏感写作中，被动语态的使用可以避免冒犯读者。在下一个例子中，不指明是谁拒绝了居民，这样可以关注动作本身，而不去指责某个特定的人。

  The residents of the shelter were turned away from your coffee shop.

  语法检查工具：大多数语法检查工具可以辨识被动语态，但无法决定被动语态的使用是否恰当，比如无法判断施动者是否不明。

28c 保持语态一致

转换语态会带来主语的转换,通常这样的做法既非必要又令人困惑。

不一致的主语和语态:Internet blogs cover an enormous range of topics. Opportunities for people to discuss pet issues are provided on these sites.

改写:Internet blogs cover an enormous range of topics and provide opportunities for people to discuss pet issues.

恰当的语态转换能帮助读者专注于单一主语。比如The candidate campaigned vigorously and was nominated on the first ballot.

练习28.1 改写:使用主动语态

把下列句子改写为主动语态,必要的时候加上主语。带星号部分的参考答案请见书后。

例子:

Contaminants are removed from water by treatment plants.

Treatment plants remove contaminants from water.

*1. Water quality is determined by many factors.

*2. Suspended and dissolved substances are contained in all natural waters.

*3. The amounts of the substances are controlled by the environment.

*4. Some dissolved substances are produced by pesticides.

*5. Sediment is deposited in water by fields, livestock feedlots, and other sources.

6. The bottom life of streams and lakes is affected by sediment.

7. Light penetration is reduced by sediment, and bottom-dwelling organisms may be smothered.

8. The quality of water in city systems is measured frequently.

9. If legal levels are exceeded by pollutants, the citizens must be notified by city officials.

10. The chlorine taste of water is disliked by many people.

练习28.2 主动语态和被动语态的转换

练习动词的两种语态,把下列句子中的主动语态和被动语态相互转换。(被动转成主动时,你可能需要加上一个主语)哪一种写法的句子看起来更有表现力,为什么？带星号部分的参考答案请见书后。

例子：

The actor was discovered in a nightclub.

A talent <u>scout</u> <u>discovered</u> the actor in a nightclub.

*1. When the Eiffel Tower was built in 1889, it was thought by the French to be ugly.

*2. At the time, many people still resisted industrial technology.

3. The tower's naked steel construction typified this technology.

4. Beautiful ornament was expected to grace fine buildings.

5. Further, a structure without solid walls could not even be called a building.

第 29 章　主谓一致

概要

在下列情况中，确保主谓一致：

- 当主谓之间插入了别的词语时（p. 245）
- 当多个主语由and连接时（p. 245）
- 当主语的各部分由or或nor连接时（p. 246）
- 有everyone和其他不定代词时（p. 246）
- 有诸如team之类的集合名词时（p. 247）
- 有who, which和that时（p. 247）
- 有news和其他以-s结尾的单数名词时（p. 248）
- 当动词在主语之前时（p. 248）
- 有is, are和其他系动词时（p. 249）
- 有头衔和被定义的词时（p. 249）

动词和它的主语在数量和人称上应当匹配，或者说一致：单数主语用单数动词，复数主语用复数动词，如下：

Daniel Inouye was the first Japanese American in Congress.
　主语　　 动词

More Japanese Americans live in Hawaii and California than elsewhere.
　　　　主语　　　　　动词

第四部分　句子成分和句型

大多数主谓一致的问题出现在主语的词尾被省略时，或者当句子各部分之间的关系不确定时。

语法检查工具：语法检查工具能抓住许多主谓一致的简单错误，例如，Addie and John is late，以及某些复杂一些的错误，例如，Is Margaret and Tom going with us?（两个句子中都应该用are），但是查不出The old group has gone their separate ways（应该是have）这样的错，对The old group have gone their separate ways这样的句子给出的修改意见也是错的，因为这句子本来就是正确的。

29a 名词和动词的词尾 -s 及 -es 作用不同

对于名词和动词来说，-s或-es词尾是相反的：它通常把名词变成复数，但总是把现在时态的动词变成单数。所以单数主语不会以-s结尾，但它的动词却会。复数名词会以-s结尾，但是它的动词却不会。主语和动词只有其一会有-s结尾。

单数主语	复数主语
The boy play**s**.	The boy**s** play.
The bird soar**s**.	The bird**s** soar.

这些规则的唯一例外是不规则的复数名词，如child/children, woman/women。不规则复数名词仍然要用复数的动词：The children play. The women sing.

（CULTURE LANGUAGE）如果你的母语或方言不是标准美式英语，主谓一致可能不容易，特别是有如下原因：

- 一些英语方言的单数动词省略-s词尾或者在复数动词上使用-s词尾。

    不标准：The voter resist change.
    标准：The voter resists change.
    标准：The voters resist change.

    动词be，不论在现在时还是过去时中，单复数形式都不同。（见p. 193）

    不标准：Taxes is high. They was raised just last year.
    标准：Taxes are high. They were raised just last year.

    have也有特别的-s形式has：

    不标准：The new tax have little chance of passing.
    标准：The new tax has little chance of passing.

- 在有些语言中，动词短语的各部分都要随主语变化，而在英语动词短语中，只有助动词be, have和do会随着主语变化。情态助动词，如can, may, should, will, would等不变化。

不标准：The tax mays pass next year.

标准：The tax may pass next year.

动词短语中的主要动词也不随主语变化。

不标准：The tax may passes next year.

标准：The tax may pass next year.

29b 即使有别的词插在主谓之间，主谓也需要保持一致

The survival of hibernating frogs in freezing temperatures is [不是 are] fascinating.

A chemical reaction inside the cells of the frogs stops [不是 stop] the formation of ice crystals.

注意：以as well as, together with, along with, 及in addition to开头的短语不会改变主语的数。

The president, together with the deans, has [不是 have] agreed to revise the catalog.

29c 由and连接的主语通常用复数动词

Frost and Roethke were contemporaries.

例外：当主语的各部分构成一个单一的思想或者指的是单个人或事物的时候，用单数动词：

Avocado and bean sprouts is a California sandwich.

当复合主语之前有形容词each或every时，动词通常用单数：

Each man, woman, and child has a right to be heard.

29d 当主语的各部分由 or 或 nor 连接时，动词与较近的部分保持一致

Either the painter or the carpenter knows the cost.

The cabinets or the bookcases are too costly.

当主语的一部分是单数而另一部分是复数时，为了避免别扭，把复数部分放在靠近动词的位置，这样动词就用复数形式：

别扭：Neither the owners nor the contractor agrees.

改写：Neither the contractor nor the owners agree.

29e 主语是 everyone 和其他不定代词时，视情况用单数或复数动词

大多数不定代词的意义是单数的，指的是一个不确定的人或事物，它们用单数动词：

Something smells.　　Neither is right.

有四个不定代词总是复数意义：both, few, many, several。

Both are correct.　　Several were invited.

有六个不定代词可能是单数意义也可能是复数意义：all, any, more, most, none, some。其动词用单数还是复数要看代词指的是什么：

All of the money is reserved for emergencies.［all 指的是 money］

All of the funds are reserved for emergencies.［all 指的是 funds］

none，即便它指的是复数名词，也可以是单数的，是为了特别强调"没有一个"的意思。None［没有一个］of the animals has a home.

（CULTURE LANGUAGE）见 p. 276 关于 few（not many）和 a few（some）之间的区别。

29f 集合名词，如 team，依其意思而用单数或复数动词

当这个群体作为一个整体而行动时，用单数动词：

The team has won five of the last six meets.

但当群体的成员不是联合行动而是各自行动时，用复数动词：

The old team have gone their separate ways.

如果team have这样的说法听起来很别扭的时候，改变一下句子的说法：The members of the old team have gone their separate ways.

集合名词number可以是单数也可以是复数。前面是a时，它是复数；前面是the时，它是单数：

A number of people are in debt.

The number of people in debt is very large.

CULTURE LANGUAGE 有一些不可数名词是集合名词，因为它们指明的是群体，如furniture，clothing，mail。这些不可数名词通常用单数动词：Mail arrives daily. 但是也有一些是用复数动词的，包括clergy，military，people，police和由形容词变来的名词如the poor，the rich，the young，the elderly之类。如果你指的是群体里的一个代表，用单数名词police officer或poor person。

29g who，which 和 that 接的动词与它们的先行词保持一致

当who，which和that用作主语时，它们指的是句子中的另一个词，称为先行词。动词与先行词保持一致。

Mayor Garber ought to listen to the people who work for her.

Bardini is the only aide who has her ear.

当句子中包含了one of the或the only one of the时，通常会出现与who和that有关的一致性问题：

Bardini is one of the aides who work unpaid. [Of the aides who work unpaid, Bardini is one.]

Bardini is the only one of the aides who knows the community. [Of the aides, only one, Bardini, knows the community.]

🌐 以one of the开头的短语中，要确保名词是复数的：Bardini is one of the aides [不是 aide] who work unpaid.

29h news 和其他一些以 -s 结尾的单数名词用单数动词

以 -s 结尾的单数名词包括 athletics, economics, linguistics, mathematics, measles, mumps, news, physics, politics 和 statistics，还有如 Athens, Wales 和 United States 等地名。

After so long a wait, the news has to be good.

Statistics is required of psychology majors.

这些词中有几个会用复数动词，但只有当它们指的是多个个体而不是活动整体或知识整体时才会用复数动词：The statistics prove him wrong.

以 -s 结尾的数词和度量词也可以是单数，当它们所指的数量是个整体的时候：

Three years is a long time to wait.

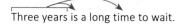
Three-fourths of the library consists of reference books.

29i 即使动词在主语之前，也要与主语保持一致

动词出现在主语之前，主要是在问句中和以 there 或 here 及 be 的某种形式开头的结构中：

Is voting a right or a privilege?

Are a right and a privilege the same thing?

There are differences between them.

29j is, are 和其他系动词与主语保持一致，而不是与主语补足语保持一致

让系动词与主语——通常是句子中的第一个成分——保持一致，而不是与作为主语补足语的名词或代词保持一致。

The child's sole support is her court-appointed guardians.

Her court-appointed guardians are the child's sole support.

29k 头衔和被定义的词用单数动词

Hakada Associates is a new firm.

Dream Days remains a favorite book.

Folks is a down-home word for *people*.

练习29.1　改写：主谓一致

如果需要，改写下列句子中的动词以保持主语和谓语动词在数量上一致。如果句子本来就是对的，标记其序号。带星号部分的参考答案请见书后。

例子：

Each of the job applicants type sixty words per minute.

Each of the job applicants types sixty words per minute.

*1. Weinstein & Associates are a consulting firm that try to make businesspeople laugh.

*2. Results from recent research shows that humor relieves stress.

*3. Reduced stress in businesses in turn reduce illness and absenteeism.

*4. In special conferences held by one consultant, each of the participants practice making others laugh.

*5. "Isn't there enough laughs within you to spread the wealth?" the consultant asks his students.

6. The consultant quotes Casey Stengel's rule that the best way to keep your management job is to separate the underlings who hate you from the ones who have not decided how they feel.

7. Such self-deprecating comments in public is uncommon among business managers, the consultant says.

8. Each of the managers in a typical firm take the work much too seriously.

9. The humorous boss often feels like the only one of the managers who have other things in mind besides profits.

10. One consultant to many companies suggest cultivating office humor with practical jokes such as a rubber fish in the water cooler.

11. When a manager or employees regularly posts cartoons on the bulletin board, office spirit usually picks up.

12. When someone who has seemed too easily distracted is entrusted with updating the cartoons, his or her concentration often improves.

13. In the face of levity, the former sourpuss becomes one of those who hides bad temper.

14. Reduced stress can reduce friction within an employee group, which then work together more productively.

15. Every one of the consultants caution, however, that humor has no place in life-affecting corporate situations such as employee layoffs.

练习29.2 调整句子以保持主谓一致

改写下面段落，把带下画线的词从复数改为单数。（你可能会需要如例句中一样给单数名词加上a或the）然后如果需要的话改变动词以使之与新的主语保持一致。第一段的答案见书后。

例子：

Siberian tigers are an endangered subspecies.

The Siberian tiger is an endangered subspecies.

*Siberian tigers are the largest living cats in the world, much bigger than their relative the Bengal tiger. *They grow to a length of nine to twelve feet, including their tails, and to a height of about three and a half feet. *They can weigh over six hundred pounds. *These carnivorous hunters live in northern China and Korea as well as in Siberia. *During the long winter of this Arctic climate, the yellowish striped <u>coats</u> get a little lighter in order to blend with the snow-covered landscape. *The <u>coats</u> also grow quite thick because the <u>tigers</u> have to withstand temperatures as low as-50°F.

<u>Siberian tigers</u> sometimes have to travel great distances to find food. <u>They</u> need about twenty pounds of food a day because of <u>their</u> size and the cold climate, but when <u>they</u> have fresh food <u>they</u> may eat as much as a hundred pounds at one time. <u>They</u> hunt mainly deer, boars, and even bears, plus smaller prey such as fish and rabbits. <u>They</u> pounce on <u>their</u> prey and grab <u>them</u> by the back of the neck. <u>Animals</u> that are not killed immediately are thrown to the ground and suffocated with a bite to the throat. Then the <u>tigers</u> feast.

代词

251

代词是指代名词的词，如she和who，需要我们特别注意，因为它们的意义完全来自它们所指代的别的词。本部分讨论代词的格（第30章）、代词与所指代的词的一致（第31章）以及清楚的指代（第32章）。

第30章 代词的格

概要

- 区分复合主语和复合宾语：She and I 与her and me（下页）
- 主语补足语中使用代词主格（p. 253）
- 根据代词在从句中的功能决定使用who还是whom（p. 254）
- 在其他结构中使用恰当的格，例如，在than或as之后或与不定式连用时（p. 256）

选择代词的正确的格，及正确的形式，如用she还是her，需要理解代词在句子中如何起作用。

- **主格**表明该代词是主语或者主语补足语。
- **宾格**表明该代词是宾语或者宾语补足语。
- **所有格**表示该代词拥有句中的一个名词或者是它的来源。

252

主格	宾格	所有格
I	me	my, mine
you	you	your, yours
he	him	his
she	her	her, hers
it	it	its
we	us	our, ours
you	you	your, yours
they	them	their, theirs
who	whom	whose
whoever	whomever	—

语法检查工具：语法检查工具能查出一些代词的格的错误，但会错过很多。例如，能查出 We asked whom would come（应该是 who），但查不出 We dreaded them coming（应该是 their）。

标准美式英语中，-self 代词不变形。它们的唯一形式就是 myself, yourself, himself, herself, itself, ourselves, yourselves, themselves。避免使用非标准的 hisself, ourself 和 theirselves。

错误：Novick presented the proposal hisself.

改写：Novick presented the proposal himself.

30a 区分复合主语和复合宾语：she and I 与 her and me

复合主语和复合宾语由两个或两个以上的名词或代词组成，其格形式与单独一个名词或代词的格形式相同。

　　　　　复合主语
She and Novick discussed the proposal.

　　　　　　　　　　　　复合宾语
The proposal disappointed her and him.

如果对正确词形没把握，可以做做下面的测试。

> **测试复合结构中的格**
>
> 1. 识别复合结构（以and, but, or, nor连接的结构）：
>   [He, Him] and [I, me] won the prize.
>   The prize went to [he, him] and [I, me].
> 2. 给复合结构中的每个部分写一个单独的句子：
>   [He, Him] won the prize. [I, Me] won the prize.
>   The prize went to [he, him]. The prize went to [I, me].
> 3. 选择"听"起来正确的代词：
>   He won the prize. I won the prize.[主格]
>   The prize went to him. The prize went to me.[宾格]
> 4. 把单独的句子再拼回来：
>   He and I won the prize.
>   The prize went to him and me.

30b 在主语补足语中使用主格：It was she.

在系动词之后，重述主语的代词（主语补足语）应该用主格：

　　　　　　　　　　　　　　主语补足语
The ones who care most are she and Novick.

　　　　主语补足语
It was they whom the mayor appointed.

如果这个结构你看起来感到别扭，就换一个更自然的语序：She and Novick are the ones who care most. The mayor appointed them.

> **练习30.1　选择代词的主格或宾格**
>
> 请从下列句子括号里的一对词中，选择恰当的主格或宾格代词。带星号部分的参考答案请见书后。
>
> 　　例子：
>
> 　　"Between you and [I, me]," the seller said, "this deal is a steal."
>
> 　　"Between you and me," the seller said, "this deal is a steal."
>
> *1. Kayla and [I, me] were competing for places on the relay team.
>
> *2. The fastest runners at our school were [she, her] and [I, me], so [we, us] expected to make the team.

3. [She, Her] and [I, me] were friends but also intense rivals.

4. The time trials went badly, excluding both [she, her] and [I, me] from the team.

5. Next season [she, her] and [I, me] are determined to earn places on the team.

30c 用 who 还是 whom 取决于代词在句子中的功能

1 ▪ 问句

在句首，用 who 做主语，whom 做宾语：

主语 →
Who wrote the policy?

宾语 ←
Whom does it affect?

要找到问句中正确的格，请按下列步骤来做：

1. 提出问题：

[Who, Whom] makes that decision?

[Who, Whom] does one ask?

2. 用人称代词回答问题。选择看起来正确的代词，并注意它的格：

[She, Her] makes that decision. She makes that decision.［主格］

One asks [she, her]. One asks her.［宾格］

3. 在问句中使用同样的格（who 或 whom）：

Who makes that decision?［主格］

Whom does one ask?［宾格］

2 ▪ 从句

在从句中，主语用 who 或 whoever，宾语用 whom 或 whomever：

主语 →
Give old clothes to whoever needs them.

宾语 ←
I don't know whom the mayor appointed.

要确定用哪种格，做做下面的测试。

1. 找到从句的位置：

Few people know [who, whom] they should ask.

They are unsure [who, whom] makes the decision.

2. 把从句重写为一个单独的句子，用人称代词替换 who, whom。选择看起来正确的代词，并注意它的格：

They should ask [she, her]. They should ask her.［宾格］

[She, her] usually makes the decision. She usually makes the decision.［主格］

3. 在从句中使用相同的格（who或whom）：

Few people know whom they should ask.［宾格］

They are unsure who makes the decision.［主格］

注意：不要受I think和she says之类的表达误导而给从句的主语用了whom而不是who。

　　　　　　　　　主语
He is the one who I think is best qualified.

在这样的结构中选择用who还是whom时，要去掉插入的短语，以便看到各部分之间真正的关系：He is the one who is best qualified.

练习30.2　选择who或whom

从下列句子括号里的一对词中，选择合适的代词形式。带星号部分的参考答案请见书后。

例子：

My mother asked me [who, whom] I was meeting.

My mother asked me whom I was meeting.

*1. The school administrators suspended Jurgen, [who, whom] they suspected of setting the fire.

*2. Jurgen had been complaining to other custodians, [who, whom] reported him.

*3. He constantly complained of unfair treatment from [whoever, whomever] happened to be passing in the halls, including pupils.

*4. "[Who, Whom] here has heard Mr. Jurgen's complaints?" the police asked.

*5. "[Who, Whom] did he complain most about?"

6. His coworkers agreed that Jurgen seemed less upset with the staff or students, most of [who, whom] he did not even know, than with the building itself.

7. "He took out his aggression on the building," claimed one coworker [who, whom] often witnessed Jurgen's behavior.

8. "He cursed and kicked the walls and [whoever, whomever] he saw nearby."

9. The coworker thought that Jurgen might have imagined people [who, whom] instructed him to behave the way he did.

10. "He's someone [who, whom] other people can't get next to," said the coworker.

30d 在其他结构中使用正确的格

1 ▪ we或us与名词连用

名词之前用we还是us取决于名词的作用：

　　　　　　　　　　　　　　　　介词
　　　　　　　　　　　　　　　▸ 宾语
Freezing weather is welcomed by us skaters.

主语 ▸
We skaters welcome freezing weather.

2 ▪ 同位语中的代词

在同位语中，代词的格取决于同位语所描述或等同的词的功能。

　　　　　　　　　　　　　　　　同位语标识对象
The class elected two representatives, DeShawn and me.

　　　　　　　　　同位语标识对象
Two representatives, DeShawn and I, were elected.

3 ▪ than或as之后的代词

当代词在一个比较中跟在than或as之后时，代词的格提示省略掉的是什么词。主格代词一定是被省略的动词的主语：

　　　　　　　　　　　　　　　主语
Some critics like Glass more than he [does].

宾格代词一定是被省略的动词的宾语：

　　　　　　　　　　　　　　　　　　　　宾语
Some critics like Glass more than [they like] him.

4 ▪ 不定式的主语和宾语

不定式的主语和宾语都用宾格。

　　　　　　　不定式的主语
The school asked him to speak.

　　　　　　　　　　不定式的宾语
Students chose to invite him.

5 ▪ 动名词之前的格

通常，如果一个代词或名词紧挨在动名词之前，用它们的所有格。

The coach disapproved of their lifting weights.

The coach's disapproving was a surprise.

练习30.3　改写：代词的格

改写下面句子中不恰当的代词形式。如果句子本来就是对的，在其序号上做标记。带星号部分的参考答案请见书后。

例子：

Convincing we veterans to vote yes will be difficult.

Convincing us veterans to vote yes will be difficult.

*1. Written four thousand years ago, *The Epic of Gilgamesh* tells of a bored king who his people thought was too harsh.

*2. Gilgamesh found a source of entertainment when he met Enkidu, a wild man who had lived with the animals in the mountains.

*3. Him and Gilgamesh wrestled to see whom was more powerful.

*4. After hours of struggle, Enkidu admitted that Gilgamesh was stronger than he.

*5. The friendship of the two strong men was sealed by them fighting.

6. Gilgamesh said, "Between you and I, mighty deeds will be accomplished, and our fame will be everlasting."

7. Among their glorious acts, Enkidu and him defeated a giant bull, Humbaba, and cut down the bull's cedar forests.

8. Their bringing back cedar logs to Gilgamesh's treeless land won great praise from the people.

9. When Enkidu died, Gilgamesh mourned his death, realizing that no one had been a better friend than him.

10. When Gilgamesh himself died many years later, his people raised a monument praising Enkidu and he for their friendship and their mighty deeds of courage.

第 31 章 代词和先行词的一致

概要

确保代词和其先行词在下列情形中保持一致：
- 当多个先行词由and连接时（下方）
- 当先行词的各部分由or或nor连接时（p. 259）
- 有everyone, person及其他不定代词时（p. 259）
- 有team之类的集合名词时（p. 261）

每个代词都要与其**先行词**在数量、人称和性上保持一致，先行词即代词所指的词。本章讨论单数和复数先行词以及代替它们的代词。

语法检查工具：语法检查工具在代词与先行词的一致上提供不了帮助，因为无法识别二者之间应有的关系。

CULTURE LANGUAGE 代词的性应该与其先行词一致，而不是与它可能修饰的名词一致：Sara asked her [not his] son. 同样，英语中的名词只有中性，除非它们特别指向男性或女性。所以book, sun和earth之类的名词用代词it：Read this book. It is inspiring.

31a 由 and 连接的多个先行词通常用复数代词

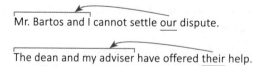

例外：当复合先行词指的是单一的概念、人或事物时，代词就是单数：

My friend and adviser offered her help.

当复合先行词跟在each或every后面时，代词是单数：

Every girl and woman took her seat.

31b 当先行词的各部分由 or 或 nor 连接时，代词与就近的部分保持一致

Tenants or owners must present their grievances.

Either the tenant or the owner will have her way.

当一个主语是复数而另一个主语是单数时，要把复数主语放在第二，否则句子会很别扭：

别扭：Neither the tenants nor the owner has yet made her case.

改写：Neither the owner nor the tenants have yet made their case.

31c 有 everyone, person 和其他先行词时，视情况用单数或复数代词

不定词——**不定代词**和**种类名词**——不特指任何具体的人或物。大多数不定代词和所有的类别名词在意义上都是单数。当它们作为先行词时，用单数代词。

Each of the animal shelters has its population of homeless pets.
  不定代词

Every worker in our shelter cares for his or her favorite animal.
  种类名词

有四个不定代词在意义上是复数：both, few, many, several。作为先行词时，它们用复数单词。

Many of the animals show affection for their caretakers.

有六个不定代词在意义上可以是单数也可以是复数：all, any, more, most, none, some。作为先行词时，如果指向单数词则用单数代词，如果指向复数词则用复数代词。

Most of the shelter's equipment was donated by its original owner.［most是指equipment］

Most of the veterinarians donate their time.［most是指veterinarians］

none即使指向复数词，也可能是单数意义，特别是当它强调"没有一个"的意思时。None［不是one］of the shelters has increased its capacity.

大多数代词一致的问题出在单数不定词上。我们常用这些词来表达"many"或"all"的意义而不是"one"，然后用复数代词来指代它们，比如在Everyone has their own locker或者A person can padlock their locker中。我们也常常想用不定词来涵盖阳性和阴性，这样可以用they等词——而不用he等阳性代词——来指向两性，如在Everyone deserves his privacy中。（关于这个很多读者认为有性别歧视的代词he的更多内容，见p. 169）

尽管有些专家能接受把they, them和their用在单数不定词上，大多数人都不认可这样做，很多老师和雇主认为这样的做法是不正确的。为安全起见，涉及单数不定词和指向它们的代词时，你有几个选择：

确保不定词的一致的几个正确做法

- 把不定词改为复数词，然后用复数代词来匹配。
  错误：Every athlete deserves their privacy.
  改写：Athletes deserve their privacy.
- 重写句子以省略代词。
  错误：Everyone is entitled to their own locker.
  改写：Everyone is entitled to a locker.
- 用he or she（him or her, his or her）来指称不定词。
  错误：Now everyone has their private space.
  改写：Now everyone has his or her private space.

然而，he or she的用法如果在几个句子中出现不止一次，很快就会显得别扭。（很多读者不接受he/she的替代写法）大多数情况下，用复数或省略代词的做法不仅能修正一致的问题，也会使句子更通顺可读。

31d 集合名词，如 team，视情况用单数或复数代词

如果一个**集合名词**指代作为一个整体的群体，用单数代词：

The committee voted to disband itself.

当提到团体中的单个成员时，用复数代词：

The old team have gone their separate ways.

如果team have . . . their这样的说法看起来很别扭，就换个说法：The members of the old team have gone their separate ways.

CULTURE LANGUAGE 在标准美式英语中，不可数名词（它们没有复数）的集合名词通常用单数代词：The mail sits in its own basket. 但是有几个不可数名词用复数代词，包括clergy，military，police，the rich和the poor：The police support their unions.

练习31.1　改写：代词和先行词的一致

改写下列句子，使代词和先行词在人称和数上一致。有些题有不止一个可能的答案。避免使用阳性代词he。（见p. 260）如果改变句子的主语，那么必要的话也要改变动词以保持一致。如果句子本来就是对的，在其序号上做标记。带星号部分的参考答案请见书后。

例子：

Each of the Boudreaus' children brought their laundry home at Thanksgiving.

All of the Boudreaus' children brought their laundry home at Thanksgiving.
Or: Each of the Boudreaus' children brought laundry home at Thanksgiving.
Or: Each of the Boudreaus' children brought his or her laundry home at Thanksgiving.

*1. Each girl raised in a Mexican American family in the Rio Grande Valley of Texas hopes that one day they will be given a *quinceañera* party for their fifteenth birthday.

*2. Such celebrations are very expensive because it entails a religious service followed by a huge party.

*3. A girl's immediate family, unless they are wealthy, cannot afford the party by themselves.

*4. The parents will ask each close friend or relative if they can help with the preparations.

*5. Surrounded by her family and attended by her friends and their escorts, the *quinceañera* is introduced as a young woman eligible for Mexican American society.

6. Almost any child will quickly astound observers with their capabilities.

7. Despite their extensive research and experience, neither child psychologists nor parents have yet figured out how children become who they are.

8. Of course, the family has a tremendous influence on the development of a child in their midst.

9. Each member of the immediate family exerts their own unique pull on the child.

10. Other relatives, teachers, and friends also can affect the child's view of the world and of themselves.

11. The workings of genetics also strongly influence the child, but it may never be fully understood.

12. The psychology community cannot agree in its views of whether nurture or nature is more important in a child's development.

13. Another debated issue is whether the child's emotional development or their intellectual development is more central.

14. Just about everyone has their strong opinion on these issues, often backed up by evidence.

15. Neither the popular press nor scholarly journals devote much of their space to the wholeness of the child.

第 32 章　代词对先行词的指向

概要

- 使代词清楚地指向一个先行词（下页）
- 把代词放在离先行词足够近的位置，以确保指代清晰（p. 264）
- 使代词指向一个确定的先行词（p. 264）
- 指向读者的时候，只用 you（p. 265）
- 保持代词的一致（p. 265）

代词应该清楚地指向它的**先行词**，即它所指代的那一个或多个名词。否则，读者会很难弄清楚代词的意思。写作的时候，要确保每个代词都指向一个清楚的、靠近的、确定的先行词。

语法检查工具：语法检查工具查不出指代不明的代词。例如，查不出来下面的那些令人困惑的例子。

🌐 CULTURE LANGUAGE　在标准美式英语中，代词需要一个清楚的就近的先行词，但不要把代词及其先行词同时作为同一个句子的主语：Jim［不是Jim he］told Mark to go alone.（见pp. 300–301）

32a 使代词清楚地指向一个先行词

如果两个名词都可以作为一个代词的先行词，那么就会指代不明：

令人困惑的句子：Emily Dickinson is sometimes compared with Jane Austen, but she led a more reclusive life.

可以用两种办法改写这样的句子：

- 用恰当的名词取代代词：

清楚的句子：Emily Dickinson is sometimes compared with Jane Austen, but Dickinson led a more reclusive life.

- 重写句子，避免重复。如果用该代词，要确保它只有一个可能的先行词。

清楚的句子：Despite occasional comparison of their lives, Emily Dickinson was more reclusive than Jane Austen.

清楚的句子：Though sometimes compared with her, Emily Dickinson led a more reclusive life than Jane Austen.

32b 把代词放在离先行词足够近的位置，以确保指代清晰

以who，which或that开头的句子通常应该紧跟在它所指的词之后：

令人困惑的句子：Jody found a dress in the attic that her aunt had worn.

清楚的句子：In the attic Jody found a dress that her aunt had worn.

32c 使代词指向一个确定的，而不是暗示的先行词

一个代词应该指向一个确定的名词或其他代词。如果代词的先行词只是由上下文暗示而没有明示，那么读者就只能猜测其意思。

1 ▪ 含义模糊的this, that, which或it

this, that, which或it应该指向一个确定的名词,而不是表达思想或情形的一整个句群。

令人困惑的句子:The faculty agreed on changing the requirements, but it took time.

清楚的句子:The faculty agreed on changing the requirements, but the agreement took time.

清楚的句子:The faculty agreed on changing the requirements, but the change took time.

令人困惑的句子:The British knew little of the American countryside, and they had no experience with the colonists' guerrilla tactics. This gave the colonists an advantage.

清楚的句子:The British knew little of the American countryside, and they had no experience with the colonists' guerrilla tactics. This ignorance and inexperience gave the colonists an advantage.

2 ▪ 带it和they的不定先行词

it和they应该有确定的名词先行词。如果先行词缺失,需要重写句子。

令人困惑的句子:In Chapter 4 of this book it describes the early flights of the Wright brothers.

清楚的句子:Chapter 4 of this book describes the early flights of the Wright brothers.

令人困惑的句子:Even in TV reality shows, they present a false picture of life.

清楚的句子:Even TV reality shows present a false picture of life.

清楚的句子:Even in TV reality shows, the producers present a false picture of life.

3 ▪ 暗含的名词

有时一个名词会由某个别的词或词组暗含，比如一个形容词（happy里暗含着happiness）、一个动词（drive里暗含着driver）或一个所有格（mother's里暗含着mother）。但是代词无法指代这样暗含的名词，只能指代确定的明示的名词。

令人困惑的句子：In Cohen's report she made claims that led to a lawsuit.

清楚的句子：In her report Cohen made claims that led to a lawsuit.

令人困惑的句子：Her reports on psychological development generally go unnoticed outside it.

清楚的句子：Her reports on psychological development generally go unnoticed outside the field.

32d 指代"你，读者"时，只能用"you"

除学术写作之外的所有正式写作中，用you清楚地指代读者是可以接受的。但是上下文必须适合这样一个意思：

不合适：In the fourteenth century you had to struggle simply to survive.

改写：In the fourteenth century one [或者 a person] had to struggle simply to survive.

作者有时候不由地就用上了you，因为很难持续使用one，a person或类似的不定词。一句一句地说下来，不定词会显得臃肿，而且会需要使用he或者he or she来达成代词和先行词的一致。（见pp. 259-261）为了避免这样的问题，可以用复数名词和代词：

原句：In the fourteenth century one had to struggle simply to survive.

改写：In the fourteenth century people had to struggle simply to survive.

32e 保持代词一致

在一个句子中或一组相关的句子中，代词应当一致。（见第31章）一方面，代词和它们的先行词一致才能连贯，另外，一个篇章内的代词也应该互相匹配。

不一致的代词：One finds when reading that your concentration improves with practice, so that I now comprehend more in less time.

改写：I find when reading that my concentration improves with practice, so that I now comprehend more in less time.

练习32.1　改写：代词的指代

下列句子中，很多代词没有清楚、确定和恰当的先行词。必要的话改写句子以纠正这样的错误。带星号部分的参考答案请见书后。

例子：

In Grand Teton National Park they have moose, elk, and trumpeter swans.

Moose, elk, and trumpeter swans live in Grand Teton National Park.

*1. "Life begins at forty" is a cliché many people live by, and this may or may not be true.

*2. Living successfully or not depends on one's definition of it.

*3. When she was forty, Pearl Buck's novel *The Good Earth* won the Pulitzer Prize.

*4. Buck was raised in a missionary family in China, and she wrote about it in her novels.

*5. In *The Good Earth* you have to struggle, but fortitude is rewarded.

6. Buck received much critical praise and earned over $7 million, but she was very modest about it.

7. Pearl Buck donated most of her earnings to a foundation for Asian American children that proves her generosity.

8. In the *Book of Romance* it reserves a chapter for the story of Elizabeth Barrett, who at forty married Robert Browning against her father's wishes.

9. In the 1840s they did not normally defy their fathers, but Elizabeth was too much in love to obey.

10. She left a poetic record of her love for Robert, and readers still enjoy reading them.

练习32.2　改写：代词的指代

改写下列段落，使每个代词清楚地指向单个、确定、恰当的先行词。带星号部分的参考答案请见书后。

　　*In Charlotte Brontë's *Jane Eyre*, she is a shy young woman that takes a job as governess. *Her employer is a rude, brooding man named Rochester. *He lives in a mysterious mansion on the English moors, which contributes an eerie quality to Jane's experience. *Eerier still are the fires, strange noises, and other unexplained happenings in the house; but Rochester refuses to discuss this. Eventually, they fall in love. On the day they are to be married, however, she learns that he has a wife hidden in the house. She is hopelessly insane and violent and must be guarded at all times, which explains his strange behavior. Heartbroken, Jane leaves the moors, and many years pass before they are reunited.

修饰语

修饰语描写或限制句子中别的词语。它们是形容词、副词，或当形容词或副词用的词群。本部分讲解怎样识别和解决修饰语形式中的问题（第33章）以及它们与句子其他部分的关系的问题（第34章）。

第 33 章　形容词和副词

概要

- 用形容词修饰名词和代词（p. 268）
- 在系动词之后使用形容词来修饰主语，用副词修饰动词（p. 268）
- 正确使用比较级和最高级形式（p. 269）
- 避免大多数双重否定（p. 271）
- 区分现在分词形容词和过去分词形容词（p. 272）
- 正确使用a, an, the和其他限定词（p. 273）

形容词修饰名词（happy child）和代词（special someone）。副词修饰动词（almost see）、形容词（very happy）、其他副词（not very），以及整个的词群（Otherwise, I'll go.）判断一个修饰语应该是形容词还是副词的唯一办法是确定它在句子中的功能。

语法检查工具：对于形容词和副词的误用，语法检查工具只能找出一部分。例如，能查出Some children suffer bad and James did not see nothing，但查不出Educating children good should be everyone's focus.

🌐 在标准美式英语中，形容词不随所修饰的名词变化来表示复数：white［不是whites］shoes, square［不是squares］spaces, better［不是betters］

chances。只有名词有复数。

33a 形容词只用来修饰名词和代词

用形容词而不是副词来修饰动词、副词或其他形容词不是标准美式英语的做法。

错误：Educating children good should be everyone's focus.

改写：Educating children well should be everyone's focus.

错误：Some children suffer bad.

改写：Some children suffer badly.

CULTURE LANGUAGE 在not和no之间做选择有点难。not是副词，所以它否定动词或形容词：They do not learn. They are not happy. They have not been in class. （了解not和动词及形容词的位置关系，见p. 281）no是形容词，它否定名词：No child likes to fail. No good school fails children. 把no放在名词或其他修饰语之前。

33b 在系动词后使用形容词修饰主语，用副词修饰动词

有些动词可以当系动词也可以不当系动词，取决于它们在句子中的意义。当动词后的词修饰主语时，该动词是系动词，那个修饰词应该是形容词：He looked happy. The milk turned sour. 而当动词后的词修饰动词时，那个修饰词应当是副词：He looked carefully. The car turned suddenly.

有两对词特别容易出错。一对是bad和badly：

The weather grew bad.
系动词 形容词

She felt bad.
系动词 形容词

Flowers grow badly in such soil.
动词 副词

另一种棘手的组合是good和well。good只能用作形容词。well可以用作副词，具有多种意思，也可以用作形容词，只表示适合或健康。

Decker felt well.　　　　Her health was good.　　　She trained well.
系动词 形容词　　　　系动词 形容词　　　　动词 副词

练习33.1　改写：形容词和副词

改写下列句子，正确使用形容词和副词。如果句子本来就是正确的，在其序号上做标记。带星号部分的参考答案请见书后。

例子：

The announcer warned loud and clear that traffic was stopped on the bridge.

The announcer warned loudly and clearly that traffic was stopped on the bridge.

*1. People who take their health serious often believe that movie-theater popcorn is a healthy snack.

*2. Nutrition information about movie popcorn may make these people feel different.

3. One large tub of movie popcorn has twelve hundred calories and sixty grams of saturated fat—both surprisingly high numbers.

4. Once people are aware of the calories and fat, they may feel badly about indulging in this classic snack.

5. People who want to eat good should think twice before ordering popcorn at the movies.

33c　正确使用形容词和副词的比较级、最高级形式

利用-er和-est词尾或者more和most 或less和least这样的词，形容词和副词可以表示品质或数量的程度。大多数修饰语有三种形式。

原级：字典中列出的原形	比较级：更高或更低程度的品质	最高级：最高或最低程度的品质
形容词		
red	redder	reddest
awful	more/less awful	most/least awful

副词

soon	sooner	soonest
quickly	more/less quickly	most/least quickly

270 　　如果光靠听还不能确定究竟用-er/-est或more/most，请查字典。如果能用词尾表示，字典会列出来。否则，就用more或most。

1 ▪ 不规则形容词和副词

不规则修饰语要靠改变原级的拼写来表示比较和最高的程度。

原级	比较级	最高级
形容词		
good	better	best
bad	worse	worst
little	littler, less	littlest, least
many		
some ｝	more	most
much		
副词		
well	better	best
badly	worse	worst

2 ▪ 双重比较

双重比较级或双重最高级同时使用了-er/-est词尾和more/most。这是冗余的。

Chang was the wisest [不是 most wisest] person in town.

He was smarter [不是 more smarter] than anyone else.

3 ▪ 逻辑比较

绝对/极限修饰语

有些形容词和副词无法进行逻辑的比较——例如，perfect, unique, dead, impossible, infinite。这些绝对词前面可以有副词，比如表示"接近"的nearly或almost，但它们无法用more或most来进行合乎逻辑的修饰（如most perfect）。

错误：He was the most unique teacher we had.

正确：He was a unique teacher.

完整性

要做合乎逻辑的比较，就必须在下列方面做到完整：

- **所做比较需要给出一个完整的关系以达到清楚明晰。**

  不清楚：Carmakers worry about their industry more than environmentalists.

  清楚：Carmakers worry about their industry more than environmentalists do.

  清楚：Carmakers worry about their industry more than they worry about environmentalists.

- **所比较的事项应该是可比的。**

  不合逻辑：The cost of a hybrid car can be greater than a gasoline-powered car.［不合理地比较成本和汽车］

  改写：The cost of a hybrid car can be greater than the cost of［或者that of］a gasoline-powered car.

关于比较的对称，见pp. 156–157。

any与any other

把某事物与同类中其他事物做比较时，用any other。把某事物与不同类的其他事物做比较时，用any。

不合逻辑：Los Angeles is larger than any city in California.［因为洛杉矶本身就是加州的一个城市，所以这句话似乎在说洛杉矶比它自己还大］

改写：Los Angeles is larger than any other city in California.

不合逻辑：Los Angeles is larger than any other city in Canada.［加拿大的城市构成了一个洛杉矶不属于的群体］

改写：Los Angeles is larger than any city in Canada.

33d 当心双重否定

在双重否定中，两个否定词，例如，no, not, none, barely, hardly或scarcely互相抵消。有些双重否定是作者有意为之，如She was not unhappy是故意低调，意指她其实很高兴。但是大多数双重否定其实是事与愿违：Jenny did not feel nothing是想说Jenny感觉到了什么，要表达相反的意思，必须去掉其中一个否定词（She felt nothing），或者把一个否定词改成肯定的说法（She did not feel anything）。

错误：The IRS cannot hardly audit all tax returns. None of its audits never touch many cheaters.

改写：The IRS cannot audit all tax returns. Its audits never touch many cheaters.

> **练习33.2　改写：双重否定**
>
> 识别并改写下列句子中的双重否定。每个错误可能有不止一种改法。如果句子本来就是对的，在其序号上做标记。带星号部分的参考答案见书后。

*1. Interest in books about the founding of the United States is not hardly consistent among Americans: it seems to vary with the national mood.

*2. Americans show barely any interest in books about the founders when things are going well in the United States.

3. However, when Americans can't hardly agree on major issues, sales of books about the Revolutionary War era increase.

4. During such periods, one cannot go to no bookstore without seeing several new volumes about John Adams, Thomas Jefferson, and other founders.

5. When Americans feel they don't have nothing in common, their increased interest in the early leaders may reflect a desire for unity.

33e 区分现在分词形容词和过去分词形容词

现在分词和过去分词都可以当形容词用：a burning building，a burned building。如上两例，二者所指时间不同。

但是，那些派生于表达情感的动词的分词，其现在分词和过去分词的意思会完全不同。现在分词修饰引起了情感的事物：That was a frightening storm（暴风雨令人害怕），而过去分词修饰体验这情感的事物：They quieted the frightened horses（马感到害怕）。

下列分词是最容易混淆的：

amazing/amazed	embarrassing/embarrassed
amusing/amused	exciting/excited
annoying/annoyed	exhausting/exhausted
astonishing/astonished	fascinating/fascinated
boring/bored	frightening/frightened
confusing/confused	frustrating/frustrated
depressing/depressed	interesting/interested

pleasing/pleased   surprising/surprised
satisfying/satisfied   tiring/tired
shocking/shocked   worrying/worried

练习33.3 改写：现在分词和过去分词

改写下列句中的形容词，以区分现在分词和过去分词。如果句子本来就是对的，在其序号上做标记。带星号部分的参考答案请见书后。

例子：

The subject was embarrassed to many people.

The subject was embarrassing to many people.

*1. Several critics found Alice Walker's *The Color Purple* to be a fascinated book.

*2. One confused critic wished that Walker had deleted the scenes set in Africa.

3. Another critic argued that although the book contained many depressed episodes, the overall effect was excited.

4. Since other readers found the book annoyed, this critic pointed out its many surprising qualities.

5. In the end most critics agreed that the book was a satisfied novel about the struggles of an African American woman.

33f 正确使用 a，an，the 和其他限定词

限定词是特别的形容词，它们总是出现在名词前面。常见的限定词有a，an 和the（称作**冠词**），以及my，their，whose，this，these，those，one，some和any。

标准美式英语的母语者在使用限定词时可以依赖直觉，但说其他语言和方言的人会感到困难。在标准美式英语中，限定词的使用取决于它们所出现的上下文及它们后面是什么样的名词。

- **专有名词**指的是某个特定的人、地或物，以大写字母开头：February, Joe Allen, Red River。大多数专有名词前面不带限定词。
- **可数名词**指明英语中可数的某物，可以有复数：girl/girls, apple/apples, child/children。单数可数名词前面总是有限定词，复数可数名词前面有时候有限定词。
- **不可数名词**指明英语中通常认为不可数的某物，没有复数形式。不可数名词有时前面有限定词。下面是一些不可数名词，按意义分组：

抽象名词：confidence, democracy, education, equality, evidence, health, information, intelligence, knowledge, luxury, peace, pollution, research, success, supervision, truth, wealth, work

食物和饮料：bread, candy, cereal, flour, meat, milk, salt, water, wine

情感：anger, courage, happiness, hate, joy, love, respect, satisfaction

自然事件和物质：air, blood, dirt, gasoline, gold, hair, heat, ice, oil, oxygen, rain, silver, smoke, weather, wood

群组：clergy, clothing, equipment, furniture, garbage, jewelry, junk, legislation, machinery, mail, military, money, police, vocabulary

学科：accounting, architecture, biology, business, chemistry, engineering, literature, psychology, science

英语二语词典会告诉你一个名词是可数还是不可数，还是二者都可以。（推荐字典见p. 173）

注意：许多名词有时候可数有时候不可数：

The library has a <u>room</u> for readers. [room是一个可数名词，意思是"有墙的区域"]

The library has <u>room</u> for reading. [room是一个不可数名词，意思是"空间"]

语法检查工具：因为部分的同一个名词可以归到不同的类别，所以语法检查工具无法提示是否有漏用或者误用的冠词或其他限定词。例如，语法检查工具能查出来Scientist developed new progress里的Scientist一词前面少了a，但它也会误以为Vegetation suffers from drought里的Vegetation之前不该省掉the。

1 ▪ a, an和the与单数可数名词连用

如果因为你之前还没有提及某事物，使得读者还不了解某单数可数名词的所指时，该单数可数名词前面要用a或an：

<u>A</u> scientist in our chemistry department developed <u>a</u> process to strengthen metals. [scientist和process是第一次被提及]

用在单数可数名词之前的the表示它对于读者有确定的所指，原因如下：

- 你之前已经提及：

A scientist in our chemistry department developed a process to strengthen metals. <u>The</u> scientist patented <u>the</u> process. [在上文已经指明该scientist和process]

- 紧挨或紧接着你说出该事物，你就指明了它是什么：

The most productive laboratory is <u>the</u> research center in <u>the</u> chemistry department. [most productive指明了laboratory, in the chemistry department

指明了research center，并且chemistry department是共用的]
- **名词所指是独一无二的事物——唯一的存在：**
  The sun rises in the east.[sun和east是独有事物]
- **名词指明的是读者都知道的机构或设施：**
  Many men and women aspire to the presidency.[presidency是大家都知道的]
  The cell phone has changed communication.[cell phone是大家都知道的设施]

指普通类别的名词之前不用the：
  Wordsworth's poetry shows his love of nature[不是the nature].
  General Sherman said that war is hell.[war指的是普通类别]
  The war in Iraq has left many wounded.[war指的是一场特定的战争]

与复数可数名词连用

a或an从来不会出现在复数可数名词之前，the从来不会出现在表示普通类别的复数名词之前，表示某类别中的特定代表的复数名词前面会用the。
  Men and women are different.[men和women指的是普通类别]
  The women formed a team.[women指的是特定的一些人]

与不可数名词连用

a或an从来不出现在不可数名词之前。the会出现在表示普通类别中的特定代表的不可数名词前。
  Vegetation suffers from drought.[vegetation指的是普通类别]
  The vegetation in the park withered or died.[vegetation指的是特定的一些植物]

与专用名词连用

a或an从来不出现在专有名词之前。the通常不出现在专有名词之前。
  Garcia lives in Boulder.

但也有例外。例如，我们通常在下列词之前用the：复数专有名词（the Murphys、the Boston Celtics），机构或组织的名字（the Department of Justice、the Sierra Club），船只（the Lusitania），海洋（the Pacific），山脉（the Alps），地区（the Middle East），河流（the Mississippi）和一些国家名（the United States、the Netherlands）。

2 ▪ 其他限定词

冠词之外的英语限定词的使用也取决于上下文和名词的类别。下列限定词可以与单数可数名词、复数可数名词或不可数名词连用，如下所示。

276 **可与任何名词连用（单数可数、复数可数、不可数）**

my, our, your, his, her, its, their, 名词所有格（boy's, boys'）

whose, which (ever), what (ever)

some, any, the other

no

<u>Their</u> account is overdrawn.［单数可数］

<u>Their</u> funds are low.［复数可数］

<u>Their</u> money is running out.［不可数］

只与单数名词连用（可数及不可数）

this, that

<u>This</u> account has some money.［可数］

<u>That</u> information may help.［不可数］

只与不可数名词和复数可数名词连用

most, enough, other, such, all, all of the, a lot of

<u>Most</u> funds are committed.［复数可数］

<u>Most</u> money is needed elsewhere.［不可数］

只与单数可数名词连用

one, every, each, either, neither, another

<u>One</u> car must be sold.［单数可数］

只与复数可数名词连用

these, those

both, many, few, a few, fewer, fewest, several

two, three 等

<u>Two</u> cars are unnecessary.［复数可数］

注意：few 的意思是"不多"或"不够"。a few 的意思是"一些""少量但够了"。

<u>Few</u> committee members came to the meeting.

<u>A few</u> members can keep the committee going.

不要把much与复数可数名词连用。

　　Many[不是 much]members want to help.

只与不可数名词连用

much, more, little, a little, less, least, a large amount of

　　Less luxury is in order.[不可数]

　　注意：little的意思是"不多"或"不够"。a little的意思是"一些""少量但够了"。

　　Little time remains before the conference.

　　The members need a little help from their colleagues.

不要把many与不可数名词连用。

　　Much[不是 many]work remains.

练习33.4　改写：冠词 (CULTURE LANGUAGE)

在每个空中，指明用a, an, the还是不要用冠词。带星号部分的参考答案请见书后。

　　例子：

　　On our bicycle trip across _____ country, we carried _____ map and plenty of _____ food and _____ water.

　　On our bicycle trip across the country, we carried a map and plenty of food and water.

　　*From _____ native American Indians who migrated from _____ Asia 20,000 years ago to _____ new arrivals who now come by _____ planes, _____ United States is _____ nation of foreigners. *It is _____ country of immigrants who are all living under _____ single flag.

　　*Back in _____ seventeenth and eighteenth centuries, at least 75% of the population came from _____ England. *However, between 1820 and 1975 more than 38 million immigrants came to this country from elsewhere in _____ Europe. Many children of _____ immigrants were self-conscious and denied their heritage; many even refused to learn _____ native language of their parents and grandparents. They tried to "Americanize" themselves. The so-called Melting Pot theory of _____ social change stressed _____ importance of blending everyone together into _____ kind of stew. Each nationality would contribute its own flavor, but _____ final stew would be something called "American."

　　This Melting Pot theory was never completely successful. In the last half of the twentieth century, _____ ethnic revival changed _____ metaphor. Many people now see _____ American society as _____ mosaic. Americans are once again proud of their heritage, and _____ ethnic differences make _____ mosaic colorful and interesting.

练习33.5　改写：形容词和副词

改写下列句子，改正形容词和副词的错误使用。如果句子本来就是对的，在其序号上做标记。带星号部分的参考答案请见书后。

例子：

Sports fans always feel happily when their team wins.

Sports fans always feel <u>happy</u> when their team wins.

*1. Americans often argue about which professional sport is better: basketball, football, or baseball.

*2. Basketball fans contend that their sport offers more action because the players are constant running and shooting.

*3. Because it is played indoors in relative small arenas, basketball allows fans to be more closer to the action than the other sports do.

*4. Football fanatics say they don't hardly stop yelling once the game begins.

*5. They cheer when their team executes a real complicated play good.

6. They roar more louder when the defense stops the opponents in a goal-line stand.

7. They yell loudest when a fullback crashes in for a score.

8. In contrast, the supporters of baseball believe that it might be the most perfect sport.

9. It combines the one-on-one duel of pitcher and batter struggling valiant with the tight teamwork of double and triple plays.

10. Because the game is played slow and careful, fans can analyze and discuss the manager's strategy.

第 34 章 错置修饰语和垂悬修饰语

概要
- 把错置修饰语重置，使之与本意要修饰的词清楚关联（下方）
- 重写句子，使垂悬修饰语与句子相关联（p. 283）

句子中词语的位置安排是它们之间关系的重要提示。如果读者无法把修饰语与它们想描述的词联系起来，就会造成不明修饰。

语法检查工具：语法检查工具无法识别大多数修饰语的问题。例如，查不出 Gasoline high prices affect usually car sales 中的错置修饰语，也查不出 The vandalism was visible passing the building 中的垂悬修饰语。

34a 重置错置修饰语

错置修饰语在句子中放错了位置，通常会使句子别扭或难懂，甚至可能使句子变得可笑。

1 ▪ 清楚的位置

读者倾向于把修饰语与它所能修饰的最近的词联系起来。其他位置会使修饰语错联系到别的词。

难懂：He served steak to the men on paper plates.

清楚：He served the men steak on paper plates.

难懂：According to the police, many dogs are killed by automobiles and trucks roaming unleashed.

清楚：According to the police, many dogs roaming unleashed are killed by automobiles and trucks.

2 ▪ only 及其他限制修饰词

限制修饰词包括 almost, even, exactly, hardly, just, merely, nearly, only, scarcely 和 simply。为了意思清晰明确，要把这样的词紧挨在它所修饰的词或词

群的前面。

不清晰：The archaeologist only found the skull on her last dig.

清晰：The archaeologist found only the skull on her last dig.

清晰：The archaeologist found the skull only on her last dig.

3 ▪ 副词和语法单元

副词位置常可在句中多处移动，但如果打断某些语法单元的话，会使句子显得别扭。

- **长的副词会打断主谓结构：**

  别扭：The city, after the hurricane, began massive rebuilding.
  （主语）（副词）（动词）

  改写：After the hurricane, the city began massive rebuilding.
  （副词）（主语）（动词）

- **副词插在动词及其宾语之间总是会显得别扭：**

  别扭：The hurricane had damaged badly many homes in the city.
  （动词）（副词）（宾语）

  改写：The hurricane had badly damaged many homes in the city.
  （动词）（副词）（宾语）

- **分离不定式，即在to和动词之间插入副词，让许多读者不喜欢：**

  别扭：The weather service expected temperatures to not rise.
  （不定式）

  改写：The weather service expected temperatures not to rise.
  （不定式）

  分离不定式有时候会显得自然可用，但也会招一些读者不喜欢：

  Several US industries expect to more than triple their use of robots.
  （不定式）

  上面的分离不定式比其他表达法更经济简练，比如 Several US industries expect to increase their use of robots by more than three times.

- **动词短语中的长副词常常显得别扭：**

　　　　　　　　　　　　助动词 ─────────── 副词 ─────
别扭：People who have osteoporosis can, by increasing their daily intake of
　　　 ───────────────── 主要动词
　　　 calcium and vitamin D, improve their bone density.

　　　　　　　　　　　　　　　 副词 ───────────
改写：By increasing their daily intake of calcium and vitamin D, people who
　　　　　　　　　　　　　　　动词短语
　　　 have osteoporosis can improve their bone density.

(CULTURE LANGUAGE) 在问句中，把单个词的副词紧接在主语之后。

　　　　　　　　　　　　　　动词短语
助动词　主语　副词　的其余部分
Will spacecraft ever be able to leave the solar system?

4 ▪ 其他副词的位置 (CULTURE LANGUAGE)

有几个副词的位置有特别的惯用法。

- **频率副词**包括 always, never, often, rarely, seldom, sometimes 和 usually。它们通常出现在句子开头，单个词的动词前面，或动词短语中的助动词之后：

　　　　　　　　　主要
助动词　副词　动词
Robots have sometimes put humans out of work.

　副词　　　动词短语
Sometimes robots have put humans out of work.

频率副词常常跟在 be 动词之后：

　动词　副词
Robots are often helpful to workers.

当 rarely, seldom 和其他否定性的频率副词在句子开头时，正常的主谓语序需要改变。（见 pp. 161–162）

副词　动词　主语
Rarely are robots simple machines.

- **程度副词**包括 absolutely, almost, certainly, completely, definitely, especially, extremely, hardly 和 only。它们的位置就在所修饰的词（形容词、别的副词，有时候也有动词）的前面：

　　　　　　　　　副词　　形容词
Robots have been especially useful in making cars.

- **方式副词**包括 badly, beautifully, openly, tightly, well 和其他描述事情是怎样完成的词。它们通常出现在动词的后面：

　　　　动词　　副词
　　Robots work <u>smoothly</u> on assembly lines.

- **副词**not 依其修饰的词而改变位置。当它修饰动词时，放在助动词之后（如果有不止一个助动词则放在第一个之后）：

　　　　　　　　主要
　　　　助动词　动词
　　Robots do <u>not</u> think.

当 not 修饰另一个副词或形容词时，放在其他修饰词的前面。

　　　　　　　　形容词
　　Robots are <u>not</u> sleek machines.

5 ▪ 形容词的顺序 (CULTURE LANGUAGE)

英语对于名词前的两到三个形容词的顺序有特别的规定。（名词前有三个以上形容词的情况很少见）多个形容词按下面的顺序排列：

限定词	观点	尺寸或形状	颜色	来源	材料	作形容词用的名词	名词
many						state	**laws**
	lovely		green	Thai			**birds**
a		square			wooden		**table**
all						business	**reports**
the			blue		litmus		**paper**

关于名词前形容词的标点，见 p. 316。

练习 34.1　改写：错置修饰语

改写下列句子，使修饰语能清楚而恰当地描写所修饰的词。带星号部分的参考答案请见书后。

例子：

Although at first I feared the sensation of flight, I came to enjoy flying over time.

Although at first I feared the sensation of flight, <u>over time</u> I came to enjoy flying.

*1. People dominate in our society who are right-handed.

*2. Hand tools, machines, and doors even are designed for right-handed people.

*3. However, nearly 15% may be left-handed of the population.

*4. Children often when they begin school prefer one hand or the other.

*5. Parents and teachers should not try to deliberately change a child's preference for the left hand.

6. Women have contributed much to American culture of great value.

7. For example, Elizabeth Pinckney during the colonial era introduced indigo, the source of a valuable blue dye.

8. Emma Willard founded the Troy Female Seminary, the first institution to provide a college-level education for women in 1821.

9. Mary Lyon founded Mount Holyoke Female Seminary as the first true women's college with directors and a campus who would sustain the college even after Lyon's death.

10. *Una* was the first US newspaper, which was founded by Paulina Wright Davis in 1853, that was dedicated to gaining women's rights.

11. Mitchell's Comet was discovered in 1847, which was named for Maria Mitchell.

12. Mitchell was the first American woman astronomer who lived from 1818 to 1889.

13. She was a member at Vassar College of the first faculty.

14. She was when elected to the American Academy of Arts and Sciences in 1848 the first woman to join the prestigious organization.

15. Mitchell said that she was persistent rather than especially capable when asked about her many accomplishments.

练习34.2　改写：副词或形容词的位置

改写下列句子，纠正副词或形容词的位置。如果句子本来就是对的，在其序号上做标记，带星号部分的参考答案请见书后。

例子：

Gasoline high prices affect usually car sales.

<u>High</u> gasoline prices <u>usually</u> affect car sales.

*1. Some years ago Detroit cars often were praised.

*2. Luxury large cars especially were prized.

3. Then a serious oil shortage led drivers to value small foreign cars that got good mileage.

4. When gasoline ample supplies returned, consumers bought again American large cars and trucks.

5. Consumers not were loyal to the big vehicles when gasoline prices dramatically rose.

34b 让垂悬修饰语与句子关联

垂悬修饰语没有合理地修饰句子中的任何成分。

垂悬：Passing the building, the vandalism became visible.

垂悬修饰语通常在句首，包含一个动词形式，暗含但没有明示主语。在上述例子中，暗含的主语是经过建筑物的某人或某物。读者会默认这个暗含的主语与句子的主语相同（本例中为vandalism），但是vandalism不能经过建筑物。该修饰语"垂悬"着，因为它没能明显地与句子的其他部分发生联系。下面是另一个例子：

垂悬：Although intact, graffiti covered every inch of the walls and windows.
　　　〔处于intact状态的是walls和windows，而不是graffiti〕

识别和改写垂悬修饰语

- **找到主语。** 如果修饰语缺少自己的主语（如when in diapers），确认它修饰的是什么。
- **把主语和该修饰语联系起来。** 确认该修饰语所描写的就是主句的主语。如果不是，该修饰语大概就是垂悬修饰语。

　　　　　修饰语　　　　主语
　垂悬：When in diapers, my mother remarried.

- **按需要改写句子。** 改写垂悬修饰语使它有自己的主语，或者改变主句的主语。
  改写a：When I was in diapers, my mother remarried.
  改写b：When in diapers, I attended my mother's second wedding.

要改写垂悬修饰语，你会需要重写整个句子。（如果只是把修饰语挪个位置，它还会是垂悬修饰语：The vandalism became visible passing the building.）选择哪种修改方式取决于你想强调句中的什么。

- 重写垂悬修饰语，使它成为一个完整的句子，有自己明确的主语和动词。读者能接受新主语和句子主语不同。

垂悬：Passing the building, the vandalism became visible.

改写：As we passed the building, the vandalism became visible.

- 把句子的主语改成该修饰语可以正确修饰的一个词。

垂悬：Trying to understand the causes, vandalism has been extensively studied.

改写：Trying to understand the causes, researchers have extensively studied vandalism.

练习34.3　改写：垂悬修饰语

改写下列句子，以去除垂悬修饰语。每个题有不止一种可能的答案。带星号部分的参考答案请见书后。

例子：

Driving north, the vegetation became more sparse.

Driving north, we noticed that the vegetation became more sparse.

或者：As we drove north, the vegetation became more sparse.

*1. Drawing conclusions from several formal studies, pets can improve people's emotional well-being.

*2. Suffering from Alzheimer's and unable to recognize her husband, one woman's ability to identify her beloved dog was unaffected.

*3. Once subject to violent outbursts, a companion dog calmed an autistic boy.

*4. Facing long hospital stays, pet-therapy dogs can cheer up patients.

*5. To understand why people with serious illnesses often respond well to animals, pet therapy is being studied.

6. After accomplishing many deeds of valor, Andrew Jackson's fame led to his election to the presidency in 1828 and 1832.

7. To aid the American Revolution, service as a mounted courier was Jackson's choice.

8. Earning the nicknames "Old Hickory" and "Sharp Knife," the War of 1812 established Jackson's military prowess.

9. Losing only six dead and ten wounded, the triumph of the Battle of New Orleans burnished Jackson's reputation.

10. Winning many military battles, the American public believed in Jackson's leadership.

句子中的错误

如果一个词群缺少某成分，或某成分太多，或含有一些不能自洽的成分，却标点为一个句子，就会让读者不明所以。

第 35 章　残缺句

概要
- 检验你的句子是否完整（p. 286）
- 改写残缺句（p. 288）
- 注意不完整句的可以接受的用法（p. 288）

残缺句是句子的一部分，却以大写字母开头以句号结尾，分离出来当作整个句子。读者会认为残缺句是严重的错误。

语法检查工具：语法检查工具能查出许多但不是所有的残缺句，也会把一些实际完整的句子标记为残缺句。

完整句 vs. 残缺句

完整句或主句
1. 包含一个主语和一个谓语（The wind blows），
2. 不是（以because, who等开头的）从句。

残缺句
1. 缺少谓语（The wind blowing），
2. 或缺少主语（And blows），
3. 或是没有与完整句相关联的一个从句（Because the wind blows）。

35a 检验你的句子是否完整

标点为句子的词群应当通过下面全部三项检测,否则就是残缺句,需要改写。

检验1:找出谓语

找出能当句子谓语的动词,有些残缺句根本就没有动词。

残缺句:Uncountable numbers of sites on the Web.

改写:Uncountable numbers of sites make up the Web.

另一些残缺句可能有一个动词形式,但不是**定式动词**。定式动词有如下词形变化。非谓语动词没有词形变化,必须带助动词才能用作句子动词。

	完整句中的定式动词	残缺句中的非谓语动词
单数	The network grows.	The network growing.
复数	Networks grow.	Networks growing.

现在时	The network grows.	
过去时	The network grew.	The network growing.
将来时	The network will grow.	

残缺句:The network taking a primary role in communication and commerce.

改写:The network is taking a primary role in communication and commerce.

CULTURE LANGUAGE 有些语言允许省略be动词的各种形式,但英语必须明确给出be动词。

残缺句:The network growing rapidly. It much larger than once anticipated.

改写:The network is growing rapidly. It is much larger than once anticipated.

检测2:找出主语

句子的主语通常在谓语的前面出现。如果没有主语,那么这个词群很可能是个残缺句。

残缺句:And has enormous popular appeal.

改写:And the Web has enormous popular appeal.

有一种完整句,即命令句中,主语you是不言自明的:[You] Try this recipe.

CULTURE LANGUAGE 有些语言允许省略句子主语,特别是当主语为代词时。但在英语中,除非是祈使句,否则总是给出句子主语:

残缺句:Web commerce has expanded dramatically. Has hurt traditional stores.

改写：Web commerce has expanded dramatically. <u>It</u> has hurt traditional stores.

检测3：确保该句子不是从句

从句通常以从属性词开头，如下所示：

从属连词			关系代词
after	provided	until	that
although	since	when	which
as	so that	whenever	who/whom
because	than	where	whoever/whomever
even if	that	whereas	
even though	though	whether	
if	till	while	
once	unless		

从句用作句子的一部分（名词或修饰语），不作为完整句用：

　　残缺句：When the government devised the Internet.

　　　改写：The government devised the Internet.

　　　改写：When the government devised the Internet, <u>no expansive computer network existed</u>.

　　残缺句：The reason that the government devised the Internet.［这个残缺句是一个名词（reason）加上它的修饰语（that . . . Internet）］

　　　改写：The reason that the government devised the Internet <u>was to provide secure links among departments and defense contractors</u>.

　　注意：以疑问词how, what, when, where, which, who, whom, whose和why开头的提问不是残缺句：Who was responsible? When did it happen?

35b 改写残缺句

几乎所有残缺句都可以用如下两种办法之一改写。改写的方法视残缺句中信息的重要性，以及你想怎样强调而定。

改写残缺句

选择1

将残缺句改写为完整句。 这种改写方法给予残缺句中的信息与其他完整句相同的地位。

残缺句：A major improvement in public health occurred with the widespread use of vaccines. Which protected children against life-threatening diseases.

改写：A major improvement in public health occurred with the widespread use of vaccines. They protected children against life-threatening diseases.

选择2

将残缺句与适当的主句合并。 这种改写方法将残缺句中的信息置于主句信息之下。

残缺句：The polio vaccine eradicated the disease from most of the globe. The first vaccine to be used widely.

改写：The polio vaccine, the first to be used widely, eradicated the disease from most of the globe.

35c 注意一些非完整句的可以接受的用法

有几个词群缺少通常的主谓结构，是非完整句，但不是残缺句，因为它们与大多数读者的期待范围一致。这样的句子包括命令句（Move along. Shut the window.）、感叹句（Oh no!）、问答句（Where next? To Kansas.），及求职简历中的描述（Weekly volunteer in soup kitchen.）。

有经验的作者有时候会利用残缺句来达到特别的效果。这样的残缺句多出现在非正式写作而不是正式写作中。但是，除非你很有经验，或者对自己的写作非常有把握，还是应该避免使用残缺句，应致力于写出清楚、完整的句子。

练习35.1　改写：残缺句

改写下列句子中的残缺句，或者把它与完整句合并，或者把它改写成完整句。如果题中没有残缺句，在其序号上做标记。带星号部分的参考答案请见书后。

例子：

Jujitsu is good for self-protection. Because it enables one to overcome an opponent without the use of weapons.

Jujitsu is good for self-protection because it enables one to overcome an opponent without the use of weapons. 或：Jujitsu is good for self-protection. It enables one to overcome an opponent without the use of weapons.

*1. Human beings who perfume themselves. They are not much different from other animals.

*2. Animals as varied as insects and dogs release pheromones. Chemicals that signal other animals.

*3. Human beings have a diminished sense of smell. And do not consciously detect most of their own species' pheromones.

*4. The human substitute for pheromones may be perfumes. Most common in ancient times were musk and other fragrances derived from animal oils.

*5. Some sources say that people began using perfume to cover up the smell of burning flesh. During sacrifices to the gods.

6. Perfumes became religious offerings in their own right. Being expensive to make, they were highly prized.

7. The earliest historical documents from the Middle East record the use of fragrances. Not only in religious ceremonies but on the body.

8. In the nineteenth century, chemists began synthesizing perfume oils. Which previously could be made only from natural sources.

9. The most popular animal oil for perfume today is musk. Although some people dislike its heavy, sweet odor.

10. Synthetic musk oil would help conserve a certain species of deer. Whose gland is the source of musk.

练习35.2　改写：残缺句

改写下列段落，消灭其中的残缺句，或者把它们与主句合并，或者把它们改写为主句。第一段的答案出现在书后。

例子：

Gymnosperms, the most advanced of nonflowering plants. They thrive in diverse environments.

Gymnosperms, the most advanced of nonflowering plants, thrive in diverse environments. Or: Gymnosperms are the most advanced of nonflowering plants. They thrive in diverse environments.

*People generally avoid eating mushrooms except those they buy in stores. *But in fact many varieties of mushrooms are edible. *Mushrooms are members of a large group of vegetation called nonflowering plants. *Including algae, mosses, ferns, and coniferous trees. *Even the giant redwoods of California. *Most of the nonflowering plants prefer moist environments. *Such as forest floors, fallen timber, and still water. *Mushrooms, for example. *They prefer moist, shady soil. *Algae grow in water.

Most mushrooms, both edible and inedible, are members of a class called basidium fungi. A term referring to their method of reproduction. The basidia produce spores. Which can develop into mushrooms. This classification including the prized meadow mushroom, cultivated commercially, and the amanitas. The amanita group contains both edible and poisonous species. Another familiar group of mushrooms, the puffballs. They are easily identified by their round shape. Their spores are contained under a thick skin. Which eventually ruptures to release the spores. The famous morels are in still another group. These pitted, spongy mushrooms called sac fungi because the spores develop in sacs.

Anyone interested in mushrooms as food should heed the US Public Health Service warning. Not to eat any wild mushrooms unless their identity and edibility are established without a doubt.

第 36 章　逗号拼接句和融合句

概要

- 把没有用and, but或其他并列连词连接的句子分开（p.291）
- 把用however, for example等连接副词或其他过渡语连接的句子分开（p.294）

一个句子的核心是含有主语和谓语的主句，要知道一个句子结束而另一个句子开始，读者会期待如下信号：

- **句号**。句号造成两个独立分开的句子：
  The ship was huge. Its mast stood eighty feet high.
- **逗号和并列连词**。它们连接句中的两个分句：
  The ship was huge, and its mast stood eighty feet high.
- **分号**，在一个句子中把两个分句分隔开：
  The ship was huge; its mast stood eighty feet high.

如果句子中的两个主句连在一起而没有第二或第三个信号，读者就会看不明白。其结果是造成逗号拼接句，即两个分句只由逗号连接。

逗号拼接句：The ship was huge, its mast stood eighty feet high.

或者结果可能是一个融合的句子（或连续句），在句子之间没有标点或连词：

融合句：The ship was huge its mast stood eighty feet high.

逗号拼接句和融合句的常见修改方法见p. 292的方框。

语法检查工具：语法检查工具能查出许多逗号拼接句，但是会漏掉大多数融合句。例如，能查出 Money is tight, we need to spend carefully，但查不出 Money is tight we need to spend carefully。语法检查工具也会误标一些其实是正确的句子，例如，Money being tighter now than before, we need to spend carefully。

在标准美式英语中，一个句子不能含一个以上主句，除非几个主句之间由逗号加并列连词分开或者由分号分开。如果你的母语没有这样的规则或者已经使你习惯于写长句，你在英语写作时可能特别需要注意纠正逗号拼接句和融合句。

36a 把没有由 and，but 或别的并列连词分开的主句分开

如果你的读者指出你的写作中有逗号拼接句和融合句，那意味着你没有在句子的主句之间做出足够的分割。用下列方法修复这样的问题。

分开句子
如果几个句子表达的思想只是松散相连，把它们分成单独的句子。
逗号拼接句：Chemistry has contributed much to our understanding of foods, many foods such as wheat and beans can be produced in the laboratory.

找出并修改逗号拼接句和融合句

下列步骤能帮助你找出并修改逗号拼接句和融合句。

1. 在草稿中用下画线一句一句标出主句。
   Sailors trained on the ship. They learned about wind and sails. Trainees who took the course ranged from high school students to Navy officers. The ship was built in 1910, it had sailed ever since. In almost a century, it had circled the globe forty times. It burned in 2001 its cabins and decks were destroyed.

2. 这些相连的句子是由句号分开的吗？
   如果是，没问题。
   如果不是，去往第三个问题。
   逗号拼接句：The ship was built in 1910, it had sailed ever since.
   　融合句：It burned in 2001 its cabins and decks were destroyed.

3. 这些相连的句子是由逗号连接的吗？
   如果是，去往第四个问题。

（续表）

逗号拼接句：The ship was built in 1910, it had sailed ever since.
如果**不是**，去往第五个问题。
　　融合句：It burned in 2001 its cabins and decks were destroyed.

4. 主句间的逗号后面有并列连词吗？
　　如果有，没问题。
　　如果没有，加上一个并列连词：and, but, or, nor, for, so, yet。
　　修改：The ship was built in 1910<u>,</u> and it had sailed ever since.

5. 这些相连的句子是由分号分开的吗？
　　如果是，没问题。
　　如果不是，加上一个分号。
　　修改：It burned in 2001<u>;</u> its cabins and decks were destroyed.
　　作为另一个修改方法，你也可以把其中一个主句变成另一个的从句。
　　修改：<u>When</u> it burned in 2001, its cabins and decks were destroyed.

　　修改：Chemistry has contributed much to our understanding of foods<u>.</u> Many foods such as wheat and beans can be produced in the laboratory.

(CULTURE LANGUAGE) 如果你在母语中已习惯于写很长的句子，在英语写作中常写出逗号拼接句，那么，把长句分开成几个单独的句子大概是最好的选择。

并列连词

如果几个主句的意思只是松散相关，又同等重要，在逗号拼接句中插入并列连词。

逗号拼接句：Some laboratory-grown foods taste good, they are nutritious.
　　修改：Some laboratory-grown foods taste good, <u>and</u> they are nutritious.
在融合句中插入逗号和并列连词：
　　融合句：Chemists have made much progress they still have a way to go.
　　修改：Chemists have made much progress<u>,</u> but they still have a way to go.

分号

如果句子间的联系不用连词就已经很紧密而明显，在其间插入分号：
逗号拼接句：Good taste is rare in laboratory-grown vegetables, they are usually bland.
　　修改：Good taste is rare in laboratory-grown vegetables<u>;</u> they are usually bland.

从属

如果一个意思不如另一个意思重要，把次要的意思放在从句中。

逗号拼接句：The vitamins are adequate, the flavor is deficient.

修改：Even though the vitamins are adequate, the flavor is deficient.

36b 把由 however，for example 等连接的主句分开

有两类非连词可以描述两个主句之间的关系：**连接副词**和其他**过渡语**。（p. 51有更长的列表）

常见连接副词和过渡语			
accordingly	for instance	in the meantime	otherwise
anyway	further	in the past	similarly
as a result	furthermore	likewise	so far
at last	hence	meanwhile	still
at length	however	moreover	that is
besides	incidentally	namely	then
certainly	in contrast	nevertheless	thereafter
consequently	indeed	nonetheless	therefore
even so	in fact	now	thus
finally	in other words	of course	to this end
for all that	in short	on the contrary	undoubtedly
for example	instead	on the whole	until now

当两个主句由连接副词或过渡语连接时，必须用句号或分号分隔。该副词或过渡语通常也由一个或多个逗号与主句分开。

逗号拼接句：Healthcare costs are higher in the United States than in many other countries, consequently health insurance is also more costly.

修改：Healthcare costs are higher in the United States than in many other countries. Consequently, health insurance is also more costly.

修改：Healthcare costs are higher in the United States than in many other countries; consequently, health insurance is also more costly.

连接副词或过渡语在句中的位置常常可以多变：

Healthcare costs are higher in the United States than in many other countries; health insurance, consequently, is also more costly.

不管连接副词和过渡语在句中什么位置，句子中都应该有句号或分号把它与其

他句子分开。

注意：连接副词和其他过渡语可以出现在句中多处，这是它们与并列连词（and，but等）及从属连词（although，because等）的重要区别。连词不能换位置。

> **练习36.1　合并句子以避免逗号拼接句和融合句**
>
> 用括号中提出的方法把下列每对句子合并成一个，不要造成逗号拼接句或融合句。带星号部分的参考答案请见书后。
>
> 例子：
>
> The sun sank lower in the sky. The colors gradually faded.（把一个句子变成另一个的从句）
>
> As the sun sank lower in the sky, the colors gradually faded.
>
> *1. Some people think that dinosaurs were the first living vertebrates Fossils of turtles go back 40 million years further.（提供逗号和并列连词）
>
> *2. Most other reptiles exist mainly in tropical regions. Turtles inhabit a variety of environments worldwide.（把一个句子变成另一个的从句）
>
> *3. Turtles do not have teeth. Their jaws are covered with a sharp, horny sheath.（提供分号）
>
> *4. Turtles cannot expand their lungs to breathe air. They make adjustments in how space is used within the shell.（提供分号和连接副词或过渡语）
>
> *5. Some turtles can get oxygen from water. They don't need to breathe air.（提供分号和连接副词或过渡语）
>
> 6. The exact origin of paper money is unknown. It has not survived as coins, shells, and other durable objects have.（把一个句子变成另一个的从句）
>
> 7. Scholars disagree over where paper money originated. Many believe it was first used in Europe.（把一个句子变成另一个的从句）
>
> 8. Perhaps goldsmiths were also bankers. Thus they held the gold of their wealthy customers.（提供分号）
>
> 9. The goldsmiths probably gave customers receipts for their gold. These receipts were then used in trade.（提供逗号和并列连词）
>
> 10. The goldsmiths were something like modern-day bankers. Their receipts were something like modern-day money.（提供分号）
>
> 11. The goldsmiths became even more like modern-day bankers. They began issuing receipts for more gold than they actually held in their vaults.（把一个句子变成另一个的从句）

12. Today's bankers owe more to their customers than they actually have in reserve. They keep enough assets on hand to meet reasonable withdrawals.（提供分号和连接副词或过渡语）

13. In economic crises, bank customers sometimes fear the loss of their money. Consequently, they demand their deposits.（提供分号）

14. Depositors' demands may exceed a bank's reserves. The bank may collapse.（提供逗号和并列连词）

15. The government now regulates banks to protect depositors. Bank failures are less frequent than they once were.（提供分号和连接副词或过渡语）

练习36.2　改写：逗号拼接句和融合句

用以下四种方法中的两种，把下列逗号拼接句或融合句连接起来：（1）把它们分开成单独的句子；（2）在句子之间插入恰当的并列连词或逗号加并列连词；（3）在句子之间插入分号和连接副词或过渡语；（4）把一个句子变成另一个的从句。

例子：

Carolyn still had a headache, she could not get the child-proof cap off the aspirin bottle.

Carolyn still had a headache because she could not get the child-proof cap off the aspirin bottle.（从属）

Carolyn still had a headache, for she could not get the child-proof cap off the aspirin bottle.（并列）

*1. Money has a long history, it goes back at least as far as the earliest records.

*2. Many of the earliest records concern financial transactions, indeed, early history must often be inferred from commercial activity.

*3. Every known society has had a system of money, though the objects serving as money have varied widely.

*4. Sometimes the objects have had real value, in modern times their value has been more abstract.

*5. Cattle, fermented beverages, and rare shells have served as money each one had actual value for the society.

6. As money, these objects acquired additional value they represented other goods.

7. Today money may be made of worthless paper, it may even consist of a bit of data in a computer's memory.

8. We think of money as valuable only our common faith in it makes it valuable.

9. That faith is sometimes fragile, consequently, currencies themselves are fragile.

10. Economic crises often shake the belief in money, indeed, such weakened faith helped cause the Great Depression of the 1930s.

11. Throughout history money and religion were closely linked, there was little distinction between government and religion.

12. The head of state and the religious leader were often the same person so that all power rested in one ruler.

13. These powerful leaders decided what objects would serve as money, their backing encouraged public faith in the money.

14. Coins were minted of precious metals the religious overtones of money were then strengthened.

15. People already believed the precious metals to be divine, their use in money intensified its allure.

练习36.3　改写：逗号拼接句和融合句

依文章意思使用最恰当的办法改写下列段落中的每一个逗号拼接句和融合句。第一段的答案请见书后。

　　*What many call the first genocide of modern times occurred during World War I, the Armenians were deported from their homes in Anatolia, Turkey. *The Turkish government assumed that the Armenians were sympathetic to Russia, with whom the Turks were at war. *Many Armenians died because of the hardships of the journey many were massacred. *The death toll was estimated at between 600,000 and 1 million.

　　Many of the deported Armenians migrated to Russia, in 1918 they established the Republic of Armenia, they continued to be attacked by Turkey, in 1920 they became the Soviet Republic of Armenia rather than surrender to the Turks. Like other Soviet republics, Armenia became independent in 1991, about 3.4 million Armenians live there now.

　　The Armenians have a long history of conquest by others. As a people, they formed a centralized state in the seventh century BC then they were ruled by the Persian empire until it was conquered by Alexander the Great. Greek and Roman rule followed, internal clan leadership marked by disunity and strife was next. In AD 640 the country was invaded by the Arabs in the eleventh century it was conquered by the Byzantines and then by the Turks, under whose control it remained until the twentieth century.

第 37 章　杂糅句（混合句）

概要
- 确保主语和谓语在意义上匹配（下方）
- 理清语法上杂糅的句子（p. 299）
- 句子的各部分，比如主语，只说一次（p. 300）

杂糅句（混合句），是包含意义上或语法上彼此不相容的部分的句子。

语法检查工具：语法检查工具能识别简单的杂糅句，如reason is because，但无法识别大多数杂糅句。

37a 使主谓在意义上相匹配

在意义上杂糅的句子中，主语被描述为做了什么不合逻辑的事情。有时这种杂糅被称作"谓语错误"，因为谓语与主语相冲突。

1 ▪ 与be的不合逻辑的等同

当be动词的某种形式连接主语和一个描写主语的词（补足语）时，主语及其补足语应该有合乎逻辑的关联。

> 杂糅句：A <u>compromise</u> between the city and the country would be the ideal <u>place</u> to live.

> 修改：A <u>community</u> that offered the best qualities of both city and country would be the ideal <u>place</u> to live.

2 ▪ is when, is where

在定义中，be的两侧都应该是名词。口语中，下定义的句子常常以when或where开头，但是在写作中应该避免这种写法。

> 杂糅句：An <u>examination</u> is <u>when you are tested</u> on what you know.

> 修改：An <u>examination</u> is a <u>test</u> of what you know.

3 ▪ reason is because

reason is because这个说法，我们常常听到，但它是冗余表达，因为because就意味着"for the reason that"。

　　杂糅句：The reason the temple requests donations is because the school needs expansion.

　　修改：The reason the temple requests donations is that the school needs expansion.

　　修改：The temple requests donations because the school needs expansion.

4 ▪ 其他杂糅的意思

谓语错误并不限于含be的句子。

　　杂糅句：The use of emission controls was created to reduce air pollution.

　　修改：Emission controls were created to reduce air pollution.

37b 理清楚语法上杂糅的句子

许多杂糅句是从一个语法想法或结构开始，却以另一个语法结构结束。

　　杂糅句：By paying more attention to impressions than facts leads us to misjudge others.

这个杂糅句把一个介词短语用作leads的主语，但是介词短语只能作为修饰语，不能作为名词，所以不能作为句子的主语。

　　改写：By paying more attention to impressions than facts, we misjudge others.

口语中常见用just because作主语的结构，但写作中应当避免。

　　杂糅句：Just because no one is watching doesn't mean we have license to break the law.

　　改写：Even when no one is watching, we don't have license to break the law.

300 在电脑上写作时，当你要把两个句子的部分连接起来，或者重写半句而另外半句不动的时候，特别容易产生杂糅句。当你不让主语和谓语动词表达最重要的意思的时候，也容易产生杂糅句。（见p. 144）

> **练习37.1　改写：杂糅句**
>
> 改写下列句子，使其各部分彼此在语法和意义上相容。每题有不止一种可能的答案。如果一个句子本来就是对的，在其序号上做标记。带星号部分的参考答案请见书后。
>
> 例子：
>
> When they found out how expensive pianos are discouraged them.
>
> When they found out how expensive pianos are, they were discouraged.
>
> 或者：Finding out how expensive pianos are discouraged them.
>
> *1. A hurricane is when the winds in a tropical depression rotate counterclockwise at more than seventy-four miles per hour.
>
> *2. Because hurricanes can destroy so many lives and so much property is why people fear them.
>
> *3. Through high winds, storm surge, floods, and tornadoes is how hurricanes have killed thousands of people.
>
> *4. Storm surge is where the hurricane's winds whip up a tide that spills over seawalls and deluges coastal islands.
>
> *5. The winds themselves are also destructive, uprooting trees and smashing buildings.
>
> 6. Many scientists observe that hurricanes in recent years they have become more ferocious and destructive.
>
> 7. However, in the last half-century, with improved communication systems and weather satellites have made hurricanes less deadly.
>
> 8. The reason is because people have more time to escape.
>
> 9. The emphasis on evacuation is in fact the best way for people to avoid a hurricane's force.
>
> 10. Simply boarding up a house's windows will not protect a family from wind, water surges, and flying debris.

37c 句子的各部分，比如主语，只说一次 (CULTURE LANGUAGE)

在有些语言中，句子的某些部分可以重复，包括任何句子中的主语或形容词性从句中的宾语或副词。而在英语中，这些部分只能在句子中明示一次。

1 ▪ 主语的重复

你可能会想在动词之前用代词重述一下主语，但是主语在句子中只需要说一次：

错误：The liquid it reached a temperature of 110℃.
改写：The liquid reached a temperature of 110℃.
错误：Gases in the liquid they escaped.
改写：Gases in the liquid escaped.

2 ▪ 形容词性从句中的重复

形容词性从句以 who, whom, whose, which, that, where, 或 when 开头。（见 pp. 209–210）开头的词取代了另一个词，主语（He is the person who called.）、动词宾语或介词宾语（He is the person whom I mentioned.），或者介词加代词（He knows the office where [in which] the meeting is.）。

不要在形容词性从句中说出这个被取代的词。

错误：The technician whom the test depended on her was burned.［whom 应该取代 her］
改写：The technician whom the test depended on was burned.

以 where 或 when 开头的形容词性从句不需要 there 或 then 之类的副词。

错误：Gases escaped at a moment when the technician was unprepared then.
改写：Gases escaped at a moment when the technician was unprepared.

注意：whom, which 和类似词语有时会被省略，但读者仍然能明白。这样的话，被取代的词不需要被明示。

错误：Accidents rarely happen to technicians the lab has trained them.［whom 被理解为：... technicians whom the lab has trained］
改写：Accidents rarely happen to technicians the lab has trained.

练习37.2　改写：重复的主语和句子其他成分

改写下列句子，去除任何不需要的词语。带星号部分的参考答案请见书后。

例子：

Scientists they use special instruments for measuring the age of artifacts.

Scientists use special instruments for measuring the age of artifacts.

*1. Archaeologists and other scientists they can often determine the age of their discoveries by means of radiocarbon dating.

*2. This technique it can be used on any material that once was living.

3. This technique is based on the fact that all living organisms they contain carbon.

4. The most common isotope is carbon 12, which it contains six protons and six neutrons.

5. A few carbon atoms are classified as the isotope carbon 14, where the nucleus consists of six protons and eight neutrons there.

第五部分
标点符号 5

第38章·句末标点

第39章·逗号

第40章·分号

第41章·冒号

第42章·撇号

第43章·引号

第44章·其他标点

第 38 章　句末标点

概要

结束句子的时候，用下列符号之一：

- 句号（下方）
- 问号（p. 305）
- 感叹号（p. 305）

句号、问号和感叹号各有特殊的用法。

语法检查工具：语法检查工具能查出遗漏的问号、用错的符号组合（比如句子末尾有问号加句号），但基本也就仅此而已。

38a 大多数句子后面，许多缩略语后面，用句号

1 ▪ 陈述句，温和的命令，以及间接疑问句

陈述句

The airline went bankrupt.　　It no longer flies.

温和的命令

Think of the possibilities.　　Please consider others.

间接疑问句

间接疑问句转述某人问了什么，但不用原问句里的原词或形式：

The judge asked why I had been driving with my lights off.

No one asked how we got home.

🌐 在标准美式英语中，间接疑问句的转述动词（asked 或 said）通常出现在从句之前，这个从句包含正常语序的主语和动词：The reporter asked <u>why the bank failed</u>，而不是问句语序 <u>why did the bank fail</u>。

2 ▪ 缩略语

如果缩略语包含小写字母或以小写字母结尾，要用句号，否则就省略。

Dr.	Mr., Mrs.	e.g.	Feb.	ft.
St.	Ms.	i.e.	p.	a.m., p.m.
PhD	BC, AD	USA	IBM	JFK
BA	AM, PM	US	USMC	AIDS

注意：当缩略语出现在句子末尾时，只用一个句号：My first class is at 8 a.m.

38b 在直接疑问句的末尾用问号，有时也用问号表示存疑

1 ▪ 直接疑问句

Who will follow her?

What is the difference between these two people?

在间接疑问句之后，用句号：We wondered who would follow her.（见p. 304）

一系列问句，每一个结尾都用一个问号：

The officer asked how many times the suspect had been arrested. Three times?
Four times? More than that?

注意：问号可以在引号内也可以在引号外，取决于它是被引用的问句的一部分，还是更大的句子的一部分。（见p. 338）

He asked, "Who will go?" ［问号是被引用的问句的一部分］

Did he say, "I will go"? ［问号是更大的句子的一部分］

2 ▪ 存疑

括号里的问号可以表示对数字或日期存疑。

The Greek philosopher Socrates was born in 470 (?) BC and died in 399 BC. ［苏格拉底的生日我们并不确切了解］

然而，不要用问句表示挖苦或反讽。

不要：Stern's friendliness (?) bothered Crane.

而要：Stern's <u>insincerity</u> bothered Crane.

38c 在强调声明、感叹词或命令的后面，用感叹号

No! We must not lose this election!

Come here immediately!

温和的感叹和命令的后面，视情况用逗号或句号：Oh, call whenever you can.

少用感叹号，哪怕是在非正式写作中。频繁使用感叹号会使人觉得语气过强。

注意：感叹号可以在引号内也可以在引号外，取决于它是引用句的一部分还是更大的句子的一部分。（见p. 338）

练习38.1　改写：句末标点

在下面段落中插入合适的句末标点（句号、问号或感叹号）。带星号部分的参考答案请见书后。

　　*When visitors first arrive in Hawaii, they often encounter an unexpected *language barrier Standard English is the language of business and government, *but many of the people speak Pidgin English Instead of an excited "Aloha" the *visitors may be greeted with an excited Pidgin "Howzit" or asked if they know *"how fo' find one good hotel" Many Hawaiians question whether Pidgin will hold children back because it prevents communication with *haoles*, or Caucasians, who run businesses Yet many others feel that Pidgin is a last defense of ethnic diversity on the islands To those who want to make Standard English the official language of the state, these Hawaiians may respond, "Just 'cause I speak Pidgin no mean I dumb" They may ask, "Why you no listen" or, in standard English, "Why don't you listen"

第 39 章　逗号

概要

正确使用逗号：

- 分隔由and, but和其他并列连词连接的主句（p. 308）
- 把大多数引入成分与主句分开（p. 309）
- 把非重要的成分与主句分开（p. 311）
- 分隔一系列项目及并列形容词（p. 315, p. 316）
- 分隔日期、地址、地名和长数字的各部分（p. 317）
- 分隔标记短语和引用语（p. 318）
- 避免常见的逗号误用，如在主语和动词之间，连词之后和必要成分前后。（p. 319）

逗号（,）是句中最常用的标点符号。它的主要用法见后面方框。

逗号的主要用法

- 分隔由and, but 或其他并列连词连接的主句。(p. 308)

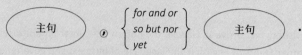

The building is finished, but it has no tenants.

- 把大多数引入成分与主句分开。(p. 309)

Unfortunately, the only tenant pulled out.

- 把非必要成分与主句分开。(p. 311)

The empty building symbolizes a weak local economy, which affects everyone.

The primary cause, the decline of local industry, is not news.

- 分隔一系列项目。(p. 315)

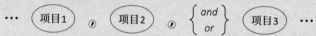

The city needs healthier businesses, new schools, and improved housing.

- 分隔并列形容词。(p. 316)

A tall, sleek skyscraper is not needed.

逗号的其他用法：
分隔日期、地址、地名和长数字的各部分。(p. 317)
分隔标记短语和引用语。(p. 318)

什么时候不用逗号，见p. 319。

语法检查工具：语法检查工具会忽视许多逗号的错误。例如，它查不出 We cooked lasagna_spinach_and apple pie 中遗漏的逗号，也查不出 The travelers were tempted by, the many shops 中多出的逗号。

39a 在连接主句的 and，but 或其他并列连词之前使用逗号

用并列连词连接词或词组时，不要用逗号：Dugain plays⌒and sings Irish⌒and English folk songs. 但是，当并列连词连接各个主句时，一定要用逗号。

Caffeine can keep coffee drinkers alert⌒and it may elevate their mood.

Caffeine was once thought to be safe⌒but now researchers warn of harmful effects.

Coffee drinkers may suffer sleeplessness⌒for the drug acts as a stimulant to the nervous system.

注意：逗号用在并列连词之前，而不是之后。Caffeine increases heart rate⌒and⌒it [不是 and, it] constricts blood vessels.

例外：有些作者会在很短而意义相关的几个主句之间省略逗号。如果你对于这样的句子中要不要用逗号没有把握，那就还是用。用逗号总是正确的。

> **练习39.1**　把互相联系的几个主句用逗号分开
>
> 在下列句子中每个连接主句的并列连词之前插入逗号。如果句子本来就是对的，在其序号上做标记。带星号部分的参考答案请见书后。
>
> 例子：
>
> I would have attended the concert and the reception but I had to baby-sit for my niece.
>
> I would have attended the concert and the reception⌒but I had to baby-sit for my niece.
>
> *1. Parents once automatically gave their children the father's last name but some no longer do.
>
> *2. Parents were once legally required to give their children the father's last name but these laws have been contested in court.
>
> *3. Parents may now give their children any last name they choose and the arguments for choosing the mother's last name are often strong and convincing.
>
> *4. Parents who choose the mother's last name may do so because they believe that the mother's importance should be recognized or because the mother's

name is easier to pronounce.

*5. The child's last name may be just the mother's or it may link the mother's and the father's with a hyphen.

6. Sometimes the first and third children will have the mother's last name and the second child will have the father's.

7. Occasionally, the mother and father combine parts of their names and a new last name is formed.

8. Critics sometimes point out that unusual names confuse others and can create difficulties for children.

9. Children with last names different from their fathers' may feel embarrassed or have identity problems since most children in the United States still bear their fathers' names.

10. Hyphenated names are awkward and difficult to pass on so some observers think they will die out in a generation or two.

39b 用逗号把大多数引入成分与主句分开

引入成分放在句子的开头，修饰接下来的主句中的一个或多个词。引入成分后通常接一个逗号。

从属从句

<u>Even when identical twins are raised apart</u>, they grow up very like each other.

非谓语动词或动词短语

<u>Explaining the similarity</u>, some researchers claim that one's genes are one's destiny.

<u>Concerned</u>, other researchers deny the claim.

介词词组

<u>In a debate that has lasted centuries</u>, scientists use identical twins to argue for or against genetic destiny.

过渡语

<u>Of course</u>, scientists can now look directly at the genes themselves to answer questions.

你可以在短的从句或介词词组后面省略逗号，只要不会造成读者的不解：When snow falls₀the city collapses. By the year 2000₀the world population had topped 6 billion. 如果是以过渡语开始的句子，也可以在过渡语后面省略逗号：Thus₀the debate about education continues.（见pp. 313–314）话说回来，这两种情况，用逗号总是对的。

注意：要区分用作修饰语的-ing词语和用作主语的-ing词语。前者几乎总是接逗号，而后者从来不接逗号。

```
 ———— 修饰语 ————      主语        动词
Studying identical twins₀ geneticists learn about inheritance.

 ———— 主语 ————  动词
Studying identical twins₀helps geneticists learn about inheritance.
```

练习39.2　用标点符号把引入成分与主句隔开

在引入成分后面插入必要的逗号。如果句子本来就是对的，在其序号上做标记。带星号部分的参考答案请见书后。

例子：

After the new library opened the old one became a student union.

After the new library opened₀ the old one became a student union.

*1. Veering sharply to the right a large flock of birds neatly avoids a high wall.

*2. Moving in a fluid mass is typical of flocks of birds and schools of fish.

*3. With the help of complex computer simulations zoologists are learning more about this movement.

*4. Because it is sudden and apparently well coordinated the movement of flocks and schools has seemed to be directed by a leader.

*5. Almost incredibly the group could behave with more intelligence than any individual seemed to possess.

6. However new studies have discovered that flocks and schools are leaderless.

7. As it turns out evading danger is really an individual response.

8. When each bird or fish senses a predator it follows individual rules for fleeing.

9. To keep from colliding with its neighbors each bird or fish uses other rules for dodging.

10. Multiplied over hundreds of individuals these responses look as if they have been choreographed.

39c 用一个或多个逗号把非重要的成分与主句隔开

句子某部分前后的逗号常常表示该成分对句子意义并非必要。这个不必要的成分可以修饰或重述它所指的词，但它并不把该词限制至某一个特定个体或群体。即便这个成分被删除，它所指的词的意思还是清楚的。

非必要成分

The company, which is located in Oklahoma, has an excellent reputation.
（因为非必要成分不限定意义，所以也叫作**非限定成分**）

相反，必要成分（或称**限定成分**）就要限定其所指词的意义：删除该成分会使意义变得太宽泛。必要成分不能用逗号与主句分开。

必要成分

The company rewards employees who work hard.
省略上例中画下画线的部分，会歪曲句子原意，句子原意是：公司并不奖励所有员工，而是只奖励努力的员工。

不同句子中的相同元素可能是重要的，也可能是无关紧要的，这取决于你的意思和上下文：

重要

Not all the bands were equally well received, however. The band playing old music held the audience's attention. The other groups created much less excitement. [playing old music可以把一个特定的乐队从所有可能的乐队中区分出来，所以信息是必不可少的]

非重要

A new band called Fats made its debut on Saturday night. The band, playing old music, held the audience's attention. [playing old music会增加这个乐队的信息，这个乐队已经被命名，读者已经很熟悉了，所以这个短语是不必要的]

验证非必要成分和必要成分

1. 识别该成分：

Hai Nguyen who emigrated from Vietnam lives in Denver.
Those who emigrated with him live elsewhere.

（续表）

> 2. 去掉该成分。句子根本意义变化了吗？
> Hai Nguyen lives in Denver. 没有。
> Those live elsewhere. 变了。[Those是谁？]
> 3. 如果意思没有变，该成分是非必要成分，应当用逗号将其与主句分开：
> Hai Nguyen◯ who emigrated from Vietnam◯ lives in Denver.
> 如果意思变了，该成分是必要成分，不应当用逗号将其与主句分开。
> Those◯who emigrated with him◯live elsewhere.

注意：当非必要成分落在句子中间时，确保用一对逗号将其与主句分开，一个在之前，一个在之后。

1 ▪ 非重要短语和从句

大多数非重要短语和从句用作形容词，也有用作副词的，但较为少见。在下面的例句中，下画线标出的词语可以省略，而不影响句意清晰。

Elizabeth Blackwell was the first woman to graduate from an American medical school◯ <u>in 1849</u>. [短语]

She was a medical pioneer◯ <u>helping to found the first medical college for women</u>. [短语]

She taught at the school◯ <u>which was affiliated with the New York Infirmary</u>. [形容词性从句]

Blackwell◯ <u>who published books and papers on medicine</u>◯ practiced pediatrics and gynecology. [形容词性从句]

She moved to England in 1869◯ <u>when she was forty-eight</u>. [副词性从句]

注意：that只用在重要从句中，从不用在非重要从句中。

错误：The tree, <u>that</u> is 120 years old, shades the house.

改正：The tree, <u>which</u> is 120 years old, shades the house.

许多作者把which用在非重要从句中。

2 ▪ 非重要同位语

同位语可以是重要的也可以是不重要的，取决于其意义和上下文。不重要的同位语仅仅给它所指的词补充信息：

Toni Morrison's fifth novel◯ *Beloved*◯ won the Pulitzer Prize in 1988. [因为fifth已经指明了小说，所以书名只是增加了一些细节]

相反，重要同位语会限定或定义其所指的词：

Morrison's novel○*The Bluest Eye*○is about an African American girl who longs for blue eyes.［Morrison写过不止一部小说，所以书名是指明目标对象的关键］

3 ▪ 其他非必要成分

就像非必要的修饰语或同位语一样，许多其他成分也对句子的结构、语调或整体的清晰有所贡献，但对其意义并不重要。与非必要修饰语或同位语不同，这些其他的非必要成分通常并不指向句子中任何确定的词语。

注意：如果这样的成分出现在句子中间，用一对逗号把它们与主句分开，逗号一个在之前，一个在之后。

独立短语

Household recycling having succeeded○ the city now wants to extend the program to businesses.

Many businesses○ their profits already squeezed○ resist recycling.

插入语和过渡语

通常用逗号把插入语和过渡语与主句分开：

The world's most celebrated holiday is○ perhaps surprisingly○ New Year's Day. ［过渡语］

Interestingly○ Americans have relatively few holidays. ［过渡语］

US workers○ for example○ receive fewer holidays than European workers do. ［插入语］

（破折号和括号也可以用来把插入语与主句分开。见pp. 339–341）

当过渡语连接几个主句时，在它前面用分号，在它后面用逗号（见p. 323）：

European workers often have long paid vacations○ indeed○ they may receive a full month after just a few years with a company.

例外：连词and和but有时候用作过渡语，但其后从来不用逗号。（见p. 308）另外一些过渡语的用法各有不同，取决于该表达及作者的判断。许多作者把我们读起来没有停顿的短语的逗号省略，例如also, hence, next, now, then和thus。同样，therefore和instead用在句子中或句子末尾的时候，也不用逗号。

US workers○ thus○ put in more work days. But○ the days themselves may be shorter.

Then○ the total hours worked would come out roughly the same.

对照短语

The substance▢ not the style▢ is important.

Substance▢ unlike style▢ cannot be faked.

反问句

They don't stop to consider others ▢do they?

Jones should be allowed to vote▢ shouldn't he?

yes和no

Yes▢ the editorial did have a point.

No▢ that can never be.

直接称呼

Cody▢ please bring me the newspaper.

With all due respect▢ sir▢ I will not.

温和的感叹

Well▢ you will never know who did it.

Oh▢ they forgot all about the baby.

练习39.3　用标点符号把必要成分和非必要成分与主句分开

用逗号把下列句子中的非必要成分与主句分开，并删除错误地把必要成分与主句分开的逗号。如果句子本来就是对的，在其序号上做标记。带星号部分的参考答案请见书后。

例子：

Elizabeth Blackwell who attended medical school in the 1840s was the first American woman to earn a medical degree.

Elizabeth Blackwell▢ who attended medical school in the 1840s▢ was the first American woman to earn a medical degree.

*1. Many colleges have started campus garden programs, that aim to teach students about the benefits of sustainable farming methods and locally grown food.

*2. These gardens which use organic farming techniques also provide fresh produce for the college cafeteria.

*3. A garden, that is big enough to grow produce for a college cafeteria, requires a large piece of land.

*4. Such a garden also needs a leader, who can choose crops that will thrive in local growing conditions.

*5. Volunteers, willing to work in the garden every week, are essential as well.

6. Some campus gardeners distribute produce to people in the community who live far from a grocery store.

7. Some urban neighborhoods are called "food deserts," because they lack grocery stores that residents can reach easily on foot.

8. The colleges may distribute produce with special trucks or "veggie wagons" that drive through the urban neighborhoods.

9. The wagons deliver produce once a week although they may make two deliveries during peak harvest time.

10. A community garden planted during the academic year will fare better in the southern states where the growing season is longer than in northern states.

39d 在一系列项目之间使用逗号

三个或更多同等重要的项目构成一个系列。这些项目可以是词、短语或句子。

Anna Spingle married at the age of seventeen, had three children by twenty-one, and divorced at twenty-two.

She worked as a cook, a baby-sitter, and a crossing guard.

有些作者会省略一个系列中并列连词之前的那个逗号（Breakfast consisted of coffee, eggs, and kippers）。不过最后的这个逗号写上是绝对不错的，而且也使读者容易看清楚最后两项是分开的。

39e 在平等修饰同一个词的多个形容词之间用逗号

平等修饰同一个词的形容词，称作并列形容词，可以用and或者逗号分开。

Spingle's scratched and dented car is old, but it gets her to work.

She has dreams of a sleek, shiny car.

如果靠近名词的那个形容词与该名词在意义上的联系比别的形容词更紧密，那么这些就不是并列形容词。

Spingle's children work at various odd jobs.

They all expect to go to a nearby⌒community college.

形容词加逗号的测试

1. 找出形容词：
   She was a faithful sincere friend.
   They are dedicated medical students.
2. 这些形容词能调换顺序而不改变意思吗？
   She was a sincere faithful friend. 能。
   They are medical dedicated students. 不能。
3. 这些形容词之间可以合理插入and吗？
   She was a faithful and sincere friend. 能。
   They are dedicated and medical students. 不能。
4. 如果两个问题的回答都是"能"，这些形容词就应该由逗号分开。
   She was a faithful, sincere friend.
5. 如果两个问题的回答都是"不能"，这些形容词就不应该由逗号分开。
   They are dedicated⌒medical students.

练习39.4　给系列项目或并列形容词加标点符号

给下列句子插入逗号，以分开并列形容词或系列项目。如果句子本来就是对的，在其序号上做标记。带星号部分的参考答案请见书后。

例子：

Quiet by day, the club became a noisy smoky dive at night.

Quiet by day, the club became a noisy, smoky dive at night.

*1. Shoes with high heels were originally designed to protect feet from mud garbage and animal waste in the streets.

*2. The first known high heels worn strictly for fashion appeared in the sixteenth century.

*3. The heels were worn by men and made of colorful silk fabrics soft suedes or smooth leathers.

*4. High-heeled shoes became popular when the short powerful King Louis XIV of France began wearing them.

*5. Louis's influence was so strong that men and women of the court priests and cardinals and even household servants wore high heels.

6. Eventually only wealthy fashionable French women wore high heels.

7. In the seventeenth and eighteenth centuries, French culture represented the

one true standard of elegance and refinement.

8. High-heeled shoes for women spread to other courts of Europe among the Europeans of North America and to almost all social classes.
9. Now high heels are common, though depending on the fashion they range from short squat thick heels to tall skinny spikes.
10. A New York boutique recently showed a pair of purple satin pumps with tiny jeweled bows and four-inch stiletto heels.

39f 在日期、地址、地名和长数字上用逗号

当这些成分出现在句中时，以逗号分开的信息也以逗号结束，如下面各例子：

日期

July 4, 1776, is the date the Declaration was signed.
The bombing of Pearl Harbor on Sunday, December 7, 1941, prompted American entry into World War II.

不要在反序的日期信息各部分之间用逗号（15 December 1992），也不要在由月份或季节和年份组成的日期信息里用逗号（December 1941）。

形容词和地名

Use the address 220 Cornell Road, Woodside, California 94062, for all correspondence.
Columbus, Ohio, is the location of Ohio State University.

不要在州名和邮政编码之间用逗号。

长数字

用逗号把长数字从右往左分隔为三个一组。对于四个数字的数字，逗号可有可无。

The new assembly plant cost $7,525,000.
A kilometer is 3,281 feet［或 3281 feet］.

🌐 **CULTURE LANGUAGE** 有些语言与标准美式英语用法不同，是用句号而不是逗号来分隔长数字。

39g 按照标准做法在引用语中使用逗号

she said, he writes 之类的词，标识出一个引用语的来源。应当用标点符号把这些**标记短语**与引用语分隔开，通常是用一个或多个逗号。

Eleanor Roosevelt said⊙ "You must do the thing you think you cannot do."

"Knowledge is power⊙" wrote Francis Bacon.

"The shore has a dual nature⊙" observes Rachel Carson⊙ "changing with the swing of the tides." ［标记短语以逗号中断引号，因此以逗号结尾］

例外：某些情形下不要在标记短语中用逗号：

- 如果标记短语在两个句子之间打断了引用语，在该短语后用分号或句号。用分号还是句号取决于原引文的标点：

    不能是："That part of my life was over," she wrote, "his words had sealed it shut."

    而应是："That part of my life was over," she wrote⊙ "His words had sealed it shut." ［She wrote 在句号处中断了引文］

    或是："That part of my life was over," she wrote⊙ "his words had sealed it shut." ［She wrote 在分号处中断了引文］

- 如果标记短语跟在以感叹号或问号结尾的引语之后，省略逗号。

    "Claude⊙" Mrs. Harrison called.

    "Why must I come home⊙" he asked.

- 如果一个完整的句子引出一个引语，用冒号：

    Her statement was clear⊙ "I will not resign."

- 当一个引语融入你自己的句子结构中时，省略逗号，包括以 that 开头的引语。

    James Baldwin insists that⊙ "one must never, in one's life, accept . . . injustices as commonplace."

    Baldwin thought that the violence of a riot⊙ "had been devised as a corrective"⊙ to his own violence.

- 引用一个标题时，省略逗号，除非该标题是非重要同位语。

    The Beatles recorded⊙ "She Loves You"⊙ in the early 1960s.

    The Beatles' first huge US hit⊙ "She Loves You⊙" appeared in 1963.

见练习43.1，p. 338，标点引用的练习。

39h 删掉不需要的逗号

如果逗号用得过多，会使句子变得不爽利甚至令人迷惑。下面是几种关于最常见的逗号误用的建议。

1 ▪ 主语和动词之间，动词和宾语之间，或介词和宾语之间，都不要逗号

不是：The returning soldiers, received a warm welcome.［主谓分离］

而是：The returning soldiers○received a warm welcome.

不是：They had chosen, to fight for their country despite, the risks.［动词chosen和它的宾语分离，介词despite和它的宾语分离］

而是：They had chosen○to fight for their country despite○the risks.

2 ▪ 大多数复合结构里没有逗号

包含两个成分的复合结构几乎从来不用逗号。唯一的例外是由并列连词连接的两个主句组成的句子：The computer network failed○but employees kept working.（见p.308）

不是：Banks, and other financial institutions（复合主语）have helped older people with money management, and investment.（介词的复合宾语）

而是：Banks○and other financial institutions have helped older people with money management○and investment.

不是：One bank created special accounts for older people, and held classes,（复合谓语）and workshops.（动词的复合宾语）

而是：One bank created special accounts for older people○and held classes○and workshops.

3 ▪ 连词后不用逗号

不是：Parents of adolescents notice increased conflict at puberty, and, they complain of bickering.

而是：Parents of adolescents notice increased conflict at puberty, and○they complain of bickering.

不是：Although, other primates leave the family at adolescence, humans do not.

而是：Although⌒other primates leave the family at adolescence, humans do not.

4 ▪ 必要成分前后不用逗号

不是：Hawthorne's work, *The Scarlet Letter,* was the first major American novel.［要想把这部小说与Hawthorne的其他作品区分开来，标题是必不可少的］

而是：Hawthorne's work⌒*The Scarlet Letter*⌒was the first major American novel.

不是：The symbols, that Hawthorne uses, have influenced other novelists.［该分句指出哪些象征是有影响力的］

而是：The symbols⌒that Hawthorne uses⌒have influenced other novelists.

不是：Published in 1850, *The Scarlet Letter* still resonates today, because of its theme of secret sin.［这一分句对于解释这部小说为何受欢迎至关重要］

而是：Published in 1850, *The Scarlet Letter* still resonates today⌒because of its theme of secret sin.

注意：就像前一个例子中的because从句，大多数副词从句是必要成分，因为它们描写的情状对于主句是必不可少的。

5 ▪ 一系列的项目前后不用逗号

逗号是用来把一个系列的内部分隔开的（p. 315），但它们不把这个系列与句子的其他部分分隔开。

不是：The skills of, hunting, herding, and agriculture, sustained the Native Americans.

而是：The skills of⌒hunting, herding, and agriculture⌒sustained the Native Americans.

6 ▪ 间接引语之前不用逗号

不是：The report concluded, that dieting could be more dangerous than overeating.

而是：The report concluded⌒that dieting could be more dangerous than overeating.

练习39.5　改写：多余的和误用的逗号

改写下列句子，去除多余的或误用的逗号。如果句子本来就是对的，在其序号上做标记。带星号部分的参考答案请见书后。

例子：

Aquifers can be recharged by rainfall, but, the process is slow.

Aquifers can be recharged by rainfall, but◯ the process is slow.

*1. Underground aquifers are deep, and sometimes broad layers of water, that are trapped between layers of rock.

*2. Porous rock, or sediment holds the water.

*3. Deep wells drilled through the top layers of solid rock, produce a flow of water.

*4. Such wells are sometimes called, artesian wells.

*5. One of the largest aquifers in North America, the Ogallala aquifer, is named after the Ogallala Indian tribe, which once lived in the region and hunted buffalo there.

6. The Ogallala aquifer underlies a region from western Texas through northern Nebraska, and has a huge capacity of fresh water, that is contained in a layer of sand and gravel.

7. But, the water in the Ogallala is being removed at a rate faster than it is being replaced.

8. Water is pumped from the aquifer for many purposes, such as drinking and other household use, industrial use, and, agricultural use.

9. Scientists estimate that, at the present consumption rate the Ogallala will be depleted in forty years.

10. Water table levels are receding from six inches to three feet a year, the amount depending on location.

练习39.6　改写：逗号

在下列段落中必要之处插入逗号，去掉任何误用或多余的逗号。带星号部分的参考答案请见书后。

*Ellis Island New York reopened for business in 1990 but now the customers are tourists not immigrants. *This spot which lies in New York Harbor was the first American soil seen, or touched by many of the nation's immigrants. *Though other places also served as ports of entry for foreigners none has the symbolic power of, Ellis Island. *Between its opening in 1892 and its closing in 1954, over

20 million people about two-thirds of all immigrants were detained there before taking up their new lives in the United States. *Ellis Island processed over 2000 newcomers a day when immigration was at its peak between 1900 and 1920.

As the end of a long voyage and the introduction to the New World Ellis Island must have left something to be desired. The "huddled masses" as the Statue of Liberty calls them indeed were huddled. New arrivals were herded about kept standing in lines for hours or days yelled at and abused. Assigned numbers they submitted their bodies to the pokings and proddings of the silent nurses and doctors, who were charged with ferreting out the slightest sign, of sickness disability or insanity. But, millions survived the examination humiliation and confusion, to take the last short boat ride to New York City, and begin new lives.

第 40 章　分号

概要

正确使用分号：

- 用分号隔开不由 and, but 或其他并列连词连接的主句（下方）
- 用分号隔开由 however, for example 或类似表达连接的主句（下页）
- 用分号隔开包含逗号的主句或系列项目（p. 325）
- 避免常见的误用：分号用在短语和从句中，分号用在系列项目和解释前（p. 325）

分号（;）分隔开平等的和平衡的多个成分——通常是多个主句，有时是系列项目。

语法检查工具：语法检查工具能查出分号使用的少数几个错误，例如，它会建议在 The set was perfect, the director had planned every detail 里的 perfect 之后用分号，这样就避免了逗号拼接句的产生。但是它也会遗漏 The set was perfect; deserted streets, dark houses, and gloomy mist 中误用的分号。（应该用冒号，见 pp. 326–327）

40a 在不由 and, but 或其他并列连词连接的主句之间使用分号

当没有并列连词连接两个主句时，句子应当由分号分开。

A new ulcer drug arrived on the market with a mixed reputation; doctors find that the drug works but worry about its side effects.

The side effects are not minor⟨;⟩ some leave the patient quite uncomfortable or even ill.

注意：这条规则防止了逗号拼接句和融合句的产生。（见pp. 290–291）

40b 在由 however, for example 等连接的主句之间使用分号

当连接副词或其他过渡语把两个主句连接在一个句子中时，应当用分号把二者分开：

An American immigrant, Levi Strauss, invented blue jeans in the 1860s⟨;⟩ eventually, his product clothed working men throughout the West.

分号在两个主句之间的位置永远不变，但连接副词或过渡语的位置可以在第二个主句中变动。不管该副词或过渡语在哪个位置，都由一个或多个逗号将其与主句分开。

Blue jeans have become fashionable all over the world⟨;⟩ however⟨,⟩ the American originators still wear more jeans than anyone else.

Blue jeans have become fashionable all over the world⟨;⟩ the American originators⟨,⟩ however⟨,⟩ still wear more jeans than anyone else.

Blue jeans have become fashionable all over the world⟨;⟩ the American originators still wear more jeans than anyone else⟨,⟩ however.

注意：这条规则防止了逗号拼接句和融合句的产生。（见pp. 294–295）

练习40.1　合并句子：相互联系的主句

把下列各组句子合并成一个只包含两个主句的句子。如括号中所示，只用分号或者用一个分号加一个连接副词或过渡语再接逗号来连接各主句。你需要增删、改词或重新安排词序。每题有不止一种可能的答案。带星号部分的参考答案请见书后。

例子：

The Albanians censored their news. We got little news from them. And what we got was unreliable. (Therefore和分号)

The Albanians censored their news⟨;⟩ therefore⟨,⟩ the little news we got from them was unreliable.

*1. Electronic instruments are prevalent in jazz. They are also prevalent in rock music. They are less common in classical music. (However和分号)

*2. Jazz and rock change rapidly. They nourish experimentation. They nourish improvisation.(分号)

*3. The notes and instrumentation of traditional classical music were established by a composer. The composer was writing decades or centuries ago. Such music does not change.(<u>Therefore</u>和分号)

*4. Contemporary classical music not only can draw on tradition. It can also respond to innovations. These are innovations such as jazz rhythms and electronic sounds.(分号)

*5. Much contemporary electronic music is more than just one type of music. It is more than just jazz, rock, or classical. It is a fusion of all three.(分号)

6. Most music computers are too expensive for the average consumer. Digital keyboard instruments can be inexpensive. They are widely available.(<u>However</u>和分号)

7. Inside the keyboard is a small computer. The computer controls a sound synthesizer. The instrument can both process and produce music.(<u>Consequently</u>和分号)

8. The person playing the keyboard presses keys or manipulates other controls. The computer and synthesizer convert these signals. The signals are converted into vibrations and sounds.(分号)

9. The inexpensive keyboards can perform only a few functions. To the novice computer musician, the range is exciting. The range includes drum rhythms and simulated instruments.(<u>Still</u>和分号)

10. Would-be musicians can orchestrate whole songs. They start from just the melody lines. They need never again play "Chopsticks."(分号)

40c 在主句之间使用分号或者在一系列含逗号的项目之间使用分号

正常情况下，逗号用来分隔由并列连词（and, but, or, nor）连接的几个主句，以及分隔系列项目。但是，当主句或系列项目含有逗号时，在它们之间使用分号会使句子更清晰易懂。

Lewis and Clark led the men of their party with consummate skill, inspiring and encouraging them, doctoring and caring for them<u>; and</u> they kept voluminous journals.

—Page Smith

The custody case involved Amy Dalton, the child(;)Ellen and Mark Dalton, the parents(;)and Ruth and Hal Blum, the grandparents.

40d 删除或替换无用的分号

分号常会被误用于本应使用别的标点或根本不需要标点的一些结构中。

1 ▪ 主句和从句之间或主句和短语之间不用分号

分号在某些需要其他标点符号或不需要标点符号的结构中经常被误用。

不是：Pygmies are in danger of extinction; because of encroaching development.

而是：Pygmies are in danger of extinction( )because of encroaching development.

不是：According to African authorities; only about 35,000 Pygmies exist today.

而是：According to African authorities(,) only about 35,000 Pygmies exist today.

2 ▪ 在一个系列之前或者在解释之前不用分号

用冒号和破折号而不是分号来引出系列、解释等。（见pp. 326–327和p. 340）

不是：Teachers have heard all sorts of reasons why students do poorly; psychological problems, family illness, too much work, too little time.

而是：Teachers have heard all sorts of reasons why students do poorly(:)psychological problems, family illness, too much work, too little time.

练习40.2　改写：分号

在下面段落里的必要之处插入分号，并删除任何误用或多余的分号，代以其他合适的标点。带星号部分的参考答案请见书后。

*The set, sounds, and actors in the movie captured the essence of horror films. *The set was ideal; dark, deserted streets, trees dipping their branches over the sidewalks, mist hugging the ground and creeping up to meet the trees, looming shadows of unlighted, turreted houses. *The sounds, too, were appropriate, especially terrifying was the hard, hollow sound of footsteps echoing throughout the film. But the best feature of the movie was its actors; all of them tall, pale, and thin to the point of emaciation. With one exception, they were dressed uniformly in gray and had gray hair. The exception was an actress who dressed only in black; as if to set off her pale yellow, nearly white, long hair; the only color in the film. The glinting black eyes of another actor stole almost every scene, indeed, they were the source of the film's mischief.

第 41 章　冒号

概要

正确使用冒号：
- 用冒号引出结论性的解释、系列或同位语，以及一些结论性的引语（下方）
- 用冒号结束公文信件的致意，分隔标题和副标题，以及分隔时间（p. 327）
- 避免冒号的误用：动词之后，介词之后，such as 或 including 之后（p. 328）

冒号（:）主要是作为引出之用的标点符号：它表示紧接其后的词语会做解释或详述。它也有几个惯例性的使用，如在时间的表示上。

语法检查工具：许多语法检查工具无法识别漏用或误用的冒号，只是忽视了之。

41a 在结论性的解释、系列或同位语，以及一些引语之前使用冒号

作为引路员，冒号之前总是有一个完整的主句。它后面可以接也可以不接主句。这是冒号与分号的一个不同，分号通常只用来分隔几个主句。（见 p. 323）

解释

Soul food has a deceptively simple definition: the ethnic cooking of African Americans.

有时候一个结论性的解释之前有 the following 或 as follows 及一个冒号：

A more precise definition might be the following: soul food draws on ingredients, cooking methods, and dishes that originated in Africa, were brought to the New World by slaves, and were modified in the Carib-bean and the American South.

注意：冒号之后的完整句子可以以大写字母开头，也可以以小写字母开头。只要全文一致即可。

系列

At least three soul food dishes are familiar to most Americans: fried chicken, barbecued spareribs, and sweet potatoes.

同位语

Soul food has one disadvantage：fat.

namely，that is 以及其他引出同位语的表达会跟在冒号之后：Soul food has one disadvantage：namely, fat.

引语

如果引出部分是个完整的句子，在引语之前使用冒号。

One soul food chef has a solution："Soul food doesn't have to be greasy to taste good. Instead of using ham hocks to flavor beans, I use smoked turkey wings. The soulful, smoky taste remains, but without all the fat."

41b 公文信件的致意之后，标题和副标题之间，以及时间的分隔之间，使用冒号

公文信件的致意
Dear Ms. Burak：

标题和副标题
Charles Dickens：An Introduction to His Novels

时间
12：26 AM　　6：00 PM

41c 删除或替换无用的冒号

只在主句末尾使用冒号，不要在下列情形使用冒号：

- 删除动词之后的冒号。

    不是：The best-known soul food dishes <u>are:</u> fried chicken and barbecued spareribs.

    而是：The best-known soul food dishes are◯fried chicken and barbecued spareribs.

- 删除介词之后的冒号。

    不是：Soul food recipes can be found <u>in:</u> mainstream cookbooks as well as specialized references.

    而是：Soul food recipes can be found in◯mainstream cookbooks as well as specialized references.

- 删除such as 或including之后的冒号。

    不是：Many Americans have not tasted delicacies <u>such as:</u> chitlins and black-eyed peas.

而是: Many Americans have not tasted delicacies <u>such as○chitlins</u> and black-eyed peas.

练习41.1　改写：冒号和分号

在下列句子中需要之处使用冒号或分号，并删除或取代错误的用法。如果一个句子本来就是对的，在其序号上做标记。带星号部分的参考答案请见书后。

例子：

Mix the ingredients as follows sift the flour and salt together, add the milk, and slowly beat in the egg yolk.

Mix the ingredients as follows⊙ sift the flour and salt together, add the milk, and slowly beat in the egg yolk.

*1. Sunlight is made up of three kinds of radiation; visible rays; infrared rays, which we cannot see; and ultraviolet rays, which are also invisible.

*2. Especially in the ultraviolet range; sunlight is harmful to the eyes.

*3. Ultraviolet rays can damage the retina: furthermore, they can cause cataracts on the lens.

*4. Infrared rays are the longest; measuring 700 nanometers and longer, while ultraviolet rays are the shortest; measuring 400 nanometers and shorter.

*5. The lens protects the eye by: absorbing much of the ultraviolet radiation and thus protecting the retina.

6. By protecting the retina, however, the lens becomes a victim; growing cloudy and blocking vision.

7. The best way to protect your eyes is: to wear hats that shade the face and sunglasses that screen out the ultraviolet rays.

8. Many sunglass lenses have been designed as ultraviolet screens; many others are extremely ineffective.

9. Sunglass lenses should screen out ultraviolet rays and be dark enough so that people can't see your eyes through them, otherwise, the lenses will not protect your eyes, and you will be at risk for cataracts later in life.

10. People who spend much time outside in the sun; really owe it to themselves to buy a pair of sunglasses that will shield their eyes.

第 42 章　撇号

概要

正确使用撇号：

- 用撇号在单个或多个词中表示所有权（p. 331）
- 避免撇号在复数名词、单数动词或人称代词所有格中常见的错误使用（p. 332）
- 用撇号在缩写中表示省略（p. 333）

撇号（'）作为一个词的一部分出现，表示拥有、一个或多个字母的省略，有时也表示复数。

撇号很容易用错。为保险起见，检查你的草稿以确保所有以-s结尾的词既没有省略需要的撇号，也没有加多余的撇号。

语法检查工具： 语法检查工具在识别撇号的错误时，通常有对有错。例如，它可能会标记出缩略词（如isnt）中遗漏的撇号，但分不出its和it's，their和they're，your和you're，whose和who's。语法检查工具能认出所有格中的一些撇号错误，但它也会误标记其实正确的复数词。与其依赖语法检查工具，不如用你的文字编辑器的Search或Find功能来找出所有以-s结尾的词语，然后检查它们以确保撇号都用对了。

撇号的用法和误用

撇号的用法

- 用撇号构成名词及不定代词的所有格。（p. 331）

单数	复数
Ms. Park'**s**	the Parks'
lawyer'**s**	lawyers'
everyone'**s**	two weeks'

- 用撇号构成缩略形式。（p. 333）

    it'**s** a girl　　shouldn'**t**
    you'**re**　　won'**t**

- 缩略语的复数、日期的复数和词形本身的复数里，撇号可要可不要。（p. 334）

    MA'**s** or MA**s**　　C'**s** or C**s**
    1960'**s** or 1960**s**　　*if*'**s** or *if***s**

（续表）

撒号的误用
- 不要用撇号加-s构成复数名词的所有格（p. 331），而要先以-s构成复数再加撇号。

不是	而是
the Kim's car	the Kims' car
boy's fathers	boys' fathers
babie's care	babies' care

- 不要用撇号去构成名词的复数。（p. 332）

不是	而是
book's are	books are
the Freed's	the Freeds

- 不要在-s结尾的动词上用撇号。（p. 333）

不是	而是
swim's	swims

- 不要用撇号构成人称代词复数的所有格。（p. 333）

不是	而是
it's toes	its toes
your's	yours

42a 用撒号表示所有

名词或不定代词以加撒号，通常再加-s，来构成所有格：the dog's hair, everyone's hope。只有几个不定代词不用撒号表示拥有：mine, yours, his, hers, its, ours, theirs和whose。

注意：记住，撒号或撒号加-s是附加成分。在撒号之前，要把所有人拼写完整，不能漏掉或添加字母。

1 ▪ 单数词：加-'s

Bill Boughton's skillful card tricks amaze children.
Some of the earth's forests are regenerating.
Everyone's fitness can be improved through exercise.

单数词的-'s词尾也适用于以-s结尾的单数词，如下方所示：

Henry James's novels reward the patient reader.
The business's customers filed suit.

例外：撒号可以单独加在以-s结尾的单数词之后，如果再加s会难以发音的话。

Moses' mother concealed him in the bulrushes.

Joan Rivers's jokes offend many people.

然而，再多加-s也绝不会错。

2 ▪ 以-s结尾的复数词，只加-'

Workers' incomes have fallen slightly over the past year.

Many students benefit from several years' work after high school.

The Jameses' talents are extraordinary.

注意单数所有格和以-s结尾的复数词的区别。单数词形通常带-s：James's，而复数词形只需要撇号：Jameses'。

3 ▪ 不以-s结尾的复数词，加-'s

Children's educations are at stake.

We need to attract the media's attention.

4 ▪ 复合词：只在最后一个字上加-'s

The brother-in-law's business failed.

Taxes are always somebody else's fault.

5 ▪ 两个或三个所有人的情况，视所有权加-'s

个体所有

Zimbale's and Mason's comedy techniques are similar. [每个喜剧演员都有自己的技巧]

联合所有

The child recovered despite their mother and father's neglect. [父母都疏忽了]

练习42.1　构成所有格

把方括号内的每个词或词群变成所有格。带星号部分的参考答案请见书后。

例子：

The [men] blood pressures were higher than the [women].

The men's blood pressures were higher than the women's.

*1. In works for adults and teens, fiction writers often explore [people] relationship to nature and the environment.

*2. For example, [Carl Hiaasen] inventive and humorous plots often revolve around endangered [species] habitats.

*3. In *Hoot*, [Hiaasen] first novel for younger readers, endangered [owls] habitat will be destroyed if a [business] plans to build a new restaurant proceed.

*4. In *Scat* two [students] investigation into a [teacher] disappearance leads to an environmental mystery.

*5. Two of [Margaret Atwood] recent novels are about several [individuals] survival following a devastating environmental crisis and a plague that has killed nearly all of the residents of a city.

6. The first of the two books, *Oryx* and *Crake*, involves characters with those names but is told from one [man] perspective, that of a character named Jimmy.

7. Gradually readers learn about [Oryx and Crake] lives and why they are not struggling for survival along with Jimmy.

8. In the second Atwood book, *The Year of the Flood*, readers encounter a similar story, but through two [women] experiences.

9. In both books, most of the [city] residents have died from an outbreak of disease, and [everyone] home is empty.

10. Some readers may be unsettled by these two [books] visions of the future.

42b 删除或取代复数名词、单数动词或人称代词所有格中误用的撇号

1 ▪ 复数名词

名词的复数通常由加-s或-es构成：boys，families，Joneses。不要用加撇号的办法去构成复数：

不是：The Jones' controlled the firm's until 2011.

而是：The Joneses controlled the firms until 2011.

2 ▪ 单数动词

以-s结尾的动词从来不加撇号：

不是：The subway break's down less often now.

而是：The subway breaks down less often now.

3 ▪ 人称代词所有格

his, hers, its, ours, yours, theirs 和 whose 是 he, she, it, we, you, they 和 who 的所有格形式,它们不加撇号。

不是:The house is her's. It's roof leaks.

而是:The house is her~~'~~s. It~~'~~s roof leaks.

不要把代词所有格与词的缩略形式弄混。

42c 使用撇号构成缩略形式

缩略形式可以用撇号取代一个或多个字母、数字或词,如下面各例:

it is	it⌀s	cannot	can⌀t
they are	they⌀re	does not	doesn⌀t
you are	you⌀re	were not	weren⌀t
who is	who⌀s	class of 2015	class of ⌀15

注意:不要混淆缩略形式与人称代词。

缩略形式	人称代词
It⌀s a book.	It~~'~~s cover is green.
They⌀re coming.	The~~i~~r car broke down.
You⌀re right.	You~~'~~r idea is good.
Who⌀s coming?	Who~~'~~se party is it?

练习42.2　改写:缩略形式和人称代词

改写下列句子,纠正缩略形式和人称代词使用上的错误。如果句子本来就是对的,在其序号上做标记。带星号部分的参考答案请见书后。

例子:

The agencies give they're employees they're birthdays off.

The agencies give th~~ei~~r employees th~~ei~~r birthdays off.

*1. Many students seek help from the college writing center when their writing papers for their classes.

*2. The writing center has expanded it's hours: it's now open until 10 PM every night.

3. The writing center also offers online tutoring to students whose schedules make face-to-face meetings difficult.

4. For online tutoring, students can submit they're papers by computer when they're ready to receive help.

5. In a survey, students who use the writing center responded that it's a good source of feedback for they're writing.

42d 缩略语、日期和词形本身的复数形式中，撇号可要可不要

有时你会见到撇号用于构成缩略语的复数（BA's）、日期的复数（1900's）和词形本身（but's）的复数。但大多数现在通行的写作指导都不建议这样使用撇号。

BAs   PhDs
1990s   2000s
The sentence has too many *buts*.
Two 3s end the zip code.

注意：词或字母本身当作一个词来用的，要将它变成斜体或标下画线（见 p. 361），但不加 -s。

练习42.3   改写：撇号

改正下面段落中撇号的误用或缩略形式和人称代词所有格之间的混用。带星号部分的参考答案请见书后。

*People who's online experiences include blogging, Web cams, and social-networking sites are often used to seeing the details of other peoples private lives. *Many are also comfortable sharing they're own opinions, photographs, and videos with family, friend's, and even stranger's. *However, they need to realize that employers and even the government can see they're information, too. *Employers commonly put applicants names through social-networking Web sites such as *MySpace* and *Facebook*. Many companies monitor their employees outbound e-mail. People can take steps to protect their personal information by adjusting the privacy settings on their social-networking pages. They can avoid posting photos of themselves that they wouldnt want an employer to see. They can avoid sending personal e-mail while their at work. Its the individuals responsibility to keep certain information private.

第 43 章　引号

概要

正确使用引号：

- 把直接引语和引语里的引语放在引号内（下方及下页）
- 把作品中的作品标题放在引号内（下页）
- 把用在特殊意义上的词放在引号内（p. 337）
- 避免引号的常见误用：自己的论文的标题，常见绰号，以及俚语（p. 337）
- 按照标准做法，把引号放在别的标点之内或之外（p. 337）

引号，不管是双引号（" "）还是单引号（' '），主要是用来把直接引语及某些特定标题收入其中。引号的另外的用法将在本书其他章节讲述。

- 用引号给 she said 及其他标记短语加标点。（pp. 318–319）
- 用省略号或方括号对引文做改动。（pp. 341–344）
- 引用文献相对于解释或总结文献。（pp. 412–418）
- 把引语融入自己的文本中。（pp. 419–422）
- 引用时避免抄袭。（pp. 425–431）
- 在 MLA 格式或 APA 格式中长段散文的引用和诗歌的引用。（pp. 485–486, p. 518）

语法检查工具：语法检查工具能帮你查出单边引号，也能帮你查找引号内外的标点。

43a 用双引号括住直接引语

直接引语以原话报告某人所说或所写：

"Life," said the psychoanalyst Karen Horney, "remains a very efficient therapist."

引用对话时，给每个说话人另起一段：

"What shall I call you? Your name?" Andrews whispered rapidly, as with a high squeak the latch of the door rose.

"Elizabeth," she said. "Elizabeth."

—Graham Greene, *The Man Within*

注意：与你的正文分隔开了的直接引语，不要用引号。关于 MLA 格式和 APA 格式各自怎样处理这种引语，请看 pp. 485–486 和 p. 518。间接引语不以原话报告某人所说或所写，不要用引号：

The psychoanalyst Karen Horney claimed that "life is a good therapist."

43b 用单引号括住引语里的引语

"In formulating any philosophy," Woody Allen writes, "the first consideration must always be: What can we know? Descartes hinted at the problem when he wrote, 'My mind can never know my body, although it has become quite friendly with my leg.'"

注意在句子末尾出现了两种不同的引号——单引号用来结束内层引文，双引号用来结束主体引文。

43c 是更大作品的一部分的作品的标题，前后要用引号

出版或发布于更大的作品中的作品，它的标题要用引号括起来。（见下面方框）用单引号标记引用的标题之内的引语，如下面方框中文章的标题。要把标题的所有标点都用引号括起来，如文章的标题。

要用引号括起来的标题

其他标题应用斜体或下画线。（见pp. 360–361）

歌曲
"The Star-Spangled Banner"

小故事
"The Gift of the Magi"

短诗
"Mending Wall"

杂志文章
"Does Scaring Work?"

论文
"Joey: A Mechanical Boy"

网站上的网页或文档
"Readers' Page" (on the site *Friends of Prufrock*)

电视片或广播节目的一集
"The Mexican Connection" (on *Sixty Minutes*)

书的小节
"The Mast Head" (Chapter 35 of *Moby-Dick*)

注意：有些学科对文献引用内部的标题不要求使用引号。关于APA格式，见p. 502。

43d 引号可用来括住用在特殊意义上的词语

On movie sets movable "wild walls" make a one-walled room seem four-walled on film.

注意：你想定义或强调的词语，用斜体或下画线标注。（见p. 361）

43e 删除不需要的引号

你的文章的标题

不是："The Death Wish in One Poem by Robert Frost"
而是：The Death Wish in One Poem by Robert Frost
或者：The Death Wish in "Stopping by Woods on a Snowy Evening"

常见的绰号

不是：As President, "Jimmy" Carter preferred to use his nickname.
而是：As President, Jimmy Carter preferred to use his nickname.

俚语或套话

如果俚语或套话用得不合适，加上引号也无益。如果用得合适，也无须加上引号。

不是：We should support the President in his "hour of need" rather than "wimp out on him."
而是：We should give the President the support he needs rather than turn away like cowards.

43f 按照标准做法把其他标点放在引号之内或之外

1 ▪ 逗号和句号：在引号之内

Swift uses irony in his essay "A Modest Proposal."

Many first-time readers are shocked to see infants described as "delicious."

"'A Modest Proposal,'" wrote one critic, "is so outrageous that it cannot be believed."

例外：当括注紧接在引文之后时，逗号或句号都要放在出处之后：

One critic calls the essay "outrageous" (Olms 26).

Partly because of "the cool calculation of its delivery"(Olms 27), the satire still chills a modern reader.

2 ▪ 冒号和分号：在引号之外

A few years ago the slogan in elementary education was "learning by playing"; now educators are concerned with teaching basic skills.

We all know the meaning of "basic skills": reading, writing, and arithmetic.

3 ▪ 破折号、问号和感叹号：只有当它们是引文的一部分的时候才放在引号内

当破折号、问号和感叹号是引文的一部分的时候，把它放在引号内。不要再用其他的标点符号，比如句号或逗号：

"But must you—"Marcia hesitated, afraid of the answer.

"Go away!" I yelled.

Did you say, "Who is she?" [当你的句子和引文都以问号或感叹号结尾时，只在引文中使用标点符号]

当破折号、问号或感叹号只针对更大的句子而不针对引文时，把它放在引号之外——还是不要再用别的标点符号：

Another evocative line in English poetry—"Now slides the silent meteor on"—comes from Alfred, Lord Tennyson.

Who said, "Now cracks a noble heart"?

The woman called me "stupid"!

练习43.1　改写：问号

在下面段落里插入必要的问号。带星号部分的参考答案请见书后。

*In one class we talked about a passage from *I Have a Dream*, the speech delivered by Martin Luther King, Jr., on the steps of the Lincoln Memorial on August 28, 1963:

* When the architects of our republic wrote the magnificent words of the Constitution and the Declaration of Independence, they were signing a promissory note to which every American was to fall heir. *This note was a promise that all men would be guaranteed the unalienable rights of life, liberty, and the pursuit of happiness.

*What did Dr. King mean by this statement? the teacher asked. *Perhaps we should define promissory note first. Then she explained that a person who signs such a note agrees to pay a specific sum of money on a particular date or on demand by the holder of the note.

One student suggested, Maybe Dr. King meant that the writers of the Constitution and Declaration promised that all people in America should be equal.

He and over 200,000 people had gathered in Washington, DC, added another student. Maybe their purpose was to demand payment, to demand those rights for African Americans.

The whole discussion was an eye-opener for those of us (including me) who had never considered that those documents make promises that we should expect our country to fulfill.

第 44 章　其他标点

概要

- 用破折号（—）把中断部分与句子隔开（下方）
- 用括号（( )）把句中的插入表达和列表标记括起来（p. 341）
- 用省略号（. . .）表示引文中的省略（p. 341）
- 方括号（[ ]）主要用来表示引文中的改动（p. 344）
- 用斜杠（/）分隔选项和诗行（p. 344）

语法检查工具：语法检查工具能查出单边括号或方括号，这样你能补齐另一半，但本章会讲述的括号的别的误用，语法检查工具通常查不出，只会忽略。

44a 用一个或多个破折号表示转换以及把一些句子成分隔开

破折号主要是表示中断的标点符号：它表示转换、插入或中断。破折号由两个连字符连成（—），或者你可以在你的文字编辑器上用一个叫作em dash 的符号。不要在破折号的前后或两个连字符之间或em dash 的前后加入额外的空格。

注意：当一个以破折号开始的中断句子的成分出现在句子中间时，确保要加上另一个破折号来标记中断的结束。看下页的第一个例子。

1 ▪ 转换和犹豫

The novel—if one can call it that—appeared in 2012.

If the book had a plot—but a plot would be conventional.

"I was worried you might think I had stayed away because I was influenced by—" He stopped and lowered his eyes.

Astonished, Howe said, "Influenced by what?"

"Well, by—" Blackburn hesitated and for an answer pointed to the table.

—Lionel Trilling

2 ▪ 非必要成分

破折号可以代替逗号来分隔修饰词、并列表达式和其他不必要的成分。破折号比逗号更强调此成分。

Though they are close together—separated by only a few blocks—the two neighborhoods could be in different countries.

当一个非必要成分还有它自己的标点时，破折号就特别有用：

The qualities Monet painted—sunlight, rich shadows, deep colors—abounded near the rivers and gardens he used as subjects.

3 ▪ 开场系列、收尾系列和解释

Shortness of breath, skin discoloration or the sudden appearance of moles, persistent indigestion, the presence of small lumps—all these may signify cancer. [开场系列]

The patient undergoes a battery of tests—imaging, blood tests, perhaps even biopsy. [收尾系列]

Many patients are disturbed by MRI imaging—by the need to keep still for long periods in an exceedingly small space. [收尾解释]

后两个例子中，可以用冒号而不是破折号。破折号更不正式。

4 ▪ 过度使用

破折号太多会使句子听起来紧张带喘气。

不要：In all his life—eighty-seven years—my great-grandfather never allowed his picture to be taken—not even once. He claimed the "black box"—the camera—would steal his soul.

而要：In all his eighty-seven years, my great-grandfather did not allow his picture to be taken even once. He claimed the "black box"—the camera—would steal his soul.

44b 用括号把句中的插入性短语和列表标记括起来

注意：括号总是成对使用，一个在要标记的内容之前，一个在之后。

1 ▪ 插入语

插入语包括解释、事实、偏离以及可能有用有趣但并非必要的例子。括号减弱插入语的重要性。（逗号加强重要性，破折号更强）

The population of Philadelphia (now about 1.5 million) has declined since 1950.

注意：不要在括号括起来的插入语前面加上逗号。插入语之后的标点符号应该放在右括号之外：

不要：The population of Philadelphia compares with that of Phoenix, (just under 1.5 million.)

而要：The population of Philadelphia compares with that of Phoenix (just under 1.5 million).

如果你用括号括起一个完整的句子，请将句子大写，并在括号内加上句号：

In general, coaches will tell you that scouts are just guys who can't coach. (But then, so are brain surgeons.)

—Roy Blount

2 ▪ 句中的列表标记

Outside the Middle East, the following countries have the largest oil reserves: (1) Venezuela (63 billion barrels), (2) Russia (57 billion barrels), and (3) Mexico (51 billion barrels).

当你在文中列表时，不要像上面一样在序号上用括号。

44c 用省略号表示引文中的省略

省略号包含间有空格的三个句号（...），通常表示引文有所省略。下文的多个例子都引自或提及下面这篇文章：

原始引文：

"At the heart of the environmentalist world view is the conviction that human physical and spiritual health depends on sustaining the planet in a relatively unaltered state. Earth is our home in the full, genetic sense, where humanity and its ancestors existed for all the millions of years of their evolution. Natural ecosystems—forests, coral reefs, marine blue waters—maintain the world exactly as we would wish it to be maintained. When we debase the global environment and extinguish the variety of life, we are dismantling a support system that is too complex to understand, let alone replace, in the foreseeable future."

—Edward O. Wilson, "Is Humanity Suicidal?"

1. 省略句中部分

Wilson writes, "Natural ecosystems ... maintain the world exactly as we would wish it to be maintained."

2. 省略句末部分，没有给出处

Wilson writes, "Earth is our home ...."［句子的句号，结束到最后一个字，放在省略号之前］

3. 省略句末部分，有出处

Wilson writes, "Earth is our home ..." (27).［句子的句号跟在出处之后］

4. 省略两个或多个句子的部分

Wilson writes, "At the heart of the environmentalist world view is the conviction that human physical and spiritual health depends on sustaining the planet ... where humanity and its ancestors existed for all the millions of years of their evolution."

5. 省略一个或多个句子

As Wilson puts it, "At the heart of the environmentalist world view is the conviction that human physical and spiritual health depends on sustaining the planet in a relatively unaltered state. ... When we debase the global environment and extinguish the variety of life, we are dismantling a support system that is too complex to understand, let alone replace, in the foreseeable future."

6. 从一个句子的中间一直省略到另一个句子的末尾

"Earth is our home .... When we debase the global environment and extinguish the variety of life, we are dismantling a support system that is too complex to understand, let alone replace, in the foreseeable future."

7. 省略句子的开头，留下一个完整的句子

a. 方括号括住的大写字母

"[H]uman physical and spiritual health," Wilson writes, "depends on sustaining the planet in a relatively unaltered state."［不需要省略号，因为H两边的括号表明该字母最初不是大写，因此句子的开头被省略了］

b. 小写字母

According to Wilson, "human physical and spiritual health depends on sustaining the planet in a relatively unaltered state."［这里不需要省略号，因为小写的h表明了句子的开头已经被省略了］

c. 来自原文的大写字母

One reviewer comments, "...Wilson argues eloquently for the environmentalist world view" (Hami 28).［这里需要省略号，因为句子被引用的部分是以大写字母开头，此外看不出原文句子的开头已经被省略了］

8. 用一个词或短语

Wilson describes the earth as "our home."［不需要省略号］

注意这些例子的特点：

- 非此不能表明你已省略了原文的时候，用省略号，如当省略了一个或多个句子时（例5和例6），或当引用的词语能形成一个完整而又不同于原文的句子时（例1—4和例7c）。
- 当显然有所省略而无须说明的时候，不需要用省略号，例如，当方括号里的大写或小写字母表明有所省略时（例7a和7b），或当一个词组显然来自一个更大的句子时（例8）。
- 把省略号放在句子句号之后，除非有括注跟在引文之后，如例3和例7c，这种时候句号跟在引文之后。

如果从诗歌里省略了一行或多行，或从散文里省略了一段或多段，用单独一整行省略号表明这个省略：

In "Song: Love Armed" from 1676, Aphra Behn contrasts two lovers' experiences of a romance:

    Love in fantastic triumph sate,
     Whilst bleeding hearts around him flowed,
   . . . .
    But my poor heart alone is harmed,
     Whilst thine the victor is, and free. (lines 1-2, 15-16)

（如上例的引文格式，请看pp. 485–486）

> **练习44.1　使用省略号**
>
> 用省略号或其他标点符号，按照题中要求引用下面段落。带星号部分的参考答案请见书后。
>
>   Women in the sixteenth and seventeenth centuries were educated in the home and, in some cases, in boarding schools. Men were educated at home, in grammar schools, and at the universities. The universities were closed to female students. For women, "learning the Bible," as Elizabeth Joceline puts it, was an impetus to learning to read. To be able to read the Bible in the vernacular was a liberating experience that freed the reader from hearing only the set passages read in the church and interpreted by the church. A Protestant woman was expected to read the scriptures daily, to meditate on them, and to memorize portions of them. In addition, a woman was expected to instruct her entire household in "learning the Bible" by holding instructional and devotional times each day for all household members, including the servants.
>
>   —Charlotte F. Otten, *English Women's Voices*, 1540–1700
>
> *1. Quote the fifth sentence, but omit everything from *that freed the reader* to the end.
>
> 2. Quote the fifth sentence, but omit the words *was a liberating experience that*.
>
> 3. Quote the first and sixth sentences.

44d　用方括号表示引文的改动

  方括号在数学公式中有特殊的作用，但它们对于各种写作的主要作用是表示：为了解释、澄清或纠正错误，你对引文有所改动。

"That Chevron station [just outside Dallas] is one of the busiest in the nation," said a company spokesperson.

  放在方括号里的sic（拉丁文，意为"以这种方式"）表示引文的原文有错，非你之过。不要把方括号里的sic用斜体或下画线标记。

According to the newspaper report, "The car slammed thru [sic] the railing and into oncoming traffic."

不要用sic取笑作者，或者用它标记显然不是标准英语的文章。

44e 在多个选择之间、诗歌各行之间，用斜线

观点
Some teachers oppose pass[/]fail courses.

诗歌
Many readers have sensed a reluctant turn away from death in Frost's lines "The woods are lovely, dark and deep, [/] But I have promises to keep" (13–14).

当用这种方式分隔诗行时，在斜线之前和之后留一个空格。（更多关于引用诗歌的内容，请看pp. 485–486）

练习44.2　改写：破折号、括号、省略号、方括号和斜线

在下面段落中插入必要的破折号、括号、省略号、方括号和斜线。有时候可能有几种不同的标点可以用。带星号部分的参考答案请见书后。

*"Let all the learned say what they can, 'Tis ready money makes the man." *These two lines of poetry by the Englishman William Somerville 1645–1742 may apply to a current American economic problem. *Non-American investors with "ready money" pour some of it as much as $1.3 trillion in recent years into the United States. *Stocks and bonds, savings deposits, service companies, factories, artworks, political campaigns the investments of foreigners are varied and grow more numerous every day. Proponents of foreign investment argue that it revives industry, strengthens the economy, creates jobs more than 3 million, they say, and encourages free trade among nations. Opponents caution that the risks associated with heavy foreign investment namely decreased profits at home and increased political influence from outside may ultimately weaken the economy. On both sides, it seems, "the learned say, 'Tis ready money makes the man or country." The question is, whose money theirs or ours?

第六部分
拼写和文字处理细节

第45章 · 拼写

第46章 · 连字符

第47章 · 大写字母

第48章 · 斜体或下画线

第49章 · 缩略语

第50章 · 数字

第 45 章 拼写

概要

- 对于典型的拼写问题要有预期,比如容易误导的发音(下方)
- 给词语加上词尾或前缀时和构成复数时,要遵循关于ie/ei的拼写规则(p.350)

你可以按照本章建议,找出并解决你的拼写问题,训练自己更好地拼写。你也可以立刻就改进你的拼写,方法是培养以下三个习惯:

- 仔细检查你的写作。
- 对你的拼写培养一种健康的怀疑态度。
- 每次对拼写没把握时,查字典。

拼写检查器:拼写检查器能找出并跟踪你的论文中的拼写错误,但是用处有限,主要因为它无法识别相似拼写的混淆,比如their/they're/there,以及principal/principle。更多关于拼写检查的内容,请看p.39。

45a 对典型拼写错误要有所预期

拼写错误通常源自误导性的发音、同一个词的不同词形,以及英式发音和美式发音的混淆。

1 ▪ 发音

在英语中,词的发音不能作为拼写的可靠指导,对于同音词,即发音相同而词形不同的词,尤其如此。下面方框中是一些同音词和近音词。(关于容易混淆的词语的更多内容,请看pp.523–535的词语用法汇编)

常见易混淆的词语

accept (to receive)	allusion (an indirect reference)
except (other than)	illusion (an erroneous belief or perception)
affect (to have an influence on)	ascent (a movement up)
effect (result)	assent (to agree, or an agreement)
all ready (prepared)	bare (unclothed)
already (by this time)	bear (to carry, or an animal)

349 board (a plane of wood)
bored (uninterested)

brake (to stop)
break (to smash)

buy (to purchase)
by (next to)

capital (the seat of government)
capitol (the building where a legislature meets)

cite (to quote an authority)
sight (the ability to see)
site (a place)

desert (to abandon)
dessert (after-dinner course)

discreet (reserved, respectful)
discrete (individual, distinct)

elicit (to draw out)
illicit (illegal or immoral)

eminent (prominent, respected)
imminent (about to occur)

fair (average, or lovely)
fare (a fee for transportation)

forth (forward)
fourth (after *third*)

hear (to perceive by ear)
here (in this place)

heard (past tense of *hear*)
herd (a group of animals)

hole (an opening)
whole (complete)

its (possessive of *it*)
it's (contraction of *it is* or *it has*)

know (to be certain)
no (the opposite of *yes*)

lead (heavy metal)
led (past tense of *lead*)

lessen (to reduce)
lesson (something learned)

meat (flesh)
meet (to encounter, or a competition)

passed (past tense of *pass*)
past (after, or a time gone by)

patience (forbearance)
patients (persons under medical care)

peace (the absence of war)
piece (a portion of something)

plain (clear)
plane (a carpenter's tool, or an airborne vehicle)

presence (the state of being at hand)
presents (gifts)

principal (most important, or the head of a school)
principle (a basic truth or law)

rain (precipitation)
reign (to rule)
rein (a strap for an animal)

raise (to lift up)
raze (to tear down)

right (correct)
rite (a religious ceremony)
write (to make letters)

road (a surface for driving)
rode (past tense of *ride*)

scene (where an action occurs)
seen (past participle of *see*)

stationary (unmoving)
stationery (writing paper)

（续表）

their (possessive of *they*)	weather (climate)
there (opposite of *here*)	whether (*if*, or introducing a choice)
they're (contraction of *they are*)	which (one of a group)
to (toward)	witch (a sorcerer)
too (also)	who's (contraction of *who is* or *who has*)
two (following *one*)	whose (possessive of *who*)
waist (the middle of the body)	your (possessive of *you*)
waste (discarded material)	you're (contraction of *you are*)
weak (not strong)	
week (Sunday through Saturday)	

2 ▪ 同一个词的不同词形

350

同一个词的名词和动词词形、名词和形容词词形常常有不同的拼写，例如，advice（名词）和advise（动词）；description（名词）和describe（动词）；height（名词）和high（形容词）；generosity（名词）和generous（形容词）。类似的不同也可以在一些不规则动词（know，knew，known）和不规则名词的复数形式（man，men）上看到。

3 ▪ 美式英语拼写和英式英语拼写 (CULTURE LANGUAGE)

当面向美国读者写作时，用美式英语拼写，而不是英式英语拼写。

美式英语	英式英语
color, humor	colour, humour
theater, center	theatre, centre
canceled, traveled	cancelled, travelled
judgment	judgement
realize, civilize	realise, civilise
connection	connexion

你的字典会把两种拼写都列出来，但会给英式英语特别标记为chiefly Brit或类似标记。

45b 遵循拼写规则

1 ▪ ie和ei

要区分ie和ei，可以用下面这个脍炙人口的顺口溜：

I before *e*, except after *c*, or when pronounced "*ay*" as in *neighbor* and *weigh*.

i before *e*	believe	thief	hygiene
ei after *c*	ceiling	conceive	perceive
ei sounded as "*ay*"	sleigh	eight	beige

例外：对于那些例外，记住下面这句话：

The weird foreigner neither seizes leisure nor forfeits height.

2 ▪ 结尾的e

当给一个以e结尾的词加词尾时，如果词尾以元音开头，要去掉这个词末尾的e：

    advise + able = advisable   surprise + ing = surprising

如果词尾以辅音开头，保留该词结尾的e。

    care + ful = careful   like + ly = likely

例外：保留清音c或g后面的e，以使辅音的发音保持清音不变成浊音：courageous, changeable。如果e前面有另一个元音，去掉辅音前的这个e：argue + ment = argument, true + ly = truly。

3 ▪ 结尾的y

当给以y结尾的词加词尾时，如果y后面接辅音，改y为i：

    beauty, beauties   worry, worried   supply, supplies

但是，如果y在元音后，如果y是专有名词的结尾，或者如果所加的词尾是ing，则保留这个y。

    day, days   Minsky, Minskys   cry, crying

4 ▪ 结尾的辅音

当给一个单音节并以辅音结尾的词加词尾时，假如该辅音跟着一个单元音，那么双写该辅音。否则，不要双写辅音。

    slap, slapping   park, parking   pair, paired

在多于一个音节的词语中，如果最后一个辅音之前有单元音，并且加上新词尾之后该辅音结束了重读音节，那么双写最后这个辅音。否则就不双写它。

refer, referring   refer, reference   relent, relented

5 ▪ 前缀

加前缀时，不要给原词加减字母：

unnecessary   disappoint   misspell

6 ▪ 复数

大多数名词以在单数词形后面加s来构成复数，以s，sh，ch或x结尾的名词复数加es。

boy, boys   kiss, kisses   church, churches

以元音加o结尾的名词通常加s构成复数。以辅音加o结尾的词通常加es构成复数。

ratio, ratios   hero, heroes

有些非常常见的名词有不规则的复数形式。

child, children   woman, women   mouse, mice

有些英语词来源于意大利语、希腊语、拉丁语或法语，它们按照原来的语言构成复数：

analysis, analyses   criterion, criteria   piano, pianos
basis, bases   datum, data   thesis, theses
crisis, crises   medium, media

这一类词中有几个名词的复数可以是规则的也可以是不规则的，例如，index，indices，indexes；curriculum，curricula，curriculums。现代更多用其规则复数形式。

复合名词的复数形式，给复合词的主要词加s。有时候该主要词不是复合词中的最后一个词：

city-states   fathers-in-law   passersby

CULTURE LANGUAGE 不可数名词没有复数形式，规则、不规则的都没有。不可数名词的例子有air，intelligence和wealth。见pp. 273–274。

练习45.1　使用正确的拼写

从方括号中选择正确的拼写，必要的话参考pp. 348–349的词汇列表，或者参考字典。带星号部分的参考答案请见书后。

例子：

The boat [passed, past] us so fast that we rocked violently in [its, it's] wake.

The boat passed us so fast that we rocked violently in its wake.

*1. Science [affects, effects] many [important, importent] aspects of our lives.

*2. Many people have a [pore, poor] understanding of the [role, roll] of scientific breakthroughs in [their, they're] health.

*3. Many people [beleive, believe] that [docters, doctors] are more [responsable, responsible] for [improvements, improvments] in health care than scientists are.

*4. But scientists in the [labratory, laboratory] have made crucial steps in the search for [knowlege, knowledge] about human health and [medecine, medicine].

*5. For example, one scientist [who's, whose] discoveries have [affected, effected] many people is Ulf Von Euler.

6. In the 1950s Von Euler's discovery of certain hormones [lead, led] to the invention of the birth control pill.

7. Von Euler's work was used by John Rock, who [developed, developped] the first birth control pill and influenced family [planing, planning].

8. Von Euler also discovered the [principal, principle] neurotransmitter that controls the heartbeat.

9. Another scientist, Hans Selye, showed what [affect, effect] stress can have on the body.

10. His findings have [lead, led] to methods of [baring, bearing] stress.

练习45.2　运用拼写检查器

用下面这段话试试你的电脑的拼写检查器。按下面原样输入这段话，运行拼写检查器，然后检查并改正电脑拼写检查器没有查出来的错误。（一共有14个错误）带星号部分的参考答案请见书后。

　　*The whether effects all of us, though it's affects are different for different people. *Some people love a fare day with warm temperatures and sunshine. *They revel in spending a hole day outside without the threat of rein. Other people prefer dark, rainy daze. They relish the opportunity to slow down and here they're inner thoughts. Most people agree, however, that to much of one kind of whether—reign, sun, snow, or clouds—makes them board.

第 46 章　连字符

概要

正确使用连字符:
- 用连字符构成复合形容词、分数和合成词(下方)
- 用连字符在行末按音节切分词语(下页)

46a 在某些复合词中使用连字符

1 ▪ 复合形容词

两三个词一起在名词前作为单个修饰语来用时,用连字符把它们连成一个整体。

She is a well-known actor.
Some Spanish-speaking students work as translators in the admission and finance offices.

当这样的复合形容词跟在名词后面时,就不需要连字符了。

The actor is well-known.
Many students are Spanish-speaking.

含有-ly副词的复合修饰语,即使用在名词前,也不需要连字符: clearly-defined。 354

当复合形容词的一部分在两个或更多的平行复合形容词中只出现一次时,连字符提示读者应当在心里把哪些词与缺失的部分连接在一起。

School-age children should have eight- or nine-o'clock bedtimes.

2 ▪ 分数和合成词

连字符连接分数的分子和分母: two-thirds, three-fourths。连字符也用来连接整个数字的各部分: twenty-one, ninety-nine。

3 ▪ 前缀和后缀

不要把连字符用在前缀上,除非下列情况:

- 前缀self-, all-和ex-: self-control, all-inclusive, ex-student。
- 在首字母的大写单词前加上前缀: un-American。
- 单词前有一个大写字母: T-shirt。
- 防止误读: de-emphasize, re-create a story。

唯一总是需要加连字符的后缀是-elect，如president-elect。

46b 使用连字符断开行末的单词

为了避免文档中出现很短的行，可以把一些词在一行的末尾和下一行的开端断开。可以把文字编辑器设置为自动在合适位置切分词语。如果手动来分，遵循下列规则：

- 只在音节之间断开——例如，win-dows，不能像wi-ndows这样断开。字典上可查到正确的切分方法。
- 不要断开单音节词。
- 第一行至少留下两个字母，第二行至少留下三个字母。如果一个词的切分不能满足这条规则，（如a-bus-er）就不要分了。
- 不要用连字符断开一个网址，因为读者会以为连字符是地址的一部分。关于网址可以怎样断开，不同的格式有不同的做法，例如，MLA格式只允许在斜线之后断开，而APA格式允许在大多数标点符号之前断开。

练习46.1　使用连字符

在必要之处插入连字符，并删除不需要的连字符。如果一个句子本来就是对的，在其序号上做标记。带星号部分的参考答案请见书后。

例子：

Elephants have twelve inch long teeth, but they have only four of them.

Elephants have twelve-inch-long teeth, but they have only four of them.

*1. The African elephant is well known for its size.

*2. Both male and female African elephants can grow to a ten-foot height.

*3. The non African elephants of south central Asia are somewhat smaller.

*4. A fourteen or fifteen year old elephant has reached sexual maturity.

*5. The elephant life span is about sixty five or seventy years.

6. A newborn elephant calf weighs two to three hundred pounds.

7. It stands about thirty three inches high.

8. A two hundred pound, thirty three inch baby is quite a big baby.

9. Unfortunately, elephants are often killed for their ivory tusks, and partly as a result they are an increasingly-endangered species.

10. African governments have made tusk and ivory selling illegal.

第 47 章　大写字母

概要

- 每个句子的第一个字母要大写（p. 356）
- 专有名词、专有形容词和用作专有名词的重要部分的词，要首字母大写（p. 356）
- 作品标题和副标题里的大多数词，要首字母大写（p. 358）
- 网络通信中的大写问题，按惯例行事（p. 359）

在大多数写作中，关于什么时候某个词首字母要大写，可以从本章所描述的惯例及桌面字典得到帮助。参考 pp. 433–434 的格式指导，了解各学科的要求。

语法检查工具：语法检查工具能查出大写字母的滥用以及句首没有大写的错误，也能查出专有名词和形容词里遗漏的大写——前提是该检查工具的词典里收有这些名词和形容词。例如，某检查工具能查出 christianity 和 europe，但查不出 china（作为国家名）或者 Stephen king。

（CULTURE LANGUAGE）每种语言对于大写有不同的惯例。比如英语是唯一一个要求大写第一人称单数（I）的语言，并且英语要求专有名词首字母大写，但大多数普通名词首字母不大写的做法也和其他一些语言不同。

47a 每句话的第一个字母要大写

No one expected the outcome.
Will inflation result?
Watch out!

引用别的作者的话时，应该保留他们原话中开头的大写字母，或者要表明你改变了原来的大写。如果可能的话，把引文并入你自己的句子，这样它的大写与你的一致：

"**P**sychotherapists often overlook the benefits of self-deception," the author argues.

The author argues that "**t**he benefits of self-deception" are not always recognized by psychotherapists.［句子中引用的短语首字母不要大写］

如果需要改变原文的大写，要用方括号表明你的改动。

"**[T]**he benefits of self-deception" are not always recognized by psychotherapists, the author argues.

The author argues that "[p]sychotherapists often overlook the benefits of self-deception."

注意：如果是一系列的问句，首字母可大写也可不大写。下面两个例子都是正确用法：

Is the population a hundred? **T**wo hundred? **M**ore?

Is the population a hundred? **t**wo hundred? **m**ore?

冒号之后的完整句子的第一个字，也是首字母可大写也可不大写。

47b 专有名词、专有形容词和用作专有名词的重要部分的词，要首字母大写

1 ▪ 专有名词和专有形容词

专有名词是特定人、地和事物的名称：Shakespeare，China，World War I。
专有形容词由专有名词形成：Shakespearean，Chinese。所有专有名词和专有形容词都要大写，但冠词（a，an，the）除外。

需要首字母大写的专有名词和专有形容词

特定的人或事物

Stephen **k**ing	**B**oulder **D**am
Napoleon **B**onaparte	the **E**mpire **S**tate **B**uilding

特定的地方和地理区域

New **Y**ork **C**ity	the **M**editerranean **S**ea
China	the **N**ortheast, the **S**outh

但是，**n**ortheast of the **c**ity, going south 不要首字母大写。

星期几，月份，节假日

Monday	**Y**om **K**ippur
May	**C**hristmas

政府办公室、部门和机构

House of **R**epresentatives	**P**olk **M**unicipal **C**ourt
Department of **D**efense	**S**equoia **H**ospital

学术机构和院系

University of **K**ansas	**D**epartment of **N**ursing
Santa **M**onica **C**ollege	**H**aven **H**igh **S**chool

但是，the **u**niversity, **c**ollege course, high **s**chool diploma 不要首字母大写。

（续表）

政治、社会、学术和其他组织及协会及成员

Democratic Party, Democrats	League of Women Voters
Sierra Club	Boston Celtics
B'nai B'rith	Chicago Symphony Orchestra

种族、民族及其语言

Native American	Germans
African American	Swahili
Caucasian	Italian
但是，blacks, whites不要首字母大写。	

宗教、其成员，及圣物

Christianity, Christians	God
Catholicism, Catholics	Allah
Judaism, Orthodox Jews	the Bible［但biblical不要首字母大写］
Islam, Muslims	the Koran, the Qur'an

历史事件、公文、时期和运动

the Vietnam War	the Renaissance
the Constitution	the Romantic Movement

2 ▪ 用作专有名词重要部分的常见名词

普通名词street, avenue, park, river, ocean, lake, company, college, country和memorial，如果它们用作专有名词的一部分，指称特定地名或机构时，首字母要大写：

Main Street	Ford Motor Company
Central Park	Madison College
Mississippi River	George Washington Memorial

3 ▪ 方位名词

方位名词，只有当它们指称某个特定区域而不是泛指方向时，首字母才大写：

Students from the West often melt in eastern humidity.

4 ▪ 关系名词

只有当关系名词在专有名词之前或者取代专有名词时，首字母才大写：

Our aunt scolded us for disrespecting Father and Uncle Jake.

5 ▪ 带人名的头衔

头衔出现在人名之前时,首字母大写。头衔出现在人名之后或者不与人名相连时,首字母不大写:

Professor Otto Osborne   Otto Osborne, a **p**rofessor
Doctor Jane Covington   Jane Covington, a **d**octor
Governor Ella Moore   Ella Moore, the **g**overnor

注意: 很多作者会把级别很高的头衔首字母大写,即使它在人名之后或单独使用: Ronald Reagan, past President of the United States。

47c 标题和副标题中的大部分词都要首字母大写

你的文章中,标题中的所有词都要首字母大写,除了这些之外:冠词(a, an, the),不定式to,并列连词(and, but等),介词(with, between等)。但是,如果这些词是标题的第一个词或最后一个词,或是在冒号或分号之后,那就要首字母大写。

"**C**ourtship **t**hrough **t**he **A**ges"   **M**anagement: **A N**ew **T**heory
A Diamond **I**s **F**orever   "**O**nce **M**ore **t**o **t**he **L**ake"
"**K**nowing **W**hom **t**o **A**sk"   **A**n **E**nd **t**o **L**ive **F**or
Learning **f**rom **L**as **V**egas   **F**ile **u**nder **A**rchitecture

注意: 关于标题中的大写,各学科有自己的规定。例如,前述规则反映的是针对英语和其他人文学科的MLA格式。而作为对照,针对社会科学的APA格式只要求在出处中把书和文章标题中的第一个词及专有名词的首字母大写。(见p. 502)

47d 网络通信中,按惯例使用大写

网络通信中,全用大写字母或者全不用大写字母的写法造成阅读困难。另外,全用大写字母写的信息令人感到粗鲁。做网络通信时请按照47a–47c中的规则使用大写字母。

> **练习47.1   改写:大写字母**
>
> 改写下列句子,改正在大写上的错误。有疑问请参考字典。如果句子本来就是对的,在其序号上做标记。带星号部分的参考答案请见书后。

例子：

The first book on the reading list is mark twain's *a connecticut yankee in king arthur's court*.

The first book on the reading list is M̲ark T̲wain's A̲ C̲onnecticut Y̲ankee in K̲ing A̲rthur's C̲ourt.

*1. San Antonio, texas, is a thriving city in the southwest.

*2. The city has always offered much to tourists interested in the roots of spanish settlement in the new world.

*3. The alamo is one of five Catholic Missions built by Priests to convert native americans and to maintain spain's claims in the area.

*4. But the alamo is more famous for being the site of an 1836 battle that helped to create the republic of Texas.

*5. Many of the nearby Streets, such as Crockett street, are named for men who died in that Battle.

6. The Hemisfair plaza and the San Antonio river link tourist and convention facilities.

7. Restaurants, Hotels, and shops line the River. the haunting melodies of "Una paloma blanca" and "malagueña" lure passing tourists into Casa rio and other mexican restaurants.

8. The university of Texas at San Antonio has expanded, and a Medical Center lies in the Northwest part of the city.

9. A marine attraction on the west side of San Antonio entertains grandparents, fathers and mothers, and children with the antics of dolphins and seals.

10. The City has attracted high-tech industry, creating a corridor between san antonio and austin.

第 48 章　斜体或下画线

概要

下列情况用斜体或下画线：

- 单独出现的作品标题（下页）
- 船只、飞机、航天器和火车的名字（p. 361）
- 不是英语的一部分的外语词（p. 361）

- 当作字符用的词或字母（p. 361）
- 偶尔，想强调的词（p. 362）

斜体和下画线表示突出或强调。现在，斜体已经在学术写作和公文写作中普遍使用。但有些倒还是推荐用下画线，问问你的导师他/她的喜好是什么。

斜体或下画线的使用，在整个文档中，不论是正文还是出处，都要前后一致。如果用斜体，确保你的斜体字母与别的字体可清晰区分。如果用下画线，标记两个或以上的词语时，要把词语之间的空格也标上下画线：<u>Criminal Statistics: Misuses of Numbers</u>。

语法检查工具：语法检查工具无法识别斜体或下画线的使用问题。自己检查，确保你正确地使用了这两种强调手段。

48a 单独出现的作品标题

在文本中，单独出版、发行或上演的作品，其标题用斜体或下画线标记。（见下面的方框）其他标题用引号标记。

用斜体或下画线标记的标题

其他标题应用引号标记。（见p. 336）

书	网站
War and Peace	*Friends of Prufrock*
And the Band Played On	*YouTube*
剧	**电脑软件**
Hamlet	*Microsoft Internet Explorer*
The Phantom of the Opera	*Google*
手册	**期刊**
The Truth about Alcoholism	*Time*
长的音乐作品	*Philadelphia Inquirer*
Tchaikovsky's Swan Lake	**出版过的演讲**
除了 *Symphony in C*	Lincoln's *Gettysburg Address*
广播电视节目	**电影和视频**
NBC Sports Hour	*Schindler's List*
Radio Lab	*How to Relax*

（续表）

长诗	视觉艺术作品
Beowulf	Michelangelo's *David*
Paradise Lost	the *Mona Lisa*

例外：法律文书、圣经、可兰经，及它们的一部分，通常不用斜体或下画线标记。

不是：We studied the *Book of Revelation* in the *Bible*.

而是：We studied the Book of Revelation in the Bible.

48b 船只、飞机、航天器和火车的名字，用斜体或下画线

| *Challenger* | *Orient Express* | *Queen Mary 2* |
| *Apollo XI* | *Montrealer* | *Spirit of St. Louis* |

48c 不是英语的一部分的外语词，用斜体或下画线

将尚未融入英语的外来语用斜体或下画线表示。词典会说明一个词是否仍被认为是英语的外来词。

The scientific name for the brown trout is *Salmo trutta*.［动植物的拉丁文学名总是斜体或下画线］

The Latin *De gustibus non est disputandum* translates roughly as "There's no accounting for taste."

48d 当作字符用的词或字母，用斜体或下画线标记

用斜体或下画线表示你把一个词或字母当作字符使用，而不是用它的意义。你所定义和解释的词就属于这一类。

The word *syzygy* refers to a straight line formed by three celestial bodies, as in the alignment of the earth, sun, and moon.

Some people say *th*, as in *thought*, with a faint *s* or *f* sound.

48e 偶尔也用斜体或下画线表示强调

斜体或下画线可以用来强调一个词或词组,特别是转述某人说了什么的时候。但是这种强调手段要少用,否则你的写作会显得过于情绪化。

48f 在网络通信中,用其他做法替代斜体或下画线

有些形式的网络通信不允许使用斜体或下画线这样的传统强调手段,原因见本章所述。如果不能使用斜体或下画线来突出书的标题或其他通常需要强调的成分,在该成分的前后输入下横线"_":*Measurements coincide with those in_Joule's Handbook_*。你也可以在要强调的词的前后加上星号:*I *will not* be able to attend.*

不要用全文大写来表示强调:太吵了。

> **练习48.1　改写:斜体或下画线**
>
> 在下列段落中,用斜体或下画线强调需要突出的词或短语,并在不必要地被强调的词或词组前画一个对钩。如果句子本来就是对的,在其序号上做标记。带星号部分的参考答案请见书后。
>
> 例子:
>
> Of Hitchcock's movies, Psycho is the scariest.
>
> Of Hitchcock's movies, *Psycho* is the scariest.
>
> *1. Of the many Vietnam veterans who are writers, Oliver Stone is perhaps the most famous for writing and directing the films Platoon and Born on the Fourth of July.
>
> *2. Tim O'Brien has written short stories for Esquire, GQ, and Massachusetts Review.
>
> *3. Going after Cacciato is O'Brien's dreamlike novel about the horrors of combat.
>
> *4. The word Vietnam is technically two words (*Viet* and *Nam*), but most American writers spell it as *one* word.
>
> *5. American writers use words or phrases borrowed from Vietnamese, such as di di mau ("go quickly") or dinky dau ("crazy").
>
> 6. Philip Caputo's *gripping* account of his service in Vietnam appears in the book A Rumor of War.
>
> 7. Caputo's book was made into a television movie, also titled *A Rumor of War*.

8. David Rabe's plays—including The Basic Training of Pavlo Hummel, Streamers, and Sticks and Bones—depict the effects of the war *not only* on the soldiers *but also* on their families.

9. Called "*the poet laureate of the Vietnam war,*" Steve Mason has published two collections of poems: Johnny's Song and Warrior for Peace.

10. The Washington Post published *rave* reviews of Veteran's Day, an autobiography by Rod Kane.

第 49 章　缩略语

概要

- 缩略语只用于读者熟悉的事物上（下页）
- 了解你的学科规范对度量单位、地名、日历名称、拉丁表达和其他词的缩写的要求（下页）
- 只在专有名词前面或后面用缩略语表示头衔（p. 365）
- 只在特定日期和数字的前面或后面才使用BC，BCE，AD，CE，AM，PM，no.和$（p. 365）
- 只在公司的官方名称中才使用Inc., Bros., Co., 或&（代替and）（p. 365）

在学术写作中，缩略语的恰当与否部分取决于学科，非技术领域比技术领域用缩略语较少。

本章的写作指导适用于非技术性文本。参考pp. 433–434列出的其中的写作规范指导，了解你所在学科的要求。

用法各有不同，但是作者们越来越多地省略两三个词组成的、全由首字母大写构成的缩略语中的句号：US，BA，USMC。关于缩略语的标点，请看pp. 304–305。

语法和拼写检查器：语法检查工具可以标记一些缩写，如ft.（代表foot）和st .（代表street）。拼写检查器将标记它不能识别的缩写。但是这两个检查器都不能判断缩写是否适合你的写作情况。

49a 大多数写作中，可以接受常见的缩略语和首字母

首字母缩略词是一个缩略语，它可以像一个词一样读出来，例如WHO、NATO、SWAT和AIDS。只要为人熟知，缩略语可以在大多数文章中使用。

机构：LSU, UCLA, TCU

组织：CIA, FBI, YMCA, AFL-CIO

公司：IBM, CBS, ITT

人：JFK, LBJ, FDR

国家：US, USA

注意：如果一个名字或者术语（如operating room）频繁出现于一篇文章，可以用它的缩略语（OR）来减少用词。第一次出现的时候给出全拼，在括号中给出缩略语，以后就可以使用缩略语了。

49b 通常把度量单位、地名、日历名称、人名和课程完全拼写出来

在大多数学术写作、普通写作和公文写作中，下面列出的词都应该给出全拼。（但在引用出处和技术写作中，前三类更多使用缩略语形式）

度量单位

The dog is thirty inches [不用in.] high.

地理名称

The publisher is in Massachusetts [不是Mass.或MA].

星期、月份和节假日

The truce was signed on Tuesday [不是Tues.], April [不是Apr.] 16.

人名

Robert [不是Robt.] Frost wrote accessible poems.

课程

I'm majoring in political science [不是poli. sci.].

49c 通常拉丁缩略语只用在引文出处和括号内的解释中

i.e.	*id est*: that is	
cf.	*confer*: compare	
e.g.	*exempli gratia*: for example	
et al.	*et alii*: and others	

etc. *et cetera*: and so forth

NB *nota bene*: note well

He said he would be gone a fortnight (i.e., two weeks).

Bloom et al., editors, *Anthology of Light Verse*

Trees, too, are susceptible to disease (e.g., Dutch elm disease).

有些作者在正式写作中避免用这样的缩略语，即使是在括号中也不用。

49d 在紧挨专有名词之前及之后的头衔中使用标准缩略语

专有名词之前	专有名词之后
Dr. Michael Hsu	Michael Hsu, MD
Mr., Mrs., Ms., Hon.,	DDS, DVM, PhD,
St., Rev., Msgr., Gen.	EdD, OSB, SJ, Sr., Jr.

Rev.，Hon.，Prof.，Rep.，Sen.，Dr. 和 St.（Saint）这样的缩略语只用在专有名词之前。

49e 只有在特定日期和数字之前或之后才使用 BC，BCE，AD，CE，AM，PM，no. 及 $

| 44 BC | AD 1492 | 11:26 AM（或 a.m.） | no. 36（或 No. 36） |
| 44 BCE | 1492 CE | 8:05 PM（或 p.m.） | $7.41 |

BC（"before Christ"），BCE（"before the common era"）及 CE（"common era"）总是跟在日期后面。相反，AD（*anno Domini*，"in the year of the Lord"的拉丁文）总是在日期的前面。

49f 只在公司的官方名称中才使用 Inc.，Bros.，Co. 或 &（and）

不是：The Santini bros. operate a large moving firm in New York City & environs.

而是：The Santini brothers operate a large moving firm in New York City and environs.

或：Santini Bros. is a large moving firm in New York City and environs.

练习49.1 改写：缩略语

对下列句子做必要的改动，纠正缩略语在非技术写作中的不当使用。如果句子本来就是对的，在其序号上做标记。带星号部分的参考答案请见书后。

例子：

One prof. lectured for five hrs.

One <u>professor</u> lectured for five <u>hours</u>.

*1. In an issue of *Science* magazine, Dr. Virgil L. Sharpton discusses a theory that could help explain the extinction of dinosaurs.

*2. About 65 mill. yrs. ago, a comet or asteroid crashed into the earth.

*3. The result was a huge crater about 10 km. (6.2 mi.) deep in the Gulf of Mex.

*4. Sharpton's new measurements suggest that the crater is 50 pct. larger than scientists had previously believed.

*5. Indeed, 20-yr.-old drilling cores reveal that the crater is about 186 mi. wide, roughly the size of Conn.

6. The space object was traveling more than 100,000 miles per hour and hit the earth with the impact of 100 to 300 megatons of TNT.

7. On impact, 200,000 cubic km. of rock and soil were vaporized or thrown into the air.

8. That's the equivalent of 2.34 bill. cubic ft. of matter.

9. The impact would have created 400-ft. tidal waves across the Atl. Ocean, temps. higher than 20,000 degs., and powerful earthquakes.

10. Sharpton theorizes that the dust, vapor, and smoke from this impact blocked the sun's rays for mos., cooled the earth, and thus resulted in the death of the dinosaurs.

第50章 数字

概要

- 按你所在领域的标准用法使用数字（下页）
- 对于日期、地址和其他信息，按惯例使用数字（p. 367）
- 句首的数字要拼写出来（p. 368）

数是用数字（28）写出来，还是用文字（twenty-eight）写出来，是个学科规范的问题：技术性学科更常用数字，非技术性学科更倾向于使用文字。在所有的学科中，引文出处中都比正文中更多地使用数字。

语法检查工具：语法检查工具能查出句首的数字，也可以设定为忽视数字或寻找数字。但是它没法告诉你对于你的写作情形来说，数字或全拼出来的单词是否用得恰当。

50a 按你所在领域的标准用法使用数字

要用两三个字才能拼出来的数，用数字。

The leap year has 366 days.
The population of Minot, North Dakota, is about 32,800.

在非技术性学术写作中，把能用一两个词拼出来的数拼出来。用连字符的数可以看成一个词。

Twelve nations signed the treaty.
The ball game drew forty-two thousand people.
Jenson lived to be ninety-nine or one hundred.

多数公文写作中，所有大于10的数都用数字：five reasons, 11 participants。在技术性的学术和公文写作中，例如，科学文章和工程文章中，多有大于10的数都用数字表示，而0–9的数，如果指的是确切的数量，也用数字：2 liters, 1 hour。（更多细节，请参考列在pp. 433–434的写作规范）

注意：百万以上的整数，用数字和文字联合表示：26 million, 2.45billion。如果一个段落里出现好几个数在一起，要么全使用数字，要么全使用文字表示，即使按惯例会要求混用。要小心，避免连续使用两个数字，因为会让人迷惑不解。改写句子以分开两个数字：

不清楚：Out of 530 101 children caught the virus.
清楚：Out of 530 children 101 caught the virus.

CULTURE LANGUAGE 在标准美式英语中，用逗号分隔开长数字（26,000），用句号作小数点（2.06）。

50b 对于日期、地址和其他信息，按照惯例来使用数字

日期和年份
June 18, 1985   AD 12
456 BC   2010

一天里的时间
9:00 AM   3:45 PM

地址
355 Clinton Avenue
Washington, DC 20036

确切的钱数
$3.5 million $4.50

小数、百分数和分数
22.5   3½
48%（或者 48 percent）

比分和统计数据
21 to 7   a ratio of 8 to 1
a mean of 26

页码、章节、卷册、场、幕、行
Chapter 9, page 123
Hamlet, act 5, scene 3

例外：只需几个词表达的整的钱数，用文字表示：seventeen dollars, sixty cents。当用 o'clock 表示一天里的时间的时候，数字也用文字表示：two o'clock，而不是 2 o'clock。

50c 把句首的数拼写出来

为了清晰，把句首的数拼写出来。如果这个数要多于两个词才能写出来，调整句子，把数放在后面的位置，这样可以用数字来表示。

不是：3.9 billion people live in Asia.

而是：The population of Asia is 3.9 billion.

> **练习50.1 改写：数字**
>
> 改写下列句子，在非技术写作中正确使用数字。如果一个句子本来就是对的，在其序号上做标记。带星号部分的参考答案请见书后。
>
> 例子：
>
> Addie paid two hundred and five dollars for used scuba gear.
>
> Addie paid $205 for used scuba gear.
>
> *1. The planet Saturn is nine hundred million miles, or nearly one billion five hundred million kilometers, from the sun.
>
> *2. A year on Saturn equals almost thirty of our years.

*3. Thus, Saturn orbits the sun only two and four-tenths times during the average human life span.

*4. It travels in its orbit at about twenty-one thousand six hundred miles per hour.

*5. 15 to 20 times denser than Earth's core, Saturn's core measures 17,000 miles across.

6. The temperature at Saturn's cloud tops is minus one hundred seventy degrees Fahrenheit.

7. In nineteen hundred thirty-three, astronomers found on Saturn's surface a huge white spot 2 times the size of Earth and 7 times the size of Mercury.

8. Saturn's famous rings reflect almost seventy percent of the sunlight that approaches the planet.

9. The ring system is almost forty thousand miles wide, beginning 8,800 miles from the planet's visible surface and ending forty-seven thousand miles from that surface.

10. The spacecraft *Cassini* traveled more than eight hundred and twenty million miles to explore and photograph Saturn.

第七部分
研究和文献记录

7

第51章·研究策略

第52章·寻找原始资料

第53章·处理原始资料

第54章·抄袭的避免和原始资料的引用

第55章·撰写论文

第56章·MLA原始资料来源的标注与格式

第57章·APA原始资料来源的标注与格式

第 51 章　研究策略

概要

- 制定计划（下方）
- 撰写研究日记（p. 371）
- 寻找可研究的主题和问题（p. 371）
- 设定关于原始资料的目标（p. 373）
- 记录带有注释的参考目录（p. 376）

和许多作者一样，你可能认为像侦探处理新案件那样处理研究性写作是很有裨益的。秘密就是你所关注的问题的答案。对答案的探求会让你思考其他人对你的主题的看法，但是你不应仅仅是简单地汇报他们的观点。在他们的观点之上，你要形成并支撑自己的观点。

如果你采取本章中所描述的步骤，你的调查将会更加富有成效和令人愉快。

51a 规划研究过程

研究性写作是一个写作过程：

- 你在由主题、目的、读者、类型和其他因素组成的特定环境下工作。（第1章）
- 你收集与主题有关的观点和信息。（第2章）
- 你关注并整理你的观点。（第3章）
- 你打草稿以探究你要表达的意思。（第4章）
- 你修改以完成你的论文。（第5章）
- 你校订以改进并完善你的论文。（第6章）

尽管本清单中的过程似乎整齐有序，但是你从经验中得知这些阶段是重叠的，例如，你可能在收集到所有所需信息之前就开始起草文章，而在打草稿时，你可能会发现一个让你重新思考研究方法的原始资料。对研究性写作过程的预期可以让你灵活自由地研究，并对各种发现持开放态度。

一份经过深思熟虑的计划和系统性的步骤有助于你在研究性写作的各种活动中坚持到底。步骤之一就是制定一份类似下面表格的将可用时间分配给必要工作的时间表。你可以估算出每一个用横线分隔的部分大概需要占用总时间的四分之一。前两个部分最无法预计，因此明智的办法就是尽早开工，以便为无法预料的事留出时间。

	研究性写作的时序步骤
_____	1. 制订计划，开始撰写研究日记（此处和下方）
_____	2. 寻找可研究的主题和问题（下方）
_____	3. 设定关于原始资料的目标（p. 373）
_____	4. 查找印刷版和电子版的原始资料（p. 378），制作带有注释的参考目录（p. 376）
_____	5. 评估并组合原始资料（p. 397, p. 409）
_____	6. 从原始资料处收集信息（p. 411），通常采用总结、改述和直接引用等方法（p. 412）
_____	7. 采取措施避免抄袭（p. 425）
_____	8. 形成主题陈述并创建论文结构（p. 435）
_____	9. 起草论文（p. 436），将总结、改述和直接引用融入自己的观点中（p. 418）
_____	10. 修改并校订论文（p. 437）
_____	11. 在论文中引用原始资料（p. 432）
_____	12. 准备引用或参考文献的清单（p. 432）
_____	13. 准备最后成稿（p. 438）
_____	交稿

51b 撰写研究日记

进行研究项目时，要随时携带笔记本或电脑，用来写研究日记，作为一个记录活动和观点的地方。（见 p. 11 撰写日记）在日记中，你可以记录你查询的原始资料、你想继续研究的线索，以及你遇到的任何困难。最重要的是，你可以记录你对原始资料的看法、线索、困难、新的研究方向、各种关系，以及任何打动你的事情。撰写研究日记这一举动可以扩展并明确你的想法。

注意：研究日记是记录并形成自己观点的地方。为避免混淆自己的观点和他人的观点，要分开记录原始资料所提及的内容，可以使用 pp. 411–412 提到的方法。

51c 寻找可研究的主题和问题

在阅读本部分内容之前，回顾一下第一章中关于寻找并缩小写作主题范围的建议（pp. 4–6）。一般来说，同样的步骤适用于任何类型的研究性论文的写作。但是，选择并限定研究性论文的主题可能会带来特殊的机会和问题。在继续主题研究之前，你要将主题转化成一个可以指导你搜寻原始资料的问题。

1 ▪ 合适的主题

寻找一个你想要了解更多的研究主题（这可能是一个你已经写过的主题，但没有任何研究成果）。以自己的观点开始研究会激发你的积极性。在你开始查验原始资料时，你就会成为对话的参与者。

在确定了主题时，你要问以下问题。每一个要求都有相应的缺陷。

- 关于主题，可用信息的原始资料是否足够？

  避免很新的主题，如最新发布的医学发现或今日新闻中的突发事件。

- 主题是否在任务所需的原始资料种类和数量方面鼓励研究的进行？

  既要**避免**完全依赖个人观点和经验的主题（如你的爱好的优点），又要**避免**只需要在一个来源中进行研究的主题（如直接而真实的传记）。

- 主题是否引导你客观地评估原始资料并做出可信的结论？

  避免完全依赖信仰或偏见的主题，例如，人类生命起源于何时或者为什么女人（或男人）更优秀。你的读者不太可能动摇他们自己的信仰。

- 主题是否符合论文的长度要求和研究与写作的时间要求？

  避免宽泛的主题，因为它有太多的来源，无法进行充分的调查，比如历史上的一个重大事件。

2 ▪ 研究问题

对主题提出一个或多个问题打开了调查的途径。在提问时，你可以思考已知的主题信息、探究未知的信息并开始形成自己的看法。（见 p. 373 使用自己现有知识的建议）

要努力缩小研究问题的范围，这样你就可以在可用的时间和空间内回答问题。How does human activity affect the environment 这个问题范围很宽泛，包含了诸如污染、资源分配、气候变化、人口增长、土地使用、生物多样性和臭氧层等问题。How can buying environmentally friendly products help the environment 或者 How, if at all, should carbon emissions be taxed 等类似问题的范围就小多了。每一个问题还要求不能用简单的"是"或"否"来回答；即便是尝试性的，答案也要求体现对正反面观点和因果关系的思考。

当你阅读和写作时，你的问题无疑会反映你对该主题知识的增加，最终它的答案将成为你的主要观点或论题陈述。（见 p. 435）

51d 设定关于原始资料的目标

开始寻找原始资料之前,你要考虑你对主题已经了解多少,你可能在哪些地方找到相关的信息。

1 ▪ 你的现有知识

发现自己对主题的了解程度可以帮助你明白自己不清楚的地方。在开始阶段,抽出时间写下你所知的主题信息:你已经获知的事实、你在其他地方听到或读到的观点,当然还有你自己的观点。使用第2章中提到的一个或多个发现技巧,从而探索并形成你的观点:撰写日记、观察四周、自由写作、头脑风暴、绘图、提问,并进行批判性思考。

探索了自己的想法后,你要列出一些自己无法回答的问题,无论是实际问题(How much do Americans spend on green products?)还是更为开放性的问题(Are green products worth the higher prices?)。这些问题将会提示你从何处着手。

2 ▪ 原始资料的种类

正如前面所述,对于许多研究项目,你要查询各种原始资料。你可以在参考目录及流行期刊的文章中或者通过网络搜索查找主题提纲(探寻与主题有关的观点的广度和深度),以此为开端。然后在你提炼观点和研究问题时,你会转向更为专业的原始资料,例如,学术书籍和期刊以及你自己的采访或调查。(见pp. 383–396,了解更多关于各种原始资料的信息)

你选择的各种原始资料很大程度上取决于你的主题。例如,关于green consumerism的论文要求使用很新的原始资料,因为对环境无害的产品对于美国市场来说是非常新鲜的。你的老师或许也会明确你要用的各种原始资料,或者你的写作任务要求也会限定你要用的各种原始资料。

来自图书馆和因特网的原始资料

与你在开放网络上找到的大多数原始资料相比,来自图书馆或图书馆网站的原始资料(主要是参考作品、书籍和期刊文章)有两大优点:图书馆的原始资料经过分类编目,易于检索;它们先后经过出版社和图书管理员的遴选,通常比较可靠。与之相反,因特网的检索系统更难以有效地使用,而且因特网上的原始资料在上传之前大多没有经过任何遴选,所以通常不大可靠。(也有许多例外,比如在线学术期刊和参考作品。但是这些原始资料可能只能通过你的

图书馆网站获得）

大多数老师期望论文写作者查找图书馆的原始资料，但是如果你能审慎使用的话，他们也接受因特网上的原始资料。即便有不足之处，因特网也可以是第一手原始资料、最新信息和不同观点的重要来源。参见pp. 397–409图书馆和因特网原始资料的评估准则。

第一手和第二手的原始资料

有第一手原始资料或者研究任务有要求时，你要使用第一手的原始资料。这些原始资料是第一手的记录，例如，文学作品、历史文件（信函、演说等）、目击证人的描述（包括现场记者的文章）、实验报告或作者完成的调查，以及你创造的原始资料（采访、实验、观察或通信）。

有些研究任务允许使用第二手原始资料。这些第二手的原始资料通常报道并分析从其他原始资料（通常是第一手原始资料）中获得的信息。比如记者关于争议事件的总结、历史学家关于一场战役的描述、评论家对于一首诗歌的解读以及心理学家对多个研究的评论。第二手的原始资料可能包含有助于引导、支撑及拓展你个人思维的总结和解释。但是，大多数研究性写作任务要求你有超越类似原始资料的自己的观点。

学术性和流行性的原始资料

著名专家的学术成就有助于提升研究的深度、权威性和特殊性。大多数老师要求学生在研究中强调学术性的原始资料。但是，流行性原始资料中包含的普通大众的观点和信息也有助于将更为学术性的方法运用到日常生活中。

- **核对标题。** 它是专业的标题还是使用了一般词汇？
- **核对出版单位。** 是学术期刊（如 *Education Forum*）或学术书籍的出版社（如 Harvard University Press）还是流行杂志（如 *Time* 或 *Newsweek*）或流行书籍的出版社（如 Little, Brown）？参见 p. 384 和 pp. 400–401 学术性和流行性原始资料的区别。
- **核对期刊文章的长度。** 学术文章一般比报刊文章长得多。
- **核对作者。** 查找可以告诉你有关作者专业知识的简要传记。
- **核对原始资料。** 学术作者在注释或参考目录中正式引用原始资料。
- **核对URL（统一资源定位符）。** 网站的URL或电子地址包括原始资料来源的缩写：学术网站通常以edu，org或gov结尾，而流行网站通常以com结尾。（参见 p. 403 在线原始资料的种类）

较老和较新的原始资料

核对出版日期。 对于大多数主题来说，较老的、已被确认的原始资料（如书籍）和最近的原始资料（如新闻、文章、采访或网站）的结合将提供背景信息和最新信息。只有历史题材或非常现代的主题要求强调某种极端的原始资料。

无偏见和有偏见的原始资料

寻找不同的观点。 试图做到无偏见的原始资料可以提供主题综述和可靠事实。带有明显偏见的原始资料给你一系列关于主题的观点，可以丰富你对主题的了解。当然，要做到发现偏见，你可能需要认真阅读原始资料（见 pp. 397–409），但是你可以从书目清单中做出推断。

- **核对作者。** 你可能听说过作者是一位受人尊敬的研究者（因而更有可能是客观的）或者是某个观点的主要倡导者（因而不大可能是客观的）。
- **核对题目。** 它可能透露一些有关观点的信息。（思考一下这些形成鲜明对比的标题："Go for the Green" 和 "Green Consumerism and the Struggle for Northern Maine"）

注意： 要特别谨慎地对待你在因特网上找到的原始资料。见 pp. 402–409。

具有有益特征的原始资料

根据题材和研究的进程，你可能要寻找有特征的原始资料，如插图（可以阐明重要概念）、参考目录（可以将你引向其他原始资料）和文献索引（可以帮你形成电子检索的关键词；见 pp. 385–386）等。

51e 记录带有注释的参考目录

为了追踪原始资料的来源和内容，你要制作一份**参考目录**，即书籍、文章、网站及其他可能的原始资料的档案。当你的档案内容充实（如10到30个原始资料）时，你可以决定哪些是最有希望的，并首先查找这些原始资料。

1 ▪ 原始资料的信息

提交论文时，你会按照要求附加一份使用过的原始资料的清单。你的清单必须用读者能够理解的格式列出找到原始资料所需的所有资料。这样，读者就可以核查或跟踪你的原始资料。（见 pp. 432–434）p. 377 中的加框文字显示了用来记录每一种原始资料的信息，这样，你之后就不用重复进行一些步骤。

注意：缜密地记录原始资料的信息有助于避免由于疏忽而导致的抄袭，因为你不大可能在论文中遗漏信息。在需要引用原始资料时，认真记录还有助于避免遗漏或混淆数字、日期或其他数据。本书描述两种文献资料的格式：MLA（p. 439）和APA（p. 497）。至于其他格式，请查询pp. 433–434列举的指导原则。

2 ▪ 注释

为参考目录做注释就是将参考目录从简单的清单转变为评估原始资料的工具。注释可以帮助你发现原始资料中可能存在的差距，并在日后帮助你决定哪些原始资料需要深度追查。在发现并评估原始资料时，你不仅要记录原始资料的出版信息，还要记录以下信息：

- 你对原始资料内容的现有认知。期刊数据库和书籍目录一般包括有助于这一部分注释的原始资料的摘要或总结。
- 你如何认为原始资料有助于你的研究。它是否提供专家意见、统计资料、重要范例或一系列的观点？它是否将主题放在一个历史、社会或经济的环境中？
- 你对原始资料的评估意见。思考原始资料的可靠性以及如何将之融入你的研究中。（参见pp. 397–410评估并综合原始资料）

制作一份参考目录所需的信息

书籍

图书馆的索书号
作者、编者、译者或其他所列人员的姓名
标题和副标题
出版数据：出版地点、出版单位名称、出版日期
其他重要信息，比如版次或卷号
媒介（印刷版、网络版等）

期刊文章

作者姓名
文章标题和副标题
期刊名称
出版数据：刊发文章的卷号和期号（如果有的话）、发行日期、文章出现的页码

媒介（印刷版、网络版等）

电子版原始资料

作者姓名
原始资料的标题和副标题
网站、期刊或其他较大作品的名称
出版数据，比如上面列举的关于书籍或文章的数据；网站的发行人或主办者；发布、修订或在线发帖的日期
其他媒介（印刷版、电影等）上的原始资料的出版数据
在线原始资料的格式（网站或网页、播客、电子邮件等）
你查询原始资料的日期
任何用来获取原始资料的数据库的名称
完整的URL（参见下方的注释）

（续表）

DOI（数字对象标识符），如果有的话（参见下方的注释） 媒介（印刷版、网络版、CD-ROM等） **其他原始资料** 作者、创作者或其他所列人员（如政府部门、唱片艺术家或拍摄者）的姓名	作品名称 格式，如未经出版的信件、现场演出或照片 出版或制作数据：出版标题，出版单位或制作者姓名，出版、发行或制作日期 识别号（如果有的话） 媒介（印刷版、打字稿等）

注意：引用电子版原始资料时，不同的文献资料格式对URL和DOI的要求有所不同。（参见p. 502 DOI）例如，MLA格式一般不要求URL和DOI，APA格式一般要求DOI（如果有的话）或主页的URL，而一些其他格式总是要求完整的URL。即便你在最后的原始资料引用中不需要完整的URL和DOI，你也要做好记录。这样，在需要再次查询时，你就可以追踪原始资料。对于通过图书馆数据库找到的原始资料，如果可以获得DOI的话，则只记录DOI，因为数据库的URL一般不能用来查找原始资料。

以下条目来自带有注释的参考目录。它显示了一名学生对原始资料的注释，包括总结、学生认为有帮助的关于原始资料特征方面的注释，以及对原始资料优缺点的评估意见。

» **带有注释和评估意见的参考文献条目**

原始资料的出版信息	Gore, Al. *Our Choice: A Plan to Solve the Climate Crisis.* Emmaus: Rodale, 2009. Print.
原始资料的总结	A sequel to Gore's *An Inconvenient Truth* that emphasizes solutions to global warming. Expands on the argument that global warming is a serious threat, with recent examples of natural disasters. Proposes ways that governments, businesses, and individuals can reduce or reverse the risks of global warming.
有帮助的特征	Includes helpful summaries of scientific studies, short essays on various subjects, and dozens of images, tables, charts, and graphs.
对原始资料的评估意见	Compelling overview of possible solutions, with lots of data that seem thorough and convincing. But the book is aimed at a general audience and doesn't have formal source citations. Can use it for broad concepts, but for data I'll have to track down Gore's scholarly sources.

第 52 章　寻找原始资料

概要

- 从图书馆网址入手（下方）
- 规划电子搜索（p. 380）
- 查阅参考作品（p. 383）
- 查阅书籍（p. 383）
- 查找期刊文章（p. 384）
- 查看网络和社交媒体（p. 388, p. 391）
- 查阅政府出版物（p. 392）
- 查找图像、音频和视频资料（p. 392）
- 通过采访、调查和观察形成自己的原始资料（p. 395）

图书馆以及连接因特网的电脑让你可以接触几乎无限量的原始资料。当然，挑战就是找到你所需要的恰当且有价值的原始资料，然后有效地使用它们。本章将告诉你如何做到这一切。

注意：查找原始资料时，你要避免寻找"高招"的冲动，也就是要避免查找两三个全面说明主题内容的完美的原始资料。你要阅读并综合众多原始资料以便形成自己的观点，而不是仅仅重复他人的观点。（见pp. 409–410）

给研究者的贴士

利用图书馆提供的两个现有资源：
- 情况介绍（介绍图书馆的资源，解释如何获取并使用图书馆的网址和印刷版书籍）
- 参考书管理员（其职责就是帮助你和其他读者驾驭图书馆资源。所有的图书馆都提供面对面的咨询，许多图书馆提供电子邮件和聊天服务。即便是有经验的研究者也经常咨询参考书管理员）

52a 从图书馆网址入手

对于学术研究来说，图书馆网址是你通向观点和信息的大门。从图书馆网址而不是诸如Google等公共搜索引擎入手。图书馆检索要比直接的网络搜索更高效且更有效果。

图书馆原始资料的优势

图书馆网址将引导你接触海量的资源，包括公开网站上没有的书籍、期刊文章和参考文献。更重要的是，你在图书馆网址上找到的每一个原始资料都经过遴选以确保其价值。例如，一篇学术期刊文章经过至少三遍连续审读：主题专家首先认为它值得在期刊上发表，然后数据库供应商相信数据库包含的期刊价值，最后学校图书馆认定值得订购该数据库。

注意：从图书馆网址入手，但不要止步于此。许多书籍、期刊和其他优秀的原始资料都没有在线上，只能在图书馆的书架找到，而且大多数老师希望研究性论文在某种程度上以这些资料为基础。在浏览图书馆在线数据库时发现了有用的实体原始资料后，你要记录下这些原始资料，然后在图书馆里查找。

公开网站上原始资料的劣势

Google 和其他搜索引擎似乎比图书馆网址更为方便用户，似乎回报很多的原始资料供你使用。但是正如前面谈到的，公开网站上的大多数原始资料都没有经过遴选，其价值无法保证。许多原始资料确实是可靠的且与你的研究有关，但是更多的原始资料并非如此。

52b 规划电子搜索

由于网站的建立方式不同，你获取图书馆资源的方式会有所不同。许多图书馆提供实体馆藏（如印刷书籍和期刊）目录和单篇文章数据库的各自单独的搜索。其他图书馆则提供可以同时搜索所有图书馆资源（包括印刷版书籍和电子版书籍、印刷版文章和电子版文章等）的集中的搜索页面。

不论是哪种情况，电子搜索需要进行规划。过于随意的搜索在获得成百上千无关原始资料的同时会遗失有益的原始资料。要熟悉你能获得的电子版原始资料的种类和每一个原始资料的不同搜索策略。在研究的早期，要花时间确定主题资料库和网站搜索引擎（见 p.381）的**关键词**。

1 ▪ 电子版原始资料的种类

图书馆网址将你引入许多种适合学术研究的电子资源。

- **图书馆的馆藏目录**，图书馆网址上可以找到，也就是列出了图书馆拥有或订阅的所有资源的数据库。根据图书馆的不同，该目录可能包含印刷版和电子版的书籍、期刊、杂志、报纸、参考作品等。它还可能包括附近其他学校图书馆或州内图书馆的馆藏目录。

- **在线数据库**包括索引、参考目录和其他参考作品。它们提供出版信息、摘要和全文，是通向期刊文章的主要路径。图书馆订购数据库，将它们上传到搜索主页或单独的数据库页面，使得它们可以通过网址获得。（你还可能在网上直接发现数据库，但是图书馆是更富有成效的起始点）
- **研究指导**，可以通过一些图书馆获得，提供某个特定主题（如20世纪英国文学或发展心理学）的图书馆资源的路径。
- **基于光盘的数据库**，包括与在线数据库相同的信息，但它们必须在图书馆的电脑终端阅读。越来越多的图书馆抛弃光盘，转而支持在线数据库。

2 ▪ 数据库和搜索引擎

为了形成有效的关键词，了解图书馆数据库、图书馆搜索引擎和公共搜索引擎的不同运行方式是很有帮助的。

- **数据库和关键词与其作者、标题和主题词的索引相匹配**。主题词反映数据库的术语目录，由已经阅读过该原始资料的人指定。通过使用自己的关键词，你可以找到这些主题词，直到你找到有用的原始资料。该原始资料的信息将列出主题词。在此主题词下，数据库将该原始资料及其他类似的原始资料编入索引中。（见p.387的例证）然后，你可以使用那些标题进行进一步的搜索。
- **图书馆的中央搜索引擎在所有图书馆的馆藏书籍和在线资源中寻找关键词**。在你完成最初的关键词搜索后，引擎将在图书馆现有资源中提供限定或扩展搜索的选择。搜索引擎不会从公开网站上获取内容。
- **网络搜索引擎在公共网站上的标题和文章中寻找关键词**。搜索结果将取决于你的关键词如何很好地描述主题以及对原始资料中所使用单词的预期。如果你过于宽泛地描述主题或者明确描述主题但却没有与相关原始资料的词相匹配，你的搜索将不会得到相关的原始资料，可能会得到许多无关的原始资料。

3 ▪ 关键词提炼

每个数据库和搜索引擎都提供了一个术语和符号系统，你可以使用它来精练你的关键字，以实现高效的搜索。基本操作将在下页的框中显示，但资源是不同的。例如，一些假设AND应该链接两个或多个关键字，而另一些则提供指定"必须包含所有的字"的选项，或"可以包含任何一个字"的选项，以及框中描述的操作的其他选项。通过查阅高级搜索页面，你可以了解搜索引擎系统。

注意：你或许需要反复试验才能形成关键词，有时候极少或没有出现原始资料，而有时候会出现上千个大多是无关的原始资料。但是这个过程不是白费时间的忙碌工作，完全不是。它教会你很多关于主题的事：你应该如何缩小关键词的范围、其他人是如何描述的、哪些是其他人认为有意思或可争议的，以及主要论点是什么。

参见pp. 389–391网络的关键词搜索范例。

382

提炼关键词的方法

大多数数据库和许多搜索引擎用**逻辑操作符**（使你可以扩展或限定关键词和搜索的术语或符号）进行运作。

- 用AND或 + 以缩小搜索范围。（只包含使用所有所给单词的原始资料）关键词green AND products要求只出现阴影部分的原始资料。

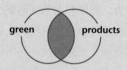

- 用NOT或 - 以缩小搜索范围。（排除不相关单词）关键词green AND products NOT guide排除了使用guide一词的原始资料。

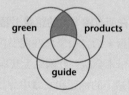

- 用OR以扩大搜索范围。（提供可替代的关键词）关键词green AND products OR goods考虑到了使用products一词同义词的原始资料。

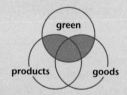

- 用括号或引号形成搜索短语。例如, (green products) 要求准确无误的词组，而不是单个单词。只有使用了green products的原始资料才会出现。
- 使用通配符允许同一单词的不同形式。比如在consum*中，通配符*表示原始资料可能包含consume, consumer, consumerism, consumption 和 consumptive, consumedly, consummate。这个例子暗示你需要考虑通配符认可的所有变体以及它是否让你的搜

（续表）

> 索范围过大。如果你只想从众多变体中寻找两到三个变体，你最好使用OR一词：consumption OR consumerism。（注意：一些系统使用?，:，或+作为通配符而不是*）
> - **确保关键词的拼写正确**。一些搜索工具会寻找相近匹配或近似匹配，但是拼写正确是让你找到相关原始资料的最佳机会。

52c 查阅参考作品

参考作品通常可以在线获得，包括百科全书、字典、参考目录、索引、地图集、年历和手册。你的研究必须超越这些原始资料，但是它们可以帮助你决定你是否真的对主题感兴趣以及主题是否符合研究论文的要求。（p. 372）对参考作品进行初步研究还可以帮助你形成电子搜索的关键词，并指导你进行有关主题的更为详细的搜索。

通过图书馆和直接上网，你会找到许多参考作品。下面的清单提供了一系列学科的网络参考目录[1]：

INFOMINE（infomine. ucr. edu）

ipl2（ipl. org）

Library of Congress（lcweb. loc. gov）

World Wide Web Virtual Library（vlib. org）

注意：基于网络的百科全书维基百科（wikipedia.org）是因特网上非常大的参考资料网址之一。和其他百科全书一样，维基百科可以提供主题的背景信息搜索。不同的是，维基百科是一个任何人都可以提供资料或进行编辑的网站。使用此类网站前，要先咨询老师此类网站上的原始资料是否可行。如果真的使用了，你必须按照pp. 397–409上的指导原则认真评估找到的任何信息。

52d 查阅书籍

图书馆的书籍目录可以在图书馆查找或者通过图书馆网址在线查找。你可以通过作者、标题、关键词或下页所示的Library of Congress Subject Headings（LCSH）的主题词查找目录。一旦你找到了书籍在LCSH的主题词，你就可以用它们来查找相似的原始资料。

---

1 部分网站因某些原因无法打开。

» 书籍目录的完整记录

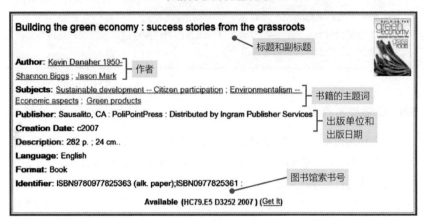

52e 查阅期刊

期刊包括实体或在线的报纸、学术期刊、杂志。报纸提供过去和现在事件的详细记录。期刊和杂志较难区分，但是它们的差异很大。大多数大学老师要求学生的研究更多地依赖期刊而非杂志。

期刊	杂志
范例	
American Anthropologist, Journal of Black Studies, Journal of Chemical Education	The New Yorker, Time, Rolling Stone, People
可得性	
主要是大学和学院的图书馆，可以在图书馆书架或在线数据库获得	公共图书馆、报摊、书店、公开网络和在线数据库
目的	
增加特定领域的知识	表达观点、通报信息或娱乐
作者	
该领域的专家	可能是也可能不是主题专家
读者	
通常是该领域的专家	普通大众或者拥有特定兴趣的小群体

原始资料引用
常常包含原始资料引用　　　　　　　极少包含原始资料引用

文章长度
通常很长，十页或十页以上　　　　　通常很短，不到十页

出版频率
季刊或更小频率　　　　　　　　　　周刊、双周刊或月刊

期号页码
可以单独标注页码（类似杂志），　　单独标注页码，每一期都从第一页
也可以按年度卷册连续标注页码，　　开始
这样期号3（该年度的第三期）的
第一页可以是p. 373。

1 ▪ 期刊数据库

期刊数据库将期刊、杂志和报纸上的文章编入索引中。通常，这些数据库包括文章的摘要或总结。它们可能也会提供文章的全文。图书馆订购许多期刊数据库并提供多种数据库的服务。大多数数据库和服务可以通过图书馆网址搜索。

注意：搜索引擎Google中可以搜索出学术文章的Google学术搜索，对跨学科的主题搜索、对学科专用数据库过于有限的主题搜索尤其有用。如果你在学术参考目录下进行搜索，Google学术搜索可以连接图书馆的馆藏书籍。但是，要记住Google学术搜索还不很详尽，可能会列举一些你无法找到全文的文章。图书馆是最佳的文章来源，所以从图书馆开始吧。

数据库的选择

你需要考虑你在查找的内容，以决定查阅哪个数据库：

- **你的研究主题是跨学科的吗？** 如果是这样，从查阅一般数据库开始，如Academic Search Complete，JSTOR，LexisNexis Academic Universe，或者CQ Researcher。一般数据库涵盖多个主题和学科，但不能提供单个主题的完整期刊索引。

- **你的研究主题关注单个学科吗？** 如果是这样，开始查阅学科专用数据库，如Historical Abstracts，MLA International Bibliography，Biological Abstracts，或Education Search Complete。学科专用数据库涵盖少量学科，但包含每个主题的大部分现有期刊。如果你不知道恰当的数据库名称，图书馆的网

址可能会按学科列举各种可能性。
- **哪些数据库最有可能包含你所需要的资源类型？** 大多数图书馆的网页能让你将数据库的搜索范围缩小到某个特定的学科。有些图书馆也提供搜索指导，为你搜索的术语列举可能有帮助的数据库。通过核对数据库的描述（有时候标注为"Help"或"Guide"）或有索引的资源清单（有时候标注为"Publications"或"Index"），你就可以发现每个数据库的重点。数据库的描述还告诉你数据库覆盖的时间段，这样你就知道自己是否还需要在图书馆查阅更久以前的实体索引。

数据库搜索

当开始搜索数据库时，你要使用自己的关键词以查找原始资料。下面的截屏解释了该步骤。你的目的在于找到至少一个适合主题的原始资料，这样你才能明白数据库本身对这些原始资料使用了什么主题词。（p. 387的截屏）选择一个或多个这类主题词用作关键词可以集中并加快你的搜索。

注意： 许多数据库允许你将搜索限定在所谓的经过同行评鉴或经过推荐的期刊。这类学术期刊上的文章在发表前经过该领域专家评鉴并由作者修改过。将搜索限定在经过同行评鉴的期刊可以帮助你应对庞大的数据库。这些数据库有可能搜索出许多无法使用的文章。

» **1. 期刊数据库的初期关键词搜索**

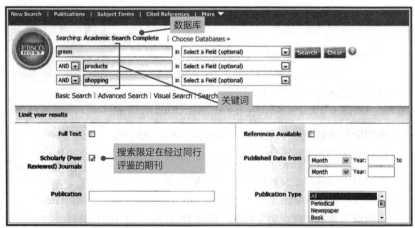

» 2. 部分关键词搜索结果

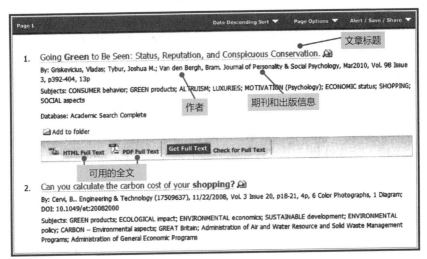

» 3. 带摘要的全文记录

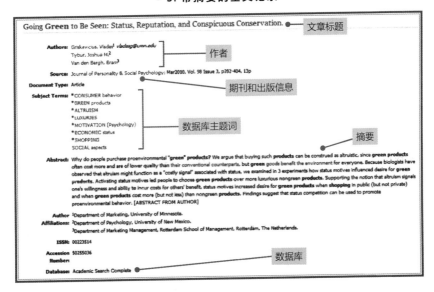

摘要的使用

上面的截图中，全文记录显示了总结文章的摘要。通过描述研究方法、结论和其他信息，摘要可以告诉你是否要继续深入文章，从而节省你的时间。但是，摘要不能代替文章。如果你想使用作品为原始资料，你必须查阅全文。

有用的数据库

以下清单包含学术图书馆通常订购的数据库。其中一些数据库涵盖大体相同的材料,因此你所在的图书馆可能不会订购清单中的全部数据库。

EBSCOhost Academic Search。涵盖社会科学、自然科学、艺术、人文的杂志和期刊的索引。许多文章都有全文。

InfoTrac Expanded Academic。Gale Group的综合期刊索引,包括社会科学、自然科学、艺术、人文等领域的综合期刊。它包括全文文章。

LexisNexis Academic。涵盖新闻、商业、法律和参考信息的索引,许多文章都有全文。它包括国际、国内和地区的报纸及新闻杂志、法律和商业出版物以及法庭案件。

ProQuest Research Library。一种涵盖自然科学、社会科学、艺术和人文学科的期刊索引,包括许多全文文章。

2 ▪ 期刊的位置

如果索引列表不包括文章全文或者不直接链接文章全文,你就需要查阅期刊。最新一期的期刊可能保存在图书馆的期刊室。过期期刊通常保存在其他地方,要么按卷装订,要么就保存在胶片上,需要用特殊机器来阅读。图书管理员会告诉你如何操作机器。

52f 搜索网络

作为一名学术研究者,你可以通过两种方式进入网络:通过图书馆网址以及诸如Bing和Google等公共搜索引擎。图书馆网址是你查找书籍和文章的主要途径。对于大多数主题来说,这些书籍和文章应该构成了大部分的原始资料。见pp. 379–380关于图书馆原始资料的讨论。这里讨论的公共网络可以带来大量的信息,但是它也有限制其对学术研究产生作用的劣势:

- **网络具有开放性**。任何有合适工具的人都可以将信息放到因特网上,即便是经过认真构思的搜索也会产生可靠性大不一样的原始资料:期刊文章、政府文件、学术数据、高中生撰写的学期论文、伪装成客观报道的商品宣传、狂热的学说等。你必须特别用心地评估因特网上的原始资料。(见pp. 402–409)

- **网络具有变化性**。没有一个搜索引擎能跟上网络信息的日常增加和删除,你今天找到的原始资料可能明天就被更新或消失了。一般来说,你不应该推迟查阅你认为可能会用到的在线原始资料。

- **网络并不包含所有资料。**大多数的书籍和许多期刊只有通过图书馆才能获得，而不是直接通过网络获得。

网络无疑要谨慎使用。它不应该是你唯一的原始资料来源。

1 ▪ 搜索引擎

为了找到网络上的原始资料，你可以使用将网址编录为索引并进行关键词搜索的搜索引擎。（见pp. 380–382）一般来说，在你还没有提炼主题或你想进行总体概述时，你要使用索引。当你已经提炼了主题并想寻找特定信息时，你要使用关键词。

现有的搜索引擎

下面的加框文字列举了目前流行的搜索引擎。在网络浏览器的地址栏或位置栏输入地址就可以进入这些搜索引擎。

网络搜索引擎

搜索引擎的特征经常变化，新的搜索引擎不断出现。至于最新的搜索引擎，参见 easysearcher.com 上收集的链接。

审核网站的名录
INFOMINE（infomine. ucr. edu）
ipl2（ipl. org）
Internet Scout Project（scout. wisc. edu/archives）

搜索引擎
Ask. com（ask. com）   Google（google. com）
Bing（bing. com）   MetaCrawler（metacrawler. com）
Dogpile（dogpile. com）   Yahoo!（yahoo. com）

注意：为了获得不错的原始资料，不能只尝试一个搜索引擎，要尝试四到五个搜索引擎。没有一个搜索引擎可以收录整个网络的原始资料，即便是最强大的引擎也不会包含任何特定时间内的半数网站。另外，大多数搜索引擎接受付费配置，给那些交费的网站靠前的位置。这些所谓的赞助链接通常会有赞助标记，但它们可能会破坏搜索引擎根据关键词排列网站的方法。

搜索记录

不论你使用哪个搜索引擎，你的网络浏览器具有让你跟踪网络原始资料和

搜索的功能:

- 使用"收藏夹"或"书签"保存网址作为链接。在靠近浏览器屏幕上方的区域点击"收藏夹"或"书签"以添加你想返回的网址。收藏夹或书签会存档,直到你将它删除。
- 使用"搜索历史"查找你曾访问过的网址。浏览器记录某个时期访问过的网址。(过了那个时期,搜索历史就会被删除)如果你忘记给网址做标记,你可以点击"搜索历史"或"前往"来查找你的搜索历史并恢复网址。

2 ▪ 搜索范例

以下的网络搜索范例解释了关键词提炼如何缩小搜索范围,从而使相关的匹配记录最大化,使无关的匹配记录最小化。一名研究绿色消费品之环境影响的学生 Justin Malik 在 Google 上使用了关键词 green products。但是正如截图1所示,搜索出超过5300万个条目,而第一页全部是销售产品的网站,包括赞助的网站和其他广告商。

» **1. 第一次Google搜索结果**

Malik 意识到他得改变策略以获得更多有用的结果。他试着组合同义词和范围更小的术语,得出 "green consumerism" 和 products。但是,提炼关键词后的

» 2. 使用提炼后的关键词得到的Google搜索结果

搜索仍旧有13万个结果。增加site:.gov将搜索范围限定在政府网站，用"green consumerism" products site:.gov进行搜索，Malik得到197个结果。（参见截屏2）他用site:.org（非营利机构）、site:.edu（教育机构）和site:.com（商业机构）代替site:.gov继续限定搜索范围。

52g 查找社交媒体

你通过交互式媒体获得的在线原始资料可以让你直接接触专家和那些观点及信息可能鼓励你研究的人。这些社交媒体包括电子邮件、博客、社交网站和讨论小组。和网络网站一样，它们是未经遴选的，因此你必须经常认真评估它们。（见pp. 407–409）

注意： 如果你的论文包括未公开的社交媒体信函（比如电子邮件或讨论小组的帖子），你得征询作者的使用许可。这样做就是告知作者他或她的观点即将在更广范围内得以传播，也让作者核实你没有歪曲他或她的观点。（见p. 395 采访）

1 ▪ 使用电子邮件

电子邮件让你和其他对主题感兴趣的人进行沟通。例如，你可能用电子邮件和学校老师进行交谈或者采访另一个州的专家以便继续采用他或她已经发表的学术文章。

2 ▪ 使用博客和社交网址

博客（网络日志）是一名或多名作者用读者可以对作者或彼此做出反应的方式、一般围绕一个共同主题、发布带有时间标记的评论的网站。你可以在blogcatalog.com上找到博客目录。

和博客有点类似，诸如Facebook等社交网站上的页面越来越多地被机构、企业、个人甚至学者用来进行相互交流。

和所有本部分讨论的其他社交媒体一样，博客和社交网站上的页面必须经过认真评估，才能用作潜在的原始资料。里面有些是关于观点和学问的可靠的原始资料，许多是有价值的书籍、文章、网站和其他原始资料，但是，还有许多仅仅是作者发牢骚和自我推销的窗口。见pp. 407–409区分好坏的贴士。

3 ▪ 使用讨论列表

讨论列表（有时候称为**专题通信服务**或**列表**）使用电子邮件联系对共同话题（通常有一个学术或技术重点）感兴趣的人。通过发送问题到合适的列表，你可以接触到许多拥有主题知识的人。关于讨论列表的目录，参见tile.net/lists。

通过查阅列表档案以确保讨论与自己的主题有关并弄清楚你的问题是否已经被人回答过，你就可以开始讨论列表的研究。当你给列表写文章时，要遵守pp. 82–83撰写电子邮件的准则。要经常按照pp. 407–409的准则评估你收到的信息。尽管许多发言人是可靠的专家，但是几乎任何一个可以连接因特网的人都能发帖子。

4 ▪ 使用网络论坛和新闻组

与讨论列表相比，网络论坛和新闻组更加公开，更不具有学术性，因此它们的信息需要更为用心的评估。**网络论坛**让参与者通过简单地选择网页链接就参与到谈话中。参见delphiforums.com的论坛目录。**新闻组**是在主题标题下成立的，例如soc代表社会议题，biz代表商务。参见groups.google.com的新闻组目录。

52h 查阅政府出版物

政府出版物提供各类数据、报告、政策文件、公共记录以及其他历史与当代信息。对于美国的政府出版物，请在www.gpoaccess.gov网站上查阅政府印刷局的美国政府出版物。Google的美国政府搜索网站（google.com/unclesam）

也很有用，因为它列举了.gov（政府）和.mil（军方）的文件。它的排名系统强调最有用的文件。许多联邦、州和地方政府机关在网站上发布重要的出版物（法律、报告、新闻稿）。在搜索引擎上使用关键词 United States federal government，你可以找到各个联邦机构的网址列表。使用州、城市或城镇的名称加上 government 一词来查找州政府和地方政府的信息。

52i 查找图像、音频和视频资料

在研究项目中，图像、音频和视频资料可以作为第一手和第二手的原始资料。绘画、广告或演讲的视频都可以是写作的主题，因此是第一手的原始资料。就主题在电台采访专家的播客或大学演讲可以作为第二手的原始资料。因为这些原始资料好多都没有经过遴选（任何人都可以发帖），因此你必须认真评估这些你在公共网络上找到的原始资料。（见pp. 402–409）

注意： 就如你引用文本资料一样，你必须在论文中完整引用每一个图像、音频和视频资料，列出其作者、标题和出版信息。另外，有些原始资料要求你征得版权所有者（原始资料来源本身或诸如视频的拍摄者或创作者等第三方）的许可。如果你要在公共网络上发表，你尤其需要获得许可。（见pp. 431–432 在线出版）为避免征询许可，你可以搜索不受版权保护的图像、音频和视频资料。例如在Google上，你可以在高级搜索中选择"Labeled for reuse"。如果有疑问，请咨询学校图书管理员。

1 ▪ 图像

pp. 68–75讨论了用图像来支撑写作。你有多种选择来找到图像：

- **在阅读文本或在线原始资料的同时寻找图像。** 你的原始资料可能包括图表、表格、照片和其他支撑观点的图像。找到你想使用的图像后，复印或下载之，以便日后使用。
- **创建自己的图像，** 如照片或图表。见pp. 69–73创建图像。
- **使用图像搜索引擎。** Google，Yahoo!和其他搜索引擎可以用来搜索图像。它们可以将搜索限定在无须重复授权的图像上。尽管搜索引擎可以找到图像的原始资料，但是结果可能是不准确或不完整的，因为被搜索的原始资料经常不包含图像描述。（引擎可搜索文档名称和任何配图文字）
- **使用公共图像数据库。** 下面列举的网站一般能进行准确搜索，因为这些网站上的图像根据图像描述、艺术家姓名和图像日期等信息归档：
Duke University，Ad*Access（library.duke.edu/digitalcollections/adaccess）。

横跨1911—1955年的印刷广告。

Library of Congress, American Memory（memory. loc. gov/ammem）。记录美国经历的地图、照片、印刷品和广告。

Library of Congress, Prints and Photographs Online Catalog（loc.gov/pictures）。图书馆馆藏中的视觉效果，包括可通过American Memory获得的视觉效果。

New york Public Library Digital Gallery（digitalgallery.nypl.org/nypldigital）。图书馆馆藏的地图、图画、照片和绘画。

Political Cartoons（politicalcartoons.com）。关于当代问题和事件的漫画。

- **使用公共图像目录**。以下网站收集了图像原始资料的链接：

Art Project（googleartproject.com）。精选来自美国和欧洲主要博物馆的美术作品。

Art Source（ilpi. com/artsource/general.html）。艺术和建筑的原始资料。

Cultural Politics: Resources for Critical Analysis（culturalpolitics.net）。流行文化的广告、时尚、杂志、玩具和其他工艺品的原始资料。

MuseumLink's Museum of Museums（museumlink.com）。链接到世界各地的博物馆。

Yale University Art Library, Image Resources（www.library.yale.edu/arts）。视觉和表演艺术的原始资料。

- **使用订阅数据库**。图书馆可能订购以下的原始资料：

ARTstor。博物馆藏品和通常用于艺术史课程的图像数据库。

Associated Press, AccuNet/AP Multimedia Archives。历史和当代新闻图像。

Grove Art Online。艺术图片和博物馆网站链接。

许多你找到的图像都可以免费复印或下载，但有些需要付费。在付费之前，咨询图书管理员，看看其他地方是否有可以免费使用的图像。

2 ▪ 音频和视频

通过网络和光盘获得的音频和视频可以给读者提供"身临其境"的体验。例如，如果你就Martin Luther King的*I Have a Dream*这个演讲的媒体反应撰写论文，而你以电子版的方式发表你的论文，你得插入该演讲以及电视和广播关于该演讲报道的链接。

- **音频档案**，比如播客、网络直播、刻录在光盘上的广播节目、采访、演讲、讲座和音乐。它们可以通过网络和图书馆获得。音频的在线原始资料来源包括国会图书馆的American Memory（参见上方）和www.podcastdirectory.com网站上的播客。
- **视频档案**保存了演出、演讲和公开展示、新闻事件和其他活动。它们可以通过网络和图书馆的DVD或蓝光光盘获得。视频的在线原始资料来源包括国会图书馆的American Memory（参见上页）、YouTube（涵盖广告、历史片段、当前事件及其他）和诸如Google（video.google.com）等搜索引擎。

52j 形成自己的原始资料

学术写作通常要求你进行第一手的研究以获得你自己的信息。例如，你可能需要分析诗歌、做实验或者采访专家。初步研究的三种常用的方法是观察、个人采访和调查。

1 ▪ 个人采访

对于研究项目来说，采访尤其有用，因为它让你提出一些与主题相匹配的问题。你可以进行现场采访、电话采访或在线采访。如果安排得开的话，现场采访是更可取的，因为你可能看到被采访者的面部表情和手势，并听到他或她的语气。

下面是采访的几条准则：

- **电话或信函预约**。告诉被采访者你打电话的原因、希望讨论的内容和采访的时间长度。在任何方面都要言而有信。
- **准备一系列开放式问题**，一小时的采访需要准备十到十二个问题。采访之前对这些问题做些研究，以发现问题的背景信息以及被采访者对这些问题发表过哪些观点。
- **关注被采访者的应答**，以便你问一些恰当的后续问题。要小心解读被采访者的应答，尤其是在进行在线采访的时候，因为你无法依靠面部表情、手势和声音语气来感知被采访者的态度。
- **做详细的笔记**。在现场采访或电话采访时，要做笔记。如果有设备并且被采访者同意的话，你可以录音。对于在线采访，可以将讨论存入文档。
- **核实要引用的语句**。在论文中引用被采访者的话语之前，要和被采访者核实，确保引文的准确性。
- **采访之后及时发感谢函**。向被采访者承诺给他或她一份最终的论文，并马上邮寄。

参见p. 493用作研究的原始资料的采访范例。

2 ▪ 调查

向确定的人群提问可以准备有关调查对象的态度、行为、背景和预期等方面的信息。使用以下的贴士来规划并进行调查：

- **确定调查目的**。调查问题应该受调查目的的支配。形成关于主题的假设（可以被检验的概括）将有助于完善调查目标。
- **明确调查对象的身份**。思考与假设有关的调查对象的类型，如男大学生或学龄前儿童。对调查对象进行采样，以便调查结果具有代表性。
- **撰写调查问题**。问题包括引导调查对象应答的封闭式问题（核对表和多项选择题、对错题或是非题）或要求进行简短描述性应答的开放式问题。要避免出现泄露你个人偏见或对主题应答形成假设的含沙射影的问题，比如 "How much more money does your father make than your mather?"
- **测试调查问题**。和几个调查对象讨论问题答案，剔除或重写调查对象认为不明确、令人不适或无法回答的问题。
- **记录调查结果**。统计答案的实际数量，包括空白问卷。
- **从原始数据中找出模式**。模式可能证实或驳斥假设。必要的话，修改假设或进行额外的研究。

参见p. 520用作研究的原始资料的调查范例。

3 ▪ 观察

观察是收集话题的新鲜信息的有效方式。你可以在受到控制的环境下观察，比如在儿童发育实验室观察游戏中的孩子。或者，你可以在更为开放的环境下观察，比如在校园咖啡厅观察学生的互动。遵循以下通过观察规划和收集信息的准则：

- **明确你要了解的东西是可以被观察的**。你可以观察人们的选择和互动，但是你需要进行采访或调查，以发现人们的态度或观点。
- **给予充足的时间**。观察需要几个时段，花费几个小时，以确保观察的可靠性。
- **记录你的观察印象**。在整个观察过程中，在纸张、电脑或移动装置上认真做笔记，记录下每个观察时段的日期、时间和地点。
- **清楚你自己的偏见**。这种意识将帮助你避免掉入只看你想看的陷阱。

第 53 章　处理原始资料

概要

- 了解批判性阅读原始资料的标准（下方）
- 评估图书馆的原始资料（p. 398）
- 评估网络原始资料和社交媒体（p. 402, p. 407）
- 从原始资料中综合信息（p. 409）
- 收集信息，认真总结、改述和引用（p. 411, p. 412）
- 将原始资料信息融入论文（p. 419）

研究性写作不仅仅是发现并汇报原始资料的内容。挑战和乐趣来自与原始资料的互动和综合原始资料。批判性地阅读原始资料将帮助你发现它们的含义，判断它们的相关性和可靠性，并建立它们之间的关系。使用原始资料拓展并支撑自己的观点使你将主题变成你自己的。

CULTURE LANGUAGE　将主题变成你自己的，需要对原始资料进行批判性思考并形成独立的观点。如果你的本土文化强调理解和尊重而不是质疑和补充已经确定的权威，那么这些目标一开始就会让你觉得不舒服。本章中的信息将帮助你处理原始资料，这样你就会凭一己之力成为专家，令人信服地向他人传递你的专业知识。

53a　评估原始资料

在开始从原始资料中收集观点和信息之前，你要浏览原始资料，以评估其内容以及你将如何使用它们。在评估每一份原始资料时，如p. 378所示，在带注释的参考目录上添加评估意见。

注意： 在评估原始资料时，你需要考虑你是如何得到它们的。你从图书馆获得的原始资料，不论是印刷版还是电子版，都经过了出版单位和图书管理员的预先审查。它们依旧需要你的批判性阅读，但你可以对它们所含的信息抱有信心。然而，对于你直接获得的在线原始资料，你无法假定它们经过了类似的预先审查，因此你必须进行细致的批判性阅读。评估网站和其他在线原始资料的特别贴士始于p. 402。

1 ▪ 相关性和可信度

不是所有你找到的原始资料都有价值：有些可能和主题无关，其他的也许不可靠。判断原始资料的相关性和可信度是评估原始资料的重要任务。如果你还没有这么做，请阅读本书第10章。它提供了回答下面加框文字中问题的答案的基础。

评估资料时需要考虑的问题

关于在线原始资料，请用p. 402和p. 407的问题进行补充。

相关性

- **原始资料是否关注主题？** 它是否聚焦于主题或少量涵盖主题？它如何与你找到的其他原始资料相比较？
- **原始资料是否符合专业需求？** 检查原始资料对主题的处理方式，可以让你有所了解，从而确保原始资料既不太肤浅又不过于专业。
- **对于主题来说，原始资料是否够新？** 它是什么时候出版的？如果主题是最新的，那么原始资料也应该是最新的。

可信度

- **原始资料来自何处？** 你是从图书馆获得还是直接从网络获得？（如果是后者，见pp. 402–409）原始资料是通俗的还是学术的？
- **作者是该领域的专家吗？** 在传记（如果原始资料包含的话）、传记参考资料或网络的关键词搜索中核查作者的资历证明。
- **作者的偏见是什么？** 作者的观点如何与其他原始资料中的观点相关联？作者强调、忽视或摈弃了哪些方面？
- **原始资料是否公正、合理且写得很好？** 它是否提供合理的推论或公正描述了对立观点？语气是否沉着客观？原始资料的组织是否具有逻辑性且没有错误？
- **即使在你不赞同作者观点的情况下，主张是否得到良好的证据支撑？** 作者是否提供了准确、相关、具有代表性且足够的证据支持他或她的主张？作者是否引用原始资料？如果是，那么它们是否可靠？

---

2 ▪ 评估图书馆的原始资料

评估通过图书馆找到的原始资料（不论是印刷版的还是图书馆网站上的），你要考虑日期、题目、总结、简介、标题、作者传记和任何原始资料的引用。以下的标准拓展了前面加框文字中最重要的贴士。接下来的几页显示了学生Justin Malik如何将这些标准运用到他在研究green consumerism时查询过的两个印刷版原始资料：一篇杂志文章和一篇期刊文章。

确认原始资料来源

检查图书馆原始资料是通俗的还是学术的。学术性的原始资料（如参考期刊和大学出版社的书籍）一般更有深度，也更可靠，但是一些通俗的原始资料（如供普通读者阅读的第一手新闻报道和书籍）通常也适于研究项目。

核查作者的专业知识

在学术出版物发表文章的作者通常是专家，其权威性得到了认证。核查原始资料以了解它是否包含作者的生平事略，核查传记等参考资料，或在网络的关键词搜索中核查作者的姓名。查找作者的其他出版物、他或她的工作和社交关系，例如，大学教师、非营利机构的研究员、一般娱乐书籍的作者或流行杂志的作者。

辨别偏见

每一位作者都有一个影响其选择和解释证据的观点。你可以从列举了参考目录和文章书籍评论的传记或者引用索引和评论索引中了解作者的偏见。但是，你还要查看原始资料本身。作者的观点如何与其他原始资料的观点相关联？作者强调、忽略或摈弃了哪些方面？当你意识到原始资料的偏见时，你可以在写作中承认并努力平衡它们。

确定原始资料是否公正、合理且写得很好

即便是带有强烈偏见的作品也应该以客观的语气展示可靠的推理，并公正地论述对立的观点。所有的原始资料都应该经过逻辑组织，都应该用清晰而正确的句子来表述。任何一个特性的缺失都应该引起警告。

分析支撑作者观点的证据

不论你是否赞同作者的观点，证据都应该准确、与论点相关、代表论点所处的语境并足以得出该论点。（见pp. 113–114）作者的原始资料本身应该是可靠的。

评估图书馆原始资料

p. 401是Justin Malik撰写green consumerism论文时查询过的两个图书馆原始资料的示范页。Malik用pp. 398–399中的问题和准则评估了原始资料。

Makower	Jackson
Origin Interview with Joel Makower published in *Vegetarian Times*, a popular magazine.	**Origin** Article by Tim Jackson published in *Journal of Industrial Ecology*, a scholarly journal sponsored by two reputable universities: MIT and Yale.
Author Gives Makower's credentials at the beginning of the interview: the author of a book on green products and of a monthly newsletter on green businesses. Quotes another source that calls Makower the "guru of green business practice."	**Author** Includes a biography at the end of the article that describes Jackson as a professor at the University of Surrey (UK) and lists his professional activities related to the environment.
Bias Describes and promotes green products. Concludes with an endorsement of a for-profit Web site that tracks and sells green products.	**Bias** Presents multiple views of green consumerism. Argues that a solution to environmental problems will involve green products and less consumption but in different ways than currently proposed.
Reasonableness and writing Presents Makower's data and perspective on distinguishing good from bad green products, using conversational writing in an informal presentation.	**Reasonableness and writing** Presents and cites opposing views objectively, using formal academic writing.
Source citations Lacks source citations for claims and data.	**Source citations** Includes more than three pages of source citations, many of scholarly and government sources and all cited within the article.
Assessment **Unreliable for academic research:** Despite Makower's reputation, the article comes from a nonscholarly source, takes a one-sided approach to consumption, and depends on statistics credited only to Makower.	**Assessment** **Reliable for academic research:** The article comes from a scholarly journal, the author is an expert in the field, he discusses many views and concedes some, and his source citations confirm evidence from reliable sources.

（续表）

Unreliable source for academic research:

An interview with Joel Makower, published in *Vegetarian Times*

Reliable source for academic research:

An article by Tim Jackson, published in the *Journal of Industrial Ecology*

3 ▪ 评估网站

帮助你评估图书馆原始资料的批判性阅读在很大程度上同样会帮助你评估可以直接登录的网站。正如你不会将 *People* 等流行杂志用作学术研究，你不会将名人的网站、粉丝的网站或八卦网站用作原始资料。但是，许多网站似乎是有价值的。这对评估提出了额外的挑战，因为它们没有经过编辑和图书管理员的先期遴选。你必须依靠自己的力量区分学术文章和企业推广，区分有效数据和虚构的统计数据，区分理由充足的观点和聪明的宣传。

下面加框文字中总结的策略可以帮助你做到这一切。在pp. 404–405，你可以见到Justin Malik如何将此策略运用到他在研究green consumerism时查询过的两个网站中。

评估网站时需要考虑的问题

用p. 398中的问题补充下列问题。

- **你查看的是什么类型的网站？**网站类型让你在哪些方面对网站的目的和内容有所期待？
- **谁是作者或主办方？**负责网站的个人或团体的可信度如何？
- **网站的目的和偏见是什么？**网站的作者或主办方的想法是什么？你发现他们有什么偏见？
- **网站的背景告诉你什么？**关于网站主题，你已经知道哪些信息可以帮助你进行评估？网站链接提供了哪些支持或其他信息？
- **网站的外观告诉你什么？**网站的设计是否经过深思熟虑并引人注目？文字是否清晰且无错？
- **网站内容的可信度如何？**网站的主张是否得到证据的良好支撑？证据是否来自可靠的原始资料？网站最近一次的更新是什么时候？

注意：评估网站文件时，你通常需要找到网站的主页，以发现作者或主办方、发表日期和其他相关信息。你阅读的页面可能含有指向主页的链接。如果没有，你可以通过编辑浏览器上地址或定位区域的URL找到。逆向操作，从后向前删除URL的末端部分直到最后一个斜线符号，然后点击回车。重复此步骤，直到你找到主页。在主页上，你还可以找到菜单选择，通常标注为"About"。它将你引向网站作者或主办方的情况说明。

确定网站类型

当你搜索网站时，你可能会遇到各种不同类型的网站。尽管它们有时候重叠，但网站类型通常可以通过内容和目的来识别。以下是你使用搜索引擎可以找到的主要的网站类型：

- **学术网站**：这些网站旨在建构知识，通常是可靠的。它们包括内含支撑数据和广泛引用学术性原始资料的研究报告。源自美国的此类网站，URL通常以edu（大学或学院）、org（非营利机构）或gov（政府部门或机构）结尾。源自其他国家的网站，URL的结尾各不相同，通常以国家代码结尾，例如，英国用uk，德国用de，韩国用kr。
- **信息网站**：个人、非营利机构、企业、学校和政府部门都有集中管理各种主题（如天文学、嘻哈音乐和动物园设计等）信息的网站。网站的URL可能以edu，org，gov，或com（商业机构）结尾。这样的网站通常没有学术网址建构知识的宗旨，可能省略支撑数据和引用材料，但是它们会提供有用的信息，有时候还包含学术性和其他原始资料的链接。
- **鼓吹性网站**：许多网站展示推广某些政策或决定的个人或团体（如美国步枪协会等）的观点。它们的URL通常以org结尾，但也可能以edu或com结尾。大多数鼓吹性网站具有强烈的偏见。一些网站包含严肃的证据和充分的研究以支持它们的立场，但其他的网站选择或歪曲证据。
- **商业网站**：企业和其他商业机构（如汽车制造商、电子产品制造商和书商）维护网站，以便自我辩解、自我推销或销售产品和服务。商业网站的URL通常以com结尾，但是有些网站以biz结尾。美国之外的商业网站通常以国家代码结尾。尽管商业网站以增加主办方的盈利为目的，但它们也包含可靠的数据。
- **个人网站**：由个人维护的网站内容五花八门，从家庭旅游日记到对政治问题的观点到关于学术发展的报告。它们的URL通常以com或edu结尾。个人网站的可靠度和它们的作者一样，但是有些网站的确提供有价值的证言、可靠的原始资料链接和其他有用的信息。个人网站通常是p. 391讨论过的博客或社交网络的页面。

注意：开放性的资讯网站允许任何人提供并编辑网站信息。诸如维基百科等享有盛誉的开放性资讯网站，其较早时期的词条很可靠，因为它们经过专家的审核与编辑，但最近的词条可能有错，甚至是误报。你得向老师询问开放性的资讯网址是不是可接受的原始资料来源。如果是，对照其他更为可靠的原始资料来源，使用以下准则认真评估这些网站。

评估网站

p. 405是Justin Malik为撰写green consumerism论文而查询的两个网站的截图。Malik用p. 398和p. 402加框文字中的问题评估了原始资料。

Allianz Knowledge Partnersite	*Center for Climate and Energy Solutions*
Author and sponsor Site sponsor is the Allianz Group, a global insurance company partnering with well-known organizations to provide information on a variety of issues. Authors of article are not climate scientists.	Listed author is an expert on sustainable technologies. (His name links to a biography.) Site sponsor is the Center for Climate and Energy Solutions, a nonprofit organization that specializes in energy, climate change, and business.
Purpose and bias Educational page on a corporate-sponsored Web site with the self-stated purpose of gathering information about global issues and making it available to an international audience.	Informational site with the stated purpose of "working to promote action and sound policy on the challenges of energy and climate change." Report expresses bias toward businesses that have lowered their carbon emissions through innovation.
Context One of many sites publishing current information on climate issues.	One of many sites publishing current research on climate issues.
Presentation Clean, professionally designed site with mostly error-free writing.	Clean, professionally designed site with error-free writing.
Content Article gives basic information about climate change and provides links to other pages that expand on its claims. Probably because of the intended general (nonscientist) audience, the pages do not include citations of scholarly research.	Report is current (date above the author's name), it describes companies that have successfully reduced carbon emissions and remained competitive, and it provides references to scholarly sources.
Assessment **Unreliable for academic research:** Despite the wealth of information in the article and its links, the material lacks the scholarly source citations necessary for its use as evidence in an academic paper.	**Reliable for academic research:** The report has an explicit bias toward companies that innovate to reduce carbon emissions, but the site sponsor is reputable and the author is an expert and cites scholarly sources.

（续表）

Unreliable source for academic research: An article published on the Web site *Allianz knowledge Partnersite*

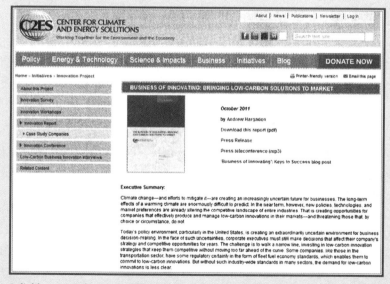

Reliable source for academic research: A report published on the Web site *Center for Climate and Energy Solutions*

确定作者或主办方

有信誉的网站通常标明作者、负责网站的团体,并提供作者和主办方的联系方式或链接。如果没有这些信息,你就不应该使用该原始资料。如果只有作者或主办方的姓名,你就可以通过关键词搜索在传记词典中或其他原始资料中发现更多的信息。要确保作者和主办方具有所展示主题方面的专业知识:例如,如果作者是个医生,他或她是哪方面的医生?

判断目的和偏见

网站的目的决定其提供的观点和信息。推断网站的目的可以告诉你如何解释在网站上看到的信息。如果一个网站意在销售产品或拥护一个特定的立场,它可能强调有利的观点和信息,而忽视甚至歪曲不利的信息或对立的观点。相反,如果一个网站意在建构知识(如学术项目或期刊),它就有可能承认不同的观点和证据。

判定网站的目的和偏见通常需要你不仅仅看首页,还要领会语言和图像所暗含的意思。首先,要在通常标注为"About"的这个页面批判性地阅读网站的自我介绍。要怀疑任何一个不提供自我信息与目的的网站。

考虑背景

对一个网站的评估应该考虑到网站本身之外的因素。这些因素中最重要的是你自己的知识。你对网站主题及他人对主题的普遍看法了解多少?该网站在何处融入整个背景环境?你从该网站中可以了解哪些你不曾知道的?

另外,你可以点击网站的链接来查看这些链接如何支持或不支持网站的可信度。例如,学术性原始资料的链接增加网站的权威性,只要该学术性原始资料真的与网站的主张有关,并支持网站的主张。

检查外观

检查网站的外观和文字表达方式可以明白其目的和可靠性。网站的所有元素支撑其目的,或者网站堆积了无关的材料和图表?文章是否书写清晰并关注目的?是否相对无错,还是包含拼写和语法错误?网站是否精心建构并维护良好,还是草率凌乱?自动弹出的广告的干扰程度如何?

分析内容

有了网站的作者、目的和背景的信息,你就可以评估其内容。网站上的观点和信息是最新的,还是过时了?(查看发布日期)它们是否有倾向性?如果有，倾向于哪个方向？观点和数据是具有权威性，还是你需要平衡或者甚至排斥它们？网站上的主张是否由源自可靠的原始资料的证据支撑？这些问题需要仔细阅读文章及其原始资料。

4 ▪ 评估其他在线原始资料

和网站一样，社交媒体和多媒体需要批判性的审查。社交媒体（包括电子邮件、博客、讨论小组、Facebook网页和开放性资讯网站）可以是可靠数据和观点的来源，但是它们也会包含错误或误导性的数据和有倾向性的观点。多媒体（包括图像、音频和视频）可以给你的观点提供有价值的支撑，但是它们也会误导或曲解。例如，用"I have a dream"在YouTube视频网站上搜索会得到Martin Luther King发表此著名演讲的视频以及人们充满恶意地说起他及其演讲的视频。

要评估社交媒体和多媒体，请提出以下问题。下面几页将对此进行解释。

评估社交媒体和多媒体需要考虑的问题

将p. 398和p. 402上的问题作为这些问题的补充。
- **谁是作者或创作者？** 他或她的可信度如何？
- **作者或创作者的目的是什么？** 你对作者或创作者发表作品的原因了解多少？
- **背景揭示了什么？** 对作品的反应（如对博客帖子或讨论话题上的其他信息的反应）体现了原始资料平衡性和可靠性的哪些方面？
- **内容价值几何？** 作者或创作者的主张是否由证据支撑？证据来自可靠的原始资料吗？
- **原始资料如何与其他原始资料相比？** 根据你所看到的可靠的资料来源，作者或创造者的声明看起来准确和公平吗？

确定作者或创作者

检查潜在原始资料的作者或创作者有助于判断该资料的可靠性。通过网站的关键词搜索或传记词典，你可以了解作者或创作者的背景信息。如果你根本无法辨别作者或创作者，你就不要使用该原始资料。

追踪作者或创作者的其他作品，你还可以了解此人的兴趣和偏见。例如，你可以核查博客作者是否引用或链接到其他出版物，在讨论小组档案中查找同一作者的其他帖子，或者获取摄影者作品的概览。

分析作者或创作者的目的

你对作者或创作者发表作品的原因了解多少？查找作者或创作者的主张、证据的使用（或缺失）以及对对立观点的处理。这些要素传递此人在该主题上的立场及普遍公正性。它们将帮助你在其他原始资料中确定该原始资料的位置。

考虑背景

社交媒体和多媒体通常难以单独评估。通过指出他人如何看待作者或创作者，而不是仅限于对他人反应的特定描述可以给你一种背景的感觉。例如，在博客或Facebook网页，要查看其他人发的评论帖。如果你发现负面或愤怒的反应，要了解其原因：有时候在线的匿名性鼓励人们对非常合理的帖子做出充满恶意的反应。

分析内容

可靠的原始资料提供论点的证据并列举证据的来源。如果你没有发现类似的支撑证据，你或许不应该使用该原始资料。但是，当原始资料对你很重要而且传记信息或背景信息显示作者或创作者是严肃可靠时，你可以请他或她指导你找到支撑信息。

文章的语气也可以暗示其目的和可靠性。大多数社交媒体中，文章语气更通俗，比其他类型的原始资料要激烈；要带着怀疑的目光看那些充满蔑视、傲慢或强烈语气的文章。

对比其他原始资料

要经常将社交媒体和多媒体原始资料与其他原始资料相比较，这样你就可以区分未经证实的单个观点和经过验证的更为主流的观点。不要仅仅因为你在其他博客上见到过就想当然地认为博客作者的信息和观点是主流的。技术使得内容可以在瞬间被其他博客获取，因此，广泛传播只显示大众兴趣而非可靠性。

要提防那些复制期刊文章、报告或其他出版物的博客。努力查找出版物的原始版本，以确保它的复制是完整而准确的，而不是经过选择性的引用或歪曲。如果你找不到原始版本，就不要将该出版物用作原始资料。

53b 合成原始资料

当你开始明白原始资料间的差异和共同之处时，你就进入研究性写作最重要的部分：为了自己的目的而建立关系。这种合成是批判性地阅读原始资料的重要步骤。通过打草稿和修改研究论文，这一步骤得以继续。当你推断出两位作者观点之间或者同一作者的两部作品之间的联系时，你就形成了关于主题的个人观点，并创建了新的知识。

随着原始资料处理过程的逐步完成，你对原始资料的合成就会变得更加详尽和富有经验。本章节均衡描述了这一步骤：从原始资料中收集信息（pp. 411–412）；决定是否总结、改述或直接引用原始资料（pp. 412–418）以及将原始资料融入自己的句子中（pp. 419–423）。除非你是分析第一手的原始资料（如诗人的作品），否则你首先要快速而有选择性地阅读原始资料，以便获得主题的总体印象并了解原始资料是如何处理主题的。不要陷入做详细笔记的困境中，但是要在研究日记（p. 371）或带有注释的参考目录（p. 376）中记录下你对原始资料的看法。

对原始资料做出反应

记下那些让你思考的原始资料可以让你发现自己对某一主题的看法。你是否同意作者的观点？你为什么同意或反对？每一个原始资料向你揭示了哪些处理主题的新方法？在你理解之前，原始资料中是否有需要你做进一步研究的地方？当你阅读其他资料时，这些资料是否提示了你应该记住的问题？

串联原始资料

当你注意到原始资料之间的关系时，要马上记录下来。两个原始资料在理论上或对事实的解释上是否有所不同？一个原始资料是否阐明另一个原始资料，可能是评论或澄清或提供附加数据？两个或多个原始资料是否支持你曾读过的理论或你自己的观点？

留意自己的见解

除了原始资料促成的观点外，你一定会有一些独立的想法：一种信念、一个突然变得清晰的混乱点、一个你从未见到其他人问过的问题。这些见解会在一些意想不到的时刻出现，所以随时在笔记本或电脑上记录下来是个不错的办法。

得出自己的结论

随着研究的继续，你在合成原始资料时形成的反应、联系和见解将引导你用主题句（见pp. 435–436）来回答最初的研究问题。它们还会引导你获得支撑论点的主要观点（你从合成原始资料中得出的结论）。这是形成论文的主要部分。一旦有了观点，就要随时记录。

利用原始资料支撑你的结论

有效的原始资料合成要求认真处理原始资料中的证据。这样，它就会顺畅地融入你的句子中，但又明显地有别于你自己的观点。打草稿时，要确保每一个段落关注一个观点，观点要有来自原始资料的证据支撑。一般来说，用自己的观点开始每一段文章，用恰当的引用提供原始资料中的证据，并以对证据的解释收尾。（避免以原始资料的引用结束一个段落；相反，用你自己的观点收尾）这样，你的论文就会将其他人的作品合成为你自己的作品。（见pp. 103–104学术写作中的段落结构）

练习53.1　合成原始资料

以下三个段落讨论了同样的问题：毒品合法化。你认为作者的观点有什么相似之处？有什么不同？写一段你自己的文章，使用这些作者的观点作为你自己对毒品合法化的观点的出发点。

> Perhaps the most unfortunate victims of drug prohibition laws have been the residents of America's ghettos. These laws have proved largely futile in deterring ghetto-dwellers from becoming drug abusers, but they do account for much of what ghetto residents identify as the drug problem. Aggressive, gun-toting drug dealers often upset law-abiding residents far more than do addicts nodding out in doorways. Meanwhile other residents perceive the drug dealers as heroes and successful role models. They're symbols of success to children who see no other options. At the same time the increasingly harsh criminal penalties imposed on adult drug dealers have led drug traffickers to recruit juveniles. Where once children started dealing drugs only after they had been using them for a few years, today the sequence is often reversed. Many children start using drugs only after working for older drug dealers for a while. Legalization of drugs, like legalization of alcohol in the 1930s, would drive the drug-dealing business off the streets and out of apartment buildings and into government-regulated, tax-paying stores. It also would force many of the gun-toting dealers out of the business and convert others into legitimate businessmen.
>
> —Ethan A. Nadelmann, "Shooting Up"

Statistics argue against legalization. The University of Michigan conducts an annual survey of twelfth graders, asking the students about their drug consumption. In 1980, 56.4% of those polled said they had used marijuana in the past twelve months, whereas in 2011 only 45.5% had done so. Cocaine use was also reduced in the same period (22.6% to 5.2%). At the same time, twelve-month use of legally available drugs—alcohol and nicotine-containing cigarettes—remained constant at about 70% and 50%, respectively. The numbers of illegal drug users haven't declined nearly enough: those teenaged marijuana and cocaine users are still vulnerable to addiction and even death, and they threaten to infect their impressionable peers. But clearly the prohibition of illegal drugs has helped, while the legal status of alcohol and cigarettes has not made them less popular.

—Sylvia Runkle, "The Case against Legalization"

I have to laugh at the debate over what to do about the drug problem. Everyone is running around offering solutions—from making drug use a more serious criminal offense to legalizing it. But there isn't a real solution. I know that. I used and abused drugs, and people, and society, for two decades. Nothing worked to get me to stop all that behavior except just plain being sick and tired. Nothing. Not threats, not ten-plus years in prison, not anything that was said to me. I used until I got through. Period. And that's when you'll win the war. When all the dope fiends are done. Not a minute before.

—Michael W. Posey, "I Did Drugs Until They Wore Me Out. Then I Stopped."

53c 从原始资料中收集信息

从原始资料中收集信息时，你可以合成许多观点。这种信息收集过程不是机械性的。相反，你在阅读的时候，会评估并组织原始资料中的信息。

研究者处理原始资料的方法各不相同，但所有方法具有共同的目标：

- **准确记录原始资料内容**。准确性将有助于预防错误的陈述与抄袭。
- **准确记录查找原始资料的方法**。这些记录是追溯研究步骤和在终稿中引用原始资料所必要的。（见pp. 376–378制定参考目录）
- **合成原始资料**。信息收集是个关键过程，引导你理解原始资料、明白它们之间的关系以及它们如何支撑你自己的观点。

为了达到这些目的，你可以做手抄笔记、在电脑或其他设备上输入笔记、解释复印或打印的原始资料或者解释下载的文件。对于任何一个项目，你可以使用所有这些方法。每种方法都有其优劣。

- **手写笔记**：如果在你遇到原始资料时手边没有电脑或复印机，手抄笔记就特别有用。但是，手抄笔记具有风险性。誊抄的过程中容易出错。很有可能出现誊抄原始资料的文字，而后将它误认为是自己的，并在文章中使用它，从而引发抄袭的情况。要注意笔记的准确性，并在引用的信息旁标注引号。
- **电子笔记**：在电脑或其他设备上输入笔记可以将原始资料精简为论文笔记，因为你可以在写作时将笔记输入草稿中。但是，电子笔记有和手写笔记一样的劣势：出错和抄袭的风险。和手写笔记一样，要力求笔记的准确性，引用的地方要用引号。
- **复印和打印**：复印印刷版的原始资料或者打印在线原始资料，其优势在于既方便又减少了在信息收集过程中出错和抄袭的风险。劣势在于复印或打印会干扰你合成原始资料这一关键工作。你不得不费力在复印件和打印件上标注原始资料的出版信息。如果你没有这些可用于终稿的信息，你就不能使用该原始资料。
- **下载**：在线研究过程中，你通常可以全文下载，下载网站页面、讨论小组的信息和其他材料。在打草稿时，你可以将原始资料信息从一个文档输入另一个文档。与复印和打印一样，下载会干扰你和原始资料之间的沟通，会很容易地使你不能把心思集中在使用原始资料时必须用到的出版信息上。更重要的是，直接输入原始资料很容易导致抄袭。你必须明确区分自己与他人的观点与文字。

53d 总结、改述和引用

决定是否总结、改述或直接引用原始资料是合成原始资料观点与你自己观点的重要步骤。当你用自己的话总结作者的论点或改述重要的范例或者当你选择一个重要段落来引用时，你就是在合成原始资料。选择总结、改述还是引用应该取决于你为什么要使用原始资料。

注意：总结、改述和引用都要求在论文中标明原始资料的引用。没有出处的总结或改述或者没有引号的引用都是抄袭。（关于抄袭见pp.425–431）

1 ▪ 总结

总结时，你用自己的话将一个展开的观点或论点浓缩成一两句话。（见pp. 89–91）当你在没有背景或支撑证据的情况下想记录作者观点的要点时，总结就很有用。下面的段落来自Justin Malik撰写green consumerism论文时使用过的原始资料：一篇关于消费及其对环境影响的学术论文。

原始引文

Such intuition is even making its way, albeit slowly, into scholarly circles, where recognition is mounting that ever-increasing pressures on ecosystems, life-supporting environmental services, and critical natural cycles are driven not only by the sheer number of resource users and the inefficiencies of their resource use, but also by the patterns of resource use themselves. In global environmental policymaking arenas, it is becoming more and more difficult to ignore the fact that the overdeveloped North must restrain its consumption if it expects the underdeveloped South to embrace a more sustainable trajectory.

—Thomas Princen, Michael Maniates, and Ken Conca,
Confronting Consumption, p. 4

在下面一句话的总结中，Malik选出作者文章中的核心，并用自己的话加以表述。

» 原始资料的总结

> Environmental consequences of consumption
> Princen, Maniates, and Conca 4
> Overconsumption may be a more significant cause of environmental problems than increasing population is.

注意Malik是如何在笔记中记录作者的姓名和页码，以避免在自己的论文中意外抄袭作者的观点。

下面的例子显示了之前的总结在草稿中的样子。第一个例子缺少适当的引用，因此是抄袭。第二个例子有适当的引用（MLA格式）。

没有标注引文的总结（抄袭）

Always seeking newer and better things, we consume without regard for the resources we use or the waste we leave behind. In fact, overconsumption may be a more significant cause of environmental problems than increasing population is.

标注恰当引文的总结（没有抄袭）

Always seeking newer and better things, we consume without regard for the resources we use or the waste we leave behind. In fact, according to Thomas Princen, Michael Maniates, and Ken Conca, overconsumption may be a more significant cause of environmental problems than increasing population is (4).

关于抄袭见pp. 425–431。

2 ▪ 改述

在你改述时，你更为紧密地遵循作者的原始表述，但是你用自己的语言和句子结构重新阐述作者的观点。在你想展示或检验作者的推理路线但又觉得原文的用词不值得直接引用时，改述是非常有用的。

下面的笔记显示了Malik如何改述p. 413中的段落。注意关于作者姓名和页码的记录：它将帮助Malik避免混淆改述与自己的观点，从而避免在论文中不经意地抄袭原始资料。

» 原始资料的彻底改述

Environmental consequences of consumption

Princen, Maniates, and Conca 4

Scholars are coming to believe that consumption is partly to blame for changes in ecosystems, reduction of essential natural resources, and changes in natural cycles. Policy makers increasingly see that developing nations will not adopt practices that reduce pollution and waste unless wealthy nations consume less. Rising population around the world does cause significant stress on the environment, but consumption is increasing even more rapidly than population.

与原文相比，这个改述使用了更为简单的句子和更为常用的术语。正如下面的对比所显示的，它实际上是对原文的翻译，只保留了那些没有合适同义词的单词，如ecosystems, natural, cycles, population和consumption。

原作者的话	Malik的改述
Such intuition is even making its way, albeit slowly, into scholarly circles, where recognition is mounting that	Scholars are coming to believe that
ever-increasing pressures on ecosystems, life-supporting environmental services, and critical natural cycles are driven not only by the sheer number of resource users and the inefficiencies of their resource use, but also by the patterns of resource use themselves.	consumption is partly to blame for changes in ecosystems, reduction of essential natural resources, and changes in natural cycles.
In global environmental policymaking arenas, it is becoming more and more difficult to ignore the fact that	Policy makers increasingly see that
overdeveloped countries must restrain their consumption if they expect underdeveloped countries to embrace a more sustainable trajectory.	developing nations will not adopt practices that reduce pollution and waste unless wealthy nations consume less.
And while global population growth still remains a huge issue in many regions around the world—both rich and poor—	Rising population around the world does cause significant stress on the environment,
per-capita growth in consumption is, for many resources, expanding eight to twelve times faster than population growth.	but consumption is increasing even more rapidly than population.

改述时应遵循的准则：

- 多次阅读原始资料以确保对原始资料的理解。然后你就发现使用自己的语言会更容易。
- 用自己的语言和句子结构重新表述主要观点。你不需要遵循原文的结构或重新陈述原文。选择并重新表述你需要的部分。如果完整的句子显得过于复杂或累赘，可以使用词组。在下面的例子中，Justin Malik更为简要地对引文进行了改述。

» **原始资料的简短改述**

> Environmental consequences of consumption
> Princen, Maniates, and Conca 4
> Consumption is increasing more rapidly than population + contributing to major ecological crises. Wealthy nations have to start consuming less.

- **注意不要歪曲意思。** 不要改变原始资料的时态或省略连接词、修饰语及其他材料。这些材料的缺失会迷惑你或者让你歪曲原始资料。
- **注意不要抄袭原始资料。** 使用自己的词和句子结构，并在笔记中提供引文。下面的例子显示了之前的改述在草稿中的样子。第一个例子缺少恰当的引用，因而是抄袭。第二个例子有恰当的引用（MLA格式）。

没有标注引文的改述（抄袭）

Always seeking newer and better things, we consume without regard for the resources we use or the waste we leave behind. In fact, overconsumption is increasing more rapidly than population and contributing to major ecological crises. Wealthy nations have to start consuming less.

标注恰当引文的改述（没有抄袭）

Always seeking newer and better things, we consume without regard for the resources we use or the waste we leave behind. In fact, according to Thomas Princen, Michael Maniates, and Ken Conca, overconsumption is increasing more rapidly than population and contributing to major ecological crises. Wealthy nations have to start consuming less (4).

关于抄袭见pp. 425–431。

CULTURE LANGUAGE 如果英语不是你的母语，而且你在改述原始资料的观点时遇到了困难，试一下这个方法：多读几遍原文再开始改述。然后，不看原文，陈述文章的要点，而不是逐句"翻译"。对照原文，检查你的文章，确保在没有使用原作者语言和句子结构的情况下自己抓住了原始资料作者的意思和重点。如果你需要一个单词的同义词，可以查字典。

3 ▪ 直接引用

你的来自原始资料的笔记可能包括许多引用,尤其是如果你依赖复印、打印或下载的话。是否在草稿中使用引用而不是总结或改述取决于原始资料是第一手的还是第二手的以及原话的重要性:

- **分析第一手原始资料时可以大量引用原文。** 第一手资料包括文学作品、目击者的报告和历史文件。引用通常既是分析的目标,也是观点的主要支撑。
- **利用第二手原始资料时可以选择性引用。** 第二手原始资料是对其他原始资料的报道或分析,例如,评论家对诗歌的看法或历史学家对多个目击者报告的综合。要优先考虑总结和改述,而不是引用。每一个引用都要经过以下加框文字的检验。大多数十来页的论文不应该有两个或三个以上、每个长度超过几行的引用。

对直接引用第二手原始资料的检验

作者的原文满足下列条件之一:
- 语言异乎寻常生动、大胆或富有创造性。
- 改述会歪曲或丢失意思。
- 在你的解释中,单词本身具有争议性。
- 引文代表并强调某个重要专家的主要意见或观点。
- 引文使你的观点更具说服力。
- 引文是图表、表格或示意图。

引文要尽可能短小:
- 它只包含与自己观点相关的资料。
- 它经过编辑,剔除了范例和其他不必要的材料,使用方括号和省略号。

(pp. 341–344)

无论是在笔记中还是在草稿中引用原始资料时,要谨慎以避免抄袭或歪曲原始资料:

- **认真记录材料。** 记下作者的准确用词、拼写、大写和标点符号。
- **每处直接引用的内容至少要校对两遍。**
- **用引号标出引用的原始资料**,这样日后就不会将它与改述或总结相混淆。确保将标点符号也转移到草稿中,除非引文很长,并与文章分开。更多关于处理长引文的建议,参见pp. 485–486(MLA格式)和p. 518(APA格式)。

- 用方括号表示增加解释性词或变更单词的大小写。(见p. 344，p. 356)
- 用省略号省略无关的材料。(见pp. 341–343)
- 在草稿中列出原始资料的来源。关于提供引用材料见pp. 432–434。

下面的笔记显示了Justin Malik如何引用p. 413中的部分文章。他用方括号和省略号让引文更加简洁。注意对作者姓名、页码以及原文前后的引号的记录。所有这一切帮助Malik避免在论文中抄袭原始资料。

» 原始资料的引用

Environmental consequences of consumption

Princen, Maniates, and Conca 4

"[E]ver-increasing pressures on ecosystems, life-supporting environmental services, and critical natural cycles are driven not only by the sheer number of resource users . . . but also by the patterns of resource use themselves."

下面的例子展示了作为草稿一部分的引文。第一个例子缺少恰当的标点符号和引用，是抄袭。第二个例子是正确的（MLA格式）。

缺少引号、省略号和引文的引用（抄袭）

Increasing consumption may be as much of a threat to the environment as increasing population. In fact, ever-increasing pressures on ecosystems, life-supporting environmental services, and critical natural cycles are driven not only by the sheer number of resource users but also by the patterns of resource use themselves.

有引号、省略号和恰当引文的引用（没有抄袭）

Increasing consumption may be as much of a threat to the environment as increasing population. According to Thomas Princen, Michael Maniates, and Ken Conca, "ever-increasing pressures on ecosystems, life-supporting environmental services, and critical natural cycles are driven not only by the sheer number of resource users . . . but also by the patterns of resource use themselves" (4).

关于抄袭见pp. 425–431。

> **练习53.2　总结和改述**
>
> 准备两份原始笔记，一份总结下一段，另一份释义前四句话（以"autonomy"这个词结尾）。一定要记录来源的作者姓名和页码。
>
> Federal organization [of the United States] has made it possible for different states to deal with the same problems in many different ways. One consequence of federalism, then, has been that people are treated differently, by law, from state to state. The great strength of this system is that differences from state to state in cultural preferences, moral standards, and levels of wealth can be accommodated. In contrast to a unitary system in which the central government makes all important decisions (as in France), federalism is a powerful arrangement for maximizing regional freedom and autonomy. The great weakness of our federal system, however, is that people in some states receive less than the best or the most advanced or the least expensive services and policies that government can offer. The federal dilemma does not invite easy solution, for the costs and benefits of the arrangement have tended to balance out.
>
> —Peter K. Eisinger et al., *American Politics*, p. 44

> **练习53.3　结合总结、改述和直接引用**
>
> 准备一份来源说明，包括转述或总结，以及直接引用，以陈述以下段落的主要思想。一定要记录来源的作者姓名和页码。
>
> Most speakers unconsciously duel even during seemingly casual conversations, as can often be observed at social gatherings where they show less concern for exchanging information with other guests than for asserting their own dominance. Their verbal dueling often employs very subtle weapons like mumbling, a hostile act which defeats the listener's desire to understand what the speaker claims he is trying to say (but is really not saying because he is mumbling!). Or the verbal dueler may keep talking after someone has passed out of hearing range—which is often an aggressive challenge to the listener to return and acknowledge the dominance of the speaker.
>
> —Peter K. Farb, *Word Play*, p. 107

53e　将原始资料融入文章中

将原始资料融入句子中是将他人的观点和信息与自己的观点和信息相结合的关键所在。源自原始资料的证据应该支撑你的结论，而不是成为你的结论：你应该不想让证据淹没你自己的观点。为了将自己的观点放在首位，你不仅仅要展示借来的材料，你也要介绍和解释它。

注意： 本节的范例在原始资料引用方面使用了MLA格式和现在时态（如disagrees）。见pp. 422–424提供引用材料的不同格式和学术学科中的动词时态。本书的其他地方还讨论了几种其他引用规则：

- 使用逗号以强调信号短语。（pp. 318–319）
- 将引号和其他标点符号放在一起。（pp. 337–338）
- 使用方括号和省略号以表示引用中的变化。（pp. 341–344）
- 夹注的标点符号和位置。（pp. 445–447）
- 确定长文和诗歌引用的格式。（MLA格式，pp. 485–486；APA格式，p. 518）

1 ▪ 引入所借用的材料

通过识别总结、改述或引用并提供自己的观点和语句与原始资料的观点和语句之间的平稳过渡来引入所借用的材料。在下面的段落中，作者没有将自己的结构与原始资料的句子融为一体：

不恰当的引文： One editor disagrees with this view and "a good reporter does not fail to separate opinions from facts" (Lyman 52).

在下面的修改稿中，作者添加了词语，将引文融入自己的句子中：

修改后的引文： One editor disagrees with this view, <u>maintaining that</u> "a good reporter does not fail to separate opinions from facts" (Lyman 52).

为了融合自己的用词和原始资料的用词，你有时候需要对引文中的词进行替换或添加，用方括号表示你所做的变更。

添加单词： "The tabloids [of England] are a journalistic case study in bad reporting," claims Lyman (52).

改变动词形式： A bad reporter, Lyman implies, is one who "[fails] to separate opinions from facts" (52).［方括号内的动词替换原句中的fail］

改变大小写： "[T]o separate opinions from facts" is the work of a good reporter (Lyman 52).［在原始文件中，to没有大写］

用名词代替代词： The reliability of a news organization "depends on [reporters'] trustworthiness," says Lyman (52).［方括号里的名词代替了原词中的their］

2 ▪ 解释所借用的材料

你需要将所借用的材料融入自己的句子，这样读者就能够毫不费力地明白它是如何帮助你得出自己的观点。如果你只是将原始资料堆放在论文中，而不解释你希望读者如何解读它，读者就得很费力地去理解你的句子以及你试图建立的句子之间的关系。例如，下面的文章迫使我们自己去弄明白作者的句子和引文表达的是对立的观点：

> **引文的堆放**：Many news editors and reporters maintain that it is impossible to keep personal opinions from influencing the selection and presentation of facts. "True, news reporters, like everyone else, form impressions of what they see and hear. However, a good reporter does not fail to separate opinions from facts" (Lyman 52).

在修改稿中，画线的添加内容告诉我们如何解读引文：

> **修改后的引文**：Many news editors and reporters maintain that it is impossible to keep personal opinions from influencing the selection and presentation of facts. <u>Yet not all authorities agree with this view. One editor grants that</u> "news reporters, like everyone else, form impressions of what they see and hear." <u>But, he insists,</u> "a good reporter does not fail to separate opinions from facts" (Lyman 52).

信号短语

在之前的那段文章中，one editor grants 和 he insists 是**信号短语**：它们告诉读者谁是来源，以及在接下来的引语中会出现什么。信号短语通常包括：原作者的姓名（或替代词，如 one editor 和 he），以及表示原作者态度或处理观点的方法的动词。

下面是一些用作信号短语的动词。这些动词都用了现在时态。这是人文学科的典型写作。在社会学科和自然学科中，过去时态或现在完成时态更为常见。见 pp. 423–424。

作者是 中立的	作者推断或 暗示	作者争辩	作者心神不宁或 态度轻蔑
comments	analyzes	claims	belittles
describes	asks	contends	bemoans
explains	assesses	defends	complains
illustrates	concludes	holds	condemns
notes	considers	insists	deplores
observes	demonstrates	maintains	deprecates
points out	finds		derides
records	predicts		disagrees
relates	proposes	作者赞同	laments
reports	reveals	admits	warns
says	shows	agrees	
sees	speculates	concedes	
thinks	suggests	concurs	
writes	supposes	grants	

改变信号短语以适应你对所借用材料的解释，这还可以让读者保持兴趣。信号短语可以放在所借用材料之前、之中或之后：

信号短语在所借用材料之前：Lyman insists that "a good reporter does not fail to separate opinions from facts" (52).

信号短语在所借用材料之中："However," Lyman insists, "a good reporter does not fail to separate opinions from facts" (52).

信号短语在所借用材料之后："[A] good reporter does not fail to separate opinions from facts," Lyman insists (52).

背景信息

你可以给信号短语添加信息，以便告诉读者你使用原始资料的原因。在大多数情况下，要在文章中提供作者的姓名，尤其当作者是位专家或者读者认识该作者时。

标明作者：Harold Lyman grants that "news reporters, like everyone else, form impressions of what they see and hear." But, Lyman insists, "a good reporter does not fail to separate opinions from facts" (52).

如果原始资料的标题提供了有关作者或引文背景的信息，你可以在文章中提及。

给出标题：Harold Lyman, in his book *The Conscience of the Journalist*, grants that "news reporters, like everyone else, form impressions of what they see and hear." But, Lyman insists, "a good reporter does not fail to separate opinions from facts" (52).

如果被引用作者的背景和经历强化或阐明引文，你可以在文章提及这些凭证。

给出凭证：Harold Lyman, a newspaper editor for more than forty years, grants that "news reporters, like everyone else, form impressions of what they see and hear." But, Lyman insists, "a good reporter does not fail to separate opinions from facts" (52).

在你只是陈述事实或者组合不同原始资料的事实和意见时，你没有必要在文章中提及作者的姓名、原始资料或凭据。在下面一段文章中，信息比原始资料重要，因此原始资料的名称只在括号里标明：

To end the abuses of the British, many colonists were urging three actions: forming a united front, seceding from Britain, and taking control of their own international relations (Wills 325–36).

3 ▪ 整合原始资料的学科格式

之前例子中用来引入和解释所借用材料的画线部分通常适用于各种学科，但是在动词时态和引用材料的格式方面，各学科有所不同。

英语和其他人文学科

英语、其他语种及相关学科的作者采用MLA格式来引用原始资料（参见第56章），通常在信号短语中使用动词的一般现在时。在讨论文学作品之外的原始资料时，现在完成时态有时候也是恰当的：

Lyman insists ... [一般现在时]。

Lyman has insisted ... [现在完成时]。

讨论文学作品时，只有在描述作者的作品和作品中的行为时要使用一般现在时：

Kate Chopin builds irony into every turn of "The Story of an Hour." For example, Mrs. Mallard, the central character, finds joy in the death of her husband, whom she loves, because she anticipates "the long procession of years that would belong to her absolutely" (23).

在撰写文学论文时，要避免时态的变化。例如，你可以缩短引文以避开引文中使用过去时态的动词：

有时态变化：Her freedom elevates her, so that "she carried herself unwittingly like a goddess of victory" (24).

没有时态变化： Her freedom elevates her, so that she walks "unwittingly like a goddess of victory" (24).

历史和其他人文学科

历史、艺术史、哲学及相关学科的作者通常在信号短语中使用动词的一般现在时态和现在完成时态：

Lincoln persisted, as Haworth has noted, in "feeling that events controlled him."[3]
What Miller calls Lincoln's "severe self-doubt"[6] undermined his effectiveness on at least two occasions.

引文右上方的数字是引用材料的芝加哥格式，用于历史和其他学科。

社会和自然科学

社会和自然科学的作者在报告研究结果时使用动词的一般现在时。在其他场合，他们在信号短语中使用一般过去时或现在完成时，引入解释、说明或其他评论时也是如此。（因此，当你撰写社会和自然科学的文章时，通常要将p. 421中所列的信号短语动词从一般现在时转为一般过去时或现在完成时）

Lin (2001) has suggested that preschooling may significantly affect children's academic performance not only in elementary school but through high school (pp. 22–23).

In an exhaustive survey of the literature published between 1990 and 2005, Walker (2006) found "no proof, merely a weak correlation, linking place of residence and rate of illness" (p. 121).

这些文章遵循第57章中讨论的APA引用材料的格式。社会学、教育学、护理学、生物学和其他许多社会和自然科学也使用APA格式或与它非常相似的格式。

练习53.4　引入并解释引文

利用下面这段的观点，并从你自己的观察和经验中举例，写一段关于焦虑的文章。从下面的段落中至少引用一段话或改写一段话到你自己的句子中。在你的段落中，确定作者的名字，并给出他的身份或资质的证明：他是一位精神病学教授和执业精神分析学家。

There are so many ways in which human beings are different from all the lower forms of animals, and almost all of them make us uniquely susceptible to feelings of anxiousness. Our imagination and reasoning powers facilitate anxiety; the anxious feeling is precipitated not by an absolute impending threat—such as the worry about an examination, a speech, travel—but rather by the symbolic and often unconscious representations. We do not have to be experiencing a potential danger. We can experience something related to it. We can recall, through our incredible memories, the original symbolic sense of vulnerability in childhood and suffer the feeling attached to that. We can even forget the original memory and be stuck with the emotion—which is then compounded by its seemingly irrational quality at this time. It is not just the fear of death which pains us, but the anticipation of it; or the anniversary of a specific death; or a street, a hospital, a time of day, a color, a flower, a symbol associated with death.

—Willard Gaylin, "Feeling Anxious," p. 23

第 54 章 抄袭的避免和原始资料的引用

概要

- 了解什么是抄袭，不要有意或无意地抄袭原始资料（下方）
- 了解你不需要标明哪些原始资料（p. 428）
- 了解你必须标明的原始资料（p. 428）
- 如果你打算发表作品，需要获得必要的许可（p. 431）
- 认真标注原始资料来源（p. 432）

作为学术写作核心的知识建构，取决于包括学生在内的每一位参与者在使用和标明原始资料时的诚信。作者或创作者的作品是他或她的知识财产。你和其他人可以借用作品中的观点甚至是词或图像，但是你必须承认你所展示的东西来自别人且属于别人。

当你在写作中标明原始资料时，你不仅仅是在赞许你查询过的作品的作者或创作者，你还展示了自己作品的依据，而这反过来增加了你作为研究者和作者的诚信。标明原始资料在学者、学生、作者和读者之间建立了建构知识所需的信任。

抄袭（plagiarism，源自拉丁语"kidnapper"一词）是将他人的作品展现为自己的作品。不论是有意还是无意，抄袭是严重的过错。它破坏了信任，损毁甚至毁坏了你作为研究者和作者的信誉。在大多数大学，学术诚信的准则要求严惩抄袭行为：扣分或给不及格、休学或开除。避免抄袭的方法就是标明来源：你所写的每一页文字都要记录你查询过的原始资料，并在文章及参考目录中引用原始资料。

CULTURE LANGUAGE 原创性、知识产权和抄袭的概念不是众所周知的。例如，在其他文化中，为了表示对学者作品的掌握或尊重，学生可能会被鼓励去复制学者的语，而不用标明原始资料。但是在美国，不论是有意还是无意，使用他人作品而不标明出处是很严重的过错。如果你对本章的准则还有疑问，请咨询你的老师。

避免抄袭的清单

了解原始资料
你是否使用了
- 自己的经历
- 常识或
- 他人的材料？

你必须对他人的材料致谢。

谨慎引用
- 检查每一处引用与原始资料完全一致。
- 插入文章中的每一处引用前后加引号。（与文章分开的引用不需要引号，见pp. 485–486和p. 518）
- 用省略号表示省略内容，用方括号表示增加内容。
- 每一处引用都要标明出处。

谨慎改述和总结
- 用自己的词和句子结构改述和总结。如果你使用了作者的词句，在引用处加上引号。
- 每一处改述或总结都标明出处。

负责任地引用原始资料
- 每一处使用他人材料的地方都要标明出处。
- 参考目录中列出所有用过的原始资料。参见第56章和第57章MLA格式和APA格式。

54a 避免有意和无意的抄袭

老师通常会分辨实为欺骗的有意抄袭和因作者缺乏组织原始资料的经验而导致的无意抄袭。

1 ▪ 有意抄袭

有意抄袭是蓄意为之：通过将他人的作品作为自己的作品上交，作者选择了欺骗。有意抄袭的学生让自己失去了有关诚信研究教育的机会。当欺骗行为被发现的时候，他们通常面临严厉的处罚，包括开除。

以下是有意抄袭的例子：

从原始资料中复制短语、句子或较长段落，不添加引号和引文出处就将它冒充为自己的作品。

总结或改述他人的观点，没有在引用时注明出处。

将从网络上复制的论文当成自己的论文上交，让朋友代写论文或从其他学生那里获得论文。

将从论文服务机构那里购买的论文当成自己的论文上交。**购买的研究结果或论文不是你自己的作品。**

2 ▪ 无意抄袭

无意抄袭不是故意的：受困于原始资料中复杂的信息和观点，作者忘了在原文前后加引号或者忘了在引文、改述或总结处标明出处。大多数老师和学校不允许无意抄袭，但是他们对无意抄袭的处理要比有意抄袭轻，至少在第一次出现无意抄袭时。

下面是无意抄袭的例子：

阅读原始资料时没有做笔记，结果无法分辨哪些是你最近学的，哪些是你已经知道的。

复制粘贴原始资料中的材料到你的文件中，却没有在其他作者的作品前后加引号。

改述时忘记添加引文出处。即使改述是用自己的语言和词表达他人的观点，你仍然需要援引该观点的原始资料。

因为你没有意识到承认他人观点的必要性而省略了他人观点的出处。

抄袭与因特网

因特网使得抄袭比以往要容易得多：只要轻点鼠标，你就可以复制并粘贴段落或整个文本到你的文档中。如果你在没有标明原始资料的情况下就这么做的话，你就是在抄袭。

> 因特网也使得发现抄袭变得容易得多。老师可以使用搜索引擎在网络的任何地方（包括学术出版物、各种网站和学期论文集）找到特定的短语或句子。和学生一样，他们可以轻松地搜索学期论文的网站，查找与他们所收论文的相似之处。他们还可以使用检测软件（这些软件可以比较学生的作品与网络上任何地方的其他作品），查找短到几个单词的匹配。
>
> 一些老师建议学生使用抄袭检测软件以确保他们的作品中没有无意抄袭，至少没有来自网络的无意抄袭。

54b 了解不需要标明出处的材料

1 ▪ 你自己的材料

用自己的话或格式表达的自己的观察、思想、事实汇编或实验结果不需要标明出处。你应该描述结论的根据，这样读者就可以评估你的思想，但是你不需要为它们引用原始资料。

2 ▪ 常识

常识由一个主题的标准信息、民间文学和常识性观察组成。

- **标准信息**包括重大历史事件（如罗马皇帝查理大帝的统治时期：公元768年至公元814年），但不包括对历史事件的评价（如历史学家认为查理大帝在扩大权力时有时候没必要那么残忍）。
- **民间文学**广为人知（如童话"白雪公主"），但是不能追溯到特定的作者。可追溯到作者的文学不是民间文学，即使它众所周知。
- **常识性观察**是大多数人都知道的事情，例如，低收入和固定收入的人非常讨厌通货膨胀。但是，某个经济学家关于通货膨胀对中国移民的影响的论证就不是常识性观察。

如果你对主题的了解不足以决定某个信息是常识的话，那么要为引用、改述或总结记录原始资料。随着你阅读了更多关于主题的文章，该信息在没有标明出处的情况下反复出现的话，该信息可能就是常识。但是如果你在研究结束时还存有疑虑，你就要标明出处。

54c 了解必须标明出处的材料

你必须对他人的独立材料（即任何既不是自己的又不属于常识的事实、观点或意见）标明出处。原始资料可以是正式的出版物或发行物，如书籍、文章、电影、采访、艺术作品、连环漫画、地图、网页或博客帖子。原始资料还可以是非正式的，如推特、Facebook上的帖子、你在广播中听到的观点，或者实际上形成你的论点的老师或同学的评论。你必须对观点或事实的总结或改述以及所引用的呈现观点或事实的语言和格式标明出处：用词、句子结构、行文组织和特殊的图表。无论你如何使用他人的材料、用了多少或使用的频率如何，你必须标明出处。

1 ▪ 使用被复制的语言：引号和引文出处

下面的例子直接抄袭了原文。没有引号或引文出处，该例子与原文用词（画线部分）相匹配，与原作者的句子结构高度一致。

原文："The character and mentality of the keepers may be of more importance in understanding prisons than the character and mentality of the kept."

抄袭：But the character of prison officials (the keepers) is of more importance in understanding prisons than the character of prisoners (the kept).

为避免抄袭，作者可以改述或引用原始资料（见p. 430中的例子）或者在标出引号和引文出处的情况下使用作者的原话（此处用的是MLA格式）：

修改稿（引用）：According to one critic of the penal system, "The character and mentality of the keepers may be of more importance in understanding prisons than the character and mentality of the kept" (Mitford 9).

即便有了引文出处，句子结构也不一样，下面的例子仍然是抄袭，因为它使用了作者的原话（画线部分）却没有用引号：

抄袭：According to one critic of the penal system, the psychology of the kept may say less about prisons than the psychology of the keepers (Mitford 9).

修改稿（引用）：According to one critic of the penal system, the psychology of "the kept" may say less about prisons than the psychology of "the keepers" (Mitford 9).

2 ▪ 使用改述或总结：你自己的词和句子结构及引文出处

下面的例子改变了原文的句子结构，但仍然使用了作者的词（画线部分），却没有引号和引文出处：

抄袭：In understanding prisons, we should know more about the character and mentality of the keepers than of the kept.

为避免抄袭，作者可以使用引号来引用原始资料（见p. 429）或使用他或她自己的词且仍然注明原始资料（因为观点是原文作者的）：

修改稿（改述）：Mitford holds that we may be able to learn more about prisons from the psychology of the prison officials than from that of the prisoners (9).

修改稿（改述）：We may understand prisons better if we focus on the personalities and attitudes of the prison workers rather than those of the inmates (9).

在接下来的例子中，作者没有用原文作者的词，但仍然抄袭了原文作者的句子结构。经过修改的改述改变了句子结构和词：

抄袭：One critic of the penal system maintains that the psychology of prison officials may be more informative about prisons than the psychology of prisoners (Mitford 9).

修改稿（改述）：One critic of the penal system maintains that we may be able to learn less from the psychology of prisoners than from the psychology of prison officials (Mitford 9).

3 ▪ 使用在线原始资料

在线原始资料可以那么轻松地获得，可以那么容易地被复制到你自己的文件中，以至于似乎它们是可以免费获得的，免除了你标明出处的义务。不是那样的。给在线原始资料标明出处要比给印刷版的原始资料标明出处棘手，但仍然是必要的：当你在印刷版文件或在线文件中使用来自在线原始资料的材料时，不论你是用什么方式找到的材料，你都必须给他人的独立材料标明出处。

当你在工作中记录了在线原始资料时，引用这些资料就容易多了：

- **每次查阅在线资料时，记录完整的出版信息**。在线原始资料每天都会发生变化，甚至会完全消失。见p. 377信息（比如出版日期）的记录。没有恰当的信息，你就不可以使用该原始资料。

- **任何复制并粘贴到文件中的文章前后都要立刻加上引号**。如果你不立刻加引号，你就有可能忘记哪些属于原始资料，哪些是你自己的。如果你不知道你用的是谁的，要重新核查原始资料，或者就干脆不用。

- **标明被链接的网站**。如果你不但使用了一个网站，而且还使用了一个或多个该网站链接的网站，你就必须标明被链接的网站。一个人使用了第二个人的作品不会减轻你引用第二个作品的责任。

练习54.1　辨别抄袭

以下编号的条目显示了引用或改写下面段落的各种尝试。仔细地将每一条目与原文进行比较。哪些尝试是抄袭的，不准确的，或两者兼而有之？哪些是可以接受的？为什么？

I would agree with the sociologists that psychiatric labeling is dangerous. Society can inflict terrible wounds by discrimination, and by confusing health with disease and disease with badness.

—George E. Vaillant, *Adaptation to Life*, p. 361

1. According to George Vaillant, society often inflicts wounds by using psychiatric labeling, confusing health, disease, and badness (361).

2. According to George Vaillant, "psychiatric labeling [such as 'homosexual' or 'schizophrenic'] is dangerous. Society can inflict terrible wounds by . . . confusing health with disease and disease with badness" (361).

3. According to George Vaillant, when psychiatric labeling discriminates between health and disease or between disease and badness, it can inflict wounds on those labeled (361).

4. Psychiatric labels can badly hurt those labeled, says George Vaillant, because they fail to distinguish among health, illness, and immorality (361).

5. Labels such as "homosexual" and "schizophrenic" can be hurtful when they fail to distinguish among health, illness, and immorality.

6. "I would agree with the sociologists that society can inflict terrible wounds by discrimination, and by confusing health with disease and disease with badness" (Vaillant 361).

54d　发表作品时获得许可

　　你在即将发表的作品中使用了印刷版或在线原始材料时，你不但必须标明原始资料，而且要遵守版权规定。

　　出版发行意味着你的作品将在班级或其他团体的小圈子外传播。它可能出现在报纸杂志等平面媒体上，也可能出现在同样是出版媒介的网络（受密码保护的网站除外，如课程网站。许多版权持有人认为这些网站是私人的）上。

　　不论你是在平面媒体上出版还是在线出版，借用某些材料或某些数量的材料都要求你获得版权持有人的许可。你可以在印刷版出版物的版权页（标题页之后）和网站上标为"Terms of Use"的页面上找到版权持有人和授权的信息。

如果你在私人网站上看不到供学生使用或出版的明确声明，你就必须寻求许可。

公平使用的法律约定使得作者可以使用一小部分受版权保护的材料而无须获得版权持有人的许可，只要作者标明原始材料。公平使用的标准因印刷版和在线原始资料而不同，不是固定的。以下是传统标准的使用准则：

- **源自印刷版原始材料的文章**：可以在未经许可的情况下从一篇文章引用五十字及以下或从一本书引用三百字及以下。从文章或书籍中引用更长文字或任何对剧本、诗歌或歌曲的引用都必须征得版权持有人的许可。
- **源自在线原始资料的文章**：可以在未经许可的情况下引用整篇文章的一小部分，例如，从三百字的文章中最多引用四十字。与印刷版文章一样，任何对在线剧本、诗歌或歌曲的引用都必须征得版权持有人的许可。
- **图像、音频和视频**：无论是印刷版原始资料还是在线原始资料，都要在获得许可后才能使用受版权保护的传播媒介：照片、图表、地图、漫画、绘画、音频、视频等。
- **链接**：将自己的网站与其他网站链接前要征得对方的许可，例如，你依靠被链接的网站为自己的主张提供内容翔实的证据，或者你将被链接网站上的多媒体元素（图像或声音或视频短片）合并到自己的网站上。

注意：虽然大多数在线原始资料都是受版权保护的，但是许多有价值的材料都没有版权保护：创作者没有提出版权要求，或者版权已经失效，这样作品的版权就是公有的。创作者没有提出版权要求的作品包括大多数的政府文件和标注为可重复使用的材料。（通过在电脑上设定搜索引擎，你就可以找到此类多媒体原始资料。见 p. 393）公有领域的原始资料包括已经去世至少五十年的作者的大多数作品。你无须获得转载许可就能使用未受版权保护的原始资料，但是你仍然必须援引原始资料。

54e 认真标注原始资料来源

每次借用他人的文字、事实或观点时，你都必须标注原始资料的来源，也就是提供一份告诉读者你借用了材料以及你从哪里借用材料的参考目录（或证明）。

大多数学术学科的编辑和老师对学术期刊和学生论文都要求特定的原始资料来源的标注格式。所有这些格式都有共同的特点：

- **文章中的引文标明材料是借用的**，并向读者指明原始资料的详细信息。
- **详细的原始资料信息**，通过脚注或尾注告诉读者如何查找原始资料。

引文和详细的信息使得读者可以找到每一个原始资料以及所借用的材料出现在

原始资料中的位置。

除了这些重要的相似之处外，各学科的原始资料来源标注格式在引文格式、原始资料信息的排列和其他个别项目上有很大的差异。每一个学科的格式反映从业者对用特定方式展现某种信息的需求。例如，在社会科学中，原始资料的时效性非常重要，其研究相互依赖相互纠正，因此社会科学的文章引用包括原始资料的出版日期。然而，在人文学科中，时效性不是那么重要，因此文章引用不包括出版日期。

各学科的原始资料来源的标注格式在格式准则中有所描述，包括下面加框文字中的格式。本书展示 *MLA Handbook for Writers of Research Papers* 和 *Publication Manual of the American Psychological Association* 中的格式。

标注原始资料来源的格式准则

人文学科

The Chicago Manual of Style. 16th ed. 2010.

A Manual for Writers of Research Papers, Theses, and Dissertations, by Kate L. Turabian, 8th ed., rev. Wayne C. Booth, Gregory G. Colomb, Joseph M. Williams, and the University of Chicago Press Editorial Staff. 2013.

MLA Handbook for Writers of Research Papers. 7th ed. 2009.（见pp. 439–483）

社会科学

American Anthropological Association. *AAA Style Guide*. 2009. www.aaanet.org/publications/style_guide.pdf

American Political Science Association. *Style Manual for Political Science*. 2006. www.apsanet.org/media/PDFs/Publications/APSAStyleManual2006.pdf

Publication Manual of the American Psychological Association. 6th ed. 2009（见pp. 497–519）

American Sociological Association. *ASA Style Guide*. 4th ed. 2010.

Linguistic Society of America. "LSA Style Sheet." Published every December in *LSA Bulletin*.

A Uniform System of Citation (law). 19th ed. 2010.

科学和数学

American Chemical Society. *ACS Style Guide: A Manual for Authors and Editors*. 3rd ed. 2006.

American Institute of Physics. *Style Manual for Guidance in the Preparation of Papers*. 4th ed. 1997. www.aip.org/pubservs/style/4thed/ALP_Style_4thed.pdf

American Medical Association Manual of Style. 10th ed. 2007.

Council of Science Editors. *Scientific Style and Format: The CSE Manual for Authors, Editors, and Publishers*. 7th ed. 2006.

向老师询问你应该使用哪种原始资料来源的标注格式。如果老师没有要求特定的格式，请使用本书中提到的适合你所撰写论文所属学科的格式。确保一篇文章使用一种原始资料的引用格式，这样你就用前后一致的格式提供所有必需的信息。

注意： 参考目录软件有助于在选定的格式中规定原始资料引用的格式。如果你在写论文时需要使用类似的软件，要咨询你的老师。软件提示你所需的信息（作者姓名、书名等），还有排列、用大写字母书写、用斜体字排版、加标点符号于格式所需的信息。但是，没有一个软件能预料原始资料信息的所有变化或完全取代你。你还需要关心并关注用所需的格式准确而完整地标明原始资料。

第 55 章　撰写论文

概要

- 用主题句聚焦材料（下方）
- 组织材料（p. 436）
- 草拟论文，包括原始资料引用（p. 436）
- 修改并编辑草稿（p. 437）
- 采用恰当的文本格式（p. 438）

和其他类型的写作一样，研究性写作包括聚焦中心思想、组织观点、在草稿中表达观点、修改并编辑草稿以及规定终稿的格式。因为研究性写作依赖于他人的作品，因此写作的各个阶段要求关注原始资料的解释、融合与引用。

本章补充并拓展了第1章至第6章中详细讨论过的写作环境和写作过程。如果你还没读它们，那么在阅读本章前，请阅读这些章节。

55a 整理并组织论文

在草稿中开始使用原始资料笔记前，你要思考论文的中心思想和组织。

1 ▪ 主题句

你的研究开始于一个与主题有关的问题。（见 pp. 372–373）尽管在研究的过程中，那个问题可能会有所变化，但是当你一旦查阅了大多数原始资料后，你应该能够回答那个问题。试着用主题句（将主题压缩成单个观点的主张）来回答那个问题。例如，下面是Justin Malik的研究问题和主题句。他的论文终稿出现在pp. 488–496：

研究问题
How can green consumerism help the environment?

主题句
Although green consumerism can help the environment, consumerism itself is the root of some of the most pressing ecological problems we face. To make a real difference, we must consume less.

（Malik的主题句由两个句子组成，第一个句子是第二个句子的基础。许多老师允许用两个或多个句子来陈述主题，只要它们构成一个观点，并且最后一个句子展示论文的关键主张。但是，有些老师要求用一个句子陈述主题。请向老师询问他或她的偏好）

在你组织并起草论文时，精准的主题句将有助于你集中思维。更多关于主题句的讨论，见pp. 16–19。

2 ▪ 组织论文

为了组织论文，你需要综合或锻造观点之间的关系。（见pp. 409–410）下面是其中一个方法：

- **根据类别排列原始信息。** 每一类信息对应论文的一个主要部分：支撑主题的你自己的重要观点。在每个类别中，你可能有与你自己不同的源视图，并且你打算讨论或反驳。
- **审核研究日记**，寻找原始资料和其他帮助你组织论文的想法之间的关系。
- **客观看待分类信息。** 如果有些类别的信息内容不够，考虑是否放弃这类信息或者进行更多的研究以补全之。如果大多数信息属于一到两个类别，考虑它们是否太宽泛，是否应该再细分。（如果这些再思考影响了主题句，要相应地加以修改）
- **在每一类信息中，辨别中心思想、支撑观点和证据。** 只有支撑观点可以来自原始资料。中心思想应该是你自己的。

更多关于组织论文的讨论，包括正式和非正式提纲的范例，见pp. 20–24。

55b 草稿、修改、校订和论文格式

1 ▪ 第一稿

草拟论文时,你没有必要循规蹈矩地按照从简介到结论这个顺序写。相反,你可以一个章节一个章节地写,从你最有信心的那个章节开始写。每一个章节应该围绕着一个有助于主题的主要观点,即你在阅读和思考原始资料时得出的结论。每一章节以陈述该主要观点为开篇,然后用笔记上的信息、总结、改述和引文加以支撑。记得要插入笔记上的原始资料信息。

- **用转接句和其他标识将各个章节融为一体**。随着论文各个章节的发展,你会发现它们之间浮现出的关系。将这些关系表述出来,并用转接句加以强调。(见pp. 43–44和pp. 50–51)标题恰当地突出了文章的组织和信号方向。这些标识有助于创建一篇条理清晰的完整文章。
- **追踪原始资料的引用**。草拟论文时,在括号内插入每一个总结、改述和引用的原始资料信息。例如(Frankel 42)指的是Frankel作品的p. 42。如果你认真地插入这些笔记,并且在后续的几稿中继续这么做的话,你就不大可能无意抄袭,在终稿中也就不会有标注原始资料来源的困难。

2 ▪ 修改论文

要先修改草稿,对文章内容和整体轮廓满意后再尝试校订句子或提炼文字。根据pp. 29–34上的建议开始修改论文,并对照下面的清单补充论文。

研究论文的修改清单

任务
草稿如何满足老师布置的任务要求?

主题句
主题句是否很好地描述了主题和观点?

结构
(为草稿列提纲可以帮助你一眼就明白论文结构。见p. 30)
所借用的材料是否始终如一地阐明和支撑(而不是引导并主导)你的观点?是否很好地体现了观点的重要性?观点的排列是否清晰?

证据
支撑论据在哪些地方比较薄弱或与读者无关?

（续表）

合理性和清晰性
读者会发现观点有多少合理性？（见pp. 114–123）你需要在哪些地方解释读者可能不明白或有争议的术语或概念？

3 ▪ 校订论文

关于校订论文，请查阅pp. 36–38的建议和清单。从一个第一次接触此论文的人的角度而不是从一个花费多个小时进行规划和研究的人的角度去阅读你的作品。查找是否有观念错误、篇章累赘、用词冗长、观点和证据间的不良转接、不必要的重复、单词用错或拼错，以及语法、标点符号或结构上的错误。总之，要检查任何可能干扰读者理解论文意思的地方。

4 ▪ 论文格式

论文的终稿应该遵照老师或所属学科论文格式准则所建议的论文格式。（见pp. 433–434）本书详细介绍了两个常见的格式：MLA（现代语言协会）格式（pp. 484–486）和APA（美国心理学协会）格式（pp. 516–519）。

在任何学科中，你可以用易读的字体、标题、插图和其他元素有效且迷人地展示你的观点。见pp. 66–75观点。

第56章 MLA原始资料来源的标注与格式

概要

- 在文内引文注释中标注原始资料（下页）
- 恰当放置引文，从而使得引文清晰但不突兀（p. 445）
- 必要时使用补充注释（p. 447）
- 准备MLA参考目录（p. 448）（见pp. 450–451格式索引）
- 遵循MLA关于页边距、行距、长引文和其他元素的准则（p. 484）
- 查阅MLA论文范例（p. 486）

英语、其他语言或一些其他人文学科使用MLA原始资料来源的标注格式。（2009年第七版的*MLA Handbook for Writers of Research Papers*一书中有所描述）

在MLA格式中，你需要两次标明所借用材料的原始资料：

- **文章中，所借用资料后括号内的简单引用引导读者查看所有被引用作品的完整目录。**文内引文注释包括作者的姓（如果文章中还没有提及的话）和所借用的材料在原始资料中的页码。

  文内引文注释

  Among African cities, says one observer, in Johannesburg "a spirit of optimism glows" (Gaddis 155).

- **在论文的最后，参考文献的目录包括每一个原始资料的完整参考目录信息。**

  参考文献的条目

  Gaddis, Anicee. "Johannesburg." *Transculturalism: How the World Is Coming Together*. Ed. Claude Grunitzky. New York: True, 2008. 154–57.

56a 在文章中使用 MLA 文内引文注释

1 ▪ 引用格式

文章中的引用原始资料必须包含足够的信息，从而使得读者可以找到以下内容：

- 参考目录中的原始资料。
- 所借用材料在原始资料中的位置。

对于任何一种原始资料，你通常可以通过提供作者的姓氏和材料所在页码（如果原始资料使用页码的话）来满足这两个要求。读者可以在参考目录中找到原始资料，并在原始资料中找到所借用的材料。

以下的格式阐释了基本的文内引文注释形式和适用于不常见原始资料（如没有作者或没有页码的资料）的引用形式。参见下页加框文字中所有格式的索引。

注意：格式1和格式2展示了在文章中直接引用和用括号表示引用之间的直接关系。如果你没有在文章中提到作者的名字，你就得在参考页码之前在括号中标注作者的姓氏（格式1）。如果你在文章中提到了作者的名字，括号中就不用包括作者的姓氏（格式2）。

> ## MLA文内引文注释
>
> 1. 你的文章中没有提到作者姓名（p. 440）
> 2. 你的文章中提到了作者姓名（p. 441）
> 3. 两个或三个作者合作的作品（p. 441）
> 4. 三个以上作者合作的作品（p. 441）
> 5. 两部或两部以上作品被引用的作者的作品（p. 441）
> 6. 匿名作品（p. 442）
> 7. 团体作者的作品（p. 442）
> 8. 非印刷版的原始资料（p. 442）
> 9. 多卷册的作品（p. 443）
> 10. 整部作品，或没有页码的作品，或没有其他参考号码的作品（p. 443）
> 11. 按段落或部分编号而不是按页码编号的作品（p. 444）
> 12. 另一个原始资料提到过的原始资料（间接的原始资料）（p. 444）
> 13. 文学作品（p. 444）
> 14. 《圣经》（p. 445）
> 15. 一次引用两部或两部以上作品（p. 445）

1. 你的文章中没有提到作者姓名

当你没有在句子中提到作者姓名时，要在括号中提供作者的姓氏和页码，两者之间没有标点符号。

> One researcher concludes that "women impose a distinctive construction on moral problems, seeing moral dilemmas in terms of conflicting responsibilities" (Gilligan 105-06).

参见格式6中原始资料没有列出作者时的使用格式，以及格式10和格式11中原始资料没有提供页码时的使用格式。

2. 你的文章中提到了作者姓名

当你已经在所引用的原始资料中提到了作者的姓名，就不要在加括号的引用中重复提及。括号中只要提供页码即可。

> Carol Gilligan concludes that "women impose a distinctive construction on moral problems, seeing moral dilemmas in terms of conflicting responsibilities" (105-06).

参见格式6中原始资料没有列出作者时的使用格式，以及格式10和格式11中原始资料没有提供页码时的使用格式。

3. 两个或三个作者合作的作品

如果原始资料有两个或三个作者，需要在文章中或在引用中列举所有人的姓氏。用and分隔两个作者的姓氏。

> As Frieden and Sagalyn observe, "The poor and the minorities were the leading

victims of highway and renewal programs" (29).

According to one study, "The poor and the minorities were the leading victims of highway and renewal programs" (Frieden and Sagalyn 29).

至于有三个作者的情况，作者之间用逗号分隔，在最后一个作者前加and。

The textbook by Wilcox, Ault, and Agee discusses the "ethical dilemmas in public relations practice" (125).

One textbook discusses the "ethical dilemmas in public relations practice" (Wilcox, Ault, and Agee 125).

4. 三个以上作者合作的作品

如果原始资料有三个以上的作者，你可以列举他们的全部姓氏或者在第一个作者的姓氏后面加et al.（拉丁语"以及其他人"的缩写）。具体选择取决于你在参考目录中的做法。（见p. 449和p. 452）

Increased competition means that employees of public relations firms may find their loyalty stretched in more than one direction (Wilcox et al. 417).

Increased competition means that employees of public relations firms may find their loyalty stretched in more than one direction (Wilcox, Cameron, Reber, and Shin 417).

5. 两部或两部以上作品被引用的作者的作品

如果你的参考目录中包括同一个作者的两部或两部以上作品，那么你的引用必须告诉读者你参考的是该作者的哪一部作品。在文章或者引文注释中给出书名。只要书名很简短，就可以在引文注释中给出完整的书名。否则，要将书名缩短到第一个、第二个或第三个主要单词（不包括A, An, 或The）。

At about age seven, children begin to use appropriate gestures with their stories (Gardner, *Arts* 144-45).

Gardner的作品全名是*The Arts and Human Development*。（见p. 452被引用作品条目）因为原始资料是一本书，所以上面例子中缩短了的书名用斜体字表示。

6. 匿名作品

如上所示，对于没有指定作者或编者（不论是个人还是组织）的作品，要使用作品标题的全称或者缩短了的标题。在参考目录中，按照标题中的首个主要单词的字母顺序来排列匿名作品（见p. 452），这样，缩短了的标题的首个单词应该是一样的。下面的引用指的是一个题为"The Right to Die"的未署名原始资料。因为原始资料是期刊文章,所以标题前后加了引号。

One article notes that a death-row inmate may demand execution to achieve a fleeting notoriety ("Right" 16).

"The Right to Die" notes that a death-row inmate may demand execution to achieve a fleeting notoriety (16).

如果两部或两部以上匿名作品的标题相同,可以在文内引文注释中用额外信息(如出版日期)来区分它们。

7. 团体作者的作品

一些作品的作者是政府机构、协会、委员会、公司或其他团体。要根据组织机构的名称来引用这类作品。如果名称很长,可以将名称融入文章中,以避免出现具有干扰性的引文注释。

A 2012 report by the Nevada Department of Education provides evidence of an increase in graduation rates (12).

8. 非印刷版的原始资料

有指定作者的作品:

你要像引用其他原始资料那样引用诸如电子书、网页、Facebook帖子或推特等非印刷版的原始资料。当参考文献的条目按照作者或其他投稿者姓名列出原始资料时,要在文本引用中使用那个姓名。下面的例子引用了电子阅读器上的一本电子书。

Writing about post-Saddam Iraq, the journalist George Packer describes the tense relationship between Kurdistan and the rest of the country (ch. 1).

注意: 前面的条目列出了章节号码,而不是电子阅读器的页码,因为不同的电子设备所显示的页码会有所不同。但是,对于有固定页码的PDF文档这类非印刷版的原始资料,要引用页码。

没有标注作者的作品:

当参考文献的条目按照标题列出作品时,要像格式6中解释的那样,在文章中引用作品的标题。下一个例子引用了完整的作品(一部DVD上的电影),并在文章中给出了标题,因此它省略了引文注释(参见格式10)。

Many decades after its release, *Citizen Kane* is still remarkable for its rich black-and-white photography.

9. 多卷册的作品

如果你只查阅了多卷册作品中的一卷，参考目录要对此加以说明。（见p. 462 格式30）你可以用对待任何一本书的方式对待它。

如果你查阅了多卷册作品中的两卷或两卷以上作品，那么在页码前列出相应的卷册（下面例子中的第5卷）。

> After issuing the Emancipation Proclamation, Lincoln said, "What I did, I did ... under a very heavy and solemn sense of responsibility" (5: 438).

数字5表示引文出自第5卷，数字438表示第5卷中的页码。当此类引文中出现作者姓名时，要将它放在卷号前，中间没有标点符号：(Lincoln 5: 438)。

如果你指的是多卷册作品中完整的一卷，没有引用具体的页码，要在卷号前加缩略词vol.，例如(vol. 4)或(Lincoln, vol. 5)。（注意姓名后的逗号）这样，读者就不会将卷号误认为页码。

10. 整部作品，或没有页码的作品，或没有其他参考号码的作品

如果你完整引用一部作品（如推特或一篇完整的文章），你可以省略页码或其他参考号码。如果引用的作品有一个作者，那么在文章中列出作者的姓名。你不再需要引文注释，但是该原始资料仍然必须出现在参考目录中。

> Boyd deals with the need to acknowledge and come to terms with our fear of nuclear technology.

当你从没有页码或其他参考号码的作品（如网络原始资料）引用特定篇章时，要使用相同的格式。

如下面的例子所示，如果文章中没有出现作者姓名，那么要把作者姓名放在引文注释中。

> Almost 20% of commercial banks have been audited for the practice (Friis).

11. 按段落或部分编号而不是按页码编号的作品

有些电子版原始资料按照段落或部分编号而不是给每一页编号。引用这些原始资料上的篇章时，要列出段落或部分的号码，将它们与页码区分开：在作者姓名之后加逗号、一个半角空格和par.（一个段落）或pars.（多个段落）或sec.或secs.。

> Twins reared apart report similar feelings (Palfrey, pars. 6-7).

12. 另一个原始资料提到过的原始资料（间接的原始资料）

当你想使用已经标有引号的引文（表示你阅读的这篇文章的作者引用了其

他人的作品）时，要尝试找到原始资料，并直接从原始资料引用。如果你找不到原始资料，那么必须标明你的引用是间接的。在下面的引文中，qtd. in说的是Boyd引用了Davino的作品。

> George Davino maintains that "even small children have vivid ideas about nuclear energy" (qtd. in Boyd 22).

然后，参考目录只列出Boyd（所查询的作品），不列出Davino。

13. 文学作品

小说、剧本和诗歌通常有许多版本，因此老师会要求你提供相关的篇章信息。不论读者查的是哪个版本，这些信息都有助于他们找到你所引用的篇章。

- **小说**：首先是页码，接着是分号，然后是作品相关部分或章节的信息。
  > Toward the end of James's novel, Maggie suddenly feels "the thick breath of the definite—which was the intimate, the immediate, the familiar, as she hadn't had them for so long" (535; pt. 6, ch. 41).

- **没有分部分的诗歌**：你可以省略页码，在引文中标注所在行的号码。为避免与页码混淆，第一次引用时在号码前加line或lines；之后就只标号码。
  > In Shakespeare's Sonnet 73 the speaker identifies with the trees of late autumn, "Bare ruined choirs, where late the sweet birds sang" (line 4). "In me," Shakespeare writes, "thou seest the glowing of such fire / That on the ashes of his youth doth lie . . ." (9-10).

  （见pp. 133–135关于诗歌的论文范例）

- **诗剧和分部分的诗歌**：省略页码，列出相关部分（幕和场［如果有的话］、篇、卷等）和所在行的号码。用阿拉伯数字标注相关部分（包括幕和场），除非你的老师特别指出要用罗马数字。
  > Later in Shakespeare's *King Lear* the disguised Edgar says, "The prince of darkness is a gentleman" (3.4.147).

- **散文体剧本**：页码后加幕和场，如果有的话。参见p.447的 *Death of a Salesman*。

14.《圣经》

你在括号中引用《圣经》段落时，超过四个字母的任何标题都要用缩略词，例如，Gen.（Genesis），1 Sam.（1 Samuel），Ps.（Psalms），Prov.（Proverbs），Matt.（Matthew），Rom.（Romans），然后用阿拉伯数字标明章节和诗篇。

> According to the Bible, at Babel God "did . . . confound the language of all the

earth" (Gen. 11.9).

15. 一次引用两部或两部以上作品

当你在一个引文注释中提及不止一部作品时，要用分号隔开参考文献。

Two recent articles point out that a computer badly used can be less efficient than no computer at all (Gough and Hall 201; Richards 162).

因为文章中的长引文会干扰读者，你可以选择在尾注或脚注中而不是在文章中引用多部作品。参见pp. 447–448。

2 ▪ 引文注释的位置和标点符号

下面的准则将帮助你确定文内引文注释的位置并标注标点符号，以便区分你自己的观点和原始资料的观点，同时让文章变得容易阅读。参见pp. 419–422 编辑引文和使用信号短语将原始资料融入你的句子中。

引文的位置

放置文内引文注释的两个目标：

- 明确引文的始末位置。
- 尽可能不让引文显得很唐突。

将引文注释放在包含所借用材料的句子成分之后，你就可实现上述两个目标。这个句子成分可以是词组或从句，可以出现在句子之前、之中或之后。如下面的例子所示，句子成分通常后接标点符号。

> The inflation rate might climb as high as 30% (Kim 164), an increase that could threaten the small nation's stability.
>
> The inflation rate, which might climb as high as 30% (Kim 164), could threaten the small nation's stability.
>
> The small nation's stability could be threatened by its inflation rate, which, one source predicts, might climb as high as 30% (Kim 164).

在最后一个例子中，所添加的one source predicts阐明Kim只需为通货膨胀率的预言负责，无须为稳定性的立场负责。

当你对原始资料的改述或总结的长度超过一个句子时，需要在第一个句子中列出作者的姓名并在最后一个句子的末尾放置引文注释，以此明确引文的范围。

> Juliette Kim studied the effects of acutely high inflation in several South American and African countries since World War II. She discovered that a major change in government accompanied or followed the inflationary period in 56%

of cases (22-23).

当你在同一段落中引用两个或两个以上原始资料时，要列出作者的姓名和引文注释，这样读者就能明白谁说了什么。在接下来的例子中，句子的开始和结尾明确标注不同的原始资料。

> Schools use computers extensively for drill-and-practice exercises, in which students repeat specific skills such as spelling words, using the multiplication facts, or, at a higher level, doing chemistry problems. But many education experts criticize such exercises for boring students and failing to engage their critical thinking and creativity. Jane M. Healy, a noted educational psychologist and teacher, takes issue with "interactive" software for children as well as drill-and-practice software, arguing that "some very popular 'educational' software . . . may be damaging to independent thinking, attention, and motivation" (20). Another education expert, Harold Wenglinsky of the Educational Testing Service, found in a well-regarded study that fourth and eighth graders who used computers frequently, including for drill and practice, actually did worse on tests than their peers who used computers less often (*Does It Compute?* 21). In a later article, Wenglinsky concludes that "the quantity of use matters far less than the quality of use." In schools, he says, high-quality computer work, involving critical thinking, is still rare ("In Search" 17).

如何给引文注释添加标点符号

通常在句子规定的标点符号前放置引文注释。如果所借用的材料是直接引用的文字，要将引文注释放在右引号和该句子规定的标点符号之间。

> Spelling argues that during the 1970s American automobile manufacturers met consumer needs "as well as could be expected" (26), but not everyone agrees with him.

以问号或感叹号结尾的引文除外。如果引文以问号或感叹号结尾，要在右引号前使用恰当的标点符号。引文后标注引用注释和句号。

> "Of what use is genius," Emerson asks, "if the organ . . . cannot find a focal distance within the actual horizon of human life?" ("Experience" 60). Mad genius is no genius.

当引文注释出现在单独成段的直接引用之后，要将引文注释放在引文结尾的标点符号之后空一格的地方。不要对引文注释使用额外的标点符号，或者在引文前后使用引号。

In Arthur Miller's *Death of a Salesman*, the most poignant defense of willie Loman comes from his wife, linda:

> He's not the finest character that ever lived. But he's a human being, and a terrible thing is happening to him. So attention must be paid. He's not to be allowed to fall into his grave like an old dog. Attention, attention must finally be paid to such a person. (56; act 1)

（这个剧本的引文注释包括幕次和页码。见 p. 445）

关于更多放置与总结、改述或引用相关的引文注释的例子，请见 p. 488 开始的研究性论文范例。

3 ▪ 在特殊场合下使用脚注或尾注

你偶尔会想用脚注或尾注代替引文注释。如果你想立刻参考多个原始资料，用一个很长的引文注释列出所有这些原始资料会很碍事。要在需要注释的文字右上角标注数字以表示引文注释，然后以相同的数字为起始撰写注释：

文章：At least five studies have confirmed these results.[1]

注释：　1. Abbott and Winger 266-68; Casner 27; Hoyenga 78-79; Marino 36; Tripp, Tripp, and Walk 179-83.

你也可以用脚注或尾注对原始资料进行评论或提供一些与文章不相融的信息：

文章：So far, no one has confirmed these results.[2]

注释：　2. Manter tried repeatedly to replicate the experiment, but he was never able to produce the high temperatures (616).

注释要缩排 0.5 英寸（1.27 厘米），在正文行输入数字，然后输入句号并空一格。如果注释以脚注形式出现，要将它放在出现引文的那一页的底部，用 4 倍行距与文章隔开，注释用双倍行距。如果注释以尾注的形式出现，要按照数字顺序将它与其他尾注一起放在文章和参考目录之间的那一页。所有尾注都要用双倍行距。

56b 准备 MLA 格式的参考目录

在论文的最后，题为"Works Cited"的清单包含所有你在论文中引用、改述或总结的原始资料。（如果老师要求你包括你查阅过却没有引用的原始资料，那么将该清单命名为"Works Consulted"）

请遵照这个参考目录的格式：

- **按照作者姓氏的字母顺序排列原始资料。**如果原始资料没有提供作者，按照文章标题中第一个主要单词的字母顺序来排列原始资料（不包括A，An，或The）。
- **用双倍行距输入参考目录。**
- **从每一条目的第二行起，文字向右缩排0.5英寸（1.27厘米）。**文字处理软件可以自动规定这种所谓的悬挂式缩进的格式。

» MLA参考文献页

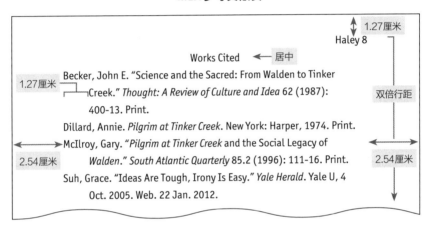

关于完整的参考目录，请参见pp. 495–496的Justin Malik的论文。

所有格式的索引出现在接下来的几页中。使用你的最佳判断力使格式适应特定的原始资料。如果你找不到与所使用原始资料完全匹配的格式，要查找并遵循匹配度最高的格式。你当然需要结合不同的格式。例如，对于有三个编者的书籍，你需要依靠格式2（两个或三个作者）和格式21（有编者的书籍）。

注意：MLA格式要求每一个原始资料都标注出版媒介，如平面媒体、网络、DVD或电视。如果你在平面杂志查询过文章，就要将出版媒介标为Print。如果你查询了网络上的文章，就要将出版媒介标为Web。下面的格式都遵循这个标准。

1 ▪ 作者

以下的格式显示了在引用任何一种原始资料时处理作者姓名的方法。

1. 一个作者

Ehrenreich, Barbara. *Dancing in the Streets: A History of Collective Joy*. New York: Metropolitan-Holt, 2006. Print.

列出作者的全名：先是姓氏，然后是逗号、名和中间名或首字母。省略头衔，如Dr.或PhD.。姓名以句号收尾。如果原始资料将编者列为作者，请参见p. 459格式21。

2. 两个或三个作者

Lifton, Robert Jay, and Greg Mitchell. *Who Owns Death: Capital Punishment, the American Conscience, and the End of Executions*. New York: Morrow, 2000. Print.

Simpson, Dick, James Nowlan, and Elizabeth O'Shaughnessy. *The Struggle for Power and Influence in Cities and States*. New York: Longman, 2011. Print.

根据书名页上的顺序列出作者姓名。只是颠倒第一个作者的姓名顺序（姓前名后）。用逗号和and隔开两个作者的姓名；用逗号隔开三个作者的姓名，并在第三个作者姓名前加and。如果原始资料将两个或三个编者列为作者，请见p. 459格式21。

3. 三个以上作者

Wilcox, Dennis L., Glen T. Cameron, Bryan H. Reber, and Jae-Hwa Shin. *Think Public Relations*. Boston: Allyn, 2010. Print.

Wilcox, Dennis L., et al. *Think Public Relations*. Boston: Allyn, 2010. Print.

MLA格式参考目录

1 ■ 作者
1. 一个作者 p. 449
2. 两个或三个作者 p. 449
3. 三个以上作者 p. 449
4. 两部或两部以上作品的作者为同一人 p. 452
5. 团体作者 p. 452
6. 作者姓名未经标注（匿名）p. 452

2 ■ 定期出版的印刷版原始资料
学术期刊上的文章
7. 有卷号和期号的期刊文章（印刷版）p. 453, p. 454
8. 只有期号的期刊文章（印刷版）p. 453
9. 期刊文章或论文的摘要（印刷版）p. 453

报纸上的文章
10. 全国性报纸上的文章（印刷版）p. 455
11. 本地报纸上的文章（印刷版）p. 455

杂志上的文章
12. 周刊或双周刊上的文章（印刷版）p. 456
13. 月刊或双月刊上的文章（印刷版）p. 456

评论、社论、读者来信、采访
14. 评论（印刷版）p. 456
15. 社论或读者来信（印刷版）p. 456
16. 采访（印刷版）p. 457

（续表）

连载文章或特刊文章
- 17. 连载文章（印刷版）p. 457
- 18. 特刊文章（印刷版）p. 457

3 ▪ 非周期性的印刷版原始资料

书籍
- 19. 书籍（印刷版）的基本格式 p. 457, p. 458
- 20. 第二版或后续版本（印刷版）p. 459
- 21. 有编者的书籍（印刷版）p. 459
- 22. 既有作者又有编者的书籍（印刷版）p. 459
- 23. 有译者的书籍（印刷版）p. 459
- 24. 文集（印刷版）p. 460
- 25. 文集中的选文（印刷版）p. 460
- 26. 同一部文集中的两篇或两篇以上选文（印刷版）p. 460
- 27. 在作品集中再版的学术文章（印刷版）p. 461
- 28. 参考书中的文章（印刷版）p. 461
- 29. 绘本或带插图的故事书（印刷版）p. 461
- 30. 多卷册的作品（印刷版）p. 462
- 31. 系列书籍（印刷版）p. 462
- 32. 再版的书籍（印刷版）p. 462
- 33. 《圣经》（印刷版）p. 462
- 34. 书名中套书名的书籍（印刷版）p. 463
- 35. 已出版的会议记录（印刷版）p. 463
- 36. 前言、卷首语、序或跋（印刷版）p. 463
- 37. 缺少出版信息或页码的书籍（印刷版）p. 463

其他非周期性的印刷版原始资料
- 38. 政府出版物（印刷版）p. 464
- 39. 手册或宣传册（印刷版）p. 464
- 40. 论文（印刷版）p. 464
- 41. 信件（印刷版）p. 465

4 ▪ 非周期性的网络原始资料

只能通过网络获得的非周期性原始资料
- 42. 有标题的短作品（网络版）p. 466, p. 467
- 43. 没有标题的短作品（网络版）p. 468
- 44. 书籍（网络版）p. 468
- 45. 完整的网站（网络版）p. 468
- 46. 报纸上的文章（网络版）p. 469
- 47. 杂志上的文章（网络版）p. 469
- 48. 政府出版物（网络版）p. 469
- 49. 参考书中的文章（网络版）p. 470
- 50. 图像（网络版）p. 470
- 51. 电视或广播节目（网络版）p. 470
- 52. 录像（网络版）p. 471
- 53. 录音（网络版）p. 471
- 54. 播客（网络版）p. 471
- 55. 博客文章（网络版）p. 472
- 56. 维基网站（网络版）p. 472

有印刷版的非周期性网络原始资料
- 57. 有印刷版出版信息的短作品（网络版）p. 472
- 58. 有印刷版出版信息的书籍（网络版）p. 472

还可以在其他媒介上获得的非周期性网络原始资料
- 59. 有其他出版信息的录音（网络版）p. 473
- 60. 有其他出版信息的电影或录像（网络版）p. 473
- 61. 有其他出版信息的图像（网络版）p. 473

URL的引用
- 62. 需要引用URL的原始资料（网络版）p. 473

5 ▪ 在线数据库里的期刊和书籍
- 63. 学术期刊上的文章（在线数据库）p. 474, p. 475

（续表）

64. 期刊文章的摘要（在线数据库）p. 476	75. 社交网站上的帖子p. 479
65. 报纸上的文章（在线数据库）p. 476	76. 推特p. 479
66. 杂志上的文章（在线数据库）p. 476	**在CD-ROM和DVD-ROM上的出版物**
67. 书籍（在线数据库）476	77. 非周期性的CD-ROM或DVD-ROM p. 479
	78. 周期性的CD-ROM或DVD-ROM p. 480
6 ▪ 直接查询的网络期刊	**8 ▪ 其他印刷版和非印刷版原始资料**
68. 学术期刊上的文章（网络版）p. 477, p. 478	79. 电视或广播节目p. 480
	80. 个人或广播、电视采访p. 481
69. 期刊文章的摘要（网络版）p. 477	81. 录音p. 481
7 ▪ 其他电子版原始资料	82. 电影、DVD或录像p. 481
数字文档	83. 绘画、照片或其他视觉艺术作品 p. 482
70. 电子阅读器上的书籍（数字版）p. 477	84. 私人照片p. 482
71. 文本文件（数字版）p. 477	85. 地图、表格、图表或示意图p. 482
72. 媒体文件（数字版）p. 479	86. 漫画或连载漫画p. 482
社交媒体	87. 广告p. 483
73. 电子邮件信息p. 479	88. 演出p. 483
74. 讨论小组上的帖子p. 479	89. 讲座、演讲、致辞或读物p. 483

452　如果作品有三个以上作者，你可以列出所有作者的姓名，但你没有必要这么做。如果你没有给出所有姓名，你只要提供第一个作者的姓名即可，之后加逗号和缩略词et al.。如果原始资料将三个以上编者列为作者，参见p. 459格式21。

4. 两部或两部以上作品的作者为同一人

Gardner, Howard. *The Arts and Human Development*. New York: Wiley, 1973. Print.

---. *Five Minds for the Future*. Boston: Harvard Business School P, 2007. Print.

只在第一个条目上列出作者的姓名。至于同一作者的第二部和其他作品，用三个连字符代替作者姓名，后接句号。注意三个连字符只能代替完全相同的姓名。如果第二部作品是作者和其他人合作的，那么两个人的姓名都要列出。

使用三个连字符的条目要紧跟在标注作者姓名的条目之后。如上所示，在同一作者的一组条目中，要按照标题中第一个主要单词的字母排列原始资料。

如果你引用了将同一编者列为作者的两个或两个以上原始资料，要在连字符后加逗号和ed.或eds.，视情况而定。（参见p. 459格式21）

5. 团体作者
Vault Technologies. *Turnkey Parking Solutions*. Salt Lake City: Mills, 2011. Print.

团体作者包括协会、委员会、机构、政府部门、公司和其他团体。当原始资料只提供团体名称而非个人姓名时，可将团体名称列为作者。

6. 作者姓名未经标注（匿名）
The Dorling Kindersley World Atlas. London: Dorling, 2010. Print.

对于没有标注作者姓名（无论是个人还是团体）的作品，要列出作品的完整标题。如果作品是一本书，将书名排成斜体。如果作品是期刊文章或其他短作品，要在标题上加引号。

"A Guardian and a Guide." *Economist* 4 Apr. 2012: 80. Print.

按照文章标题中第一个主要单词的字母顺序来排列作品（不包括A, An，或The）。

2 ▪ 定期出版的印刷版原始资料

定期出版的印刷版原始资料包括定期（按季度、月、周或天）出版的学术期刊、报纸和杂志。以下清单改编自 *MLA Handbook for Writers of Research Papers*。按照它们在所引用作品条目中的出现顺序，清单详细列举了定期出版的印刷版原始资料中的可能要素。

- **作者**。列出作者的姓氏、名和中间名或首字母。如要引用一个以上作者的文章、同一作者的两篇文章、团体作者的文章或匿名文章，请参见格式2—6。
- **文章标题**，用引号标出。列出标题和副标题。标题用句号收尾，句号放在右引号之前。
- **定期出版的印刷版资料名称**，排成斜体。省略名称开头的A, An或The。不要用句号收尾。
- **出版信息**。对卷号、期号和出版日期的处理方法取决于你所引用的定期出版的印刷版资料的种类，参见格式7—18。（至于期刊和杂志的区别，见p. 384）如果你包括了出版月份，要用月份的缩略词，除非是May, June或July。
- **文章所在的页码**，没有pp.。
- **出版媒介**：在Print后加句号。

学术期刊上的文章
7. 有卷号和期号的期刊文章（印刷版）
Bee, Robert. "The Importance of Preserving Paper-Based Artifacts in a Digital

Age." *Library Quarterly* 78.2 (2008): 174-94. Print.

参见p. 454中印刷版期刊文章的基本格式和所需信息在期刊中的位置。

8. 只有期号的期刊文章（印刷版）

Rae, Ian. "The Case for Digital Poetics." *Canadian Literature* 204 (2010): 134-37, Print.

如果学术期刊只有期号，没有卷号，要在期刊名称后加期号。

9. 期刊文章或论文的摘要（印刷版）

Lever, Janet. "Sex Differences in the Games Children Play." *Social Problems* 23.2 (1996): 478-87. *Psychological Abstracts* 63.5 (1996): item 1431. Print.

印刷版期刊文章的格式

（续表）

① ②
Bee, Robert. "The Importance of Preserving Paper-Based Artifacts in a Digital Age."
③ ④ ⑤ ⑥ ⑦
Library Quarterly 78.2 (2008): 179-94. Print.

① **作者姓名**。按照姓氏、逗号、名、中间名或首字母的顺序，列出作者的全名。省略头衔。姓名以句号收尾。

② **文章标题**，用引号标示。列出完整的标题和副标题，用冒号分隔。标题以句号收尾，句号放在右引号前。

③ **期刊名称**，用斜体字标示，省略标题起始部分的A, An或The。不要用句号收尾。

④ **卷号和期号**，用阿拉伯数字表示，用句号分隔。期号后不用加句号。

⑤ **出版年份**，用括号标示，后接冒号。

⑥ **文章所在页码**，不要用pp.标示。为清晰起见，最后一个数字只提供所需的数位，通常是两位数。

⑦ **媒介**。列出文章的出版媒介Print，以句号收尾。

对于期刊文章的摘要，首先根据格式7提供文章的出版信息，然后列出摘要的信息。如果摘要的出版者按照条目而非页码列举摘要，则要在数字前加item。如果摘要所在期刊的名称没有标明你的原始资料是摘要，则要在原始出版信息后加Abstract。参见p. 476格式64。

对于*Dissertation Abstracts*（*DA*）或*Dissertation Abstracts International*（*DAI*）上的摘要，要列出作者姓名、标题、Diss.（"Dissertation"的缩写）、授予作者学位的机构、论文日期以及在*DA*或*DAI*上的出版信息。

> Steciw, Steven K. "Alterations to the Pessac Project of Le Corbusier." Diss. U of Cambridge, England, 1986. *DAI* 46.10 (1986): 565C. Print.

还可参见pp. 464–465格式40（论文）、p. 476格式64（在线数据库上的摘要）和p. 477格式69（网络上的摘要）。

注意：大多数老师希望你查阅全文，并从全文而不是摘要中引用原始资料。参见p. 387。

报纸上的文章
10. 全国性报纸上的文章（印刷版）

> Rosenberg, Karen. "Building Blocks of Meaning, Retranslated." *New York Times* 4 May 2012, natl. ed.: C28+. Print.

列出作者姓名、文章标题和报纸在其首页上的名称（但是没有A, An，或The）。

在报纸名称之后，列出发行的日、月、年。（除 May、June 和 July 外，其他月份均须用缩略词）如果报纸在首页上方列出了版次，要在日期后加上版次（参见上面例子中的 natl.ed.）。如果报纸分成标有字母的不同版面，要按照报纸的做法在页码前标出版面名称：如上面例子中的 C28+。（加号表示文章将在后面的页面继续）如果报纸分成标有数字或标题的不同版面，要在冒号前加上版面名称，如 sec. 1: 3 或 Business Day sec.: 4+。用出版媒介 Print 收尾。

11. 地方性报纸上的文章（印刷版）

Gilbert, Ellen. "Senior Adults and Fourth Graders Collaborate on Community Garden." *Town Topics* [Princeton] 18 Apr. 2011: 1+. Print.

如果发行城市没有出现在地方性报纸的首页，要在报纸名称的后面用方括号标出城市名称。不要将城市名称排成斜体。

杂志上的文章

12. 周刊或双周刊上的文章（印刷版）

Simon, Taryn. "A Living Man Declared Dead." *New Yorker* 23 Apr. 2012. 56-61. Print.

列出作者姓名、文章标题和杂志名称。在杂志名称后列出发行的日、月、年。（除 May、June 和 July 外，其他月份均须用缩略词）日期不要放在括号里，不要提供卷号或期号。列出文章所在页码和媒介 Print。

13. 月刊或双月刊上的文章（印刷版）

Harmon, Katherine. "The Patient Scientist." *Scientific American* Jan. 2012: 54-59. Print.

在杂志名称后列出发行的月和年。（除 May、June 和 July 外，其他月份均须用缩略词）日期不要放在括号里，不要提供卷号或期号。列出文章所在页码和媒介 Print。

评论、社论、读者来信、采访

14. 评论（印刷版）

Glasswell, Kathryn, and George Kamberelis. "Drawing and Redrawing the Map of Writing Studies." Rev. of *Handbook of Writing Research*, by Charles A. MacArthur, Steve Graham, and Jill Fitzgerald. *Reading Research Quarterly* 42.2 (2007): 304-23. Print.

Rev. 是 "Review" 一词的缩略词。在作品名称、逗号和 by 后列出被评论的作品的作者姓名。如果评论本身没有标题，则在评论者的姓名之后列出 Rev. of 和被评论的作品名称。

15. 社论或读者来信（印刷版）
社论

"The Risk from Chemical Plants." Editorial. *New York Times* 4 May 2012, natl. ed.: A22. Print.

对于没有标注作者姓名的社论，先列出社论标题，然后在标题之后加上Editorial一词。对于标注了作者姓名的社论，先列出作者姓名，之后的格式如上所示。

读者来信

Stasi, Dom. "Climate and Heresy." Letter. *Scientific American* Mar. 2011: 8. Print.

如果有标题的话，在标题之后加上Letter一词。或者在作者姓名之后加上Letter一词。

16. 采访（印刷版）

Aloni, Shulamit. Interview. *Palestine-Israel Journal of Politics, Economics, and Culture* 14.4 (2007): 63-68. Print.

首先列出被采访者的姓名。如果采访没有标题（如示例），在被采访者姓名之后加上Interview一词。（如果有标题的话，用采访标题代替Interview一词）你也可以加上采访者的姓名，如果你知道的话。关于引用广播采访或你自己完成的采访参见p. 481的格式80。

连载文章或特刊文章
17. 连载文章（印刷版）

Kleinfeld, N. R. "Living at an Epicenter of Diabetes, Defiance, and Despair." *New York Times* 10 Jan. 2006, natl. ed.: A1+. Print. Pt. 2 of a series, Bad Blood, begun 9 Jan. 2006.

在pp. 453–456列举的格式（学术期刊、报纸或杂志）之后列出连载的文章。如果愿意，可以在条目的末尾加上描述，以表明此文是系列的一部分。

18. 特刊文章（印刷版）

Rubini, Monica, and Michela Menegatti. "Linguistic Bias in Personnel Selection." *Celebrating Two Decades of Linguistic Bias Research*. Ed. Robbie M. Sutton and Karen M. Douglas. Spec. issue of *Journal of Language and Social Psychology* 27.2 (2008): 168-81. Print.

先列出特刊文章的作者姓名和文章标题，然后是特刊的名称。在特刊名称后加上Ed.和特刊编辑的姓名。在期刊名称前加上Spec. issue of。参照p. 453和p. 456期刊或杂志的恰当格式用发行信息收尾。

3 ▪ 非周期性的印刷版原始资料

非周期性的印刷版原始资料是那些不定期出版的作品，如书籍、政府出版物和手册。要引用一个作者、多个作者和其他不同作品，参见格式1—6。

书籍

19. 书籍（印刷版）的基本格式

Shteir, Rachel. *The Steal: A Cultural History of Shoplifting*. New York: Penguin, 2011. Print.

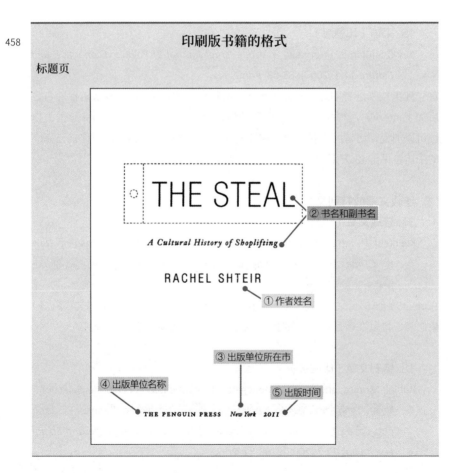

（续表）

① ② ③ ④ ⑤
Shteir, Rachel. *The Steal: A Cultural History of Shoplifting.* New York: Penguin, 2011.
⑥
Print.

① **作者姓名**。按照姓氏、逗号、名、中间名或首字母的顺序，列出作者的全名。省略头衔。姓名以句号收尾。
② **书名**，用斜体字标示。列出完整的书名和副标题，用冒号分隔。以句号收尾。
③ **出版单位所在市**，在出版单位之前，后接冒号。如果书名页列举了不止一座城市，只用第一座城市。
④ **出版单位名称**。缩短大多数出版单位的名称（UP表示大学出版社，Little表示Little, Brown）。书名页上有版本名称和出版单位名称时，要将它们都列出来。
⑤ **出版时间**。如果书名页上没有日期，可以到书名页的下一页查找。以句号收尾。
⑥ **媒介**。列出书籍的媒介Print，以句号收尾。

上面显示了书籍的基本格式以及必要信息在书中的位置。当需要其他信息时，要将它放在作者姓名和标题之间，或者是标题和出版信息之间。具体格式，如下所示。

要引用电子书籍，请参见格式44（网络上的书籍）、格式58（有印刷版出版信息的网络书籍）、格式67（在线数据库上的书籍）和格式70（电子阅读器上的书籍）。

20. 第二版或后续版本（印刷版）

Bolinger, Dwight L. *Aspects of Language.* 3rd ed. New York: Harcourt, 1981. Print.

对于第一版之后的任何版本，要在书名后加上版次。（如果书名后有编者的姓名，要将版次放在编者姓名之后。参见格式25）至于标注了作者姓名或日期而不是版次的版本，要使用恰当的名称。例如，Rev. ed.表示"Revised edition"。

21. 有编者的书籍（印刷版）

Holland, Merlin, and Rupert Hart-Davis, eds. *The Complete Letters of Oscar Wilde.* New York: Holt, 2000. Print.

处理编者姓名的方式与处理作者姓名的方式相同（格式1—4），但是要在最后一名编辑的姓名之后加上逗号、缩略词ed.（一名编者）或eds.（两名或多名编者）。

22. 既有作者又有编者的书籍（印刷版）

Mumford, Lewis. *The City in History*. Ed. Donald L. Miller. New York: Pantheon, 1986. Print.

引用作者的文字时，先列出作者的姓名，然后是书名、Ed.（只用单数，表示"Edited by"）和编者的姓名。引用编者的文字时，采用格式21（有编者的书籍），在书名之后加上By和作者的姓名。

Miller, Donald L., ed. *The City in History*. By Lewis Mumford. New York: Pantheon, 1986. Print.

23. 有译者的书籍（印刷版）

Alighieri, Dante. *The Inferno*. Trans. John Ciardi. New York: NAL, 1971. Print.

与之前的例子一样，在引用作者文字时，先列出作者的姓名，然后是书名、Trans.（表示"Translated by"）和译者的姓名。

引用译者的文字时，先列出译者的姓名，然后是逗号、trans.、书名、By和作者姓名。

Ciardi, John, trans. *The Inferno*. By Dante Alighieri. New York: NAL, 1971. Print.

如果你引用的某位作者的书籍既有译者又有编者，则按照书名页上的顺序列出译者和编者的姓名。

24. 文集（印刷版）

Kennedy, X. J., and Dana Gioia, eds. *Literature: An Introduction to Fiction, Poetry, Drama, and Writing*. 11th ed. New York: Longman, 2010. Print.

只有在引用编者的文字或者你的老师允许格式26所示的交叉参考时才能引用整本文集。列出编者的姓名（后接ed.或eds.），然后是文集的名称。

25. 文集中的选文（印刷版）

Mason, Bobbie Ann. "Shiloh." *Literature: An Introduction to Fiction, Poetry, Drama, and Writing*. Ed. X. J. Kennedy and Dana Gioia. 11th ed. New York: Longman, 2010. 569-78. Print.

上面这个例子在格式24文集这一条目中添加如下信息：选文的作者、选文的题目（用引号标出）和该选文的起止页码（不需要用缩略词pp.）。如果你愿意，你也可以在选文的题目之后添加该作品的原始出版信息。参见p. 462格式32。

如果你引用的作品来自一名作者的作品集（没有编者），要使用以下格式：

Auden, W. H. "Family Ghosts." *The Collected Poetry of W. H. Auden*. New York:

Random, 1945. 132-33. Print.

26. 同一部文集中的两篇或两篇以上选文（印刷版）

Bradstreet, Anne. "The Author to Her Book." Kennedy and Gioia 647.

Kennedy, X. J., and Dana Gioia, eds. *Literature: An Introduction to Fiction, Poetry, Drama, and Writing.* 11th ed. New York: Longman, 2010. Print.

Merwin, W. S. "For the Anniversary of My Death." Kennedy and Gioia 834-35.

Stevens, Wallace. "Thirteen Ways of Looking at a Blackbird." Kennedy and Gioia 838-39.

当你从同一部文集中引用不止一篇选文时，你的老师可能会允许你列出完整的文集信息（比如Kennedy and Gioia这一条目），然后在其他的条目中进行简单的交叉参考，从而避免重复。因此，Bradstreet，Merwin和Stevens这三个例子中，"Kennedy and Gioia"以及书中的相应页码代替了完整的出版信息。注意，每一个条目都按照恰当的字母顺序出现在参考目录中。因为一些特定的条目交叉参考了Kennedy和Gioia的文集，所以它们不需要列出媒介。

27. 在作品集中再版的学术文章（印刷版）

Molloy, Francis C. "The Suburban Vision in John O'Hara's Short Stories." *Critique: Studies in Modern Fiction* 25.2 (1984): 101-13. Rpt. in *Short Story Criticism: Excerpts from Criticism of the Works of Short Fiction Writers.* Ed. David Segal. Vol. 15. Detroit: Gale, 1989. 287-92. Print.

如果你引用的作品是以前在其他地方（如学术期刊）出版过的学术文章，要提供该文章以前的完整出版信息，后接Rpt. in（表示"Reprinted in"）和该文章的原始资料信息。

28. 参考书中的文章（印刷版）

"Reckon." *Merriam-Webster's Collegiate Dictionary.* 11th ed. 2008. Print.

Wenner, Manfred W. "Arabia." *The New Encyclopaedia Britannica: Macropaedia.* 15th ed. 2007. Print.

列出该文章的标题（如第一个例子），除非该文章是署名的（第二个例子）。至于按照字母顺序排列条目的作品，你无须列出卷号或页码。对于广泛使用并经常修订的作品（如上所示），你可以省略编者的姓名和所有出版信息（版次、出版年份和媒介除外）。

对于专业作品，要列出所有的出版信息。这类作品的主题和读者范围较窄，可能只有一个版本。

"Fortune." *Encyclopedia of Indo-European Culture*. Ed. J. P. Mallory and Douglas Q. Adams. London: Fitzroy, 1997. Print.

参见格式49（p. 470）网络上的参考书和格式77（p. 479）CD-ROM或DVD-ROM上的参考书。

29. 绘本或带插图的故事书（印刷版）

Wilson, G. Willow. *Cairo*. Illus. M. K. Perker. New York: Vertigo-DC Comics, 2005. Print.

引用带插图的故事书或绘本作者的文字时，要按照上述例子列出作者姓名、书名、Illus.（表示"Illustrated by"）和插图画家的姓名。引用插图画家的图片时，先列出他或她的姓名，然后是逗号和illus.（表示"illustrator"）。在书名和By之后，列出书的作者姓名。

Williams, Garth, illus. *Charlotte's Web*. By E. B. White. 1952. New York: Harper, 1999. Print.

30. 多卷册作品（印刷版）

Lincoln, Abraham. *The Collected Works of Abraham Lincoln*. Ed. Roy P. Basler. Vol. 5. New Brunswick: Rutgers UP, 1953. Print. 8 vols.

如果你只引用了多卷册作品中的一卷，在出版信息前列出卷号（如前面例子中的Vol. 5）。你可以在条目的最后添加总卷数（例子中的8 vols.）。

如果你引用了多卷册作品中的两卷或两卷以上作品，在出版信息前列出该作品的总卷数（下面例子中的8 vols.）。你的文内引文注释将显示你引用的哪一卷作品。（参见p. 443）

Lincoln, Abraham. *The Collected Works of Abraham Lincoln*. Ed. Roy P. Basler. 8 vols. New Brunswick: Rutgers UP, 1953. Print.

如果你引用的是经历了很多年才出齐的多卷册作品，要将出版的起止年份作为出版日期。

31. 系列书籍（印刷版）

Bergman, Ingmar. *The Seventh Seal*. New York: Simon, 1995. Print. Mod. Film Scripts Ser. 12.

在条目的最后列出该系列作品的名称（不加引号，也不排成斜体），后接系列号（如果有的话）和句号。modern和series这些常见词要用缩略词。

32. 再版的书籍（印刷版）

James, Henry. *The Bostonians.* 1886. New York: Penguin, 2001. Print.

再版的书籍包括用新书名重新发行的书籍以及最初以精装本发行的平装版书籍。在书名后列出原始出版信息，然后提供你所使用的原始资料的完整出版信息。如果原来的书名与再版的书名不一样，要在条目的最后在Rpt. of（表示"Reprint of"）之后添加原来的书名和出版日期。

33.《圣经》（印刷版）

The Bible. Print. King James Vers.

The Holy Bible. Trans. Ronald Youngblood et al. Grand Rapids: Zondervan, 1984. Print. New Intl. Vers.

引用标准版本的《圣经》（第一个例子）时，不要将书名或版本名称排成斜体。你不需要提供出版信息。对于《圣经》的某一版本（第二个例子），将书名排成斜体，再列出编者和/或译者的姓名、完整的出版信息，最后加上版本名称。

34. 书名中套书名的书籍（印刷版）

Eco, Umberto. *Postscript to* The Name of the Rose. Trans. William Weaver. New York: Harcourt, 1983. Print.

当一本书的书名中包含了另一本书的书名（例子中的The Name of the Rose）时，不要将第二个书名排成斜体。当书名中包含了引文或通常用引号标注的作品标题时，要保留引号，并用斜体字表示书名和标题。

35. 已出版的会议记录（印刷版）

Stimpson, Bill, ed. *2010 AWEA Annual Conference and Exhibition*. Proc. of Amer. Wind Energy Assn. Conf., 3-6 June 2010, New York. Red Hook: Curran, 2011. Print.

引用已出版的会议日程（proceedings of a conference）时，要使用书籍的格式（格式21）。在书名和出版数据之间，添加会议信息，如会议名称、时间和地点。你可以省略已经出现在原始资料标题中的此类信息。要像处理文集中的选文那样处理会议的特定发言（格式25）。

36. 前言、卷首语、序或跋（印刷版）

Donaldson, Norman. Introduction. *The Claverings*. By Anthony Trollope. New York: Dover, 1977. vii-xv. Print.

前言、卷首语、序或跋通常由书籍作者之外的人撰写。引用这类作品时，列出作品的名称，不要用引号，也不要排成斜体，如上面例子中的Introduction。（如果作品有自己的标题，要给标题加上引号，并将它放在作者姓名和书名之间）书名后接By和书的作者姓名。列出引文的起止页码。（在上面的例子中，小写的罗马数字指的是书籍的文前部分，通常在正文第一页之前）

当前言或卷首语的作者为书的作者时，只要在书名后面列出作者的姓氏即可：

Gould, Stephen Jay. Prologue. *The Flamingo's Smile: Reflections in Natural History*. By Gould. New York: Norton, 1985. 13-20. Print.

37. 缺少出版信息或页码的书籍（印刷版）

Carle, Eric. *The Very Busy Spider*. New York: Philomel, 1984. N. pag. Print.

有些书籍没有编页码，也没有列出出版社或出版地点。引用类似书籍时，要尽可能多地提供此类信息，用缩略词表示缺失的信息：N. p.表示没有出版地点；n. p.表示没有出版单位；n. d.表示没有出版日期；N. pag.表示没有页码。

其他非周期性的印刷版原始资料

38. 政府出版物（印刷版）

United Nations. Dept. of Economic and Social Affairs. *World Youth Report 2011: Youth and Climate Change*. New York: United Nations, 2012. Print.

United States. Cong. House. Committee on Agriculture, Nutrition, and Forestry. *Food and Energy Act of 2008*. 110th Cong., 2nd sess. Washington: GPO, 2008. Print.

Wisconsin. Dept. of Public Instruction. *Bullying Prevention Program*. Madison: Wisconsin Dept. of Public Instruction, 2010. Print.

如果政府出版物没有将某个人列为作者或编者，要如上所示，将恰当的机构作为作者。按照以下顺序列出信息，中间用句号分隔：政府名称、机构名称（可以是缩略词）、出版物名称和印刷信息。对于国会出版物（第二个例子），要在标题前列出参议院或众议院的名称和相关的委员会名称，在标题后列出国会会议的次数和名称。在第二个例子中，GPO表示US Government Printing Office。

如果政府出版物将某个人列为作者或编者，则按照有作者或编者的书籍处理原始资料：

Kim, Jiyul. *Cultural Dimensions of Strategy and Policy*. Carlisle: US Army War Coll., Strategic Studies Inst., 2009. Print.

参见格式48（p.469）引用你在网络上找到的政府出版物。

39. 手册或宣传册（印刷版）

Understanding Childhood Obesity. Tampa: Obesity Action Coalition. 2012. Print.
大多数手册或宣传册可以像书籍那样处理。在上面的例子中，手册没有列出作者，因此先列出标题。如果你的原始资料有作者，要先列出他或她的姓名，然后列出标题和出版信息。

40. 论文（印刷版）

McFaddin, Marie Oliver. *Adaptive Reuse: An Architectural Solution for Poverty and Homelessness*. Diss. U of Maryland, 2007. Ann Arbor: UMI, 2007. Print.

像处理书籍那样处理已出版的论文，但是要在论文题目之后插入Diss.（表示"Dissertation"）、授予学位的机构和年份。

对于未出版的论文，给论文题目加上引号而不是将它排成斜体，并省略出版信息。

Wilson, Stuart M. "John Stuart Mill as a Literary Critic." Diss. U of Michigan, 1990. Print.

41. 信件（印刷版）

Buttolph, Mrs. Laura E. Letter to Rev. and Mrs. C. C. Jones. 20 June 1857. *The Children of Pride: A True Story of Georgia and the Civil War*. Ed. Robert Manson Myers. New Haven: Yale UP, 1972. 334-35. Print.

列出写信人名下的已出版的信件，需要说明原始资料是一封信函，收信人是谁，写信日期是何时。其他信息的处理方式和文集中的选文一样（p.460格式25）。（参见p.456格式15读者给期刊编辑的信件格式）

和已出版信件一样，对于图书馆或档案馆收藏的未出版的信件，要说明写信人、收信人和日期。然后提供媒介：MS（表示"manuscript"）或TS（表示"typescript"）。以档案馆的名称和地址收尾。

James, Jonathan E. Letter to his sister. 16 Apr. 1970. MS. Jonathan E. James Papers. South Dakota State Archive, Pierre.

对于你收到的信件，要列出写信人的姓名、说明收信人是你、提供日期并添加媒介MS或TS。

Silva, Elizabeth. Letter to the author. 6 Apr. 2012. MS.

引用电子邮件信息或讨论小组的帖子，请参见格式73—74。（p.479）

4 ▪ 非周期性的网络原始资料

本部分展示如何引用你在网络上找到的非周期性原始资料。这些原始资料可能只出版一次或偶尔出版，或者它们可能频繁更新，但这种更新是不定期的。（大多数在线杂志和报纸属于后者。参见p. 469）有些非周期性网络原始资料只能在网上获得（p. 466）；其他的原始资料也可以在其他媒介中获得（pp. 472–473）。参见格式63—67（p. 476）引用你在在线数据库中找到的期刊和书籍，以及格式68—69（p. 477）引用你在网络上找到的学术期刊。

在引用网络原始资料时，MLA格式不要求URL（电子地址），除非在没有URL的情况下，难以找到原始资料，或者它会和另一个原始资料搞混。参见格式62（p. 473）引用URL时使用的格式。

注意：*MLA Handbook for Writers of Research Papers*没有将非周期性的网络原始资料范例列为特定的类别。为便于参考，以下的格式分辨并解释了常见的网络原始资料。如果你没有发现你需要的格式，查询pp. 450–451的格式索引，以便发现你可以改编格式的相似的原始资料类型。如果你的原始资料没有包括完整引用所需的所有信息，发现并列出你所能找到的信息。

只能通过网络获得的非周期性原始资料

许多非周期性网络原始资料只能在线获得。以下清单改编自*MLA Handbook for Writers of Research Papers*，列出了在非周期网络出版物中可能出现的元素，并按照它们在被引用作品条目中的出现顺序排列：

- **作者或其他对原始资料负责的人（如编者、译者或表演者）的姓名**。作者姓名的处理方式参见格式1—6（pp. 449–452）对于其他类型的供稿人，参见格式21—23（编者和译者）以及格式79、格式81—82和格式88（表演者、导演等）。
- **所引用作品的标题**。文章的标题和重大作品的分册，要加引号。书名或其他独立出版的原始资料，要排成斜体。
- **网站名称**，要用斜体字。
- **所引用的版本或版次**。如果有的话，请遵照格式20（p. 459）。如*Index of History Periodicals*. 2nd ed.
- **网站的发行人或主办人**，后接逗号。如果你找不到发行人或主办人，要使用N.p.（表示"No publisher"）。（见p. 469 Corbett这个例子）
- **电子版出版物、最新版本或最新帖子的日期**。如果日期包括月份，要使用缩略词，May, June和July除外。如果没有日期，要使用n.d.（表示"no

date"）。（见p. 469 Corbett这个例子）
- 出版媒介：Web。
- 你的浏览日期：按照日、月、年的顺序列出日期。所有的月份都要缩写，May，June和July除外。

对于有些网络原始资料，你可能想包括本清单中没有列出的信息，如录音的作者和表演者的姓名。（参见格式53）

42. 有标题的短作品（网络版）

Murray, Amanda. "The Birth of Hip-Hop: Innovation against the Odds." *The Lemelson Center for the Study of Invention and Innovation*. Smithsonian Inst., Natl. Museum of Amer. Hist., Oct. 2010. Web. 11 Apr. 2012.

参见下面对此条目和网站所需信息位置的分析。

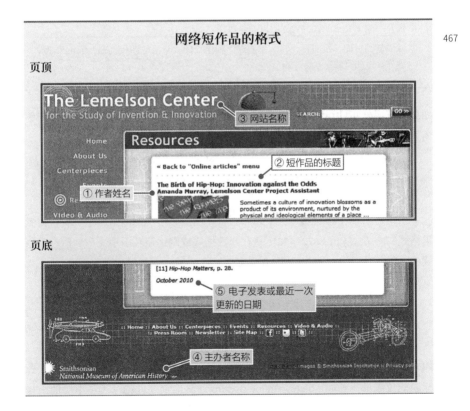

Murray, Amanda. ①"The Birth of Hip-Hop: Innovation against the Odds." ② *The Lemelson Center for the Study of Invention and Innovation.* ③ Smithsonian Inst., Natl. Museum ④ of Amer. Hist., Oct. 2010. ⑤ Web. ⑥ 11 Apr. 2012. ⑦

① **作者姓名**。按照姓氏、逗号、名、中间名或首字母的顺序列出全名。省略头衔。以句号收尾。如果你在网页上方看不到作者姓名,请查看网页下方。如果网页上没有列出作者的姓名,用短作品的标题为开始。

② **短作品的标题**,用引号标示。句号放在右引号前。

③ **网站名称**,用斜体字标示,以句号收尾。

④ **主办者名称**,以逗号收尾。

⑤ **电子发表或最近一次更新的日期**。对于包含了月和日的日期,要按照日、月、年的顺序列出日期。所有的月份都要缩写,May, June和July除外。以句号收尾。

⑥ **媒介**。列出文章的媒介Web,以句号收尾。

⑦ **你浏览的日期**,按照日、月、年的顺序列出日期。月份要缩写,May, June和July除外。以句号收尾。

468 如果你引用的短作品没有作者,可遵循格式6(p. 452)匿名原始资料,以标题为开始。具体如下所示。

"Clean Energy." *Union of Concerned Scientists: Citizens and Scientists for Environmental Solutions*. Union of Concerned Scientists, 2012. Web. 11 Mar. 2012.

引用还出现在其他媒介上(如印刷版)的篇幅短小的网络原始资料,请参见格式57—61。(pp. 472–473)从在线数据库或网络期刊引用文章,请参见格式63—66和格式68—69。(pp. 474–478)

43. 没有标题的短作品(网络版)

Cyberbullying Research Center. Home page. Cyberbullying Research Center, 2012. Web. 15 May 2012.

如果你从网站(如网站的主页或博客的帖子)上引用没有标题的短作品,要在标题的位置插入Home page, Online posting或其他描述性的标志。不要加引号或排成斜体。

44. 书籍（网络版）

Herodotus. *The Histories*. Ed. A. D. Godley. *Perseus Digital Library*. Dept. of Classics, Tufts U, 10 Apr. 2012. Web. 2 May 2012.

此类电子书的信息遵照格式21（p. 459）有编者的印刷版书籍，用网址名称、主办人、日期、媒介（Web）和浏览日期代替印刷版的出版信息。

引用其他类型的电子书，请参见格式58（有印刷版出版信息的网络书籍）、格式67（数据库中的书籍）和格式70（电子阅读器上的书籍）。

45. 完整的网站（网络版）

Crane, Gregory, ed. *The Perseus Digital Library*. Dept. of Classics, Tufts U, 10 Apr. 2012. Web. 21 July 2012.

引用完整的网站（如学术项目或基金会网站）时，要列出编者、作者或编译者（如果有的话）的姓名，网站名称，主办人，发表的日期或最近的更新日期，媒介（Web）和你浏览的日期。

如果原始资料没有作者或编者的姓名，要以网站名称为开始：

Union of Concerned Scientists: Citizens and Scientists for Environmental Solutions. Union of Concerned Scientists, 2012. Web. 11 Mar. 2012.

如果原始资料没有主办人，要使用缩略词N.p.（表示"No publisher"）。如果没有发表日期，要使用缩略词n.d.。下面的原始资料没有主办人和发表日期：

Corbett, John. *STARN: Scots Teaching and Resource Network*. N.p., n.d. Web. 26 Nov. 2011.

46. 报纸上的文章（网络版）

Angier, Natalie. "Insights from the Youngest Minds." *New York Times*. New York Times, 1 May 2012. Web. 8 May 2012.

即使在线报纸有印刷版，也应该将它看成非周期性的原始资料，因为在线的内容经常变化，而且具有不可预测性。如格式10或11所示，（p. 455）列出作者姓名、文章标题和报纸名称，然后提供出版者的名称和日期。以出版媒介（Web）和你浏览的日期收尾。如果你需要引用网络报纸的评论、社论、读者来信、采访或系列文章，要使用此格式改编印刷版期刊的格式。（格式14—17，pp. 456–457）

参见格式65引用在线数据库上的报纸文章。

47. 杂志上的文章（网络版）

Solnit, Rebecca. "America's Real Hunger Games." *Salon*. Salon Media Group, 1 May 2012. Web. 7 June 2012.

即使在线杂志有印刷版，也应该将它看成非周期性的原始资料，因为在线的内容经常变化，而且具有不可预测性。如格式12或13所示，（p. 456）列出作者姓名、文章标题和杂志名称，然后提供出版者的名称和日期。以出版媒介（Web）和你浏览的日期收尾。如果你需要引用网络杂志的评论、社论、读者来信、采访或系列文章或特刊文章，要使用此格式改编印刷版期刊的格式。（格式14—18，pp. 456–457）

参见格式66引用在线数据库上的杂志文章。

48. 政府出版物（网络版）

United States. Dept. of Education. "Why Teach." *Teach*. US Dept. of Education, n.d. Web. 1 Mar. 2012.

参见格式38印刷版政府出版物的例子，为在线出版物提供同样的信息，出版信息用Web代替Print，并添加你浏览的日期。上述例子包括政府和部门名称、原始资料的标题（用引号标示）、网站名称（用斜体字标示）、主办人的名称、n.d.（因为没有发表日期）、媒介（Web）和浏览日期。

49. 参考书中的文章（网络版）

"Yi Dynasty." *Encyclopaedia Britannica Online*. Encyclopaedia Britannica, 2012. Web. 7 Apr. 2012.

这类原始资料没有标注作者姓名，所以以文章的标题为开始，接下来的信息处理方式和其他网络原始资料一样。如果参考文章列出了作者姓名，要将它放在文章标题之前，参见格式42。

对于你找到的已出版的参考书，或者在CD-ROM或DVD-ROM上找到的参考书，请分别参见格式28（p. 461）和格式77（p. 479）。

50. 图像（网络版）

引用只能在网络上获得的图像，要列出艺术家或创作者的姓名、作品名称、作品完成日期（如果有的话）、图像类型的描述性词语（有别于图像或网站的名称）、网站名称、主办人、网站日期、媒介（Web）和你浏览的日期。以下例子展示了各种可能性。

艺术品：

Simpson, Rick. *Overload. Museum of Computer Art*. Museum of Computer Art, 2008. Web. 1 Apr. 2012.

照片：

Touboul, Jean. *Desert 1*. 2002. Photograph. *Artmuse.net*. Jean Touboul, 2007. Web. 14 Nov. 2011.

广告：

FreeCreditReport.com. Advertisement. *Facebook*. Facebook, 2012. Web. 6 May 2012.

地图、图表、表格或示意图：

"Greenhouse Effect." Diagram. *Earthguide*. Scripps Inst. of Oceanography, 2008. Web. 17 July 2012.

另请参见格式61（p. 473）引用在电脑和其他媒介上出现的图像，格式72（p. 479）引用数字文档中的图像，和格式83—87（pp. 482–483）引用不在网络上的图像。

51. 电视或广播节目（网络版）

Norris, Michele, host. *All Things Considered*. Natl. Public Radio, 6 Apr. 2012. Web. 21 Apr. 2012.

电视和广播的网络与节目的网站通常包括作为节目的一部分而播出的内容以及只能在网络上看到的内容。不论是哪种内容的原始资料，引用时要列出其标题或作者姓名。确定除作者以外的任何人的角色（例子中的host）。提供网站名称、主办人、日期、媒介（Web）和你浏览的日期。你还可以如格式53所示，在标题之后列出其他供稿人（及其作用）。

另请参见格式79（p. 480）引用不在网络上的电视或广播节目。

52. 录像（网络版）

CBS News, prod. "1968 King Assassination Report." *YouTube*. YouTube, 3 Apr. 2008. Web. 22 Feb. 2012.

列出网络上视频的标题或所引用作品的作者姓名（例子中制作视频的机构）。确定除了作者以外的任何人的角色（例子中的prod.）。提供视频标题、网站名称、主办人、日期、媒介（Web）和你浏览的日期。你还可以如格式53所示，在标题之后列出其他供稿人（及其作用）。

另请参见格式54引用录像的播客，格式60（p. 473）引用网络和其他媒介（如DVD）上的录像或电影，格式82（pp. 481–482）引用不在网络上的电影、DVD或录像。

53. 录音（网络版）

Beglarian, Eve. *Five Things*. Perf. Beglarian et al. *Earbud Music: Eve Beglarian*. N.p., 23 Oct. 2001. Web. 8 Mar. 2012.

标出音乐录音的标题或所引用作品的作者姓名（例子中的作曲家）。（如果作曲家的姓名放在标题之后，则需在作曲家姓名之前加By。参见下一个例子）前面的例子还提供了作品名称、演奏者姓名、网站名称、主办人（此处为未知，用N.p.代替）、日期、媒介（Web）和浏览日期。

同样的格式可用于你在网络上找的口头语言的录音：

Wasserstein, Wendy, narr. "Afternoon of a Faun." By Wasserstein. *The Borzoi Reader Online*. Knopf, 2001. Web. 14 Feb. 2012.

另请参见下一个格式引用声音播客，格式59引用出现在网络和其他媒介（如光盘）上的录音，格式81（p. 481）引用不在网络上的录音。

54. 播客（网络版）

Glass, Ira. "Retraction." *This American Life*. Chicago Public Media, 16 Mar. 2012. Web. 14 Apr. 2012.

前面的例子来自广播节目的播客，列出了节目中故事的作者、故事的题目（用引号标示）、节目名称（用斜体字标示）、网站名称、主办人、日期、媒介（Web）和浏览日期。如果播客没有列出作者或其他创作者，要以标题为开始。

55. 博客文章（网络版）

Marshall, Joshua Micah. "Big Money." *Talking Points Memo*. TPM Media, 26 Apr. 2012. Web. 21 May 2012.

对于博客文章，要列出作者姓名、文章标题或网站名称、主办人（没有的话，用N.p.表示）、发表日期、媒介（Web）和你浏览的日期。参见格式43（p. 468）引用没有标题的博客文章。

56. 维基网站（网络版）

"Podcast." *Wikipedia*. Wikimedia, n.d. Web. 20 Nov. 2012.

对于维基网站文章，要遵照这个例子：列出文章标题、网站名称、主办人、发表日期（例子中标示为n.d.，因为该维基网站文章没有标注日期）、媒介（Web）和浏览日期。如果你引用整个维基网站，需以网站名称为开始。

有印刷版的非周期性网络原始资料

一些你在网络上找到的原始资料可能是书籍、诗歌、短故事或其他可以从印刷版扫描的作品。引用类似的原始资料，要以作者、标题及其他信息为开始，格式要与原始资料类型相适应。（参见格式19—41）然后，你可以提供平面出版信息：出版地点、出版者和出版日期。在条目的最后，提供所使用网站的名称、版本号或版次、你使用的媒介（Web）和浏览日期。不用将"Print"作为媒介。

57. 有印刷版出版信息的短作品（网络版）

Wheatley, Phillis. "On Virtue." *Poems on Various Subjects, Religious and Moral.* London, 1773. N. pag. *American Verse Project.* Web. 21 July 2012.

这首诗的印刷版信息遵照格式25文集中的选文格式（p. 460），但是省略了出版者的名称，因为该文集在1900年前出版。印刷版信息以N.pag.收尾，因为原始资料没有页码。

58. 有印刷版出版信息的书籍（网络版）

Sassoon, Siegfried. *Counter-Attack and Other Poems.* New York: Dutton, 1918. *Google Books.* Web. 6 Mar. 2012.

这本电子书的信息遵照格式19印刷版书籍的格式（p. 457），添加了网络发表的信息（*Google Books*）、媒介（Web）和浏览日期。参见格式44（网络上的书籍）、格式67（在线数据库上的书籍）和格式70（电子阅读器上的书籍）。

还可以在其他媒介上获得的非周期性网络原始资料

一些你在网络上找到的图像、电影和录音之前可能在其他媒介上发表过，然后经过扫描和电子化处理放到网络上。引用此类原始资料，一般要提供原始的出版信息和网络发表信息。就像引用原作似的开始列出条目信息，参照格式79—89（pp. 480–483）以获得恰当的格式。然后提供所使用网络的名称、所使用的媒介（Web）和你浏览的日期，而不是提供原始的出版媒介。

59. 有其他出版信息的录音（网络版）

"Rioting in Pittsburgh." CBS Radio, 1968. *Vincent Voice Library*. Web. 7 Dec. 2011.

对于有原始出版信息的网络录音，引用格式遵照格式81（p. 481），添加网络发表信息。

60. 有其他出版信息的电影或录像（网络版）

Coca-Cola. Advertisement. Dir. Haskell Wexler. 1971. *American Memory*. Lib. of Cong. Web. 8 Apr. 2012.

对于有原始出版信息的网络电影或视频，引用格式遵照格式82（pp. 481–482），添加网络发表信息。

61. 有其他出版信息的图像（网络版）

Pollock, Jackson. *Lavender Mist: Number 1*. 1950. Natl. Gallery of Art, Washington. *WebMuseum*. Web. 7 Apr. 2012.

Keefe, Mike. "World Education Rankings." Cartoon. *Denver Post* 5 Apr. 2012. *PoliticalCartoons.com*. Web. 9 May 2012.

对于有原始出版信息的网络图像，引用格式遵照格式83—87（pp. 482–483），添加网络发表信息。

URL的引用

62. 需要引用URL的原始资料（网络版）

Joss, Rich. "Dispatches from the Ice: The Second Season Begins." *Antarctic Expeditions*. Smithsonian Natl. Zoo and Friends of the Natl. Zoo, 26 Oct. 2007. Web. 26 Sept. 2012. <http://nationalzoo.si.edu/ConservationAndScience/AquaticEcosystems/Antarctica/Expedition/FieldNew/2-FieldNews.cfm>.

MLA格式不要求在参考目录中列出URL。但是如果老师有要求的话，你就应该列出URL。在没有URL的情况下，读者可能找不到原始资料时，你也需要提供URL。例如，使用搜索引擎查找前面例子中的标题"Dispatches from the Ice"，会得到超过十个的结果。其中一个链接到正确的网站，但是文件却不对。

参考目录中，在浏览日期和句号之后，提供URL。URL的前后要加尖括号，以句号收尾。用斜线而不是连字符分隔URL。

5 ▪ 在线数据库中的期刊和书籍

本部分涵盖你通过在线数据库阅读的学术期刊、报纸、杂志和书籍。引用在线数据库上的材料与引用印刷版材料类似,在使用媒介上稍作改变。下面的清单改编自 *MLA Handbook for Writers of Research Papers*,按照在线期刊和书籍中各种可能元素在所引用作品条目中的出现顺序对它们加以详细说明:

- **作者姓名**。列出作者的姓氏、名和中间名或首字母。对于有一个以上作者的作品、同一作者的两部作品、团体作者的作品,或者没有标注作者的作品,请参见格式2—6。对于有编者或译者的作品,参见格式21—23。
- **期刊文章的标题,用引号标示**。列出标题和副标题。右引号前加句号,以此结束标题的引用。
- **期刊或书籍的名称,用斜体字标示**。对于期刊名称,参照p. 454上的格式。对于书名,参照p. 458上的格式。
- **发表信息**。参照印刷版出版物的格式:期刊、杂志和报纸参照格式7—18,书籍参照格式19—37。如果你想列出发表月份,那么月份要缩写,除非是May, June和July。
- **期刊文章所在的页码,不用pp.**。如果文章没有标注页码,则用n. pag.代替。
- **数据库名称,用斜体字标示**,如果你是通过在线数据库找到原始资料的话。
- **出版媒介**:Web,后接句号。
- **你浏览的日期**:按照日、月、年的顺序。除了May, June和July外,其他月份都要缩写。

63. 学术期刊上的文章(在线数据库)

Penuel, Suzanne. "Missing Fathers: *Twelfth Night* and the Reformation of Mourning." *Studies in Philology* 107.1 (2010): 74-96. *Academic Search Complete*. Web. 10 Apr. 2012.

参见下页方框中关于之前这个条目和数据库所需信息位置的分析。

在线数据库中学术期刊的引用格式

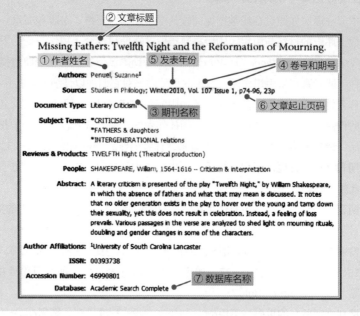

Penuel, Suzanne. "Missing Fathers: *Twelfth Night* and the Reformation of Mourning." *Studies in Philology* 107.1 (2010): 74-96. *Academic Search Complete*. Web. 10 Apr. 2012.

① 作者姓名。按照姓氏、逗号、名、中间名或首字母的顺序列出作者全名。省略头衔。以句号收尾。

② 文章标题，用引号标示。句号放在右引号前，以此收尾。（注意：例子中的剧本名称Twelfth Night在所引用的文章标题中用斜体字标示）

③ 期刊名称，用斜体字标示。省略标题起始部分的A, An或The。不要用句号收尾。

④ 卷号和期号，用阿拉伯数字表示，用句号分隔。期号后不加句号。

⑤ 发表年份，用括号标示，后接冒号。

⑥ 文章起止页码，不用加pp.。为清晰起见，最后一个数字通常只提供两位数。如果文章没有页码，标示n.pag.。

⑦ 数据库名称，用斜体字标示，以句号收尾。

⑧ 媒介。提供文章所在的媒介：Web，后接句号。

⑨ 你浏览的日期，按照日、月、年的顺序。除了May, June和July外，其他月份都要缩写。以句号收尾。

64. 期刊文章的摘要（在线数据库）

Penuel, Suzanne. "Missing Fathers: *Twelfth Night* and the Reformation of Mourning." *Studies in Philology* 107.1 (2010): 74-96. Abstract. *Academic Search Complete*. Web. 10 Apr. 2012.

在线数据库摘要的处理方式与数据库期刊文章一样，但是要在出版信息和数据库名称之间添加Abstract。（如果期刊名称明确表示所引作品是摘要的话，你可以省略这一标记）

65. 报纸上的文章（在线数据库）

Winslow, Ron. "No Easy Cure for Diabetic Children." *Wall Street Journal* 30 Apr. 2012, eastern ed.: A1+. *LexisNexis Academic*. Web. 10 Sept. 2012.

按照格式10或11（p. 455）列举作者姓名、文章标题、报纸名称、发表日期、版次（如果有的话）和页码。添加数据库名称、媒介（Web）和你浏览的日期。

66. 杂志上的文章（在线数据库）

Tucker, Abigail. "Inside the Box." *Smithsonian* Mar. 2012: 78-79. *ProQuest Research Library*. Web. 2 Aug. 2012.

按照格式12或13（p. 456）列举作者姓名、文章标题、杂志名称、发表日期和页码。添加数据库名称、媒介（Web）和你浏览的日期。

67. 书籍（在线数据库）

Hazo, Samuel. *Like a Man Gone Mad: Poems in a New Century*. Syracuse: Syracuse UP, 2010. *Ebrary*. Web. 5 June 2012.

在线数据库书籍的处理方式与印刷版书籍一样，遵照格式19—23，添加电子版的出版信息、数据库的名称、媒介（Web）和你浏览的日期。

另请参见格式44（网络书籍）、格式58（有印刷版出版信息的网络书籍）和格式70（电子阅读器中的书籍）。

6 ▪ 直接查阅的网络期刊

你直接在网络上找到的期刊可能只在线发表，也可能平面出版。不论哪一种情况，引用格式都是一样的：以恰当的平面格式为开始（p. 453），但要用Wed代替"Print"，并添加你浏览的日期。因为许多网络期刊都没有页码，你可以如p. 478上的条目所示代之以n.pag.。

477　你直接在网络上找到的报纸和杂志通常不是期刊（因为它们的内容经常变化，而且具有不可预测性），因此它们被包含在格式46和格式47中。

68. 学术期刊上的文章（网络版）

Polletta, Francesca. "Just Talk: Public Deliberation after 9/11." *Journal of Public Deliberation* 4.1 (2008): n. pag. Web. 7 Apr. 2012.

参见p. 478中关于此条目及网络期刊所需信息位置的分析。如果你需要引用网络期刊评论、社论、读者来信、采访、系列文章或特刊文章，则要使用同样的格式改编印刷版期刊的格式。（格式14—18, pp. 456–457）

对于在线数据库上的期刊文章，参见格式63。

69. 期刊文章的摘要（网络版）

Polletta, Francesca. "Just Talk: Public Deliberation after 9/11." *Journal of Public Deliberation* 4.1 (2008): n. pag. Abstract. Web. 7 Apr. 2012.

网络摘要的处理方式与网络期刊文章一样，但是得在出版信息和媒介之间添加Abstract。（如果期刊名称明确表示所引作品是摘要的话，你可以省略这一标记）参见格式64引用在线数据库上的摘要。

7 ▪ 其他电子版原始资料

数字文档

你可能需要引用不在网络上的数字文档，包括你下载或通过仪器获得的各种电子阅读器上的书籍、PDF文件、JPEG图像或MP3格式的录音。采用恰当的格式列举你所引用的原始资料（如格式19对于书籍的引用），但是要用你使用的文档格式代替媒介。如果你不知道文档格式，在媒介处标注Digital file。

70. 电子阅览器上的书籍（数字版）

Packer, George. *Interesting Times: Writings from a Turbulent Decade.* New York: Farrar, 2010. Kindle file.

列举其他类型的电子书，请参见格式44（网络书籍）、格式58（有印刷版出版信息的网络书籍）或者格式67（在线数据库上的书籍）。

71. 文本文件（数字版）

Berg, John K. "Estimates of Persons Driving While Intoxicated." *Law Enforcement Today* 22 Apr. 2011. PDF file.

Fernandez, Carlos. "Travels in Mexico." 2012. *Microsoft Word* file.

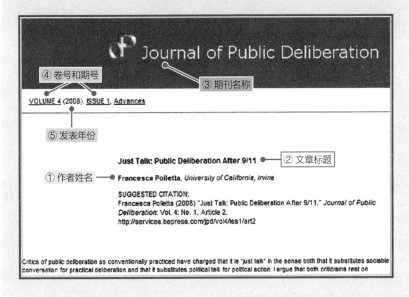

① ② ③
Polletta, Francesca. "Just Talk: Public Deliberation after 9/11." *Journal of Public*
④ ⑤ ⑥ ⑦ ⑧
Deliberation 4.1 (2008): n. pag. Web. 7 Apr. 2012.

① **作者姓名**。按照姓氏、逗号、名、中间名或首字母的顺序列出作者全名。省略头衔。以句号收尾。
② **文章标题**，用引号标示。列出完整的标题和副标题，用冒号分隔。句号放在右引号前，以此收尾。
③ **期刊名称**，用斜体字标示。省略名称起始部分的A, An或The。不要用句号收尾。
④ **卷号和期号**，用阿拉伯数字表示，用句号分隔。期号后不加句号。
⑤ **发表年份**，用括号标示，后接冒号。
⑥ **文章起止页码**，不用加缩略词pp.。如果文章没有页码，要标示为n.pag.。为清晰起见，最后一个数字通常只提供两位数。（如pp. 626–642）
⑦ **媒介**。列出文章的媒介：Web，后接句号。
⑧ **你浏览的日期**。按照日、月、年的顺序。除了May, June和July外，其他月份都要缩写。以句号收尾。

479

72. 媒体文件（数字版）

Springsteen, Bruce. "This Life." *Working on a Dream*. Columbia, 2009. MP3 file.
Girls playing basketball. Personal photograph by Granger Goetz. 2011. JPEG file.

社交媒体

73. 电子邮件信息

Bailey, Natasha. "Re: Cairo." Message to the author. 27 Mar. 2012. E-mail.

对于电子邮件，要列出写信人的姓名；电子邮件的主题栏上的标题（如果有的话），用引号标示；Message to the author（或除你之外的收信人姓名）；信息的日期；和媒介E-mail。你不需要列举你浏览电子邮件的日期。

74. 讨论小组上的帖子

Williams, Frederick. "Circles as Primitive." *The Math Forum @ Drexel*. Drexel U, 28 Feb. 2008. E-mail.

引用讨论小组的帖子，要采用与博客文章一样的格式。（格式55，p. 472）上面这个例子显示了一个讨论列表上的帖子。它包含作者姓名、帖子的标题、讨论列表的名称、主办者、发帖日期和媒介（E-mail）。如果帖子没有标题，代之以Online posting。你不需要添加浏览日期。

75. 社交网站上的帖子

Aneke, Chinwe. Online comment. *Girls Inc*. Facebook, 18 Apr. 2012. Web. 6 May 2012.

引用社交网站上的帖子，要列出作者姓名、帖子类型和页标题。后接主办者、发帖日期、媒介和你浏览的日期。

76. 推特

Bittman, Mark (bittman). "Don't blame the potato for Pringles: http://nyti.ms/w5YMFf." 21 Feb. 2012, 8:04 p.m. Tweet.

引用推特，要列出作者姓名，后接使用者姓名。（如果两者都有，而且两者不是同一人）要完整列出推特，使用作者的大小写格式。最后添加日期、时间和媒介（Tweet）。

在CD-ROM或DVD-ROM上的出版物

77. 非周期性的CD-ROM或DVD-ROM

Nunberg, Geoffrey. "Usage in the Dictionary." *The American Heritage Dictionary of the English Language*. 4th ed. Boston: Houghton, 2000. CD-ROM.

和印刷版书籍一样，单次发行的CD-ROM可以是百科全书、字典、书籍和其他只出版一次的原始资料。遵循格式19—37印刷版书籍的样式（pp. 457–464）列举此类资料，但是用CD-ROM或DVD-ROM代替Print。如果光盘的供应商和作品的出版商不一样，要在媒介后添加供应商的发行地、名称和发行日期。

另请参见格式28（p. 461）和格式49（p. 470）引用印刷版和网络上的参考书。

78. 周期性的CD-ROM或DVD-ROM

Kolata, Gina. "Gauging Body Mass Index in a Changing Body." *New York Times* 28 June 2005, natl. ed.: D1+. CD-ROM. *New York Times Ondisc*. UMI-ProQuest. Sept. 2005.

CD-ROM和DVD-ROM上的数据库是定期发行的，如每半年一次或每年一次。此类数据库里的期刊、报纸和其他出版物一般也有印刷版，所以你的所引用作品条目应该提供两个格式的信息。以印刷版的信息开始，按照格式7—18（pp. 453–457）列举此类原始资料，然后媒介用CD-ROM或DVD-ROM代替Print，后接数据库名称、供应商名称和数据库的发行信息。

8 ▪ 其他印刷版和非印刷版原始资料

本部分涵盖的原始资料类型不在电脑上，一般也不属于印刷版的原始资料。当你通过电子媒介或平面媒介找到这些原始资料时，它们中大多数的引用格式与本章其他地方谈到的引用格式相似。参见格式16（p. 457）引用平面采访。参见格式50—53（pp. 470–471）引用只能在网络上获得的图像、电视和广播节目、录像和录音。参见格式59—61（p. 473）引用可以在网络和其他媒介上获得的此类原始资料。参见格式72引用数字文档里的此类原始资料。

79. 电视或广播节目

"Moment of Truth." By Shonda Rhimes and Zakiyyah Alexander. Dir. Chandra Wilson. *Grey's Anatomy*. ABC. KGO, San Francisco, 26 Apr. 2012. Television.

先列出节目名称，除非你引用的是某个人或某些人的作品。上面的例子引用了一期节目的名称（用引号标示）以及作者和导演的姓名（分别用By和Dir.标示）。然后用斜体字标示节目名称、网络名称、呼号、地方台所在城市、日期和媒介

(Television)。如果你列出为整个节目而不是某一集工作的人，请在节目名称后面加上他们的名字。

80. 个人或广播、电视采访

Wang, Charlotte. Personal interview. 12 Mar. 2012.

Rudolph, Maya. Interview by Terry Gross. *Fresh Air*. Natl. Public Radio. WGBH, Boston, 10 Mar. 2012. Radio.

先列出被采访者的姓名。对于你自己进行的采访，明确Personal interview或者媒介（如Telephone interview或者E-mail interview），然后提供采访日期。对于你听到或看到的采访，要提供采访标题（如果有的话）或者Interview（如果没有采访标题）。添加采访者的姓名（如果能确认的话）。然后根据原始资料种类（此处为广播节目）采用恰当的格式，以媒介（此处为Radio）收尾。

81. 录音

Rubenstein, Artur, perf. Piano Concerto no. 2 in B-flat. By Johannes Brahms. Cond. Eugene Ormandy. Philadelphia Orch. RCA, 1972. LP.

Springsteen, Bruce. "This Life." *Working on a Dream*. Columbia, 2009. CD.

先列出所引用作品的作者姓名。确定作者身份，除非他或她是作曲家，例如，第一个例子中的perf.（"performer"）。如果引用的作品有明确的类型、作品编号和调（第一个例子），作品名称不需要用引号或斜体字标示。如果你引用的是歌曲或歌词（第二个例子），则用引号标示作品名称，用斜体字标示唱片的名称。然后，在By之后列出作曲家或作者的姓名（如果之前没有标注的话）和其他你想提及的参与者的姓名。最后提供录音的制作者、发行日期和媒介：第一个例子中的LP和第二个例子中的CD。

82. 电影、DVD或录像

The Joneses. Screenplay by Chris Tyrrell and Stacey Cruwys. Dir. Chris Tyrrell. Bjort. 2010. Film.

先列出作品名称，除非你引用的是某个人的作品。（参见p. 482中的例子）一般来说，要确认并提供导演的姓名。如果你认为合适，可以列举其他参与者的姓名。对于电影来说，以发行商、发行日期和媒介（Film）收尾。

对于DVD或录像带，要包括原始发行日期（如果有的话）、发行商的名称、发行日期和媒介（DVD或Videocassette）：

Balanchine, George, chor. *Serenade*. Perf. San Francisco Ballet. Dir. Hilary Bean.

1991. PBS Video, 2006. DVD.

83. 绘画、照片或其他视觉艺术作品

Arnold, Leslie. *Seated Woman*. N.d. Oil on canvas. DeYoung Museum, San Francisco.

Sugimoto, Hiroshi. *Pacific Ocean, Mount Tamalpais*. 1994. Photograph. Private collection.

对于你目睹的艺术品，要列出艺术家的姓名、作品名称（用斜体字标示）、创作日期（如果日期未知，用N.d标注），然后提供作品的媒介（如Oil on canvas 或Photograph）和作品持有方的名字和地址（如果有的话。如果没有，则使用Private collection）。

如果你见到的只是复制品，那么要提供所使用原始资料的完整出版信息。省略作品自身的媒介，代之以复制媒介品（如下面例子中的Print）。如果你查看的是实际作品，则可以省略此类信息。

Hockney, David. *Place Furstenberg, Paris*. 1985. Coll. Art Gallery, New Paltz. *David Hockney: A Retrospective*. Ed. Maurice Tuchman and Stephanie Barron. Los Angeles: Los Angeles County Museum of Art, 1988. 247. Print.

84. 私人照片

American white pelicans on Lake Winnebago. Personal photograph by the author. 3 Apr. 2012.

对于你自己或他人的私人照片，要提供照片主题（不用引号或斜体字标示）、摄影者姓名和日期。（最新版的 *MLA Handbook for Writers of Research Papers* 没有包括私人照片，因此，此格式来自之前的版本）

85. 地图、表格、图表或示意图

"The Sonoran Desert." Map. *Sonoran Desert: An American Deserts Handbook*. By Rose Houk. Tucson: Western Natl. Parks Assn., 2000. 12. Print.

列出插图的标题，除非原始资料已经标明插图作者。如果插图来自另一个出版物，则用引号标示插图的标题。如果插图是单独出版的，则用斜体字标示插图的标题。然后添加作品的描述（Map, Chart等）、出版信息和媒介（此处为Print）。

86. 漫画或连载漫画

Trudeau, Garry. "Doonesbury." Comic strip. *San Francisco Chronicle* 1 Sept. 2012: E6. Print.

列出艺术家的姓名、作品名称（用引号标示）、作品描述（Cartoon 或 Comic strip）、出版信息和媒介（此处为 Print）。

87. 广告

Fusion Hybrid by Ford. Advertisement. *New Yorker* 23 Apr. 2012: 91. Print.

列出产品或公司名称、类型（Advertisement）、出版信息和媒介（Print，Television，Radio 等）。

88. 演出

Muti, Riccardo, cond. Chicago Symphony Orch. Symphony Center, Chicago. 5 May 2012. Performance.

The New Century. By Paul Rudnick. Dir. Nicholas Martin. Mitzi E. Newhouse Theater, New York. 6 May 2009. Performance.

对于现场演出，可参考引用电影的格式。（格式82）先列出作品的名称（第二个例子），除非你引用的是某个人的作品（第一个例子）。在标题之后，提供参与者的相关信息、演出剧院、演出城市和演出日期。以媒介（Performance）收尾。

89. 演讲、讲座、致辞或读物

Fontaine, Claire. "Economics." Museum of Contemporary Art. North Miami. 5 June 2011. Address.

列出发言人的姓名、标题（如果有的话，用引号标示）、会议名称（如果有的话）、主办方的名称、发言的地点和日期。最后以发言类型的描述词（Lecture，Speech，Address，Reading）收尾。

虽然MLA格式没有提供引用课堂讲座的明确例子，但是你可以根据原始资料的类型改述之前的格式。

Cavanaugh, Carol. Class lecture on mentors. Lesley U. 4 Apr. 2012. Lecture.

> **练习56.1** 撰写所引用作品条目
>
> 从以下信息中准备作品引用条目。遵循本章中给出的MLA格式，除非你的导师指定了不同的格式。按字母顺序排列完成的条目，不要编号。带星号部分的参考答

案请见书后。

*1. An article titled "Who's Responsible for the Digital Divide?" in the March 2011 issue of the journal *Information Society*, volume 27, issue2. The article appeared on pages 92-104. The authors are Dmitry Epstein, Erik C. Nisbet, and Tarleton Gillespie. You found the article on April 19, 2012, using the online database *Academic Search Complete*.

*2. A Web article with no listed author on the Web site *Digital Divide Institute*. The sponsor of the site is DigitalDivide.org. The title of the article is "Banking the Unbanked" and the site is dated 2010. You consulted the site on April 20, 2012.

*3. A print book titled *Technology and Social Inclusion: Rethinking the Digital Divide* by Mark Warschauer. The book was published in 2003 by MIT Press in Cambridge, Massachusetts.

*4. An article in the newspaper the *New York Times*, published in the national edition on December 13, 2010, on page B3. The author is Teddy Wayne. The title is "Digital Divide Is a Matter of Income." You accessed the source through the database *LexisNexis Academic* on April 19, 2012.

5. A government report you consulted online on April 20, 2012. The author is the National Telecommunications and Information Administration, an agency within the United States Department of Commerce.The title of the report is "A Nation Online: Entering the Broadband Age." It was published on the NTIA Web site in September 2004.

6. An e-mail interview you conducted with Naomi Lee on April 23, 2012.

7. A blog posting to the Web site *Code for America* by Lauren Dyson.The title is "How Will Gov 2.0 Address the Digital Divide?" The posting is dated February 15, 2011. The sponsor of the site is Code for America. You consulted the source on April 21, 2012.

56c 用 MLA 格式撰写论文

MLA Handbook for Writers of Research Papers 为非常简单的文件格式提供了指导准则，涉及了几个要素。至于字体、标题、目录、图像及其他MLA格式没有详细说明的特征，请参见pp. 66–75。

下方的例子显示了论文第一页和最后一页的格式。至于参考目录的格式，请参见p. 448。

» **MLA论文第一页**

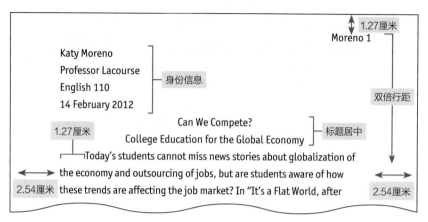

» **MLA论文最后一页**

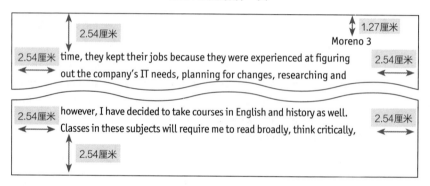

页边距：论文每一页的四边留出1英寸（2.54厘米）的页边距。

行距和缩进：全文双倍行距，段落首行缩进0.5英寸（1.27厘米）。（见下方和p.486中对诗歌和长散文的处理方式）

分页：从第一页开始给论文编号，按顺序编到最后一页（包括参考目录）。用阿拉伯数字（1，2，3）标示在右上角距页边0.5英寸（1.27厘米）处。在页码前标出你的姓氏，以免散页搞混。

身份信息和论文标题：MLA格式不要求论文有书名页。相反，你得分行列出你的姓名、老师姓名、课程名称、日期。将这些身份信息置于首页左上方距页边1英寸（2.54厘米）处，和页边距对齐且双倍行距。

再次双倍行距，并将论文标题居中。不要将题目排成斜体、不要加下画线、不要排成粗体、不要放大字体或加引号。按照p.358的准则用大写字母输入标题单词。标题的各行之间以及标题和正文之间均要双倍行距。

诗歌和长散文的引用：单行诗歌的引用格式与其他引文格式相同：将诗歌插入文中，前后用引号标示。你也可以插入两行或三行的诗歌，它们之间用斜线分隔，再空一格。

An example of Robert Frost's incisiveness is in two lines from "Death of the Hired Man": "Home is the place where, when you have to go there / They have to take you in" (119-20).

三行以上的诗歌需要单独引用。引文的前后要双倍行距。引文要向右缩进1英寸（2.54厘米）。**不要加引号**。

In "The Author to Her Book," written in 1678, Anne Bradstreet characterizes her book as a child. In these lines from the poem, she captures a parent's and a writer's frustration with the imperfections of her offspring:

> I washed thy face, but more defects I saw,
> and rubbing off a spot, still made a flaw.
> I stretched thy joints to make thee even feet,
> Yet still thou run'st more hobbling than is meet. (13-16)

四行以上的散文引用，也要单独排版。和之前的诗歌例子一样，双倍行距，向右缩进1英寸（2.54厘米）。**不要加引号**。

In the influential *Talley's Corner* from 1967, Elliot Liebow observes that "unskilled" construction work requires more skill than is generally assumed:

> A healthy, sturdy, active man of good intelligence requires from two to four weeks to break in on a construction job. . . . It frequently happens that his foreman or the craftsman he services is not willing to wait that long for him to get into condition or to learn at a glance the difference in size between a rough 2 × 8 and a finished 2 × 10. (62)

引用一整段文字或一个段落的部分文字时，不要采用段落缩进。只有在引用两段或两段以上文字时才将段落缩进0.25英寸（0.635厘米）。

56d 用 MLA 格式写成的论文范例

p. 488开始的论文范例在总体格式、文中夹注和参考目录方面遵循了MLA格式的准则。页边空白处的注释突出了论文特点：深灰方框的文字处理格式和原始资料引用；浅灰方框的文字处理论文内容。

注意：因为范文讨论的是新近的话题，因此许多原始资料来自因特网，没有采用页码或其他参考编号,因而,原始资料的文内引文注释没有给出参考编号。在一篇纯粹依赖印刷版期刊、书籍和其他传统原始资料的论文中,大多数的文内引文注释要提供页码。

提纲注释

有些老师要求学生提交论文终稿的提纲。关于建构提纲的建议,请参见 pp. 21–24。以下是用完整句子撰写的范文的正式提纲。注意主题句放置在正式标题或句子提纲之前。

Thesis statement: Although green consumerism can help the environment, consumerism itself is the root of some of the most pressing ecological problems we face. To make a real difference, we must consume less.

I. Green products claiming to help the environment both appeal to and confuse consumers.

    A. The market for ecologically sound products is enormous.

    B. Determining whether or not a product is as green as advertised can be a challenge.

II. Green products don't solve the high rate of consumption that truly threatens the environment.

    A. Overconsumption is a significant cause of three of the most serious environmental problems.

        1. It depletes natural resources.

        2. It contributes to pollution, particularly from the greenhouse gases responsible for global warming.

        3. It produces a huge amount of solid waste.

    B. The availability of greener products has not reduced the environmental effects of consumption.

III. Since buying green products does not reduce consumption, other solutions must be found for environmental problems.

    A. Experts have proposed many far-reaching solutions, but they require concerted government action and could take decades to implement.

    B. For shorter-term solutions, individuals can change their own behavior as consumers.

        1. Precycling may be the greenest behavior that individuals can adopt.

            a. Precycling means avoiding purchase of products that use raw

    materials and excessive packaging.
  b. More important, precycling means avoiding purchases of new products whenever possible.
2. For unavoidable purchases, individuals can buy green products and influence businesses to embrace ecological goals.

Malik 1

Justin Malik
Ms. Rossi
English 112-02
18 April 2012

身份信息：作者姓名、老师姓名、课程名称、日期

The False Promise of Green Consumerism

标题居中

They line the aisles of just about any store. They seem to dominate television and print advertising. Chances are that at least a few of them belong to you. From organic jeans to household cleaners to hybrid cars, products advertised as environmentally friendly are readily available and are so popular they're trendy. It's easy to see why Americans are buying these things in record numbers. The new wave of "green" consumer goods makes an almost irresistible promise: we can save the planet by shopping.

全文双倍行距

引言：用例子引出话题（第一段）和背景信息（第二段）

Saving the planet does seem to be urgent. Thanks partly to former vice president Al Gore, who sounded the alarm in 2006 with *An Inconvenient Truth* and again in 2009 with *Our Choice*, the threat of global warming has become a regular feature in the news media and a recurring theme in popular culture. Unfortunately, as Gore himself points out, climate change is just one of many environmental problems competing for our attention: the rainforests are vanishing, our air and our water are dangerously polluted, alarming numbers of species are facing extinction, and landfills are overflowing (*Our Choice* 32). All the bad news can be overwhelming, and most people feel powerless to halt the damage. Thus it is reassuring that we may be able to help by making small changes in what we buy—

引文格式：没有使用文中夹注，因为作者和书名都已在文中提及，而且讨论引用了整部作品

引文格式：同一个作者两部作品中的一部的标题格式

Malik 2

but that is not entirely true. Although green consumerism can help the environment, consumerism itself is the root of some of the most pressing ecological problems we face. To make a real difference, we must consume less.

The market for items perceived as ecologically sound is enormous. Experts estimate that spending on green products already approaches $500 billion a year in the United States (Bhanoo). Shoppers respond well to new options, whether the purchase is as minor as a bottle of chemical-free dish soap or as major as a front-loading washing machine. Not surprisingly, many businesses are responding by offering as many new eco-products as they can. Jack Neff reports in *Advertising Age* that the recent growth of green products is a "revolution" in marketing. He cites a market research report by Datamonitor: between 2007 and 2009, the number of new packaged goods labeled as green increased by 600%, and sales of organic food and beverages outpaced other options despite the higher costs (1). These new products are offered for sale at supermarkets and at stores like Walmart, Target, Home Depot, Starbucks, and Pottery Barn. It seems clear that green consumerism has grown into a mainstream interest.

Determining whether or not a product is as green as advertised can be a challenge. Claims vary: a product might be labeled as organic, biodegradable, energy efficient, recycled, carbon neutral, renewable, or just about anything that sounds environmentally positive. However, none of these terms carries a universally accepted meaning, and no enforceable labeling regulations exist (Dahl A248). Some of the new product options offer clear environmental benefits: for instance, LED lightbulbs last fifty times longer than regular bulbs and draw about 15% of the electricity ("Lightbulbs" 26, 27), and paper made from recycled fibers saves many trees. But other "green" products just as clearly do little or nothing to help the environment: a disposable razor made with less plastic is still a disposable razor, destined for a landfill after only a few uses.

Distinguishing truly green products from those that are not so green merely scratches the surface of a much larger issue. The products aren't the problem; it's our high rate of consumption that poses the real threat to the environment. We seek what's newer and better—whether cars, clothes, phones, computers, televisions, shoes, or gadgets—and they all require resources to make, ship, and use them. Political scientists Thomas Princen, Michael Maniates, and Ken Conca maintain that overconsumption is a leading force behind several ecological crises, warning that

> ever-increasing pressures on ecosystems, life-supporting environmental services, and critical natural cycles are driven not only by the sheer number of resource users . . . but also by the patterns of resource use themselves. (4)

Those patterns of resource use are disturbing. In just the last century, gross world product (the global output of consumer goods) grew at five times the rate of population growth—a difference explained by a huge rise in consumption per person. (See fig. 1.) Such growth might be good for the economy, but it is bad for the environment. As fig. 1 shows, it is accompanied by the depletion of natural resources, increases in the carbon emissions that cause global warming, and increases in the amount of solid waste disposal.

> 消费的环境影响。（接下来的四段）作者综合了六处原始资料的信息来形成自己的观点

> 超过三行的引文要单独引用，不需要引号。参见p. 486

> 省略号表示对引文的删减

> 所示引文的引用格式：放在句号之后。文中提及原始资料作者，因此不用在文内引文注释中列出作者姓名

> 文章提及并讨论了图表

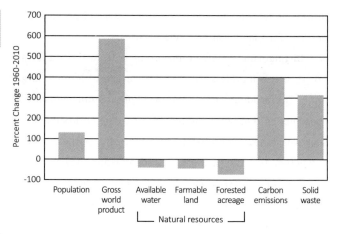

Fig 1. Global population, consumption, and environmental impacts, 1960-2010. Data from United Nations Development Programme; *Human Development Report: Changing Today's Consumption Patterns—For Tomorrow's Human Development* (New York: Oxford UP, 1998; print; 4); and from Earth Policy Inst.; "Data Center"; *Earth Policy Institute*; EPI, 12 Jan. 2011; Web; 16 Mar. 2011.

The first negative effect of overconsumption, the depletion of resources, occurs because the manufacture and distribution of any consumer product depends on the use of water, land, and raw materials such as wood, metal, and oil. Paul Hawken, a respected environmentalist, explains that just in the United States "[i]ndustry moves, mines, extracts, shovels, burns, wastes, pumps, and disposes of 4 *million pounds of material* in order to provide one average. . . family's needs for a year" (qtd. in DeGraaf, Wann, and Naylor 85; emphasis added). The United Nations Development Programme's 1998 *Human Development Report* (still the most comprehensive study of the environmental impacts of consumerism) warns that many regions in the world don't have enough water, productive soil, or forests to meet the basic needs of their populations (4). More recent data from the Earth Policy Institute show that as manufacturing and per-person consumption continue to rise, the supply of resources needed for survival continues to decline. Thus heavy consumption poses a threat not only to the environment but also to the well-being of

Malik 5

the human race.

    In addition to using up scarce natural resources, manufacturing and distributing products harm the earth by spewing pollution into the water, soil, and air. The most worrisome aspect of that pollution may be its link to global warming. As Al Gore explains, the energy needed to power manufacturing and distribution comes primarily from burning fossil fuels, a process that releases carbon dioxide and other greenhouse gases into the air. Those gases build up and trap heat in the earth's atmosphere. The result, most scientists now believe, is increasing global temperatures that will raise sea levels, expand deserts, and cause more frequent floods and hurricanes (*Inconvenient* 26-27, 81, 118-19, 184). As the bar chart in fig. 1 shows, carbon emissions, like production of consumer goods in general, are rising at rates out of proportion with population growth. The more we consume, the more we contribute to global warming.

    As harmful as they are, gradual global warming and the depletion of resources half a world away can be difficult to comprehend or appreciate. A more immediate environmental effect of our buying habits can be seen in the volumes of trash those habits create. The US Environmental Protection Agency found that in a single year (2010), US residents, corporations, and institutions produced 250 million tons of municipal solid waste, amounting to "4.43 pounds per person per day" (1). Nearly a third of that trash came just from the wrappers, cans, bottles, and boxes used for shipping consumer goods. Yet the mountains of trash left over from consumption are only a part of the problem. In industrial countries overall, 90% of waste comes not from what gets thrown out, but from the manufacturing processes of converting natural resources into consumer products (DeGraaf, Wann, and Naylor 198). Nearly everything we buy creates waste in production, comes in packaging that gets discarded immediately, and ultimately ends up in landfills that are already overflowing.

Malik 6

> 绿色消费的环境影响

Unfortunately, the growing popularity of green products has not reduced the environmental effects of consumption. A study conducted by economists Jeff Rubin and Benjamin Tal found that while eco-friendly and energy-efficient products have become more available, "consumption is growing by ever-increasing amounts." The authors give the example of automobiles: in the last generation, cars have become much more energy efficient, but the average American now drives 2500 more miles a year, for a net gain in energy use (4-5). At the same time, per-person waste production in the United States has risen by more than 20% (United States 2). Greener products may reduce our cost of consumption and even reduce our guilt about consumption, but they do not reduce consumption and its effects.

> 引文格式：文中提及作者姓名，所以只有页码

> 引文格式：文中没有提及美国政府的原始资料

> 作者根据之前的数据得出的结论

> 消费问题的解决之道（下面三段）

If buying green won't solve the problems caused by overconsumption, what will? Politicians, environmentalists, and economists have proposed an array of far-reaching ideas, including creating a financial market for carbon credits and offsets, aggressively taxing consumption and pollution, offering financial incentives for environmentally positive behaviors, and even abandoning market capitalism altogether (de Bias). However, all of these are "top-down" solutions that require concerted government action. Gaining support for any one of them, putting it into practice, and getting results could take decades. In the meantime, the environment would continue to deteriorate. Clearly, short-term solutions are also essential.

> 长期的解决之道

> 引文格式：只有作者的姓名，因为网络上的学术文章没有页码或其他参考编号

> 短期的解决之道：改变个人行为。

> 常识性定义和作者自己的例子不需要标注原始资料来源

The most promising short-term solution is for individuals to change their own behavior as consumers. The greenest behavior that individuals can adopt may be precycling, the term widely used for avoiding purchases of products that involve the use of raw materials. Precycling includes choosing eco-friendly products made of recycled or nontoxic materials (such as aluminum-free deodorants and fleece made from soda bottles) and avoiding items wrapped in excessive pack-aging (such as kitchen tools

Malik 7

strapped to cardboard and printer cartridges sealed in plastic clamshells). More important, though, precycling means not buying new things in the first place. Renting and borrowing, when possible, save money and resources; so do keeping possessions in good repair and not replacing them until absolutely necessary. Goodquality used items, from clothing to furniture to electronics, can be obtained for free, or very cheaply, through online communities like *Craigslist* and *Freecycle*, from thrift stores and yard sales, or by trading with friends and relatives. When consumers choose used goods over new, they can help to reduce demand for manufactured products that waste energy and resources, and they can help to keep unwanted items out of the waste stream.

Avoiding unnecessary purchases brings personal benefits as well. Brenda Lin, an environmental activist, explained in an e-mail interview that frugal living not only saves money but also provides pleasure:

> You'd be amazed at what people throw out or give away: perfectly good computers, oriental rugs, barely used sports equipment, designer clothes, you name it. . . . It's a game for me to find what I need in other people's trash or at Goodwill. You should see the shock on people's faces when I tell them where I got my stuff. I get almost as much enjoyment from that as from saving money and helping the environment at the same time.

Lin's experience relates to a study of the personal and social consequences of consumerism by the sociologist Juliet B. Schor. Schor found that the more people buy, the less happy they tend to feel because of the stress of working longer hours to afford their purchases (11-12). Researching the opposite effect, Schor conducted interviews with hundreds of Americans who had drastically reduced their spending so that they would be less

Malik 8

dependent on paid work. For these people, she discovered, a deliberately lower standard of living improved quality of life by leaving more time to spend with family and pursue personal interests (136-42). Reducing consumption, it turns out, does not have to translate into sacrifice.

For unavoidable purchases like food and light bulbs, buying green can make a difference by influencing corporate decisions. Some ecologists and economists believe that as more shoppers choose earth-friendly products over their traditional counterparts—or boycott products that are clearly harmful to the environment—more manufacturers and retailers will look for ways to limit the environmental effects of their industrial practices and the goods they sell (de Blas; Gore, *Inconvenient* 314). Indeed, as environmental business consultant Joel Makower and his coauthors point out, Coca-Cola, Walmart, Procter and Gamble, Dell, and other major companies have already taken up sustainability initiatives in response to market pressure. In the process, the companies have discovered that environmentally minded practices tend to raise profits and strengthen customer loyalty (5-6). By giving industry solid, bottom-line reasons to embrace ecological goals, consumer demand for earth-friendly products can magnify the effects of individual action.

Careful shopping can help the environment, but green doesn't necessarily mean "Go." All consumption depletes resources, increases the likelihood of global warming, and creates waste, so even eco-friendly products must be used in moderation. As individuals, we can each play a small role in helping the environment—and help ourselves at the same time—by not buying anything we don't really need, even if it seems environmentally sound. Reducing our personal impact on the earth is a small price to pay for preserving a livable planet for future generations.

Malik 9

Works Cited

Bhanoo, Sindya N. "Products That Are Earth-and-Profit Friendly." *New York Times*. New York Times, 11 June 2010. Web. 23 Mar. 2012.

Dahl, Richard. "Green Washing: Do You Know What You're Buying?" *Environmental Health Perspectives* 18.6 (2010): A246-52. *Academic Search Complete*. Web. 23 Mar. 2012.

de Blas, Alexandra. "Making the Shift: From Consumerism to Sustainability." *Ecos* 153 (2010): n. pag. Web. 25 Mar. 2012.

DeGraaf, John, David Wann, and Thomas H. Naylor. *Affluenza: The All-Consuming Epidemic*. 2nd ed. San Francisco: Berrett-Koehler, 2005. Print.

Earth Policy Inst. "Data Center." *Earth Policy Institute*. EPI, 12 Jan. 2011. Web. 16 Mar. 2012.

Gore, Al. *An Inconvenient Truth: The Planetary Emergency of Global Warming and What We Can Do about It*. Emmaus: Rodale, 2006. Print.

---. *Our Choice: A Plan to Solve the Climate Crisis*. Emmaus: Rodale, 2009. Print.

"Lightbulbs." *Consumer Reports* Oct. 2010: 26-28. Print.

Lin, Brenda. Message to the author. 21 Mar. 2012. E-mail.

Makower, Joel, et al. *State of Green Business 2011*. GreenBiz.com. GreenBiz Group, 2011. Web. 25 Mar. 2012.

Neff, Jack. "Green-Marketing Revolution Defies Economic Turndown." *Advertising Age* 20 Apr. 2009: 1+. *Academic Search Complete*. Web. 25 Mar. 2012.

Princen, Thomas, Michael Maniates, and Ken Conca. Introduction. *Confronting Consumption*. Ed. Princen, Maniates, and Conca. Cambridge: MIT P, 2002. 1-20. Print.

Rubin, Jeff, and Benjamin Tal. "Does Energy Efficiency Save Energy?" *StrategEcon*. CIBC World Markets, 27 Nov. 2007. Web. 23 Apr. 2012.

Schor, Juliet B. *The Overspent American: Upscaling, Downshifting,*

Malik 10

496 一个团体作者的印刷版书籍	*and the New Consumer*. New York: Basic, 1998. Print. United Nations Development Programme. *Human Development Report: Changing Today's Consumption Patterns—For Tomorrow's Human Development*. New York: Oxford UP, 1998. Print.
没有标注作者的美国政府的资料，所以将政府机构名称视为作者	United States. Environmental Protection Agency. Solid Waste and Emergency Response. *Municipal Solid Waste Generation, Recycling, and Disposal in the United States: Facts and Figures for 2010*. US Environmental Protection Agency, Dec. 2011. Web. 4 Apr. 2012.

497

第57章　APA 原始资料来源的标注与格式

概要

- 在文内引文注释中标注原始资料（下页）
- 准备APA格式的参考目录（p. 500）（见p. 503格式索引）
- 遵照关于页边距、行距、长引文和其他元素的APA格式准则（p. 516）
- 查阅APA格式的论文范例（p. 519）

心理学和其他社会科学的格式指导是 *Publication Manual of the American Psychological Association*（2010年第6版）。美国心理学协会在www.apastyle.org/learn/faqs/index.aspx（因某些原因可能会无法访问）网站上提供常见问题的答案。

在APA格式中，你要两次标明每一个原始资料：

- 在文章中，所借用的原始资料后简单的文内引文注释引导读者查看你所参考作品的完整目录。
- 在论文的最后，参考文献包括每一个原始资料的完整的书目信息。

参考文献中的每一个条目有至少一个对应的文内引文注释，每一个文内引文注释都有一个对应的参考文献条目。

57a 在文章中使用 APA 文内引文注释

在APA原始资料来源的标注格式中，文章正文中的文内引文注释让读者去参考文章最后的原始资料清单。参见下方中不同类型原始资料的格式索引。

注意：当你在一个段落中不止一次引用同一原始资料时，只要引文明确你所参考的原始资料，APA格式不要求你在第一次引用之后重复标注日期。如果原始资料清单包含同一作者的一部以上作品，那么每次引用都要标注日期。

1. 你的文章中没有提到作者姓名

One critic of Milgram's experiments questioned whether the researchers behaved morally toward their subjects (Baumrind, 1988).

如果你没有在文章中提到作者姓名，要在括号内列出作者的姓氏、原始资料的日期，有时候需要如下所示的页码。用逗号分隔各要素。将引文放在恰当的位置，这样可以清晰表示正在标注的是哪些原始资料，而且引文可以尽可能顺畅地融入你的句子结构中。（参见pp. 445–446指导准则）

APA文内引文注释

1. 你的文章中没有提到作者姓名, p. 497
2. 你的文章中提到了作者姓名, p. 498
3. 有两个作者的作品, p. 498
4. 有三个到五个作者的作品, p. 499
5. 有六个或六个以上作者的作品, p. 499
6. 团队作者的作品, p. 499
7. 没有作者的作品或匿名作品, p. 499
8. 同一作者的两部或两部以上作品中的一部, p. 500
9. 不同作者的两部或两部以上作品, p. 500
10. 间接原始资料, p. 500
11. 电子版原始资料, p. 500

APA格式要求对直接引用加注页码或其他识别数字，对段落推荐加注识别数字，除非无法获得识别数字：

In the view of one critic of Milgram's experiments (Baumrind, 1988), the subjects "should have been fully informed of the possible effects on them" (p. 34).

在数字前使用恰当的缩略词，例如，p.表示页码，para.表示段落。识别数字可以如前面的例子所示单独标注在括号内，也可以与作者姓名和日期标注在一起。另请参见p. 500格式11。

2. 你的文章中提到了作者姓名

Baumrind (1988) insisted that the subjects in Milgram's study "should have been fully informed of the possible effects on them" (p. 34).

当你在文章中提到了作者的姓名，就不用在文内引文注释中重复作者姓名。在作者姓名之后用括号标注原始资料的日期。在所借用材料之后标注原始资料所在页码或段落（如例子中所示），或者将它和日期标注在一起：(1988, p. 34)。

3. 有两个作者的作品

Bunning and Ellis (2010) revealed significant communication differences between teachers and students.

One study (Bunning & Ellis, 2010) revealed significant communication differences between teachers and students.

在文章中，两个作者之间用and连接。在文内引文注释中，两个作者之间用&连接。

4. 有三个到五个作者的作品

Pepinsky, Dunn, Rentl, and Corson (1999) demonstrated the biases evident in gestures.

第一次引用三到五个作者的作品时，需列出所有作者的姓名。

在第二次和接下来的引用中，通常只提供第一个作者的姓名，后接et al.（拉丁语的缩略词）：

In the work of Pepinsky et al. (1999), the Loaded gestures included head shakes and eye contact.

但是，同一年出版的两个或多个原始资料可能会以同样的格式表示——例如，两个引用都缩写为Pepinsky et al., 1999。在这种情况下，尽可能多地列出作者的姓氏，以区分原始资料，然后接et al., 例如, (Pepinsky, Dunn, et al., 1999)和(Pepinsky, Bradley, et al., 1999)。

5. 有六个或六个以上作者的作品

One study (McCormack et al., 2012) explored children's day-to-day experience of living with a speech impairment.

对于六个或六个以上作者的作品，即便是在第一次引用的时候，也只需提供第一个作者的姓名，后接et al.。如果在同一年中发表的两个或两个以上的来源缩写为相同的形式，则按格式4所解释的提供额外的姓氏。

6. 团体作者的作品

The students' later work improved significantly (Lenschow Research, 2011).

对于以机构、中介、公司或其他团体为作者的作品，可将团体名称视作一个人的姓名。如果团体的名称很长，且其缩略词为大家所熟知，你可以在第二次和接下来的引用中使用缩略词。例如，你可以将美国心理学协会缩写为APA。

7. 没有作者的作品或匿名作品

One article ("Leaping the Wall," 2012) examines Internet freedom and censorship in China.

对于没有标注作者的作品，可以在原来标注作者姓名的地方代之以标题的前两个或三个单词（不包括A, An或The）。用斜体字标注书名和期刊名称，用引号标注文章标题，标题中的重要词需要大写。（但是在参考目录中，文章标题不加引号，只需将期刊标题的首字母大写。参见p. 502）

对于作者为"匿名"的作品，在文内引文注释中标注"Anonymous"：(Anonymous, 2012)。

8. 同一作者的两部或两部以上作品中的一部

At about age seven, most children begin to use appropriate gestures to reinforce their stories (Gardner, 1973a).

当你引用同一作者的两部或两部以上作品中的一部时，出版日期将告知读者你指的是哪部作品，只要你的参考目录只包括作者在那一年出版的一个资料来源。如果你的参考目录列出该作者**在同一年中**出版了不止一部作品，那么作品需要按字母顺序标出。（参见p. 504）文内引文注释应该在出版日期后标注恰当的字母。

9. 不同作者的两部或两部以上作品

Two studies (Marconi & Hamblen, 1999; Torrence, 2010) found that monthly safety meetings can dramatically reduce workplace injuries.

按照作者姓氏的字母顺序排列原始资料。原始资料之间用分号隔开。

10. 间接的原始资料

Supporting data appeared in a study by Wong (as cited in Gallivan, 2012).

"as cited in"这个短语表示Wong的研究是在Gallivan的作品中发现的。只有Gallivan这个姓氏出现在参考目录中。

11. 电子版原始资料

Ferguson and Hawkins (2011) did not anticipate the "evident hostility" of participants (para. 6).

电子原始资料的引用和印刷版原始资料相似，通常列出作者的姓氏和出版日期。引用或改述按段落编号而非按页编号的电子版原始资料时，要提供段落号码，并在段落号码前加para.。如果原始资料不是按页或段落编号，而是编号中包含了标题，那么要标注出现引文的标题和段落号码，例如，(Endter & Decker, 2012, Method section, para. 3)。当原始资料没有按页或段落编号，或者没有提供惯常的标题，则省略参考号码。

57b 准备APA格式的参考目录

在APA格式中，文内引文注释将读者引向文章最后的原始资料清单，将此清单命名为"References"，并在清单中包含论文中引用过的原始资料的完整出版信息。将此清单作为单独的一部分放在论文最后，接着之前论文的页码给这部分内容编上页码。

下面的例子显示了APA格式中参考目录首页的格式：

》APA参考列表

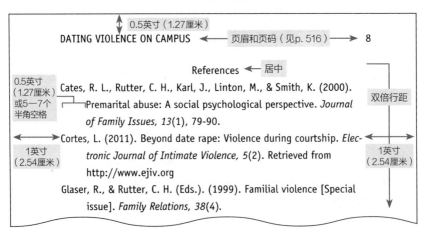

排列顺序：按照作者姓氏的字母顺序排列原始资料。如果没有作者，则按照标题中第一个主要单词的字母顺序排列。

行距：如范例所示，参考目录中的所有内容均需双倍行距，除非老师要求

使用单倍行距。（如果条目使用单倍行距，两个条目之间则需使用双倍行距）

缩进：如范例所示，每一个条目均从左边距处开始，从第二行开始向右缩进5—7个半角空格或0.5英寸（1.27厘米）。文字处理软件可以自动形成这种所谓的悬挂式缩进。

标点符号：用句号和一个半角空格分隔各个部分（作者姓名、出版日期、书名和出版信息）。不要在包含DOI和URL的参考目录中使用句号。（见p. 508）

作者姓名：对于有七个以下（含七个）作者的作品，先列出所有作者的姓氏，用逗号分隔作者姓名和姓名的各个部分。即使原始资料中完整列出了名和中间名，也只使用它们的首字母。最后一个作者的姓名前使用&符号。参见格式3（p. 504）八个或八个以上作者的处理方式。

出版日期：在作者姓名之后用括号标示出版日期，后接句号。虽然对于一些原始资料（如杂志和报纸文章）来说，出版日期包括月份，有时候也包括出版日，但一般来说，出版日期只是指出版年份。

书名：书名或标题的第一个单词的首字母、副标题的第一个单词的首字母和专有名词需要大写，其他单词都需要小写。期刊名称中的所有重要单词的首字母均需要大写。书名和期刊名要用斜体字标示。文章标题不需要用斜体字标示或使用引号。

出版城市和州：对于非周期性的原始资料（如书籍或政府出版物），要提供出版城市、逗号、所在州的两个字母的邮政缩写和冒号。如果出版社为大学且其名称中包含了所在州的名称，如University of Arizona，则省略州名。

出版社名称：对于非周期性的原始资料，在出版地点和冒号之后列出出版社的名称。许多出版社的名称需要用缩写（如用Morrow表示William Morrow）并省略Co., Inc.和Publishers等词。但是，对于协会、社团和大学出版社（如Harvard University Press），要使用全称，并且不要省略出版社名称中的Books或Press。

页码：在书籍和报纸的页码前标注缩略词p.或pp.。对于期刊或杂志，则不要使用缩略词p.或pp.。对于包含首末页的页码，要列出完整数字，如pp. 667–668。

DOI（数字对象标识符）：许多出版社给期刊文章和其他文件配置了DOI。DOI充当文本的唯一标识符和链接。如果有DOI，任何印刷版或电子版原始资料的引用均需要包含它。（参见p. 509格式18的范例）DOI后不要加句号。

p. 503是APA格式的索引。如果你找不到原始资料的格式，试着找一个接近的格式，并提供详尽的信息，这样读者就可以追溯原始资料。通常，你需要组合多个格式，以便准确引用原始资料。

1 ▪ 作者

1. 一个作者

Rodriguez, R. (1982). *A hunger of memory: The education of Richard Rodriguez.*
    Boston, MA: Godine.

开头的R.代替了作者的名字,尽管原始资料中列出了作者的全名。在这个书名中,只大写了标题和副标题的首字母和专有名词。

APA格式参考目录

1. 作者
  1. 一个作者 p. 502
  2. 两到七个作者 p. 503
  3. 八个或八个以上作者 p. 504
  4. 团体作者 p. 504
  5. 作者未标注(匿名)p. 504
  6. 同一个作者在同一年里出版的两个或多个作品 p. 504

2. 周期性的印刷版原始资料:期刊、报纸、杂志
  7. 期刊文章(印刷版)p. 505, p. 506
  8. 期刊文章的摘要(印刷版)p. 505
  9. 报纸文章(印刷版)p. 505
  10. 杂志文章(印刷版)p. 505
  11. 评论(印刷版)p. 507

3. 印刷版书籍
  12. 书籍的基本格式(印刷版)p. 507
  13. 有编者的书籍(印刷版)p. 507
  14. 有译者的书籍(印刷版)p. 507
  15. 再版的书籍(印刷版)p. 507
  16. 多卷册的作品(印刷版)p. 507
  17. 经过编辑的书籍中的文章或章节(印刷版)p. 508

4. 网络和其他电子版原始资料
  18. 有DOI(数字对象标识符)的期刊文章(网络版)p. 509, p. 510
  19. 没有DOI的期刊文章(网络版)p. 509
  20. 在线数据库中没有DOI的期刊文章(网络版)p. 509
  21. 期刊文章的摘要(网络版)p. 509
  22. 报纸文章(网络版)p. 509
  23. 杂志文章(网络版)p. 511
  24. 只出现在网络上的期刊内容(网络版)p. 511
  25. 评论(网络版)p. 511
  26. 组织或政府网站上的报道或其他资料(网络版)p. 511
  27. 书籍(网络版)p. 512
  28. 参考书中的文章(网络版)p. 512
  29. 维基网站上的文章(网络版)p. 512
  30. 毕业论文(网络版)p. 512
  31. 播客(网络版)p. 513
  32. 电影或视频录像(网络版)p. 513
  33. 视觉资料(网络版)p. 513
  34. 博客或讨论小组上的帖子(网络版)p. 513
  35. 个人通信(文内引用)p. 513

5. 其他原始资料
  36. 报告(印刷版)p. 513
  37. 政府出版物(印刷版)p. 514
  38. 毕业论文(印刷版)p. 514
  39. 采访(印刷版)p. 514
  40. 电影 p. 515
  41. 音乐录音 p. 515
  42. 电视连续剧或一集电视剧 p. 515

2. 两到七个作者
Nesselroade, J. R., & Baltes, P. B. (1999). *Longitudinal research in behavioral studies*. New York, NY: Academic Press.

对于两到七个作者的作品,要用逗号分隔作者的姓名,最后一个作者的姓名之前加&符号。

3. 八个或八个以上作者
Wimple, P. B., Van Eijk, M., Potts, C. A., Hayes, J., Obergau, W. R., Smith, H., . . . Zimmer, S. (2001). *Case studies in moral decision making among adolescents*. San Francisco, CA: Jossey-Bass.

对于八个或八个以上作者的作品,要列出前六个作者的姓名,后接省略号(三个句号),然后列出最后一个作者的姓名。

4. 团体作者
Lenschow Research. (2011). *Trends in secondary curriculum*. Baltimore, MD: Arrow Books.

对于团体作者的作品,例如,研究团体、委员会、政府机构或公司,要将团体名称视作作者姓氏。在参考目录中,按照第一个主要单词(不包括The,A或An)的字母顺序排列作品。

5. 作者未标注(匿名)
Merriam-Webster's collegiate dictionary (11th ed.). (2008). Springfield, MA: Merriam-Webster.

The Conversation. (2012, April 16). *Time, 179*(15), 6.

对于没有标注作者姓名的作品,要列出作品的标题,并按照第一个主要单词(不包括The,A或An)的字母顺序排列作品。

对于作者标注为"匿名"的作品,要用Anonymous代替作者姓名,并将之作为姓名按照字母顺序排序。

Anonymous. (2012). *Teaching research, researching teaching*. New York, NY: Alpine Press.

6. 同一个作者在同一年里出版的两个或多个作品
Gardner, H. (1973a). *The arts and human development*. New York, NY: Wiley.

Gardner, H. (1973b). *The quest for mind: Piaget Lévi-Strauss, and the structuralist movement*. New York, NY: Knopf.

在引用同一个作者在同一年里出版的两个或多个作品时，要按照作品名称中首个主要单词的字母顺序排列作品，在出版日期后加字母以示区分。在文章中引用原始资料时，要使用出版日期和字母。（见p. 500）

引用同一个作者在不同年份出版的两个或多个作品时，要按照出版日期的先后排列原始资料，最早出版的作品排在第一位。

2 ▪ 周期性的印刷版原始资料：期刊、报纸、杂志

7. 期刊文章（印刷版）

Hirsh, A. T., Gallegos, J. C., Gertz, K. J., Engel, J. M., & Jensen, M. P. (2010). Symptom burden in individuals with cerebral palsy. *Journal of Rehabilitation Research & Development*, 47, 863-876.

参见p. 506中关于印刷版期刊文章和所需信息位置的基本格式的说明。

注意：有些期刊在一年内出版的各期的页码是连续编号的，因此每一期期刊的首页接着前一期的页码编号，如首页为p. 132或p. 416。对于这样的期刊，要如上所示在期刊名称后加注期号。页码足以将读者引向你所使用的期刊。其他期刊和大多数杂志的每一期都是以p. 1开始，对于这些期刊和杂志，要将期号放在括号内，紧跟在卷号后，不用斜体字标注。参见格式10。

8. 期刊文章的摘要（印刷版）

Emery, R. E. (2006). Marital turmoil: Interpersonal conflict and the children of discord and divorce. *Psychological Bulletin, 92*, 310-330. Abstract retrieved from *Psychological Abstracts*, 2007, 69, Item 1320.

当你引用文章摘要而不是文章本身时，要列出文章的完整出版信息，后接Abstract retrieved from和摘要选集的信息，包括名称、出版日期、卷号和期号、页码或其他参考编号（范例中的Item 1320）。

9. 报纸文章（印刷版）

Rosenberg, K. (2012, May 4). Building blocks of meaning, retranslated. *The New York Times*, pp. C28-C29.

在出版年份后加月和日。如果报纸名称中有The，不能省略该单词。页码前加p.或pp.。

10. 杂志文章（印刷版）

Wallace-Wells, B. (2012, April 16). Return of the radical. *Time, 179*(15), 38-42.

列出杂志的完整发行日期：年，后接逗号，月和日（如果有的话）。即使文章出现在不连续编页的杂志上，也要列出起止页码，无须用pp.。如果杂志有卷号和期号，要提供这些信息，因为各期杂志都是单独编页的。（参见格式7的注意事项）

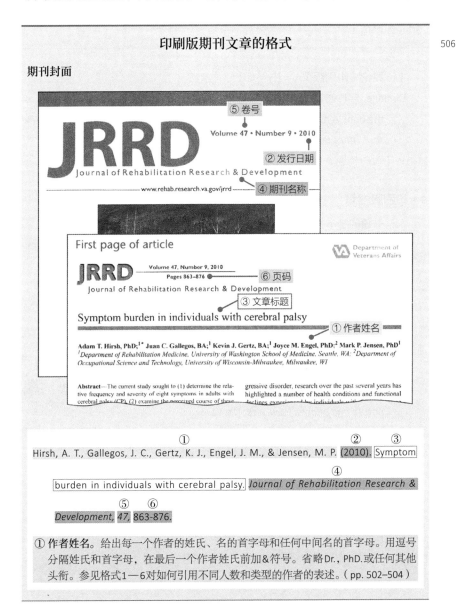

> ② 发行日期，用括号标示，后接句号。
>
> ③ 文章标题。列出完整的标题和副标题，用冒号分隔。标题和副标题第一个单词的首字母要大写。无须用引号标示标题。
>
> ④ 期刊名称，用斜体字标示。所有重要单词均要大写，以逗号收尾。
>
> ⑤ 卷号，用斜体字标示，后接逗号。见p.505何时需要包括期号。
>
> ⑥ 文章的起止页码，不用加缩略词pp.。不要省略任何数字。

11. 评论（印刷版）

Dinnage, R. (1987, November 29). Against the master and his men [Review of the book *A mind of her own: The life of Karen Horney,* by S. Quinn]. *The New York Times Book Review*, 10-11.

如果评论没有标题，则将方括号内的信息作为标题，保留方括号。

3 ▪ 印刷版书籍

12. 书籍的基本格式（印刷版）

Ehrenreich, B. (2007). *Dancing in the streets: A history of collective joy.* New York, NY: Holt.

根据格式1—4，列出作者姓名。然后列出完整的书名（包括副标题）。书名用斜体字标示。书名和副标题中第一个单词的首字母大写。以出版城市和州以及出版社名称收尾。（见p.502如何处理这些要素）

13. 有编者的书籍（印刷版）

Dohrenwend, B. S., & Dohrenwend, B. P. (Eds.). (1999). *Stressful life events: Their nature and effects*. New York, NY: Wiley.

将编者视作作者，列出其姓名，但是要在姓氏后接Ed.（一个编者）或Eds.（一个以上编者）。注意右括号前后的句号。

14. 有译者的书籍（印刷版）

Trajan, P. D. (1927). *Psychology of animals* (H. Simone, Trans.). Washington, DC: Halperin.

在书名之后列出左括号、译者的姓名，后接逗号、Trans.、右括号和句号。

15. 再版的书籍（印刷版）

Bolinger, D. L. (1981). *Aspects of language* (3rd ed.). New York, NY: Harcourt Brace Jovanovich.

版次在书名之后，用括号标示，后接句号。

16. 多卷册的作品（印刷版）

Lincoln, A. (1953). *The collected works of Abraham Lincoln* (R. P. Basler, Ed.). (Vol. 5). New Brunswick, NJ: Rutgers University Press.

Lincoln, A. (1953). *The collected works of Abraham Lincoln* (R. P. Basler, Ed.). (Vols. 1-8). New Brunswick, NJ: Rutgers University Press.

上面的第一个条目引用了一套8卷册作品中的一卷（第5卷）。上面的第二个条目引用了全部8卷作品。在括号内标注Vol.或Vols.，括号后接句号。如果没有编者的姓名，这部分内容直接标注在作品名称之后：*The collected works of Abraham Lincoln* (Vol. 5)。

17. 经过编辑的书籍中的文章或章节（印刷版）

Paykel, E. S. (1999). Life stress and psychiatric disorder: Applications of the clinical approach. In B. S. Dohrenwend & B. P. Dohrenwend (Eds.), *Stressful life events: Their nature and effects* (pp. 239-264). New York, NY: Wiley.

将选集的出版日期（范例中的1999）作为文章或章节的出版日期。在文章或章节的标题和句号之后，标注In和编者姓名（按正常顺序）、(Eds.)和逗号、选集名称和标示在括号内的文章起止页码。

4 ▪ 网络和其他电子版原始资料

在APA格式中，大多数电子版参考文献的列举方式和印刷版参考文献一样：以作者、日期、标题为开始。然后，你要添加如何检索原始资料的信息。

- 如果有DOI（数字对象标识符）的话，要提供原始资料的DOI而不是URL（统一资源定位符）。你可以在原始资料中找到DOI，或者点击"Article"或"Cross-Ref"找到DOI。参见格式18、格式23和格式25关于DOI的范例。
- 在无法获得DOI时，要列出URL。在以Retrieved from为开始的句子中提供URL。对于大多数原始资料，要使用原始资料所在网站主页的URL。（参见格式19和格式22）只有难以在主页上找到原始资料时，才使用完整的URL。（参见格式32）
- 不要在DOI或URL之后添加句号。

- 只在标点符号（如句号或斜线）前将DOI或URL断开分成两行标注。（但是在http://中，要在两个斜线后断开）不要用连字符连接URL或DOI。
- 通常不用提供你的浏览日期。只有在原始资料可能有所变化或缺少出版日期或版本编号的情况下才需提供浏览日期。

如果你找不到某个特殊原始资料的格式，可以在p. 503格式索引中查找类似的原始资料类型并加以改编。如果原始资料不包含完整引用所需的全部信息，查找并列举你能找到的信息。

18. 有DOI（数字对象标识符）的期刊文章（网络版）

Kelley-Weeder, S., Phillips, K., & Rounseville, S. (2011). Effectiveness of public health programs for decreasing alcohol consumption. *Patient Intelligence, 3*, 29-38. doi:10.2147/PI.S12431

见p. 510有DOI的网络或数据库文章以及原始资料所需信息位置的基本格式。

19. 没有DOI的期刊文章（网络版）

Polletta, F. (2008). Just talk: Public deliberation after 9/11. *Journal of Public Deliberation, 4*(1). Retrieved from http://services.bepress.com/jpd

当网络上的期刊文章没有DOI时，要在以Retrieved from为开始的句子中列出期刊主页的URL。URL后不用添加句号。

20. 在线数据库中没有DOI的期刊文章（网络版）

Rosen, I. M., Maurer, D. M., & Darnall, C. R. (2008). Reducing tobacco use in adolescents. *American Family Physician, 77*, 483-490. Retrieved from http://www.aafp.org/online/en/home/publications/journals/afp.html

如果数据库文章有DOI，采用格式18或格式23。如果没有，则用搜索引擎找到期刊的主页，再如上所示列出该主页的URL。

如果你找不到期刊的主页，则要如下面的例子所示，在检索句中列入数据库的名称：

Smith, E. M. (1926, March). Equal rights—internationally! *Life and Labor Bulletin, 4*, 1-2. Retrieved from Women and Social Movements in the United States, 1600-2000, database.

21. 期刊文章的摘要（网络版）

Polletta, F. (2008). Just talk: Public deliberation after 9/11.*Journal of Public

Deliberation, *4*(1). Abstract retrieved from http://services.bepress.com/jpd

22. 报纸文章（网络版）

Angier, N. (2012, May 1). Insights from the youngest minds. *The New York Times.*
Retrieved from http://www.nytimes.com

在检索语句中列出报纸主页的URL。如果你是在在线数据库中找到的文章，则参见格式20。

① 作者姓名。列出每一个作者的姓氏、名的首字母和任何中间名的首字母。用逗号分隔姓氏和首字母，在最后一个作者的姓氏前用&符号。省略Dr.，PhD.或任何其他头衔。参见格式1—4（pp. 502–504）引用单个和多个作者。

② 发行日期，用括号标示，后接句号。

③ 文章标题。列出完整的标题和副标题，用冒号分隔。标题和副标题第一个单词的首字母要大写。无须用引号标示标题。

④ 期刊名称，用斜体字标示。所有重要单词均需大写，以逗号收尾。

⑤ 卷号，用斜体字标示，后接逗号。参见p. 505何时包括期号。

⑥ 文章起止页码，不用加缩略词pp.。不要省略任何数字。

⑦ 检索信息，DOI（如此例）或URL（格式19）。如何引用从数据库中检索到的没有DOI的文章参见格式20。

23. 杂志文章（网络版）

Hamzelou, J. (2011, April 17). How antidepressants boost growth of new brain cells. *New Scientist*, *203* (24), 15. doi:10.1038/mp.2011.26

如果杂志文章包括DOI，则列出DOI。否则的话，要如格式22报纸文章所示，在检索句中列出杂志主页的URL。如果你是在在线数据库中找到的文章，则参见格式20。

24. 只出现在网络上的期刊内容（网络版）

Weisberg, J. (2012, May 2). Can self-exposure be private? [Supplemental material]. *The New Yorker*. Retrieved from http://www.newyorker.com

如果你引用来自期刊网站的材料（该期刊的印刷版不包含此材料），要在标题之后添加［Supplemental material］，并提供期刊所在主页的URL。

25. 评论（网络版）

Bond, M. (2008, December 18). Does genius breed success? [Review of the book *Outliers: The story of success,* by M. Gladwell]. *Nature*, *456*, 785. doi:10.1038/456874a

在线评论的引用格式与印刷版评论一样（格式11，p. 507），以检索信息收尾（此例中，以DOI收尾）。

26. 组织或政府网站上的报告或其他资料（网络版）

Zickuhr, K., & Smith, A. (2012, April 13). *Digital differences*. Retrieved from the Pew Internet & American Life Project website: http://www.pewinternet.org

独立网络文件标题的处理格式与书籍标题一样。在Zickuhr和Smith的示例中，当发布组织不是作为作者列出时，在检索语句中提供发布组织的名称。

如果难以在组织的主页上确定所引用文件的位置，则要在检索句中提供完整的URL：

> Union of Concerned Scientists. (2012). *Clean vehicles*. Retrieved from http://www.ucsusa.org/clean_vehicles

如果所引用的文件没有标注日期，在发行日期的位置标注缩略词n.d.，并在检索句中提供你浏览的日期：

> U.S. Department of Education, (n.d.). *Teach*. Retrieved April 23, 2012, from http://www.teach.gov

27. 书籍（网络版）

> Reuter, P. (Ed.). (2010). *Understanding the demand for illegal drugs*. Retrieved from http://books.nap.edu/catalog.php?record_id=12976

对于在网络或在线数据库中获得的电子版书籍，要用DOI（如果有的话）代替出版社所在的城市、州和名称（参见格式18）或如上所示用检索句代之。参见格式14—17（pp. 507–508）不同书籍的引用：有译者的书籍、第一版之后的版本、多卷册书籍、经过编辑的书籍中的文章或章节。

如果引用电子阅读器上的电子书，则需在方括号内添加格式：

> Freud, S. (1920). *Dream psychology: Psychoanalysis for beginners* (M. D. Eder, Trans.). [iPad version]. Retrieved from http://www.apple.com/itunes

28. 参考书中的文章（网络版）

> Wood, R. (1998). Community organization. In W. A. Swatos, Jr. (Ed.), *Encyclopedia of religion and society*. Retrieved from http://hirr.hartsem.edu/ency/commorg.htm

如果你引用的条目没有标注作者，则先标出文章标题，然后是出版日期。如果原始资料有DOI的话，则使用DOI而不是URL。

29. 维基网站上的文章（网络版）

> Clinical neuropsychology. (2012, April 22). Retrieved May 15, 2012, from Wikipedia: http://en.wikipedia.org/wiki/Clinical_neuropsychology

对于可能有所变化的原始资料（如此例中的维基网站），要列出你的检索日期。

30. 毕业论文（网络版）

商业数据库中的毕业论文：

McFaddin, M. O. (2007). *Adaptive reuse: An architectural solution for poverty and homelessness* (Doctoral dissertation). Available from ProQuest Dissertations and Theses database. (ATT 1378764)

如果毕业论文来自商业数据库，要在检索句中列出数据库的名称，然后在括号内标注附加号或订单号。

机构数据库中的毕业论文：

Chang, J. K. (2003). *Therapeutic intervention in treatment of injuries to the hand and wrist* (Doctoral dissertation). Retrieved from http://medsci.archive.liasu.edu/61724

如果毕业论文来自机构数据库，要在检索句中列出URL。

且见格式38（p. 514）以获得印刷版论文的例子。

31. 播客（网络版）

Glass, I. (Producer). (2012, March 16). Retraction [Audio podcast]. *This American life*. Retrieved from http://thisamericanlife.org

32. 电影或视频录像（网络版）

CBS News (Producer). (1968, April 4). *1968 King assassination report* [Video file]. Retrieved from http://www.youtube.com/watch?v=cm0BbxgxKvo

如果难以在网站主页上确定所引用电影或视频的位置，则要如例所示在检索句中提供完整的URL。

33. 视觉资料（网络版）

United Nations Population Fund (Cartographer). (2009). *Percent of population living on less than $1.25 per day* [Demographic map]. Retrieved from http://www.unfpa.org

34. 博客或讨论小组上的帖子（网络版）

Sharma, A. (2012, April 15). How effective is lifestyle management of obesity? [Web log post]. Retrieved from http://www.drsharma.ca

只有在博客或讨论小组上的帖子可以被其他人检索到时才需在参考目录中列出这些帖子。（上面例子中的原始资料可以通过搜索主页的URL检索到［现今可能因某些原因无法检索到]）在帖子标题之后添加[Web log post]，[Electronic mailing list message]或[Online forum comment]。如果博客或讨论小组的名称不是URL的一部分，则需要在检索句中标出。

35. 个人通信（文内引用）

At least one member of the research team has expressed reservations about the design of the study (L. Kogod, personal communication, February 6, 2012).

别人无法检索到的个人电子邮件或其他在线帖子只需要在文中引用，不需要在参考目录中列出。

5 ▪ 其他原始资料

36. 报告（印刷版）

Gerald, K. (2003). *Medico-moral problems in obstetric care* (Report No. NP-71). St. Louis, MO: Catholic Hospital Association.

印刷版报告的处理格式和书籍一样，但是要在标题之后在括号内列出报告编号，两者之间没有标点符号。

对于来自Educational Resources Information Center（ERIC）的报告，要在条目最后在括号内提供ERIC文件号：

Jolson, M. K. (2011). *Music education for preschoolers* (Report No. TC-622). New York, NY: Teachers College, Columbia University. (ERIC Document Reproduction Service No. ED264488)

37. 政府出版物（印刷版）

Hawaii. Department of Education. (2012). *Kauai district schools, profile 2011-12*. Honolulu, HI: Author.

Stiller, A. (2010). *Historic preservation and tax incentives*. Washington, DC: U.S. Department of the Interior.

如果政府出版物没有标注作者，要将发行机构作为出版物的作者。如果该机构既是作者又是发行者，要如第一个例子那样用Author代替发行者名称。

对于诸如法庭裁决、法律和听证会上的证词等法律资料，APA格式推荐使用和传统法律引用一致的格式。以下关于国会听证会的例子包括了完整标题、国会的期号、官方出版物中听证会记录稿的起始页码和听证会的日期。

Medicare payment for outpatient physical and occupational therapy services: Hearing before the Committee on Ways and Means, House of Representatives,

110th Cong. 3 (2007).

38. 毕业论文（印刷版）

DAI (*Dissertation Abstracts International*) 上的毕业论文：

Steciw, S. K. (1986). Alterations to the Pessac project of Le Corbusier. *Dissertation Abstracts International, 46*(6), 565C.

未发表的毕业论文：

Hernandez, A. J. (2005). *Persistent poverty: Transient work and workers in today's labor market* (Unpublished doctoral dissertation). University of Illinois, Urbana-Champaign.

39. 采访（印刷版）

Schenker, H. (2007). No peace without third-party intervention [Interview with Shulamit Aloni]. *Palestine-Israel Journal of Politics, Economics, and Culture, 14*(4), 63-68.

在采访者姓名之后列出已出版的采访，并提供标题（如果有的话），无须排成斜体或用引号标示。如果没有标题或者标题没有显示采访的格式或被采访者（如例所示），则需在方括号内添加注释。对于采访出现的原始资料类型（此处为期刊），要以出版信息收尾。

对于你自己完成的采访，不需要列在参考目录中。只需在文章中用括号标出即可，如格式35（p.513）个人通信所示。

40. 电影

American Psychological Association (Producer). (2001). *Ethnocultural psychotherapy* [DVD]. Available from http://www.apa.org/videos

Tyrrell, C. (Director). (2010). *The Joneses* [Motion picture]. United States: Bjort Productions.

先列出所引用作品的制作团体的名称或制片人的姓名，再在圆括号内标出所承担的角色。（如果你引用整部电影，要如第一个例子所示，以制作团体或制片人的名字为开始）电影片名之后，在方括号内添加媒介：[Motion picture]（电影），[DVD]或[Videocassette]。对于发行量很大的作品（第二个例子），提供影片的首映国和制片商。对于发行量不是很大的作品（第一个例子），则提供发行商的地址或URL。

41. 音乐录音

Springsteen, B. (2002). Empty sky. On *The rising* [CD]. New York, NY: Columbia.

先列出作者或作曲者的姓名。(如果你引用另一位艺术家录制的作品唱片,则在作品名称后提供此信息,例如,[Recorded by E. Davila])在方括号内标注媒介([CD],[LP]等),以灌制唱片的城市、州和唱片公司收尾。

42. 电视连续剧或一集电视剧

Rhimes, S. (Executive producer). (2012). *Grey's anatomy* [Television series]. New York, NY: ABC.

Alexander, Z. (Writer), & Wilson, C. (Director). (2012). Moment of truth [Television series episode]. In S. Rhimes (Executive producer), *Grey's anatomy*. New York, NY: ABC.

对于电视连续剧,先列出制片人的姓名,并在括号内明确他或她的角色。在连续剧的片名之后添加[Television series],并提供城市和电视公司名称。对于一集电视剧,先列出作者和导演的姓名,并在括号内明确每个人的角色。在这一集的片名之后添加[Television series episode],并提供连续剧信息(以In开始,然后是制片人姓名及角色,列出连续剧的片名,以城市和电视公司名称收尾)。

57c 用 APA 格式撰写论文

使用以下准则和范例用APA格式准备文件。对于格式的任何修改,要咨询老师。

注意:参考目录的APA格式,参见pp. 501–502。对于字体、目录、表格和图表及其他文件设计元素,参见pp. 66–75。

页边距:上下左右均留出1英寸(2.54厘米)的页边距。

行距和缩进:全文双倍行距。(表格和图表中的数据、标记和其他元素可以单倍行距)段落和整段引文向右缩进0.5英寸(1.27厘米)或5—7个半角空格。

页码编号:从标题页开始编号,连续编号一直到文章结束(包括参考目录)。如范例所示,在每一页上方距页边0.5英寸(1.27厘米)处列出页眉。页眉最右边是页码,最左边是完整或缩写后的标题。标题要全部大写。只有在标题页,标题的前面标注Running head和冒号。其他页上省略此信息。

标题页:包括完整的标题、你的姓名、课程名称、老师姓名和日期。(参见下方）在该页的上半部分输入标题，后接身份信息。标题和身份信息均水平居中，双倍行距。

» **APA 标题页**

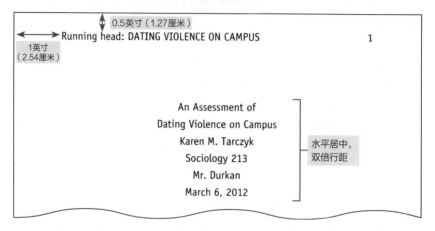

摘要：总结主题、研究方法、发现和结论（最多120个单词）。（参见下方）摘要需单独一页。

» **APA 摘要**

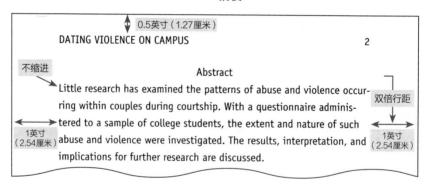

正文：先重复论文的标题，然后是引言（不做标记）。（参见下页）引言描述研究问题、研究方法、相关的背景信息（如相关的研究）和研究目的。

» APA正文的第一页

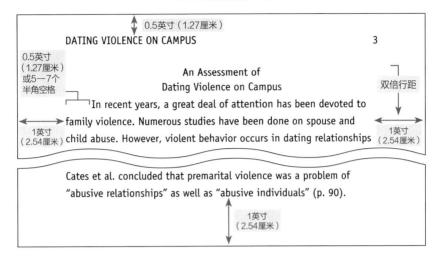

引言之后,标记为Method的部分详细讨论了你是如何进行研究的,包括对研究主题、使用材料或工具(如问卷调查)和步骤的描述。在p. 520的图释中,Method是第一级标题,Sample是第二级标题。

» APA 正文的后面一页

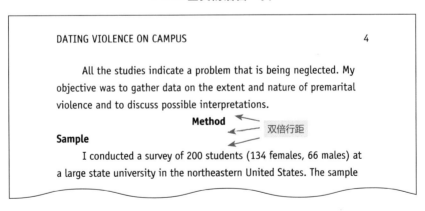

格式标题(必要的话,包括第三级标题)如下所示:

一级标题

二级标题

  三级标题。用标准的段落缩进把这个标题插入正文段落。

Results（标示为第一级标题）总结你收集的数据，解释你是如何分析数据的，并用表格、曲线图和图表形式详细展示这些数据。

Discussion（标示为第一级标题）解释数据并展示结论。（当讨论非常简短时，你可以合并这部分和前面那部分内容，标示为Results and Discussion）

参考目录另起一页，包括所有的原始资料。参见pp. 501–502的解释和范例。

长引文： 40个单词（含40个单词）以下的引文可以直接在文中引用，前后用引号标示。40个单词以上的引文需要独立成段，向右缩进0.5英寸（1.27厘米）或5个半角空格，双倍行距。

Echoing the opinions of other Europeans at the time, Freud (1961) had a poor view of Americans:

> The Americans are realty too bad. . . . Competition is much more pungent with them, not succeeding means civil death to every one, and they have no private resources apart from their profession, no hobby, games, love or other interests of a cultured person. And success means money. (p. 86)

这样的引文**不需要用引号标示**。

插图： 在表格、曲线图或图表中酌情标注数据。（对于表格格式，见p. 521的范例）每一个插图要另起一页。每一种插图要连续编号，彼此区分。文章中要对所有表格有所引证，例如，（see Figure 3）。通常，插图要紧跟在文本提示之后。（更多关于插图的信息，参见pp. 68–75）

57d APA 格式的论文范例

以下节选自一篇社会学论文，用APA的文件和格式说明了一篇研究论文的要素。

［扉页］

| 经过缩写的标题和页码 | Running head: DATING VIOLENCE ON CAMPUS　　　　　　1 |

An Assessment of

Dating Violence on Campus

Karen M. Tarczyk

Sociology 213

Mr. Durkan

March 6, 2012

| 所有信息均需要双倍行距：标题、姓名、课程名称、老师姓名、日期 |

[新页面]

DATING VIOLENCE ON CAMPUS   2

Abstract

Little research has examined the patterns of abuse and violence occurring within couples during courtship. With a questionnaire administered to a sample of college students, the extent and nature of such abuse and violence were investigated. The results, interpretations, and implications for further research are discussed.

> 摘要：对主题、研究方法、结论的总结
>
> 全文双倍行距

[新页面]

DATING VIOLENCE ON CAMPUS   3

An Assessment of
Dating Violence on Campus

> 正文首页重复标题

In recent years, a great deal of attention has been devoted to family violence. Numerous studies have been done on spouse and child abuse. However, violent behavior occurs in dating relationships as well, yet the problem of dating violence has been relatively ignored by sociological research. It should be examined further because the premarital relationship is one context in which individuals learn and adopt behaviors that surface in marriage.

> 引言：陈述作者要研究的问题

The sociologist James Makepeace (1989) contended that courtship violence is a "potential mediating link" between violence in one's family of orientation and violence in one's later family of procreation (p. 103). Studying dating behaviors at Bemidji State University in Minnesota, Makepeace reported that one-fifth of the respondents had had at least one encounter with dating violence. He then extended these percentages to students nationwide, suggesting the existence of a major hidden social problem.

> 引文格式：文中提及作者
>
> 引文格式：引文所在页码

More recent research supports Makepeace's. Cates, Rutter, Karl, Linton, and Smith (2000) found that 22.3% of respondents at Oregon State University had been either the victim or the perpetrator of premarital violence. Another study (Cortes, 2011)

> 引文格式：有五个作者的原始资料，文中提及作者
>
> 引文格式：文中没有提及作者

found that so-called date rape, while much more publicized and discussed, was reported by many fewer woman respondents (2%) than was other violence during courtship (21%).

[介绍仍在继续]

All these studies indicate a problem that is being neglected. My objective was to gather data on the extent and nature of premarital violence and to discuss possible interpretations.

Method

> 第一级和第二级标题

Sample

> Method部分：讨论研究是如何进行的

I conducted a survey of 200 students (134 females, 66 males) at a large state university in the northeastern United States. The sample consisted of students enrolled in an introductory sociology course.

[方法的解释仍在继续]

The Questionnaire

A questionnaire exploring the personal dynamics of relationships was distributed during regularly scheduled class. The survey had three sections.

[方法的解释仍在继续]

Section 3 required participants to provide information about their current dating relationships. Levels of stress and frustration, communication between partners, and patterns of decision making were examined. These variables were expected to influence the amount of violence in a relationship. The next part of the survey was adopted from Murray Strauss's Conflict Tactics Scales (1992). These scales contain 19 items designed to measure conflict and the means of conflict resolution, including reasoning, verbal aggression, and actual violence. The final page of the questionnaire contained general questions on the couple's use of alcohol, sexual activity, and overall satisfaction with the relationship.

Results

The questionnaire revealed significant levels of verbal

aggression and threatened and actual violence among dating couples. A high number of students, 50% (62 of 123 subjects), reported that they had been the victim of verbal abuse, either being insulted or sworn at.In addition, almost 14% of respondents (17 of 123) admitted being threatened with some type of violence, and more than 14% (18 of 123) reported being pushed, grabbed, or shoved. (See Table 1.)

［结果的解释仍在继续］

［表独立在一页上］

Table 1
Incidence of Courtship Violence

Type of violence	Number of students reporting	Percentage of sample
Insulted or swore	62	50.4
Threatened to hit or throw something	17	13.8
Threw something	8	6.5
Pushed, grabbed, or shoved	18	14.6
Slapped	8	6.5
Kicked, bit, or hit with fist	7	5.7
Hit or tried to hit with something	2	1.6
Threatened with a knife or gun	1	0.8
Used a knife or gun	1	0.8

Discussion

Violence within premarital relationships has been relatively ignored. The results of the present study indicate that abuse and force do occur in dating relationships. Although the percentages are small, so was the sample. Extending them to the entire campus population of 5,000 would mean significant numbers. For example, if the nearly 6% incidence of being kicked, bitten, or hit with a fist is typical, then 300 students might have experienced this type of violence.

［讨论仍在继续］

If the courtship period is characterized by abuse and violence, what accounts for it? The other sections of the survey examined some variables that appear to influence the relationship. Level of stress and frustration, both within the relationship and in the respondent's life, was one such variable. The communication level between partners, both the frequency of discussion and the frequency of agreement, was another.

［讨论仍在继续］

The method of analyzing the data in this study, utilizing frequency distributions, provided a clear overview. However, more tests of significance and correlation and a closer look at the social and individual variables affecting the relationship are warranted. The courtship period may set the stage for patterns of married life. It merits more attention.

［新页面］

DATING VIOLENCE ON CAMPUS 8

References

参考目录（另起一页）

Cates, R. L., Rutter, C. H., Karl, J., Linton, M., & Smith, K. (2000). Premarital abuse: A social psychological perspective. *Journal of Family Issues, 13*, 79-90.

印刷版期刊上的文章

Cortes, L. (2011). Beyond date rape: Violence during courtship. *Electronic Journal of Intimate Violence, 5*(2). Retrieved from http://www.ejiv.org

没有DOI的在线期刊文章

Glaser, R., & Rutter, C. H. (Eds.). (1999). Familial violence [Special issue]. *Family Relations, 38*(4).

Makepeace, J. M. (1989). Courtship violence among college students. *Family Relations, 28*(6), 97-103.

Strauss, M. L. (1992). *Conflict Tactics Scales*. New York, NY: Sociological Tests.

书籍（大写Tactics Scales两个单词的首字母，因为它是专有名词的一部分）

词语用法汇编

本词表将容易给写作者造成困扰的词或词组汇总，并提供注解。标准美式英语的推荐用法基于现行通用的词典和用法指南。标记有nonstandard（非标准）的条目，在言谈及写作中，特别是写作中，需要避免。标记有colloquial（口头语）和slang（俚语）的条目，会在言谈及一些非正式写作中出现，但在大学或公司的正式写作中最好避免。（标记有colloquial的词语和词组包括那些被许多词典标记为informal［非正式］的词或词组）

注意：正文中有两个词表可以是本词表的补充：带介词的成语，如part from及part with（pp. 176–177）；以及发音相同或相似但是拼写不同的词语，如heard和herd（pp. 348–349）。

a, an Use *a* before words beginning with consonant sounds, including those spelled with an initial pronounced *h* and those spelled with vowels that are sounded as consonants: *a historian, a one-o'clock class, a university*. Use *an* before words that begin with vowel sounds, including those spelled with an initial silent *h*: *an organism, an L, an honor*.

The article before an abbreviation depends on how the abbreviation is to be read: *She was once an AEC undersecretary* (AEC is to be read as three separate letters). *Many Americans opposed a SALT treaty* (SALT is to be read as one word, *salt*).

See also pp. 274–75 on the uses of *a/an* versus *the*.

accept, except *Accept* is a verb meaning "receive." *Except* is usually a preposition or conjunction meaning "but for" or "other than"; when it is used as a verb, it means "leave out." *I can accept all your suggestions except the last one. I'm sorry you excepted my last suggestion from your list.*

advice, advise *Advice* is a noun, and *advise* is a verb: *Take my advice; do as I advise you.*

affect, effect Usually *affect* is a verb, meaning "to influence," and *effect* is a noun, meaning "result": *The drug did not affect his driving; in fact, it seemed to have no effect at all.* But *effect* occasionally is used as a verb meaning "to bring about": *Her efforts effected a change.* And *affect* is used in psychology as a noun meaning "feeling or emotion": *One can infer much about affect from behavior.*

aggravate *Aggravate* should not be used in its colloquial meaning of "irritate" or "exasperate" (for example, *We were aggravated by her constant arguing*). *Aggravate* means "make worse": *The President was irritated by the Senate's indecision because he feared any delay might aggravate the unrest in the Middle East.*

agree to, agree with *Agree to* means "consent to," and *agree with* means "be in accord with": *How can they* agree to *a treaty when they don't* agree with *each other about the terms?*

all ready, already *All ready* means "completely prepared," and *already* means "by now" or "before now": *We were* all ready *to go to the movie, but it had* already *started.*

all right *All right* is always two words. *Alright* is a common error.

all together, altogether *All together* means "in unison" or "gathered in one place." *Altogether* means "entirely." *It's not* altogether *true that our family never spends vacations* all together.

allusion, illusion An *allusion* is an indirect reference, and an *illusion* is a deceptive appearance: *Paul's constant* allusions *to Shakespeare created the* illusion *that he was an intellectual.*

almost, most *Almost* means "nearly"; *most* means "the greater number (or part) of." In formal writing, *most* should not be used as a substitute for *almost*: *We see each other* almost [not *most*] *every day.*

a lot *A lot* is always two words, used informally to mean "many." *Alot* is a common misspelling.

among, between In general, use *among* for relationships involving more than two people or for comparing one thing to a group to which it belongs. *The four of them agreed* among *themselves that the choice was* between *New York and Los Angeles.*

amount, number Use *amount* with a singular noun that names something not countable (a noncount noun): *The* amount of food *varies.* Use *number* with a plural noun that names more than one of something countable (a plural count noun): *The* number of calories *must stay the same.*

and/or *And/or* indicates three options: one or the other or both (*The decision is made by the mayor* and/or the council). If you mean all three options, *and/or* is appropriate. Otherwise, use *and* if you mean both, *or* if you mean either.

ante-, anti- The prefix *ante-* means "before" (*antedate, antebellum*); *anti-* means "against" (*antiwar, antinuclear*). Before a capital letter or *i, anti-* takes a hyphen: *anti-Freudian, anti-isolationist.*

anxious, eager *Anxious* means "nervous" or "worried" and is usually followed by *about*. *Eager* means "looking forward" and is usually followed by *to*. *I've been* anxious about *getting blisters. I'm* eager [not *anxious*] to *get new running shoes.*

anybody, any body; anyone, any one *Anybody* and *anyone* are indefinite pronouns; *any body* is a noun modified by *any*; *any one* is a pronoun or adjective modified by *any*. *How can* anybody *communicate with* any body *of government? Can* anyone *help Amy? She has more work than* any one *person can handle.*

any more, anymore *Any more* means "no more"; *anymore* means "now."

Both are used in negative constructions. *He doesn't want any more. She doesn't live here anymore.*

are, is Use *are* with a plural subject (*books are*), *is* with a singular subject (*book is*).

as *As* may be vague or ambiguous when it substitutes for *because, since,* or *while*: *As the researchers asked more questions, their money ran out.* (Does *as* mean "while" or "because"?) *As* should never be used as a substitute for *whether* or *who*. *I'm not sure whether* [not *as*] *we can make it. That's the man who* [not *as*] *gave me directions.*

as, like In formal speech and writing, *like* should not introduce a full clause (with a subject and a verb) because it is a preposition. The preferred choice is *as* or *as if*: *The plan succeeded as* [not *like*] *we hoped. It seemed as if* [not *like*] *it might fail. Other plans like it have failed.*

assure, ensure, insure *Assure* means "to promise": *He assured us that we would miss the traffic. Ensure* and *insure* are often used interchangeably to mean "make certain," but some reserve *insure* for matters of legal and financial protection and use *ensure* for more general meanings: *We left early to ensure that we would miss the traffic. It's expensive to insure yourself against floods.*

awful, awfully Strictly speaking, *awful* means "awe-inspiring." As intensifiers meaning "very" or "extremely" (*He tried awfully hard*), *awful* and *awfully* should be avoided in formal speech or writing.

a while, awhile *Awhile* is an adverb; *a while* is an article and a noun. *I will be gone awhile* [not *a while*]. *I will be gone for a while* [not *awhile*].

bad, badly In formal speech and writing, *bad* should be used only as an adjective; the adverb is *badly*. *He felt bad because his tooth ached badly.* In *He felt bad*, the verb *felt* is a linking verb and the adjective *bad* describes the subject. See also p. 268.

being as, being that Colloquial for *because*, the preferable word in formal speech or writing: *Because* [not *Being as*] *the world is round, Columbus never did fall off the edge.*

beside, besides *Beside* is a preposition meaning "next to." *Besides* is a preposition meaning "except" or "in addition to" as well as an adverb meaning "in addition." *Besides, several other people besides you want to sit beside Dr. Christensen.*

better, had better *Had better* (meaning "ought to") is a verb modified by an adverb. The verb is necessary and should not be omitted: *You had better* [not just *better*] *go.*

between, among See *among, between.*

bring, take Use *bring* only for movement from a farther place to a nearer one and *take* for any other movement. *First take these books to the library for renewal; then take them to Mr. Daniels. Bring them back to me when he's finished.*

but, hardly, scarcely These words are negative in their own right; using *not* with any of them produces a double negative (see p. 271). We *have but* [not *haven't got but*] *an hour before our plane leaves. I could hardly* [not *couldn't hardly*] *make out her face.*

but, however, yet Each of these words is adequate to express contrast. Don't combine them. *He had finished, yet* [not *but yet*] *he continued.*

can, may Strictly, *can* indicates capacity or ability, and *may* indicates permission or possibility: *If I may talk with you a moment, I believe I can solve your problem.*

censor, censure To *censor* is to edit or remove from public view on moral or other grounds; to *censure* is to give a formal scolding. *The lieutenant was censured by Major Taylor for censoring the letters her soldiers wrote home from boot camp.*

cite, sight, site *Cite* is a verb usually meaning "quote," "commend," or "acknowledge": *You must cite your sources. Sight* is both a noun meaning "the ability to see" or "a view" and a verb meaning "perceive" or "observe": *What a sight you see when you sight Venus through a strong telescope. Site* is a noun meaning "place" or "location" or a verb meaning "situate": *The builder sited the house on an unlikely site.*

climatic, climactic *Climatic* comes from *climate* and refers to the weather: *Recent droughts may indicate a climatic change. Climactic* comes from *climax* and refers to a dramatic high point: *During the climactic duel between Hamlet and Laertes, Gertrude drinks poisoned wine.*

complement, compliment To *complement* something is to add to, complete, or reinforce it: *Her yellow blouse complemented her black hair.* To *compliment* something is to make a flattering remark about it: *He complimented her on her hair. Complimentary* can also mean "free": *complimentary tickets.*

conscience, conscious *Conscience* is a noun meaning "a sense of right and wrong"; *conscious* is an adjective meaning "aware" or "awake." *Though I was barely conscious, my conscience nagged me.*

continual, continuous *Continual* means "constantly recurring": *Most movies on television are continually interrupted by commercials. Continuous* means "unceasing": *Some cable channels present movies continuously without commercials.*

could of See *have, of.*

credible, creditable, credulous *Credible* means "believable": *It's a strange story, but it seems credible to me. Creditable* means "deserving of credit" or "worthy": *Steve gave a creditable performance. Credulous* means "gullible": *The credulous Claire believed Tim's lies.* See also *incredible, incredulous.*

criteria The plural of *criterion* (meaning "standard for judgment"): *Our criteria are strict. The most important criterion is a sense of humor.*

data The plural of *datum* (meaning "fact"). Though *data* is often used as a singular noun, many readers prefer the plural verb, and it is always correct: *The data fail* [not *fails*] *to support the hypothesis.*

device, devise   *Device* is the noun, and *devise* is the verb: *Can you devise some device for getting his attention?*

different from, different than   *Different from* is preferred: *His purpose is different from mine.* But *different than* is widely accepted when a construction using *from* would be wordy: *I'm a different person now than I used to be* is preferable to *I'm a different person now from the person I used to be.*

differ from, differ with   To *differ from* is to be unlike: *The twins differ from each other only in their hairstyles.* To *differ with* is to disagree with: *I have to differ with you on that point.*

discreet, discrete   *Discreet* (noun form *discretion*) means "tactful": *What's a discreet way of telling Maud to be quiet? Discrete* (noun form *discreteness*) means "separate and distinct": *Within a computer's memory are millions of discrete bits of information.*

disinterested, uninterested   *Disinterested* means "impartial": *We chose Pete, as a disinterested third party, to decide who was right.* Uninterested means "bored" or "lacking interest": *Unfortunately, Pete was completely uninterested in the question.*

don't   *Don't* is the contraction for *do not,* not for *does not: I don't care, you don't care,* and *he doesn't* [not *don't*] *care.*

due to the fact that   Wordy for *because.*

eager, anxious   See *anxious, eager.*

effect   See *affect, effect.*

elicit, illicit   *Elicit* is a verb meaning "bring out" or "call forth." *Illicit* is an adjective meaning "unlawful." *The crime elicited an outcry against illicit drugs.*

emigrate, immigrate   *Emigrate* means "to leave one place and move to another": *The Chus emigrated from Korea. Immigrate* means "to move into a place where one was not born": *They immigrated to the United States.*

ensure   See *assure, ensure, insure.*

enthused   Used colloquially as an adjective meaning "showing enthusiasm." The preferred adjective is *enthusiastic: The coach was enthusiastic* [not *enthused*] *about the team's prospects.*

et al., etc.   Use *et al.,* the Latin abbreviation for "and other people," only in source citations: *Jones et al.* Avoid *etc.,* the Latin abbreviation for "and other things," in formal writing, and do not use it to refer to people or to substitute for precision, as in *The government provides health care, etc.*

everybody, every body; everyone, every one   *Everybody* and *everyone* are indefinite pronouns: *Everybody* [*Everyone*] *knows Tom steals. Every one* is a pronoun modified by *every,* and *every body* a noun modified by *every.*

Both refer to each thing or person of a specific group and are typically followed by *of*: *The game commissioner has stocked every body of fresh water in the state with fish, and now every one of our rivers is a potential trout stream.*

everyday, every day *Everyday* is an adjective meaning "used daily" or "common"; *every day* is a noun modified by *every*: *Everyday problems tend to arise every day.*

everywheres Nonstandard for *everywhere*.

except See *accept, except*.

except for the fact that Wordy for *except that*.

explicit, implicit *Explicit* means "stated outright": *I left explicit instructions*. *Implicit* means "implied, unstated": *We had an implicit understanding.*

farther, further *Farther* refers to additional distance (*How much farther is it to the beach?*), and *further* refers to additional time, amount, or other abstract matters (*I don't want to discuss this any further*).

fewer, less *Fewer* refers to individual countable items (a plural count noun), *less* to general amounts (a noncount noun, always singular). *Skim milk has fewer calories than whole milk. We have less milk left than I thought.*

flaunt, flout *Flaunt* means "show off": *If you have style, flaunt it*. *Flout* means "scorn" or "defy": *Hester Prynne flouted convention and paid the price.*

flunk A colloquial substitute for *fail*.

fun As an adjective, *fun* is colloquial and should be avoided in most writing: *It was a pleasurable* [not *fun*] *evening*.

further See *farther, further*.

get This common verb is used in many slang and colloquial expressions: *get lost, that really gets me, getting on*. *Get* is easy to overuse: watch out for it in expressions such as *it's getting better* (substitute *improving*) and *we got done* (substitute *finished*).

good, well *Good* is an adjective, and *well* is nearly always an adverb: *Larry's a good dancer. He and Linda dance well together*. *Well* is properly used as an adjective only to refer to health: *You look well*. (*You look good*, in contrast, means "Your appearance is pleasing.")

good and Colloquial for "very": *I was very* [not *good and*] *tired*.

had better See *better, had better*.

had ought The *had* is unnecessary and should be omitted: *He ought* [not *had ought*] *to listen to his mother*.

hanged, hung Though both are past-tense forms of *hang*, *hanged* is used to refer to executions and *hung* is used for all other meanings: *Tom Dooley* was hanged [not hung] from a white oak tree. I hung [not hanged] the picture you gave me.

hardly See *but, hardly, scarcely*.

have, of Use *have*, not *of*, after helping verbs such as *could, should, would, may, must,* and *might*: *You should have* [not *should of*] *told me*.

he, she; he/she Convention has allowed the use of *he* to mean "he or she": *After the infant learns to creep, he progresses to crawling.* However, many writers today consider this usage inaccurate and unfair because it seems to exclude females. The construction *he/she*, one substitute for *he*, is awkward and objectionable to most readers. The better choice is to make the pronoun plural, to rephrase, or, sparingly, to use *he or she*. For instance: *After infants learn to creep, they progress to crawling. After learning to creep, the infant progresses to crawling. After the infant learns to creep, he or she progresses to crawling.* See also pp. 169 and 259–60.

herself, himself See *myself, herself, himself, yourself*.

hisself Nonstandard for *himself*.

hopefully *Hopefully* means "with hope": *Freddy waited hopefully for a glimpse of Eliza.* The use of *hopefully* to mean "it is to be hoped," "I hope," or "let's hope" is now very common; but try to avoid it in writing because many readers continue to object strongly to the usage. *I hope* [not *Hopefully*] *the law will pass*.

idea, ideal An *idea* is a thought or conception. An *ideal* (noun) is a model of perfection or a goal. *Ideal* should not be used in place of *idea*: *The idea* [not *ideal*] *of the play is that our ideals often sustain us*.

if, whether Use *whether* rather than *if* when you are expressing an alternative: *If I laugh hard, people can't tell whether I'm crying or not*.

illicit See *elicit, illicit*.

illusion See *allusion, illusion*.

immigrate, emigrate See *emigrate, immigrate*.

implicit See *explicit, implicit*.

imply, infer Writers or speakers *imply*, meaning "suggest": *Jim's letter implies he's having a good time.* Readers or listeners *infer*, meaning "conclude": *From Jim's letter I infer he's having a good time*.

incredible, incredulous *Incredible* means "unbelievable," while *incredulous* means "unbelieving": *When Nancy heard Dennis's incredible story, she was frankly incredulous.* See also *credible, creditable, credulous*.

individual, person, party *Individual* should refer to a single human being in contrast to a group or should stress uniqueness: *The US Constitution places strong emphasis on the rights of the individual.* For other meanings *person* is preferable: *What person* [not *individual*] *wouldn't want the security promised in that advertisement? Party* means "group" (*Can you seat a* *party of four for dinner?*) and should not be used to refer to an individual except in legal documents. See also *people, persons*.

infer   See *imply, infer*.

in regards to   Nonstandard for *in regard to, as regards,* or *regarding*.

insure   See *assure, ensure, insure*.

irregardless   Nonstandard for *regardless*.

is, are   See *are, is*.

is because   See *reason is because*.

is when, is where   These are faulty constructions in sentences that define: *Adolescence is a stage* [not *is when a person is*] *between childhood and adulthood. Socialism is a system in which* [not *is where*] *government owns the means of production.* See also pp. 298–99.

its, it's   *Its* is the pronoun *it* in the possessive case: *That plant is losing its leaves. It's* is a contraction for *it is* or *it has: It's* [*It is*] *likely to die. It's* [*It has*] *got a fungus.* Many people confuse *it's* and *its* because possessives are most often formed with *-'s;* but the possessive *its,* like *his* and *hers,* never takes an apostrophe.

kind of, sort of, type of   In formal speech and writing, avoid using *kind of* or *sort of* to mean "somewhat": *He was rather* [not *kind of*] *tall. Kind, sort,* and *type* are singular and take singular modifiers and verbs: *This kind of dog is easily trained.* Agreement errors often occur when these singular nouns are combined with the plural adjectives *these* and *those: These kinds* [not *kind*] *of dogs are easily trained. Kind, sort,* and *type* should be followed by *of* but not by *a: I don't know what type of* [not *type* or *type of a*] *dog that is.*

  Use *kind of, sort of,* or *type of* only when the word *kind, sort,* or *type* is important: *That was a strange* [not *strange sort of*] *statement.*

lay, lie   *Lay* means "put" or "place" and takes a direct object: *We could lay the tablecloth in the sun.* Its main forms are *lay, laid, laid. Lie* means "recline" or "be situated" and does not take an object: *I lie awake at night. The town lies east of here.* Its main forms are *lie, lay, lain.* (See also pp. 217–18.)

leave, let   *Leave* and *let* are interchangeable only when followed by *alone; leave me alone* is the same as *let me alone.* Otherwise, *leave* means "depart" and *let* means "allow": *Jill would not let Sue leave.*

less   See *fewer, less*.

lie, lay   See *lay, lie*.

like, as   See *as, like*.

like, such as   Strictly, *such as* precedes an example that represents a larger subject, whereas *like* indicates that two subjects are comparable. *Steve has recordings of many great saxophonists such as Ben Webster and Lee Konitz. Steve wants to be a great jazz saxophonist like Ben Webster and Lee*

Konitz.

literally This word means "actually" or "just as the words say," and it should not be used to qualify or intensify expressions whose words are not to be taken at face value. The sentence *He was literally climbing the walls* describes a person behaving like an insect, not a person who is restless or anxious. For the latter meaning, *literally* should be omitted.

lose, loose *Lose* means "mislay": *Did you lose a brown glove? Loose* means "unrestrained" or "not tight": *Ann's canary got loose. Loose* also can function as a verb meaning "let loose": *They loose the dogs on intruders.*

lots, lots of Colloquial substitutes for *very many, a great many*, or *much*. Avoid *lots* and *lots of* in college or business writing.

may, can See *can, may*.

may be, maybe *May be* is a verb, and *maybe* is an adverb meaning "perhaps": *Tuesday may be a legal holiday. Maybe we won't have classes.*

may of See *have, of*.

media *Media* is the plural of *medium* and takes a plural verb: *All the news media are increasingly visual.* The singular verb is common, even in the media, but many readers prefer the plural verb, and it is always correct.

might of See *have, of*.

moral, morale As a noun, *moral* means "ethical conclusion" or "lesson": *The moral of the story escapes me. Morale* means "spirit" or "state of mind": *Victory improved the team's morale.*

most, almost See *almost, most*.

must of See *have, of*.

myself, herself, himself, yourself The *-self* pronouns refer to or intensify another word or words: *Paul helped himself; Jill herself said so.* The *-self* pronouns are often used colloquially in place of personal pronouns, but that use should be avoided in formal speech and writing: *No one except me* [not *myself*] *saw the accident. Our delegates will be Susan and you* [not *yourself*]. See also p. 252 on the unchanging forms of the *-self* pronouns in standard American English.

nowheres Nonstandard for *nowhere*.

number See *amount, number*.

of, have See *have, of*.

off of *Of* is unnecessary. Use *off* or *from* rather than *off of: He jumped off* [or *from*, not *off of*] *the roof.*

OK, O.K., okay All three spellings are acceptable, but avoid this colloquial term in formal speech and writing.

on the other hand This transitional expression of contrast should be preceded by its mate, *on the one hand*: *On the one hand, we hoped for snow. On the other hand, we worried that it would harm the animals*. However, the two combined can be unwieldy, and a simple *but, however, yet,* or *in contrast* often suffices: *We hoped for snow. However, we worried that it would harm the animals.*

owing to the fact that   Wordy for *because*.

party   See *individual, person, party*.

people, persons   In formal usage, *people* refers to a general group: *We the people of the United States. . . . Persons* refers to a collection of individuals: *Will the person or persons who saw the accident please notify. . . .* Except when emphasizing individuals, prefer *people* to *persons*. See also *individual, person, party*.

per   Except in technical writing, an English equivalent is usually preferable to the Latin *per*: *$10 an* [not *per*] *hour; sent by* [not *per*] *parcel post; requested in* [not *per* or *as per*] *your letter*.

percent (per cent), percentage   Both these terms refer to fractions of one hundred. *Percent* always follows a number (*40 percent of the voters*), and the word is often used instead of the symbol (%) in nontechnical writing. *Percentage* stands alone (*the percentage of voters*) or follows an adjective (*a high percentage*).

person   See *individual, person, party*.

persons   See *people, persons*.

phenomena   The plural of *phenomenon* (meaning "perceivable fact" or "unusual occurrence"): *Many phenomena are not recorded. One phenomenon is attracting attention.*

plenty   A colloquial substitute for *very*: *The reaction occurred very* [not *plenty*] *fast*.

plus   *Plus* is standard as a preposition meaning "in addition to": *His income plus mine is sufficient*. But *plus* is colloquial as a conjunctive adverb: *Our organization is larger than theirs; moreover* [not *plus*], *we have more money*.

precede, proceed   The verb *precede* means "come before": *My name precedes yours in the alphabet*. The verb *proceed* means "move on": *We were told to proceed to the waiting room*.

prejudice, prejudiced   *Prejudice* is a noun; *prejudiced* is an adjective. Do not drop the *-d* from *prejudiced*: *I knew that my parents were prejudiced* [not *prejudice*].

pretty   Overworked as an adverb meaning "rather" or "somewhat": *He was somewhat* [not *pretty*] *irked at the suggestion*.

principal, principle   *Principal* is an adjective meaning "foremost" or "major," a noun meaning "chief official," or, in finance, a noun meaning "capital sum." *Principle* is a noun only, meaning "rule" or "axiom." *Her principal reasons for confessing were her principles of right and wrong.*

proceed, precede   See *precede, proceed.*

question of whether, question as to whether   Both are wordy substitutes for *whether.*

raise, rise   *Raise* means "lift" or "bring up" and takes a direct object: *The Kirks raise cattle.* Its main forms are *raise, raised, raised. Rise* means "get up" and does not take an object: *They must rise at dawn.* Its main forms are *rise, rose, risen.* (See also pp. 217–18.)

real, really   In formal speech and writing, *real* should not be used as an adverb; *really* is the adverb and *real* an adjective. *Popular reaction to the announcement was really* [not *real*] *enthusiastic.*

reason is because   This colloquial and redundant expression should be avoided in formal speech and writing. Use a *that* clause after *reason is*: *The reason he is absent is that* [not *is because*] *he is sick.* Or: *He is absent because he is sick.* (See also p. 299.)

respectful, respective   *Respectful* means "full of (or showing) respect": *Be respectful of other people. Respective* means "separate": *The French and the Germans occupied their respective trenches.*

rise, raise   See *raise, rise.*

scarcely   See *but, hardly, scarcely.*

sensual, sensuous   *Sensual* suggests sexuality; *sensuous* means "pleasing to the senses." *Stirred by the sensuous scent of meadow grass and flowers, Cheryl and Paul found their thoughts growing increasingly sensual.*

set, sit   *Set* means "put" or "place" and takes a direct object: *He sets the pitcher down.* Its main forms are *set, set, set. Sit* means "be seated" and does not take an object: *She sits on the sofa.* Its main forms are *sit, sat, sat.* (See also pp. 217–18.)

shall, will   *Will* is the future-tense helping verb for all persons: *I will go, you will go, they will go.* The main use of *shall* is for first-person questions requesting an opinion or consent: *Shall I order a pizza? Shall we dance? Shall* can also be used for the first person when a formal effect is desired (*I shall expect you around three*), and it is occasionally used with the second or third person to express the speaker's determination (*You shall do as I say*).

should of   See *have, of.*

sight, site, cite   See *cite, sight, site.*

since   *Since* mainly relates to time: *I've been waiting since noon.* But *since* is also often used to mean "because": *Since you ask, I'll tell you.* Revise sentences in which the word could have either meaning, such as *Since I studied physics, I have been planning to major in engineering.*

sit, set See *set, sit*.

site, cite, sight See *cite, sight, site*.

so Avoid using *so* alone or as a vague intensifier: *He was so late.* So needs to be followed by *that* and a clause that states a result: *He was so late that I left without him.*

somebody, some body; someone, some one *Somebody* and *someone* are indefinite pronouns; *some body* is a noun modified by *some*; and *some one* is a pronoun or an adjective modified by *some*. *Somebody ought to invent a shampoo that will give hair some body. Someone told Janine she should choose some one plan and stick with it.*

sometime, sometimes, some time *Sometime* means "at an indefinite time in the future": *Why don't you come up and see me sometime? Sometimes* means "now and then": *I still see my old friend Joe sometimes. Some time* means "a span of time": *I need some time to make the payments.*

somewheres Nonstandard for *somewhere*.

sort of, sort of a See *kind of, sort of, type of*.

such Avoid using *such* as a vague intensifier: *It was such a cold winter. Such* should be followed by *that* and a clause that states a result: *It was such a cold winter that Napoleon's troops had to turn back.*

such as See *as, like*.

supposed to, used to In both these expressions, the *-d* is essential: *I used to* [not *use to*] *think so. He's supposed to* [not *suppose to*] *meet us.*

sure Colloquial when used as an adverb meaning *surely*: *James Madison sure was right about the need for the Bill of Rights.* If you merely want to be emphatic, use *certainly*: *Madison certainly was right.* If your goal is to convince a possibly reluctant reader, use *surely*: *Madison surely was right.*

sure and, sure to; try and, try to *Sure to* and *try to* are the correct forms: *Be sure to* [not *sure and*] *buy milk. Try to* [not *Try and*] *find some decent tomatoes.*

take, bring See *bring, take*.

than, then *Than* is a conjunction used in comparisons, *then* an adverb indicating time: *Holmes knew then that Moriarty was wilier than he had thought.*

that, which *That* introduces an essential clause: *We should use the lettuce that Susan bought* (*that Susan bought* limits the lettuce to a particular lettuce). *Which* can introduce both essential and nonessential clauses, but many writers reserve *which* only for nonessential clauses: *The leftover lettuce, which is in the refrigerator, would make a good salad* (*which is in the refrigerator* simply provides more information about the lettuce we already know of). Essential clauses (with *that* or *which*) are not set off by commas; nonessential clauses (with *which*) are. See also pp. 312–13.

that, which, who Use *that* for animals, things, and sometimes collective or anonymous people: *The rocket that failed cost millions. Infants that walk need constant tending.* Use *which* only for animals and things: *The river, which flows south, divides two countries.* Use *who* only for people and for animals with names: *Dorothy is the girl who visits Oz. Her dog, Toto, who accompanies her, gives her courage.*

their, there, they're *Their* is the possessive form of *they*: *Give them their money. There* indicates place (*I saw her standing there*) or functions as an expletive (*There is a hole behind you*). *They're* is a contraction for *they are*: *They're going fast.*

theirselves Nonstandard for *themselves*.

them In standard American English, *them* does not serve as an adjective: *Those* [not *Them*] *people want to know*.

then, than See *than, then*.

these kind, these sort, these type, those kind See *kind of, sort of, type of*.

this, these *This* is singular: *this car* or *This is the reason I left. These* is plural: *these cars* or *These are not valid reasons.*

thru A colloquial spelling of *through* that should be avoided in all academic and business writing.

to, too, two *To* is a preposition; *too* is an adverb meaning "also" or "excessively"; and *two* is a number. *I too have been to Europe two times.*

too Avoid using *too* as a vague intensifier: *Monkeys are too mean*. When you do use *too*, explain the consequences of the excessive quality: *Monkeys are too mean to make good pets*.

toward, towards Both are acceptable, though *toward* is preferred. Use one or the other consistently.

try and, try to See *sure and, sure to; try and, try to*.

type of See *kind of, sort of, type of*. Don't use *type* without *of*: *It was a family type of* [not *type*] *restaurant*. Or better: *It was a family restaurant.*

uninterested See *disinterested, uninterested*.

unique *Unique* means "the only one of its kind" and so cannot sensibly be modified with words such as *very* or *most*: *That was a unique* [not *a very unique* or *the most unique*] *movie*.

usage, use *Usage* refers to conventions, most often those of a language: *Is "hadn't ought" proper usage? Usage* is often misused in place of the noun *use*: *Wise use* [not *usage*] *of insulation can save fuel.*

use, utilize *Utilize* can be used to mean "make good use of": *Many teachers utilize computers for instruction.* But for all other senses of "place in service" or "employ," prefer *use*.

used to See *supposed to, used to*.

wait for, wait on In formal speech and writing, *wait for* means "await" (*I'm waiting for Paul*) and *wait on* means "serve" (*The owner of the store herself waited on us*).

ways Colloquial as a substitute for *way*: *We have only a little way* [not *ways*] *to go.*

well See *good, well.*

whether, if See *if, whether.*

which, that See *that, which.*

which, who, that See *that, which, who.*

who, whom *Who* is the subject of a sentence or clause (*We don't know who will come*). *Whom* is the object of a verb or preposition (*We do not know whom we invited*). (See also pp. 254–55.)

who's, whose *Who's* is the contraction of *who is* or *who has*: *Who's* [*Who is*] *at the door? Jim is the only one who's* [*who has*] *passed. Whose* is the possessive form of *who*: *Whose book is that?*

will, shall See *shall, will.*

would be Often used instead of *is* or *are* to soften statements needlessly: *One example is* [not *would be*] *gun-control laws. Would* can combine with other verbs for the same unassertive effect: *would ask, would seem, would suggest,* and so on.

would have Avoid this construction in place of *had* in clauses that begin with *if* and state a condition contrary to fact: *If the tree had* [not *would have*] *withstood the fire, it would have been the oldest in town.* See also p. 236.

would of See *have, of.*

you In all but very formal writing, *you* is generally appropriate as long as it means "you, the reader." In all writing, avoid indefinite uses of *you*, such as *In one ancient tribe your first loyalty was to your parents.* See also p. 265.

your, you're *Your* is the possessive form of *you*: *Your dinner is ready. You're* is the contraction of *you are*: *You're bound to be late.*

yourself See *myself, herself, himself, yourself.*

版权所有
文章

Ali: "Postcard from Kashmir," from *The Half-Inch Himalayas* © 1987 by Agha Shahid Ali. Reprinted with permission of Wesleyan University Press.

Allianz SE: From Allianz Knowledge. www.knowledge.allianz.com. Used by permission.

Crawford: © *Vegetarian Times*, 2005. Reprinted with permission.

Center for Climate and Energy Solutions (C2ES): From www.c2es.org. Copyright © 2011 Center for Climate and Energy Solutions (C2ES). All rights reserved.

Reprinted by permission.

EBSCO and American Psychological Association: Screen capture copyright © 2012, EBSCO Publishing, Inc. All rights reserved. Abstract from "Going Green to Be Seen: Status, Reputation, and Conspicuous Conservation," by Vladas Griskevicius et al., *Journal of Personality & Social Psychology*, March 2010, Vol. 98, Issue 3, pp. 392–404. Reprinted by permission.

EBSCO: Copyright © 2012, EBSCO Publishing, Inc. All rights reserved.

Eisinger et al.: From *American Politics: The People and the Polity* by Peter K. Eisinger et al., New York: Little, Brown and Company, 1978. Reprinted by permission of Peter K. Eisinger.

Hirsh et al.: "Symptom burden in individuals with cerebral palsy" by A.T. Hirsh et al., *Journal of Rehabilitation Research & Development*, 2010;47(9):863–76.

Jackson: From "Live Better by Consuming Less?" by Tim Jackson, *Journal of Industrial Ecology*, 9.1-2. Copyright © 2005, John Wiley & Sons. Reprinted by permission of John Wiley & Sons Ltd.

Kelly-Weeder et al.: Abstract reprinted from Patient Intelligence, 2011: 3, S. Kelly-Weeder, K. Phillips and S. Rounseville, "Effectiveness of public health programs for decreasing alcohol consumption," pp. 29–38, copyright © 2011, with permission from Dove Medical Press Ltd.

Kuralt: From "San Angelo, Texas" in *Dateline America* by Charles Kuralt. Copyright © 1979 Houghton Mifflin Harcourt Publishing Company, reprinted by permission of the publisher. This material may not be reproduced in any form or by any means without the prior written permission of the publisher.

Lemelson Center: "The Birth of Hip-Hop: Innovation against the Odds," by Amanda Murray, Lemelson Center, National Museum of American History, Smithsonian Institute. Reprinted by permission.

Merriam-Webster: Definition of "reckon" reprinted by permission from *Merriam-Webster's Collegiate® Dictionary*, 11th Edition, © 2012 by Merriam-Webster, Incorporated (*www.Merriam-Webster.com*).

Nadelmann: From "Shooting Up" by Ethan A. Nadelmann as appeared in *The New Republic*, June 13, 1988. Reprinted by permission of the author.

Shteir: From *The Steal: A Cultural History of Shoplifting* by Rachel Shteir, copyright © 2011 by Rachel Shteir. Used by permission of The Penguin Press, a division of Penguin Group (USA) Inc. and the author.

Sowell: "Student Loans," from *Is Reality Optional?* by Thomas Sowell. Copyright © 1993 by Thomas Sowell. Reprinted by permission of Thomas Sowell and Creators Syndicate, Inc.

Tuchman: From *The Decline of Quality* by Barbara Tuchman. Copyright © 1980 Barbara Tuchman. Reprinted by permission of Russell & Volkening as agents for the author's estate.

University of Chicago Press: *The Library Quarterly*, 78.2. Copyright © 2008 University of Chicago Press. Reprinted by permission of the publisher, University of Chicago Press.

Woodward: From "Life after Death?" by Kenneth L. Woodward. From *Newsweek*, July 14, 1976. © 1976 The Newsweek/Daily Beast Company LLC. All rights reserved. Used by permission and protected by the copyright laws of the United States. The printing, copying, redistribution, or retransmission of the material without express written permission is prohibited.

照片

Page 64, bottom: © Universal/courtesy Everett Collection. **Page 71, bottom**: United States Department of Agriculture. **Page 72, top**: NASA/Johnson Space Center. **Page 72, bottom**: Jeff Malet Photography/Newscom. **Page 74, left**: Advertising Archives. **Page 74, right**: Electrolux. **Page 75, bottom**: © Bill Aron/PhotoEdit. **Page 95, bottom**: Ad Council. **Page 98**: Steve Simon Photography.

带星号练习题答案

练习11.1, p. 108
Possible revision

The stereotype that women talk more on cell phones than men do turns out to be false. In a five-year survey of 1021 cell phone owners, a major wireless company found that men spend 35% more time on their phones.

练习12.3, p. 119

1. A reasonable generalization.
2. An unreasonable generalization that cannot be inferred from the evidence.

练习12.4, p. 119
Possible answers

1. **Premise:** Anyone who has opposed pollution controls may continue to do so.
   Premise: The mayor has opposed pollution controls.
   Conclusion: The mayor may continue to do so.
   The statement is valid and true.
2. **Premise:** Corporate Web sites are sponsored by for-profit entities.
   Premise: Information from for-profit entities is unreliable.
   Conclusion: Information on corporate Web sites is unreliable.
   The statement is untrue because the second premise is untrue.

练习12.5, p. 120
Possible answers

1. Primarily emotional appeal. Ethical appeal: knowledgeable, concerned, reasonable (at least in the two uses of *may*), slightly sarcastic (*most essential of skills*).
2. Primarily rational appeal. Ethical appeal: knowledgeable, reasonable.

练习12.6, p. 124
Possible answers

1. Sweeping generalization and begged question.
   A revision: A successful marriage demands a degree of maturity.
2. Hasty generalization and non sequitur.
   A revision: Students' persistent complaints about the unfairness of the grading system should be investigated.
3. Reductive fallacy.
   A revision: The United States got involved in World War II for many complex reasons. The bombing of Pearl Harbor was a triggering incident.
4. Either/or fallacy and hasty generalization.
   A revision: People watch television for many reasons, but some watch because they are too lazy to talk or read or because they want mindless escape from their lives.
5. Reductive fallacy and begged question.
   A revision: Racial tension may occur when people with different backgrounds live side by side.

练习15.1, p. 146
Possible answers

1. <u>Many heroes helped</u> to emancipate the slaves.
2. <u>Harriet Tubman</u>, an escaped slave herself, <u>guided</u> hundreds of other slaves to freedom on the Underground Railroad.

练习15.2, p. 148

Possible answers
1. Pat Taylor strode into the packed room, greeting students called "Taylor's Kids" and nodding to their parents and teachers.
2. This wealthy Louisiana oilman had promised his "Kids" free college educations because he was determined to make higher education available to all qualified but disadvantaged students.

练习15.3, p. 151

Possible answers
1. Because soldiers admired their commanding officers, they often gave them nicknames containing the word *old*, even though not all of the commanders were old.
2. General Thomas "Stonewall" Jackson was also called "Old Jack," although he was not yet forty years old.

练习15.4, p. 154

Possible answers
1. Genaro González is a successful writer whose stories and novels have been published to critical acclaim.
2. Although he loves to write, he has also earned a doctorate in psychology.

练习15.5, p. 154

Possible revision

Sir Walter Raleigh personified the Elizabethan Age, the period of Elizabeth I's rule of England, in the last half of the sixteenth century. Raleigh was a courtier, a poet, an explorer, and an entrepreneur. Supposedly, he gained Queen Elizabeth's favor by throwing his cloak beneath her feet at the right moment, just as she was about to step over a puddle.

练习16.1, p. 157

Possible answers
1. The ancient Greeks celebrated four athletic contests: the Olympic Games at Olympia, the Isthmian Games near Corinth, the Pythian Games at Delphi, and the Nemean Games at Cleonae.
2. Each day the games consisted of either athletic events or ceremonies and sacrifices to the gods.
3. In the years between the games, competitors were taught wrestling, javelin throwing, and boxing.
4. Competitors ran sprints, participated in spectacular chariot and horse races, and ran long distances while wearing full armor.
5. The purpose of such events was to develop physical strength, to demonstrate skill and endurance, and to sharpen the skills needed for war.

练习16.2, p. 158

Possible answers
1. People can develop post-traumatic stress disorder (PTSD) after experiencing a dangerous situation and fearing for their survival.
2. The disorder can be triggered by a wide variety of events, such as combat, a natural disaster, or a hostage situation.

练习17.1, p. 162

Possible revision

After being dormant for many years, the Italian volcano Vesuvius exploded on August 24 in the year AD 79. The ash, pumice, and mud from the volcano buried two towns—Herculaneum and the more famous Pompeii—which lay undiscovered until

1709 and 1748, respectively.

练习 18.1, p. 170

Possible answers

1. Acquired immune deficiency syndrome (AIDS) is a <u>serious threat</u> all over the world.
2. The disease <u>is transmitted</u> primarily by sexual intercourse, exchange of bodily fluids, shared needles, and blood transfusions.
3. Those who think the disease is limited to <u>homosexuals</u>, <u>drug users</u>, and foreigners are quite mistaken.
4. <u>Statistics</u> suggest that in the United States one in every five hundred college students carries the HIV virus that causes AIDS.
5. <u>People</u> with HIV or full-blown AIDS do not deserve <u>others' exclusion</u> or callousness. Instead, <u>they need</u> all the compassion, medical care, and financial assistance due <u>the seriously ill</u>.

练习 18.2, p. 170

Possible answers

1. When <u>people apply</u> for a job, <u>they</u> should represent <u>themselves</u> with the best possible résumé.
2. A person applying for a job as a <u>mail carrier</u> should appear to be honest and responsible.
3. <u>Applicants</u> for a position as an in-home nurse should also represent <u>themselves</u> as honest and responsible.
4. Of course, <u>the applicant</u> should also have a background of capable nursing.
5. The business <u>executive</u> who is scanning a stack of résumés will, of necessity, read them all quickly.

练习 18.3, p. 174

1. Maxine Hong Kingston was <u>awarded</u> many prizes for her first two books, *The Woman Warrior* and *China Men*.
2. Kingston <u>cites</u> her mother's tales about ancestors and ancient Chinese customs as the sources of these memoirs.
3. Two of King's <u>progenitors</u>, her great-grandfathers, are focal points of *China Men*.
4. Both men led <u>rebellions</u> against <u>oppressive</u> employers: a sugarcane farmer and a railroad-construction engineer.
5. In her childhood Kingston was greatly <u>affected</u> by her mother's tale about a pregnant aunt who was ostracized by villagers. [*Ostracized* is correct.]

练习 18.4, p. 175

1. AIDS is a serious health <u>problem</u>.
2. Once the virus has entered the <u>blood</u> system, it <u>destroys</u> T-cells.

练习 18.6, p. 178

1. Children are waiting longer to become independent <u>of</u> their parents.
2. According <u>to</u> US Census data for young adults ages eighteen to twenty-four, 57% of men and 4<u>7%</u> of women live full-time with their parents.

练习 18.7, p. 178

1. The Eighteenth Amendment <u>to</u> the Constitution <u>of</u> the United States was ratified <u>in</u> 1919.
2. It prohibited the "manufacture, sale, or transportation <u>of</u> intoxicating liquors."

练习 18.9, p. 180

Possible answers

1. The <u>disasters</u> of the war have shaken the small nation <u>severely</u>.
2. Prices for food have <u>risen markedly</u>, and citizens <u>suspect</u> that others are <u>profiting</u> on

the black market.
3. Medical supplies are so scarce that even very sick civilians cannot get treatment.
4. With most men fighting or injured or killed, women have had to work hard and take men's places in farming and manufacturing.
5. Finally, the war's high cost has destroyed the nation's economy.

练习19.1, p. 182

1. The first ice cream, eaten in China in about 2000 BC, was lumpier than modern ice cream.
2. The Chinese made their ice cream of milk, spices, and overcooked rice and packed it in snow to solidify.

练习20.1, p. 188

Possible answers

1. If sore muscles after exercising are a problem for you, there are some things you can do to ease the discomfort.
2. First, apply cold immediately to reduce inflammation.
3. Cold constricts blood vessels and keeps blood away from the injured muscles.
4. Avoid heat for the first day.
5. Applying heat within the first twenty-four hours can increase muscle soreness and stiffness.

练习20.2, p. 188

Possible answers

After much thought, he concluded that carcinogens could be treated like automobiles. Instead of giving in to a fear of cancer, we should balance the benefits we receive from potential carcinogens (such as plastic and pesticides) against the damage they do.

练习21.1, p. 193

1. The gingko tree, which is one of the world's oldest trees, is large and picturesque.
2. Gingko trees may grow to over a hundred feet in height.
3. Their leaves look like fans and are about three inches wide.
4. The leaves turn yellow in the fall.
5. Because it tolerates smoke, low temperatures, and low rainfall, the gingko appears in many cities.

练习21.2, p. 194

1. You can reduce stress by making a few simple changes.
2. Get up fifteen minutes earlier than you ordinarily do:
3. Eat a healthy breakfast, and eat it slowly so that you enjoy it.
4. Do your more unpleasant tasks early in the day.
5. Every day, do at least one thing you really enjoy.

练习21.3, p. 197

1. Just about everyone has heard the story of the Trojan Horse.
2. This incident happened at the city of Troy and was planned by the Greeks.
3. The Greeks built a huge wooden horse with a hollow space big enough to hold many men.
4. At night, they rolled the horse to the gate of Troy and left it there filled with soldiers.
5. In the morning, the Trojans were surprised to see the enormous horse.

练习22.1, p. 200
1. The horse / has a long history of service to humanity but today is mainly a show and sport animal.
2. A member of the genus *Equus*, the domestic horse / shares its lineage with the ass and the zebra.
3. The domestic horse and its relatives / are all plains-dwelling herd animals.
4. The modern horse / evolved in North America.
5. It / migrated to other parts of the world and then became extinct in the Americas.

练习22.2, p. 202
1. The number of serious crimes in the United States decreased. (S, V)
2. A decline in serious crimes occurred each year. (S, V)
3. The Crime Index measures serious crime. (S, V, DO)
4. The FBI invented the index. (S, V, DO)
5. The four serious violent crimes are murder, robbery, forcible rape, and aggravated assault. (S, V, SC, SC, SC, SC)

练习22.3, p. 205
1. Milo Addica and Will Rokos cowrote the screenplay for *Monster's Ball*.
2. Marc Foster directed the film.

练习23.1, p. 208
1. With its many synonyms, or words with similar meanings, English can make choosing the right word a difficult task.
   (prepositional phrase; appositive phrase; prepositional phrase; participial phrase)
2. Borrowing words from other languages such as French and Latin, English acquired an unusual number of synonyms.
   (participial phrase; prepositional phrase; appositive phrase; prepositional phrase)
3. Having so many choices, how does a writer decide between *motherly* and *maternal* or among *womanly*, *feminine*, and *female*?
   (participial phrase; prepositional phrase; prepositional phrase)
4. Some people prefer longer and more ornate words to avoid the flatness of short words.
   (infinitive phrase; prepositional phrase)
5. During the Renaissance a heated debate occurred between the Latinists, favoring Latin words, and the Saxonists, preferring Anglo-Saxon words derived from Germanic roots.
   (prepositional phrase; participle; prepositional phrase; participial phrase; participial phrase; participial phrase; prepositional phrase)

练习 23.2, p. 211

1. The Prophet Muhammad, <u>who was the founder of Islam</u>, was born about 570 CE in the city of Mecca. [ADJ over "who was the founder of Islam"]
2. He grew up in the care of his grandfather and an uncle <u>because both of his parents had died</u>. [ADV]
3. His family was part of a powerful Arab tribe <u>that lived in western Arabia</u>. [ADJ]
4. When Muhammad <u>was about forty years old</u>, he had a vision <u>while he was in a cave outside Mecca</u>. [ADV, ADV]
5. He believed that God had selected him to be <u>the prophet</u> of a true religion for the Arab people. [N]

练习 24.1, p. 213

1. [main clause] Our world has many sounds, but [main clause] they all have one thing in common. [Compound.]
2. [main clause] The one thing [subordinate clause] that all sounds share is [subordinate clause] that they are produced by vibrations. [Complex.]
3. [main clause] The vibrations make the air move in waves, and [main clause] these sound waves travel to the ear. [Compound.]
4. [subordinate clause] When sound waves enter the ear, [main clause] the auditory nerves convey them to the brain, and [main clause] the brain interprets them. [Compound-complex.]
5. [main clause] Sound waves can also travel through other material, such as water and even the solid earth. [Simple.]

练习 25.1, p. 217

1. The world population has <u>grown</u> by two-thirds of a billion people in less than a decade. [Past participle.]
2. Recently it <u>broke</u> the 7 billion mark. [Past tense.]
3. Experts have <u>drawn</u> pictures of a crowded future. [Past participle.]
4. They predict that the world population may have <u>slid</u> up to as much as 10 billion by the year 2050. [Past participle.]
5. Though the food supply <u>rose</u> in the last decade, the share to each person <u>fell</u>. [Both past tense.]

练习 25.2, p. 218

1. Yesterday afternoon the child <u>lay</u> down for a nap.
2. The child has been <u>raised</u> by her grandparents.

练习 25.3, p. 220

1. A teacher sometimes <u>asks</u> too much of a student.
2. In high school I was once <u>punished</u> for being sick.
3. I had <u>missed</u> a week of school because of a serious case of the flu.
4. I <u>realized</u> that I would fail a test unless I had a chance to make up the class work.
5. I <u>discussed</u> the problem with the teacher.

练习 25.4, p. 224

1. For as long as I can remember, I <u>have</u> been writing stories.
2. While I <u>was</u> living with my grandparents one summer, I wrote mystery stories.

练习25.5, p. 225
1. A report from the Bureau of the Census has <u>confirmed</u> a widening gap between rich and poor.
2. As suspected, the percentage of people below the poverty level did <u>increase</u> over the last decade.

练习25.6, p. 227
1. Sentence correct.
2. People supporting this program hope that students will at least postpone <u>dropping</u> out of school.

练习25.7, p. 229
1. American movies treat everything from going out with [correct] someone to making up [correct] an ethnic identity, but few people <u>look into their significance</u>.
2. While some viewers stay away from [correct] topical films, others <u>turn up at the theater</u> simply because a movie has sparked debate.

练习26.1, p. 234
　　The 1960 presidential race between Richard Nixon and John F. Kennedy was the first to feature a televised debate. [Sentence correct.] Despite his extensive political experience, Nixon <u>perspired</u> heavily and <u>looked</u> haggard and uneasy in front of the camera. By contrast, Kennedy <u>projected</u> cool <u>poise</u> and <u>provided</u> crisp answers that made him seem fit for the office of President.

练习26.2, p. 234
　　E. B. White's famous children's novel *Charlotte's Web* is a wonderful story of friendship and loyalty. [Sentence correct.] Charlotte, the wise and motherly spider, <u>decides</u> to save her friend Wilbur, the young and childlike pig, from being butchered by <u>his</u> owner. She <u>makes</u> a plan to weave words into her web that <u>describe</u> Wilbur.

练习26.3, p. 236
1. Diaries that Adolf Hitler <u>was supposed</u> to have written <u>had surfaced</u> in Germany.
2. Many people <u>believed</u> that the diaries <u>were</u> authentic <u>because</u> a well-known historian <u>had declared</u> them so.

练习26.4, p. 237
1. When an athlete <u>turns</u> professional, he or she commits to a grueling regimen of mental and physical training.
2. If athletes <u>were</u> less committed, they <u>would disappoint</u> teammates, fans, and themselves.
3. If professional athletes <u>are</u> very lucky, they may play until age forty.
4. Unless an athlete achieves celebrity status, he or she <u>will have</u> few employment choices after retirement.
5. If professional sports <u>were</u> less risky, athletes <u>would have</u> longer careers and more choices after retirement.

练习27.1, p. 239
1. If John Hawkins <u>had known</u> of all the dangerous side effects of smoking tobacco, would he have introduced the dried plant to England in 1565?
2. Hawkins noted that if a Florida Indian man <u>were</u> to travel for several days, he <u>would smoke</u> tobacco to satisfy his hunger and thirst.

练习28.1, p. 242
Possible answers
1. Many <u>factors</u> <u>determine</u> water quality.
2. All natural <u>waters</u> <u>contain</u> suspended and dissolved substances.
3. The <u>environment</u> <u>controls</u> the amounts of the substances.

4. Pesticides produce some dissolved substances.
5. Fields, livestock feedlots, and other sources deposit sediment in water.

练习28.2，p. 242
Possible answers
1. When engineers built the Eiffel Tower in 1889, the French thought it to be ugly.
2. At that time, industrial technology was still resisted by many people.

练习29.1，p. 249
1. Weinstein & Associates is a consulting firm that tries to make businesspeople laugh.
2. Results from recent research show that humor relieves stress.
3. Reduced stress in businesses in turn reduces illness and absenteeism.
4. In special conferences held by one consultant, each of the participants practices making others laugh.
5. "Aren't there enough laughs within you to spread the wealth?" the consultant asks his students.

练习29.2，p. 250
The Siberian tiger is the largest living cat in the world, much bigger than its relative the Bengal tiger. It grows to a length of nine to twelve feet, including its tail, and to a height of about three and a half feet. It can weigh over six hundred pounds. This carnivorous hunter lives in northern China and Korea as well as in Siberia. During the long winter of this Arctic climate, the yellowish striped coat gets a little lighter in order to blend with the snow-covered landscape. The coat also grows quite thick because the tiger has to withstand temperatures as low as −50°F.

练习30.1，p. 253
1. Kayla and I were competing for places on the relay team.
2. The fastest runners at our school were she and I, so we expected to make the team.

练习30.2，p. 255
1. The school administrators suspended Jurgen, whom they suspected of setting the fire.
2. Jurgen had been complaining to other custodians, who reported him.
3. He constantly complained of unfair treatment from whoever happened to be passing in the halls, including pupils.
4. "Who here has heard Mr. Jurgen's complaints?" the police asked.
5. "Whom did he complain most about?"

练习30.3，p. 257
1. Sentence correct.
2. Sentence correct.
3. He and Gilgamesh wrestled to see who was more powerful.
4. Sentence correct.
5. The friendship of the two strong men was sealed by their fighting.

练习31.1，p. 261
Possible answers
1. Each girl raised in a Mexican American family in the Rio Grande valley of Texas hopes that one day she will be given a *quinceañera* party for her fifteenth birthday.
2. Such a celebration is very expensive because it entails a religious service followed by a huge party. [*Or:* Such celebrations are very expensive because they entail a religious service followed by a huge party.]
3. A girl's immediate family, unless it is wealthy, cannot afford the party by itself.
4. The parents will ask each close friend or relative if he or she can help with the preparations. [*Or:* The parents will ask close friends or relatives if they can help with the

preparations.]
5. Sentence correct.

练习32.1，p. 266

Possible answers

1. "Life begins at forty" is a cliché many people live by, and this <u>saying</u> may or may not be true.
2. Living successfully or not depends on one's definition of <u>success</u>.
3. When <u>Pearl Buck</u> was forty, her novel *The Good Earth* <u>won the</u> Pulitzer Prize.
4. <u>Buck was raised in a missionary</u> family in China, and she wrote about <u>the country</u> in her novels.
5. In *The Good Earth* <u>the characters</u> have to struggle, but fortitude is rewarded.

练习32.2，p. 266

Possible revision

In Charlotte Brontë's *Jane Eyre,* <u>Jane</u> is a shy young woman <u>who</u> takes a job as governess. Her employer is a rude, <u>brooding</u> man named <u>Rochester</u>. [Sentence correct.] He lives in a mysterious mansion on the English moors, <u>and both the mansion and the moors</u> contribute an eerie quality to Jane's experience. Eerier still are the fires, strange noises, and other unexplained happenings in the house; but Rochester refuses to discuss <u>them</u>.

练习33.1，p. 269

1. People who take their health <u>seriously</u> often believe that movie-theater popcorn is a healthy snack.
2. Nutrition information about movie popcorn may make these people feel <u>differently</u>.

练习33.2，p. 271

1. Interest in books about the founding of the United States is <u>not</u> [*or* <u>is hardly</u>] consistent among Americans: it seems to vary with the national <u>mood</u>.
2. Sentence correct.

练习33.3，p. 272

1. Several critics found Alice Walker's *The Color Purple* to be a <u>fascinating</u> book.
2. Sentence correct.

练习33.4，p. 277

From <u>the</u> native American Indians who migrated from <u>Asia</u> 20,000 years ago to <u>the</u> new <u>arrivals</u> who now come by <u>planes</u>, the United States <u>is a</u> nation of foreigners. It <u>is a</u> country of immigrants who <u>are</u> all living under a single flag.

Back in <u>the</u> seventeenth and eighteenth <u>centuries</u>, at least 75% of the population came <u>from</u> England. However, between 1820 and 1975 more than 38 million immigrants came to this country from elsewhere <u>in</u> Europe.

练习33.5，p. 277

1. Americans often argue about which professional sport is <u>best</u>: basketball, football, or baseball.
2. Basketball fans contend that their sport offers more action because the players are <u>constantly</u> running and shooting.
3. <u>Because it</u> is played indoors in <u>relatively</u> small arenas, basketball allows fans to be closer to the action than the other <u>sports</u> do.
4. <u>Football</u> fanatics say they <u>hardly</u> stop yelling once the game begins.
5. They cheer when their team executes a <u>really</u> complicated play <u>well</u>.

练习34.1，p. 282

1. People <u>who are right-handed</u> dominate in our society.
2. Hand <u>tools</u>, machines, and <u>even</u> doors are designed for right-handed people.

3. However, nearly 15% of the population may be left-handed.
4. When they begin school, children often prefer one hand or the other.
5. Parents and teachers should not try deliberately to change a child's preference for the left hand.

练习34.2, p. 282
1. Some years ago Detroit cars were often praised.
2. Large luxury cars were especially prized.

练习34.3, p. 284
Possible answers
1. Drawing conclusions from several formal studies, researchers believe that pets can improve people's emotional well-being.
2. Suffering from Alzheimer's and unable to recognize her husband, one woman could still identify her beloved dog.
3. Once subject to violent outbursts, an autistic boy was calmed by a companion dog.
4. When patients face long hospital stays, pet-therapy dogs can cheer them up.
5. To understand why people with serious illnesses often respond well to animals, researchers are studying pet therapy.

练习35.1, p. 288
Possible answers
1. Human beings who perfume themselves are not much different from other animals.
2. Animals as varied as insects and dogs release pheromones, chemicals that signal other animals.
3. Human beings have a diminished sense of smell and do not consciously detect most of their own species' pheromones.
4. No sentence fragment.
5. Some sources say that people began using perfume to cover up the smell of burning flesh during sacrifices to the gods.

练习35.2, p. 289
Possible answers
  People generally avoid eating mushrooms except those they buy in stores. But in fact many varieties of mushrooms are edible. Mushrooms are members of a large group of vegetation called nonflowering plants, including algae, mosses, ferns, and coniferous trees, even the giant redwoods of California. Most of the nonflowering plants prefer moist environments, such as forest floors, fallen timber, and still water. Mushrooms, for example, prefer moist, shady soil. Algae grow in water.

练习36.1, p. 295
Possible answers
1. Some people think that dinosaurs were the first living vertebrates, but fossils of turtles go back 40 million years further.
2. Although most other reptiles exist mainly in tropical regions, turtles inhabit a variety of environments worldwide.
3. Turtles do not have teeth; their jaws are covered with a sharp, horny sheath.
4. Turtles cannot expand their lungs to breathe air; as a result, they make adjustments in how space is used within the shell.
5. Some turtles can get oxygen from water; therefore, they don't need to breathe air.

练习36.2, p. 296
Possible answers
1. Money has a long history. It goes back at least as far as the earliest records.
  Money has a long history; it goes back at least as far as the earliest records.

2. Many of the earliest records concern financial transactions. Indeed, early history must often be inferred from commercial activity.

Many of the earliest records concern financial transactions; indeed, early history must often be inferred from commercial activity.

3. Sentence correct.
4. Sometimes the objects have had real value; however, in modern times their value has been more abstract.

Although sometimes the objects have had real value, in modern times their value has been more abstract.

5. Cattle, fermented beverages, and rare shells have served as money, and each one had actual value for the society.

Cattle, fermented beverages, and rare shells have served as money. Each one had actual value for the society.

练习36.3, p. 297

Possible answers

What many call the first genocide of modern times occurred during World War I, when the Armenians were deported from their homes in Anatolia, Turkey. The Turkish government assumed that the Armenians were sympathetic to Russia, with whom the Turks were at war. Many Armenians died because of the hardships of the journey, and many were massacred. The death toll was estimated at between 600,000 and 1 million.

练习37.1, p. 300

Possible answers

1. A hurricane occurs when the winds in a tropical depression rotate counterclockwise at more than seventy-four miles per hour.
2. Because hurricanes can destroy so many lives and so much property, people fear them.
3. Through high winds, storm surge, floods, and tornadoes, hurricanes have killed thousands of people.
4. Storm surge occurs when the hurricane's winds whip up a tide that spills over seawalls and deluges coastal islands.
5. Sentence correct.

练习37.2, p. 301

1. Archaeologists and other scientists can often determine the age of their discoveries by means of radiocarbon dating.
2. This technique can be used on any material that once was living.

练习38.1, p. 306

When visitors first arrive in Hawaii, they often encounter an unexpected language barrier. Standard English is the language of business and government, but many of the people speak Pidgin English. Instead of an excited "Aloha!" the visitors may be greeted with an excited Pidgin "Howzit!" or asked if they know "how fo' find one good hotel."

练习39.1, p. 308

1. Parents once automatically gave their children the father's last name, but some no longer do.
2. Parents were once legally required to give their children the father's last name, but these laws have been contested in court.
3. Parents may now give their children any last name they choose, and the arguments for choosing the mother's last name are often strong and convincing.
4. Sentence correct.
5. The child's last name may be just the mother's, or it may link the mother's and the father's with a hyphen.

练习 39.2, p. 310

1. Veering sharply to the right, a large flock of birds neatly avoids a high wall.
2. Sentence correct.
3. With the help of complex computer simulations, zoologists are learning more about this movement.
4. Because it is sudden and apparently well coordinated, the movement of flocks and schools has seemed to be directed by a leader.
5. Almost incredibly, the group could behave with more intelligence than any individual seemed to possess.

练习 39.3, p. 315

1. Many colleges have started campus garden programs that aim to teach students about the benefits of sustainable farming methods and locally grown food.
2. These gardens, which use organic farming techniques, also provide fresh produce for the college cafeteria.
3. A garden that is big enough to grow produce for a college cafeteria requires a large piece of land.
4. Such a garden also needs a leader who can choose crops that will thrive in local growing conditions.
5. Volunteers willing to work in the garden every week are essential as well.

练习 39.4, p. 316

1. Shoes with high heels were originally designed to protect feet from mud, garbage, and animal waste in the streets.
2. Sentence correct.
3. The heels were worn by men and made of colorful silk fabrics, soft suedes, or smooth leathers.
4. High-heeled shoes became popular when the short, powerful King Louis XIV of France began wearing them.
5. Louis's influence was so strong that men and women of the court, priests and cardinals, and even household servants wore high heels.

练习 39.5, p.321

1. Underground aquifers are deep and sometimes broad layers of water that are trapped between layers of rock.
2. Porous rock or sediment holds the water.
3. Deep wells drilled through the top layers of solid rock produce a flow of water.
4. Such wells are sometimes called artesian wells.
5. Sentence correct.

练习 39.6, p. 322

Ellis Island, New York, reopened for business in 1990, but now the customers are tourists, not immigrants. This spot, which lies in New York Harbor, was the first American soil seen or touched by many of the nation's immigrants. Though other places also served as ports of entry for foreigners, none has the symbolic power of Ellis Island. Between its opening in 1892 and its closing in 1954, over 20 million people, about two-thirds of all immigrants, were detained there before taking up their new lives in the United States. Ellis Island processed over 2000 [or 2,000] newcomers a day when immigration was at its peak between 1900 and 1920.

练习 40.1, p. 324

Possible answers

1. Electronic instruments are prevalent in jazz and rock music; however, they are less common in classical music.
2. Jazz and rock change rapidly; they nourish experimentation and improvisation.

3. The notes and instrumentation of traditional classical music were established by a composer writing decades or centuries ago; therefore, such music does not change.
4. Contemporary classical music not only can draw on tradition; it can also respond to innovations such as jazz rhythms and electronic sounds.
5. Much contemporary electronic music is more than just jazz, rock, or classical; it is a fusion of all three.

练习40.2, p. 326

The set, sounds, and actors in the movie captured the essence of horror films. The set was ideal: dark, deserted streets; trees dipping their branches over the sidewalks; mist hugging the ground and creeping up to meet the trees; looming shadows of unlighted, turreted houses. The sounds, too, were appropriate; especially terrifying was the hard, hollow sound of footsteps echoing throughout the film.

练习41.1, p. 328

1. Sunlight is made up of three kinds of radiation: visible rays; infrared rays, which we cannot see; and ultraviolet rays, which are also invisible.
2. Especially in the ultraviolet range, sunlight is harmful to the eyes.
3. Ultraviolet rays can damage the retina; furthermore, they can cause cataracts on the lens.
4. Infrared rays are the longest, measuring 700 nanometers and longer, while ultraviolet rays are the shortest, measuring 400 nanometers and shorter.
5. The lens protects the eye by absorbing much of the ultraviolet radiation and thus protecting the retina.

练习42.1, p. 332

1. In works for adults and teens, fiction writers often explore people's relationship to nature and the environment.
2. For example, Carl Hiaasen's inventive and humorous plots often revolve around endangered species' habitats.
3. In *Hoot*, Hiaasen's first novel for younger readers, endangered owls' habitat will be destroyed if a business's plans to build a new restaurant proceed.
4. In *Scat* two students' investigation into a teacher's disappearance leads to an environmental mystery.
5. Two of Margaret Atwood's recent novels are about several individuals' survival following a devastating environmental crisis and a plague that has killed nearly all of the residents of a city.

练习42.2, p. 333

1. Many students seek help from the college writing center when they're writing papers for their classes.
2. The writing center has expanded its hours: it's now open until 10 PM every night.

练习42.3, p. 334

People whose online experiences include blogging, Web cams, and social-networking sites are often used to seeing the details of other people's private lives. Many are also comfortable sharing their own opinions, photographs, and videos with family, friends, and even strangers. However, they need to realize that employers and even the government can see their information, too. Employers commonly put applicants' names through social-networking Web sites such as *MySpace* and *Facebook*.

练习43.1, p. 338

In one class we talked about a passage from *I Have a Dream*, the speech delivered by Martin Luther King, Jr., on the steps of the Lincoln Memorial on August 28, 1963:

> When the architects of our republic wrote the magnificent words of the Constitution and the Declaration of Independence, they were signing a promissory

note to which every American was to fall heir. This note was a promise that all men would be guaranteed the unalienable rights of life, liberty, and the pursuit of happiness.

⁽"⁾What did Dr. King mean by this statement?⁽"⁾ the teacher asked. ⁽"⁾Perhaps we should define ⁽"⁾promissory note⁽"⁾ first.⁽"⁾

练习44.1, p. 343

1. "To be able to read the Bible in the vernacular was a liberating experience⟨...⟩"

练习44.2, p. 345

"Let all the learned say what they can, ⟨/⟩ 'Tis ready money makes the man." These two lines of poetry by the Englishman William Somerville ⟨(⟩1645–1742⟨)⟩ may apply to a current American economic problem. Non-American investors with "ready money" pour some of it⟨—⟩as much as $1.3 trillion in recent years⟨—⟩into the United States. Stocks and bonds, savings deposits, service companies, factories, artworks, political campaigns⟨—⟩ the investments of foreigners are varied and grow more numerous every day.

练习45.1, p. 352

1. Science affects many important aspects of our lives.
2. Many people have a poor understanding of the role of scientific breakthroughs in their health.
3. Many people believe that doctors are more responsible for improvements in health care than scientists are.
4. But scientists in the laboratory have made crucial steps in the search for knowledge about human health and medicine.
5. For example, one scientist whose discoveries have affected many people is Ulf Von Euler.

练习45.2, p. 353

The weather affects all of us, though its effects are different for different people. Some people love a fair day with warm temperatures and sunshine. They revel in spending a whole day outside without the threat of rain.

练习46.1, p. 355

1. Sentence correct.
2. Sentence correct.
3. The non⊖African elephants of south⊖central Asia are somewhat smaller.
4. A fourteen⊖ or fifteen⊖year-old elephant has reached sexual maturity.
5. The elephant life span is about sixty⊖five or seventy years.

练习47.1, p. 359

1. San Antonio, Texas, is a thriving city in the Southwest.
2. The city has always offered much to tourists interested in the roots of Spanish settlement of the New World.
3. The Alamo is one of five Catholic missions built by priests to convert Native Americans and to maintain Spain's claims in the area.
4. But the Alamo is more famous for being the site of an 1836 battle that helped to create the Republic of Texas.
5. Many of the nearby streets, such as Crockett Street, are named for men who died in that battle.

练习48.1, p. 362

1. Of the many Vietnam veterans who are writers, Oliver Stone is perhaps the most famous for writing and directing the films *Platoon* and *Born on the Fourth of July*.
2. Tim O'Brien has written short stories for *Esquire*, *GQ*, and *Massachusetts Review*.
3. *Going after Cacciato* is O'Brien's dreamlike novel about the horrors of combat.

4. The word *Vietnam* is technically two words (*Viet* and *Nam*), but most American writers spell it as ✓one word. [*Viet* and *Nam* were correctly highlighted.]
5. American writers use words or phrases borrowed from Vietnamese, such as *di di mau* ("go quickly") or *dinky dau* ("crazy").

练习49.1，p. 365

1. Sentence correct.
2. About 65 million years ago, a comet or asteroid crashed into the earth.
3. The result was a huge crater about 10 kilometers (6.2 miles) deep in the Gulf of Mexico.
4. Sharpton's new measurements suggest that the crater is 50 percent larger than scientists had previously believed.
5. Indeed, 20-year-old drilling cores reveal that the crater is about 186 miles wide, roughly the size of Connecticut.

练习50.1，p. 368

1. The planet Saturn is 900 million miles, or nearly 1.5 billion kilometers, from the sun.
2. Sentence correct.
3. Thus, Saturn orbits the sun only 2.4 times during the average human life span.
4. It travels in its orbit at about 21,600 miles per hour.
5. Fifteen to twenty times denser than Earth's core, Saturn's core measures seventeen thousand miles across.

练习56.1，p. 483

The entries below follow the order of the exercise and so are not alphabetized.

Epstein, Dmitry, Erik C. Nisbet, and Tarleton Gillespie. "Who's Responsible for the Digital Divide?" *Information Society* 27.2 (2011): 92-104. *Academic Search Complete.* Web. 19 Apr. 2012.

"Banking the Unbanked." *Digital Divide Institute.* DigitalDivide.org, 2010. Web. 20 Apr. 2012.

Warschauer, Mark. *Technology and Social Inclusion: Rethinking the Digital Divide.* Cambridge: MIT P, 2003. Print.

Wayne, Teddy. "Digital Divide Is a Matter of Income." *New York Times* 13 Dec. 2010, natl. ed.: B3. *LexisNexis Academic.* Web. 19 Apr. 2012.

索引

A
a, an
    capitalization in titles, 358–59
    choosing between, 523
    rules for use of, 274–75
a, an, the, 182, 274–75
Abbreviations
    a vs. *an* with, 523
    acceptable, 363
    apostrophe with, 334
    appropriate, 363
    BC, BCE, AD, CE, AM, PM, No.,
        $, 365
    in business names, 365
    for calendar designations, 364
    grammar/style and spelling
        checkers for, 363
    Inc., Bros., Co., &, 365
    Latin, 364
    for names of people, places,
        courses, 364
    in online communication, 107,
        164–65
    period with, 304–05, 363
    plurals of, 334
    with specific dates and numbers, 365
    for titles with names, 363–64
    for units of measurement, 364
abide by, abide in, 176
Absolute modifiers, 270
Absolute phrases
    comma with, 313
    defined, 208, 313
Absolute statements, 122
Abstracts
    documenting: APA style, 505, 509,
        514; MLA style, 453, 455, 476
    in one's own paper, 517
    as research sources, 387
Abstract words, 175–76
Academic community, joining, 78–83
Academic integrity, 80–82
Academic sites, MLA style, 468, 469
Academic writing. *See also* Critical
        thinking and reading; Research
        writing
    approaches to, 100–11
    audience for, 101
    content and structure of, 104–05
    conventions of, 104–08
    designing, 104–08, 124–25
    directness in, 106
    expectations for, 100–11
    features of, 107

    formality in, 105–08
    genre in, 101–02
    goals and requirements of,
        100–11
    integrity in, 80–82
    language for, 105–08
    organization in, 105
    person and pronouns in, 107
    plagiarism in, 105
    purpose in, 100–01
    in research writing, 397–424
    in response to texts, 102–04, 124–25
    standard American English in,
        105–08
    structure and content of, 104–05
    synthesis in, 103–04, 409–10
    thesis statement and support in,
        105
    voice in, 105–08
accept, except, 348, 523
Accessibility, considering, 68
accordingly, punctuation with,
        294–95
according to, 176
accords with, 176
accuse of, 176
accustomed to, 176
Acknowledgment of opposition,
        118–19
Acknowledgment of sources. *See also*
        Plagiarism
    in academic writing, 80
    disciplines' styles for, 432–34
    necessity for, 425–34
    using APA style, 497–516
    using MLA style, 439–83
Acronyms
    acceptability of, 363–64
    defined, 363–64
    period omitted from, 304
Active reading, 87–89
Active voice
    in basic sentence pattern, 204
    consistency in use of, 241–42
    defined, 185, 240
    formation of, 240
    vs. passive voice, 145–46, 184–85,
        240–41
    as preferred form, 145–46, 240–41
AD, BC, 365
adapt from, to, 176
Address (electronic)
    Digital Object Identifiers (DOIs),
        508–09

Address (electronic) (*continued*)
  URLs (uniform resource locators), 354, 402, 465–66, 473–74, 508–15
Address (lecture), MLA style for, 483
Address (street, city, state)
  in business letters, 136–38
  commas in, 317
  numerals instead of words in, 367
Ad hominem fallacy, 122
Adjective clauses
  defined, 209–10
  repetition in, 301
Adjectives
  vs. adverbs, 194, 268–69
  adverbs to modify, 194
  capitalization of proper, 356–57
  comma with two or more, 316
  comparative and superlative forms of, 194
  coordinate, 316
  defined, 161, 267, 281
  forms of, 194, 269–71
  grammar checkers for, 267, 268
  hyphens in compound, 353–54
  infinitives and infinitive phrases as, 207
  irregular, 270
  after linking verbs, 268–69
  to modify nouns and pronouns, 194, 268
  to modify subjects, 268–69
  not to negate, 268
  order of, 281–82
  with plural nouns, 267
  prepositional phrases as, 206
  present and past participles as, 272–73
  for sentence variety, 161–62
  subordinate clauses as, 209–10
  verbals and verbal phrases as, 206–07
Ad populum fallacy, 122
Adverb clauses, 210–11, 321
Adverbs
  vs. adjectives, 194, 268–69
  comparative and superlative forms of, 194
  defined, 161, 228, 267, 279
  forms of, 194, 269–71
  grammar checkers for, 267
  with grammatical units, 278–81
  infinitives and infinitive phrases as, 207
  irregular, 270
  after linking verbs, 268–69
  -ly ending with, 194
  to modify verbs, adjectives, adverbs, word groups, 267, 268
  negative, and word order, 162
  placement of, 278–81

prepositional phrases as, 206
for sentence variety, 161–62
subordinate clauses as, 210–11
in two-word verbs, 228–29
verbals and verbal phrases as, 206–07
Advertisements. *See* Illustrations and artworks
advice, advise, 523
a few, few, 276
affect, effect, 348, 523
afraid of, 176
African American Vernacular English, 164
Afterword, MLA style, 463
aggravate, 523
Agreement of pronouns and antecedents
  with antecedents joined by *and,* 258–59
  with antecedents joined by *or* or *nor,* 259
  with collective nouns, 261
  explanation of, 258
  and generic *he,* 260
  grammar checkers for, 258
  with indefinite words, 259–61
Agreement of subjects and verbs
  explanation of, 243
  grammar checkers for, 243
  with indefinite pronouns, 246–47
  with intervening words, 245
  with inverted word order, 248
  with linking verbs, 249
  -s and *-es* endings and, 244–45
  with singular nouns ending in *-s,* 248
  with subjects joined by *and,* 245
  with subjects joined by *or* or *nor,* 246
  with *who, which,* or *that,* 247–48
  with words being described or defined, 249
agree on, to, with, 176
agree to, agree with, 523
Aircraft, italics or underlining for names of, 361
a little, little, 276
all, 246–47, 260
all ready, already, 348, 523
all right, 524
all together, altogether, 524
allusion, illusion, 348, 524
Allusions, 97
Almanacs, MLA style, 461
almost, most, 524
a lot, 524
already, all ready, 348
AM, PM, 365
among, between, 524
amount, number, 524

Ampersands (&), 365, 501
an, a
    capitalization in titles, 358–59
    choosing between, 523
    rules for use of, 274–75
Analogies, false, 123
Analysis
    in critical reading of literature, 130–32
    in critical reading of research sources, 397–409
    in critical thinking and reading, 92, 96–98
    in essay development, 15
    in paragraph development, 55
    of visuals, 96–98
    as writing assignment, 7
    of writing situation, 2–4
and
    ampersand (&) for, 365, 501
    antecedents of pronouns joined by, 258–59
    commas with, 149, 307–08, 314
    as coordinating conjunction, 149, 196
    main clauses not joined by, 291–93
    parallelism with, 155–56
    semicolons with, 323, 325
    subjects joined by, 245, 320
and/or, 524
angry with, 176
Annotated bibliographies, 376–78
Anonymous or unsigned works
    APA style: parenthetical citations, 499–500; reference list, 504
    MLA style: parenthetical citations, 442; works cited, 452, 456, 468
ante-, anti-, 524
Antecedents
    agreement of pronouns and, 258–61
    collective nouns as, 247
    defined, 258
    indefinite words as, 259–61
    reference of pronouns to, 263–66
    of *who, which, that,* and verb agreement, 247–48
Anthologies or collections
    APA style, 508
    MLA style, 460–61
anti-, ante-, 524
anxious, eager, 524
any
    vs. *any other*, 271
    pronoun with, 259–61
    verb with, 246–47
anybody
    vs. *any body*, 524
    pronoun with, 259–61
    verb with, 246–47
any more, anymore, 524

anyone
    vs. *any one*, 524
    pronoun with, 259–61
    verb with, 246–47
anything
    pronoun with, 259–61
    verb with, 246–47
anyway, 294–95
APA style, 497–522
    for document format, 516–19
    index to documentation models: parenthetical citations, 497; reference list, 503
    parenthetical citations: index to, 498; models of, 497–500
    reference list: guidelines for, 500–16; index to, 503; models of, 500–16
    sample research paper using, 519–22
Apostrophes, 329–34
    with compound words, 331
    with contractions, 333
    to form plurals of abbreviations, dates, and words and characters named as words, 334
    to form possessive case, 191, 331–32
    grammar checkers for, 329–30
    misused to form plural nouns, singular verbs, or possessive personal pronouns, 332–33
Appeal, of literary work, 132
Appeals
    ethical, 118
    as evidence, 114
    explanation of, 114
    inappropriate, 118
    rational and emotional, 117–18
    to reader's fear or pity, 121
Appositives
    case of pronoun in, 256
    colon to introduce, 327
    defined, 208, 256, 313, 327
    punctuation of, 313
Appropriate words. *See also* Language; Words
    colloquial language, 165–66
    dialect and nonstandard English, 164
    explanation of, 163–64
    grammar checkers for, 164
    indirect and pretentious writing, 166
    labels, 169–70
    sexist and other biased language, 167–69
    slang, 165
    standard American English, 163–64
    technical words, 166

are, is, 524
Arguments
　acknowledging opposing views in, 118–19
　appropriate appeals in, 117–18
　assumptions in, 114
　claims in, 112–13, 114, 398
　critical thinking and reading for, 84–99
　deductive reasoning in, 116–17
　defined, 111
　elements of, 3, 111–14
　evidence in, 113–14
　fallacies in, 120–24
　finding common ground, 118–19
　inductive reasoning in, 115
　organization of, 124–25
　oversimplifications in, 122–23
　reasonable, 114–23
　Rogerian, 119
　sample of, 125–28, 133–35
　writing, 111–28
　as writing assignment, 7
Art. *See* Illustrations and artworks
Articles (*a, an, the*)
　a vs. *an*, 523
　capitalization in titles, 358–59
　careless omission of, 182
　defined, 273
　grammar checkers for, 274
　rules for use of, 274–75
Articles in periodicals
　documenting: APA style, 505–11; MLA style, 453–57, 461, 469, 474–76, 480
　finding bibliographic information for, 453–56, 454, 474
　in online databases, 385–88, 474–76
　peer-reviewed or refereed, 384, 386
　reprinted in a collection, 461
　as research sources, 384–88
　titles, quotation marks for, 336
　in working bibliographies, 377
Artworks. *See* Illustrations and artworks
as
　vs. *like*, 525
　misuse for *because, since, while, whether, who*, 524–25
　parallelism with, 156–57
　pronoun after, 256
as a result, punctuation with, 294–95
as . . . as, 196–97
ascent, assent, 348
Assignments
　reading, 78
　writing, 6–7, 31, 79
Associations, capitalization of names of, 357

Assumptions
　interpreting, in critical reading, 92–93, 98
　used in argument, 114
assure, ensure, insure, 525
at, in, on, 177–78
at last, punctuation with, 294–95
at length, punctuation with, 294–95
Audience
　for academic writing, 101
　anticipating objections of, 118–19
　consideration of, 3, 7–9
　of essays, 31
　for illustrations, 96
　for public writing, 141–42
　purpose and, 6–7
　questions about, 3, 8
　subject and, 4
　vision loss, designing for readers with, 68
　for Web compositions, 75–76
Audiovisual works. *See* Films, DVDs, and video recordings; Illustrations and artworks; Sound recordings
Authors
　APA style: parenthetical citations, 497–500; reference list, 502–16
　determining in online sources, 399, 408
　information about, in critical reading, 85
　MLA style: list of works cited, 448–84; parenthetical citations, 439–48
　providing names of, in signal phrases, 422
Auxiliary verbs. *See* Helping verbs (auxiliary verbs)
aware of, 176
awful, awfully, 525
a while, awhile, 525

B
Background information, in signal phrases, 422
bad, badly, 268, 525
Bandwagon fallacy, 122
Bar charts, 70. *See also* Illustrations and artworks
bare, bear, 348
based on, 176
BC, AD, 365
BCE, CE, 365
be
　forms of, 145, 192–93, 232–33
　as helping verb, 193, 222
　illogical equation with, 298
　as linking verb, 268
　omission of, 286
　past participle and forms of, 222, 240

present participle and forms of, 222
-s forms of, 219–20
in subjunctive mood, 238–39
as weak verb, 145
bear, bare, 348
Begging the question, 121
Beginnings of sentences
for emphasis, 146–48
variety and, 161–62
being as, being that, 525
Beliefs
as claim in argument, 112–13
critical thinking and, 92–93
beside, besides, 525
besides, 51, 294–95
better, had better, 525
between, among, 524
Biased language, 118, 167–70, 260
Bible
capitalization of, 357
MLA style: list of works cited, 462–63; parenthetical citation, 445
no italics or underlining for, 361
Bibliographies. *See also* APA style; MLA style
annotated, 376–78
guides to preparation of, 433–34
as research sources, 376
working, 376–78
Block quotations
APA style, 518
MLA style, 485–86
Blogs. *See also* Social media
documenting: APA style, 513; MLA style, 468, 472
evaluating, 407–09
permission for using, 431–32
as research sources, 391
writing, 75–76
board, bored, 349
Body
of argument, 124
of business letter, 136–37
of essay, 20, 43
Bookmarks/Favorites, 389
Book reviews
APA style, 507, 511
MLA style, 456, 469, 474
Books
documenting, electronic: APA style, 512; MLA style, 468, 472–73, 476–77
documenting, print: APA style, 507–08; MLA style, 457–64
finding bibliographic information for, 458
as research sources, 383–84
subdivisions of, quotation marks for, 336

titles of: capitalization of, 358–59; italics or underlining for, 360
in working bibliographies, 377–78
Boolean operators, in keywords, 382
bored, board, 349
Borrowed material
interpretation of, 420–22
introduction of, 420
both
pronoun with, 259–61
verb with, 246–47
both . . . and
as correlative conjunction, 196–97
parallelism with, 156
Brackets
for changes in quotations, 344, 356
function of, 339
grammar checkers for, 339
with *sic,* 344
Brainstorming, 13–14
brake, break, 349
bring, take, 525
Brochures, MLA style, 464
Bros., 365
Browsers, 389
Business firms, abbreviations for names of, 365
Business writing. *See* Public writing
but
commas with, 307–08, 314
as coordinating conjunction, 149, 196
main clauses not joined by, 291–93
parallelism with, 155–56
semicolons with, 323, 325
but, hardly, scarcely, 525
but, however, yet, 525
buy, by, 349

C

can, may, 224, 525
capable of, 176
Capitalization
of *a, an, the* in titles, 358–59
brackets for altered, 356
after colons, 327
of compass directions, 357
of days, months, holidays, 357
as element of document design, 67
of first word in sentence, 356
of government agencies, 357
grammar checkers for, 355–56
of historical events, documents, periods, movements, 357
hyphen following, 354
of languages, 357
obtaining information about, 355–56
in online communication, 107, 164–65, 359

Capitalization *(continued)*
 of organizations and associations, 357
 with parentheses, 341
 of persons, 356–57
 of places, 356–57
 of proper nouns and adjectives, 356–57
 of questions in series, 356
 in quoted material, 356, 420
 of races and nationalities, 357
 for readers with vision loss, 68
 of regions, 357
 of relationships, 358
 of religions and religious terms, 357
 of titles of persons, 358
 of titles of works: APA style, 502; guidelines for, 358–59
Captions, 70–72, 74
Careless plagiarism, 80–81, 427
Cartoons. *See* Illustrations and artworks
Case of pronouns
 in appositive, 256
 in compound subject or object, 252–53
 defined, 251–52
 before gerund, 257
 grammar checkers for, 252
 with infinitive, 256–57
 pronoun function and, 251–52
 as subject complement, 253–54
 after *than* or *as*, 256
 we vs. *us* with noun, 256
 who vs. *whom*, 254–55
Cause-and-effect analysis
 in essay development, 15
 in paragraph development, 57
 transitional expressions for, 51
CD-ROMs
 documenting: APA style, 515; MLA style, 479–80
 periodicals on, 480
 reference works on, 479–80
CE, BCE, 365
censor, censure, 519
Central idea. *See also* Thesis and thesis statement
 topic sentences, 45
certainly, punctuation with, 294–95
certain of, 177
cf., 364
Characters in literary works, 131
charge for, with, 177
Charts. *See* Illustrations and artworks
The Chicago Manual of Style, 433
Chronological organization, 21, 48
Citation of sources, 425–34, 437. *See also* APA style; MLA style

cite, sight, site, 349, 526
Claims
 in argument, 112–13, 124–25
 supporting, 398
 in thesis statement, 18
Clarity
 completeness for, 181–82
 conciseness for, 183–87
 of draft, 37
 emphasis for, 144–46
 exact words for, 171–80
 parallelism for, 155–57
 reference of pronouns to antecedents, 263
Classification
 in essay development, 15
 in paragraph development, 55–56
Clauses
 adjective, 209–10, 301
 adverb, 210–11
 comma between, 292, 293, 307–08
 comma splices with, 290–95
 comma with introductory, 309–10
 conciseness of, 186–87
 coordination between, 149–51
 defined, 209–10
 fused sentences with, 291–95
 main. *See* Main (independent) clauses
 nonessential vs. essential, 311–14, 320–21
 noun, 210–11
 semicolon with, 294, 323, 325
 as sentence fragment, 221, 287
 simplifying, 186–87
 subordinate, 209–11. *See also* Subordinate (dependent) clauses
Clichés
 avoiding, 180
 defined, 180
 grammar checkers for, 171
 list of, 180
 no quotation marks for, 337
 style checkers for, 180
Climactic organization, 21, 48
climatic, climactic, 526
Close of business letter, 136–37
Clustering, 14–15
Co., 365
Coherence. *See also* Consistency; Unity
 defined, 24
 of essays, 24–25, 31
 of paragraphs, 46–52
Collaboration
 in community work, 142
 guidelines for, 32–34

for revisions, 28–29, 32–34,
    34–36
  using computers, 28, 32
Collective nouns
  agreement of pronouns with, 261
  agreement of verbs with, 247
  defined, 191, 247, 261
Colloquial language
  appropriate use for, 165–66
  grammar checkers for, 164
Colons, 326–28
  in business letter salutation, 327
  capitalization after, 356
  vs. dash, 340
  function of, 326
  grammar checkers for, 326
  as introducer, 326–27
  misuse of, 328
  with quotation marks, 337
  vs. semicolon, 326
  before subtitle, 327
  in time of day, 327
Color
  as design element, 68
  selecting for readers with vision
    loss, 68
  of visuals, 97
Combining sentences
  for conciseness, 187
  for variety, 160–61
Comic strips. See Illustrations and
  artworks
Commands
  construction of, 204
  exclamation point with, 305–06
  period with, 304
  verbs to begin, 187
Commas, 306–21. See also Commas,
  misuse of
  with absolute phrases, 313
  with adjectives, 316
  with conjunctive adverbs, 294
  with coordinating conjunctions,
    149–50, 308
  vs. dash, 340
  in dates, addresses, place names,
    long numbers, 317–18
  with direct address, 314
  function of, 306–08
  grammar checkers for, 308
  with *he said* and other signal
    phrases, 318–19
  with interjections, 314
  with introductory elements,
    309–10
  between items in series, 315
  with main clauses joined by *and,
    but*, etc., 307–08
  main uses of, 307

with nonessential elements,
    311–14
  vs. parentheses, 341
  with parenthetical expressions,
    313, 341
  with phrases of contrast, 314
  with prepositional phrases, 310
  with quotation marks, 337–38
  with quotations, 318–19
  with tag questions, 314
  with transitional expressions, 310
  with verbals or verbal phrases, 309
  with *yes* and *no*, 314
Commas, misuse of, 319–21
  around essential elements,
    320–21
  around series, 321
  in comma splices, 290–95
  in compound subjects, predicates,
    etc., 319–20
  after conjunctions, 320
  before indirect quotations, 321
  with other punctuation in
    quotations, 318
  between prepositions and objects,
    319
  between subjects and verbs, 319
  between verbs and objects, 319
Comma splices, 290–95
  defined, 290–91
  grammar checkers for, 291
  with main clauses not joined by
    and, but, etc., 291–93
  with main clauses related by
    however, for example, etc.,
    294–95
  revision of, 291–95
Comment function, 28, 32
Common knowledge, 428
Commonly confused words, grammar
    checkers for, 171
Common nouns, 191, 358
Communication in academic setting,
    82–83. See also Social media
Community work, 141–42
  audience, 141–42
  collaboration in, 142
  newsletters, 142
  purpose, 141–42
  writing for, 141–42
Comparative form of adjectives and
    adverbs, 194, 269–71
Comparison and contrast
  in essay development, 15
  in paragraph development, 56
  point-by-point, 56
  subject-by-subject, 56
  transitional expressions for, 51
  as writing assignment, 6

558 Comparisons
   complete, 270–71
   double, 270
   logical, 270–71
   parallelism in, 156–57
Compass directions, 358
complement, compliment, 526
Complements
   defined, 210
   object complements, 202
   subject complements, 210–11, 251–54
Complete compounds, 181–82
Complete predicates, 198
Complete sentences, 181–82, 286–87
Complete subjects, 198
Complex sentences, 212
Compound adjectives, 353–54
Compound-complex sentences, 213
Compound constructions, 155–57. *See also specific compounds*
   comma with, 307–08
   complete, 181–82
   defined, 181, 319
   parallelism in, 156–57
   pronoun case in, 252–53
   semicolon with, 323
Compound numbers, 354
Compound objects, 252–53
Compound predicates
   defined, 198
   no comma in, 319–20
Compounds, complete, 181–82
Compound sentences, 212
Compound subjects
   defined, 198
   no comma in, 319–20
   verb with, 198
Compound words
   apostrophe with possessives of, 331
   defined, 353–54
   forming plurals of, 352
   hyphens in, 353–54
Computerized databases. *See* Databases, electronic
Computerized sources. *See* Sources
Computers. *See also* Internet; Web sites
   AutoSummarize function, 91
   brainstorming on, 13–14
   collaborating on, 28, 32
   Comment function, 28, 32
   dashes on, 339
   databases on. *See* Databases, electronic
   designing documents on, 63–76
   drafting on, 26–27, 32
   editing on, 38–40
   file management on, 32
   formatting source citations on, 434
   freewriting on, 12–13
   grammar and style checkers on, 38–40. *See also entries for specific grammar and style issues*
   HTML on, 74
   idea mapping on, 14–15
   for information gathering, 412
   for invention and development, 11–14
   journals on, 11–12
   for keeping notes, 412
   library catalog on, 380
   research with. *See* Research writing
   résumé databases on, 138
   revising on, 32
   sources on. *See* Sources
   spelling checkers on, 348, 363
   summaries using, 91
   Track Changes function, 31, 34
   using the Web on, 388–91, 397–409
Computer services. *See* Databases, electronic
Computer software
   to format source citations, 434
   grammar and style checkers, 38–40
   spelling checkers, 38–40
   titles of, italics or underlining for, 360
   word processors, 31
Conciseness, 183–87
   avoiding jargon for, 187
   combining sentences for, 187
   cutting empty words and phrases for, 185
   cutting repetition for, 186
   deleting unnecessary words for, 183–87
   focusing on subject and verb for, 183–85
   grammar checkers for, 183
   reducing modifiers for, 186–87
   using active voice for, 184–85
   using strong verbs for, 184–85
Concluding elements, dashes with, 340
Conclusions
   of argument, 124
   of essay, 20, 31, 61–62
   guidelines for, 61
Concrete words, 175–76
concur in, with, 177
Conditional sentences
   defined, 239
   sequence of verb tenses in, 235–36
   subjunctive mood in, 238–39
Conference proceedings, MLA style, 463

Conjunctions
  adverbial. *See* Conjunctive adverbs
  capitalization in titles, 358–59
  coordinating. *See* Coordinating conjunctions
  correlative. *See* Correlative conjunctions
  subordinating. *See* Subordinating conjunctions
  types of, 195–96
Conjunctive adverbs
  and comma splices, 294
  comma with, 294
  vs. coordinating and subordinating conjunctions, 294–95
  defined, 149, 294, 323
  list of, 294
  semicolon with main clauses related by, 294
Connotation
  defined, 173–74
  grammar checkers for, 171
conscience, conscious, 526
consequently, punctuation with, 294–95
Consistency. *See also* Agreement of pronouns and antecedents; Agreement of subjects and verbs; Coherence; Unity
  in paragraph, 49–50
  in pronouns, 265–66
  in use of italics or underlining, 360
  in verb mood, 239
  in verb tense, 233
  in verb voice, 241–42
Consonants, final, 351
contend for, with, 177
Content, in academic writing, 104–05
Context
  determining for online sources, 402, 404, 408
  determining in critical thinking, 93
  of illustrations, 93, 97
continual, continuous, 526
Contractions, apostrophes for, 333
Contrary-to-fact sentences
  sequence of verb tenses in, 236
  subjunctive mood for, 238–39
Contrast. *See* Comparison and contrast
Conventions, of academic writing, 10
Coordinate adjectives, 316
Coordinating conjunctions
  comma with, 307–08, 320
  vs. conjunctive adverbs, 295
  for correcting comma splices or fused sentences, 291–93
  defined, 149, 155, 196, 290, 320, 323
  list of, 196

  parallelism with, 155–56
  punctuation with, 307–08, 320
Coordination
  defined, 149–50
  effective, 150–51
  excessive or faulty, 151
  grammar checkers for, 150
  parallelism with, 155–57
  to relate equal ideas, 149–51
Copyright
  fair use and, 432
  Web compositions and, 430–31
Corporate or group authors
  APA style: parenthetical citations, 499; reference list, 503–04
  MLA style: list of works cited, 452; parenthetical citations, 442
Correctness, of draft, 37
Correlative conjunctions
  defined, 150, 156, 196
  list of, 196
  parallelism with, 156
  use of, 150
could of, 528
Count nouns
  defined, 191, 273
  determiners with, 273–77
Country names, abbreviation of, 363–64
Courses of instruction, abbreviations of, 364
Credentials of source author, in signal phrase, 422
credible, creditable, credulous, 526
criteria, 526
Critical thinking and reading, 84–99
  and academic writing, 100–01, 111–28
  active reading for, 84–89
  analysis in, 92, 96–98
  and argument, 100–01, 111–14
  evaluating for, 93–94, 397–409
  with illustrations, 94–99
  interpreting for, 92–93, 98–99
  and literature, 129–32
  with online sources, 407–09
  previewing for, 85–87, 94–95
  rereading for, 88–89
  and research sources, 397–409
  response in, 91–94
  for revision, 30
  sample essay, 108–10
  summarizing for, 89–91
  synthesis in, 93, 103–04, 409–10
  techniques of, 100–08, 124–25
  with visuals, 94–99
  with Web sites and pages, 397–409
Critical writing, 108–10
Critique, of texts, 108–10

索引 581

Culture-language issues. *See also* pp. 592–93
  academic writing, structure of, 105
  adjective order, 281–82
  adjectives for adverbs, 268
  adjectives with plural nouns, 267
  adverb position, 280
  adverbs, negative, and word order, 161–62
  American vs. British spelling, 350
  appealing to readers, 9
  appropriate words, 164
  argument, 111
  articles (*a, an, the*), 181, 273–77
  at, in, on, 177–78
  capitalization, 356
  collaboration, 34
  collective nouns, 247
  comma splices, 291, 293
  conciseness, 183
  coordinating conjunctions, 196
  count nouns, 273
  critical reading, 34, 84, 397
  defined, 164
  determiners, 273–77
  dialects, 108, 164
  dictionaries, 173, 274
  direct vs. indirect approaches, 304
  discovering ideas, 11
  editing, 34
  expert opinions, 425
  expletive constructions, 187, 205
  exploratory writing, 11
  for, since, 232
  freewriting, 12–13
  fused sentences, 291, 293
  gender of nouns and pronouns, 258
  gerund or infinitive after verb, 207, 225–27
  helping verbs and main verbs, 220–24
  indirect questions, 304
  intellectual property, 425
  introductory paragraphs, 59
  invisible writing, 13
  irregular verb forms, 217
  journal writing, 12
  main clauses, 291, 293
  modal verbs, 223–24
  Ms., Miss, Mrs., 169
  noncount nouns, 247, 261, 352
  nonstandard dialects, 164
  no to negate nouns, 268
  not to negate verbs and adjectives, 268
  noun plurals, 261
  numbers, periods or commas with, 318, 367
  omitted *be,* 286
  omitted helping verbs, 220–21
  omitted *it* and *there* in expletive constructions, 187
  omitted *-s* and *-ed* verb endings, 219, 244
  omitted subjects or verbs, 220–21, 286, 287
  organization of essay, 20
  paragraphing, 43
  paraphrasing, 416
  passive voice, 201, 222, 240
  past participles, formation of, 217
  past tense, 217
  periods vs. commas with numbers, 318, 367
  plagiarism, 425
  plural nouns after *one of the,* 248
  prepositions, 177–78, 195
  present perfect tense, 232
  present vs. past participles as adjectives, 207, 272–73
  progressive tenses, 232–33
  pronoun-antecedent agreement, 261, 263
  pronoun case, 252
  pronoun gender, 258
  public writing, 135
  redundant phrases, 186
  reference of pronouns to antecedents, 248
  repetition of sentence parts, 300–01
  research topic development, 397
  revision of comma splices, 291, 293
  revision of essays, 34, 43
  -s and *-ed* verb endings, 219
  -s and *-es* subject and verb endings, 244
  -self pronouns, 252
  standard American English, 108, 164
  structure of academic writing, 105
  subjects of sentences, 198
  subject-verb agreement, 244
  subordinating conjunctions, 196
  thesis sentences or statements, 18
  titles of address, 169
  transitional expressions, 52
  transitive verbs in passive voice, 222
  transitive vs. intransitive verbs, 201
  verb forms, 217
  verbs plus particles (two-word verbs), 228–29
  verbs with *to* or *for,* 202
  verb tense sequence, 230
  vocabulary development, 87
  voice, 240
  wordiness, avoiding, 183
  word meanings, 87

word order in sentences, 200, 278–82, 304
Cumulative sentences, 147–48

D

-d, -ed, 206, 214, 218, 219–20
Dangling modifiers, 153, 283–84
Dashes
   vs. colons, 340
   vs. commas, 340
   with concluding series and explanations, 340
   forming and spacing, 339
   function of, 339
   to indicate hesitations, 340
   with introductory series, 340
   with nonessential elements, 340
   overuse of, 340
   with parenthetical expressions, 340
   with quotation marks, 338
   with shifts, 340
data, 526
Databases, electronic
   CD-ROMs for, 380–81
   documenting: APA style, 508–10; MLA style, 474–76
   finding bibliographic information for, 474–76
   kinds of, 380–81
   library catalogs, 380
   listed in annotated and working bibliographies, 377
   periodicals and periodical indexes, 385–87
   as research sources, 380–81
   vs. search engines, 381
   searching, 380–82, 385–87
   selection of, 385
   subscription, 380–81, 384–88
   of visuals, 393–94
Date of access
   APA style, 508
   MLA style, 473
Dates
   apostrophe for plurals of, 334
   BC and *AD* with, 365
   BCE and *CE* with, 365
   commas in, 317–18
   numerals vs. words for, 367
   retrieval, APA style, 508
Days of week
   abbreviations for, 364
   capitalization of, 357
Decimals, 367
Deduction (deductive reasoning), 116–17
Defined terms
   italics or underlining for, 361–62
   singular verbs with, 249
Definitions
   in essay development, 15
   in paragraph development, 54–55
   as writing assignment, 6
Demonstrative pronouns, 191
Denotation, 173–74
Dependent clauses. *See* Subordinate (dependent) clauses
dependent on, 177
Description
   in essay development, 15
   in paragraph development, 53
Descriptive titles, 34
Descriptors. *See* Keywords
desert, dessert, 349
Design, document. *See* Document design and format
Desktop publishing, 63–76
Details, 162
Determiners
   defined, 273
   grammar checkers for, 274
   uses of, 273–77
Development
   of academic writing, 10–15, 31, 79
   of paragraphs, 45–46, 53–59
device, devise, 526
Diagrams. *See* Illustrations and artworks
Dialect. *See also* Culture-language issues
   defined, 105, 164
   nonstandard, 163–64
   Standard American English as, 105–08, 163–64
   uses of, 163–64
Diction. *See* Words
Dictionaries
   for adjective and adverb forms, 270
   for capitalization, 355
   documenting: APA style, 504; MLA style, 461, 470, 479–80
   ESL, 173, 178, 274
   foreign words in, 361
   list of, 171–73
   for meanings, 173–74
   online and print versions, 171–73
   sample entry, 172
   for verb forms, 214–15, 217
differ about, over, 177
different from, different than, 526
differ from, with, 177, 526
Digital Object Identifiers (DOIs), 508–09
Direct address, comma with, 314
Direct discourse. *See* Direct quotations
Direct objects. *See also* Objects
   case of, 252–53
   defined, 201, 279
   transitive verbs and, 201

Direct questions. *See also* Indirect
    quotations
  formation of, 203
  question mark for, 305
Direct quotations. *See also* Indirect
    quotations
  accuracy of, 417
  acknowledging source of, 429
  avoiding plagiarism with, 425
  brackets for changes in, 344
  capitalization in, 356
  care in obtaining, 81–82
  changes in, 341–43, 417
  colon before, 326
  comma with, 318–19
  and copyright, 430–31
  criteria for using, 417
  defined, 132, 335
  of dialog, 335–36
  documenting, 429
  ellipsis mark for omissions from,
    341–43
  fair use of, 432
  and information gathering, 416–18
  integrating, in a paper, 419–24
  long prose quotations, format of:
    APA style, 518; MLA style, 485–86
  omissions from, 341–43
  vs. paraphrase and summary,
    412–19, 429
  of poetry, MLA style, 485–86
  quotation marks with, 335–36
  within quotations, 335–36
  she said and other signal phrases
    with, 318–19, 421
  sic in, 344
  slash with, 344–45
  tests for, 417
  verb tenses for introducing, 421, 423
Disabilities, considering readers with
    vision loss, 68
disappointed by, in, with, 177
discreet, discrete, 349, 527
Discussion, as writing assignment, 6
Discussion groups, online. *See also*
    Social media
  author's permission, obtaining, 431–32
  documenting: APA style, 513; MLA
    style, 479
  evaluating, 407–09
  for opposing views in arguments, 119
  as research sources, 391–92
disinterested, uninterested, 527
Dissertation Abstracts, 455, 514
Dissertations
  APA style, 512, 514
  MLA style, 453, 455, 464–65
Division (analysis)
  in essay development, 15
  in paragraph development, 55
Division of words, hyphen for,
    354
do, as helping verb, 193, 203, 223
Documentation of sources
  APA style, 497–516
  avoiding plagiarism and,
    425–34
  computer software for, 434
  defined, 432
  MLA style, 439–83
  necessity for, 432–34
  style guides for, 433–34
Document design and format
  APA style: document format, 65,
    516–19; reference-list format,
    522
  for business letters, 136–37
  for business memos, 139–41
  charts, 69–71
  color, 68, 97
  for community work, 141–42
  computers for, 63–76
  discipline-appropriate formats,
    64–65
  elements of, 66–68
  emphasis in, 65, 66
  flow in, 65
  grouping in, 65
  headings: APA style, 518;
    general, 67, 75
  highlighting, 67
  identification, 485
  illustrations, 68–75
  line graphs, 70–71
  lists, 67–68
  margins and spacing: APA style,
    516; general, 66; MLA style,
    484–85
  MLA style: document format, 64,
    484–86; works-cited format,
    448–84
  multimodal writing, 68–75
  for newsletters, 142
  paging: APA style, 516; MLA
    style, 485
  pie charts, 69–70
  for poetry and long prose
    quotations: APA style, 518;
    MLA style, 485–86
  principles of design, 65
  for résumés, 138–40
  spacing in, 66, 67
  standardizing in, 65
  tables, 69
  type styles and sizes, 67
  for Web compositions, 75–76
  white space, 65
DOI (Digital Object Identifier), APA
    style, 508–09
Dollar sign (*$*), 365

don't, 527
Dots, to indicate omission from quotation (ellipsis mark), 341–43
Double comparisons, 270
Double negatives, 271–72
Doublespeak, 166
Double-talk, 166
Doubt, question mark for, 305
Downloading research sources, pros and cons, 412
Drafting
　on computers, 26–27, 32
　of essays, 26–29
　maintaining momentum for, 27
　of research papers, 436–37
　of thesis statement, 16–18, 435–36
Drafts
　edited, 36–40, 437–38
　final, 40–42
　first, 26–29, 436–37
　outlines of, 30
　revised, 28–42, 437
due to the fact that, 527
DVDs. *See* Films, DVDs, and video recordings

E

-e, final, 350–51
each
　pronoun with, 259–61
　verb with, 246–47
eager, anxious, 524
EBSCOhost Academic Search, 387
-ed, -d, 206, 214, 218, 219–20
Edited works
　APA style, 508
　MLA style, 459
Editing
　in academic writing, 36–40, 80
　checklist for, 37
　on a computer, 38–40
　by peers, 28, 32–34
　research papers, 437–38
Editions, later
　APA style, 507
　MLA style, 459
Editorials, MLA style, 456, 469, 474
effect, affect, 348, 523
e.g., 364
either
　as determiner, 276
　pronoun with, 259–61
　verb with, 246–47
either . . . or
　as correlative conjunction, 196
　parallelism with, 156
Either/or fallacy, 123
ei vs. *ie*, 350

Electronic addresses
　Digital Object Identifiers (DOIs), 508–09
　URLs (uniform resource locators), 354, 402, 465–66, 473–74, 508–15
Electronic books, documenting. *See also* Books
　APA style, 512
　MLA style, 468, 472–73, 476–77
Electronic communication. *See also* Blogs; Discussion groups, online; E-mail; social networking sites
　in academic setting, 82–83
　avoiding shortcuts of, 64–65
Electronic mail. *See* E-mail
Electronic sources. *See* Sources; Web sites
elicit, illicit, 349, 527
Ellipsis marks
　forming and spacing, 341
　function of, 341
　to indicate omissions from quotations, 341–43
E-mail. *See also* Social media
　in academic setting, 82–83
　avoiding shortcuts in, 164–65
　business memos, 137–41
　capitalization in, 359
　documenting: APA style, 513; MLA style, 479
　interviews through, 395
　italics or underlining and, 362
　permission to use, 391
　as research source, 391
Em dashes, 340
emigrate, immigrate, 527
eminent, imminent, 349
Emotional appeals, 117–18
Emphasis
　active voice for, 145–46
　avoiding nouns made from verbs for, 145
　coordination for, 149–51
　in document design, 65, 66
　exclamation point for, 305–06
　focusing on subject and verb for, 144–46, 183–85
　grammar checkers for, 144
　in illustrations, 96, 97
　italics or underlining for, 67, 362
　order of information in sentences for, 146–48
　strong verbs for, 145–46
　subordination for, 152–53
Empty words and phrases, 185
Encyclopedias
　documenting: APA style, 512; MLA style, 461, 470, 479–80
　as research sources, 383

End punctuation marks
  grammar checkers for, 304
  uses of, 304–06
English, integrating borrowed
  material in, 423
English as a second language. *See*
  Culture-language issues
enough, as determiner, 276
ensure, insure, assure, 525
enthused, 527
Envelopes with business letters,
  136–37
-er, as adjective or adverb ending,
  269–71
ERIC, APA style, 512–13
-es. See -s, -es
ESL. *See* Culture-language issues
Essays. *See also* Research writing
  arguments, 125–28
  audience for, 3, 7–9
  collaboration on, 28, 30, 32–34,
    34–36
  conclusions for, 61–62
  developing subject for, 10–15
  drafting, 26–29
  editing and proofreading, 36–40
  finding subject for, 4–6
  format for, 63–76
  introductions for, 59–60
  organizing, 20–25
  peer editing of, 28, 32–34
  purpose of, 6–7
  quotation marks for titles of, 336
  relating paragraphs within, 43–44
  responding to texts in, 102–04
  revising, 28–42
  sample, 41–42
  thesis of, 16–25
  unity and coherence of, 24–25
  writing critically about, 108–10
Essential elements
  defined, 311, 320
  modifiers, 311
  no commas with, 311, 320–21
  vs. nonessential, 311–14
  test for, 312
-est, as adjective or adverb ending,
  269–71
et al., 364, 441, 449, 452, 527
etc., 364, 527
Ethical appeals, 118
Etiquette, communications in
  academic setting, 83–84
Euphemisms, 166
Evaluation
  of blog postings, 391, 407–09
  in critical thinking and reading,
    93–94
  guidelines for, 397–409
  of library sources, 398–401
  of multimedia sources, 407–09
  of online sources, 407–09
  of research sources, 81, 84–99,
    397–409
  of thesis statement, 18–19
  of visuals, 93
  of Web sources, 397–409
  as writing assignment, 7
Evasions, 120–22
even so, punctuation with, 294–95
everybody
  vs. *every body*, 527
  pronoun with, 259–61
  verb with, 246–47
everyday, every day, 527
everyone
  vs. *every one*, 527
  pronoun with, 259–61
  verb with, 246–47
everything
  pronoun with, 259–61
  verb with, 246–47
everywheres, 527
Evidence, in argument, 113–14
Exact words. *See also* Language; Words
  concrete and specific, 175–76
  denotation and connotation, 173–74
  dictionaries and thesauruses for,
    171–73
  figurative language, 179–80
  grammar checkers for, 171
  idioms, 176–79
  vs. trite expressions (clichés), 180
Examples
  in essay development, 15
  as evidence, 113
  in paragraph development, 53–54
except, accept, 348, 523
except for the fact that, 527
Exclamation points
  with quotation marks, 338
  use of, 118, 305–06
Expert opinions, 114
Expletive constructions
  conciseness by eliminating, 186–87
  necessity of *it* or *there* in, 186–87,
    205
  use of, 186–87
explicit, implicit, 527

F

Facebook, 82, 391, 407
Facts
  as claims in arguments, 113
  as evidence, 113
fair, fare, 349
Fair use, 432
Fallacies
  evasions as, 120–22
  explanation of, 120–24
  oversimplifications as, 122–23
False analogy, 123

False authority, 121
familiar with, 177
farther, further, 528
Faulty predication, 298–99
few
   pronoun with, 259–61
   verb with, 246–47
few, a few, 276
fewer, less, 528
Figurative language (figures of speech), 179–80
Figures. *See* Illustrations and artworks
Films, DVDs, and video recordings
   documenting: APA style, 513, 515; MLA style, 471, 473, 481–82
   evaluating, 407–09
   fair use of, 432
   italics or underlining for titles of, 361
   as research sources, 392–94
Final drafts, 40–42
finally, 51, 294–95
Finite verbs, 286
First drafts, 26–29, 436–37
First-level headings, 67
First person (*I, we*)
   in academic writing, 107
   and grammatical agreement, 243
   point of view, in literary works, 131
flaunt, flout, 528
Flow, in document design, 65
flunk, 528
Folk literature, 428
Fonts, 67, 75
Footnotes or endnotes, MLA style, 447–48
for
   comma with, 307–08
   as coordinating conjunction, 196
   as preposition, 195
   vs. *since*, 178, 232
for all that, punctuation with, 294–95
Foreign words
   italics or underlining for, 361
   Latin abbreviations, 364
   as source of English words, 352
Foreword, MLA style, 463
for example, punctuation with, 294–95, 323–24
for instance, punctuation with, 294–95
Formalist criticism, 130
Formal outlines
   constructing, 23–24
   for essay, 23–24
   for research papers, 486–87
   for revision, 23–24
   sentence, 486–87
   topic, 23–24, 486–87

Formal vs. informal usage
   in academic writing, 105–08
   in e-mail, 82–83
   in research sources, 408–09
Format, document. *See* Document design and format
forth, fourth, 349
Fractions
   hyphens in, 354
   numerals vs. words for, 367
Fragments, sentence, 285–88. *See* Sentence fragments
Freewriting, 12–13
Full-text resources, 384
fun, 528
further, farther, 528
furthermore, punctuation with, 294–95
further, punctuation with, 294–95
Fused sentences
   defined, 290–91
   grammar checkers for, 291
   revision of, 291–95
Future perfect progressive tense, 231
Future perfect tense, 231
Future progressive tense, 231
Future tense, 231

G

Gender
   of pronouns, 258
   and sexist language, 167–69, 260
Gender-specific terms, grammar checkers for, 164
Generalizations
   hasty, 122
   in inductive and deductive reasoning, 115
   stereotypes as, 167–69
   sweeping, 122–23
General-to-specific organization, 21, 48
General vs. specific, 20–21, 175–76
General words, 175–76
Generic *he*, 169, 260. *See also* Sexist language
Generic nouns, and pronoun agreement, 259–61
Genres
   in academic writing, 31, 101–02
   for writing assignments, 9–10
Geographical names
   abbreviation of, 364
   capitalization of, 356–57
   commas in, 317
Gerunds and gerund phrases
   defined, 207, 257
   possessives before, 257
   after verbs, 207, 225–27
get, 528
Glatt Plagiarism Services, 427
go, 215

good and, 528
good, well, 268, 269, 528
Google, 389–91
Google Scholar, 385
Government agencies,
    capitalization of, 357
Government publications
    documenting: APA style, 499,
        503–04, 511, 514; MLA style,
        442, 452, 464, 469
    as research sources, 392
Grammar and style checkers, 38–40.
    *See also entries for specific
    grammar and style issues*
Graphic narrative works, MLA style,
    461–62
Graphics or graphic files. *See*
    Illustrations and artworks
Graphs. *See* Illustrations and artworks
Grouping, in document design, 65
Group or corporate authors
    APA style: parenthetical citation,
        499; reference list, 503–04
    MLA style: list of works cited, 452;
        parenthetical citation, 442

H

had better, better, 525
had ought, 528
Handwritten research notes, pros
    and cons, 412
hanged, hung, 528
Hanging indents
    in APA reference list, 501
    creating, on word processor, 448
    in MLA works-cited list, 448
hardly, scarcely, but, 525
Hasty generalizations, 122
have
    forms of, 193
    as helping verb, 145, 193, 219–20,
        223
    -s form of, 219–20
    with verbs ending in *-ed* or *-d*,
        219–20, 223
have, of, 528
he
    case forms of, 252–53
    generic, 169, 260
    vs. *him*, 252–53
    with indefinite antecedent, 260
    with *-s, -es* verb ending, 219–20
    sexist language and, 169, 260, 528
he, she; he/she, 260, 528
Headings
    APA style, 518
    in document design, 67, 75
    and page breaks, 67
    parallelism in, 157
    on Web pages, 75
hear, here, 349

heard, herd, 349
Helping verbs (auxiliary verbs)
    with *be* or *been* as main verb,
        221–22
    combined with main verbs,
        220–24
    defined, 193
    grammar checkers for, 220–21
    list of, 193
    with main verbs ending in *-ing*,
        221
    modal, 223–24
    omitted, 220–21
    in passive voice, 222, 240
    with past participles, 221–23, 240
    in perfect tenses, 223
    with present participles, 221–22
    in progressive tenses, 221–22
    in questions, 203
    required, for finite verbs, 286
hence, punctuation with, 294–95
herd, heard, 349
here, hear, 349
here is, here are, and agreement of
    verb, 249
herself, himself, yourself, myself, 531
her vs. *she*, 252–53
Hesitations, dashes for, 340
himself, yourself, myself, herself, 531
him vs. *he*, 252–53
hisself, 528
Historical events and periods,
    capitalization of, 357
History, integrating borrowed
    material in, 423
Hits, in electronic searches, 389–91
hole, whole, 349
Holidays
    abbreviation of, 364
    capitalization of, 357
Homonyms
    defined, 173, 348
    list of, 348–49
hopefully, 529
however, punctuation with, 149,
    294–95, 323–24
however, yet, but, 525
Humanities
    integrating borrowed material in,
        423
    MLA style: documentation, 439–83;
        document format, 484–86;
        sample paper, 488–96
    style guides for, 433
hung, hanged, 528
Hyphens
    to attach prefixes and suffixes,
        354
    in compound adjectives, 353–54
    in fractions and compound
        numbers, 354

in numbers, 367
in URLs (electronic addresses), 474, 508
use in forming dash, 339
in word division, 354

I

I
  case forms of, 252
  vs. *me*, 252–53
idea, ideal, 529
Idea mapping, 14–15
Ideas
  coordination to relate equal, 149–51
  discovering, 10–15
  emphasizing, 148–54
  organizing, 20–25
identical with, identical to, 177
Idioms, 176–79
  with compound constructions, 156
  in expressions of time or place, 177–78
  grammar checkers for, 171
  list of, 176–77
  two-word verbs as, 228–29
  using, 176–79
i.e., 364
ie vs. *ei,* 350
if
  in conditional sentences, 235–36
  subjunctive after, 238–39
  as subordinating conjunction, 196
if, whether, 529
illicit, elicit, 349, 527
illusion, allusion, 348, 524
Illustrated books, MLA style, 461–62
Illustration or support. *See also* Examples
  in essay development, 15
  in paragraph development, 53–54
Illustrations and artworks
  acknowledging sources of, 69, 73, 393, 429, 430–31
  advertisements, MLA style, 470, 483
  in APA style, 513, 519
  captions for, 70–72, 74
  cartoons, MLA style, 473, 482–83
  charts: documenting, MLA style, 470, 482; using, 69–71, 519, 521
  comic strips, MLA style, 482–83
  copyrights of, 393, 430–31
  creating, 68–75
  critical viewing of, 94–99
  diagrams: documenting, MLA style, 470, 482; using, 71
  in document design, 4, 68–75
  in document format: APA style, 519, 521; MLA style, 69–72, 73, 490
  documenting: APA style, 513; MLA style, 461–62, 470, 473, 477, 482–83
  evaluating, 94–99
  figures, 69–71
  finding online, 392–94
  graphs: documenting, MLA style, 470, 482; using, 70–71, 519
  maps, MLA style, 470, 482
  in MLA style, 470, 473, 477
  online databases of, 393–94
  paintings, MLA style, 482
  permission for using, 393, 432
  photographs: documenting, MLA style, 470, 477, 482; using, 71–72
  pie charts, 69–70
  responsible use of, 73
  sources of, 73, 392–94
  tables: APA style for, 519, 521; using, 69
  titles of, italics or underlining for, 361
  using, 68–75, 392–94
  visuals: documenting, APA style, 513; MLA style, 470, 473, 477
  in Web compositions, 74, 76, 430–31
Imagery, in literary works, 131
Images. *See* Illustrations and artworks
immigrate, emigrate, 527
imminent, eminent, 349
impatient at, of, for, with, 177
Imperative mood
  defined, 238
  omission of *you* with, 238, 287
  punctuation and, 304, 305–06
  shifts between indicative and, 239
implicit, explicit, 527
Implied nouns, 265
imply, infer, 529
in, at, on, 177–78
Inc., 365
incidentally, punctuation with, 294–95
including, no colon after, 328
Incomplete sentences. *See* Sentence fragments
in contrast, punctuation with, 294–95
incredible, incredulous, 529
indeed, punctuation with, 294–95
Indefinite pronouns
  alternatives to *he* with, 260
  defined, 191, 246, 331
  list of, 246, 259
  possessives of, 330, 331
  pronoun agreement with, 259–61
  verb agreement with, 246–47
Indefinite words, and pronoun agreement, 259–61

Independent clauses. *See* Main (independent) clauses
independent of, 177
Indicative mood
  defined, 237–38
  shifts between imperative and, 239
Indirect objects. *See also* Objects
  case of, 251–52
  defined, 200–01
Indirect questions, 304
Indirect quotations. *See also* Direct quotations
  defined, 335
  no comma before, 321
Indirect sources
  APA style, 500
  MLA style, 444
individual, person, party, 529
Individual possession, possessive case to indicate, 331–32
Induction (inductive reasoning), 115
Inexact language, grammar checkers for, 171
in fact, punctuation with, 294–95
infer from, 177
infer, imply, 529
inferior to, 177
Infinitives and infinitive phrases
  case of pronouns with, 256–57
  defined, 207, 257, 279
  split, 279–80
  subjects or objects of, 256–57
  after verbs, 207, 225–27
INFOMINE, 6, 389
Informal (scratch) outlines, 21–22
Informal vs. formal usage, 105–08
Information gathering
  on computers, 412
  critical reading for, 84–99, 397–409
  direct quotation in, 416–18
  methods of, 411–12
  paraphrasing in, 414–16
  in research process, 411–12
  risk of plagiarism during, 411–12
  summarizing in, 413–14
  synthesis in, 409–10
Information service. *See* Databases, electronic
InfoTrac Expanded Academic, 385
-ing
  in gerunds, 207
  helping verbs with verbs ending in, 221
  in present participles, 192–93, 206, 221–22
  in progressive tenses, 221–22, 232–33
in other words, punctuation with, 294–95
in regards to, 529

in short, punctuation with, 294–95
Inside addresses, of business letters, 136–37
Instant messaging, revising shortcuts of, 107, 164–65
instead, punctuation with, 294–95
Insulting words, 118
insure, assure, ensure, 525
Integrating borrowed material
  in English and some other humanities, 423
  in history and some other humanities, 423
  interpretation and, 420–22
  introduction and, 420
  with signal phrases, 421
  in social and natural sciences, 423–24
  verbs and verb tenses for, 421, 423
Integrity
  in academic community, 78, 80–82
  in academic writing, 78, 425
Intellectual property, 425
Intensive pronouns, 191
Interjections
  defined, 197, 305, 314
  punctuation of, 305–06, 314
Internet. *See also* Blogs; Discussion groups, online; E-mail; Social media; Sources; Web sites
  acknowledging sources found on, 427, 430–31
  addresses. *See* URLs (uniform resource locators)
  advantages and disadvantages of, 388
  copyright and, 430–31
  evaluating sources on, 397–409
  plagiarism and, 427
  research sources on, 379–83, 388–91, 397–409
  search engines for, 388–91
  searching, 379–83, 388–91
Interpretation
  of borrowed material, 420–22
  in critical thinking and reading, 98
  of illustrations, 98
  of visuals, 98
  as writing assignment, 7
Interrogative pronouns, 191
Interviews
  documenting: APA style, 514–15; MLA style, 457, 469, 474, 481
  as research tool, 395
in the meantime, punctuation with, 294–95
in the past, punctuation with, 294–95
Intransitive verbs, 200, 218

Introductions
  to argument, 124
  to books and other sources, MLA style, 463
  of essays, 20, 31
  guidelines for writing, 59–60
Introductory elements
  commas with, 309–10
  dashes with, 340
  defined, 309
Invention
  computers for, 11–14
  techniques for, 10–15
Inverted word order, 248
Invisible writing, on computer, 13
involved in, with, 177
ipl2, 389
irregardless, 529
Irregular adjectives, 270
Irregular adverbs, 270
Irregular verbs
  defined, 214–15
  dictionary for, 214–15
  grammar checkers for, 216
  list of common, 215–16
is, are, 524
is because, 299
is when, is where, 298–99, 529
it
  case forms of, 252
  indefinite reference of, 264–65
  with -s, -es verb ending, 219–20
  vague reference of, 264–65
Italics
  consistent and appropriate use of, 360
  for defined words, 361–62
  for emphasis, 67, 362
  for foreign words, 361
  grammar checkers for, 360
  for names of ships, aircraft, spacecraft, trains, 361
  in online communication, 362
  for titles of works, 360–61
  vs. underlining, 360
  for words or characters named as words, 361–62
it is
  conciseness by eliminating, 186–87
  necessity of *it* in, 186–87
  uses of, 186–87
its, it's, 333, 349, 529

J
Jargon, 187
Job-application letters, 138
Joint possession, possessive case to indicate, 332
Journalist's questions, for essay development, 15

Journals
  on computer, 11–12
  defined, 11
  for essay development, 11–12
  reading, 11–12, 129–30
  research, 371
  scholarly. *See* Articles in periodicals; Periodicals
JSTOR, 385
just because, 299

K
Keywords
  Boolean operators for, 382
  for catalog searches, 382
  for database searches, 382
  defined, 381
  developing, 382
  for Internet searches, 382, 389–91
  in résumés, 138–39
  sample search using, 389–91
  for search engines, 382, 389–91
  trial and error with, 382, 389–91
kind of, sort of, type of, 530
Knightcite, 434
know, no, 349

L
Labels
  biased language and, 169–70
  for lists, 341
Language. *See also* Foreign words; Words
  of academic writing, 80
  appropriate, 80, 163–80
  colloquial, 165–66
  exact, 171–80
  figurative, 179–80
  formal vs. informal, 105–08
  nonstandard. *See* Culture-language issues
  sexist, 167–69
  specialized, 8
  standard. *See* Standard American English
Languages, capitalization of names of, 357
Latin abbreviations, 364
lay, lie, 217–18, 530
least, less, 269–71
leave, let, 530
Lectures
  italics or underlining for titles of, 361
  MLA style, 483
Legends, 69–71
Length
  of paragraphs, 52
  of reading material, 85
  of sentences, 159
lessen, lesson, 349
less, fewer, 528

less, least, 269–71
let, leave, 530
Letters (of alphabet)
  apostrophe for omission of, 333
  in formal outline, 23
Letters (correspondence). *See also* E-mail
  business, 136–37, 327
  documenting: APA style, 513; MLA style, 464–65
  e-mail, 479
  job application, 138
Letters to editor, MLA style, 456–57, 469, 474
LexisNexis Academic, 385, 387
Libraries
  books in, 383–84
  catalogs in, 380, 383–84
  databases from, 380–81, 384–88
  electronic sources from, 380, 384–88
  evaluating sources in, 398–401
  periodicals in, 384–88
  reference librarians, 379
  reference works in, 384–88
  research guides, 380–81
  as Web gateway for research, 379–80
  Web sites of, 379–80, 385
Library of Congress Subject Headings (LCSH), 383–84
Library subscription services
  APA style, 509
  MLA style, 474–76
lie, lay, 217–18, 530
like, as, 525
like, such as, 530
likewise, punctuation with, 294–95
Limiting modifiers, 279
Linking verbs
  adjectives vs. adverbs after, 268–69
  agreement with subjects, 249
  defined, 201, 253, 268, 286
  list of, 201
List of works cited. *See also* APA style; Bibliographies; Parenthetical text citations
  MLA style, 448–84, 495–96
Lists. *See also* Series
  in document design, 67–68
  parallelism in, 67, 157
  parentheses with labels for, 341
Listservs. *See* Discussion groups, online
literally, 530
Literary analysis
  documentation in, MLA style, 444–45, 472
  format of quotations in, MLA style, 485–86
Literature and literary works
  analyzing, 129–30
  critical approaches to, 130–32
  critical reading of, 129–32
  documenting, in MLA style, 133, 444–45
  elements of, 129–32
  forms of, 132
  meaning of, 130
  sample essays on, 133–35
  titles of: italics or underlining for, 360–61; quotation marks for, 336
little, a little, 276
Logical comparisons, 270–71
Logical fallacies, 120–24
Logic, and deductive reasoning, 117
Long quotations, format of
  in APA style, 518
  in MLA style, 485–86
  no quotation marks with, 485, 518
lose, loose, 530
lots, lots of, 530
-ly ending, adverbs with and without, 194

M

Magazines. *See* Articles in periodicals; Periodicals
Main (independent) clauses
  comma splices with, 291–95
  defined, 150, 209–10, 234, 290, 318, 323, 327
  fused, 291–95
  linked with comma and coordinating conjunction, 149, 291–93, 307–08
  for main ideas, 160
  related by conjunctive adverbs (with semicolon), 294–95
  vs. sentence fragments, 221–22
  vs. subordinate clauses, 152–53, 209–10
  tense sequence with, 234–35
Main verbs, 193, 203, 220–24, 245
make, as helping verb, 145
Manual for Writers of Research Papers, Theses, and Dissertations, A (Turabian), 433
Manuscripts. *See* Document design and format
many
  vs. *much,* 276–77
  pronoun with, 259–61
  verb with, 246–47
Mapping, 14–15
Maps. *See* Illustrations and artworks
Margins and spacing
  in academic papers: APA style, 516; MLA style, 484–85
  in business correspondence, 137
  in document design, 66, 484–85

Mathematics, style guides for, 434
may be, maybe, 530
may, can, 224, 525
may of, 528
Meanings of words
    connotation, 173–74
    denotation, 173–74
meanwhile, punctuation with, 294–95
Measurement units, 364
meat, meet, 349
media, 530
Media files, MLA style, 477
Medium of publication
    APA style, 515
    MLA style, 448, 466, 469, 473
meet, meat, 349
Memos, business, 139–41
Menus on Web pages, 75
MetaCrawler, 389
Metaphor, 179
me vs. *I,* 252–53
might of, 528
Misplaced modifiers
    defined, 278
    grammar checkers for, 278
    with *only* and other limiting modifiers, 279
    and order of adjectives, 281–82
    and position of adverbs, 278–81
    in separated subject-verb, 279
    and split infinitives, 279–80
    unclear placement, 278–79
Miss, Mrs., Ms., 136, 169
Mixed sentences
    defined, 298
    in grammar, 299–300
    in meaning, 298–99
    repeated sentence parts, 300–01
MLA Handbook for Writers of Research Papers, 439–96. *See also* MLA style
MLA style
    for document format, 484–86
    for footnotes or endnotes, 447–48
    indexes to documentation models: parenthetical citations, 440; works cited, 450–51
    for list of works cited: format of, 448–49; guidelines for, 448–49; index to, 450–51; models of, 448–84
    for parenthetical citations: index to, 440; models of, 439–45; placement and punctuation of, 445–47
    for poetry and long prose quotations, 485–86
    sample paper, 64, 488–96
Modal verbs, 223–24. *See also* Helping verbs (auxiliary verbs)

Modern Language Association style. *See* MLA style
Modifiers
    absolute, 270
    absolute phrases as, 208
    adjectives and adverbs, 267–77
    conciseness of, 186–87
    dangling, 153, 278, 283–84
    defined, 186
    grammar checkers for, 267, 268, 278
    misplaced, 278–82
    nonessential vs. essential, 311–14
    position of, 278–84
    prepositional phrases as, 205–08
    reducing, 186–87
    subordinate clauses as, 209–11
    verbals and verbal phrases as, 206–07, 219–20
Money amounts
    dollar signs with, 365
    numerals vs. words for, 367
Months of year
    abbreviation of, 364
    capitalization of, 357
Mood of verbs
    consistency of, 239
    defined, 237–38
    forms for, 237–39
    grammar checkers for, 238
    subjunctive, 238–39
moral, morale, 531
more
    in comparative forms, 269–71
    as determiner, 276
    pronoun with, 259–61
    verb with, 246–47
moreover, punctuation with, 294–95
most
    as determiner, 276
    pronoun with, 259–61
    in superlative forms, 269–71
    verb with, 246–47
most, almost, 524
Motion pictures. *See* Films, DVDs, and video recordings
Movies. *See* Films, DVDs, and video recordings
Mrs., Miss, Ms., 169
Ms., Miss, Mrs., 169
much
    pronoun with, 259–61
    verb with, 246–47
much vs. *many,* 276–77
Multilingual writers, tips for. *See* Culture-language issues
Multimedia sources. *See also* Films, DVDs, and video recordings; Illustrations and artworks; Sound recordings; Web sites
    creating and using, 72–75, 94–99, 393–94, 430–31

Multimedia sources (*continued*)
    documenting: APA style, 513, 515;
        MLA style, 480–81
    evaluating, 407–09
    in multimodal compositions, 69–75
    as research sources, 393–94
Multimodal writing, 68–75
Multivolume works
    APA style, 507–08
    MLA style: list of works cited, 462;
        parenthetical citations, 443
*MuseumLink's Museum of
    Museums*, 394
Musical works. *See also* Sound
    recordings
    documenting: APA style, 515; MLA
        style, 471, 473, 477, 481
    titles of: italics or underlining for
        longer works, 361; quotation
        marks for songs, 336
myself, herself, himself, yourself, 531

N

namely, punctuation with, 294–95,
    327
Names of persons
    abbreviation of, 364
    capitalization of, 357
    titles before and after, 136, 358
Narration
    in essay development, 15
    in paragraph development, 53–54
    in visuals, 96, 97
Narrators
    in literature, 131
    in paragraphs, 53–54
Nationalities, capitalization of, 357
Natural sciences, integrating
    borrowed material in, 423–24
NB, 364
n.d. (no date)
    APA style, 511
    MLA style, 464, 466, 468, 469, 482
neither
    pronoun with, 259–61
    verb with, 246–47
neither . . . nor
    as correlative conjunction, 196
    parallelism with, 156
Networks, computer. *See* Internet;
    Web sites
nevertheless, punctuation with, 294–95
Newsgroups. *See* Discussion groups,
    online
Newsletters, 142
Newspapers. *See* Articles in
    periodicals; Periodicals
*New York Public Library Digital
    Gallery*, 393
Nicknames, no quotation marks for,
    337

no
    comma with, 314
    vs. *know*, 349
    to negate a noun, 268
no. (abbreviation), 365
nobody
    pronoun with, 259–61
    verb with, 246–47
No date in source. *See n.d.* (no date)
No city of publication. *See n.p.* (no
    place of publication or no
    publisher)
Noncount nouns
    defined, 191, 273–74
    determiners with, 275
    list of, 273–74
    no plurals with, 261, 352
    pronouns with, 261
    verbs with, 247
none
    pronoun with, 259–61
    verb with, 246–47
Nonessential elements
    commas with, 311–14
    dashes with, 340
    defined, 311, 319, 340
    vs. essential elements, 311–14
    parentheses with, 341
    test for, 312
nonetheless, punctuation with, 294–95
Nonperiodical sources,
        documenting
    APA style, 507–08, 511–16
    MLA style, 457–65, 477–83
Nonprint sources
    APA style, 508–13, 515
    MLA style, 442–43, 465–83
Non sequiturs, 121
Nonstandard English. *See*
    Culture-language issues;
    Standard American English
no one
    pronoun with, 259–61
    verb with, 246–47
No pagination. *See n. pag.*
No place of publication. *See n.p.*
    (no place of publication or no
    publisher)
No publisher. *See n.p.* (no place of
    publication or no publisher)
nor
    and agreement of pronoun, 259
    and agreement of verb, 246
    as coordinating conjunction, 196
    parallelism with, 155–56
not
    to negate a verb or adjective, 268
    position of, 281
not . . . but
    as correlative conjunction, 150, 196
    parallelism with, 156

Note cards. *See* Information gathering
Note taking
　in classes, 78
　research sources. *See*
　　Information gathering
nothing
　pronoun with, 259–61
　verb with, 246–47
not only . . . but also
　as correlative conjunction, 196
　parallelism with, 156
Noun clauses, 210–11
Nouns
　a, an, the, and other determiners with, 182, 273–77
　adjectives to modify, 194, 268
　apostrophe with possessive, 191, 331–32
　capitalization of proper, 356–57
　collective, 191, 247
　common, 191
　count, 191, 273
　defined, 145
　effective use of, 145
　gerunds and gerund phrases as, 207
　implied, 265
　infinitives and infinitive phrases as, 207
　made from verbs, 145, 183–84
　noncount, 191, 273–74, 276
　plurals of, 331
　possessive, 191
　proper. *See* Proper nouns
　subordinate clauses as, 209–10, 210–11
　types of, 191
Novels
　MLA style: in list of works cited, 472; in parenthetical citations, 444
　reading and writing about, 129–33
nowheres, 531
now, punctuation with, 294–95
n.p. (no place of publication or no publisher), MLA style, 463–64, 466, 469, 471, 472
n. pag. (no pagination)
　APA style, 500
　MLA style, 443, 463–64, 472, 474
Number
　defined, 49
　pronoun-antecedent agreement in, 258–61
　shifts in, 49
　subject-verb agreement in, 243–44
number, amount, 524
Numbers
　abbreviations with, 365
　commas in, 317
　grammar checkers for, 367

hyphens in, 354, 367
numerals vs. words for, 366–68
spelled out at beginnings of sentences, 367
Numerals. *See* Numbers

O

Object complements, 202
Objective case
　defined, 251
　pronoun forms for, 251–52
Objective narrators, in literary works, 131
Objects
　appositive describing, pronoun case in, 256
　compound, 252–53
　defined, 210, 251
　direct, 201, 251–57
　indirect, 200–01, 251–57
　of infinitives, 256–57
　objective case for, 251–57
　of prepositions, 206, 251–52
　of verbs, 200–02, 251–52
Objects of prepositions
　case of, 251–52
　defined, 206
oblivious of, to, 177
Observations
　for essay development, 12
　as primary research source, 396
occupied by, in, with, 177
of course, punctuation with, 294–95
off of, 531
of, have, 528
oh, 197
OK, O.K., okay, 531
Omissions
　from compound constructions, 182
　from contractions, 333
　from direct quotations, 341–43, 417
　of needed words, 182
　from *there is* or *it is* constructions, 186–87
Omniscient narrators, in literary works, 131
on, at, in, 177–78
one
　pronoun with, 259–61
　verb with, 246–47
one of the, agreement problems with, 248
Online courses, taking, 79
Online papers, posted on the Web, 75–76
Online sources. *See* Sources
only, placement of, 279
on the contrary, punctuation with, 294–95
on the other hand, 531

索引　　　　595

on the whole, punctuation with, 294–95
Opinions
　as claims in argument, 112–13, 114
　critical thinking and, 92
　expert, 114
opposed to, 177
Opposing views, 118–19, 124
Opposition, acknowledging, in argument, 118–19, 124
or
　and agreement of pronoun, 259
　and agreement of verb, 246
　as coordinating conjunction, 196
　parallelism with, 155–56
Oral presentations
　documenting, MLA style, 483
　italics or underlining for titles of, 361
Organization
　of academic papers, 20–25, 31, 79, 105
　of arguments, 124–25
　of paragraphs, 48
　of research papers, 436
　of Web pages, 75–76
Organization names
　abbreviation of, 363–64
　capitalization of, 357
otherwise, punctuation with, 294–95
Outlines
　constructing, 21–24
　of drafts, 30
　of essays, 21–24
　formal, 23–24, 486–87
　format for, 486–87
　informal, 21–22
　parallelism in, 24, 157
　of research papers, 486–87
　as revision aid, 30
　sample, 486–87
　scratch, 21–22
　sentence vs. topic, 486–87
　topic, 23–24
　tree diagram, 22
Oversimplification, 122–23
owing to the fact that, 531

P

p., pp., 502
Page numbers
　documenting: APA style, 498, 502; MLA style, 440, 453–57, 460–61, 464–65, 476
　of journals vs. magazines, 384
　none: APA style, 500; MLA style, 443, 463–64, 472, 474
　in one's own papers: APA style, 516; MLA style, 485

in periodicals: APA style, 505–07; MLA style, 454
Pagination. *See n. pag.* (no pagination); Page numbers
Pamphlets
　MLA style, 464
　titles of, italics or underlining for, 361
par., para., or *pars.* (paragraph)
　APA style, 498, 500
　MLA style, 444
Paragraph numbers, documenting
　APA style, 498, 500
　MLA style, 444
Paragraphs
　in body of essay, 43–44
　central idea in, 45–46
　checklist for revising, 44
　coherence of, 46–52
　concluding, 61–62
　consistency in, 49–50
　development of, 53–59
　functions of, 43
　indention of, 65
　introductory, 59–60
　length of, 52
　organization of, 48
　parallelism in, 44, 48
　pronouns in, 49
　related in essay, 43–44
　repetition and restatement in, 48–49
　summarizing, 89–91
　topic sentence of, 45–46
　transitional expressions in and between, 50–52
　unity of, 45–46
Parallelism
　with coordinating conjunctions, 155–56
　with correlative conjunctions, 156–57
　defined, 48, 155
　grammar checkers for, 155
　in lists, 67
　with lists, headings, and outlines, 24, 67, 157
　in paragraphs, 44, 48
　use of, 155–57
Paraphrases
　academic integrity and, 82
　acknowledging sources of, 425, 429–30
　avoiding plagiarism with, 425, 429–30
　defined, 132, 414
　documenting, 425, 429–30
　examples of, 414, 416, 429–30
　in information gathering, 82, 414–16
　integrating, in paper, 419–24

vs. summaries and direct
    quotations, 412–19, 429–30
  vs. translations, 416
Parentheses
  around complete sentences, 341
  capitalization with, 341
  vs. commas or dashes, 341
  function of, 339
  grammar checkers for, 339
  for labels of lists and outlines, 341
  with other punctuation, 341
  for parenthetical expressions, 341
Parenthetical expressions
  commas for, 313, 341
  dashes for, 340
  defined, 313, 341
  parentheses for, 341
Parenthetical text citations
  APA style: index to, 498; models
    of, 497–500
  MLA style: index to, 440; models
    of, 439–45; placement and
    punctuation of, 445–47
part from, with, 177
Participles and participial phrases.
    See also Past participles;
    Present participles
  as adjectives, 206–07
  defined, 206
  of irregular verbs, 207, 214–17
  present vs. past, 272–73
Particles, in two-word verbs, 228–29
Parts of speech, 190–97
party, individual, person, 529
passed, past, 349
Passive sentences, 204
Passive voice
  vs. active voice, 184–85, 240–41
  consistency in use of, 241–42
  defined, 184, 201, 204, 222, 240
  formation of, 204, 222, 240–41
  grammar checkers for, 183, 241
  transitive verbs in, 201, 222, 240
  unemphatic, 145–46
  uses of, 240–41
  wordiness and, 184–85, 240
  word order in, 204
past, passed, 349
Past participles
  as adjectives, 206–07
  be forms with, 222, 232–33, 240
  defined, 206, 214, 221, 272
  formation of, 214–16, 215
  have forms with, 223, 232
  of irregular verbs, 207, 214–17
  in participial phrases, 206–07
  in passive voice, 222, 240
  in perfect tenses, 232
  vs. present participle, as
    adjective, 272–73
Past perfect progressive tense, 231

Past perfect tense, 231, 235
Past progressive tense, 231
Past tense
  defined, 192, 214, 231
  -ed or *-d* ending of verbs, 219–20
  formation of, 192, 214–16
  with irregular verbs, 214–17
  and tense sequence, 235
  was, 219–20
Past-tense form, 192, 214–16
patience, patients, 349
Patterns of development
  for essays, 15
  for paragraphs, 53–59
peace, piece, 349
Peer editing, 28, 32–34
Peer-reviewed journals, 386
people, persons, 531
per, 531
percent (per cent), percentage, 531
Percentages, 367
Perfect tenses
  defined, 223, 231, 232
  and tense sequence, 235
  uses of, 232
Performances, MLA style, 483
Periodical databases
  documenting: APA style, 508–10;
    MLA style, 474–76
  as research sources, 380–81, 385
  searching, 380–82, 385–87
  selecting, 385
  using, 385–87
Periodicals. *See also* Articles in
    periodicals
  databases, 385–87
  database searches for, 386
  documenting. *See* Articles in
    periodicals
  electronic, 384–88
  finding and using, 384–88
  journals vs. magazines, 384
  pagination of, 454, 505–07
  peer-reviewed or refereed, 386
  as research sources, 384–88
  titles of, italics or underlining for,
    361
  in working bibliographies, 377
Periodic sentences, 147–48
Periods
  in abbreviations, 304–05, 363
  correcting comma splices with,
    290–91, 291–93
  correcting fused sentences with,
    290–91, 291–93
  ending sentences with, 304
  grammar checkers for, 304
  with parentheses, 341
  with quotation marks, 337–38
  used in ellipsis mark to show
    omission from quotation, 341

Permission, obtaining
　for material used in one's own
　　work, 391, 431–32
　for postings on social media, 391,
　　431–32
　for use of visuals and multimedia,
　　393, 431–32
person, individual, party, 529
Person (first, second, third)
　in academic writing, 107
　defined, 50
　and point of view, in literary
　　works, 131
　pronoun-antecedent agreement in,
　　50, 258
　shifts in, 50
　subject-verb agreement in, 243
Personal pronouns
　agreement with antecedents, 258–61
　cases of, 251–57
　vs. contractions, 333
　defined, 191
　list of, 191
　possessives of, 333
persons, people, 531
Perspectives, gaining new, 78, 81
phenomena, 532
Photocopying research sources, pros
　and cons, 412
Photographs. *See* Illustrations and
　artworks
Phrases
　absolute, 208, 313
　appositive, 208, 313
　conciseness of, 186–87
　defined, 152, 160, 206, 312
　empty, 185
　essential, 311–14, 320–21
　as modifiers, 205–08
　nonessential, 311–14, 340
　prepositional. *See* Prepositional
　　phrases
　redundant, 186
　simplifying, 186–87
　subordination with, 152–53
　types of, 206–08
　verb, 220–24
　verbal. *See* Verbals and verbal
　　phrases
piece, peace, 349
Place
　in, at, on in expressions of, 177
　transitional expressions to
　　indicate, 47
Place names
　abbreviation of, 364
　capitalization of, 356–57
　commas in, 317
Plagiarism
　academic integrity and avoiding,
　　80–81
　avoiding, 80–81, 425–34
　careless, 80–81, 427
　checklist for avoiding, 426
　with computer notes, 412
　defined, 425
　deliberate, 80, 426–27
　detecting, on the Internet, 427
　with downloaded sources, 412
　with handwritten notes, 412
　and intellectual property, 425
　with Internet sources, 427, 430–31
　vs. necessary acknowledgments,
　　428–30
　with paraphrases, 429–30
　with photocopied or printed-out
　　sources, 412
　with quotations, 429
　with summaries, 91, 429–30
　vs. using common knowledge, 428
　vs. using your own independent
　　material, 428
PlagiServe, 427
plain, plane, 349
Plain form of verbs
　defined, 192, 203, 214
　in forming past tense and past
　　participle, 214–16
　in forming simple present tense,
　　192
　forms of *do* with, 223
plane, plain, 349
Plays
　acts and scenes of, 444–45, 447
　fair use of, 432
　MLA style: list of works cited, 483;
　　parenthetical citations, 444–45,
　　447–48
　reading and writing about,
　　129–33
　titles of, italics or underlining for,
　　360
plenty, 532
Plots of literary works, 130
Plurals. *See also* Agreement of
　pronouns and antecedents;
　Agreement of subjects and verbs
　apostrophe with possessives of,
　　331
　defined, 191
　determiners with, 275, 276
　formation of, 351–52
　misuse of apostrophe to form,
　　332–33
　of nouns, 332–33, 351–52
　in pronoun-antecedent
　　agreement, 258–61
　in subject-verb agreement, 243–44
　of words and characters named as
　　words, 334
plus, 532
PM, AM, 365

Podcasts
  documenting: APA style, 513; MLA style, 471–72
  evaluating, 407–09
  listing in working bibliography, 377
  as research sources, 394
Poetry
  ellipsis mark for omissions from, 343
  fair use of, 432
  MLA style: formatting quotations from, 485–86; parenthetical citations for, 444–45; works-cited entry for, 472
  reading and writing about, 129–35, 133–35
  slash between lines of, 344–45, 485
  titles of: italics or underlining for long, 361; quotation marks for short, 336
Point-by-point comparison and contrast, 56
Point of view
  in illustrations, 96
  in literary works, 131
Political Cartoons, 393
Positive forms of adjectives and adverbs, 194
Possessive case
  apostrophes to indicate, 191, 331–32
  forming, 330–32
  before gerunds, 257
  grammar checkers for, 329–30
  of nouns and indefinite pronouns, 191, 331–32
  of personal pronouns, 251–52, 333
Possessive nouns, 191
Post hoc fallacy, 123
Postponed subjects, sentences with, 204–05
precede, proceed, 532
Predicate. *See also* Objects; Subject complements; Verbs
  agreement of subject with, 243–49
  complete, 198
  in complete sentences, 286–87, 290–91
  compound, 319–20
  defined, 144, 198, 209, 285
  patterns, 200–202
  in sentences with mixed grammar, 299–300
  in sentences with mixed meaning (faulty predication), 298–99
  simple, 198–99
  verbal phrases in, 206–07
Predicate adjectives. *See* Subject complements

Predicate nouns. *See* Subject complements
Predication, faulty, 298–99
Preface, MLA style, 463
Prefixes
  with capitalized words, 354
  hyphens to attach, 354
  spelling with, 351
prejudice, prejudiced, 532
Premises, 116–17
Prepositional phrases
  as adjectives, 206
  as adverbs, 206
  commas with, 310
  defined, 195, 206, 310
  uses of, 206
Prepositions
  at, in, on, 177–78
  capitalization in titles, 358–59
  defined, 195, 228, 328
  for, since, 178, 232
  grammar checkers for, 171
  idioms with, 177–78
  list of, 195
  no colons with, 328
  objects of, 206, 251–52
  in two-word verbs, 228–29
presence, presents, 349
Presenting writing. *See* Document design and format
Present participles
  as adjectives, 206, 272–73
  be forms with, 221–22, 232–33
  defined, 192, 221, 272
  formation of, 192–93
  helping verbs with, 221–22
  in participial phrases, 206
  vs. past participles as adjectives, 272–73
  in progressive tenses, 221–22, 232–33
Present perfect progressive tense, 231
Present perfect tense, 231
Present progressive tense, 231
presents, presence, 349
Present tense
  defined, 231
  plain form of verbs in, 192
  -s, -es ending of verb, 219–20
  uses of, 230–32
Pretentious writing, 166
pretty, 532
Previewing
  in reading critically, 85–87
  in viewing visuals critically, 94–95
Primary sources
  defined, 132, 374
  one's own knowledge as, 373
  for research, 374
  vs. secondary sources, 374
  in writing about literature, 132

principal, principle, 349, 532
Principal parts of verbs, 214–17
Printing out research sources, pros and cons, 412
Prints and Photographs Online Catalog, 393
Print sources, documenting
  APA style, 502–08, 514
  MLA style, 448–65, 482–83
prior to, 177
Privacy, communications in academic setting, 83
Problem-solution organization, 21
proceed, precede, 532
Proceedings of a conference, MLA style, 463
Process
  critical reading and viewing, 84–99
  research writing, 435–38
  writing, 2–42
Process analysis
  in essay development, 15
  in paragraph development, 57–58
Progressive tenses
  defined, 221, 232
  formation of, 221–22, 231
  helping verbs in, 221–22
  -ing forms of verbs, 222, 232–33
  uses of, 232–33
Pronoun-antecedent agreement. *See* Agreement of pronouns and antecedents
Pronouns
  adjectives to modify, 194, 268
  agreement with antecedents, 258–61
  cases of, 251–57
  defined, 49, 191
  demonstrative, 191
  gender of, 258
  grammar checkers for, 252, 258, 263
  indefinite. *See* Indefinite pronouns
  intensive, 191
  interrogative, 191
  misuse of apostrophe with possessive, 333
  in paragraphs, 49
  personal. *See* Personal pronouns
  reflexive, 191
  relative. *See* Relative pronouns
  as subject complements, 251–52
  types of, 191
Pronunciation, spelling and, 348
Proofreading
  of direct quotations, 417
  for grammar and style errors, 40–41
  as part of writing process, 40–41, 182
  for spelling errors, 38–40

Proper adjectives
  capitalization of, 356–57
  defined, 356–57
Proper nouns
  articles with, 275
  capitalization of, 356–57
  common nouns as essential parts of, 358
  defined, 191, 273, 356–57
ProQuest, 387, 480
Prose, formatting long quotations from
  APA style, 518
  MLA style, 485–86
proud of, 177
Publication Manual of the American Psychological Association. See APA style
Publications, government. *See* Government publications
Public writing, 135–42
  for business, 136–37
  for community work, 141–42
  format, 135–42
  guidelines, 135–42
  for job applications, 138–39
  letters, 136–37
  memos, 139–41
  résumés, 138–40
  in Web compositions, 75–76
Published proceedings of a conference, MLA style, 463
Punctuation. *See also specific punctuation marks*
  of absolute phrases, 313
  of appositives, 313, 327
  with conjunctive adverbs, 294–95, 323–24
  with coordinating conjunctions, 149–50, 307–08, 315
  at ends of sentences, 304–06
  grammar checkers for, 304, 308, 323, 326, 329–30, 335, 339
  of introductory elements, 309–10
  of linked main clauses, 290–95, 307–08, 323, 325
  of nonessential elements, 311–14, 340
  in online communication, 107, 164–65
  with parenthetical citations, 445–47
  of parenthetical expressions, 341
  of possessive case, 331–32
  of prepositional phrases, 310
  of quotations. *See* Direct quotations
  in or with series, 315, 325, 327, 340
  of subordinate clauses, 311–14

of titles of works, 327
of verbals and verbal phrases,
    311–14
Purpose
  conveyed by writing
    assignments, 3, 6–7
  determining: in evaluating online
    sources, 404, 408; in viewing
    illustrations, 96
  document design to match, 65–73
  of essays, 3, 6–7
  and organization, 21
  and revision, 30, 31
  in thesis statement, 19
  of writing assignments, 3, 6–7

Q
Question marks
  with quotation marks, 338
  use of, 203
*question of whether, question as to
    whether*, 532
Questions
  about audience, 8
  capitalization in series, 356
  construction of, 203
  for developing essay subject, 15
  direct, 305
  indirect, 304
  journalist's, 15
  for literary analysis, 130–32
  for patterns of development, 15
  research, 371–73
  tag, 314
  who vs. *whom* in, 254–55
Quotation marks
  avoiding unnecessary, 337
  commas with, 318–19
  for direct quotations, 335–36, 429
  double, 335–36
  function of, 335
  grammar checkers for, 335
  with other punctuation, 338
  not with quotations set off from
    one's text, APA style, 518; MLA
    style, 485–86
  single, 335
  for titles of works, 336
  for words used in special sense, 337
Quotations, direct. *See* Direct
    quotations

R
Races of people, capitalization of, 357
Radio programs. *See* Television and
    radio programs
rain, reign, rein, 349
raise, raze, 349
raise, rise, 217–18, 532

Rational appeals, 117–18
raze, raise, 349
Readers. *See* Audience
Reading
  active, 87–89
  assignments, 78
  critical, 84–99, 397–409
  of illustrations, 95–96
  previewing for, 85–87
  of research sources, 397–409
  for revision, 30
  skimming, 85–87
Reading journals, 11–12, 129–30
Readings, MLA style, 483
real, really, 532
Reasonable arguments
  acknowledging opposition in,
    118–19
  appropriate appeals in, 117–18
  avoiding fallacies in, 120–24
  elements of, 114–23
  logical thinking in, 114–17
reason is because, 299, 532
Red herring, 121
Reductive fallacy, 123
Refereed journals, 386
Reference librarians, 379
Reference list, APA style, 500–16,
    522. *See also* Bibliographies;
    MLA style; Parenthetical text
    citations
Reference of pronouns
  appropriate *you*, 265
  to clear antecedent, 263
  to close antecedent, 264
  to implied nouns, 265
  to indefinite *it, they*, 264–65
  to specific antecedent, 264–65
  specific *this, that, which, it*, 264
  that vs. *which* vs. *who*, 534
References, parenthetical. *See*
    Parenthetical text citations
Reference works
  documenting: APA style, 512;
    MLA style, 461, 470
  as research sources, 383
  style guides, 433–34
  on the Web, 383
Reflexive pronouns, 191
Refworks, 434
Regular verbs
  defined, 214
  vs. irregular verbs, 214–16
  tenses of, 231. *See also* Tenses
reign, rein, rain, 349
related to, 177
Relative pronouns
  in adjective clauses, 209–10
  cases of, 254–55
  defined, 191

Relative pronouns (*continued*)
    list of, 191, 287
    reference of, 264–65
    in sentence fragments, 287
    verb agreement with, 247–48
Relevance
    of evidence, 129
    of sources, 398
Reliability, of sources, 398
Reliable narrators, in literary works, 131
Religions and their followers, capitalization of, 357
Repetition
    for paragraph coherence, 48–49
    unnecessary, 186, 300–01
Reports
    APA style, 511, 513–14
    as writing assignment, 6
Reprinted articles, MLA style, 461
Republished books, MLA style, 462, 472–73
Research guides, 380–81
Research journals, 371
Research questions, 371–73
Research writing
    annotated bibliographies for, 376–78
    APA style: documentation, 497–516; format, 516–19; parenthetical citations, 497–500; reference list, 500–16; sample paper, 519–22
    avoiding plagiarism in, 425–34
    bibliographies in: APA style, 500–16; MLA style, 448–84
    books for, 383–84
    citing sources in, 432–34
    critical reading of sources for, 397–409
    direct quotations in, 416–18
    discussion groups for, 391–92, 407–09
    documentation in, 432–34
    drafting, 436–37
    electronic searches for, 379–83
    electronic sources for, 374, 380–92
    evaluating sources for, 397–409
    examples of: APA style, 519–22; MLA style, 488–96
    formatting, 438
    gathering information for, 411–12
    goals for, 373–76
    government publications for, 392
    integrating borrowed material in, 419–24
    interviews for, 395
    keywords for, 382
    library for, 379–81, 384–88
    MLA style: documentation, 439–83; format, 448–49, 484–86; list of works cited: format of, 448–49; models of, 448–84; parenthetical citations, 439–48; sample paper, 488–96

    multimedia sources for, 377, 392–96
    one's own sources for, 395–96
    online sources for, 374, 380–81, 383, 388–91
    organizing, 436
    outlines for, 486–87
    paraphrases in, 414–16, 429–30
    periodical articles, 384–88
    planning, 370–71
    primary sources for, 374, 395–96
    question for, 371–73
    quotations in, 426, 428–31
    reference works for, 383
    research journals, 371
    revising, 437
    scheduling, 370–71
    secondary sources for, 374
    social media for, 391–92
    sources for, 378–96
    style guides for, 433–34
    subjects for, 371–72
    summaries in, 412–19, 429–30
    synthesizing sources for, 409–10
    thesis statements for, 435–36
    visuals for, 392–94
    Web sources for, 388–91, 397–409
    working bibliographies for, 376–78
    writing process for, 370–78, 435–38
    in writing situation, 3
respectful, respective, 532
Responding to texts. *See* Academic writing
Restatements, for paragraph coherence, 48–49
Restrictive elements, 311–14. *See also* Essential elements
Résumés, 138–40
Retrieval statements, APA style, 508–13
Return-address heading, 136–37
Reviews
    APA style, 507, 511
    MLA style, 456, 469, 474
Revision
    in academic writing, 29–33, 80
    checklists for, 31, 44, 437
    collaborating for, 28, 30, 32–34
    computers for, 32
    critical reading, 30
    file management during, 32
    outlines as tool for, 24
    of paragraphs, 44
    of research papers, 437
    sample, 34–36
    of thesis statement, 18–19
    Track Changes function, 31
    using word processor, 32
rewarded by, for, with, 177
right, rite, write, 349
rise, raise, 217–18, 532

road, rode, 349
Rogerian argument, 119
Run-on sentences (fused sentences), 290–95

S

-'s
  for plurals of abbreviations and words and characters used as words, 334
  for possessives, 331–32
-s, -es
  for noun plurals, 191
  possessive of words ending in, 330–31
  verb agreement with subjects ending in, 244–45
  as verb ending, 192, 219–20
Salutations of business letters
  colon after, 327
  format of, 136–37, 327
Sample documents
  annotated bibliography, 367
  argument, 125–28, 133–35
  blog post, 76
  business letter, 137
  critical response to a text, 108–10
  e-mail, 83, 141
  final draft, 41–42
  first draft, 28–29
  informative essay, 24–25
  literary analysis, 132–35
  memo, 141
  newsletter, 142
  outline, 23, 486–87
  personal narrative, 76
  research paper: APA style, 519–22; MLA style, 488–96
  response to a reading, 41–42
  résumé: print, 139; scannable, 140
  revised draft, 34–36
  Web site, 75
Sans-serif type, 67
Sarcasm, 118
scarcely, but, hardly, 525
Scene numbers, numerals for, 445
scene, seen, 349
Scholarly article reprinted in a collection, 461
Scholarly projects, MLA style, 468
Sciences
  integrating borrowed material in, 423–24
  style guides for, 433–34
Sciences, social. *See* Social sciences
Scientific Style and Format: The CSE Manual for Authors, Editors, and Publishers, 434
Scope, in thesis statement, 18
Scores, sports, 367
Scratch (informal) outlines, 21–22

Search engines
  vs. databases, 381
  defined, 388
  for finding visuals, 393–94
  keyword searches of, 382
  list of, 389
  sample, 389–91
  sample search with, 389–91
  using, 382, 388–91
Searches, electronic, 379–83, 388–91
Search histories, 389
second, 51
Secondary sources
  defined, 132, 374
  vs. primary sources, 374
  for research, 374
  in writing about literature, 132
Second-level headings
  APA style, 518
  in document design, 67
Second person (*you*), 107, 243
seen, scene, 349
-self, -selves, 192
Semicolons, 322–25
  vs. colon, 326
  with coordinating conjunctions, 149
  correcting comma splices with, 291–93, 292
  grammar checkers for, 323
  with *however, for example,* etc., 323–24
  misuse of, 325
  with quotation marks, 337
  to separate main clauses, 323–24, 325
  in series, 325
sensual, sensuous, 532
Sentence combining
  for conciseness, 187
  for variety, 160–61
Sentence-combining exercises
  beginnings and endings, 148–49
  comma splices and fused sentences, 295–96
  parallelism, 158
  related main clauses, 324–25
Sentence fragments, 285–88
  acceptable uses of, 288
  vs. complete sentences, 285–88
  defined, 285
  grammar/style checkers with, 285
  in online communication, 107, 164–65
  revising, 288
  subject omitted in, 287
  subordinate clause as, 287
  tests for, 286–87
  verbal phrases as, 221
  verbs omitted in, 286
Sentence outlines, 24, 486–87

Sentences. *See also* Sentence fragments
    beginning of, 146–48
    capitalization of first word in, 356
    commands, 204
    completeness of, 181–82, 285–88
    complex, 212
    compound, 212
    compound-complex, 213
    conciseness of, 183–87
    conditional, 235–36, 238–39
    coordination in, 149–51
    cumulative, 147–48
    defined, 198
    details in, 162
    elements of, 198–99, 285
    expletive, 186–87, 205
    fused, 290–95
    length of, 159
    linked within paragraphs, 43–44
    mixed, 298–301
    numbers at beginning of, 367
    order of information in, 146–48
    outlines, 24, 486–87
    parentheses around complete, 341
    patterns, 200–02
    periodic, 147–48
    with postponed subjects, 204–05
    predicates of, 198–202
    punctuation at end of, 304–06
    questions, 203
    repeated parts in, 300–01
    vs. sentence fragments, 285–88
    simple, 212
    subjects of, 198–99
    subordination in, 152–53
    thesis. *See* Thesis and thesis statement
    topic, 45
    transitional expressions to link, 50–52
    types of, 203–05, 212–13
    variety in, 159–62
Sequence of tenses
    in conditional sentences, 235–36
    defined, 234
    with past or past perfect tense in main clause, 235
Series
    capitalization of questions in, 356
    colon to introduce, 327
    comma in, 315
    dashes before or after, 340
    defined, 315
    misuse of comma around, 321
    misuse of semicolon before, 325
    MLA style, 457, 462
Serif type, 67
Service learning, 141–42
set, sit, 217–18, 533
Setting of literary work, 131

several
    pronoun with, 259–61
    verb with, 246–47
Sexist language
    avoiding, 167–69, 260
    generic *he* in, 169, 260
    grammar checkers for, 164
shall, will, 533
she
    case forms of, 252–53
    vs. *her*, 252–53
    with *-s, -es* verb ending, 219–20
she, he; he/she, 260, 528
Shifts
    dashes to indicate, 340
    in mood, 239
    in number, 49
    in person, 50
    in pronouns, 49, 265–66
    in tense, 49, 233
    in voice, 241–42
Ship names, italics or underlining for, 361
Short stories, quotation marks for titles of, 336
should of, 528
sic, 344
sight, site, cite, 349, 526
Signal phrases
    commas with, 318–19
    for interpreting borrowed material, 421
    with quotations, 318–19, 421
    verbs for, 421, 423
Signatures in business letters, 136–37
similarly, punctuation with, 294–95
similar to, 177
Similes, 179
Simple future tense, 231
Simple past tense, 231
Simple predicate, 198–99
Simple present tense, 192, 231
Simple sentences, 212
Simple subjects, 198
since
    vs. *for*, 178, 232
    for time and cause, 533
Singular
    defined, 191
    in pronoun-antecedent agreement, 258–61
    in subject-verb agreement, 243–44
sit, set, 533
sit, set, 217–18
site, cite, sight, 349, 526
Slang
    appropriate use of, 165
    defined, 165
    grammar checkers for, 164
    no quotation marks for, 337

Slashes
 function of, 339
 between options, 344
 to separate lines of poetry, 344–45, 485
 spaces with, 344–45
 in URLs (electronic addresses), 474, 508
Snob appeal, 122
so
 commas with, 307
 as coordinating conjunction, 196
 as vague intensifier, 533
Social media. *See also* Blogs; Discussion groups, online; E-mail; Social-networking sites
 documenting, MLA style, 479
 evaluating sources on, 407–09
 as research sources, 391–92
Social networking sites. *See also* Social media
 documenting, MLA style, 479
 evaluating sources on, 407–09
 Facebook, 82, 391, 407
 as research sources, 391–92
 Twitter, 82
Social sciences
 APA style, 497–516; documentation, 497–516; document format, 516–19; parenthetical citations, 497–500; reference list, 500–16; sample paper, 519–22
 integrating borrowed material in, 423–24
 sample paper in, 519–22
 style guides for, 433–34
so far, punctuation with, 294–95
Software. *See* Computer software
some
 pronoun with, 259–61
 verb with, 246–47
somebody
 pronoun with, 259–61
 vs. *some body*, 533
 verb with, 246–47
someone
 pronoun with, 259–61
 vs. *some one*, 533
 verb with, 246–47
something
 pronoun with, 259–61
 verb with, 246–47
sometime, sometimes, some time, 533
somewheres, 533
Songs. *See* Sound recordings
sort of, type of, kind of, 530
Sound recordings. *See also* Musical works
 acknowledging, 394
 documenting: APA style, 515; MLA style, 471, 473, 477, 481
 evaluating, 407–09
 fair use of, 432
 as research sources, 394
 titles of: italics or underlining for longer works, 360; quotation marks for songs, 336
 in Web compositions, 432
Sources. *See also* Primary sources; Secondary sources
 acknowledgment of, 80, 425–34, 439–83
 annotated bibliographies of, 376–78
 audio, 394
 books, 383–84
 citing to avoid plagiarism, 432–34
 copyrighted, 430–31
 databases, 380–82, 385–87
 direct quotation from, 426, 428–31
 documenting: APA style, 497–516; MLA style, 439–83; style guides for, 433–34
 electronic searches for, 379–83, 384–88
 evaluating, 397–409
 fair treatment of, 81
 fair use of, 432
 gathering information from, 411–12
 goals for, 373–76
 government publications, 392
 impartial vs. biased, 375
 integrating material from, 419–24
 Internet, 388–92
 interviews, 395
 keywords for finding, 382
 library vs. Internet, 374, 379–80
 management of, 81–82
 multimedia, 73, 392–94
 observations, 396
 older vs. newer, 375
 paraphrases of, 414–16
 periodicals, 384–88
 permission for using, 393
 plagiarism vs. acknowledgment of, 91, 412, 425–34
 primary vs. secondary, 132, 374
 quotations from, 416–18
 reference works, 383
 research guides for, 380
 scholarly vs. popular, 374–80
 social media, 391–92
 summaries of, 412–14
 synthesizing, 409–10, 412
 using, 419–24
 video, 394
 visuals, 392–94
 Web, 388–91
 working bibliographies of, 376–78

Spacecraft, italics or underlining for names of, 361
Spacing, within documents, 66, 67–68
Spatial organization, 21, 48
Specific-to-general organization, 21
Specific words, 175–76
Speculation, tense sequence with, 236
Speech, parts of, 190–97
Speeches
　italics or underlining for titles of, 361
　MLA style, 483
Spelling, 348–52
　American vs. British, 350
　anticipation of problems with, 348–50
　computer checkers for, 38–40, 348
　for different forms of same word, 350
　of homonyms, 348–49
　improving, 348
　in online communication, 107, 164–65
　pronunciation and, 348
　rules for, 350–52
Split infinitives, 279–80
Standard American English. *See also* Culture-language issues
　in academic writing, 105–08, 163
　defined, 106, 163
　vs. other dialects and languages, 105–08, 164
Standardization in document design, 65
stationary, stationery, 349
Statistics
　as evidence, 113
　numbers vs. words in, 367
Stereotypes
　in argument, 122
　eliminating, 167–70
still, punctuation with, 294–95
Stories
　quotation marks for titles of, 336
　reading and writing about, 129–33
Structure of essays, in academic writing, 104–05
Student writing, examples of. *See* Sample documents
Style and grammar checkers, 38–40. *See also entries for specific style and grammar issues*
Subject-by-subject comparison and contrast, 56
Subject complements
　defined, 251
　noun clauses as, 210–11

pronouns as, 253–54
　subjective case for, 251–52
Subject headings, discovering using keyword searches, 385
Subjective case
　defined, 251
　pronoun forms for, 251–57
Subjects of papers
　arguments, 112
　finding appropriate, 4–6
　limiting, 5
　organization and, 20–21
　research papers, 371–72
Subjects of sentences
　active vs. passive voice and, 240–41
　agreement between verb and, 243–49
　appositive describing, pronoun case of, 256
　complement of. *See* Subject complements
　complete, 198
　compound, 252–53, 319–20
　conciseness and, 183–84
　defined, 144, 198, 209, 251, 285
　emphasis and, 144–46
　misuse of comma between verb and, 319
　omission of, 287
　postponed, 204–05
　in sentences with mixed grammar, 299–300
　in sentences with mixed meaning, 298–99
　separation from verb, 279
　simple, 198
　subjective case for, 251–57
Subject-verb agreement. *See* Agreement of subjects and verbs
Subjunctive mood
　defined, 238
　formation of, 238–39
　grammar checkers for, 238
　uses of, 238–39
Subordinate (dependent) clauses
　as adjectives, 209–10
　as adverbs, 210–11
　commas with, 309
　correcting comma splices with, 293
　defined, 152, 160, 209–10, 234, 254, 285, 293, 309, 312
　excessive use of, 153–54
　made into modifiers, 199
　vs. main clauses, 209–10
　as nouns, 210–11
　relative pronouns and, 209–10, 287
　as sentence fragments, 287
　subordinating conjunctions and, 195–96, 209–11, 287

subordination and, 152–53
tense sequence with, 234–36
types of, 209–11
who vs. *whom* in, 254–55
Subordinating conjunctions
 defined, 195
 list of, 196, 287
 use of, 195–96, 209–11
Subordination
 effective, 153
 to emphasize main ideas, 152–53, 293
 excessive or faulty, 153–54
 grammar checkers for, 152
 for variety, 160
Subscription services. *See* Databases, electronic
Subtitles
 capitalization in, 358–59
 colons with, 328
such
 as demonstrative pronoun, 191
 as determiner, 276
 as vague intensifier, 533
such as
 vs. *like*, 530
 no colon after, 328
Suffixes, hyphen to attach, 354
Suggestive titles, 34
Summaries
 academic integrity and, 82
 as aid to reading comprehension, 89–91
 in critical reading, 89–91
 defined, 89, 412–13
 examples of, 90–91
 in information gathering, 82, 413–14
 vs. paraphrase and direct quotation, 412–19, 429–30
 plagiarism, avoiding in, 426, 429–30
 writing, 89–91, 413–14
 as writing assignment, 6
Superfluous commas, 319–21. *See also* Commas, misuse of
superior to, 177
Superlative forms of adjectives and adverbs, 194, 269–71
supposed to, used to, 533
sure, 533
sure and, sure to, 534
Surveys, 395–96
Sweeping generalizations, 122–23
Syllogisms, 116–17
Symbolism, in literary works, 131
Synonyms, 173
Synthesis
 in academic writing, 80, 103–04
 in critically viewing visuals, 93

in critical thinking and reading, 93
in research writing, 409–10, 412
in responding to texts, 103–04

T
Tables
 APA style, 521
 creating and using, 69
Tag questions, comma with, 314
take, bring, 525
Taking notes. *See* Information gathering
Technical words, 166
Technical writing
 abbreviations in, 363
 documentation in, 433–34
 numbers in, 367
 words in, 166
Television and radio programs
 documenting: APA style, 515; MLA style, 470–71, 480–81
 titles of: italics or underlining for programs, 361; quotation marks for episodes, 336
Tenses
 in conditional sentences, 235–36
 consistency in, 233
 defined, 230
 future, 231
 past 231
 perfect, 231, 232
 present, 230–32
 progressive, 221–22, 232–33
 sequence of, 234–36
 shifts in, 49
Term papers. *See* Research writing
Terms, defined
 italics or underlining for, 361–62
 singular verbs with, 249
Text files, MLA style, 477
Text messaging, avoiding shortcuts of, 107, 164–65
Text-to-speech computer programs, 38
than
 parallelism with, 156–57
 pronoun after, 256
 vs. *then*, 534
that
 as demonstrative pronoun, 191
 direct quotations preceded by, 319
 in essential clauses, 312–13, 534
 reference of, 264
 as relative pronoun, 287
 in sentence fragments, 287
 subjunctive after, 238
 vague references of, 264
 verbs with, 247–48
 vs. *which*, 534
 vs. *which* and *who*, 534

that is, punctuation with, 294–95, 327
the
    capitalization in titles, 358–59
    rules for use of, 274–75
Theater. *See* Plays
their, there, they're, 333, 349
their, there, they're, 534
theirselves, 534
them
    misuse as adjective, 534
    vs. *they*, 253–54
Theme, in literary works, 132
then, than, 534
the only one of the, 248
there, they're, their, 333, 349
there, they're, their, 534
thereafter, punctuation with, 294–95
therefore, punctuation with, 294–95
there is, there are
    and agreement of verb, 248
    conciseness by eliminating, 186–87
    necessity of *there* in, 186–87
    overuse of, 186–87
Thesauruses, 173
these, this, 534
these kind, these sort, these type, those kind, 530
Thesis and thesis statement
    argumentative, 17
    of arguments, 112–13, 124–25
    defined, 16
    developing, 16–19
    of essays, 16–19, 31
    evaluating, 18–19
    explanatory, 17
    expressed in two or more sentences, 435–36
    functions, 16
    outlines and, 21–24
    of research papers, 435–36
    revising, 18–19
they
    to avoid generic *he*, 260
    case forms of, 252
    indefinite reference of, 264–65
    vs. *them*, 253–54
they're, their, there, 333, 349, 534
Third-level headings
    APA style, 518
    in document design, 67
Third person *(he, she, it, they)*
    in academic writing, 107
    and grammatical agreement, 243
    point of view, in literary works, 131
    with *-s, -es* verb ending, 219–20

this
    as demonstrative pronoun, 191
    vs. *these*, 534
    vague reference of, 264
those kind, these kind, these sort, these type, 530
throw, 216
thru, 534
thus, punctuation with, 294–95
Time
    AM or *PM* with, 365
    colon used to punctuate, 327
    for or *since* in expressions of, 178, 232
    in, at, on in expressions of, 177
    numerals vs. words for, 367
    organization by, 21
    transitional expressions to indicate, 51
Titles of papers
    capitalization of, 358–59
    creating, 34
    format of: APA style, 516; MLA style, 485
    no quotation marks for, 336
    questions about, 31
    subject indicated by, 34
Titles of persons
    abbreviations for, 365
    in business letters, 136
    capitalization of, 358
    Ms., Miss, Mrs., 136, 169
Titles of works. *See also* Titles of papers
    APA style: parenthetical citations, 499; reference list, 502
    capitalization in, 358–59
    colons before subtitles in, 328
    commas with, 313
    italics or underlining for, 360–61
    MLA style: finding, 454, 458; list of works cited, 448–84; parenthetical citations, 439–45
    quotation marks for, 336
    verb agreement with, 249
Titles within titles, MLA style, 463
to
    with infinitives, 207, 225–27
    after verb, 225–27
to, too, two, 349, 534
Tone
    in argument, 118
    audience and, 7–8
    in academic communication, 82
    of e-mails, 82
    of essays, 31
    evaluating in online sources, 408
    of literary works, 131

too, 534
Topic outlines, 23–24, 486–87
Topic sentences, 45
Topics of papers. *See* Subjects of papers
to this end, punctuation with, 294–95
toward, towards, 534
Train names, italics or underlining for, 361
Transitional expressions
 for coherence, 50–52
 with commas, 294, 310, 313, 323–24
 in comma splices, 294–95
 defined, 294, 310, 313, 323
 list of, 51, 294
 with semicolons, 294, 323–24
 for sentence beginnings, 161
Transitive verbs
 defined, 200, 218
 in passive voice, 201, 222, 240–41
Translated works
 APA style, 507
 MLA style, 459–60
Tree diagrams, 22
Trite expressions
 avoiding, 180
 list of, 180
 style checkers for, 180
try and, try to, 534
Turnitin, 427
Tweet, documenting, 479
Twitter. See also Social media
 in academic communication, 82–83
 documenting, 479
two, too, to, 349
Two-word verbs
 grammar checkers for, 228
 particles with, 228–29
Type fonts, 67, 75
type of, 534
type of, kind of, sort of, 530

U

Underlining
 consistent and appropriate use of, 360
 for defined words, 361–62
 for emphasis, 67, 362
 for foreign words, 361
 grammar checkers for, 360
 vs. italics, 360
 for names of ships, aircraft, spacecraft, trains, 361
 in online communication, 362
 for titles of works, 360–61
 for words or characters named as words, 361–62

undoubtedly, punctuation with, 294–95
uninterested, disinterested, 527
unique, 535
Unity. *See also* Coherence
 defined, 24, 45
 of essays, 24–25, 31
 of paragraphs, 45–46
 in thesis statement, 19
unless
 in conditional sentences, 235–36
 subjunctive after, 238
Unpublished material, copyrighted sources in, 431–32
Unreliable narrators, in literary works, 131
Unsigned works. *See* Anonymous or unsigned works
Unstated premises, 117
until now, punctuation with, 294–95
URLs (uniform resource locators)
 breaking: APA style, 508; MLA style, 474; no hyphenation, 354
 documenting: APA style, 508–15; MLA style, 465–66, 473–74
 in evaluating sources, 402
 in Web sources, 465–66, 473–74, 508–15
us vs. *we*, 256
Usage
 in academic writing, 105–08
 biased, 118, 167–69, 260
 colloquial, 165–66
 and dialects, 163–64
 glossary of, 523–35
 nonstandard, 163–64, 268, 271
 sexist, 167–69
 slang, 165
 Standard American English, 105–08, 163
 technical, 166
usage, use, 535
use, utilize, 535
used to, supposed to, 533
Usenet newsgroups. *See* Discussion groups, online
us vs. *we*, 256

V

Valid deductive reasoning, 117
Variety in sentences
 adding details for, 162
 grammar checkers for, 159
 length for, 159
 sentence combining for, 160–61
 subordination for, 160

Variety in sentences (*continued*)
varying beginnings for, 161–62
varying structure for, 159–62
varying word order for, 162
Verbals and verbal phrases
as adjectives, 206–08
as adverbs, 206–08
commas with, 309
defined, 206–08
gerunds, 207, 225–27, 257
infinitives, 207, 225–27, 256–57, 279–80
as nouns, 206–08
participles, 206–07, 272–73
in sentence fragments, 221, 286
types of, 206–08
uses of, 206–08
Verbs. *See also* Tenses
active vs. passive, 204, 222, 240–41
adverbs to modify, 194, 267, 268
agreement with subjects, 243–49
conciseness and, 184–85
in conditional sentences, 235–36
-*d* and -*ed* forms of, 192, 219–20
direct objects of, 201, 251–52
effective use of, 144–46
emphasis and, 144–46
finite, 286
forms of, 192–93, 214–29
gerund vs. infinitive after, 225–27
grammar checkers for, 183, 216, 219–21, 225–26, 228, 230, 238, 241, 243
helping verbs (auxiliary verbs), 193, 220–24
indirect objects of, 200–01, 251–52
intransitive, 200, 218
for introducing borrowed material, 421
irregular, 192–93, 207, 214–17
linking, 201, 249, 268–69
main, 193, 220–24
misuse of apostrophes with, 333
misuse of commas between subject and, 319
modal, 223–24
mood, 237–39
no colons after, 328
nouns made from, 145, 183–84
objects of, 200–02, 251–52
omission of, 220–21, 286
with particles, 228–29
plain forms of, 192
principal parts of, 214–17
regular, 214
-*s* and -*es* forms of, 192, 219–20, 244–45
in signal phrases, 421, 423
strong, 145

tenses of, 230–36
to or *for* after, 202
transitive, 200, 218
two-word, 228–29
voice of, 145–46, 184–85, 240–41
weak, 145, 184
Video recordings. *See* Films, DVDs, and video recordings
Vision loss, considering readers with, 68
Visual art. *See* Illustrations and artworks
Visual literacy, 94–99
Voice, of verbs
active vs. passive, 145–46, 184–85, 240–41
consistency in, 241–42
emphasis and conciseness with, 145–46, 184–85
Voice, of writer
defined, 8–9
of essays, 31
in thesis statement, 16, 19
Volumes of books
APA style, 507–08
MLA style, 443, 462
Volumes of periodicals
APA style, 505–07
MLA style, 454

W

waist, waste, 349
wait at, for, in, on, 177, 535
ways, 535
we
case forms of, 252
vs. *us* with a noun, 256
weak, week, 349
Weasel words, 166
weather, whether, 349
Web. *See* Web sites
Webcasts, 394
Web compositions. *See* Web sites
Web forums. *See* Discussion groups, online
Web logs. *See* Blogs
Web sites. *See also* Sources
acknowledging sources from, 427, 430–31
addresses. *See* URLs (uniform resource locators)
advantages and disadvantages of, 388
color in, 68, 75
copyright and, 432
creating, 75–76
critical reading of, 397–409
vs. databases, 381
documenting sources from: APA style, 508–15; MLA style, 465–75

downloading material from, 412
evaluating sources from, 397–409
finding bibliographic information for, 467
fonts for, 75
government publications on, 392
keyword searches of, 382, 389–91
library vs. search engine for access, 379–80
navigation on, 75
papers posted on, 75–76
permission for use of material on, 432
plagiarism and, 427
printed documents vs., 75–76
as research sources, 397–409
search engines for, 388–91
searching, 388–91
short works, untitled, 468
sound recordings on, 472, 473, 481
spacing on, 75, 76
titles: italics or underlining for sites, 360; quotation marks for pages or documents, 336
types of, 402–03
visuals on, 74, 75–76
well, *good*, 268, 269, 528
what, 191
when, in conditional sentences, 235–36
whether
   vs. *if*, 349, 529
   vs. *weather*, 349
whether . . . or, 196
which
   as interrogative pronoun, 191
   in nonessential clauses, 313, 534
   as relative pronoun, 191, 287
   vs. *that*, 312–13, 534
   vague reference of, 264
   verbs with, 247–48
   vs. *who* and *that*, 534
   vs. *witch*, 349
who
   case forms of, 252
   as interrogative pronoun, 191
   reference of, 264
   as relative pronoun, 191, 287
   verbs with, 254–55
   vs. *which* and *that*, 534
   vs. *whom*, 254–55
who, *whom*, 535
whoever, 191
whoever, *whomever*, 191
whole, *hole*, 349
whom vs. *who*, 254–55
whose, *who's*, 333, 349, 535
Wikipedia
   MLA style, 472
   as reference work, 383, 406

Wikis
   documenting: APA style, 512; MLA style, 472
   as reference work, 383, 404, 406
will, *shall*, 533
witch, *which*, 349
Word division, 354
Wordiness, avoiding, 183–87
   combining sentences, 187
   cutting repetition, 186
   eliminating jargon, 187
   eliminating *there is* or *it is*, 186–87
   for emphasis, 144, 183–86
   grammar checkers for, 183
   reducing clauses and phrases, 186–87
   rewriting jargon, 187
   using active voice, 184–85
   using effective subjects and verbs, 183–85
   using strong verbs, 184–85
Word order
   with adjectives, 281–82
   with adverbs, 278–81
   inverted, and subject-verb agreement, 162
   subject-verb, 200–02
   variety in, 162
Word processors. *See* Computers
Words
   abstract, 175–76
   appropriate, 163–80
   in arguments, 118
   biased, 118, 167–69
   clichés, 180
   colloquial, 165–66
   commonly confused, 348–49
   compound, 331, 352, 353–54
   concise. *See* Conciseness
   concrete, 175–76
   connotations, 173–74
   denotations, 173–74
   dialect, 163–64
   double-talk (doublespeak), 166
   emotional, 118
   empty, 185
   euphemisms, 166
   exact, 171–80
   figurative language, 179–80
   foreign, 361
   formal vs. informal, 105–08
   general, 175–76
   grammar checkers for, 164, 171
   homonyms, 173
   idioms, 176–79
   indirect, 166
   insulting, 118
   jargon, 187

Words (*continued*)
  nonstandard. *See* Culture-language issues
  pretentious, 166
  repetition, 48–49, 186, 300–01
  sarcastic, 118
  sexist, 167–69
  slang, 165
  specialized, 166
  standard. *See* Standard American English
  strong verbs, 145
  technical, 166
  trite, 180
  unnecessary, 183–87
  weasel, 166
Words used as words
  apostrophes with, 334
  italics or underlining for, 361–62
  plurals of, 334
  quotation marks for, 337
Working bibliographies, 376–78
Works cited. *See also* APA style; Bibliographies; Parenthetical text citations
  MLA style list of works cited, 448–84, 495–96
Works of art. *See* Illustrations and artworks
World Wide Web. *See* Sources; Web sites
would be, 535
would have, 535
would of, 528
wow, 197
write, right, rite, 349
Writer's block, 26–27

Writing process
  collaboration in, 28, 30, 32–34, 34–36
  development of, 2–10
  development of thesis statement, 16–19, 435–36
  drafting, 26–29
  editing, 36–40
  invention, 10–15
  organization, 20–25
  proofreading, 40–41, 182
  for research papers, 370–78
  revision, 28–42, 437
  summarizing for, 89–91
Writing situation, 100–11

Y
-y, final, 351
yes, comma with, 314
yet
  comma with, 307
  as coordinating conjunction, 196
  parallelism with, 155–56
yet, but, however, 525
you
  appropriate use of, 107, 265, 535
  case forms of, 252
  omission in commands, 287
your, you're, 333, 349
your, you're, 535
yourself, myself, herself, himself, 531
YouTube, 394, 466

Z
Zip codes, commas with, 317
Zotero, 434

语言文化提示

CULTURE LANGUAGE 图标贯穿本手册始终,它标记那些为母语或方言不是标准美式英语的学生准备的话题。这些话题可能令人挠头,因为它们来自标准美式英语的规则,而这些规则可能与别的语言或方言很不一样。许多话题也涉及重要的文化假设。

不管你的语言背景是什么,作为大学生,你在学习美国高等教育的文化,以及这个文化使用和由其塑造的语言,这个过程很有挑战性,即便对标准美式英语的母语者来说也是一样。它要求我们不仅能够写得清楚和正确,还要掌握那些发展、展示和支持我们的想法的通常做法。如果你正在努力学习标准美式英语,并习惯于其他语言的通常做法,那么这个挑战就更大了。下面几种习惯能帮助你成功:

- **读**。除了课程作业,还要阅读报纸、杂志及英文书。读得越多,你的写作就越流畅、越准确。
- **写**。坚持写日记,每天练习英文写作。
- **说和听**。好好利用听和说英语的机会。
- **提问**。你的老师、写作中心的指导老师还有同学们,都能帮助你发现和解决写作中的问题。
- **不要苛求完美**。谁也不能写得完美,追求完美可能反而会让你无法顺畅地表达自己。不要把错误看作失败,而要看成学习的机会。
- **先修改,再编辑**。先关注每篇文章的思想、论证和组织,然后再关注语法和单词。关于修改和编辑的对照清单,请看pp.31–37。
- **设置编辑的优先级**。首先专注于干扰文章清晰度的错误,例如,词序或主谓一致的问题。下面的索引能帮助你找到你需要学习的主题,并且引导你到相应的讲解部分。标有*的页码提供了自测练习。

Academic writing, 105, 108, *108, 164
Adjective(s)
 clauses, repetition in, 301, *301
 no, with a noun, 268
 no plurals for, 267
 order of, 281, *282
 participles as, 272, *272
Adverb(s)
 introductory, word order after, 161–62
 not, with a verb or adjective, 268, 281
 position of, 161–62, 280–81
Argument, taking a position in, 111
Articles (*a, an, the*), 273–75, *277
Audience, 9, 16, 34, 60, 111, 135
Business writing, 135
Capital letters, 356
Collaboration, 34
Comma splices
 revision of, 291
 and sentence length, 293
Determiners (*a, an, the, some, few, a few,* etc.), 273–77, *277
Dictionaries, ESL, 173
Fluency, in writing, 11, 12, 13
Forms of address (*Mrs., Miss, Ms.*), 169
Idioms, 177, *178
Intellectual property, 425
Introductions, 60
Nonstandard dialect, 164
Nouns
 collective: pronouns with, 261; verbs with, 247
 noncount: form of, 273, 352; list of, 273–74; pronouns with, 261; verbs with, 247
 plural: forms of, 273, 352; with *one of the,* 248
Numbers, punctuation of, 318, 367
Omissions
 helping or linking verb, 286
 subject of sentence, 287
 there or *it* at sentence beginning, 205
Organization, 20, 43, 52, 60
Paragraphs, 20, 43
Paraphrasing, 416
Plagiarism, 425
Prepositions
 for vs. *since,* 178, 232
 idioms with, 177–78, *178
 in vs. *at* vs. *on,* 177
 meanings of, 195
 to or *for* needed after some verbs, 202
Pronouns
 with collective and noncount nouns, 261

 matching antecedent in gender, 258
 needless repetition with, 263, 300–01, *301
 -self forms of, 252
Questions
 forming indirect, 304
 position of adverbs in, 280
Reading, critical, 84, 87, 397
Redundancy
 and implied meaning, 186
 in sentence parts, 300–01, *301
Research writing, originality in, 397, 425
Spelling
 British vs. American, 350
 noncount nouns, no plurals of, 352
Standard American English, 108, 164
Subject of sentence
 agreement with verb, 244–45, 247
 needless repetition of, 198, 263, 300–01, *301
 omission of, in fragments, 287
Subordinating conjunctions, 196
Thesis statement, 16
Transitional expressions, 52
Verbs
 agreement with subjects, 244–45, 247
 with collective nouns, 247
 gerund vs. infinitive with, 225–27, *227
 helping (*be, have, can,* etc.), 220–24, *224, *225
 with indirect objects, 202
 intransitive, 201
 irregular, 217
 with noncount nouns, 247
 participles of, 222, 272, *272
 passive voice of, 201, 222, 240
 perfect tenses of, 223, 232
 progressive tenses of, 221–22, 232–33
 -s and *-ed* endings of, 219–20, *220
 tense formation of, 230
 transitive, 201, 222, 240
 two-word, particles with, 228–29, *229
Wordiness, vs. incorrect grammar, 183
Word order
 adjectives and adverbs, 161–62, 280–81, *282
 questions, 280, 304
 subject-verb-object, 200Editing